Place-of-Service Codes for Professional Claims

Listed below are the Place-of-Service codes. The list contains the code, name, and description. These codes should be used on professional claims to specify the entity where service(s) were rendered. Check with your individual payer (eg, Medicare, Medicaid, other private insurance) to determine whether a particular code will be recognized for payment purposes. The codes are maintained by the Centers for Medicare and Medicaid Services (CMS). More information regarding the review and modification process as well as updates to the code set can be found at the CMS Web site http://cms.hhs.gov/states/posdata.pdf. If you would like to comment on a code(s) or description(s), please send your request to posinfo@cms.hhs.gov.

Place of Service Code(s)	Place of Service Name	Place of Service Description
01-02	Unassigned	N/A
03	School	A facility whose primary purpose is education.
04	Homeless Shelter	A facility or location whose primary purpose is to provide temporary housing to homeless individuals (eg, emergency shelters, individual or family shelters).
05	Indian Health Service Free-standing Facility	A facility or location, owned and operated by the Indian Health Service, that provides diagnostic, therapeutic (surgical and non-surgical), and rehabilitation services to American Indians and Alaska Natives who do not require hospitalization.
06	Indian Health Service Provider-based Facility	A facility or location, owned and operated by the Indian Health Service, that provides diagnostic, therapeutic (surgical and non-surgical), and rehabilitation services rendered by, or under the supervision of, physicians to American Indians and Alaska Natives admitted as inpatients or outpatients.
07	Tribal 638 Free-standing Facility	A facility or location owned and operated by a federally recognized American Indian or Alaska Native tribe or tribal organization under a 638 agreement, that provides diagnostic, therapeutic (surgical and non-surgical), and rehabilitation services to tribal members who do not require hospitalization.
08	Tribal 638 Provider-based Facility	A facility or location owned and operated by a federally recognized American Indian or Alaska Native tribe or tribal organization under a 638 agreement, that provides diagnostic, therapeutic (surgical and non-surgical), and rehabilitation services to tribal members admitted as inpatients or outpatients.
09-10	Unassigned	N/A
11	Office	Location, other than a hospital, skilled nursing facility (SNF), military treatment facility, community health center, State or local public health clinic, or intermediate care facility (ICF), where the health professional routinely provides health examinations, diagnosis, and treatment of illness or injury on an ambulatory basis.
12	Home	Location, other than a hospital or other facility, where the patient receives care in a private residence.
13-14	Unassigned	N/A
15	Mobile Unit	A facility/unit that moves from place-to-place equipped to provide preventive, screening, diagnostic, and/or treatment services.
16-19	Unassigned	N/A
20	Urgent Care Facility	Location, distinct from a hospital emergency room, an office, or a clinic, whose purpose is to diagnose and treat illness or injury for unscheduled, ambulatory patients seeking immediate medical attention.
21	Inpatient Hospital	A facility, other than psychiatric, that primarily provides diagnostic, therapeutic (both surgical and nonsurgical), and rehabilitation services by, or under, the supervision of physicians to patients admitted for a variety of medical conditions.
22	Outpatient Hospital	A portion of a hospital that provides diagnostic, therapeutic (both surgical and nonsurgical), and rehabilitation services to sick or injured persons who do not require hospitalization or institutionalization.
23	Emergency Room — Hospital	A portion of a hospital where emergency diagnosis and treatment of illness or injury is provided.
24	Ambulatory Surgical Center	A freestanding facility, other than a physician's office, where surgical and diagnostic services are provided on an ambulatory basis.
25	Birthing Center	A facility, other than a hospital's maternity facilities or a physician's office, that provides a setting for labor, delivery, and immediate post-partum care as well as immediate care of new-born infants.
26	Military Treatment Facility	A medical facility operated by one or more of the Uniformed Services. Military Treatment Facility (MTF) also refers to certain former U.S. Public Health Service (USPHS) facilities now designated as Uniformed Service Treatment Facilities (USTF).
27-30	Unassigned	N/A
31	Skilled Nursing Facility	A facility that primarily provides inpatient skilled nursing care and related services to patients who require medical, nursing, or rehabilitative services but does not provide the level of care or treatment available in a hospital.

32	Nursing Facility	A facility that primarily provides to residents skilled nursing care and related services for the rehabilitation of injured, disabled, or sick persons, or, on a regular basis, health-related care services above the level of custodial care to other than mentally retarded individuals.
33	Custodial Care Facility	A facility that provides room, board, and other personal assistance services, generally on a long-term basis, and which does not include a medical component.
34	Hospice	A facility, other than a patient's home, in which palliative and supportive care for terminally ill patients and their families are provided.
35-40	Unassigned	N/A
41	Ambulance — Land	A land vehicle specifically designed, equipped, and staffed for lifesaving and transporting the sick or injured.
42	Ambulance — Air or Water	An air or water vehicle specifically designed, equipped, and staffed for lifesaving and transporting the sick or injured.
43-49	Unassigned	N/A
50	Federally Qualified Health Center	A facility located in a medically underserved area that provides Medicare beneficiaries preventive primary medical care under the general direction of a physician.
51	Inpatient Psychiatric Facility	A facility that provides inpatient psychiatric services for the diagnosis and treatment of mental illness on a 24-hour basis, by or under the supervision of a physician.
52	Psychiatric Facility — Partial Hospitalization	A facility for the diagnosis and treatment of mental illness that provides a planned therapeutic program for patients who do not require full time hospitalization, but who need broader programs than are possible from outpatient visits to a hospital-based or hospital-affiliated facility.
53	Community Mental Health Center	A facility that provides the following services: outpatient services, including specialized outpatient services for children, the elderly, individuals who are chronically ill, and residents of the CMHC's mental health services area who have been discharged from inpatient treatment at a mental health facility; 24 hour a day emergency care services; day treatment, other partial hospitalization services, or psychosocial rehabilitation services; screening for patients being considered for admission to State mental health facilities to determine the appropriateness of such admission; and consultation and education services.
54	Intermediate Care Facility/Mentally Retarded	A facility that primarily provides health-related care and services above the level of custodial care to mentally retarded individuals but does not provide the level of care or treatment available in a hospital or SNF.
55	Residential Substance Abuse Treatment Facility	A facility that provides treatment for substance (alcohol and drug) abuse to live-in residents who do not require acute medical care. Services include individual and group therapy and counseling, family counseling, laboratory tests, drugs and supplies, psychological testing, and room and board.
56	Psychiatric Residential Treatment Center	A facility or distinct part of a facility for psychiatric care which provides a total 24-hour therapeutically planned and professionally staffed group living and learning environment.
57-59	Unassigned	N/A
60	Mass Immunization Center	A location where providers administer pneumococcal pneumonia and influenza virus vaccinations and submit these services as electronic media claims, paper claims, or using the roster billing method. This generally takes place in a mass immunization setting, such as a public health center, pharmacy, or mall but may include a physician office setting.
61	Comprehensive Inpatient Rehabilitation Facility	A facility that provides comprehensive rehabilitation services under the supervision of a physician to inpatients with physical disabilities. Services include physical therapy, occupational therapy, speech pathology, social or psychological services, and orthotics and prosthetics services.
62	Comprehensive Outpatient Rehabilitation Facility	A facility that provides comprehensive rehabilitation services under the supervision of a physician to outpatients with physical disabilities. Services include physical therapy, occupational therapy, and speech pathology services.
63-64	Unassigned	N/A
65	End-Stage Renal Disease Treatment Facility	A facility other than a hospital, which provides dialysis treatment, maintenance, and/or training to patients or caregivers on an ambulatory or home-care basis.
66-70	Unassigned	N/A
71	State or Local Public Health Clinic	A facility maintained by either State or local health departments that provides ambulatory primary medical care under the general direction of a physician.
72	Rural Health Clinic	A certified facility which is located in a rural medically underserved area that provides ambulatory primary medical care under the general direction of a physician.
73-80	Unassigned	N/A
81	Independent Laboratory	A laboratory certified to perform diagnostic and/or clinical tests independent of an institution or a physician's office.
82-98	Unassigned	N/A
99	Other Place of Service	Other place of service not identified above.

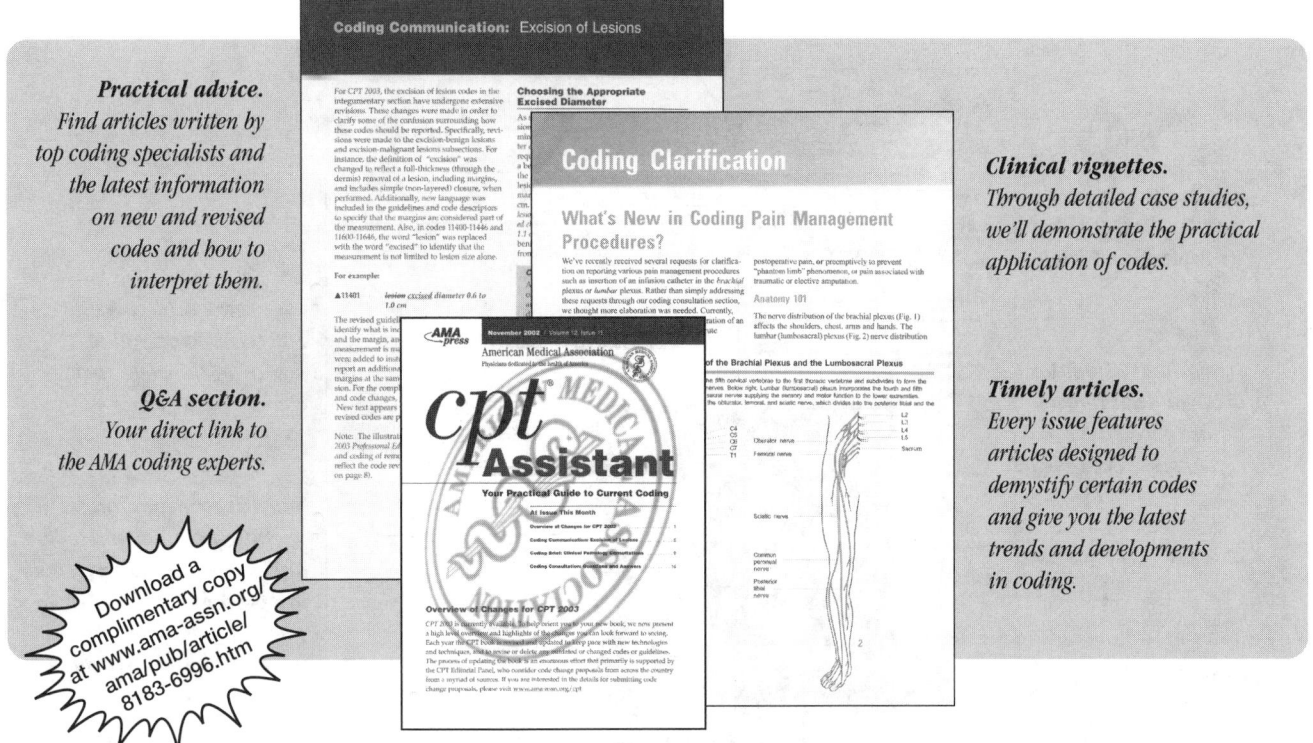

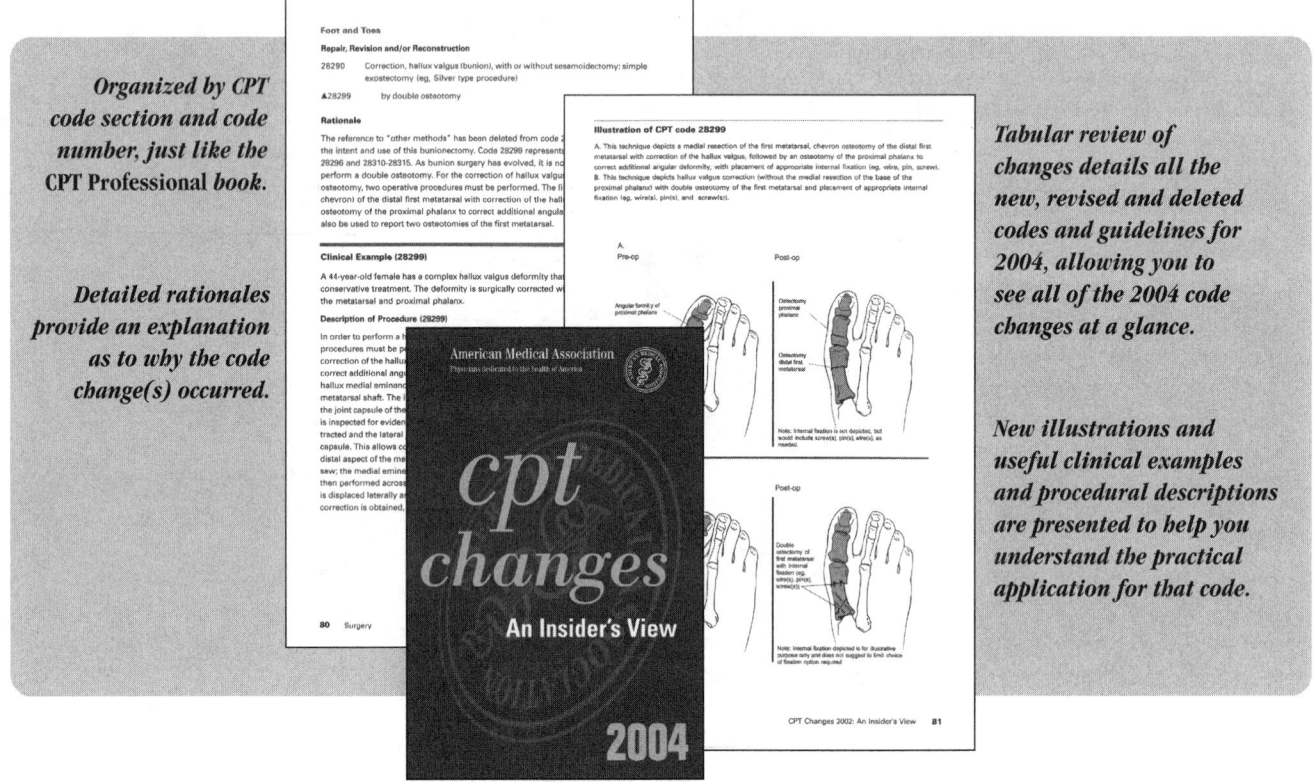

American Medical Association

Physicians dedicated to the health of America

Current Procedural Terminology

cpt®

2004

Michael Beebe, MS
Joyce A. Dalton
Catherine Duffy, RHIT, BS
Martha Espronceda, BA
Desiree D. Evans
Ron Friedmann, BS, RHIA
Rejina L. Glenn
Gloria Green, BA
DeHandro Hayden, BS
Elizabeth Lumakovska, RHIT, BS
Marie L. Mindeman, BA, RHIT
Karen E. O'Hara, BS, CCS-P
Mary R. O'Heron, RHIA, CCS-P
Danielle Pavloski, BS, RHIT, CCS-P
Dan Reyes, BA
Desiree Rozell, MPA
Lianne Stancik, RHIT
Jennifer Trajkovski, BS, RHIT
Ada Walker
Joan Zacharias, RHIT

AMA press

Standard ISBN: 1-57947-420-9
ISSN: 0276-8283

1st Edition printed 1966
2nd Edition printed 1970
3rd Edition printed 1973
4th Edition printed 1977
Revised: 1978, 1979, 1980, 1981, 1982, 1984, 1985,
1986, 1987, 1988, 1989, 1990, 1991, 1992, 1993, 1994,
1995, 1996, 1997, 1998, 1999, 2000, 2001, 2002, 2003

For questions regarding the use of CPT codes, please contact the American Medical Association CPT Information and Education Services at 800 634-6922.

To purchase additional CPT products, contact the American Medical Association Customer Service at 800 621-8335.

To request a license for distribution of products containing or reprinting CPT, please see our Web site at *www.ama-assn.org/cpt* or contact the American Medical Association CPT Intellectual Property Services, 515 N. State Street, Chicago, Illinois 60610, 312 464-5022.

AC25:OP054104:10/03

Foreword

Current Procedural Terminology, Fourth Edition (CPT®) is a listing of descriptive terms and identifying codes for reporting medical services and procedures performed by physicians. The purpose of the terminology is to provide a uniform language that will accurately describe medical, surgical, and diagnostic services, and will thereby provide an effective means for reliable nationwide communication among physicians, patients, and third parties. *CPT 2004* is the most recent revision of a work that first appeared in 1966.

CPT descriptive terms and identifying codes currently serve a wide variety of important functions in the field of medical nomenclature. The *CPT* book is useful for administrative management purposes such as claims processing and for the development of guidelines for medical care review. The uniform language is also applicable to medical education and outcomes, health services and quality research by providing a useful basis for local, regional, and national utilization comparisons. The *CPT* book is the most widely accepted nomenclature for the reporting of physician procedures and services under government and private health insurance programs. In 2000 the CPT Code Set was designated by the Department of Health and Human Services as the national coding standard for physician and other health care professional services and procedures under the Health Insurance Portability and Accountability Act (HIPAA). This means that for all financial and administrative health care transactions sent electronically, the CPT Code Set will need to be used.

The changes that appear in this revision have been prepared by the CPT Editorial Panel with the assistance of physicians representing all specialties of medicine, and with important contributions from many third party payors and governmental agencies.

The American Medical Association trusts that this revision will continue the usefulness of its predecessors in identifying, describing, and coding medical, surgical, and diagnostic services.

Michael D. Maves, MD, MBA
Executive Vice President, CEO

Acknowledgments

Publication of the annual *CPT* book represents many challenges and opportunities. From reconciling the many differences of opinion about the best way to describe a procedure, to the last details on placement of a semicolon, many individuals and organizations devote their energies and expertise to the preparation of this revision.

The editorial staff wishes to express sincere thanks to the many national medical specialty societies, health insurance organizations and agencies, and to the many individual physicians and other health professionals who have made contributions.

Thanks are due to Robert A. Musacchio, PhD, Sr VP, American Medical Association; Claudia Bonnell, Blue Cross and Blue Shield Association; Nelly Leon-Chisen, American Hospital Association; Thomas Musco, Health Insurance Association of America; and Sue Bowman, RHIA, American Health Information Management Association, for their invaluable assistance in enhancing the CPT Code Set.

And finally, our gratitude to AMA Press of the American Medical Association for their assistance in producing the books, diskettes, and CD-ROMs that contain the CPT Code Set: Anthony J. Frankos, Vice President, Business Products; Mike Desposito, Publisher; Elise Schumacher, Senior Acquisition Editor; J. D. Kinney, Director of Marketing; Jean Roberts, Director, Production and Manufacturing; Erin Kalitowski, Marketing Manager; Pat Lee, Technical Developmental Editor; Rosalyn Carlton, Senior Production Coordinator; Boon Ai Tan, Senior Production Coordinator; Ronnie Summers, Senior Print Coordinator; and Todd Feinstein, Application Developer.

American Occupational Therapy Association
Linda Botten, OTR, CHT, ATP
American Optometric Association
Mike Todd, OD
American Orthopaedic Association
Robert H. Haralson III, MD
American Orthopaedic Foot and Ankle Society
Walter J. Pedowitz, MD
American Osteopathic Association
Boyd R. Buser, DO
American Pediatric Surgical Association
John P. Crow, MD
American Physical Therapy Association
Rhea Cohn, PT
American Podiatric Medical Association
Robert D. Sowell, DPM
American Psychiatric Association
Chester W. Schmidt, Jr, MD
American Psychological Association
Antonio Puente, PhD
American Roentgen Ray Society
Geraldine B. McGinty, MD
American Society for Aesthetic Plastic Surgery
Paul R. Weiss, MD
American Society for Dermatologic Surgery
Pamela K. Phillips, MD
American Society for Gastrointestinal Endoscopy
Maurits J. Wiersema, MD
Klaus Mergener, MD**
American Society for Reproductive Medicine
John T. Queenan, Jr, MD
American Society for Surgery of the Hand
Daniel J. Nagle, MD
American Society for Therapeutic Radiology and Oncology
Paul E. Wallner, DO
American Society of Abdominal Surgeons
Louis F. Alfano, Jr, MD
American Society of Anesthesiologists
H. J. Przybylo, MD
American Society of Cataract and Refractive Surgery
Stephen S. Lane, MD
American Society of Clinical Oncology
Dean Gesme, MD
American Society of Clinical Pathologists
Mark S. Synovec, MD
American Society of Colon and Rectal Surgeons
David A. Margolin, MD
American Society of Cytopathology
David C. Hoak, MD
American Society of General Surgeons
Charles Drueck, MD
American Society of Hematology
Samuel M. Silver, MD, PhD
American Society of Neuroradiology
Robert A. Murray, MD
American Society of Ophthalmic Plastic and Reconstructive Surgery
David M. Reifler, MD
American Society of Plastic Surgeons
Raymond V. Janevicius, MD
American Speech-Language Hearing Association
R. Wayne Holland, EdD
American Thoracic Society
Scott Manaker, MD
American Urological Association
Jeffrey A. Dann, MD
Association of University Radiologists
Bob W. Gayler, MD
College of American Pathologists
Stephen N. Bauer, MD
Congress of Neurological Surgeons
R. Patrick Jacob, MD
Contact Lens Association of Ophthalmologists
Charles B. Slonim, MD, FACS
Endocrine Society
Richard A. Dickey, MD*
National Association of Social Workers
Nelda Spyres, ACSW, LCSW
North American Spine Society
Francis P. Lagattuta, MD
Radiologic Society of North America
Richard E. Fulton, MD
Renal Physicians Association
Richard J. Hamburger, MD
Society for Investigative Dermatology
Stephen P. Stone, MD
Society for Radiologists in Ultrasound
Robert L. Bree, MD
Society of American Gastrointestinal Endoscopic Surgeons
Eric G. Weiss, MD
Society of Critical Care Medicine
George A. Sample, MD
Society of Interventional Radiology
Gary S. Dorfman, MD
Society of Nuclear Medicine
Kenneth A. McKusick, MD
Society of Thoracic Surgeons
Keith S. Naunheim, MD
United States and Canadian Academy of Pathology
Beverly P. Nelson, MD

*New Advisors October 2002
**New Advisors June 2003

AMA Health Care Professionals Advisory Committee (HCPAC)

Tracy R. Gordy, MD, Co-Chair
AMA CPT Editorial Panel
Helene Fearon, PT, Co-Chair
Linda Botten, OTR, CHT, ATP
American Occupational Therapy Association
Patrick J. Cafferty, PA-C
American Academy of Physician Assistants
Rhea Cohn, PT
American Physical Therapy Association
R. Wayne Holland, EdD
American Speech-Language Hearing Association
Stephen S. Lane, MD
American Society of Cataract and Refractive Surgery
Craig S. Little, DC
American Chiropractic Association
Antonio Puente, PhD
American Psychological Association
Robert D. Sowell, DPM
American Podiatric Medical Association
Nelda Spyres, ACSW, LCSW
National Association of Social Workers
Ann M. Thrailkill, RN
American Nurses Association
Mike Todd, OD
American Optometric Association
Jane V. White, PhD, RD, FADA
American Dietetic Association

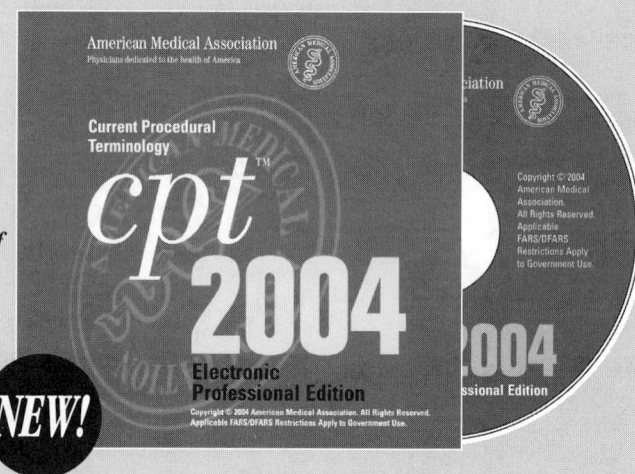

Contents

Introduction

Current Procedural Terminology, Fourth Edition (*CPT*®) is a set of codes, descriptions, and guidelines intended to describe procedures and services performed by physicians and other health care providers. Each procedure or service is identified with a five-digit code. The use of CPT codes simplifies the reporting of services.

Inclusion of a descriptor and its associated five-digit code number in the *CPT* book is based on the procedure being consistent with contemporary medical practice and being performed by many practitioners in clinical practice in multiple locations. Inclusion in the *CPT* book does not represent endorsement by the American Medical Association of any particular diagnostic or therapeutic procedure. Inclusion or exclusion of a procedure does not imply any health insurance coverage or reimbursement policy.

The main body of the material is listed in six sections. Each section is divided into subsections with anatomic, procedural, condition, or descriptor subheadings. The procedures and services with their identifying codes are presented in numeric order with one exception—the entire **Evaluation and Management** section (99201-99499) appears at the beginning of the listed procedures. These items are used by most physicians in reporting a significant portion of their services.

Section Numbers and Their Sequences

Evaluation and Management 99201-99499

Anesthesiology 00100-01999, 99100-99140

Surgery 10021-69990

Radiology (Including Nuclear Medicine and Diagnostic Ultrasound) 70010-79999

Pathology and Laboratory 80048-89356

Medicine (except Anesthesiology) 90281-99199, 99500-99602

The first and last code numbers and the subsection name of the items appear at the top of most pages (eg, "11055-11313 Surgery/Integumentary System"). The continuous pagination of the *CPT* book is found on the lower, outer margin of each page along with the section name.

Instructions for Use of the *CPT* Book

Select the name of the procedure or service that accurately identifies the service performed. Do not select a CPT code that merely approximates the service provided. If no such procedure or service exists, then report the service using the appropriate unlisted procedure or service code. In surgery, it may be an operation; in medicine, a diagnostic or therapeutic procedure; in radiology, a radiograph. Other additional procedures performed or pertinent special services are also listed. When necessary, any modifying or extenuating circumstances are added. Any service or procedure should be adequately documented in the medical record.

It is important to recognize that the listing of a service or procedure and its code number in a specific section of this book does not restrict its use to a specific specialty group. Any procedure or service in any section of this book may be used to designate the services rendered by any qualified physician or other qualified health care professional.

Format of the Terminology

Current Procedural Terminology (CPT) has been developed as stand-alone descriptions of medical procedures. However, some of the procedures in the *CPT* book are not printed in their entirety, but refer back to a common portion of the procedure listed in a preceding entry. This is evident when an entry is followed by one or more indentations. This is done in an effort to conserve space.

Example

25100 Arthrotomy, wrist joint; with biopsy

25105 with synovectomy

Note that the common part of code 25100 (that part before the semicolon) should be considered part of code 25105. Therefore, the full procedure represented by code 25105 should read:

25105 Arthrotomy, wrist joint; for synovectomy

Requests to Update the CPT Nomenclature

The effectiveness of the *Current Procedural Terminology* (*CPT*®) nomenclature depends on constant updating to reflect changes in medical practice. This can only be accomplished through the interest and timely suggestions of practicing physicians, medical specialty societies, state medical associations, and other organizations and agencies. Accordingly, the American Medical Association welcomes correspondence, inquiries, and suggestions concerning old and new procedures, as well as other matters such as codes and indices.

To submit a suggestion to add, delete, or revise procedures contained in the *CPT* book, please contact:

CPT Editorial Research & Development
American Medical Association
515 North State Street
Chicago, Illinois 60610

Coding change request forms are also available at the AMA/CPT website www.ama-assn.org/ama/pub/article/3866-3846.html.

All proposed changes of the *CPT* book will be considered by the CPT Editorial Panel with consultation of appropriate medical specialty societies.

Guidelines

Specific "Guidelines" are presented at the beginning of each of the six sections. These guidelines define items that are necessary to appropriately interpret and report the procedures and services contained in that section. For example, in the **Medicine** section, specific instructions are provided for handling unlisted services or procedures, special reports, and supplies and materials provided. Guidelines also provide explanations regarding terms that apply only to a particular section. For instance, **Radiology Guidelines** provide a definition of the unique term, "radiological supervision and interpretation." While in **Anesthesia**, a discussion of reporting time is included.

Add-on Codes

Some of the listed procedures are commonly carried out in addition to the primary procedure performed. These additional or supplemental procedures are designated as "add-on" codes with a "✚" symbol, and are listed in Appendix D of the *CPT* book. Add-on codes in *CPT 2004* can be readily identified by specific descriptor nomenclature which includes phrases such as "each additional" or "(List separately in addition to primary procedure)".

The "add-on" code concept in *CPT 2004* applies only to add-on procedures/services performed by the same physician. Add-on codes describe additional intra-service work associated with the primary procedure (eg, additional digit(s), lesion(s), neurorrhaphy(s), vertebral segment(s), tendon(s), joint(s)).

Add-on codes are always performed in addition to the primary service/procedure, and must never be reported as a stand-alone code. All add-on codes found in the *CPT* book are exempt from the multiple procedure concept (see modifier '-51' definition included in **Appendix A**).

Modifiers

A modifier provides the means by which the reporting physician can indicate that a service or procedure that has been performed has been altered by some specific circumstance but not changed in its definition or code. The judicious application of modifiers obviates the necessity for separate procedure listings that may describe the modifying circumstance. Modifiers may be used to indicate to the recipient of a report that:

- A service or procedure has both a professional and technical component.
- A service or procedure was performed by more than one physician and/or in more than one location.
- A service or procedure has been increased or reduced.
- Only part of a service was performed.
- An adjunctive service was performed.
- A bilateral procedure was performed.
- A service or procedure was provided more than once.
- Unusual events occurred.

Example

A physician providing diagnostic or therapeutic radiology services, ultrasound or nuclear medicine services in a hospital would add the modifier '-26' to report the professional component.

73090-26 = Professional component only for an x-ray of the forearm

Example

Two surgeons may be required to manage a specific surgical problem. When two surgeons work together as primary surgeons performing distinct part(s) of a procedure, each surgeon should report his/her distinct operative work by adding the modifier '-62' to the procedure code and any associated code(s) for that procedure as long as both surgeons continue to work together as primary surgeons. Each surgeon should report the co-surgery once using the same procedure code. The modifier '-62' would be applicable. For instance, a neurological surgeon and an otolaryngologist are working as co-surgeons in performing transphenoidal excision of a pituitary neoplasm.

61548-62 = Hypophysectomy or excision of pituitary tumor, transnasal or transseptal approach, nonstereotactic + two surgeons modifier

AND the second surgeon would report:

61548-62 = Hypophysectomy or excision of pituitary tumor, transnasal or transseptal approach, nonstereotactic + two surgeons modifier

If additional procedure(s) (including add-on procedure(s)) are performed during the same surgical session, separate code(s) may also be reported with the modifier '-62' added. **Note:** If a co-surgeon acts as an assistant in the performance of additional procedure(s) during the same surgical session, those services may be reported using separate procedure code(s) with the modifier '-80' or modifier '-82' added, as appropriate. A complete listing of modifiers is found in Appendix A.

Unlisted Procedure or Service

It is recognized that there may be services or procedures performed by physicians that are not found in the *CPT* book. Therefore, a number of specific code numbers have been designated for reporting unlisted procedures. When an unlisted procedure number is used, the service or procedure should be described. Each of these unlisted procedural code numbers (with the appropriate accompanying topical entry) relates to a specific section of the book and is presented in the Guidelines of that section.

Special Report

A service that is rarely provided, unusual, variable, or new may require a special report in determining medical appropriateness of the service. Pertinent information should include an adequate definition or description of the nature, extent, and need for the procedure; and the time, effort, and equipment necessary to provide the service. Additional items which may be included are: complexity of symptoms, final diagnosis, pertinent physical findings, diagnostic and therapeutic procedures, concurrent problems, and follow-up care.

Code Changes

A summary listing of additions, deletions, and revisions applicable to the *CPT* book is found in **Appendix B**. New procedure numbers added to the CPT book are identified throughout the text with the symbol "●" placed before the code number. In instances where a code revision has resulted in a substantially altered procedure descriptor, the symbol "▲" is placed before the code number. The symbols "► ◄" are used to indicate new and revised text other than the procedure descriptors. CPT add-on codes are annotated by a "✚" symbol and are listed in **Appendix D**. The "⊘" symbol is used to identify codes that are exempt from the use of modifier '-51', but have not been designated as CPT add-on procedures/services. A list of codes exempt from modifier '-51' usage is included in **Appendix E**.

Alphabetical Reference Index

An expanded alphabetical index is found in the back of the book. It includes listings by procedure and anatomic site. Procedures and services commonly known by their eponyms or other designations are also included.

CPT in Electronic Formats

CPT 2004 procedure codes and descriptors are also available on diskettes and CD-ROM in various formats. For more information call 800 621-8335.

Visit CPT on the AMA Website
www.ama-assn.org/go/cpt

CPT Assistant Newsletter and *CPT Changes: An Insider's View* References

References Contained within *CPT 2004* Professional

The symbol "➲" below many codes throughout the book has been included to indicate that the American Medical Association (AMA) has published reference material on that particular code.

The "➲" symbol refers to two AMA publications — the *CPT Assistant* monthly newsletter and *CPT Changes: An Insider's View*, an annual book with all of the coding changes for the current year.

How to Read the References

Example

✚ **34808** Endovascular placement of iliac artery occlusion device (List separately in addition to code for primary procedure)

➲ *CPT Assistant* Dec 00:1; *CPT Changes: An Insider's View* 2001

This reference indicates that in the *CPT Assistant* newsletter, December 2000 issue, page 1, and in *CPT Changes: An Insider's View* 2001 edition, material is available that may assist in understanding the application of the code.

How to Obtain the Referenced Publications

CPT Assistant annual subscriptions can be purchased by calling the AMA's Customer Service Department at 800 621-8335. Individual back issues are available for purchase and immediate download at **www.ama-assn.org/go/cpt/online**.

Current and past editions of *CPT Changes: An Insider's View* can be purchased by calling the AMA's Customer Service Department at 800 621-8335, or online at **www.amapress.com**.

CPT 2004 Book Features

Summary of Additions, Deletions, and Revisions Included in Appendix B

Appendix B contains code numbers and indicates whether a code was added, revised, or deleted. Deleted language appears with a ~~strikethrough~~, while new text appears underlined. This gives users a quick reference to the changes, without having to refer to the previous edition for the original code language.

"Bleed" Tabs for Sections

The "bleed" tabs along the edge of the pages give users a visual reference to the sections of the CPT book.

The following features appear only in the *CPT* Professional Edition.

Place-of-Service Codes

The *CPT* book now contains the list of Place-of-Service codes. These codes are used on professional claims to specify the entity where service(s) are rendered. Users are required to check with their individual payers to determine whether a particular code will be recognized for payment purposes.

Color to Indicate Changed Text

Green text indicates a change. We continue to use the ► ◄ to indicate specific words or sections that contain changes, but by using color, the changed text is easier to notice.

Color "Bleeds" for Sections

Color bleeds on each page of the book make it even easier to navigate through the book, giving users a visual guide. The thumb notches remain for those who prefer the tactile approach.

Thumb Notched Pages

Separate "thumb notches" make it easy to locate the various sections of the book.

Illustrations

The CPT Professional book contains many anatomical and procedural illustrations to help users visualize the codes.

Note: In 2003, Appendix C (Update to Short Descriptors) was deleted. Because of this, Appendices D, E, and F, now are C, D, and E, respectively.

Evaluation and Management (E/M) Services Guidelines

In addition to the information presented in the **Introduction,** several other items unique to this section are defined or identified here.

Classification of Evaluation and Management (E/M) Services

The E/M section is divided into broad categories such as office visits, hospital visits, and consultations. Most of the categories are further divided into two or more subcategories of E/M services. For example, there are two subcategories of office visits (new patient and established patient) and there are two subcategories of hospital visits (initial and subsequent). The subcategories of E/M services are further classified into levels of E/M services that are identified by specific codes. This classification is important because the nature of physician work varies by type of service, place of service, and the patient's status.

The basic format of the levels of E/M services is the same for most categories. First, a unique code number is listed. Second, the place and/or type of service is specified, eg, office consultation. Third, the content of the service is defined, eg, comprehensive history and comprehensive examination. (See "Levels of E/M Services," page 2, for details on the content of E/M services.) Fourth, the nature of the presenting problem(s) usually associated with a given level is described. Fifth, the time typically required to provide the service is specified. (A detailed discussion of time is provided on page 3.)

Definitions of Commonly Used Terms

Certain key words and phrases are used throughout the E/M section. The following definitions are intended to reduce the potential for differing interpretations and to increase the consistency of reporting by physicians in differing specialties.

New and Established Patient

Solely for the purposes of distinguishing between new and established patients, **professional services** are those face-to-face services rendered by a physician and reported by a specific CPT code(s). A new patient is one who has not received any professional services from the physician or another physician of the same specialty who belongs to the same group practice, within the past three years.

An established patient is one who has received professional services from the physician or another physician of the same specialty who belongs to the same group practice, within the past three years.

In the instance where a physician is on call for or covering for another physician, the patient's encounter will be classified as it would have been by the physician who is not available.

No distinction is made between new and established patients in the emergency department. E/M services in the emergency department category may be reported for any new or established patient who presents for treatment in the emergency department.

Chief Complaint

A concise statement describing the symptom, problem, condition, diagnosis or other factor that is the reason for the encounter, usually stated in the patient's words.

Concurrent Care

Concurrent care is the provision of similar services, eg, hospital visits, to the same patient by more than one physician on the same day. When concurrent care is provided, no special reporting is required. Modifier '-75' has been deleted.

Counseling

Counseling is a discussion with a patient and/or family concerning one or more of the following areas:

- diagnostic results, impressions, and/or recommended diagnostic studies;
- prognosis;
- risks and benefits of management (treatment) options;
- instructions for management (treatment) and/or follow-up;

- importance of compliance with chosen management (treatment) options;
- risk factor reduction; and
- patient and family education.

(For psychotherapy, see 90804-90857)

Family History

A review of medical events in the patient's family that includes significant information about:

- the health status or cause of death of parents, siblings, and children;
- specific diseases related to problems identified in the Chief Complaint or History of the Present Illness, and/or System Review;
- diseases of family members which may be hereditary or place the patient at risk.

History of Present Illness

A chronological description of the development of the patient's present illness from the first sign and/or symptom to the present. This includes a description of location, quality, severity, timing, context, modifying factors and associated signs and symptoms significantly related to the presenting problem(s).

Levels of E/M Services

Within each category or subcategory of E/M service, there are three to five levels of E/M services available for reporting purposes. Levels of E/M services are **not** interchangeable among the different categories or subcategories of service. For example, the first level of E/M services in the subcategory of office visit, new patient, does not have the same definition as the first level of E/M services in the subcategory of office visit, established patient.

The levels of E/M services include examinations, evaluations, treatments, conferences with or concerning patients, preventive pediatric and adult health supervision, and similar medical services, such as the determination of the need and/or location for appropriate care. Medical screening includes the history, examination, and medical decision-making required to determine the need and/or location for appropriate care and treatment of the patient (eg, office and other outpatient setting, emergency department, nursing facility, etc.). The levels of E/M services encompass the wide variations in skill, effort, time, responsibility and medical knowledge required for the prevention or diagnosis and treatment of illness or injury and the promotion of optimal health. Each level of E/M services may be used by all physicians.

The descriptors for the levels of E/M services recognize seven components, six of which are used in defining the levels of E/M services. These components are:

- history;
- examination;
- medical decision making;
- counseling;
- coordination of care;
- nature of presenting problem; and
- time.

The first three of these components (history, examination, and medical decision making) are considered the **key** components in selecting a level of E/M services. (See "Determine the Extent of History Obtained," page 5.)

The next three components (counseling, coordination of care, and the nature of the presenting problem) are considered **contributory** factors in the majority of encounters. Although the first two of these contributory factors are important E/M services, it is not required that these services be provided at every patient encounter.

Coordination of care with other providers or agencies without a patient encounter on that day is reported using the case management codes.

The final component, time, is discussed in detail (see page 3).

Any specifically identifiable procedure (ie, identified with a specific CPT code) performed on or subsequent to the date of initial or subsequent "E/M Services" should be reported separately.

The actual performance and/or interpretation of diagnostic tests/studies ordered during a patient encounter are not included in the levels of E/M services. Physician performance of diagnostic tests/studies for which specific CPT codes are available may be reported separately, in addition to the appropriate E/M code. The physician's interpretation of the results of diagnostic tests/studies (ie, professional component) with preparation of a separate distinctly identifiable signed written report may also be reported separately, using the appropriate CPT code with the modifier '-26' appended.

The physician may need to indicate that on the day a procedure or service identified by a CPT code was performed, the patient's condition required a significant separately identifiable E/M service above and beyond other services provided or beyond the usual preservice and postservice care associated with the procedure that was performed. The E/M service may be caused or prompted by the symptoms or condition for which the procedure and/or service was provided. This circumstance may be reported by adding the modifier '-25' to the appropriate level of E/M service. As such, different diagnoses are not required for reporting of the procedure and the E/M services on the same date.

Nature of Presenting Problem

A presenting problem is a disease, condition, illness, injury, symptom, sign, finding, complaint, or other reason for encounter, with or without a diagnosis being established at the time of the encounter. The E/M codes recognize five types of presenting problems that are defined as follows:

Minimal: A problem that may not require the presence of the physician, but service is provided under the physician's supervision.

Self-limited or minor: A problem that runs a definite and prescribed course, is transient in nature, and is not likely to permanently alter health status OR has a good prognosis with management/compliance.

Low severity: A problem where the risk of morbidity without treatment is low; there is little to no risk of mortality without treatment; full recovery without functional impairment is expected.

Moderate severity: A problem where the risk of morbidity without treatment is moderate; there is moderate risk of mortality without treatment; uncertain prognosis OR increased probability of prolonged functional impairment.

High severity: A problem where the risk of morbidity without treatment is high to extreme; there is a moderate to high risk of mortality without treatment OR high probability of severe, prolonged functional impairment.

Past History

A review of the patient's past experiences with illnesses, injuries, and treatments that includes significant information about:

- prior major illnesses and injuries;
- prior operations;
- prior hospitalizations;
- current medications;
- allergies (eg, drug, food);
- age appropriate immunization status;
- age appropriate feeding/dietary status.

Social History

An age appropriate review of past and current activities that includes significant information about:

- marital status and/or living arrangements;
- current employment;
- occupational history;
- use of drugs, alcohol, and tobacco;
- level of education;
- sexual history;
- other relevant social factors.

System Review (Review of Systems)

An inventory of body systems obtained through a series of questions seeking to identify signs and/or symptoms which the patient may be experiencing or has experienced. For the purposes of CPT the following elements of a system review have been identified:

- Constitutional symptoms (fever, weight loss, etc.)
- Eyes
- Ears, Nose, Mouth, Throat
- Cardiovascular
- Respiratory
- Gastrointestinal
- Genitourinary
- Musculoskeletal
- Integumentary (skin and/or breast)
- Neurological
- Psychiatric
- Endocrine
- Hematologic/Lymphatic
- Allergic/Immunologic

The review of systems helps define the problem, clarify the differential diagnosis, identify needed testing, or serves as baseline data on other systems that might be affected by any possible management options.

Time

The inclusion of time in the definitions of levels of E/M services has been implicit in prior editions of *CPT.* The inclusion of time as an explicit factor beginning in *CPT 1992* is done to assist physicians in selecting the most appropriate level of E/M services. It should be recognized that the specific times expressed in the visit code descriptors are averages, and therefore represent a range of times which may be higher or lower depending on actual clinical circumstances.

Time is **not** a descriptive component for the emergency department levels of E/M services because emergency department services are typically provided on a variable intensity basis, often involving multiple encounters with several patients over an extended period of time. Therefore, it is often difficult for physicians to provide accurate estimates of the time spent face-to-face with the patient.

Studies to establish levels of E/M services employed surveys of practicing physicians to obtain data on the amount of time and work associated with typical E/M services. Since "work" is not easily quantifiable, the codes must rely on other objective, verifiable measures that correlate with physicians' estimates of their "work". It has been demonstrated that physicians' estimations of **intraservice time** (as explained on the next page), both within and across specialties, is a variable that is predictive of the "work" of E/M services. This same research has shown there is a strong relationship between intra-service time and total time for E/M services. Intra-service time, rather than total time, was chosen for inclusion with the codes because of its relative ease of measurement and because of its direct correlation with measurements of the total amount of time and work associated with typical E/M services.

Intra-service times are defined as **face-to-face** time for office and other outpatient visits and as **unit/floor** time for hospital and other inpatient visits. This distinction is necessary because most of the work of typical office visits takes place during the face-to-face time with the patient, while most of the work of typical hospital visits takes place during the time spent on the patient's floor or unit.

Face-to-face time (office and other outpatient visits and office consultations): For coding purposes, face-to-face time for these services is defined as only that time that the physician spends face-to-face with the patient and/or family. This includes the time in which the physician performs such tasks as obtaining a history, performing an examination, and counseling the patient.

Physicians also spend time doing work before or after the face-to-face time with the patient, performing such tasks as reviewing records and tests, arranging for further services, and communicating further with other professionals and the patient through written reports and telephone contact.

This **non-face-to-face** time for office services—also called pre- and post-encounter time—is not included in the time component described in the E/M codes. However, the pre- and post-face-to-face work associated with an encounter was included in calculating the total work of typical services in physician surveys.

Thus, the face-to-face time associated with the services described by any E/M code is a valid proxy for the total work done before, during, and after the visit.

Unit/floor time (hospital observation services, inpatient hospital care, initial and follow-up hospital consultations, nursing facility): For reporting purposes, intra-service time for these services is defined as unit/floor time, which includes the time that the physician is present on the patient's hospital unit and at the bedside rendering services for that patient. This includes the time in which the physician establishes and/or reviews the patient's chart, examines the patient, writes notes and communicates with other professionals and the patient's family.

In the hospital, pre- and post-time includes time spent off the patient's floor performing such tasks as reviewing pathology and radiology findings in another part of the hospital.

This pre- and post-visit time is not included in the time component described in these codes. However, the pre- and post-work performed during the time spent off the floor or unit was included in calculating the total work of typical services in physician surveys.

Thus, the unit/floor time associated with the services described by any code is a valid proxy for the total work done before, during, and after the visit.

Unlisted Service

An E/M service may be provided that is not listed in this section of *CPT*. When reporting such a service, the appropriate "Unlisted" code may be used to indicate the service, identifying it by "Special Report", as discussed in the following paragraph. The "Unlisted Services" and accompanying codes for the E/M section are as follows:

99429 Unlisted preventive medicine service

99499 Unlisted evaluation and management service

Special Report

An unlisted service or one that is unusual, variable, or new may require a special report demonstrating the medical appropriateness of the service. Pertinent information should include an adequate definition or description of the nature, extent, and need for the procedure; and the time, effort, and equipment necessary to provide the service. Additional items which may be included are complexity of symptoms, final diagnosis, pertinent physical findings, diagnostic and therapeutic procedures, concurrent problems, and follow-up care.

Clinical Examples

Clinical examples of the codes for E/M services are provided to assist physicians in understanding the meaning of the descriptors and selecting the correct code. The clinical examples are listed in Appendix C. Each example was developed by physicians in the specialties shown.

The same problem, when seen by physicians in different specialties, may involve different amounts of work. Therefore, the appropriate level of encounter should be reported using the descriptors rather than the examples.

The examples have been tested for validity and approved by the CPT Editorial Panel. Physicians were given the examples and asked to assign a code or assess the amount of time and work involved. Only those examples that were rated consistently have been included in Appendix C.

Table 1
Categories and Subcategories of Service

Category/Subcategory	Code Numbers
Office or Other Outpatient Services	
New Patient	99201-99205
Established Patient	99211-99215
Hospital Observation Discharge Services	99217
Hospital Observation Services	99218-99220
Hospital Observation or Inpatient Care Services (Including Admission and Discharge Services)	99234-99236
Hospital Inpatient Services	
Initial Hospital Care	99221-99223
Subsequent Hospital Care	99231-99233
Hospital Discharge Services	99238-99239
Consultations	
Office Consultations	99241-99245
Initial Inpatient Consultations	99251-99255
Follow-up Inpatient Consultations	99261-99263
Confirmatory Consultations	99271-99275
Emergency Department Services	99281-99288
Pediatric Patient Transport	99289-99290
Critical Care Services	
Adult (over 24 months of age)	99291-99292
Pediatric	99293-99294
Neonatal	99295-99296
Intensive Care (Low Birth Weight)	99298-99299
Nursing Facility Services	
Comprehensive Nursing Facility Assessments	99301-99303
Subsequent Nursing Facility Care	99311-99313
Nursing Facility Discharge Services	99315-99316
Domiciliary, Rest Home or Custodial Care Services	
New Patient	99321-99323
Established Patient	99331-99333
Home Services	
New Patient	99341-99345
Established Patient	99347-99350
Prolonged Services	
With Direct Patient Contact	99354-99357
Without Direct Patient Contact	99358-99359
Standby Services	99360
Case Management Services	
Team Conferences	99361-99362
Telephone Calls	99371-99373
Care Plan Oversight Services	99374-99380
Preventive Medicine Services	
New Patient	99381-99387
Established Patient	99391-99397
Individual Counseling	99401-99404
Group Counseling	99411-99412
Other	99420-99429
Newborn Care	99431-99440
Special E/M Services	99450-99456
Other E/M Services	99499

Instructions for Selecting a Level of E/M Service

Identify the Category and Subcategory of Service

The categories and subcategories of codes available for reporting E/M services are shown in Table 1 above.

Review the Reporting Instructions for the Selected Category or Subcategory

Most of the categories and many of the subcategories of service have special guidelines or instructions unique to that category or subcategory. Where these are indicated, eg, "Inpatient Hospital Care," special instructions will be presented preceding the levels of E/M services.

Review the Level of E/M Service Descriptors and Examples in the Selected Category or Subcategory

The descriptors for the levels of E/M services recognize seven components, six of which are used in defining the levels of E/M services. These components are:

- history;
- examination;
- medical decision making;
- counseling;
- coordination of care;
- nature of presenting problem; and
- time.

The first three of these components (ie, history, examination, and medical decision making) should be considered the **key** components in selecting the level of E/M services. An exception to this rule is in the case of visits which consist predominantly of counseling or coordination of care (See numbered paragraph 3, page 7.)

The nature of the presenting problem and time are provided in some levels to assist the physician in determining the appropriate level of E/M service.

Determine the Extent of History Obtained

The extent of the history is dependent upon clinical judgment and on the nature of the presenting problems(s). The levels of E/M services recognize four types of history that are defined as follows:

Problem focused: chief complaint; brief history of present illness or problem.

Expanded problem focused: chief complaint; brief history of present illness; problem pertinent system review.

Detailed: chief complaint; extended history of present illness; problem pertinent system review extended to include a review of a limited number of additional systems; **pertinent** past, family, and/or social history **directly related to the patient's problems.**

Comprehensive: chief complaint; extended history of present illness; review of systems which is directly related to the problem(s) identified in the history of the present illness plus a review of all additional body systems; **complete** past, family, and social history.

The comprehensive history obtained as part of the preventive medicine evaluation and management service is not problem-oriented and does not involve a chief complaint or present illness. It does, however, include a comprehensive system review and comprehensive or interval past, family, and social history as well as a comprehensive assessment/history of pertinent risk factors.

Determine the Extent of Examination Performed

The extent of the examination performed is dependent on clinical judgment and on the nature of the presenting problem(s). The levels of E/M services recognize four types of examination that are defined as follows:

Problem focused: a limited examination of the affected body area or organ system.

Expanded problem focused: a limited examination of the affected body area or organ system and other symptomatic or related organ system(s).

Detailed: an extended examination of the affected body area(s) and other symptomatic or related organ system(s).

Comprehensive: a general multi-system examination or a complete examination of a single organ system. **Note:** The comprehensive examination performed as part of the preventive medicine evaluation and management service is multisystem, but its extent is based on age and risk factors identified.

For the purposes of these CPT definitions, the following body areas are recognized:

- Head, including the face
- Neck
- Chest, including breasts and axilla
- Abdomen
- Genitalia, groin, buttocks
- Back
- Each extremity

For the purposes of these CPT definitions, the following organ systems are recognized:

- Eyes
- Ears, Nose, Mouth, and Throat
- Cardiovascular
- Respiratory
- Gastrointestinal
- Genitourinary
- Musculoskeletal
- Skin
- Neurologic
- Psychiatric
- Hematologic/Lymphatic/Immunologic

Determine the Complexity of Medical Decision Making

Medical decision making refers to the complexity of establishing a diagnosis and/or selecting a management option as measured by:

- the number of possible diagnoses and/or the number of management options that must be considered;
- the amount and/or complexity of medical records, diagnostic tests, and/or other information that must be obtained, reviewed, and analyzed; and
- the risk of significant complications, morbidity, and/or mortality, as well as comorbidities, associated with the patient's presenting problems(s), the diagnostic procedure(s) and/or the possible management options.

Four types of medical decision making are recognized: straightforward; low complexity; moderate complexity; and high complexity. To qualify for a given type of decision making, two of the three elements in Table 2 on the following page must be met or exceeded.

Comorbidities/underlying diseases, in and of themselves, are not considered in selecting a level of E/M services *unless* their presence significantly increases the complexity of the medical decision making.

Select the Appropriate Level of E/M Services Based on the Following

1. For the following categories/subcategories, **all of the key components,** ie, history, examination, and medical decision making, must meet or exceed the stated requirements to qualify for a particular level of E/M service: office, new patient; hospital observation services; initial hospital care; office consultations; initial inpatient consultations; confirmatory consultations; emergency department services; comprehensive nursing facility assessments; domiciliary care, new patient; and home, new patient.

Table 2
Complexity of Medical Decision Making

Number of Diagnoses or Management Options	Amount and/or Complexity of Data to be Reviewed	Risk of Complications and/or Morbidity or Mortality	Type of Decision Making
minimal	minimal or none	minimal	**straightforward**
limited	limited	low	**low complexity**
multiple	moderate	moderate	**moderate complexity**
extensive	extensive	high	**high complexity**

2. For the following categories/subcategories, **two of the three key components** (ie, history, examination, and medical decision making) must meet or exceed the stated requirements to qualify for a particular level of E/M services: office, established patient; subsequent hospital care; follow-up inpatient consultations; subsequent nursing facility care; domiciliary care, established patient; and home, established patient.

3. When counseling and/or coordination of care dominates (more than 50%) the physician/patient and/or family encounter (face-to-face time in the office or other outpatient setting or floor/unit time in the hospital or nursing facility), then **time** may be considered the key or controlling factor to qualify for a particular level of E/M services. This includes time spent with parties who have assumed responsibility for the care of the patient or decision making whether or not they are family members (eg, foster parents, person acting in locum parentis, legal guardian). The extent of counseling and/or coordination of care must be documented in the medical record.

Notes

Evaluation and Management

Office or Other Outpatient Services

The following codes are used to report evaluation and management services provided in the physician's office or in an outpatient or other ambulatory facility. A patient is considered an outpatient until inpatient admission to a health care facility occurs.

To report services provided to a patient who is admitted to a hospital or nursing facility in the course of an encounter in the office or other ambulatory facility, see the notes for initial hospital inpatient care (page 11) or comprehensive nursing facility assessments (page 22).

For services provided by physicians in the emergency department, see 99281-99285.

For observation care, see 99217-99220.

For observation or inpatient care services (including admission and discharge services), see 99234-99236.

New Patient

99201 **Office or other outpatient visit** for the evaluation and management of a new patient, which requires these three key components:

- **a problem focused history;**
- **a problem focused examination; and**
- **straightforward medical decision making.**

Counseling and/or coordination of care with other providers or agencies are provided consistent with the nature of the problem(s) and the patient's and/or family's needs.

Usually, the presenting problems are self limited or minor. Physicians typically spend 10 minutes face-to-face with the patient and/or family.

99202 **Office or other outpatient visit** for the evaluation and management of a new patient, which requires these three key components:

- **an expanded problem focused history;**
- **an expanded problem focused examination; and**
- **straightforward medical decision making.**

Counseling and/or coordination of care with other providers or agencies are provided consistent with the nature of the problem(s) and the patient's and/or family's needs.

Usually, the presenting problem(s) are of low to moderate severity. Physicians typically spend 20 minutes face-to-face with the patient and/or family.

99203 **Office or other outpatient visit** for the evaluation and management of a new patient, which requires these three key components:

- **a detailed history;**
- **a detailed examination; and**
- **medical decision making of low complexity.**

Counseling and/or coordination of care with other providers or agencies are provided consistent with the nature of the problem(s) and the patient's and/or family's needs.

Usually, the presenting problem(s) are of moderate severity. Physicians typically spend 30 minutes face-to-face with the patient and/or family.

99204 **Office or other outpatient visit** for the evaluation and management of a new patient, which requires these three key components:

- **a comprehensive history;**
- **a comprehensive examination; and**
- **medical decision making of moderate complexity.**

Counseling and/or coordination of care with other providers or agencies are provided consistent with the nature of the problem(s) and the patient's and/or family's needs.

Usually, the presenting problem(s) are of moderate to high severity. Physicians typically spend 45 minutes face-to-face with the patient and/or family.

99205 **Office or other outpatient visit** for the evaluation and management of a new patient, which requires these three key components:

- **a comprehensive history;**
- **a comprehensive examination; and**
- **medical decision making of high complexity.**

Counseling and/or coordination of care with other providers or agencies are provided consistent with the nature of the problem(s) and the patient's and/or family's needs.

Usually, the presenting problem(s) are of moderate to high severity. Physicians typically spend 60 minutes face-to-face with the patient and/or family.

Established Patient

99211 **Office or other outpatient visit** for the evaluation and management of an established patient, that may not require the presence of a physician. Usually, the presenting problem(s) are minimal. Typically, 5 minutes are spent performing or supervising these services.

99212 **Office or other outpatient visit** for the evaluation and management of an established patient, which requires at least two of these three key components:

- **a problem focused history;**
- **a problem focused examination;**
- **straightforward medical decision making.**

Counseling and/or coordination of care with other providers or agencies are provided consistent with the nature of the problem(s) and the patient's and/or family's needs.

Usually, the presenting problem(s) are self limited or minor. Physicians typically spend 10 minutes face-to-face with the patient and/or family.

99213 **Office or other outpatient visit** for the evaluation and management of an established patient, which requires at least two of these three key components:

- **an expanded problem focused history;**
- **an expanded problem focused examination;**
- **medical decision making of low complexity.**

Counseling and coordination of care with other providers or agencies are provided consistent with the nature of the problem(s) and the patient's and/or family's needs.

Usually, the presenting problem(s) are of low to moderate severity. Physicians typically spend 15 minutes face-to-face with the patient and/or family.

99214 **Office or other outpatient visit** for the evaluation and management of an established patient, which requires at least two of these three key components:

- **a detailed history;**
- **a detailed examination;**
- **medical decision making of moderate complexity.**

Counseling and/or coordination of care with other providers or agencies are provided consistent with the nature of the problem(s) and the patient's and/or family's needs.

Usually, the presenting problem(s) are of moderate to high severity. Physicians typically spend 25 minutes face-to-face with the patient and/or family.

99215 **Office or other outpatient visit** for the evaluation and management of an established patient, which requires at least two of these three key components:

- **a comprehensive history;**
- **a comprehensive examination;**
- **medical decision making of high complexity.**

Counseling and/or coordination of care with other providers or agencies are provided consistent with the nature of the problem(s) and the patient's and/or family's needs.

Usually, the presenting problem(s) are of moderate to high severity. Physicians typically spend 40 minutes face-to-face with the patient and/or family.

Hospital Observation Services

The following codes are used to report evaluation and management services provided to patients designated/admitted as "observation status" in a hospital. It is not necessary that the patient be located in an observation area designated by the hospital.

If such an area does exist in a hospital (as a separate unit in the hospital, in the emergency department, etc.), these codes are to be utilized if the patient is placed in such an area.

For definitions of key components and commonly used terms, please see **Evaluation and Management Services Guidelines.**

Typical times have not yet been established for this category of services.

Observation Care Discharge Services

Observation care discharge of a patient from "observation status" includes final examination of the patient, discussion of the hospital stay, instructions for continuing care, and preparation of discharge records. For observation or inpatient hospital care including the admission and discharge of the patient on the same date, see codes 99234-99236 as appropriate.

99217 **Observation care discharge** day management (This code is to be utilized by the physician to report all services provided to a patient on discharge from "observation status" if the discharge is on other than the initial date of "observation status." To report services to a patient designated as "observation status" or "inpatient status" and discharged on the same date, use the codes for Observation or Inpatient Care Services [including Admission and Discharge Services, 99234-99236 as appropriate.])

Initial Observation Care

New or Established Patient

The following codes are used to report the encounter(s) by the supervising physician with the patient when designated as "observation status." This refers to the initiation of observation status, supervision of the care plan for observation and performance of periodic reassessments. For observation encounters by other physicians, see Office or Other Outpatient Consultation codes (99241-99245).

To report services provided to a patient who is admitted to the hospital after receiving hospital observation care services on the same date, see the notes for initial hospital inpatient care (page 11). For a patient admitted to the hospital on a date subsequent to the date of observation status, the hospital admission would be reported with the appropriate Initial Hospital Care codes (99221-99223). For a patient admitted and discharged from observation or inpatient status on the same date, the services should be reported with codes 99234-99236 as appropriate. Do not report observation discharge (99217) in conjunction with a hospital admission.

When "observation status" is initiated in the course of an encounter in another site of service (eg, hospital emergency department, physician's office, nursing facility) all evaluation and management services provided by the supervising physician in conjunction with initiating "observation status" are considered part of the initial observation care when performed on the same date. The observation care level of service reported by the supervising physician should include the services related to initiating "observation status" provided in the other sites of service as well as in the observation setting.

Evaluation and management services on the same date provided in sites that are related to initiating "observation status" should NOT be reported separately.

These codes may not be utilized for post-operative recovery if the procedure is considered part of the surgical "package." These codes apply to all evaluation and management services that are provided on the same date of initiating "observation status."

99218 **Initial observation care,** per day, for the evaluation and management of a patient which requires these three key components:

- **a detailed or comprehensive history;**
- **a detailed or comprehensive examination; and**
- **medical decision making that is straightforward or of low complexity.**

Counseling and/or coordination of care with other providers or agencies are provided consistent with the nature of the problem(s) and the patient's and/or family's needs.

Usually, the problem(s) requiring admission to "observation status" are of low severity.

99219 **Initial observation care,** per day, for the evaluation and management of a patient, which requires these three key components:

- **a comprehensive history;**
- **a comprehensive examination; and**
- **medical decision making of moderate complexity.**

Counseling and/or coordination of care with other providers or agencies are provided consistent with the nature of the problem(s) and the patient's and/or family's needs.

Usually, the problem(s) requiring admission to "observation status" are of moderate severity.

99220 **Initial observation care,** per day, for the evaluation and management of a patient, which requires these three key components:

- **a comprehensive history;**
- **a comprehensive examination; and**
- **medical decision making of high complexity.**

Counseling and/or coordination of care with other providers or agencies are provided consistent with the nature of the problem(s) and the patient's and/or family's needs.

Usually, the problem(s) requiring admission to "observation status" are of high severity.

Hospital Inpatient Services

The following codes are used to report evaluation and management services provided to hospital inpatients. Hospital inpatient services include those services provided to patients in a "partial hospital" setting. These codes are to be used to report these partial hospitalization services. See also psychiatry notes in the full text of *CPT.*

For definitions of key components and commonly used terms, please see **Evaluation and Management Services Guidelines.** For Hospital Observation Services, see 99218-99220. For a patient admitted and discharged from observation or inpatient status on the same date, the services should be reported with codes 99234-99236 as appropriate.

Initial Hospital Care

New or Established Patient

The following codes are used to report the first hospital inpatient encounter with the patient by the admitting physician.

For initial inpatient encounters by physicians other than the admitting physician, see initial inpatient consultation codes (99251-99255) or subsequent hospital care codes (99231-99233) as appropriate.

When the patient is admitted to the hospital as an inpatient in the course of an encounter in another site of service (eg, hospital emergency department, observation status in a hospital, physician's office, nursing facility) all evaluation and management services provided by that physician in conjunction with that admission are considered part of the initial hospital care when performed on the same date as the admission. The inpatient care level of service reported by the admitting physician should include the services related to the admission he/she provided in the other sites of service as well as in the inpatient setting.

Evaluation and management services on the same date provided in sites that are related to the admission "observation status" should NOT be reported separately. For a patient admitted and discharged from observation or inpatient status on the same date, the services should be reported with codes 99234-99236 as appropriate.

99221 **Initial hospital care,** per day, for the evaluation and management of a patient which requires these three key components:

- **a detailed or comprehensive history;**
- **a detailed or comprehensive examination; and**
- **medical decision making that is straightforward or of low complexity.**

Counseling and/or coordination of care with other providers or agencies are provided consistent with the nature of the problem(s) and the patient's and/or family's needs.

Usually, the problem(s) requiring admission are of low severity. Physicians typically spend 30 minutes at the bedside and on the patient's hospital floor or unit.

99222 **Initial hospital care,** per day, for the evaluation and management of a patient, which requires these three key components:

- **a comprehensive history;**
- **a comprehensive examination; and**
- **medical decision making of moderate complexity.**

Counseling and/or coordination of care with other providers or agencies are provided consistent with the nature of the problem(s) and the patient's and/or family's needs.

Usually, the problem(s) requiring admission are of moderate severity. Physicians typically spend 50 minutes at the bedside and on the patient's hospital floor or unit.

99223 **Initial hospital care,** per day, for the evaluation and management of a patient, which requires these three key components:

- **a comprehensive history;**
- **a comprehensive examination; and**
- **medical decision making of high complexity.**

Counseling and/or coordination of care with other providers or agencies are provided consistent with the nature of the problem(s) and the patient's and/or family's needs.

Usually, the problem(s) requiring admission are of high severity. Physicians typically spend 70 minutes at the bedside and on the patient's hospital floor or unit.

Subsequent Hospital Care

All levels of subsequent hospital care include reviewing the medical record and reviewing the results of diagnostic studies and changes in the patient's status, (ie, changes in history, physical condition and response to management) since the last assessment by the physician.

99231 **Subsequent hospital care,** per day, for the evaluation and management of a patient, which requires at least two of these three key components:

- **a problem focused interval history;**
- **a problem focused examination;**
- **medical decision making that is straightforward or of low complexity.**

Counseling and/or coordination of care with other providers or agencies are provided consistent with the nature of the problem(s) and the patient's and/or family's needs.

Usually, the patient is stable, recovering or improving. Physicians typically spend 15 minutes at the bedside and on the patient's hospital floor or unit.

99232 **Subsequent hospital care,** per day, for the evaluation and management of a patient, which requires at least two of these three key components:

- **an expanded problem focused interval history;**
- **an expanded problem focused examination;**
- **medical decision making of moderate complexity.**

Counseling and/or coordination of care with other providers or agencies are provided consistent with the nature of the problem(s) and the patient's and/or family's needs.

Usually, the patient is responding inadequately to therapy or has developed a minor complication. Physicians typically spend 25 minutes at the bedside and on the patient's hospital floor or unit.

99233 **Subsequent hospital care,** per day, for the evaluation and management of a patient, which requires at least two of these three key components:

- **a detailed interval history;**
- **a detailed examination;**
- **medical decision making of high complexity.**

Counseling and/or coordination of care with other providers or agencies are provided consistent with the nature of the problem(s) and the patient's and/or family's needs.

Usually, the patient is unstable or has developed a significant complication or a significant new problem. Physicians typically spend 35 minutes at the bedside and on the patient's hospital floor or unit.

Observation or Inpatient Care Services (Including Admission and Discharge Services)

The following codes are used to report observation or inpatient hospital care services provided to patients admitted and discharged on the same date of service. When a patient is admitted to the hospital from observation status on the same date, the physician should report only the initial hospital care code. The initial hospital care code reported by the admitting physician should include the services related to the observation status services he/she provided on the same date of inpatient admission.

When "observation status" is initiated in the course of an encounter in another site of service (eg, hospital emergency department, physician's office, nursing facility) all evaluation and management services provided by the supervising physician in conjunction with initiating "observation status" are considered part of the initial observation care when performed on the same date. The observation care level of service should include the services related to initiating "observation status" provided in the other sites of service as well as in the observation setting when provided by the same physician.

For patients admitted to observation or inpatient care and discharged on a different date, see codes 99218-99220 and 99217, or 99221-99223 and 99238-99239.

99234 **Observation or inpatient hospital care,** for the evaluation and management of a patient including admission and discharge on the same date which requires these three key components:

- **a detailed or comprehensive history;**
- **a detailed or comprehensive examination; and**
- **medical decision making that is straightforward or of low complexity.**

Counseling and/or coordination of care with other providers or agencies are provided consistent with the nature of the problem(s) and the patient's and/or family's needs.

Usually the presenting problem(s) requiring admission are of low severity.

99235 **Observation or inpatient hospital care,** for the evaluation and management of a patient including admission and discharge on the same date which requires these three key components:

- **a comprehensive history;**
- **a comprehensive examination; and**
- **medical decision making of moderate complexity.**

Counseling and/or coordination of care with other providers or agencies are provided consistent with the nature of the problem(s) and the patient's and/or family's needs.

Usually the presenting problem(s) requiring admission are of moderate severity.

99236 **Observation or inpatient hospital care,** for the evaluation and management of a patient including admission and discharge on the same date which requires these three key components:

- **a comprehensive history;**
- **a comprehensive examination; and**
- **medical decision making of high complexity.**

Counseling and/or coordination of care with other providers or agencies are provided consistent with the nature of the problem(s) and the patient's and/or family's needs.

Usually the presenting problem(s) requiring admission are of high severity.

Hospital Discharge Services

The hospital discharge day management codes are to be used to report the total duration of time spent by a physician for final hospital discharge of a patient. The codes include, as appropriate, final examination of the patient, discussion of the hospital stay, even if the time spent by the physician on that date is not continuous, instructions for continuing care to all relevant caregivers, and preparation of discharge records, prescriptions and referral forms. For a patient admitted and discharged from observation or inpatient status on the same date, the services should be reported with codes 99234-99236 as appropriate.

99238 **Hospital discharge day management;** 30 minutes or less

99239 more than 30 minutes

(These codes are to be utilized by the physician to report all services provided to a patient on the date of discharge, if other than the initial date of inpatient status. To report services to a patient who is admitted as an inpatient, and discharged on the same date, see codes 99234-99236 for observation or inpatient hospital care including the admission and discharge of the patient on the same date. To report concurrent care services provided by a physician(s) other than the attending physician, use subsequent hospital care codes (99231-99233) on the day of discharge.)

(For Observation Care Discharge, use 99217)

(For observation or inpatient hospital care including the admission and discharge of the patient on the same date, see 99234-99236)

(For Nursing Facility Care Discharge, see 99315, 99316)

(For discharge services provided to newborns admitted and discharged on the same date, use 99435)

Consultations

A consultation is a type of service provided by a physician whose opinion or advice regarding evaluation and/or management of a specific problem is requested by another physician or other appropriate source.

A physician consultant may initiate diagnostic and/or therapeutic services at the same or subsequent visit.

The written or verbal request for a consult may be made by a physician or other appropriate source and documented in the patient's medical record. The consultant's opinion and any services that were ordered or performed must also be documented in the patient's medical record and communicated by written report to the requesting physician or other appropriate source.

A "consultation" initiated by a patient and/or family, and not requested by a physician, is not reported using the initial consultation codes but may be reported using the codes for confirmatory consultation or office visits, as appropriate.

If a confirmatory consultation is required, eg, by a third party payor, the modifier '-32', mandated services, should also be reported.

Any specifically identifiable procedure (ie, identified with a specific CPT code) performed on or subsequent to the date of the initial consultation should be reported separately.

If subsequent to the completion of a consultation, the consultant assumes responsibility for management of a portion or all of the patient's condition(s), the follow-up consultation codes should not be used. In the hospital setting, the consulting physician should use the appropriate inpatient hospital consultation code for the initial encounter and then subsequent hospital care codes (not follow-up consultation codes). In the office setting, the appropriate established patient code should be used.

There are four subcategories of consultations: office, initial inpatient, follow-up inpatient, and confirmatory. See each subcategory for specific reporting instructions.

For definitions of key components and commonly used terms, please see **Evaluation and Management Services Guidelines**.

Office or Other Outpatient Consultations

New or Established Patient

The following codes are used to report consultations provided in the physician's office or in an outpatient or other ambulatory facility, including hospital observation services, home services, domiciliary, rest home, custodial care, or emergency department (see consultation definition, above). Follow-up visits in the consultant's office or other outpatient facility that are initiated by the physician consultant are reported using office visit codes for established patients (99211-99215). If an additional request for an opinion or advice regarding the same or a new problem is received from the attending physician and documented in the medical record, the office consultation codes may be used again.

99241 **Office consultation** for a new or established patient, which requires these three key components:

- **a problem focused history;**
- **a problem focused examination; and**
- **straightforward medical decision making.**

Counseling and/or coordination of care with other providers or agencies are provided consistent with the nature of the problem(s) and the patient's and/or family's needs.

Usually, the presenting problem(s) are self limited or minor. Physicians typically spend 15 minutes face-to-face with the patient and/or family.

99242 **Office consultation** for a new or established patient, which requires these three key components:

- **an expanded problem focused history;**
- **an expanded problem focused examination; and**
- **straightforward medical decision making.**

Counseling and/or coordination of care with other providers or agencies are provided consistent with the nature of the problem(s) and the patient's and/or family's needs.

Usually, the presenting problem(s) are of low severity. Physicians typically spend 30 minutes face-to-face with the patient and/or family.

99243 **Office consultation** for a new or established patient, which requires these three key components:

- **a detailed history;**
- **a detailed examination; and**
- **medical decision making of low complexity.**

Counseling and/or coordination of care with other providers or agencies are provided consistent with the nature of the problem(s) and the patient's and/or family's needs.

Usually, the presenting problem(s) are of moderate severity. Physicians typically spend 40 minutes face-to-face with the patient and/or family.

99244 **Office consultation** for a new or established patient, which requires these three key components:

- **a comprehensive history;**
- **a comprehensive examination; and**
- **medical decision making of moderate complexity.**

Counseling and/or coordination of care with other providers or agencies are provided consistent with the nature of the problem(s) and the patient's and/or family's needs.

Usually, the presenting problem(s) are of moderate to high severity. Physicians typically spend 60 minutes face-to-face with the patient and/or family.

99245 Office consultation for a new or established patient, which requires these three key components:

- **a comprehensive history;**
- **a comprehensive examination; and**
- **medical decision making of high complexity.**

Counseling and/or coordination of care with other providers or agencies are provided consistent with the nature of the problem(s) and the patient's and/or family's needs.

Usually, the presenting problem(s) are of moderate to high severity. Physicians typically spend 80 minutes face-to-face with the patient and/or family.

Initial Inpatient Consultations

New or Established Patient

The following codes are used to report physician consultations provided to hospital inpatients, residents of nursing facilities, or patients in a partial hospital setting. Only one initial consultation should be reported by a consultant per admission.

99251 **Initial inpatient consultation** for a new or established patient, which requires these three key components:

- **a problem focused history;**
- **a problem focused examination; and**
- **straightforward medical decision making.**

Counseling and/or coordination of care with other providers or agencies are provided consistent with the nature of the problem(s) and the patient's and/or family's needs.

Usually, the presenting problem(s) are self limited or minor. Physicians typically spend 20 minutes at the bedside and on the patient's hospital floor or unit.

99252 **Initial inpatient consultation** for a new or established patient, which requires these three key components:

- **an expanded problem focused history;**
- **an expanded problem focused examination; and**
- **straightforward medical decision making.**

Counseling and/or coordination of care with other providers or agencies are provided consistent with the nature of the problem(s) and the patient's and/or family's needs.

Usually, the presenting problem(s) are of low severity. Physicians typically spend 40 minutes at the bedside and on the patient's hospital floor or unit.

99253 **Initial inpatient consultation** for a new or established patient, which requires these three key components:

- **a detailed history;**
- **a detailed examination; and**
- **medical decision making of low complexity.**

Counseling and/or coordination of care with other providers or agencies are provided consistent with the nature of the problem(s) and the patient's and/or family's needs.

Usually, the presenting problem(s) are of moderate severity. Physicians typically spend 55 minutes at the bedside and on the patient's hospital floor or unit.

99254 **Initial inpatient consultation** for a new or established patient, which requires three key components:

- **a comprehensive history;**
- **a comprehensive examination; and**
- **medical decision making of moderate complexity.**

Counseling and/or coordination of care with other providers or agencies are provided consistent with the nature of the problem(s) and the patient's and/or family's needs.

Usually, the presenting problem(s) are of moderate to high severity. Physicians typically spend 80 minutes at the bedside and on the patient's hospital floor or unit.

99255 **Initial inpatient consultation** for a new or established patient, which requires these three key components:

- **a comprehensive history;**
- **a comprehensive examination; and**
- **medical decision making of high complexity.**

Counseling and/or coordination of care with other providers or agencies are provided consistent with the nature of the problem(s) and the patient's and/or family's needs.

Usually, the presenting problem(s) are of moderate to high severity. Physicians typically spend 110 minutes at the bedside and on the patient's hospital floor or unit.

Follow-Up Inpatient Consultations

Established Patient

Follow-up consultations are visits to complete the initial consultation OR subsequent consultative visits requested by the attending physician.

A follow-up consultation includes monitoring progress, recommending management modifications or advising on a new plan of care in response to changes in the patient's status.

If the physician consultant has initiated treatment at the initial consultation, and participates thereafter in the patient's management, the codes for subsequent hospital care should be used (99231-99233).

The following codes are used to report follow-up consultations provided to hospital inpatients or nursing facility residents only. For consultative services provided in other settings, the codes for office or other outpatient consultations should be reported (99241-99245).

99261 **Follow-up inpatient consultation** for an established patient, which requires at least two of these three key components:

- **a problem focused interval history;**
- **a problem focused examination;**
- **medical decision making that is straightforward or of low complexity.**

Counseling and/or coordination of care with other providers or agencies are provided consistent with nature of the problem(s) and the patient's and/or family's needs.

Usually, the patient is stable, recovering or improving. Physicians typically spend 10 minutes at the bedside and on the patient's hospital floor or unit.

99262 **Follow-up inpatient consultation** for an established patient which requires at least two of these three key components:

- **an expanded problem focused interval history;**
- **an expanded problem focused examination;**
- **medical decision making of moderate complexity.**

Counseling and/or coordination of care with other providers or agencies are provided consistent with the nature of the problem(s) and the patient's and/or family's needs.

Usually, the patient is responding inadequately to therapy or has developed a minor complication. Physicians typically spend 20 minutes at the bedside and on the patient's hospital floor or unit.

99263 **Follow-up inpatient consultation** for an established patient which requires at least two of these three key components:

- **a detailed interval history;**
- **a detailed examination;**
- **medical decision making of high complexity.**

Counseling and/or coordination of care with other providers or agencies are provided consistent with the nature of the problem(s) and the patient's and/or family's needs.

Usually, the patient is unstable or has developed a significant complication or a significant new problem. Physicians typically spend 30 minutes at the bedside and on the patient's hospital floor or unit.

Confirmatory Consultations

New or Established Patient

The following codes are used to report the evaluation and management services provided to patients when the consulting physician is aware of the confirmatory nature of the opinion sought (eg, when a second/third opinion is requested or required on the necessity or appropriateness of a previously recommended medical treatment or surgical procedure).

Confirmatory consultations may be provided in any setting.

A physician consultant providing a confirmatory consultation is expected to provide an opinion and/or advice only. Any services subsequent to the opinion are coded at the appropriate level of office visit, established patient, or subsequent hospital care. If a confirmatory consultation is required, eg, by a third party payor, the modifier '-32', mandated services, should also be reported. (See also Consultation notes, page 13.) Typical times have not yet been established for this subcategory of services.

99271 **Confirmatory consultation** for a new or established patient, which requires these three key components:

- **a problem focused history;**
- **a problem focused examination; and**
- **straightforward medical decision making.**

Counseling and/or coordination of care with other providers or agencies are provided consistent with the nature of the problem(s) and the patient's and/or family's needs.

Usually, the presenting problem(s) are self limited or minor.

99272 **Confirmatory consultation** for a new or established patient, which requires these three key components:

- **an expanded problem focused history;**
- **an expanded problem focused examination; and**
- **straightforward medical decision making.**

Counseling and/or coordination of care with other providers or agencies are provided consistent with the nature of the problem(s) and the patient's and/or family's needs.

Usually, the presenting problem(s) are of low severity.

99273 **Confirmatory consultation** for a new or established patient, which requires these three key components:

- **a detailed history;**
- **a detailed examination; and**
- **medical decision making of low complexity.**

Counseling and/or coordination of care with other providers or agencies are provided consistent with the nature of the problem(s) and the patient's and/or family's needs.

Usually, the presenting problem(s) are of moderate severity.

99274 **Confirmatory consultation** for a new or established patient, which requires these three key components:

- **a comprehensive history;**
- **a comprehensive examination; and**
- **medical decision making of moderate complexity.**

Counseling and/or coordination of care with other providers or agencies are provided consistent with the nature of the problem(s) and the patient's and/or family's needs.

Usually, the presenting problem(s) are of moderate to high severity.

99275 **Confirmatory consultation** for a new or established patient, which requires these three key components:

- **a comprehensive history;**
- **a comprehensive examination; and**
- **medical decision making of high complexity.**

Counseling and/or coordination of care with other providers or agencies are provided consistent with the nature of the problem(s) and the patient's and/or family's needs.

Usually, the presenting problem(s) are of moderate to high severity.

Emergency Department Services

New or Established Patient

The following codes are used to report evaluation and management services provided in the emergency department. No distinction is made between new and established patients in the emergency department.

An emergency department is defined as an organized hospital-based facility for the provision of unscheduled episodic services to patients who present for immediate medical attention. The facility must be available 24 hours a day.

For critical care services provided in the emergency department, see Critical Care notes and 99291, 99292.

For evaluation and management services provided to a patient in an observation area of a hospital, see 99217-99220.

For observation or inpatient care services (including admission and discharge services), see 99234-99236.

99281 **Emergency department visit** for the evaluation and management of a patient, which requires these three key components:

- **a problem focused history;**
- **a problem focused examination; and**
- **straightforward medical decision making.**

Counseling and/or coordination of care with other providers or agencies are provided consistent with the nature of the problem(s) and the patient's and/or family's needs.

Usually, the presenting problem(s) are self limited or minor.

99282 **Emergency department visit** for the evaluation and management of a patient, which requires these three key components:

- **an expanded problem focused history;**
- **an expanded problem focused examination; and**
- **medical decision making of low complexity.**

Counseling and/or coordination of care with other providers or agencies are provided consistent with the nature of the problem(s) and the patient's and/or family's needs.

Usually, the presenting problem(s) are of low to moderate severity.

99283 **Emergency department visit** for the evaluation and management of a patient, which requires these three key components:

- **an expanded problem focused history;**
- **an expanded problem focused examination; and**
- **medical decision making of moderate complexity.**

Counseling and/or coordination of care with other providers or agencies are provided consistent with the nature of the problem(s) and the patient's and/or family's needs.

Usually, the presenting problem(s) are of moderate severity.

99284 **Emergency department visit** for the evaluation and management of a patient, which requires these three key components:

- **a detailed history;**
- **a detailed examination; and**
- **medical decision making of moderate complexity.**

Counseling and/or coordination of care with other providers or agencies are provided consistent with the nature of the problem(s) and the patient's and/or family's needs.

Usually, the presenting problem(s) are of high severity, and require urgent evaluation by the physician but do not pose an immediate significant threat to life or physiologic function.

99285 **Emergency department visit** for the evaluation and management of a patient, which requires these three key components within the constraints imposed by the urgency of the patient's clinical condition and/or mental status:

- **a comprehensive history;**
- **a comprehensive examination; and**
- **medical decision making of high complexity.**

Counseling and/or coordination of care with other providers or agencies are provided consistent with the nature of the problem(s) and the patient's and/or family's needs.

Usually, the presenting problem(s) are of high severity and pose an immediate significant threat to life or physiologic function.

Other Emergency Services

In physician directed emergency care, advanced life support, the physician is located in a hospital emergency or critical care department, and is in two-way voice communication with ambulance or rescue personnel outside the hospital. The physician directs the performance of necessary medical procedures, including but not limited to: telemetry of cardiac rhythm; cardiac and/or pulmonary resuscitation; endotracheal or esophageal obturator airway intubation; administration of intravenous fluids and/or administration of intramuscular, intratracheal or subcutaneous drugs; and/or electrical conversion of arrhythmia.

99288 **Physician direction of** emergency medical systems (EMS) emergency care, advanced life support

Pediatric Critical Care Patient Transport

The following codes 99289 and 99290 are used to report the physical attendance and direct face-to-face care by a physician during the interfacility transport of a critically ill or critically injured pediatric patient. For the purpose of reporting codes 99289 and 99290, face-to-face care begins when the physician assumes primary responsibility of the pediatric patient at the referring hospital/facility, and ends when the receiving hospital/facility accepts responsibility for the pediatric patient's care. Only the time the physician spends in direct face-to-face contact with the patient during the transport should be reported. Pediatric patient transport services involving less than 30 minutes of face-to-face physician care should not be reported using codes 99289, 99290. Procedure(s) or service(s) performed by other members of the transporting team may not be reported by the supervising physician.

The following services are included when performed during the pediatric patient transport by the physician providing critical care and may not be reported separately: routine monitoring evaluations (eg, heart rate, respiratory rate, blood pressure, and pulse oximetry), the interpretation of cardiac output measurements (93561, 93562), chest x-rays (71010, 71015, 71020), pulse oximetry (94760, 94761, 94762), blood gases and information data stored in computers (eg, ECGs, blood pressures, hematologic data) (99090), gastric intubation (43752, 91105), temporary transcutaneous pacing (92953), ventilatory management (94656, 94660, 94662) and vascular access procedures (36000, 36400, 36405, 36406, 36410, 36415, 36540, 36600). Any services performed which are not listed above should be reported separately.

Critical care is the direct delivery by a physician(s) of medical care for a critically ill or critically injured patient. A critical illness or injury acutely impairs one or more vital organ systems such that there is a high probability of imminent or life threatening deterioration in the patient's condition. Critical care involves high complexity decision making to assess, manipulate, and support vital system function(s) to treat single or multiple vital organ system failure and/or to prevent further life threatening deterioration of the patient's condition. Examples of vital organ system failure include, but are not limited to: central nervous system failure, circulatory failure, shock, renal, hepatic, metabolic, and/or respiratory failure.

Providing medical care to a critically ill, injured, or post-operative patient qualifies as a critical care service only if both the illness or injury and the treatment being provided meet the above requirements.

The direction of emergency care to transporting staff by a physician located in a hospital or other facility by two-way communication is not considered direct face-to-face care and should not be reported with codes 99289, 99290. Physician directed emergency care through outside voice communication to transporting staff personnel is reported with code 99288.

The emergency department services codes (99281-99285), initial hospital care codes (99221-99223), hourly critical care codes (99291, 99292), or initial date neonatal intensive care code (99295) are only reported after the patient has been admitted to the emergency department, the inpatient floor or the critical care unit of the receiving facility.

Code 99289 is used to report the first 30-74 minutes of direct face-to-face time with the transport pediatric patient and should be reported only once on a given date. Code 99290 is used to report each additional 30 minutes provided on a given date. Face-to-face services less than 30 minutes should not be reported with these codes.

99289 Critical care services delivered by a physician, face-to-face, during an interfacility transport of critically ill or critically injured pediatric patient, 24 months of age or less; first 30-74 minutes of hands on care during transport

+ 99290 each additional 30 minutes (List separately in addition to code for primary service)

(Use 99290 in conjunction with 99289)

(Critical care of less than 30 minutes total duration should be reported with the appropriate E/M code)

Critical Care Services

Critical care is the direct delivery by a physician(s) of medical care for a critically ill or critically injured patient. A critical illness or injury acutely impairs one or more vital organ systems such that there is a high probability of imminent or life threatening deterioration in the patient's condition. Critical care involves high complexity decision making to assess, manipulate, and support vital system function(s) to treat single or multiple vital organ system failure and/or to prevent further life threatening deterioration of the patient's condition. Examples of vital organ system failure include, but are not limited to: central nervous system failure, circulatory failure, shock, renal, hepatic, metabolic, and/or respiratory failure. Although critical care typically requires interpretation of multiple physiologic parameters and/or application of advanced technology(s), critical care may be provided in life threatening situations when these elements are not present. Critical care may be provided on multiple days, even if no changes are made in the treatment rendered to the patient, provided that the patient's condition continues to require the level of physician attention described above.

Providing medical care to a critically ill, injured, or post-operative patient qualifies as a critical care service only if both the illness or injury and the treatment being provided meet the above requirements. Critical care is usually, but not always, given in a critical care area, such as the coronary care unit, intensive care unit, pediatric intensive care unit, respiratory care unit, or the emergency care facility.

►Inpatient◄ critical care services provided to infants 31 days up through 24 months of age are reported with pediatric critical care codes 99293 and 99294. The pediatric critical care codes are reported as long as the infant/young child qualifies for critical care services during the hospital stay ►through 24 months of age. Inpatient◄ critical care services provided to neonates (30 days of age or less) are reported with the neonatal critical care codes 99295 and 99296. The neonatal critical care codes are reported as long as the neonate qualifies for critical care services ►during the hospital stay◄ through the 30th postnatal day. The reporting of the pediatric and neonatal critical care services is not based on time or the type of unit (eg, pediatric or neonatal critical care unit) and it is not dependent upon the type of provider delivering the care. ►To report critical care services provided in the outpatient setting (eg, emergency department or office), for neonates and pediatric patients up through 24 months of age, use the hourly Critical Care codes 99291-99292. If the same physician provides critical care services for a neonatal or pediatric patient in both the outpatient and inpatient settings on the same day, report only the appropriate Neonatal or Pediatric Critical Care code (99293-99296) for all critical care services provided on that day.◄ For additional instructions on reporting these services, see the Neonatal and Pediatric Critical Care section and codes 99293-99296.

Services for a patient who is not critically ill but happens to be in a critical care unit are reported using other appropriate E/M codes.

Critical care and other E/M services may be provided to the same patient on the same date by the same physician.

The following services are included in reporting critical care when performed during the critical period by the physician(s) providing critical care: the interpretation of cardiac output measurements (93561, 93562), chest x-rays (71010, 71015, 71020), pulse oximetry (94760, 94761, 94762), blood gases, and information data stored in computers (eg, ECGs, blood pressures, hematologic data (99090)); gastric intubation (43752, 91105); temporary transcutaneous pacing (92953); ventilatory management (94656, 94657, 94660, 94662); and vascular access procedures (36000, 36410, 36415, 36540, 36600). Any services performed which are not listed above should be reported separately.

Codes 99291-99292 should be reported for the physician's attendance during the transport of critically ill or critically injured patients over 24 months of age to or from a facility or hospital. For physician transport services of critically ill or critically injured pediatric patients 24 months of age or less see 99289, 99290.

The critical care codes 99291 and 99292 are used to report the total duration of time spent by a physician providing critical care services to a critically ill or critically injured patient, even if the time spent by the physician on that date is not continuous. For any given period of time spent providing critical care services, the physician must devote his or her full attention to the patient and, therefore, cannot provide services to any other patient during the same period of time.

Time spent with the individual patient should be recorded in the patient's record. The time that can be reported as critical care is the time spent engaged in work directly related to the individual patient's care whether that time was spent at the immediate bedside or elsewhere on the floor or unit. For example, time spent on the unit or at the nursing station on the floor reviewing test results or imaging studies, discussing the critically ill patient's care with other medical staff or documenting critical care services in the medical record would be reported as critical care, even though it does not occur at the bedside. Also, when the patient is unable or clinically incompetent to participate in discussions, time spent on the floor or unit with family members or surrogate decision makers obtaining a medical history, reviewing the patient's condition or prognosis, or discussing treatment or limitation(s) of treatment may be reported as critical care, provided that the conversation bears directly on the management of the patient.

Time spent in activities that occur outside of the unit or off the floor (eg, telephone calls, whether taken at home, in the office, or elsewhere in the hospital) may not be reported as critical care since the physician is not immediately available to the patient. Time spent in activities that do not directly contribute to the treatment of the patient may not be reported as critical care, even if they are performed in the critical care unit (eg, participation in administrative meetings or telephone calls to discuss other patients). Time spent performing separately reportable procedures or services should not be included in the time reported as critical care time.

Code 99291 is used to report the first 30-74 minutes of critical care on a given date. It should be used only once per date even if the time spent by the physician is not continuous on that date. Critical care of less than 30 minutes total duration on a given date should be reported with the appropriate E/M code.

Code 99292 is used to report additional block(s) of time, of up to 30 minutes each beyond the first 74 minutes. (See table below.)

The following examples illustrate the correct reporting of critical care services:

Total Duration of Critical Care	Codes
less than 30 minutes (less than 1/2 hour)	appropriate E/M codes
30-74 minutes (1/2 hr. - 1 hr. 14 min.)	99291 X 1
75-104 minutes (1 hr. 15 min. - 1 hr. 44 min.)	99291 X 1 AND 99292 X 1
105-134 minutes (1 hr. 45 min. - 2 hr. 14 min.)	99291 X 1 AND 99292 X 2
135 - 164 minutes (2 hr. 15 min. - 2 hr. 44 min.)	99291 X 1 AND 99292 X 3
165 - 194 minutes (2 hr. 45 min. - 3 hr. 14 min.)	99291 X 1 AND 99292 X 4
194 minutes or longer (3 hr. 14 min. - etc.)	99291 and 99292 as appropriate (see illustrated reporting examples above)

99291 **Critical care, evaluation and management** of the critically ill or critically injured patient; first 30-74 minutes

+ 99292 each additional 30 minutes (List separately in addition to code for primary service)

(Use 99292 in conjunction with 99291)

►Inpatient◄ Neonatal and Pediatric Critical Care Services

The following codes (99293-99296) are used to report services provided by a physician directing the ►inpatient◄ care of a critically ill neonate/infant. The same definitions for critical care services apply for the adult, child, and neonate.

The initial day neonatal critical care code (99295) can be used in addition to codes 99360, 99436 or 99440 as appropriate, when the physician is present for the delivery ►(99360 or 99436)◄ and newborn resuscitation ►(99440)◄ is required. Other procedures performed as a necessary part of the resuscitation ►(eg, endotracheal intubation (31500)) are also reported separately when performed as part of the pre-admission delivery room care. In order to report these procedures separately, they must be performed as a necessary component of the resuscitation and not simply as a convenience before admission to the neonatal intensive care unit.◄

Codes 99295, 99296 are used to report services provided by a physician directing the ►inpatient◄ care of a critically ill neonate through the first 30 days of life. They represent care starting with the date of admission (99295) and subsequent day(s) (99296) and may be reported only once per day, per patient. Once the neonate is no longer considered to be critically ill, the Intensive Low Birth Weight Services codes for those with present body weight of less than 2500 grams (99298, 99299) or the codes for Subsequent Hospital Care (99231-99233) for those with present body weight over 2500 grams should be utilized.

Codes 99293, 99294 are used to report services provided by a physician directing the ►inpatient◄ care of a critically ill infant or young child from 31 days of postnatal age up through 24 months of age. They represent care starting with the date of admission (99293) and subsequent day(s) (99294) and may be reported by a single physician only once per day, per patient in a given setting. The critically ill or critically injured child older than ►24 months of age◄ would be reported with hourly critical care service codes (99291, 99292). Once an infant is no longer considered to be critically ill but continues to require intensive care, the Intensive Low Birth Weight Services codes (99298, 99299) should be used to report services for infants with present body weight of less than 2500 grams. When the present body weight of those infants exceeds 2500 grams, the Subsequent Hospital Care (99231-99233) codes should be utilized. ►To report critical care services provided in the outpatient setting (eg, emergency department or office), for neonates and pediatric patients up through 24 months of age, use the hourly Critical Care codes 99291-99292. If the same physician provides critical care services for a neonatal or pediatric patient in both the outpatient and inpatient settings on the same day, report only the appropriate Neonatal or Pediatric Critical Care code (99293-99296) for all critical care services provided on that day.◄

Care rendered under 99293-99296 includes management, monitoring, and treatment of the patient including respiratory, pharmacologic control of the circulatory system, enteral and parenteral nutrition, metabolic and hematologic maintenance, parent/family counseling, case management services, and personal direct supervision of the health care team in the performance of cognitive and procedural activities.

The pediatric and neonatal critical care codes include those procedures listed above for the hourly critical care codes (99291, 99292). In addition, the following procedures are also included in the bundled (global) pediatric and neonatal critical care service codes (99293-99296): umbilical venous (36510) and umbilical arterial (36660) catheters, central (36555) or peripheral vessel catheterization (36000), other arterial catheters (36140, 36620), oral or nasogastric tube placement (43752), endotracheal intubation (31500), lumbar puncture (62270), suprapubic bladder aspiration (51000), bladder catheterization (53670), initiation and management of mechanical ventilation (94656, 94657) or continuous positive airway pressure (CPAP) (94660), surfactant administration, intravascular fluid administration (90780, 90781), transfusion of blood components (36430, 36440), vascular punctures (36420, 36600), invasive or non-invasive electronic monitoring of vital signs, bedside pulmonary function testing (94375), and/or monitoring or interpretation of blood gases or oxygen saturation (94760-94762). Any services performed which are not listed above should be reported separately.

For additional instructions, see descriptions listed for 99293-99296

►Inpatient◄ Pediatric Critical Care

▲99293 **Initial inpatient pediatric critical care,** 31 days up through 24 months of age, per day, for the evaluation and management of a critically ill infant or young child

▲99294 **Subsequent inpatient pediatric critical care,** 31 days up through 24 months of age, per day, for the evaluation and management of a critically ill infant or young child

►Inpatient◄ Neonatal Critical Care

▲99295 **Initial inpatient neonatal critical care,** per day, for the evaluation and management of a critically ill neonate, 30 days of age or less

This code is reserved for the date of admission for neonates who are critically ill. Critically ill neonates require cardiac and/or respiratory support (including ventilator or nasal CPAP when indicated), continuous or frequent vital sign monitoring, laboratory and blood gas interpretations, follow-up physician reevaluations, and constant observation by the health care team under direct physician supervision. Immediate preoperative evaluation and stabilization of neonates with life threatening surgical or cardiac conditions are included under this code. Neonates with life threatening surgical or cardiac conditions are included under this code.

Care for neonates who require an intensive care setting but who are not critically ill is reported using the initial hospital care codes (99221-99223).

▲99296 **Subsequent inpatient neonatal critical care,** per day, for the evaluation and management of a critically ill neonate, 30 days of age or less

A critically ill neonate will require cardiac and/or respiratory support (including ventilator or nasal CPAP when indicated), continuous or frequent vital sign monitoring, laboratory and blood gas interpretations, follow-up physician re-evaluations throughout a 24-hour period, and constant observation by the health care team under direct physician supervision.

(99297 has been deleted. To report, use 99296)

Intensive (Non-Critical) Low Birth Weight Services

Codes 99298-99299 are used to report services subsequent to the day of admission provided by a physician directing the continuing intensive care of the low birth weight (LBW) or very low birth weight (VLBW) infant who no longer meets the definition of critically ill. They represent subsequent day(s) of care and may be reported only once per day, per patient. Low birth weight services are reported for those neonates less than 2500 grams who do not meet the definition of critical care but continue to require intensive observation and frequent services and interventions only available in an intensive care setting. The level and frequency of services required for the LBW and the VLBW infant exceed those available in less intensive hospital areas or medical floors. Codes 99298-99299 are global 24-hour codes with the same services bundled as outlined under codes 99293-99296.

For additional instructions, see descriptions listed for 99298-99299.

99298 **Subsequent intensive care,** per day, for the evaluation and management of the recovering very low birth weight infant (present body weight less than 1500 grams)

Infants with present body weight less than 1500 grams who are no longer critically ill continue to require intensive cardiac and respiratory monitoring, continuous and/or frequent vital sign monitoring, heat maintenance, enteral and/or parenteral nutritional adjustments, laboratory and oxygen monitoring and constant observation by the health care team under direct physician supervision.

99299 **Subsequent intensive care,** per day, for the evaluation and management of the recovering low birth weight infant (present body weight of 1500-2500 grams)

Infants with present body weight of 1500-2500 grams who are no longer critically ill continue to require intensive cardiac and respiratory monitoring, continuous and/or frequent vital sign monitoring, heat maintenance, enteral and/or parenteral nutritional adjustments, laboratory and oxygen monitoring, and constant observation by the health care team under direct physician supervision.

Nursing Facility Services

The following codes are used to report evaluation and management services to patients in Nursing Facilities (formerly called Skilled Nursing Facilities (SNFs), Intermediate Care Facilities (ICFs) or Long Term Care Facilities (LTCFs)).

These codes should also be used to report evaluation and management services provided to a patient in a psychiatric residential treatment center (a facility or a distinct part of a facility for psychiatric care, which provides a 24-hour therapeutically planned and professionally staffed group living and learning environment). If procedures such as medical psychotherapy are provided in addition to evaluation and management services, these should be reported in addition to the evaluation and management services provided.

Nursing facilities that provide convalescent, rehabilitative, or long term care are required to conduct comprehensive, accurate, standardized, and reproducible assessments of each resident's functional capacity using a Resident Assessment Instrument (RAI). All RAIs include the Minimum Data Set (MDS), Resident Assessment Protocols (RAPs) and utilization guidelines. The MDS is the primary screening and assessment tool; the RAPs trigger the identification of potential problems and provide guidelines for follow-up assessments.

Physicians have a central role in assuring that all residents receive thorough assessments and that medical plans of care are instituted or revised to enhance or maintain the residents' physical and psychosocial functioning.

Two subcategories of nursing facility services are recognized: Comprehensive Nursing Facility Assessments and Subsequent Nursing Facility Care. Both subcategories apply to new or established patients. Comprehensive Assessments may be performed at one or more sites in the assessment process: the hospital, observation unit, office, nursing facility, domiciliary/non-nursing facility or patient's home.

For definitions of key components and commonly used terms, please see **Evaluation and Management Services Guidelines.**

Comprehensive Nursing Facility Assessments

New or Established Patient

When the patient is admitted to the nursing facility in the course of an encounter in another site of service (eg, hospital emergency department, physician's office), all evaluation and management services provided by that physician in conjunction with that admission are considered part of the initial nursing facility care when performed on the same date as the admission or readmission. The nursing facility care level of service reported by the admitting physician should include the services related to the admission he/she provided in the other sites of service as well as in the nursing facility setting.

Hospital discharge or observation discharge services performed on the same date of nursing facility admission or readmission may be reported separately. For a patient discharged from inpatient status on the same date of nursing facility admission or readmission, the hospital discharge services should be reported with codes 99238-99239 as appropriate. For a patient discharged from observation status on the same date of nursing facility admission or readmission, the observation care discharge services should be reported with code 99217. For a patient admitted and discharged from observation or inpatient status on the same date, see codes 99234-99236.

(For nursing facility care discharge, see 99315, 99316)

More than one comprehensive assessment may be necessary during an inpatient confinement.

99301 **Evaluation and management** of a new or established patient involving an annual nursing facility assessment which requires these three key components:

- **a detailed interval history;**
- **a comprehensive examination; and**
- **medical decision making that is straightforward or of low complexity.**

Counseling and/or coordination of care with other providers or agencies are provided consistent with the nature of the problem(s) and the patient's and/or family's needs.

Usually, the patient is stable, recovering or improving. The review and affirmation of the medical plan of care is required. Physicians typically spend 30 minutes at the bedside and on the patient's facility floor or unit.

99302 **Evaluation and management** of a new or established patient involving a nursing facility assessment which requires these three key components:

- **a detailed interval history;**
- **a comprehensive examination; and**
- **medical decision making of moderate to high complexity.**

Counseling and/or coordination of care with other providers or agencies are provided consistent with the nature of the problem(s) and the patient's and/or family's needs.

Usually, the patient has developed a significant complication or a significant new problem and has had a major permanent change in status.

The creation of a new medical plan of care is required. Physicians typically spend 40 minutes at the bedside and on the patient's facility floor or unit.

99303 **Evaluation and management** of a new or established patient involving a nursing facility assessment at the time of initial admission or readmission to the facility, which requires these three key components:

- **a comprehensive history;**
- **a comprehensive examination; and**
- **medical decision making of moderate to high complexity.**

Counseling and/or coordination of care with other providers or agencies are provided consistent with the nature of the problem(s) and the patient's and/or family's needs.

The creation of a medical plan of care is required. Physicians typically spend 50 minutes at the bedside and on the patient's facility floor or unit.

Subsequent Nursing Facility Care

New or Established Patient

The following codes are used to report the services provided to residents of nursing facilities who do not require a comprehensive assessment, and/or who have not had a major, permanent change of status.

All levels include reviewing the medical record, noting changes in the resident's status since the last visit, and reviewing and signing orders.

99311 **Subsequent nursing facility care,** per day, for the evaluation and management of a new or established patient, which requires at least two of these three key components:

- **a problem focused interval history;**
- **a problem focused examination;**
- **medical decision making that is straightforward or of low complexity.**

Counseling and/or coordination of care with other providers or agencies are provided consistent with the nature of the problem(s) and the patient's and/or family's needs.

Usually, the patient is stable, recovering or improving. Physicians typically spend 15 minutes at the bedside and on the patient's facility floor or unit.

99312 **Subsequent nursing facility care,** per day, for the evaluation and management of a new or established patient, which requires at least two of these three key components:

- **an expanded problem focused interval history;**
- **an expanded problem focused examination;**
- **medical decision making of moderate complexity.**

Counseling and/or coordination of care with other providers or agencies are provided consistent with the nature of the problem(s) and the patient's and/or family's needs.

Usually, the patient is responding inadequately to therapy or has developed a minor complication. Physicians typically spend 25 minutes at the bedside and on the patient's facility floor or unit.

99313 **Subsequent nursing facility care,** per day, for the evaluation and management of a new or established patient, which requires at least two of these three key components:

- **a detailed interval history;**
- **a detailed examination;**
- **medical decision making of moderate to high complexity.**

Counseling and/or coordination of care with other providers or agencies are provided consistent with the nature of the problem(s) and the patient's and/or family's needs.

Usually, the patient has developed a significant complication or a significant new problem. Physicians typically spend 35 minutes at the bedside and on the patient's facility floor or unit.

Nursing Facility Discharge Services

The nursing facility discharge day management codes are to be used to report the total duration of time spent by a physician for the final nursing facility discharge of a patient. The codes include, as appropriate, final examination of the patient, discussion of the nursing facility stay, even if the time spent by the physician on that date is not continuous. Instructions are given for continuing care to all relevant caregivers, and preparation of discharge records, prescriptions and referral forms.

99315 Nursing facility discharge day management; 30 minutes or less

99316 more than 30 minutes

Domiciliary, Rest Home (eg, Boarding Home), or Custodial Care Services

The following codes are used to report evaluation and management services in a facility which provides room, board and other personal assistance services, generally on a long-term basis. The facility's services do not include a medical component.

For definitions of key components and commonly used terms, please see **Evaluation and Management Services Guidelines.**

Typical times have not yet been established for this category of services.

New Patient

99321 **Domiciliary or rest home visit** for the evaluation and management of a new patient which requires these three key components:

- **a problem focused history;**
- **a problem focused examination; and**
- **medical decision making that is straightforward or of low complexity.**

Counseling and/or coordination of care with other providers or agencies are provided consistent with the nature of the problem(s) and the patient's and/or family's needs.

Usually, the presenting problem(s) are of low severity.

99322 **Domiciliary or rest home visit** for the evaluation and management of a new patient, which requires these three key components:

- **an expanded problem focused history;**
- **an expanded problem focused examination; and**
- **medical decision making of moderate complexity.**

Counseling and/or coordination of care with other providers or agencies are provided consistent with the nature of the problem(s) and the patient's and/or family's needs.

Usually, the presenting problem(s) are of moderate severity.

99323 **Domiciliary or rest home visit** for the evaluation and management of a new patient, which requires these three key components:

- **a detailed history;**
- **a detailed examination; and**
- **medical decision making of high complexity.**

Counseling and/or coordination of care with other providers or agencies are provided consistent with the nature of the problem(s) and the patient's and/or family's needs.

Usually, the presenting problem(s) are of high complexity.

Established Patient

99331 **Domiciliary or rest home visit** for the evaluation and management of an established patient, which requires at least two of these three key components:

- **a problem focused interval history;**
- **a problem focused examination;**
- **medical decision making that is straightforward or of low complexity.**

Counseling and/or coordination of care with other providers or agencies are provided consistent with the nature of the problem(s) and the patient's and/or family's needs.

Usually, the patient is stable, recovering or improving.

99332 **Domiciliary or rest home visit** for the evaluation and management of an established patient, which requires at least two of these three key components:

- **an expanded problem focused interval history;**
- **an expanded problem focused examination;**
- **medical decision making of moderate complexity.**

Counseling and/or coordination of care with other providers or agencies are provided consistent with the nature of the problem(s) and the patient's and/or family's needs.

Usually, the patient is responding inadequately to therapy or has developed a minor complication.

99333 **Domiciliary or rest home visit** for the evaluation and management of an established patient, which requires at least two of these three key components:

- **a detailed interval history;**
- **a detailed examination;**
- **medical decision making of high complexity.**

Counseling and/or coordination of care with other providers or agencies are provided consistent with the nature of the problem(s) and the patient's and/or family's needs.

Usually, the patient is unstable or has developed a significant complication or a significant new problem.

Home Services

The following codes are used to report evaluation and management services provided in a private residence.

For definitions of key components and commonly used terms, please see **Evaluation and Management Services Guidelines.**

New Patient

99341 **Home visit** for the evaluation and management of a new patient, which requires these three key components:

- **a problem focused history;**
- **a problem focused examination; and**
- **straightforward medical decision making.**

Counseling and/or coordination of care with other providers or agencies are provided consistent with the nature of the problem(s) and the patient's and/or family's needs.

Usually, the presenting problem(s) are of low severity. Physicians typically spend 20 minutes face-to-face with the patient and/or family.

99342 **Home visit** for the evaluation and management of a new patient, which requires these three key components:

- **an expanded problem focused history;**
- **an expanded problem focused examination; and**
- **medical decision making of low complexity.**

Counseling and/or coordination of care with other providers or agencies are provided consistent with the nature of the problem(s) and the patient's and/or family's needs.

Usually, the presenting problem(s) are of moderate severity. Physicians typically spend 30 minutes face-to-face with the patient and/or family.

99343 **Home visit** for the evaluation and management of a new patient, which requires these three key components:

- **a detailed history;**
- **a detailed examination; and**
- **medical decision making of moderate complexity.**

Counseling and/or coordination of care with other providers or agencies are provided consistent with the nature of the problem(s) and the patient's and/or family's needs.

Usually, the presenting problem(s) are of moderate to high severity. Physicians typically spend 45 minutes face-to-face with the patient and/or family.

99344 **Home visit** for the evaluation and management of a new patient, which requires these three components:

- **a comprehensive history;**
- **a comprehensive examination; and**
- **medical decision making of moderate complexity.**

Counseling and/or coordination of care with other providers or agencies are provided consistent with the nature of the problem(s) and the patient's and/or family's needs.

Usually, the presenting problem(s) are of high severity. Physicians typically spend 60 minutes face-to-face with the patient and/or family.

99345 **Home visit** for the evaluation and management of a new patient, which requires these three key components:

- **a comprehensive history;**
- **a comprehensive examination; and**
- **medical decision making of high complexity.**

Counseling and/or coordination of care with other providers or agencies are provided consistent with the nature of the problem(s) and the patient's and/or family's needs.

Usually, the patient is unstable or has developed a significant new problem requiring immediate physician attention. Physicians typically spend 75 minutes face-to-face with the patient and/or family.

Established Patient

99347 **Home visit** for the evaluation and management of an established patient, which requires at least two of these three key components:

- **a problem focused interval history;**
- **a problem focused examination;**
- **straightforward medical decision making.**

Counseling and/or coordination of care with other providers or agencies are provided consistent with the nature of the problem(s) and the patient's and/or family's needs.

Usually, the presenting problem(s) are self limited or minor. Physicians typically spend 15 minutes face-to-face with the patient and/or family.

99348 **Home visit** for the evaluation and management of an established patient, which requires at least two of these three key components:

- **an expanded problem focused interval history;**
- **an expanded problem focused examination;**
- **medical decision making of low complexity.**

Counseling and/or coordination of care with other providers or agencies are provided consistent with the nature of the problem(s) and the patient's and/or family's needs.

Usually, the presenting problem(s) are of low to moderate severity. Physicians typically spend 25 minutes face-to-face with the patient and/or family.

99349 **Home visit** for the evaluation and management of an established patient, which requires at least two of these three key components:

- **a detailed interval history;**
- **a detailed examination;**
- **medical decision making of moderate complexity.**

Counseling and/or coordination of care with other providers or agencies are provided consistent with the nature of the problem(s) and the patient's and/or family's needs.

Usually, the presenting problem(s) are moderate to high severity. Physicians typically spend 40 minutes face-to-face with the patient and/or family.

99350 **Home visit** for the evaluation and management of an established patient, which requires at least two of these three key components:

- **a comprehensive interval history;**
- **a comprehensive examination;**
- **medical decision making of moderate to high complexity.**

Counseling and/or coordination of care with other providers or agencies are provided consistent with the nature of the problem(s) and the patient's and/or family's needs.

Usually, the presenting problem(s) are of moderate to high severity. The patient may be unstable or may have developed a significant new problem requiring immediate physician attention. Physicians typically spend 60 minutes face-to-face with the patient and/or family.

Prolonged Services

Prolonged Physician Service With Direct (Face-To-Face) Patient Contact

Codes 99354-99357 are used when a physician provides prolonged service involving direct (face-to-face) patient contact that is beyond the usual service in either the inpatient or outpatient setting. This service is reported in addition to other physician services, including evaluation and management services at any level. Appropriate codes should be selected for supplies provided or procedures performed in the care of the patient during this period.

Codes 99354-99357 are used to report the total duration of face-to-face time spent by a physician on a given date providing prolonged service, even if the time spent by the physician on that date is not continuous.

Code 99354 or 99356 is used to report the first hour of prolonged service on a given date, depending on the place of service.

Either code also may be used to report a total duration of prolonged service of 30-60 minutes on a given date. Either code should be used only once per date, even if the time spent by the physician is not continuous on that date. Prolonged service of less than 30 minutes total duration on a given date is not separately reported because the work involved is included in the total work of the evaluation and management codes.

Code 99355 or 99357 is used to report each additional 30 minutes beyond the first hour, depending on the place of service. Either code may also be used to report the final 15-30 minutes of prolonged service on a given date.

Prolonged service of less than 15 minutes beyond the first hour or less than 15 minutes beyond the final 30 minutes is not reported separately.

The following examples illustrate the correct reporting of prolonged physician service with direct patient contact in the office setting:

Total Duration of Prolonged Services	Code(s)
less than 30 minutes (less than 1/2 hour)	Not reported separately
30-74 minutes (1/2 hr. - 1 hr. 14 min.)	99354 X 1
75-104 minutes (1 hr. 15 min. - 1 hr. 44 min.)	99354 X 1 AND 99355 X 1
105-134 minutes (1 hr. 45 min. - 2 hr. 14 min.)	99354 X 1 AND 99355 X 2
135-164 minutes (2 hr. 15 min. - 2 hr. 44 min.)	99354 X 1 AND 99355 X 3
165-194 minutes (2 hr. 45 min. - 3 hr. 14 min.)	99354 X 1 AND 99355 X 4

+ 99354 Prolonged physician service in the office or other outpatient setting requiring direct (face-to-face) patient contact beyond the usual service (eg, prolonged care and treatment of an acute asthmatic patient in an outpatient setting); first hour (List separately in addition to code for office or other outpatient Evaluation and Management service)

(Use 99354 in conjunction with codes 99201-99215, 99241-99245, 99301-99350)

+ 99355 each additional 30 minutes (List separately in addition to code for prolonged physician service)

(Use 99355 in conjunction with code 99354)

+ 99356 Prolonged physician service in the inpatient setting, requiring direct (face-to-face) patient contact beyond the usual service (eg, maternal fetal monitoring for high risk delivery or other physiological monitoring, prolonged care of an acutely ill inpatient); first hour (List separately in addition to code for inpatient Evaluation and Management service)

(Use 99356 in conjunction with codes 99221-99233, 99251-99255, 99261-99263)

+ 99357 each additional 30 minutes (List separately in addition to code for prolonged physician service)

(Use 99357 in conjunction with code 99356)

Prolonged Physician Service Without Direct (Face-To-Face) Patient Contact

Codes 99358 and 99359 are used when a physician provides prolonged service not involving direct (face-to-face) care that is beyond the usual service in either the inpatient or outpatient setting.

This service is to be reported in addition to other physician service, including evaluation and management services at any level.

Codes 99358 and 99359 are used to report the total duration of non-face-to-face time spent by a physician on a given date providing prolonged service, even if the time spent by the physician on that date is not continuous. Code 99358 is used to report the first hour of prolonged service on a given date regardless of the place of service.

It may also be used to report a total duration of prolonged service of 30-60 minutes on a given date. It should be used only once per date even if the time spent by the physician is not continuous on that date.

Prolonged service of less than 30 minutes total duration on a given date is not separately reported.

Code 99359 is used to report each additional 30 minutes beyond the first hour regardless of the place of service. It may also be used to report the final 15-30 minutes of prolonged service on a given date.

Prolonged service of less than 15 minutes beyond the first hour or less than 15 minutes beyond the final 30 minutes is not reported separately.

+ 99358 **Prolonged evaluation and management service** before and/or after direct (face-to-face) patient care (eg, review of extensive records and tests, communication with other professionals and/or the patient/family); first hour (List separately in addition to code(s) for other physician service(s) and/or inpatient or outpatient Evaluation and Management service)

+ 99359 each additional 30 minutes (List separately in addition to code for prolonged physician service)

(Use 99359 in conjunction with code 99358)

(To report telephone calls, see 99371-99373)

Physician Standby Services

Code 99360 is used to report physician standby service that is requested by another physician and that involves prolonged physician attendance without direct (face-to-face) patient contact. The physician may not be providing care or services to other patients during this period. This code is not used to report time spent proctoring another physician. It is also not used if the period of standby ends with the performance of a procedure subject to a "surgical" package by the physician who was on standby.

Code 99360 is used to report the total duration of time spent by a physician on a given date on standby. Standby service of less than 30 minutes total duration on a given date is not reported separately.

Second and subsequent periods of standby beyond the first 30 minutes may be reported only if a full 30 minutes of standby was provided for each unit of service reported.

99360 **Physician standby service,** requiring prolonged physician attendance, each 30 minutes (eg, operative standby, standby for frozen section, for cesarean/high risk delivery, for monitoring EEG)

(For hospital mandated on call services, see 99026, 99027)

(99360 may be reported in addition to 99431, 99440 as appropriate)

(99360 may not be reported in addition to 99436)

Case Management Services

Physician case management is a process in which a physician is responsible for direct care of a patient, and for coordinating and controlling access to or initiating and/or supervising other health care services needed by the patient.

Team Conferences

99361 **Medical conference** by a physician with interdisciplinary team of health professionals or representatives of community agencies to coordinate activities of patient care (patient not present); approximately 30 minutes

99362 approximately 60 minutes

Telephone Calls

99371 **Telephone call** by a physician to patient or for consultation or medical management or for coordinating medical management with other health care professionals (eg, nurses, therapists, social workers, nutritionists, physicians, pharmacists); simple or brief (eg, to report on tests and/or laboratory results, to clarify or alter previous instructions, to integrate new information from other health professionals into the medical treatment plan, or to adjust therapy)

99372 intermediate (eg, to provide advice to an established patient on a new problem, to initiate therapy that can be handled by telephone, to discuss test results in detail, to coordinate medical management of a new problem in an established patient, to discuss and evaluate new information and details, or to initiate new plan of care)

99373 complex or lengthy (eg, lengthy counseling session with anxious or distraught patient, detailed or prolonged discussion with family members regarding seriously ill patient, lengthy communication necessary to coordinate complex services of several different health professionals working on different aspects of the total patient care plan)

Care Plan Oversight Services

Care Plan Oversight Services are reported separately from codes for office/outpatient, hospital, home, nursing facility or domiciliary services. The complexity and approximate physician time of the care plan oversight services provided within a 30-day period determine code selection. Only one physician may report services for a given period of time, to reflect that physician's sole or predominant supervisory role with a particular patient. These codes should not be reported for supervision of patients in nursing facilities or under the care of home health agencies unless they require recurrent supervision of therapy.

The work involved in providing very low intensity or infrequent supervision services is included in the pre- and post-encounter work for home, office/outpatient and nursing facility or domiciliary visit codes.

99374 **Physician supervision** of a patient under care of home health agency (patient not present) in home, domiciliary or equivalent environment (eg, Alzheimer's facility) requiring complex and multidisciplinary care modalities involving regular physician development and/or revision of care plans, review of subsequent reports of patient status, review of related laboratory and other studies, communication (including telephone calls) for purposes of assessment or care decisions with health care professional(s), family member(s), surrogate decision maker(s) (eg, legal guardian) and/or key caregiver(s) involved in patient's care, integration of new information into the medical treatment plan and/or adjustment of medical therapy, within a calendar month; 15-29 minutes

99375 30 minutes or more

99377 **Physician supervision** of a hospice patient (patient not present) requiring complex and multidisciplinary care modalities involving regular physician development and/or revision of care plans, review of subsequent reports of patient status, review of related laboratory and other studies, communication (including telephone calls) for purposes of assessment or care decisions with health care professional(s), family member(s), surrogate decision maker(s) (eg, legal guardian) and/or key caregiver(s) involved in patient's care, integration of new information into the medical treatment plan and/or adjustment of medical therapy, within a calendar month; 15-29 minutes

99378 30 minutes or more

99379 **Physician supervision** of a nursing facility patient (patient not present) requiring complex and multidisciplinary care modalities involving regular physician development and/or revision of care plans, review of subsequent reports of patient status, review of related laboratory and other studies, communication (including telephone calls) for purposes of assessment or care decisions with health care professional(s), family member(s), surrogate decision maker(s) (eg, legal guardian) and/or key caregiver(s) involved in patient's care, integration of new information into the medical treatment plan and/or adjustment of medical therapy, within a calendar month; 15-29 minutes

99380 30 minutes or more

Preventive Medicine Services

The following codes are used to report the preventive medicine evaluation and management of infants, children, adolescents and adults.

The extent and focus of the services will largely depend on the age of the patient.

If an abnormality/ies is encountered or a preexisting problem is addressed in the process of performing this preventive medicine evaluation and management service, and if the problem/abnormality is significant enough to require additional work to perform the key components of a problem-oriented E/M service, then the appropriate Office/Outpatient code 99201-99215 should also be reported. Modifier '-25' should be added to the Office/Outpatient code to indicate that a significant, separately identifiable Evaluation and Management service was provided by the same physician on the same day as the preventive medicine service. The appropriate preventive medicine service is additionally reported.

An insignificant or trivial problem/abnormality that is encountered in the process of performing the preventive medicine evaluation and management service and which does not require additional work and the performance of the key components of a problem-oriented E/M service should not be reported.

The "comprehensive" nature of the Preventive Medicine Services codes 99381-99397 reflects an age and gender appropriate history/exam and is NOT synonymous with the "comprehensive" examination required in Evaluation and Management codes 99201-99350.

Codes 99381-99397 include counseling/anticipatory guidance/risk factor reduction interventions which are provided at the time of the initial or periodic comprehensive preventive medicine examination. (Refer to codes 99401-99412 for reporting those counseling/anticipatory guidance/risk factor reduction interventions that are provided at an encounter separate from the preventive medicine examination.)

Immunizations and ancillary studies involving laboratory, radiology, other procedures, or screening tests identified with a specific CPT code are reported separately. For immunizations, see 90471-90474 and 90476-90749.

New Patient

99381 **Initial comprehensive preventive medicine** evaluation and management of an individual including an age and gender appropriate history, examination, counseling/anticipatory guidance/risk factor reduction interventions, and the ordering of appropriate immunization(s), laboratory/diagnostic procedures, new patient; infant (age under 1 year)

99382 early childhood (age 1 through 4 years)

99383 late childhood (age 5 through 11 years)

99384 adolescent (age 12 through 17 years)

99385 18-39 years

99386 40-64 years

99387 65 years and over

Established Patient

99391 **Periodic comprehensive preventive medicine** reevaluation and management of an individual including an age and gender appropriate history, examination, counseling/anticipatory guidance/risk factor reduction interventions, and the ordering of appropriate immunization(s), laboratory/diagnostic procedures, established patient; infant (age under 1 year)

99392 early childhood (age 1 through 4 years)

99393 late childhood (age 5 through 11 years)

99394 adolescent (age 12 through 17 years)

99395 18-39 years

99396 40-64 years

99397 65 years and over

Counseling and/or Risk Factor Reduction Intervention

New or Established Patient

These codes are used to report services provided to individuals at a separate encounter for the purpose of promoting health and preventing illness or injury.

Preventive medicine counseling and risk factor reduction interventions provided as a separate encounter will vary with age and should address such issues as family problems, diet and exercise, substance abuse, sexual practices, injury prevention, dental health, and diagnostic and laboratory test results available at the time of the encounter.

These codes are not to be used to report counseling and risk factor reduction interventions provided to patients with symptoms or established illness. For counseling individual patients with symptoms or established illness, use the appropriate office, hospital or consultation or other evaluation and management codes. For counseling groups of patients with symptoms or established illness, use 99078.

Preventive Medicine, Individual Counseling

99401 **Preventive medicine counseling** and/or risk factor reduction intervention(s) provided to an individual (separate procedure); approximately 15 minutes

99402 approximately 30 minutes

99403 approximately 45 minutes

99404 approximately 60 minutes

Preventive Medicine, Group Counseling

99411 **Preventive medicine counseling** and/or risk factor reduction intervention(s) provided to individuals in a group setting (separate procedure); approximately 30 minutes

99412 approximately 60 minutes

Other Preventive Medicine Services

99420 **Administration and interpretation** of health risk assessment instrument (eg, health hazard appraisal)

99429 **Unlisted preventive** medicine service

Newborn Care

The following codes are used to report the services provided to newborns in several different settings.

For newborn hospital discharge services provided on a date subsequent to the admission date of the newborn, use 99238.

For discharge services provided to newborns admitted and discharged on the same date, use 99435.

99431 **History and examination** of the normal newborn infant, initiation of diagnostic and treatment programs and preparation of hospital records. (This code should also be used for birthing room deliveries.)

99432 **Normal newborn care** in other than hospital or birthing room setting, including physical examination of baby and conference(s) with parent(s)

99433 **Subsequent hospital care,** for the evaluation and management of a normal newborn, per day

99435 **History and examination** of the normal newborn infant, including the preparation of medical records. (This code should only be used for newborns assessed and discharged from the hospital or birthing room on the same date.)

99436 **Attendance** at delivery (when requested by delivering physician) and initial stabilization of newborn

(99436 may be reported in addition to 99431)

(99436 may not be reported in addition to 99440)

99440 **Newborn resuscitation:** provision of positive pressure ventilation and/or chest compressions in the presence of acute inadequate ventilation and/or cardiac output

Special Evaluation and Management Services

The following codes are used to report evaluations performed to establish baseline information prior to life or disability insurance certificates being issued. This service is performed in the office or other setting, and applies to both new and established patients. When using these codes, no active management of the problem(s) is undertaken during the encounter.

If other evaluation and management services and/or procedures are performed on the same date, the appropriate E/M or procedure code(s) should be reported in addition to these codes.

Basic Life and/or Disability Evaluation Services

99450 **Basic life** and/or disability examination that includes:

- **measurement of height, weight and blood pressure;**
- **completion of a medical history following a life insurance pro forma;**
- **collection of blood sample and/or urinalysis complying with "chain of custody" protocols; and**
- **completion of necessary documentation/certificates.**

Work Related or Medical Disability Evaluation Services

99455 **Work related** or medical disability examination by the treating physician that includes:

- **completion of a medical history commensurate with the patient's condition;**
- **performance of an examination commensurate with the patient's condition;**
- **formulation of a diagnosis, assessment of capabilities and stability, and calculation of impairment;**
- **development of future medical treatment plan; and**
- **completion of necessary documentation/certificates and report.**

99456 **Work related** or medical disability examination by other than the treating physician that includes:

- **completion of a medical history commensurate with the patient's condition;**
- **performance of an examination commensurate with the patient's condition;**
- **formulation of a diagnosis, assessment of capabilities and stability, and calculation of impairment;**
- **development of future medical treatment plan; and**
- **completion of necessary documentation/certificates and report.**

►(Do not report 99455, 99456 with 99080 for the completion of Workman's Compensation forms)◄

Other Evaluation and Management Services

99499 **Unlisted evaluation and management** service

Anesthesia Guidelines

Services involving administration of anesthesia are reported by the use of the anesthesia five digit procedure code (00100-01999) plus modifier codes (defined under "Anesthesia Modifiers" later in these Guidelines).

The reporting of anesthesia services is appropriate by or under the responsible supervision of a physician. These services may include but are not limited to general, regional, supplementation of local anesthesia, or other supportive services in order to afford the patient the anesthesia care deemed optimal by the anesthesiologist during any procedure. These services include the usual preoperative and postoperative visits, the anesthesia care during the procedure, the administration of fluids and/or blood and the usual monitoring services (eg, ECG, temperature, blood pressure, oximetry, capnography, and mass spectrometry). Unusual forms of monitoring (eg, intra-arterial, central venous, and Swan-Ganz) are not included.

Items used by all physicians in reporting their services are presented in the **Introduction.** Some of the commonalities are repeated here for the convenience of those physicians referring to this section on **Anesthesia.** Other definitions and items unique to anesthesia are also listed.

To report sedation with or without analgesia (conscious sedation) provided by a physician also performing the service for which conscious sedation is being provided, see codes 99141, 99142.

To report regional or general anesthesia provided by a physician also performing the services for which the anesthesia is being provided, see modifier '-47,' Anesthesia by Surgeon, in Appendix A.

Time Reporting

Time for anesthesia procedures may be reported as is customary in the local area. Anesthesia time begins when the anesthesiologist begins to prepare the patient for the induction of anesthesia in the operating room or in an equivalent area and ends when the anesthesiologist is no longer in personal attendance, that is, when the patient may be safely placed under postoperative supervision.

Physician's Services

Physician's services rendered in the office, home, or hospital, consultation, and other medical services are listed in the section entitled **Evaluation and Management Services** (99200 series) found in the front of the book, beginning on page 1. "Special Services and Reporting" (99000 series) are presented in the **Medicine** section.

Materials Supplied by Physician

Supplies and materials provided by the physician (eg, sterile trays, drugs) over and above those usually included with the office visit or other services rendered may be listed separately. List drugs, tray supplies, and materials provided. Identify as 99070.

Separate or Multiple Procedures

►When multiple surgical procedures are performed during a single anesthetic administration, the anesthesia code representing the most complex procedure is reported. The time reported is the combined total for all procedures.◄

Special Report

A service that is rarely provided, unusual, variable, or new may require a special report in determining medical appropriateness of the service. Pertinent information should include an adequate definition or description of the nature, extent, and need for the procedure; and the time, effort, and equipment necessary to provide the service. Additional items which may be included are:

- complexity of symptoms;
- final diagnosis;
- pertinent physical findings;
- diagnostic and therapeutic procedures;
- concurrent problems;
- follow-up care.

Anesthesia Modifiers

All anesthesia services are reported by use of the anesthesia five digit procedure code (00100-01999) plus the addition of a physical status modifier. The use of other optional modifiers may be appropriate.

Physical Status Modifiers

Physical Status modifiers are represented by the initial letter 'P' followed by a single digit from 1 to 6 defined below.

P1-A normal healthy patient.

P2-A patient with mild systemic disease.

P3-A patient with severe systemic disease.

P4-A patient with severe systemic disease that is a constant threat to life.

P5-A moribund patient who is not expected to survive without the operation.

P6-A declared brain-dead patient whose organs are being removed for donor purposes.

The above six levels are consistent with the American Society of Anesthesiologists (ASA) ranking of patient physical status. Physical status is included in CPT to distinguish among various levels of complexity of the anesthesia service provided.

Example: 00100-P1

Qualifying Circumstances

More than one may be selected.

Many anesthesia services are provided under particularly difficult circumstances, depending on factors such as extraordinary condition of patient, notable operative conditions, and/or unusual risk factors. This section includes a list of important qualifying circumstances that significantly impact on the character of the anesthesia service provided. These procedures would not be reported alone but would be reported as additional procedure numbers qualifying an anesthesia procedure or service.

+ 99100 Anesthesia for patient of extreme age, under 1 year and over 70 (List separately in addition to code for primary anesthesia procedure)

(For procedure performed on infants less than 1 year of age at time of surgery, see 00326, 00834, 00836)

+ 99116 Anesthesia complicated by utilization of total body hypothermia (List separately in addition to code for primary anesthesia procedure)

+ 99135 Anesthesia complicated by utilization of controlled hypotension (List separately in addition to code for primary anesthesia procedure)

+ 99140 Anesthesia complicated by emergency conditions (specify) (List separately in addition to code for primary anesthesia procedure)

(An emergency is defined as existing when delay in treatment of the patient would lead to a significant increase in the threat to life or body part.)

Anesthesia

Head

00100 Anesthesia for procedures on salivary glands, including biopsy

00102 Anesthesia for procedures involving plastic repair of cleft lip

00103 Anesthesia for reconstructive procedures of eyelid (eg, blepharoplasty, ptosis surgery)

00104 Anesthesia for electroconvulsive therapy

00120 Anesthesia for procedures on external, middle, and inner ear including biopsy; not otherwise specified

00124 otoscopy

00126 tympanotomy

00140 Anesthesia for procedures on eye; not otherwise specified

00142 lens surgery

00144 corneal transplant

00145 vitreoretinal surgery

00147 iridectomy

00148 ophthalmoscopy

00160 Anesthesia for procedures on nose and accessory sinuses; not otherwise specified

00162 radical surgery

00164 biopsy, soft tissue

00170 Anesthesia for intraoral procedures, including biopsy; not otherwise specified

00172 repair of cleft palate

00174 excision of retropharyngeal tumor

00176 radical surgery

00190 Anesthesia for procedures on facial bones or skull; not otherwise specified

00192 radical surgery (including prognathism)

00210 Anesthesia for intracranial procedures; not otherwise specified

00212 subdural taps

00214 burr holes, including ventriculography

00215 cranioplasty or elevation of depressed skull fracture, extradural (simple or compound)

00216 vascular procedures

00218 procedures in sitting position

00220 cerebrospinal fluid shunting procedures

00222 electrocoagulation of intracranial nerve

Neck

00300 Anesthesia for all procedures on the integumentary system, muscles and nerves of head, neck, and posterior trunk, not otherwise specified

00320 Anesthesia for all procedures on esophagus, thyroid, larynx, trachea and lymphatic system of neck; not otherwise specified, age 1 year or older

00322 needle biopsy of thyroid

(For procedures on cervical spine and cord, see 00600, 00604, 00670)

00326 Anesthesia for all procedures on the larynx and trachea in children less than 1 year of age

(Do not report 00326 in conjunction with code 99100)

00350 Anesthesia for procedures on major vessels of neck; not otherwise specified

00352 simple ligation

(For arteriography, use 01916)

Thorax (Chest Wall and Shoulder Girdle)

00400 Anesthesia for procedures on the integumentary system on the extremities, anterior trunk and perineum; not otherwise specified

00402 reconstructive procedures on breast (eg, reduction or augmentation mammoplasty, muscle flaps)

00404 radical or modified radical procedures on breast

00406 radical or modified radical procedures on breast with internal mammary node dissection

00410 electrical conversion of arrhythmias

00450 Anesthesia for procedures on clavicle and scapula; not otherwise specified

00452 radical surgery

00454 biopsy of clavicle

00470 Anesthesia for partial rib resection; not otherwise specified

00472 thoracoplasty (any type)

00474 radical procedures (eg, pectus excavatum)

Intrathoracic

00500 Anesthesia for all procedures on esophagus

00520 Anesthesia for closed chest procedures; (including bronchoscopy) not otherwise specified

00522 needle biopsy of pleura

00524 pneumocentesis

▲00528 mediastinoscopy and diagnostic thoracoscopy not utilizing one lung ventilation

(For tracheobronchial reconstruction, use 00539)

●00529 mediastinoscopy and diagnostic thoracoscopy utilizing one lung ventilation

00530 Anesthesia for permanent transvenous pacemaker insertion

00532 Anesthesia for access to central venous circulation

00534 Anesthesia for transvenous insertion or replacement of pacing cardioverter-defibrillator

(For transthoracic approach, use 00560)

00537 Anesthesia for cardiac electrophysiologic procedures including radiofrequency ablation

00539 Anesthesia for tracheobronchial reconstruction

00540 Anesthesia for thoracotomy procedures involving lungs, pleura, diaphragm, and mediastinum (including surgical thoracoscopy); not otherwise specified

00541 utilizing one lung ventilation

00542 decortication

►(00544 has been deleted. To report, use 00542)◄

00546 pulmonary resection with thoracoplasty

00548 intrathoracic procedures on the trachea and bronchi

00550 Anesthesia for sternal debridement

00560 Anesthesia for procedures on heart, pericardial sac, and great vessels of chest; without pump oxygenator

00562 with pump oxygenator

00563 with pump oxygenator with hypothermic circulatory arrest

00566 Anesthesia for direct coronary artery bypass grafting without pump oxygenator

00580 Anesthesia for heart transplant or heart/lung transplant

Spine and Spinal Cord

00600 Anesthesia for procedures on cervical spine and cord; not otherwise specified

(For myelography and diskography, see radiological procedures 01905)

00604 procedures with patient in the sitting position

00620 Anesthesia for procedures on thoracic spine and cord; not otherwise specified

00622 thoracolumbar sympathectomy

00630 Anesthesia for procedures in lumbar region; not otherwise specified

00632 lumbar sympathectomy

00634 chemonucleolysis

00635 diagnostic or therapeutic lumbar puncture

00640 Anesthesia for manipulation of the spine or for closed procedures on the cervical, thoracic or lumbar spine

00670 Anesthesia for extensive spine and spinal cord procedures (eg, spinal instrumentation or vascular procedures)

Upper Abdomen

00700 Anesthesia for procedures on upper anterior abdominal wall; not otherwise specified

00702 percutaneous liver biopsy

00730 Anesthesia for procedures on upper posterior abdominal wall

00740 Anesthesia for upper gastrointestinal endoscopic procedures, endoscope introduced proximal to duodenum

00750 Anesthesia for hernia repairs in upper abdomen; not otherwise specified

00752 lumbar and ventral (incisional) hernias and/or wound dehiscence

00754 omphalocele

00756 transabdominal repair of diaphragmatic hernia

00770 Anesthesia for all procedures on major abdominal blood vessels

00790 Anesthesia for intraperitoneal procedures in upper abdomen including laparoscopy; not otherwise specified

00792 partial hepatectomy or management of liver hemorrhage (excluding liver biopsy)

00794 pancreatectomy, partial or total (eg, Whipple procedure)

00796 liver transplant (recipient)

(For harvesting of liver, use 01990)

00797 gastric restrictive procedure for morbid obesity

Lower Abdomen

00800 Anesthesia for procedures on lower anterior abdominal wall; not otherwise specified

00802 panniculectomy

00810 Anesthesia for lower intestinal endoscopic procedures, endoscope introduced distal to duodenum

00820 Anesthesia for procedures on lower posterior abdominal wall

00830 Anesthesia for hernia repairs in lower abdomen; not otherwise specified

00832 ventral and incisional hernias

(For hernia repairs in the infant 1 year of age or younger, see 00834, 00836)

00834 Anesthesia for hernia repairs in the lower abdomen not otherwise specified, under 1 year of age

(Do not report 00834 in conjunction with code 99100)

00836 Anesthesia for hernia repairs in the lower abdomen not otherwise specified, infants less than 37 weeks gestational age at birth and less than 50 weeks gestational age at time of surgery

(Do not report 00836 in conjunction with code 99100)

00840 Anesthesia for intraperitoneal procedures in lower abdomen including laparoscopy; not otherwise specified

00842 amniocentesis

00844 abdominoperineal resection

00846 radical hysterectomy

00848 pelvic exenteration

(00850 has been deleted. To report, use 01961)

00851 tubal ligation/transection

(00855 has been deleted. To report, use 01963)

(00857 has been deleted. To report, use 01968, 01969)

00860 Anesthesia for extraperitoneal procedures in lower abdomen, including urinary tract; not otherwise specified

00862 renal procedures, including upper 1/3 of ureter, or donor nephrectomy

00864 total cystectomy

00865 radical prostatectomy (suprapubic, retropubic)

00866 adrenalectomy

00868 renal transplant (recipient)

(For donor nephrectomy, use 00862)

(For harvesting kidney from brain-dead patient, use 01990)

(00869 has been deleted. To report, use 00921)

00870 cystolithotomy

00872 Anesthesia for lithotripsy, extracorporeal shock wave; with water bath

00873 without water bath

00880 Anesthesia for procedures on major lower abdominal vessels; not otherwise specified

00882 inferior vena cava ligation

(00884 has been deleted. To report, use 01930)

Perineum

00902 Anesthesia for; anorectal procedure

00904 radical perineal procedure

00906 vulvectomy

00908 perineal prostatectomy

00910 Anesthesia for transurethral procedures (including urethrocystoscopy); not otherwise specified

00912 transurethral resection of bladder tumor(s)

00914 transurethral resection of prostate

00916 post-transurethral resection bleeding

00918 with fragmentation, manipulation and/or removal of ureteral calculus

00920 Anesthesia for procedures on male genitalia (including open urethral procedures); not otherwise specified

00921 vasectomy, unilateral/bilateral

00922 seminal vesicles

00924 undescended testis, unilateral or bilateral

00926 radical orchiectomy, inguinal

00928 radical orchiectomy, abdominal

00930 orchiopexy, unilateral or bilateral

00932 complete amputation of penis

00934 radical amputation of penis with bilateral inguinal lymphadenectomy

00936 radical amputation of penis with bilateral inguinal and iliac lymphadenectomy

00938 insertion of penile prosthesis (perineal approach)

Anesthesia

00940 Anesthesia for vaginal procedures (including biopsy of labia, vagina, cervix or endometrium); not otherwise specified

00942 colpotomy, vaginectomy, colporrhaphy, and open urethral procedures

00944 vaginal hysterectomy

(00946 has been deleted. To report, use 01960)

00948 cervical cerclage

00950 culdoscopy

00952 hysteroscopy and/or hysterosalpingography

(00955 has been deleted. To report, use 01967)

Pelvis (Except Hip)

01112 Anesthesia for bone marrow aspiration and/or biopsy, anterior or posterior iliac crest

01120 Anesthesia for procedures on bony pelvis

01130 Anesthesia for body cast application or revision

01140 Anesthesia for interpelviabdominal (hindquarter) amputation

01150 Anesthesia for radical procedures for tumor of pelvis, except hindquarter amputation

01160 Anesthesia for closed procedures involving symphysis pubis or sacroiliac joint

01170 Anesthesia for open procedures involving symphysis pubis or sacroiliac joint

● **01173** Anesthesia for open repair of fracture disruption of pelvis or column fracture involving acetabulum

01180 Anesthesia for obturator neurectomy; extrapelvic

01190 intrapelvic

Upper Leg (Except Knee)

01200 Anesthesia for all closed procedures involving hip joint

01202 Anesthesia for arthroscopic procedures of hip joint

01210 Anesthesia for open procedures involving hip joint; not otherwise specified

01212 hip disarticulation

01214 total hip arthroplasty

01215 revision of total hip arthroplasty

01220 Anesthesia for all closed procedures involving upper 2/3 of femur

01230 Anesthesia for open procedures involving upper 2/3 of femur; not otherwise specified

01232 amputation

01234 radical resection

01250 Anesthesia for all procedures on nerves, muscles, tendons, fascia, and bursae of upper leg

01260 Anesthesia for all procedures involving veins of upper leg, including exploration

01270 Anesthesia for procedures involving arteries of upper leg, including bypass graft; not otherwise specified

01272 femoral artery ligation

01274 femoral artery embolectomy

Knee and Popliteal Area

Surgical endoscopy/arthroscopy always includes a diagnostic endoscopy/arthroscopy.

01320 Anesthesia for all procedures on nerves, muscles, tendons, fascia, and bursae of knee and/or popliteal area

01340 Anesthesia for all closed procedures on lower 1/3 of femur

01360 Anesthesia for all open procedures on lower 1/3 of femur

01380 Anesthesia for all closed procedures on knee joint

01382 Anesthesia for diagnostic arthroscopic procedures of knee joint

01390 Anesthesia for all closed procedures on upper ends of tibia, fibula, and/or patella

01392 Anesthesia for all open procedures on upper ends of tibia, fibula, and/or patella

01400 Anesthesia for open or surgical arthroscopic procedures on knee joint; not otherwise specified

01402 total knee arthroplasty

01404 disarticulation at knee

01420 Anesthesia for all cast applications, removal, or repair involving knee joint

01430 Anesthesia for procedures on veins of knee and popliteal area; not otherwise specified

01432 arteriovenous fistula

01440 Anesthesia for procedures on arteries of knee and popliteal area; not otherwise specified

01442 popliteal thromboendarterectomy, with or without patch graft

01444 popliteal excision and graft or repair for occlusion or aneurysm

Lower Leg (Below Knee, Includes Ankle and Foot)

Surgical endoscopy/arthroscopy always includes a diagnostic endoscopy/arthroscopy.

01462 Anesthesia for all closed procedures on lower leg, ankle, and foot

01464 Anesthesia for arthroscopic procedures of ankle and/or foot

01470 Anesthesia for procedures on nerves, muscles, tendons, and fascia of lower leg, ankle, and foot; not otherwise specified

01472 repair of ruptured Achilles tendon, with or without graft

01474 gastrocnemius recession (eg, Strayer procedure)

01480 Anesthesia for open procedures on bones of lower leg, ankle, and foot; not otherwise specified

01482 radical resection (including below knee amputation)

01484 osteotomy or osteoplasty of tibia and/or fibula

01486 total ankle replacement

01490 Anesthesia for lower leg cast application, removal, or repair

01500 Anesthesia for procedures on arteries of lower leg, including bypass graft; not otherwise specified

01502 embolectomy, direct or with catheter

01520 Anesthesia for procedures on veins of lower leg; not otherwise specified

01522 venous thrombectomy, direct or with catheter

Shoulder and Axilla

Surgical endoscopy/arthroscopy always includes a diagnostic endoscopy/arthroscopy.

Includes humeral head and neck, sternoclavicular joint, acromioclavicular joint, and shoulder joint.

01610 Anesthesia for all procedures on nerves, muscles, tendons, fascia, and bursae of shoulder and axilla

01620 Anesthesia for all closed procedures on humeral head and neck, sternoclavicular joint, acromioclavicular joint, and shoulder joint

01622 Anesthesia for diagnostic arthroscopic procedures of shoulder joint

01630 Anesthesia for open or surgical arthroscopic procedures on humeral head and neck, sternoclavicular joint, acromioclavicular joint, and shoulder joint; not otherwise specified

01632 radical resection

01634 shoulder disarticulation

01636 interthoracoscapular (forequarter) amputation

01638 total shoulder replacement

01650 Anesthesia for procedures on arteries of shoulder and axilla; not otherwise specified

01652 axillary-brachial aneurysm

01654 bypass graft

01656 axillary-femoral bypass graft

01670 Anesthesia for all procedures on veins of shoulder and axilla

01680 Anesthesia for shoulder cast application, removal or repair; not otherwise specified

01682 shoulder spica

Upper Arm and Elbow

Surgical endoscopy/arthroscopy always includes a diagnostic endoscopy/arthroscopy.

01710 Anesthesia for procedures on nerves, muscles, tendons, fascia, and bursae of upper arm and elbow; not otherwise specified

01712 tenotomy, elbow to shoulder, open

01714 tenoplasty, elbow to shoulder

01716 tenodesis, rupture of long tendon of biceps

01730 Anesthesia for all closed procedures on humerus and elbow

01732 Anesthesia for diagnostic arthroscopic procedures of elbow joint

01740 Anesthesia for open or surgical arthroscopic procedures of the elbow; not otherwise specified

01742 osteotomy of humerus

01744 repair of nonunion or malunion of humerus

01756 radical procedures

01758 excision of cyst or tumor of humerus

01760 total elbow replacement

01770 Anesthesia for procedures on arteries of upper arm and elbow; not otherwise specified

01772 embolectomy

01780 Anesthesia for procedures on veins of upper arm and elbow; not otherwise specified

01782 phleborrhaphy

Forearm, Wrist, and Hand

01810 Anesthesia for all procedures on nerves, muscles, tendons, fascia, and bursae of forearm, wrist, and hand

01820 Anesthesia for all closed procedures on radius, ulna, wrist, or hand bones

01829 Anesthesia for diagnostic arthroscopic procedures on the wrist

01830 Anesthesia for open or surgical arthroscopic/endoscopic procedures on distal radius, distal ulna, wrist, or hand joints; not otherwise specified

01832 total wrist replacement

01840 Anesthesia for procedures on arteries of forearm, wrist, and hand; not otherwise specified

01842 embolectomy

01844 Anesthesia for vascular shunt, or shunt revision, any type (eg, dialysis)

01850 Anesthesia for procedures on veins of forearm, wrist, and hand; not otherwise specified

01852 phleborrhaphy

01860 Anesthesia for forearm, wrist, or hand cast application, removal, or repair

Radiological Procedures

(01904 has been deleted. To report, use 01905)

01905 Anesthesia for myelography, diskography, vertebroplasty

(01906 has been deleted. To report, use 01905)

(01908 has been deleted. To report, use 01905)

(01910 has been deleted. To report, use 01905)

(01912 has been deleted. To report, use 01905)

(01914 has been deleted. To report, use 01905)

01916 Anesthesia for diagnostic arteriography/venography

(Do not report 01916 in conjunction with therapeutic codes 01924-01926, 01930-01933)

(01918 has been deleted. To report, use 01916)

01920 Anesthesia for cardiac catheterization including coronary angiography and ventriculography (not to include Swan-Ganz catheter)

(01921 has been deleted. To report, see 01924-01926)

01922 Anesthesia for non-invasive imaging or radiation therapy

01924 Anesthesia for therapeutic interventional radiologic procedures involving the arterial system; not otherwise specified

01925 carotid or coronary

01926 intracranial, intracardiac, or aortic

01930 Anesthesia for therapeutic interventional radiologic procedures involving the venous/lymphatic system (not to include access to the central circulation); not otherwise specified

01931 intrahepatic or portal circulation (eg, transcutaneous porto-caval shunt (TIPS))

01932 intrathoracic or jugular

01933 intracranial

Burn Excisions or Debridement

01951 Anesthesia for second and third degree burn excision or debridement with or without skin grafting, any site, for total body surface area (TBSA) treated during anesthesia and surgery; less than four percent total body surface area

01952 between four and nine percent of total body surface area

+ 01953 each additional nine percent total body surface area or part thereof (List separately in addition to code for primary procedure)

(Use 01953 in conjunction with code 01952)

Obstetric

● 01958 Anesthesia for external cephalic version procedure

01960 Anesthesia for vaginal delivery only

01961 Anesthesia for cesarean delivery only

01962 Anesthesia for urgent hysterectomy following delivery

01963 Anesthesia for cesarean hysterectomy without any labor analgesia/anesthesia care

01964 Anesthesia for abortion procedures

01967 Neuraxial labor analgesia/anesthesia for planned vaginal delivery (this includes any repeat subarachnoid needle placement and drug injection and/or any necessary replacement of an epidural catheter during labor)

+ 01968 Anesthesia for cesarean delivery following neuraxial labor analgesia/anesthesia (List separately in addition to code for primary procedure performed)

(Use 01968 in conjunction with code 01967)

+ 01969 Anesthesia for cesarean hysterectomy following neuraxial labor analgesia/anesthesia (List separately in addition to code for primary procedure performed)

(Use 01969 in conjunction with code 01967)

Other Procedures

01990 Physiological support for harvesting of organ(s) from brain-dead patient

01991 Anesthesia for diagnostic or therapeutic nerve blocks and injections (when block or injection is performed by a different provider); other than the prone position

01992 prone position

(Do not report code 01991or 01992 in conjunction with 99141)

01995 Regional intravenous administration of local anesthetic agent or other medication (upper or lower extremity)

(For intra-arterial or intravenous therapy for pain management, see 90783, 90784)

01996 Daily hospital management of epidural or subarachnoid continuous drug administration

(Report code 01996 for daily hospital management of continuous epidural or subarachnoid drug administration performed after insertion of an epidural or subarachnoid catheter)

01999 Unlisted anesthesia procedure(s)

Notes

Surgery Guidelines

Items used by all physicians in reporting their services are presented in the **Introduction.** Some of the commonalities are repeated here for the convenience of those physicians referring to this section on **Surgery.** Other definitions and items unique to Surgery are also listed.

Physicians' Services

Physicians' services rendered in the office, home, or hospital, consultations, and other medical services are listed in the section entitled **Evaluation and Management Services** (99200 series) found in the front of the book, beginning on page 9. "Special Services and Reports" (99000 series) is presented in the **Medicine** section.

CPT Surgical Package Definition

The services provided by the physician to any patient by their very nature are variable. The CPT codes that represent a readily identifiable surgical procedure thereby include, on a procedure-by-procedure basis, a variety of services. In defining the specific services "included" in a given CPT surgical code, the following services are always included in addition to the operation per se:

- local infiltration, metacarpal/metatarsal/digital block or topical anesthesia;
- subsequent to the decision for surgery, one related E/M encounter on the date immediately prior to or on the date of procedure (including history and physical);
- immediate postoperative care, including dictating operative notes, talking with the family and other physicians;
- writing orders;
- evaluating the patient in the postanesthesia recovery area;
- typical postoperative follow-up care.

Follow-Up Care for Diagnostic Procedures

Follow-up care for diagnostic procedures (eg, endoscopy, arthroscopy, injection procedures for radiography) includes only that care related to recovery from the diagnostic procedure itself. Care of the condition for which the diagnostic procedure was performed or of other concomitant conditions is not included and may be listed separately.

Follow-Up Care for Therapeutic Surgical Procedures

Follow-up care for therapeutic surgical procedures includes only that care which is usually a part of the surgical service. Complications, exacerbations, recurrence, or the presence of other diseases or injuries requiring additional services should be separately reported.

Materials Supplied by Physician

Supplies and materials provided by the physician (eg, sterile trays/drugs), over and above those usually included with the procedure(s) rendered are reported separately. List drugs, trays, supplies, and materials provided. Identify as 99070 or specific supply code.

Reporting More Than One Procedure/Service

When a physician performs more than one procedure/service on the same date, same session or during a post-operative period (subject to the "surgical package" concept), several CPT modifiers may apply. (See Appendix A for definition.)

-27 Multiple Outpatient Hospital E/M Encounters on the Same Date

For hospital outpatient reporting purposes, utilization of hospital resources related to separate and distinct E/M encounters performed in multiple outpatient hospital settings on the same date may be reported by adding the modifier '-27' to each appropriate level outpatient and/or emergency department E/M code(s). This modifier provides a means of reporting circumstances involving evaluation and management services provided by physician(s) in more than one (multiple) outpatient hospital setting(s) (eg, hospital emergency department, clinic). **Note:** This modifier is not to be used for physician reporting of multiple E/M services performed by the same physician on the same date. For physician reporting of all outpatient evaluation and management services provided by the same physician on the same date and performed in multiple outpatient setting(s) (eg, hospital emergency department, clinic), see **Evaluation and Management, Emergency Department,** or **Preventive Medicine Services** codes.

-51 Multiple Procedures

When multiple procedures/services (other than evaluation and management) are performed at the same session, report the most significant procedure first, with all other procedures listed with the '-51' modifier appended. For a list of procedures exempt from the use of the '-51' modifier, see Appendices D and E.

-58 Staged or Related Procedure or Service by the Same Physician During the Postoperative Period

When a procedure(s) is prospectively planned as a staged procedure, or when the secondary and subsequent procedure(s) is more extensive, or to indicate therapy following a diagnostic surgical procedure, use the '-58' modifier with the staged procedure(s).

-59 Distinct Procedural Service

For procedure(s)/service(s) not ordinarily performed or encountered on the same day by the same physician, but appropriate under certain circumstances (eg, different site or organ system, separate excision or lesion), use the '-59' modifier.

-76 Repeat Procedure by Same Physician

When a procedure or service is repeated by the same physician subsequent to the original service, use the '-76' modifier.

-77 Repeat Procedure by Another Physician

When a procedure is repeated by another physician subsequent to the original service, use the '-77' modifier.

-78 Return to the Operating Room for a Related Procedure During the Postoperative Period

When a procedure, related to the initial procedure, requires a return to the operating room during the postoperative period of that initial procedure, use the '-78' modifier.

-79 Unrelated Procedure or Service by the Same Physician During the Postoperative Period

When a procedure, unrelated to the initial procedure, is performed by the same physician during the postoperative period of the initial procedure, use the '-79' modifier.

-91 Repeat Clinical Diagnostic Laboratory Test

In the course of treatment of the patient, it may be necessary to repeat the same laboratory test on the same day to obtain subsequent (multiple) test results. Under these circumstances, the laboratory test performed can be identified by its usual procedure number and the addition of the modifier '-91'. **Note:** This modifier may not be used when tests are rerun to confirm initial results; due to testing problems with specimens or equipment; or for any other reason when a normal, one-time, reportable result is all that is required. This modifier may not be used when other code(s) describe a series of test results (eg, glucose tolerance tests, evocative/suppression testing). This modifier may only be used for laboratory test(s) performed more than once on the same day on the same patient.

Separate Procedure

Some of the procedures or services listed in *CPT* that are commonly carried out as an integral component of a total service or procedure have been identified by the inclusion of the term "separate procedure." The codes designated as "separate procedure" should not be reported in addition to the code for the total procedure or service of which it is considered an integral component.

However, when a procedure or service that is designated as a "separate procedure" is carried out independently or considered to be unrelated or distinct from other procedures/services provided at that time, it may be reported by itself, or in addition to other procedures/services by appending the modifier '-59' to the specific "separate procedure" code to indicate that the procedure is not considered to be a component of another procedure, but is a distinct, independent procedure. This may represent a different session or patient encounter, different procedure or surgery, different site or organ system, separate incision/excision, separate lesion, or separate injury (or area of injury in extensive injuries).

Subsection Information

Several of the subheadings or subsections have special needs or instructions unique to that section. Where these are indicated (eg, "Maternity Care and Delivery"), special **"Notes"** will be presented preceding those procedural terminology listings, referring to that subsection specifically. If there is an "Unlisted Procedure" code number (see below) for the individual subsection, it will also be shown. Those subsections within the **Surgery** section that have **"Notes"** are as follows:

Removal of Skin Tags 11200-11201

Shaving of Lesions 11300-11313

Excision—Benign Lesions 11400-11471

Excision—Malignant Lesions 11600-11646

Repair (Closure) 12001-13160

Adjacent Tissue Transfer or Rearrangement 14000-14350

Free Skin Grafts 15000-15400

Flaps (Skin and/or Deep Tissue) 15570-15999

Burns, Local Treatment 16000-16036

Destruction, Benign Lesions 17000-17250

Destruction, Malignant Lesions 17260-17286

Mohs Micrographic Surgery 17304-17310

Musculoskeletal 20000-29999

Wound Exploration—Trauma 20100-20103

Grafts (or Implants) 20900-20999

Spine: Excision 22100-22116

Spine: Osteotomy 22210-22226

Spine: Fracture/Dislocation 22305-22328

Spine: Arthrodesis 22548-22812

Spinal Instrumentation 22840-22855

Casting and Strapping 29000-29750

Cardiovascular System 33010-37799

Pacing Cardioverter-Pacemaker or Defibrillator 33200-33249

Venous—CABG 33510-33516

Arterial—Venous—CABG 33517-33530

Arterial—CABG 33533-33545

Arteries and Veins 34001-35907

Endovascular Repair of Abdominal Aortic Aneurysm 34800-34826

Endovascular Repair of Illiac Aneurysm 34900

Transluminal Angioplasty 35450-35476

Transluminal Atherectomy 35480-35495

Composite Grafts 35681-35683

Vascular Injection Procedures: Intravenous 36000-36015

►**Central Venous Access Procedures** . . 36555-36597◄

Intra-Arterial/Intra-Aortic 36100-36299, 37250-37251

Endoscopy 31505-31579, 32601-32665, 43200-43272, 44360-44397, 45300-45387, 46600-46615, 47550-47556

Herniotomy 49491-49611

Urodynamics 51725-51797

Endoscopy

- **Urinary** 50945-50980, 51990-52400
- **Testis** 54690-54699
- **Female Genital** 58550-58579, 58660-58679
- **Endocrine** 60650-60659

Ureter and Pelvis 52320-52355

Maternity Care and Delivery 59000-59899

Surgery of Skull Base 61580-61619

Neurostimulators (Intracranial) 61850-61888, 62263-62319

Neurostimulators (Spinal) 63650-63688

Neurostimulators (Peripheral Nerve) . 64553-64595

Secondary Implants(s) 65125-65175

Removal Cataract 66830-66999

Prophylaxis 67141-67145

Operating Microscope 69990

Unlisted Service or Procedure

A service or procedure may be provided that is not listed in this edition of *CPT*. When reporting such a service, the appropriate "Unlisted Procedure" code may be used to indicate the service, identifying it by "Special Report" as discussed in the section below. The "Unlisted Procedures" and accompanying codes for **Surgery** are as follows:

15999 Unlisted procedure, excision pressure ulcer

17999 Unlisted procedure, skin, mucous membrane and subcutaneous tissue

19499 Unlisted procedure, breast

20999 Unlisted procedure, musculoskeletal system, general

21089 Unlisted maxillofacial prosthetic procedure

21299 Unlisted craniofacial and maxillofacial procedure

21499 Unlisted musculoskeletal procedure, head

21899 Unlisted procedure, neck or thorax

22899 Unlisted procedure, spine

22999 Unlisted procedure, abdomen, musculoskeletal system

23929	Unlisted procedure, shoulder
24999	Unlisted procedure, humerus or elbow
25999	Unlisted procedure, forearm or wrist
26989	Unlisted procedure, hands or fingers
27299	Unlisted procedure, pelvis or hip joint
27599	Unlisted procedure, femur or knee
27899	Unlisted procedure, leg or ankle
28899	Unlisted procedure, foot or toes
29799	Unlisted procedure, casting or strapping
29999	Unlisted procedure, arthroscopy
30999	Unlisted procedure, nose
31299	Unlisted procedure, accessory sinuses
31599	Unlisted procedure, larynx
31899	Unlisted procedure, trachea, bronchi
32999	Unlisted procedure, lungs and pleura
33999	Unlisted procedure, cardiac surgery
36299	Unlisted procedure, vascular injection
37501	Unlisted vascular endoscopy procedure
37799	Unlisted procedure, vascular surgery
38129	Unlisted laparoscopy procedure, spleen
38589	Unlisted laparoscopy procedure, lymphatic system
38999	Unlisted procedure, hemic or lymphatic system
39499	Unlisted procedure, mediastinum
39599	Unlisted procedure, diaphragm
40799	Unlisted procedure, lips
40899	Unlisted procedure, vestibule of mouth
41599	Unlisted procedure, tongue, floor of mouth
41899	Unlisted procedure, dentoalveolar structures
42299	Unlisted procedure, palate, uvula
42699	Unlisted procedure, salivary glands or ducts
42999	Unlisted procedure, pharynx, adenoids, or tonsils
43289	Unlisted laparoscopy procedure, esophagus
43499	Unlisted procedure, esophagus
43659	Unlisted laparoscopy procedure, stomach
43999	Unlisted procedure, stomach
44238	Unlisted laparoscopy procedure, intestine (except rectum)
44239	Unlisted laparoscopy procedure, rectum
44799	Unlisted procedure, intestine
44899	Unlisted procedure, Meckels diverticulum and the mesentery
44979	Unlisted laparoscopy procedure, appendix
45999	Unlisted procedure, rectum
46999	Unlisted procedure, anus
47379	Unlisted laparoscopic procedure, liver
47399	Unlisted procedure, liver
47579	Unlisted laparoscopy procedure, biliary tract
47999	Unlisted procedure, biliary tract
48999	Unlisted procedure, pancreas
49329	Unlisted laparoscopy procedure, abdomen, peritoneum and omentum
49659	Unlisted laparoscopy procedure, hernioplasty, herniorrhaphy, herniotomy
49999	Unlisted procedure, abdomen, peritoneum and omentum
50549	Unlisted laparoscopy procedure, renal
50949	Unlisted laparoscopy procedure, ureter
53899	Unlisted procedure, urinary system
54699	Unlisted laparoscopy procedure, testis
55559	Unlisted laparoscopy procedure, spermatic cord
55899	Unlisted procedure, male genital system
58578	Unlisted laparoscopy procedure, uterus
58579	Unlisted hysteroscopy procedure, uterus
58679	Unlisted laparoscopy procedure, oviduct, ovary
58999	Unlisted procedure, female genital system (nonobstetrical)
►**59897**	Unlisted fetal invasive procedure, including ultrasound guidance◄
59898	Unlisted laparoscopy procedure, maternity care and delivery
59899	Unlisted procedure, maternity care and delivery
60659	Unlisted laparoscopy procedure, endocrine system
60699	Unlisted procedure, endocrine system
64999	Unlisted procedure, nervous system
66999	Unlisted procedure, anterior segment of eye
67299	Unlisted procedure, posterior segment
67399	Unlisted procedure, ocular muscle
67599	Unlisted procedure, orbit
67999	Unlisted procedure, eyelids
68399	Unlisted procedure, conjunctiva
68899	Unlisted procedure, lacrimal system
69399	Unlisted procedure, external ear
69799	Unlisted procedure, middle ear
69949	Unlisted procedure, inner ear
69979	Unlisted procedure, temporal bone, middle fossa approach

Special Report

A service that is rarely provided, unusual, variable, or new may require a special report in determining medical appropriateness of the service. Pertinent information should include an adequate definition or description of the nature, extent, and need for the procedure, and the time, effort, and equipment necessary to provide the service. Additional items which may be included are:

- complexity of symptoms;
- final diagnosis;
- pertinent physical findings (such as size, locations, and number of lesion(s), if appropriate);
- diagnostic and therapeutic procedures (including major and supplementary surgical procedures, if appropriate);
- concurrent problems;
- follow-up care.

Surgical Destruction

Surgical destruction is a part of a surgical procedure and different methods of destruction are not ordinarily listed separately unless the technique substantially alters the standard management of a problem or condition. Exceptions under special circumstances are provided for by separate code numbers.

Notes

Surgery

General

(10000-10020 have been deleted. To report see 10060, 10061)

10021 Fine needle aspiration; without imaging guidance

10022 with imaging guidance

(For radiological supervision and interpretation, see 76003, 76360, 76393, 76942)

(For percutaneous needle biopsy other than fine needle aspiration, see 20206 for muscle, 32400 for pleura, 32405 for lung or mediastinum, 42400 for salivary gland, 47000, 47001 for liver, 48102 for pancreas, 49180 for abdominal or retroperitoneal mass, 60100 for thyroid, 62269 for spinal cord)

(For evaluation of fine needle aspirate, see 88172, 88173)

Integumentary System

Skin, Subcutaneous and Accessory Structures

Incision and Drainage

(For excision, see 11400, et seq)

10040 Acne surgery (eg, marsupialization, opening or removal of multiple milia, comedones, cysts, pustules)

10060 Incision and drainage of abscess (eg, carbuncle, suppurative hidradenitis, cutaneous or subcutaneous abscess, cyst, furuncle, or paronychia); simple or single

10061 complicated or multiple

10080 Incision and drainage of pilonidal cyst; simple

10081 complicated

(For excision of pilonidal cyst, see 11770-11772)

10120 Incision and removal of foreign body, subcutaneous tissues; simple

10121 complicated

(To report wound exploration due to penetrating trauma without laparotomy or thoracotomy, see 20100-20103, as appropriate)

(To report debridement associated with open fracture(s) and/or dislocation(s), use 11010-11012, as appropriate)

10140 Incision and drainage of hematoma, seroma or fluid collection

(If imaging guidance is performed, see 76360, 76393, 76942)

10160 Puncture aspiration of abscess, hematoma, bulla, or cyst

(If imaging guidance is performed, see 76360, 76393, 76942)

10180 Incision and drainage, complex, postoperative wound infection

(For secondary closure of surgical wound, see 12020, 12021, 13160)

Excision—Debridement

(For dermabrasions, see 15780-15783)

(For nail debridement, see 11720-11721)

(For burn(s), see 16000-16035)

11000 Debridement of extensive eczematous or infected skin; up to 10% of body surface

+ 11001 each additional 10% of the body surface (List separately in addition to code for primary procedure)

(Use 11001 in conjunction with code 11000)

11010 Debridement including removal of foreign material associated with open fracture(s) and/or dislocation(s); skin and subcutaneous tissues

11011 skin, subcutaneous tissue, muscle fascia, and muscle

11012 skin, subcutaneous tissue, muscle fascia, muscle, and bone

11040 Debridement; skin, partial thickness

11041 skin, full thickness

11042 skin, and subcutaneous tissue

11043 skin, subcutaneous tissue, and muscle

11044 skin, subcutaneous tissue, muscle, and bone

(Do not report 11040-11044 in addition to 97601, 97602)

Paring or Cutting

11055 Paring or cutting of benign hyperkeratotic lesion (eg, corn or callus); single lesion

11056 two to four lesions

11057 more than four lesions

Biopsy

►During certain surgical procedures in the integumentary system, such as excision, destruction, or shave removals, the removed tissue is often submitted for pathologic examination. The obtaining of tissue for pathology during the course of these procedures is a routine component of such procedures. This obtaining of tissue is not considered a separate biopsy procedure and is not separately reported. The use of a biopsy procedure code (eg, 11100, 11101) indicates that the procedure to obtain tissue for pathologic examination was performed independently, or was unrelated or distinct from other procedures/services provided at that time. Such biopsies are not considered components of other procedures when performed on different lesions or different sites on the same date, and are to be reported separately.◄

(For biopsy of conjunctiva, use 68100; eyelid, use 67810)

▲**11100** Biopsy of skin, subcutaneous tissue and/or mucous membrane (including simple closure), unless otherwise listed; single lesion

+ **11101** each separate/additional lesion (List separately in addition to code for primary procedure)

(Use 11101 in conjunction with code 11100)

Removal of Skin Tags

Removal by scissoring or any sharp method, ligature strangulation, electrosurgical destruction or combination of treatment modalities including chemical or electrocauterization of wound, with or without local anesthesia.

11200 Removal of skin tags, multiple fibrocutaneous tags, any area; up to and including 15 lesions

+ **11201** each additional ten lesions (List separately in addition to code for primary procedure)

(Use 11201 in conjunction with code 11200)

Shaving of Epidermal or Dermal Lesions

Shaving is the sharp removal by transverse incision or horizontal slicing to remove epidermal and dermal lesions without a full-thickness dermal excision. This includes local anesthesia, chemical or electrocauterization of the wound. The wound does not require suture closure.

11300 Shaving of epidermal or dermal lesion, single lesion, trunk, arms or legs; lesion diameter 0.5 cm or less

11301 lesion diameter 0.6 to 1.0 cm

11302 lesion diameter 1.1 to 2.0 cm

11303 lesion diameter over 2.0 cm

11305 Shaving of epidermal or dermal lesion, single lesion, scalp, neck, hands, feet, genitalia; lesion diameter 0.5 cm or less

11306 lesion diameter 0.6 to 1.0 cm

11307 lesion diameter 1.1 to 2.0 cm

11308 lesion diameter over 2.0 cm

11310 Shaving of epidermal or dermal lesion, single lesion, face, ears, eyelids, nose, lips, mucous membrane; lesion diameter 0.5 cm or less

11311 lesion diameter 0.6 to 1.0 cm

11312 lesion diameter 1.1 to 2.0 cm

11313 lesion diameter over 2.0 cm

Excision—Benign Lesions

Excision (including simple closure) of benign lesions of skin (eg, neoplasm, cicatricial, fibrous, inflammatory, congenital, cystic lesions), includes local anesthesia. See appropriate size and area below. For shave removal, see 11300 et seq., and for electrosurgical and other methods see 17000 et seq.

Excision is defined as full-thickness (through the dermis) removal of a lesion, including margins, and includes simple (non-layered) closure when performed. Report separately each benign lesion excised. Code selection is determined by measuring the greatest clinical diameter of the apparent lesion plus that margin required for complete excision (lesion diameter plus the most narrow margins required equals the excised diameter). The margins refer to the most narrow margin required to adequately excise the lesion, based on the physician's judgment. The measurement of lesion plus margin is made prior to excision. The excised diameter is the same whether the surgical defect is repaired in a linear fashion, or reconstructed (eg, with a skin graft).

The closure of defects created by incision, excision, or trauma may require intermediate or complex closure. Repair by intermediate or complex closure should be reported separately. For excision of benign lesions requiring more than simple closure, ie, requiring intermediate or complex closure, report 11400-11446 in addition to appropriate intermediate (12031-12057) or complex closure (13100-13153) codes. For reconstructive closure, see 14000-14300, 15000-15261, 15570-15770. See page 51 for definition of intermediate or complex closure.

11400 Excision, benign lesion including margins, except skin tag (unless listed elsewhere), trunk, arms or legs; excised diameter 0.5 cm or less

11401 excised diameter 0.6 to 1.0 cm

11402 excised diameter 1.1 to 2.0 cm

11403 excised diameter 2.1 to 3.0 cm

11404 excised diameter 3.1 to 4.0 cm

11406 excised diameter over 4.0 cm

(For unusual or complicated excision, add modifier '-22')

11420 Excision, benign lesion including margins, except skin tag (unless listed elsewhere), scalp, neck, hands, feet, genitalia; excised diameter 0.5 cm or less

11421 excised diameter 0.6 to 1.0 cm

11422 excised diameter 1.1 to 2.0 cm

11423 excised diameter 2.1 to 3.0 cm

11424 excised diameter 3.1 to 4.0 cm

11426 excised diameter over 4.0 cm

(For unusual or complicated excision, add modifier '-22')

11440 Excision, other benign lesion including margins (unless listed elsewhere), face, ears, eyelids, nose, lips, mucous membrane; excised diameter 0.5 cm or less

11441 excised diameter 0.6 to 1.0 cm

11442 excised diameter 1.1 to 2.0 cm

11443 excised diameter 2.1 to 3.0 cm

11444 excised diameter 3.1 to 4.0 cm

11446 excised diameter over 4.0 cm

(For unusual or complicated excision, add modifier '-22')

(For eyelids involving more than skin, see also 67800 et seq)

11450 Excision of skin and subcutaneous tissue for hidradenitis, axillary; with simple or intermediate repair

11451 with complex repair

11462 Excision of skin and subcutaneous tissue for hidradenitis, inguinal; with simple or intermediate repair

11463 with complex repair

11470 Excision of skin and subcutaneous tissue for hidradenitis, perianal, perineal, or umbilical; with simple or intermediate repair

11471 with complex repair

(When skin graft or flap is used for closure, use appropriate procedure code in addition)

(For bilateral procedure, add modifier '-50')

Excision—Malignant Lesions

Excision (including simple closure) of malignant lesions of skin (eg, basal cell carcinoma, squamous cell carcinoma, melanoma) includes local anesthesia. (See appropriate size and body area below.) For destruction of malignant lesions of skin, see destruction codes 17260-17286.

Excision is defined as full-thickness (through the dermis) removal of a lesion including margins, and includes simple (non-layered) closure when performed. Report separately each malignant lesion excised. Code selection is determined by measuring the greatest clinical diameter of the apparent lesion plus that margin required for complete excision (lesion diameter plus the most narrow margins required equals the excised diameter). The margins refer to the most narrow margin required to adequately excise the lesion, based on the physician's judgment. The measurement of lesion plus margin is made prior to excision. The excised diameter is the same whether the surgical defect is repaired in a linear fashion, or reconstructed (eg, with a skin graft).

The closure of defects created by incision, excision, or trauma may require intermediate or complex closure. Repair by intermediate or complex closure should be reported separately. For excision of malignant lesions requiring more than simple closure, ie, requiring intermediate or complex closure, report 11600-11646 in addition to appropriate intermediate (12031-12057) or complex closure (13100-13153) codes. For reconstructive closure, see 14000-14300, 15000-15261, 15570-15770. See page 51 for definition of intermediate or complex closure.

When frozen section pathology shows the margins of excision were not adequate, an additional excision may be necessary for complete tumor removal. Use only one code to report the additional excision and re-excision(s) based on the final widest excised diameter required for complete tumor removal at the same operative session. To report a re-excision procedure performed to widen margins at a subsequent operative session, see codes 11600-11646, as appropriate. Append the modifier '-58' if the re-excision procedure is performed during the postoperative period of the primary excision procedure.

11600 Excision, malignant lesion including margins, trunk, arms, or legs; excised diameter 0.5 cm or less

11601 excised diameter 0.6 to 1.0 cm

11602 excised diameter 1.1 to 2.0 cm

11603 excised diameter 2.1 to 3.0 cm

11604 excised diameter 3.1 to 4.0 cm

11606 excised diameter over 4.0 cm

11620 Excision, malignant lesion including margins, scalp, neck, hands, feet, genitalia; excised diameter 0.5 cm or less

11621 excised diameter 0.6 to 1.0 cm

11622 excised diameter 1.1 to 2.0 cm

11623 excised diameter 2.1 to 3.0 cm

11624 excised diameter 3.1 to 4.0 cm

11626 excised diameter over 4.0 cm

11640 Excision, malignant lesion including margins, face, ears, eyelids, nose, lips; excised diameter 0.5 cm or less

11641 excised diameter 0.6 to 1.0 cm

11642 excised diameter 1.1 to 2.0 cm

11643 excised diameter 2.1 to 3.0 cm

11644 excised diameter 3.1 to 4.0 cm

11646 excised diameter over 4.0 cm

(For eyelids involving more than skin, see also 67800 et seq)

Nails

(For drainage of paronychia or onychia, see 10060, 10061)

11719 Trimming of nondystrophic nails, any number

11720 Debridement of nail(s) by any method(s); one to five

11721 six or more

11730 Avulsion of nail plate, partial or complete, simple; single

+ 11732 each additional nail plate (List separately in addition to code for primary procedure)

(Use 11732 in conjunction with code 11730)

11740 Evacuation of subungual hematoma

11750 Excision of nail and nail matrix, partial or complete, (eg, ingrown or deformed nail) for permanent removal;

11752 with amputation of tuft of distal phalanx

(For skin graft, if used, use 15050)

11755 Biopsy of nail unit (eg, plate, bed, matrix, hyponychium, proximal and lateral nail folds) (separate procedure)

11760 Repair of nail bed

11762 Reconstruction of nail bed with graft

11765 Wedge excision of skin of nail fold (eg, for ingrown toenail)

▸Pilonidal Cyst◂

11770 Excision of pilonidal cyst or sinus; simple

11771 extensive

11772 complicated

(For incision of pilonidal cyst, see 10080, 10081)

Introduction

11900 Injection, intralesional; up to and including seven lesions

11901 more than seven lesions

(11900, 11901 are not to be used for preoperative local anesthetic injection)

(For veins, see 36470, 36471)

(For intralesional chemotherapy administration, see 96405, 96406)

11920 Tattooing, intradermal introduction of insoluble opaque pigments to correct color defects of skin, including micropigmentation; 6.0 sq cm or less

11921 6.1 to 20.0 sq cm

+ 11922 each additional 20.0 sq cm (List separately in addition to code for primary procedure)

(Use 11922 in conjunction with code 11921)

11950 Subcutaneous injection of filling material (eg, collagen); 1 cc or less

11951 1.1 to 5.0 cc

11952 5.1 to 10.0 cc

11954 over 10.0 cc

11960 Insertion of tissue expander(s) for other than breast, including subsequent expansion

(For breast reconstruction with tissue expander(s), use 19357)

11970 Replacement of tissue expander with permanent prosthesis

11971 Removal of tissue expander(s) without insertion of prosthesis

11975 Insertion, implantable contraceptive capsules

11976 Removal, implantable contraceptive capsules

11977 Removal with reinsertion, implantable contraceptive capsules

11980 Subcutaneous hormone pellet implantation (implantation of estradiol and/or testosterone pellets beneath the skin)

11981 Insertion, non-biodegradable drug delivery implant

11982 Removal, non-biodegradable drug delivery implant

11983 Removal with reinsertion, non-biodegradable drug delivery implant

Repair (Closure)

Use the codes in this section to designate wound closure utilizing sutures, staples, or tissue adhesives (eg, 2-cyanoacrylate), either singly or in combination with each other, or in combination with adhesive strips. Wound closure utilizing adhesive strips as the sole repair material should be coded using the appropriate E/M code.

Definitions

The repair of wounds may be classified as Simple, Intermediate, or Complex.

Simple repair is used when the wound is superficial; eg, involving primarily epidermis or dermis, or subcutaneous tissues without significant involvement of deeper structures, and requires simple one layer closure. This includes local anesthesia and chemical or electrocauterization of wounds not closed.

Intermediate repair includes the repair of wounds that, in addition to the above, require layered closure of one or more of the deeper layers of subcutaneous tissue and superficial (non-muscle) fascia, in addition to the skin (epidermal and dermal) closure. Single-layer closure of heavily contaminated wounds that have required extensive cleaning or removal of particulate matter also constitutes intermediate repair.

Complex repair includes the repair of wounds requiring more than layered closure, viz., scar revision, debridement, (eg, traumatic lacerations or avulsions), extensive undermining, stents or retention sutures. Necessary preparation includes creation of a defect for repairs (eg, excision of a scar requiring a complex repair) or the debridement of complicated lacerations or avulsions. Complex repair does not include excision of benign (11400-11446) or malignant (11600-11646) lesions.

Instructions for listing services at time of wound repair:

1. The repaired wound(s) should be measured and recorded in centimeters, whether curved, angular, or stellate.

2. When multiple wounds are repaired, add together the lengths of those in the same classification (see above) and from all anatomic sites that are grouped together into the same code descriptor. For example, add together the lengths of intermediate repairs to the trunk and extremities. Do not add lengths of repairs from different groupings of anatomic sites (eg, face and extremities). Also, do not add together lengths of different classifications (eg, intermediate and complex repairs).

When more than one classification of wounds is repaired, list the more complicated as the primary procedure and the less complicated as the secondary procedure, using modifier '-51'.

3. Decontamination and/or debridement: Debridement is considered a separate procedure only when gross contamination requires prolonged cleansing, when appreciable amounts of devitalized or contaminated tissue are removed, or when debridement is carried out separately without immediate primary closure. (For extensive debridement of soft tissue and/or bone, see 11040-11044.)

(For extensive debridement of soft tissue and/or bone, not associated with open fracture(s) and/or dislocation(s) resulting from penetrating and/or blunt trauma, see 11040-11044.)

(For extensive debridement of subcutaneous tissue, muscle fascia, muscle, and/or bone associated with open fracture(s) and/or dislocation(s), see 11010-11012.)

4. Involvement of nerves, blood vessels and tendons: Report under appropriate system (Nervous, Cardiovascular, Musculoskeletal) for repair of these structures. The repair of these associated wounds is included in the primary procedure unless it qualifies as a complex wound, in which case modifier '-51' applies.

Simple ligation of vessels in an open wound is considered as part of any wound closure.

Simple "exploration" of nerves, blood vessels or tendons exposed in an open wound is also considered part of the essential treatment of the wound and is not a separate procedure unless appreciable dissection is required. If the wound requires enlargement, extension of dissection (to determine penetration), debridement, removal of foreign body(s), ligation or coagulation of minor subcutaneous and/or muscular blood vessel(s) of the subcutaneous tissue, muscle fascia, and/or muscle, not requiring thoracotomy or laparotomy, use codes 20100-20103, as appropriate.

Repair—Simple

Sum of lengths of repairs for each group of anatomic sites.

12001 Simple repair of superficial wounds of scalp, neck, axillae, external genitalia, trunk and/or extremities (including hands and feet); 2.5 cm or less

12002 2.6 cm to 7.5 cm

12004 7.6 cm to 12.5 cm

12005 12.6 cm to 20.0 cm

12006 20.1 cm to 30.0 cm

12007 over 30.0 cm

12011 Simple repair of superficial wounds of face, ears, eyelids, nose, lips and/or mucous membranes; 2.5 cm or less

12013 2.6 cm to 5.0 cm

12014 5.1 cm to 7.5 cm

12015 7.6 cm to 12.5 cm

12016 12.6 cm to 20.0 cm

12017 20.1 cm to 30.0 cm

12018 over 30.0 cm

12020 Treatment of superficial wound dehiscence; simple closure

12021 with packing

(For extensive or complicated secondary wound closure, use 13160)

Repair—Intermediate

Sum of lengths of repairs for each group of anatomic sites.

12031 Layer closure of wounds of scalp, axillae, trunk and/or extremities (excluding hands and feet); 2.5 cm or less

12032 2.6 cm to 7.5 cm

12034 7.6 cm to 12.5 cm

12035 12.6 cm to 20.0 cm

12036 20.1 cm to 30.0 cm

12037 over 30.0 cm

12041 Layer closure of wounds of neck, hands, feet and/or external genitalia; 2.5 cm or less

12042 2.6 cm to 7.5 cm

12044 7.6 cm to 12.5 cm

12045 12.6 cm to 20.0 cm

12046 20.1 cm to 30.0 cm

12047 over 30.0 cm

12051 Layer closure of wounds of face, ears, eyelids, nose, lips and/or mucous membranes; 2.5 cm or less

12052 2.6 cm to 5.0 cm

12053 5.1 cm to 7.5 cm

12054 7.6 cm to 12.5 cm

12055 12.6 cm to 20.0 cm

12056 20.1 cm to 30.0 cm

12057 over 30.0 cm

Repair—Complex

Reconstructive procedures, complicated wound closure.

Sum of lengths of repairs for each group of anatomic sites.

(For full thickness repair of lip or eyelid, see respective anatomical subsections)

13100 Repair, complex, trunk; 1.1 cm to 2.5 cm

(For 1.0 cm or less, see simple or intermediate repairs)

13101 2.6 cm to 7.5 cm

+ 13102 each additional 5 cm or less (List separately in addition to code for primary procedure)

(Use 13102 in conjunction with code 13101)

13120 Repair, complex, scalp, arms, and/or legs; 1.1 cm to 2.5 cm

(For 1.0 cm or less, see simple or intermediate repairs)

13121 2.6 cm to 7.5 cm

+ 13122 each additional 5 cm or less (List separately in addition to code for primary procedure)

(Use 13122 in conjunction with code 13121)

13131 Repair, complex, forehead, cheeks, chin, mouth, neck, axillae, genitalia, hands and/or feet; 1.1 cm to 2.5 cm

(For 1.0 cm or less, see simple or intermediate repairs)

13132 2.6 cm to 7.5 cm

+ 13133 each additional 5 cm or less (List separately in addition to code for primary procedure)

(Use 13133 in conjunction with code 13132)

13150 Repair, complex, eyelids, nose, ears and/or lips; 1.0 cm or less

(See also 40650-40654, 67961-67975)

13151 1.1 cm to 2.5 cm

13152 2.6 cm to 7.5 cm

+ 13153 each additional 5 cm or less (List separately in addition to code for primary procedure)

(Use 13153 in conjunction with code 13152)

13160 Secondary closure of surgical wound or dehiscence, extensive or complicated

(For packing or simple secondary wound closure, see 12020, 12021)

Adjacent Tissue Transfer or Rearrangement

For full thickness repair of lip or eyelid, see respective anatomical subsections.

Excision (including lesion) and/or repair by adjacent tissue transfer or rearrangement (eg, Z-plasty, W-plasty, V-Y plasty, rotation flap, advancement flap, double pedicle flap). When applied in repairing lacerations, the procedures listed must be developed by the surgeon to accomplish the repair. They do not apply when direct closure or rearrangement of traumatic wounds incidentally result in these configurations.

Skin graft necessary to close secondary defect is considered an additional procedure. ►For purposes of code selection, the term "defect" includes the primary and secondary defects. The primary defect resulting from the excision and the secondary defect resulting from flap design to perform the reconstruction are measured together to determine the code.◄

14000 Adjacent tissue transfer or rearrangement, trunk; defect 10 sq cm or less

14001 defect 10.1 sq cm to 30.0 sq cm

14020 Adjacent tissue transfer or rearrangement, scalp, arms and/or legs; defect 10 sq cm or less

14021 defect 10.1 sq cm to 30.0 sq cm

14040 Adjacent tissue transfer or rearrangement, forehead, cheeks, chin, mouth, neck, axillae, genitalia, hands and/or feet; defect 10 sq cm or less

14041 defect 10.1 sq cm to 30.0 sq cm

14060 Adjacent tissue transfer or rearrangement, eyelids, nose, ears and/or lips; defect 10 sq cm or less

14061 defect 10.1 sq cm to 30.0 sq cm

(For eyelid, full thickness, see 67961 et seq)

14300 Adjacent tissue transfer or rearrangement, more than 30 sq cm, unusual or complicated, any area

14350 Filleted finger or toe flap, including preparation of recipient site

Free Skin Grafts

Identify by size and location of the defect (recipient area) and the type of graft; includes simple debridement of granulations or recent avulsion.

When a primary procedure such as orbitectomy, radical mastectomy, or deep tumor removal requires skin graft for definitive closure, see appropriate anatomical subsection for primary procedure and this section for skin graft.

Use 15000 for initial wound preparation.

Use 15100-15261 for autogenous skin grafts. For autogenous tissue-cultured skin grafts, use 15100-15121. These codes include harvesting of keratinocytes and their subsequent application. Procedures are coded by recipient site. Use codes 15342 and 15343 for application of skin substitute/neodermis. Use modifier '-58' for staged application procedure(s).

Repair of donor site requiring skin graft or local flaps is to be added as an additional procedure.

Codes 15000, 15001, 15350, 15351, 15400, 15401 describe burn and wound preparation and management procedures. The following definition should be applied to codes 15000, 15001, 15100, 15101, 15120, 15121 when determining the involvement of body size. The measurement of 100 sq cm is applicable to adults and children age 10 and over, percentages apply to infants and children under the age of 10.

(For microvascular flaps, see 15756-15758)

15000 Surgical preparation or creation of recipient site by excision of open wounds, burn eschar, or scar (including subcutaneous tissues); first 100 sq cm or one percent of body area of infants and children

(For appropriate skin grafts, see 15050-15261; list the free graft separately by its procedure number when the graft, immediate or delayed, is applied)

+ 15001 each additional 100 sq cm or each additional one percent of body area of infants and children (List separately in addition to code for primary procedure)

(Use code 15001 in conjunction with code 15000)

(For excision of benign lesions, see 11400-11471)

(For excision of malignant lesions, see 11600-11646)

(For excision with alloplastic dressing, use 15000 only)

(For excision with immediate skin grafting use 15050-15261 in addition to 15000)

(For excision with immediate allograft placement use 15350 in addition to 15000)

(For excision with immediate xenograft placement use 15400 in addition to 15000)

15050 Pinch graft, single or multiple, to cover small ulcer, tip of digit, or other minimal open area (except on face), up to defect size 2 cm diameter

15100 Split graft, trunk, arms, legs; first 100 sq cm or less, or one percent of body area of infants and children (except 15050)

+ 15101 each additional 100 sq cm, or each additional one percent of body area of infants and children, or part thereof (List separately in addition to code for primary procedure)

(Use 15101 in conjunction with code 15100)

15120 Split graft, face, scalp, eyelids, mouth, neck, ears, orbits, genitalia, hands, feet and/or multiple digits; first 100 sq cm or less, or one percent of body area of infants and children (except 15050)

+ 15121 each additional 100 sq cm, or each additional one percent of body area of infants and children, or part thereof (List separately in addition to code for primary procedure)

(Use 15121 in conjunction with code 15120)

(For eyelids, see also 67961 et seq)

15200 Full thickness graft, free, including direct closure of donor site, trunk; 20 sq cm or less

+ 15201 each additional 20 sq cm (List separately in addition to code for primary procedure)

(Use 15201 in conjunction with code 15200)

15220 Full thickness graft, free, including direct closure of donor site, scalp, arms, and/or legs; 20 sq cm or less

+ 15221 each additional 20 sq cm (List separately in addition to code for primary procedure)

(Use 15221 in conjunction with code 15220)

15240 Full thickness graft, free, including direct closure of donor site, forehead, cheeks, chin, mouth, neck, axillae, genitalia, hands, and/or feet; 20 sq cm or less

(For finger tip graft, use 15050)

(For repair of syndactyly, fingers, see 26560-26562)

+ 15241 each additional 20 sq cm (List separately in addition to code for primary procedure)

(Use 15241 in conjunction with code 15240)

15260 Full thickness graft, free, including direct closure of donor site, nose, ears, eyelids, and/or lips; 20 sq cm or less

+ 15261 each additional 20 sq cm (List separately in addition to code for primary procedure)

(Use 15261 in conjunction with code 15260)

(For eyelids, see also 67961 et seq)

(Repair of donor site requiring skin graft or local flaps, to be added as additional separate procedure)

15342 Application of bilaminate skin substitute/neodermis; 25 sq cm

+ 15343 each additional 25 sq cm (List separately in addition to code for primary procedure)

(Use 15343 in conjunction with code 15342)

15350 Application of allograft, skin; 100 sq cm or less

(For staged tissue graft implantation, use modifier '-58')

+ 15351 each additional 100 sq cm (List separately in addition to code for primary procedure)

(Use 15351 in conjunction with code 15350)

15400 Application of xenograft, skin; 100 sq cm or less

+ 15401 each additional 100 sq cm (List separately in addition to code for primary procedure)

(Use 15401 in conjunction with code 15400)

Flaps (Skin and/or Deep Tissues)

Regions listed refer to recipient area (not donor site) when flap is being attached in transfer or to final site.

Regions listed refer to donor site when tube is formed for later or when "delay" of flap is prior to transfer.

Procedures 15570-15738 do not include extensive immobilization (eg, large plaster casts and other immobilizing devices are considered additional separate procedures).

Repair of donor site requiring skin graft or local flaps is considered an additional separate procedure.

(For microvascular flaps, see 15756-15758)

15570 Formation of direct or tubed pedicle, with or without transfer; trunk

15572 scalp, arms, or legs

15574 forehead, cheeks, chin, mouth, neck, axillae, genitalia, hands or feet

15576 eyelids, nose, ears, lips, or intraoral

15600 Delay of flap or sectioning of flap (division and inset); at trunk

15610 at scalp, arms, or legs

15620 at forehead, cheeks, chin, neck, axillae, genitalia, hands, or feet

15630 at eyelids, nose, ears, or lips

15650 Transfer, intermediate, of any pedicle flap (eg, abdomen to wrist, Walking tube), any location

(For eyelids, nose, ears, or lips, see also anatomical area)

(For revision, defatting or rearranging of transferred pedicle flap or skin graft, see 13100-14300)

(Procedures 15732-15738 are described by donor site of the muscle, myocutaneous, or fasciocutaneous flap)

15732 Muscle, myocutaneous, or fasciocutaneous flap; head and neck (eg, temporalis, masseter muscle, sternocleidomastoid, levator scapulae)

15734 trunk

15736 upper extremity

15738 lower extremity

Other Flaps and Grafts

Repair of donor site requiring skin graft or local flaps should be reported as an additional procedure.

15740 Flap; island pedicle

15750 neurovascular pedicle

15756 Free muscle or myocutaneous flap with microvascular anastomosis

(Do not report code 69990 in addition to code 15756)

15757 Free skin flap with microvascular anastomosis

(Do not report code 69990 in addition to code 15757)

15758 Free fascial flap with microvascular anastomosis

(Do not report code 69990 in addition to code 15758)

15760 Graft; composite (eg, full thickness of external ear or nasal ala), including primary closure, donor area

15770 derma-fat-fascia

15775 Punch graft for hair transplant; 1 to 15 punch grafts

15776 more than 15 punch grafts

(For strip transplant, use 15220)

Other Procedures

15780 Dermabrasion; total face (eg, for acne scarring, fine wrinkling, rhytids, general keratosis)

15781 segmental, face

15782 regional, other than face

15783 superficial, any site, (eg, tattoo removal)

15786 Abrasion; single lesion (eg, keratosis, scar)

+ 15787 each additional four lesions or less (List separately in addition to code for primary procedure)

(Use 15787 in conjunction with code 15786)

15788 Chemical peel, facial; epidermal

15789 dermal

15792 Chemical peel, nonfacial; epidermal

15793 dermal

15810 Salabrasion; 20 sq cm or less

15811 over 20 sq cm

15819 Cervicoplasty

15820 Blepharoplasty, lower eyelid;

15821 with extensive herniated fat pad

15822 Blepharoplasty, upper eyelid;

15823 with excessive skin weighting down lid

(For bilateral blepharoplasty, add modifier '-50')

15824 Rhytidectomy; forehead

(For repair of brow ptosis, use 67900)

15825 neck with platysmal tightening (platysmal flap, P-flap)

15826 glabellar frown lines

15828 cheek, chin, and neck

15829 superficial musculoaponeurotic system (SMAS) flap

(For bilateral rhytidectomy, add modifier '-50')

15831 Excision, excessive skin and subcutaneous tissue (including lipectomy); abdomen (abdominoplasty)

15832 thigh

15833 leg

15834 hip

15835 buttock

15836 arm

15837 forearm or hand

15838 submental fat pad

15839 other area

(For bilateral procedure, add modifier '-50')

15840 Graft for facial nerve paralysis; free fascia graft (including obtaining fascia)

(For bilateral procedure, add modifier '-50')

15841 free muscle graft (including obtaining graft)

15842 free muscle flap by microsurgical technique

(Do not report code 69990 in addition to code 15842)

15845 regional muscle transfer

(For intravenous fluorescein examination of blood flow in graft or flap, use 15860)

(For nerve transfers, decompression, or repair, see 64831-64876, 64905, 64907, 69720, 69725, 69740, 69745, 69955)

15850 Removal of sutures under anesthesia (other than local), same surgeon

15851 Removal of sutures under anesthesia (other than local), other surgeon

15852 Dressing change (for other than burns) under anesthesia (other than local)

15860 Intravenous injection of agent (eg, fluorescein) to test vascular flow in flap or graft

15876 Suction assisted lipectomy; head and neck

15877 trunk

15878 upper extremity

15879 lower extremity

Pressure Ulcers (Decubitus Ulcers)

15920 Excision, coccygeal pressure ulcer, with coccygectomy; with primary suture

15922 with flap closure

15931 Excision, sacral pressure ulcer, with primary suture;

15933 with ostectomy

15934 Excision, sacral pressure ulcer, with skin flap closure;

15935 with ostectomy

15936 Excision, sacral pressure ulcer, in preparation for muscle or myocutaneous flap or skin graft closure;

15937 with ostectomy

(For repair of defect using muscle or myocutaneous flap, use code(s) 15734 and/or 15738 in addition to 15936, 15937. For repair of defect using split skin graft, use codes 15100 and/or 15101 in addition to 15936, 15937)

15940 Excision, ischial pressure ulcer, with primary suture;

15941 with ostectomy (ischiectomy)

15944 Excision, ischial pressure ulcer, with skin flap closure;

15945 with ostectomy

15946 Excision, ischial pressure ulcer, with ostectomy, in preparation for muscle or myocutaneous flap or skin graft closure

(For repair of defect using muscle or myocutaneous flap, use code(s) 15734 and/or 15738 in addition to 15946. For repair of defect using split skin graft, use codes 15100 and/or 15101 in addition to 15946)

15950 Excision, trochanteric pressure ulcer, with primary suture;

15951 with ostectomy

15952 Excision, trochanteric pressure ulcer, with skin flap closure;

15953 with ostectomy

15956 Excision, trochanteric pressure ulcer, in preparation for muscle or myocutaneous flap or skin graft closure;

15958 with ostectomy

(For repair of defect using muscle or myocutaneous flap, use code(s) 15734 and/or 15738 in addition to 15956, 15958. For repair of defect using split skin graft, use codes 15100 and/or 15101 in addition to 15956, 15958)

15999 Unlisted procedure, excision pressure ulcer

(For free skin graft to close ulcer or donor site, see 15000 et seq)

Burns, Local Treatment

Procedures 16000-16036 refer to local treatment of burned surface only.

List percentage of body surface involved and depth of burn.

For necessary related medical services (eg, hospital visits, detention) in management of burned patients, see appropriate services in **Evaluation and Management** and **Medicine** sections.

(For skin graft, see 15100-15650)

16000 Initial treatment, first degree burn, when no more than local treatment is required

16010 Dressings and/or debridement, initial or subsequent; under anesthesia, small

16015 under anesthesia, medium or large, or with major debridement

16020 without anesthesia, office or hospital, small

16025 without anesthesia, medium (eg, whole face or whole extremity)

16030 without anesthesia, large (eg, more than one extremity)

16035 Escharotomy; initial incision

+ 16036 each additional incision (List separately in addition to code for primary procedure)

(Use 16036 in conjunction with code 16035)

(For debridement, curettement of burn wound, see 16010-16030)

Destruction

Destruction means the ablation of benign, premalignant or malignant tissues by any method, with or without curettement, including local anesthesia, and not usually requiring closure.

Any method includes electrosurgery, cryosurgery, laser and chemical treatment. Lesions include condylomata, papillomata, molluscum contagiosum, herpetic lesions, warts (ie, common, plantar, flat), milia, or other benign, premalignant (eg, actinic keratoses), or malignant lesions.

(For destruction of lesion(s) in specific anatomic sites, see 40820, 46900-46917, 46924, 54050-54057, 54065, 56501, 56515, 57061, 57065, 67850, 68135)

(For paring or cutting of benign hyperkeratotic lesions (eg, corns or calluses), see 11055-11057)

(For sharp removal or electrosurgical destruction of skin tags and fibrocutaneous tags, see 11200, 11201)

(For cryotherapy of acne, use 17340)

(For initiation or follow-up care of topical chemotherapy (eg, 5-FU or similar agents), see appropriate office visits)

(For shaving of epidermal or dermal lesions, see 11300-11313)

Destruction, Benign or Premalignant Lesions

17000 Destruction (eg, laser surgery, electrosurgery, cryosurgery, chemosurgery, surgical curettement), all benign or premalignant lesions (eg, actinic keratoses) other than skin tags or cutaneous vascular proliferative lesions; first lesion

+ 17003 second through 14 lesions, each (List separately in addition to code for first lesion)

(Use 17003 in conjunction with code 17000)

⊘ 17004 Destruction (eg, laser surgery, electrosurgery, cryosurgery, chemosurgery, surgical curettement), all benign or premalignant lesions (eg, actinic keratoses) other than skin tags or cutaneous vascular proliferative lesions; 15 or more lesions

(Do not report 17004 in conjunction with codes 17000-17003)

17106 Destruction of cutaneous vascular proliferative lesions (eg, laser technique); less than 10 sq cm

17107 10.0 to 50.0 sq cm

17108 over 50.0 sq cm

17110 Destruction (eg, laser surgery, electrosurgery, cryosurgery, chemosurgery, surgical curettement), of flat warts, molluscum contagiosum, or milia; up to 14 lesions

17111 15 or more lesions

(For destruction of common or plantar warts, see 17000, 17003, 17004)

17250 Chemical cauterization of granulation tissue (proud flesh, sinus or fistula)

(17250 is not to be used with removal or excision codes for the same lesion)

Destruction, Malignant Lesions, Any Method

17260 Destruction, malignant lesion (eg, laser surgery, electrosurgery, cryosurgery, chemosurgery, surgical curettement), trunk, arms or legs; lesion diameter 0.5 cm or less

17261 lesion diameter 0.6 to 1.0 cm

17262 lesion diameter 1.1 to 2.0 cm

17263 lesion diameter 2.1 to 3.0 cm

17264 lesion diameter 3.1 to 4.0 cm

17266 lesion diameter over 4.0 cm

17270 Destruction, malignant lesion (eg, laser surgery, electrosurgery, cryosurgery, chemosurgery, surgical curettement), scalp, neck, hands, feet, genitalia; lesion diameter 0.5 cm or less

17271 lesion diameter 0.6 to 1.0 cm

17272 lesion diameter 1.1 to 2.0 cm

17273 lesion diameter 2.1 to 3.0 cm

17274 lesion diameter 3.1 to 4.0 cm

17276 lesion diameter over 4.0 cm

17280 Destruction, malignant lesion (eg, laser surgery, electrosurgery, cryosurgery, chemosurgery, surgical curettement), face, ears, eyelids, nose, lips, mucous membrane; lesion diameter 0.5 cm or less

17281 lesion diameter 0.6 to 1.0 cm

17282 lesion diameter 1.1 to 2.0 cm

17283 lesion diameter 2.1 to 3.0 cm

17284 lesion diameter 3.1 to 4.0 cm

17286 lesion diameter over 4.0 cm

Mohs Micrographic Surgery

Mohs micrographic surgery, for the removal of complex or ill-defined skin cancer, requires a single physician to act in two integrated, but separate and distinct capacities: surgeon and pathologist. If either of these responsibilities are delegated to another physician who reports his services separately, these codes are not appropriate. If repair is performed, use separate repair, flap, or graft codes. If a biopsy of a suspected skin cancer is performed on the same day as Mohs surgery because there was no prior pathology confirmation of a diagnosis, then report diagnostic skin biopsy (11100, 11101) and frozen section pathology (88331) with modifier '-59' to distinguish from the subsequent definitive surgical procedure of Mohs surgery.

⊘ **17304** Chemosurgery (Mohs micrographic technique), including removal of all gross tumor, surgical excision of tissue specimens, mapping, color coding of specimens, microscopic examination of specimens by the surgeon, and complete histopathologic preparation including the first routine stain (eg, hematoxylin and eosin, toluidine blue); first stage, fresh tissue technique, up to 5 specimens

(If additional special pathology procedures, stains or immunostains are required, use 88311-88314, 88342)

⊘ **17305** second stage, fixed or fresh tissue, up to 5 specimens

⊘ **17306** third stage, fixed or fresh tissue, up to 5 specimens

⊘ **17307** additional stage(s), up to 5 specimens, each stage

+ **17310** each additional specimen, after the first 5 specimens, fixed or fresh tissue, any stage (List separately in addition to code for primary procedure)

(Use 17310 in conjunction with codes 17304-17307)

Other Procedures

17340 Cryotherapy (CO_2 slush, liquid N_2) for acne

17360 Chemical exfoliation for acne (eg, acne paste, acid)

17380 Electrolysis epilation, each 1/2 hour

(For actinotherapy, use 96900)

17999 Unlisted procedure, skin, mucous membrane and subcutaneous tissue

Breast

Incision

19000 Puncture aspiration of cyst of breast;

+ **19001** each additional cyst (List separately in addition to code for primary procedure)

(Use 19001 in conjunction with code 19000)

(If imaging guidance is performed, see 76095, 76096, 76393, 76942)

19020 Mastotomy with exploration or drainage of abscess, deep

19030 Injection procedure only for mammary ductogram or galactogram

(For radiological supervision and interpretation, see 76086, 76088)

►(For catheter lavage of mammary ducts for collection of cytology specimens, use Category III codes 0046T, 0047T)◄

Excision

19100 Biopsy of breast; percutaneous, needle core, not using imaging guidance (separate procedure)

(For fine needle aspiration, use 10021)

(For image guided breast biopsy, see 19102, 19103, 10022)

19101 open, incisional

19102 percutaneous, needle core, using imaging guidance

(For placement of percutaneous localization clip, use 19295)

19103 percutaneous, automated vacuum assisted or rotating biopsy device, using imaging guidance

(For imaging guidance performed in conjunction with 19102, 19103, see 76095, 76096, 76360, 76393, 76942)

(For placement of percutaneous localization clip, use 19295)

19110 Nipple exploration, with or without excision of a solitary lactiferous duct or a papilloma lactiferous duct

19112 Excision of lactiferous duct fistula

19120 Excision of cyst, fibroadenoma, or other benign or malignant tumor, aberrant breast tissue, duct lesion, nipple or areolar lesion (except 19140), open, male or female, one or more lesions

19125 Excision of breast lesion identified by preoperative placement of radiological marker, open; single lesion

+ 19126 each additional lesion separately identified by a preoperative radiological marker (List separately in addition to code for primary procedure)

(Use 19126 in conjunction with code 19125)

19140 Mastectomy for gynecomastia

19160 Mastectomy, partial;

19162 with axillary lymphadenectomy

19180 Mastectomy, simple, complete

(For immediate or delayed insertion of implant, use 19340 or 19342)

(For gynecomastia, use 19140)

19182 Mastectomy, subcutaneous

19200 Mastectomy, radical, including pectoral muscles, axillary lymph nodes

19220 Mastectomy, radical, including pectoral muscles, axillary and internal mammary lymph nodes (Urban type operation)

19240 Mastectomy, modified radical, including axillary lymph nodes, with or without pectoralis minor muscle, but excluding pectoralis major muscle

19260 Excision of chest wall tumor including ribs

19271 Excision of chest wall tumor involving ribs, with plastic reconstruction; without mediastinal lymphadenectomy

19272 with mediastinal lymphadenectomy

Introduction

19290 Preoperative placement of needle localization wire, breast;

+ 19291 each additional lesion (List separately in addition to code for primary procedure)

(Use 19291 in conjunction with code 19290)

(For radiological supervision and interpretation, see 76095, 76096, 76942)

+ 19295 Image guided placement, metallic localization clip, percutaneous, during breast biopsy (List separately in addition to code for primary procedure)

(Use 19295 in conjunction with codes 19102, 19103)

Repair and/or Reconstruction

19316 Mastopexy

19318 Reduction mammaplasty

19324 Mammaplasty, augmentation; without prosthetic implant

19325 with prosthetic implant

(For flap or graft, use also appropriate number)

19328 Removal of intact mammary implant

19330 Removal of mammary implant material

19340 Immediate insertion of breast prosthesis following mastopexy, mastectomy or in reconstruction

19342 Delayed insertion of breast prosthesis following mastopexy, mastectomy or in reconstruction

(For supply of implant, use 99070)

(For preparation of custom breast implant, use 19396)

19350 Nipple/areola reconstruction

19355 Correction of inverted nipples

19357 Breast reconstruction, immediate or delayed, with tissue expander, including subsequent expansion

19361 Breast reconstruction with latissimus dorsi flap, with or without prosthetic implant

19364 Breast reconstruction with free flap

(Do not report code 69990 in addition to code 19364)

(19364 includes harvesting of the flap, microvascular transfer, closure of the donor site, and inset shaping the flap into a breast)

19366 Breast reconstruction with other technique

(For operating microscope, use 69990)

(For insertion of prosthesis, use also 19340 or 19342)

19367 Breast reconstruction with transverse rectus abdominis myocutaneous flap (TRAM), single pedicle, including closure of donor site;

19368 with microvascular anastomosis (supercharging)

(Do not report code 69990 in addition to code 19368)

19369 Breast reconstruction with transverse rectus abdominis myocutaneous flap (TRAM), double pedicle, including closure of donor site

19370 Open periprosthetic capsulotomy, breast

19371 Periprosthetic capsulectomy, breast

19380 Revision of reconstructed breast

19396 Preparation of moulage for custom breast implant

Other Procedures

►(For microwave thermotherapy of the breast, use Category III code 0061T)◄

19499 Unlisted procedure, breast

Musculoskeletal System

Cast and strapping procedures appear at the end of this section.

The services listed below include the application and removal of the first cast or traction device only. Subsequent replacement of cast and/or traction device may require an additional listing.

Definitions

The terms "closed treatment," "open treatment," and "percutaneous skeletal fixation" have been carefully chosen to accurately reflect current orthopaedic procedural treatments.

Closed treatment specifically means that the fracture site is not surgically opened (exposed to the external environment and directly visualized). This terminology is used to describe procedures that treat fractures by three methods: 1) without manipulation 2) with manipulation 3) with or without traction.

Open treatment is used when the fractured bone is either (1) surgically opened (exposed to the external environment) and the fracture (bone ends) visualized and internal fixation may be used or (2) the fractured bone is opened remote from the fracture site in order to insert an intramedullary nail across the fracture site (the fracture site is not opened and visualized).

Percutaneous skeletal fixation describes fracture treatment which is neither open nor closed. In this procedure, the fracture fragments are not visualized, but fixation (eg, pins) is placed across the fracture site, usually under x-ray imaging.

The type of fracture (eg, open, compound, closed) does not have any coding correlation with the type of treatment (eg, closed, open, or percutaneous) provided.

The codes for treatment of fractures and joint injuries (dislocations) are categorized by the type of manipulation (reduction) and stabilization (fixation or immobilization). These codes can apply to either open (compound) or closed fractures or joint injuries.

Skeletal traction is the application of a force (distracting or traction force) to a limb segment through a wire, pin, screw, or clamp that is attached (eg, penetrates) to bone.

Skin traction is the application of a force (longitudinal) to a limb using felt or strapping applied directly to skin only.

External fixation is the usage of skeletal pins plus an attaching mechanism/device used for temporary or definitive treatment of acute or chronic bony deformity.

Codes for obtaining autogenous bone grafts, cartilage, tendon, fascia lata grafts or other tissues through separate incisions are to be used only when the graft is not already listed as part of the basic procedure.

Re-reduction of a fracture and/or dislocation performed by the primary physician may be identified by the addition of the modifier '-76' to the usual procedure number to indicate "Repeat Procedure by Same Physician." (See guidelines.)

Codes for external fixation are to be used only when external fixation is not already listed as part of the basic procedure.

All codes for suction irrigation have been deleted. To report, list only the primary surgical procedure performed (eg, sequestrectomy, deep incision).

Manipulation is used throughout the musculoskeletal fracture and dislocation subsections to specifically mean the attempted reduction or restoration of a fracture or joint dislocation to its normal anatomic alignment by the application of manually applied forces.

►(For computer assisted musculoskeletal surgical navigational orthopedic procedures, report 0054T-0056T)◄

General

Incision

20000 Incision of soft tissue abscess (eg, secondary to osteomyelitis); superficial

20005 deep or complicated

Wound Exploration—Trauma (eg, Penetrating Gunshot, Stab Wound)

20100-20103 relate to wound(s) resulting from penetrating trauma. These codes describe surgical exploration and enlargement of the wound, extension of dissection (to determine penetration), debridement, removal of foreign body(s), ligation or coagulation of minor subcutaneous and/or muscular blood vessel(s), of the subcutaneous tissue, muscle fascia, and/or muscle, not requiring thoracotomy or laparotomy. If a repair is done to major structure(s) or major blood vessel(s) requiring thoracotomy or laparotomy, then those specific code(s) would supersede the use of codes 20100-20103. To report Simple, Intermediate, or Complex repair of wound(s) that do not require enlargement of the wound, extension of dissection, etc., as stated above, use specific Repair code(s) in the Integumentary System section.

20100 Exploration of penetrating wound (separate procedure); neck

20101 chest

20102 abdomen/flank/back

20103 extremity

Surgery: Musculoskeletal System

Excision

20150 Excision of epiphyseal bar, with or without autogenous soft tissue graft obtained through same fascial incision

(For aspiration of bone marrow, use 38220)

20200 Biopsy, muscle; superficial

20205 deep

20206 Biopsy, muscle, percutaneous needle

(If imaging guidance is performed, see 76360, 76393, 76942)

(For fine needle aspiration, use 10021 or 10022)

(For evaulation of fine needle aspirate, see 88172-88173)

(For excision of muscle tumor, deep, see specific anatomic section)

20220 Biopsy, bone, trocar, or needle; superficial (eg, ilium, sternum, spinous process, ribs)

20225 deep (eg, vertebral body, femur)

(For bone marrow biopsy, use 38221)

(For radiologic supervision and interpretation, see 76003, 76360, 76393)

▲**20240** Biopsy, bone, open; superficial (eg, ilium, sternum, spinous process, ribs, trochanter of femur)

20245 deep (eg, humerus, ischium, femur)

20250 Biopsy, vertebral body, open; thoracic

20251 lumbar or cervical

(For sequestrectomy, osteomyelitis or drainage of bone abscess, see anatomical area)

Introduction or Removal

(For injection procedure for arthrography, see anatomical area)

20500 Injection of sinus tract; therapeutic (separate procedure)

20501 diagnostic (sinogram)

(For radiological supervision and interpretation, use 76080)

20520 Removal of foreign body in muscle or tendon sheath; simple

20525 deep or complicated

20526 Injection, therapeutic (eg, local anesthetic, corticosteroid), carpal tunnel

▲**20550** Injection(s); single tendon sheath, or ligament, aponeurosis (eg, plantar "fascia")

▲**20551** single tendon origin/insertion

▲**20552** Injection(s); single or multiple trigger point(s), one or two muscle(s)

20553 single or multiple trigger point(s), three or more muscle(s)

(If imaging guidance is performed, see 76003, 76393, 76942)

20600 Arthrocentesis, aspiration and/or injection; small joint or bursa (eg, fingers, toes)

20605 intermediate joint or bursa (eg, temporomandibular, acromioclavicular, wrist, elbow or ankle, olecranon bursa)

20610 major joint or bursa (eg, shoulder, hip, knee joint, subacromial bursa)

(If imaging guidance is performed, see 76003, 76360, 76393, 76942)

20612 Aspiration and/or injection of ganglion cyst(s) any location

(To report multiple ganglion cyst aspirations/injections, use 20612 and append modifier '-59')

20615 Aspiration and injection for treatment of bone cyst

20650 Insertion of wire or pin with application of skeletal traction, including removal (separate procedure)

⃠ **20660** Application of cranial tongs, caliper, or stereotactic frame, including removal (separate procedure)

20661 Application of halo, including removal; cranial

20662 pelvic

20663 femoral

20664 Application of halo, including removal, cranial, 6 or more pins placed, for thin skull osteology (eg, pediatric patients, hydrocephalus, osteogenesis imperfecta), requiring general anesthesia

20665 Removal of tongs or halo applied by another physician

20670 Removal of implant; superficial, (eg, buried wire, pin or rod) (separate procedure)

20680 deep (eg, buried wire, pin, screw, metal band, nail, rod or plate)

⃠ **20690** Application of a uniplane (pins or wires in one plane), unilateral, external fixation system

⃠ **20692** Application of a multiplane (pins or wires in more than one plane), unilateral, external fixation system (eg, Ilizarov, Monticelli type)

20693 Adjustment or revision of external fixation system requiring anesthesia (eg, new pin(s) or wire(s) and/or new ring(s) or bar(s))

20694 Removal, under anesthesia, of external fixation system

Replantation

20802 Replantation, arm (includes surgical neck of humerus through elbow joint), complete amputation

20805 Replantation, forearm (includes radius and ulna to radial carpal joint), complete amputation

20808 Replantation, hand (includes hand through metacarpophalangeal joints), complete amputation

20816 Replantation, digit, excluding thumb (includes metacarpophalangeal joint to insertion of flexor sublimis tendon), complete amputation

20822 Replantation, digit, excluding thumb (includes distal tip to sublimis tendon insertion), complete amputation

20824 Replantation, thumb (includes carpometacarpal joint to MP joint), complete amputation

20827 Replantation, thumb (includes distal tip to MP joint), complete amputation

20838 Replantation, foot, complete amputation

Grafts (or Implants)

Codes for obtaining autogenous bone, cartilage, tendon, fascia lata grafts, or other tissues through separate ►skin/fascial◄ incisions ►should be reported separately unless the code descriptor references the harvesting of the graft or implant (eg, includes obtaining graft).◄

Do not append modifier '-62' to bone graft codes 20900-20938.

(For spinal surgery bone graft(s) see codes 20930-20938)

⊘ **20900** Bone graft, any donor area; minor or small (eg, dowel or button)

⊘ **20902** major or large

⊘ **20910** Cartilage graft; costochondral

⊘ **20912** nasal septum

(For ear cartilage, use 21235)

⊘ **20920** Fascia lata graft; by stripper

⊘ **20922** by incision and area exposure, complex or sheet

⊘ **20924** Tendon graft, from a distance (eg, palmaris, toe extensor, plantaris)

⊘ **20926** Tissue grafts, other (eg, paratenon, fat, dermis)

(Codes 20930-20938 are reported in addition to codes for the definitive procedure(s) without modifier '-51')

⊘ **20930** Allograft for spine surgery only; morselized

⊘ **20931** structural

⊘ **20936** Autograft for spine surgery only (includes harvesting the graft); local (eg, ribs, spinous process, or laminar fragments) obtained from same incision

⊘ **20937** morselized (through separate skin or fascial incision)

⊘ **20938** structural, bicortical or tricortical (through separate skin or fascial incision)

(For needle aspiration of bone marrow for the purpose of bone grafting, use 38220)

Other Procedures

20950 Monitoring of interstitial fluid pressure (includes insertion of device, eg, wick catheter technique, needle manometer technique) in detection of muscle compartment syndrome

20955 Bone graft with microvascular anastomosis; fibula

20956 iliac crest

20957 metatarsal

20962 other than fibula, iliac crest, or metatarsal

(Do not report code 69990 in addition to codes 20955-20962)

20969 Free osteocutaneous flap with microvascular anastomosis; other than iliac crest, metatarsal, or great toe

20970 iliac crest

20972 metatarsal

20973 great toe with web space

(Do not report code 69990 in addition to codes 20969-20973)

(For great toe, wrap-around procedure, use 26551)

⊘ **20974** Electrical stimulation to aid bone healing; noninvasive (nonoperative)

⊘ **20975** invasive (operative)

20979 Low intensity ultrasound stimulation to aid bone healing, noninvasive (nonoperative)

● **20982** Ablation, bone tumor(s) (eg, osteoid osteoma, metastasis) radiofrequency, percutaneous, including computed tomographic guidance

20999 Unlisted procedure, musculoskeletal system, general

Head

Skull, facial bones and temporomandibular joint.

Incision

(For drainage of superficial abscess and hematoma, use 20000)

(For removal of embedded foreign body from dentoalveolar structure, see 41805, 41806)

21010 Arthrotomy, temporomandibular joint

Excision

21015 Radical resection of tumor (eg, malignant neoplasm), soft tissue of face or scalp

21025 Excision of bone (eg, for osteomyelitis or bone abscess); mandible

21026 facial bone(s)

21029 Removal by contouring of benign tumor of facial bone (eg, fibrous dysplasia)

21030 Excision of benign tumor or cyst of maxilla or zygoma by enucleation and curettage

21031 Excision of torus mandibularis

21032 Excision of maxillary torus palatinus

21034 Excision of malignant tumor of maxilla or zygoma

21040 Excision of benign tumor or cyst of mandible, by enucleation and/or curettage

(21041 has been deleted. For enucleation and/or curettage of benign cysts or tumors of mandible not requiring osteotomy, use 21040)

(For excision of benign tumor or cyst of mandible requiring osteotomy, see 21046-21047)

21044 Excision of malignant tumor of mandible;

21045 radical resection

(For bone graft, use 21215)

21046 Excision of benign tumor or cyst of mandible; requiring intra-oral osteotomy (eg, locally aggressive or destructive lesion(s))

21047 requiring extra-oral osteotomy and partial mandibulectomy (eg, locally aggressive or destructive lesion(s))

21048 Excision of benign tumor or cyst of maxilla; requiring intra-oral osteotomy (eg, locally aggressive or destructive lesion(s))

21049 requiring extra-oral osteotomy and partial maxillectomy (eg, locally aggressive or destructive lesion(s))

21050 Condylectomy, temporomandibular joint (separate procedure)

21060 Meniscectomy, partial or complete, temporomandibular joint (separate procedure)

21070 Coronoidectomy (separate procedure)

Introduction or Removal

(For application or removal of caliper or tongs, see 20660, 20665.) Codes 21076-21089 describe professional services for the rehabilitation of patients with oral, facial or other anatomical deficiencies by means of prostheses such as an artificial eye, ear, or nose or intraoral obturator to close a cleft. Codes 21076-21089 should only be used when the physician actually designs and prepares the prosthesis (ie, not prepared by an outside laboratory).

21076 Impression and custom preparation; surgical obturator prosthesis

21077 orbital prosthesis

21079 interim obturator prosthesis

21080 definitive obturator prosthesis

21081 mandibular resection prosthesis

21082 palatal augmentation prosthesis

21083 palatal lift prosthesis

21084 speech aid prosthesis

21085 oral surgical splint

21086 auricular prosthesis

21087 nasal prosthesis

21088 facial prosthesis

21089 Unlisted maxillofacial prosthetic procedure

21100 Application of halo type appliance for maxillofacial fixation, includes removal (separate procedure)

21110 Application of interdental fixation device for conditions other than fracture or dislocation, includes removal

(For removal of interdental fixation by another physician, see 20670-20680)

21116 Injection procedure for temporomandibular joint arthrography

(For radiological supervision and interpretation, use 70332. Do not report 76003 in addition to 70332)

Repair, Revision, and/or Reconstruction

(For cranioplasty, see 21179, 21180 and 62116, 62120, 62140-62147)

21120 Genioplasty; augmentation (autograft, allograft, prosthetic material)

21121 sliding osteotomy, single piece

21122 sliding osteotomies, two or more osteotomies (eg, wedge excision or bone wedge reversal for asymmetrical chin)

21123 sliding, augmentation with interpositional bone grafts (includes obtaining autografts)

21125 Augmentation, mandibular body or angle; prosthetic material

21127 with bone graft, onlay or interpositional (includes obtaining autograft)

21137 Reduction forehead; contouring only

21138 contouring and application of prosthetic material or bone graft (includes obtaining autograft)

21139 contouring and setback of anterior frontal sinus wall

21141 Reconstruction midface, LeFort I; single piece, segment movement in any direction (eg, for Long Face Syndrome), without bone graft

21142 two pieces, segment movement in any direction, without bone graft

21143 three or more pieces, segment movement in any direction, without bone graft

21145 single piece, segment movement in any direction, requiring bone grafts (includes obtaining autografts)

21146 two pieces, segment movement in any direction, requiring bone grafts (includes obtaining autografts) (eg, ungrafted unilateral alveolar cleft)

21147 three or more pieces, segment movement in any direction, requiring bone grafts (includes obtaining autografts) (eg, ungrafted bilateral alveolar cleft or multiple osteotomies)

21150 Reconstruction midface, LeFort II; anterior intrusion (eg, Treacher-Collins Syndrome)

21151 any direction, requiring bone grafts (includes obtaining autografts)

21154 Reconstruction midface, LeFort III (extracranial), any type, requiring bone grafts (includes obtaining autografts); without LeFort I

21155 with LeFort I

21159 Reconstruction midface, LeFort III (extra and intracranial) with forehead advancement (eg, mono bloc), requiring bone grafts (includes obtaining autografts); without LeFort I

21160 with LeFort I

21172 Reconstruction superior-lateral orbital rim and lower forehead, advancement or alteration, with or without grafts (includes obtaining autografts)

(For frontal or parietal craniotomy performed for craniosynostosis, use 61556)

21175 Reconstruction, bifrontal, superior-lateral orbital rims and lower forehead, advancement or alteration (eg, plagiocephaly, trigonocephaly, brachycephaly), with or without grafts (includes obtaining autografts)

(For bifrontal craniotomy performed for craniosynostosis, use 61557)

21179 Reconstruction, entire or majority of forehead and/or supraorbital rims; with grafts (allograft or prosthetic material)

21180 with autograft (includes obtaining grafts)

(For extensive craniectomy for multiple suture craniosynostosis, use only 61558 or 61559)

21181 Reconstruction by contouring of benign tumor of cranial bones (eg, fibrous dysplasia), extracranial

21182 Reconstruction of orbital walls, rims, forehead, nasoethmoid complex following intra- and extracranial excision of benign tumor of cranial bone (eg, fibrous dysplasia), with multiple autografts (includes obtaining grafts); total area of bone grafting less than 40 sq cm

21183 total area of bone grafting greater than 40 sq cm but less than 80 sq cm

21184 total area of bone grafting greater than 80 sq cm

(For excision of benign tumor of cranial bones, see 61563, 61564)

21188 Reconstruction midface, osteotomies (other than LeFort type) and bone grafts (includes obtaining autografts)

21193 Reconstruction of mandibular rami, horizontal, vertical, C, or L osteotomy; without bone graft

21194 with bone graft (includes obtaining graft)

21195 Reconstruction of mandibular rami and/or body, sagittal split; without internal rigid fixation

21196 with internal rigid fixation

21198 Osteotomy, mandible, segmental;

21199 with genioglossus advancement

21206 Osteotomy, maxilla, segmental (eg, Wassmund or Schuchard)

21208 Osteoplasty, facial bones; augmentation (autograft, allograft, or prosthetic implant)

21209 reduction

21210 Graft, bone; nasal, maxillary or malar areas (includes obtaining graft)

(For cleft palate repair, see 42200-42225)

21215 mandible (includes obtaining graft)

21230 Graft; rib cartilage, autogenous, to face, chin, nose or ear (includes obtaining graft)

21235 ear cartilage, autogenous, to nose or ear (includes obtaining graft)

21240 Arthroplasty, temporomandibular joint, with or without autograft (includes obtaining graft)

21242 Arthroplasty, temporomandibular joint, with allograft

21243 Arthroplasty, temporomandibular joint, with prosthetic joint replacement

21244 Reconstruction of mandible, extraoral, with transosteal bone plate (eg, mandibular staple bone plate)

21245 Reconstruction of mandible or maxilla, subperiosteal implant; partial

21246 complete

21247 Reconstruction of mandibular condyle with bone and cartilage autografts (includes obtaining grafts) (eg, for hemifacial microsomia)

21248 Reconstruction of mandible or maxilla, endosteal implant (eg, blade, cylinder); partial

21249 complete

21255 Reconstruction of zygomatic arch and glenoid fossa with bone and cartilage (includes obtaining autografts)

21256 Reconstruction of orbit with osteotomies (extracranial) and with bone grafts (includes obtaining autografts) (eg, micro-ophthalmia)

21260 Periorbital osteotomies for orbital hypertelorism, with bone grafts; extracranial approach

21261 combined intra- and extracranial approach

21263 with forehead advancement

21267 Orbital repositioning, periorbital osteotomies, unilateral, with bone grafts; extracranial approach

21268 combined intra- and extracranial approach

21270 Malar augmentation, prosthetic material

(For malar augmentation with bone graft, use 21210)

21275 Secondary revision of orbitocraniofacial reconstruction

21280 Medial canthopexy (separate procedure)

(For medial canthoplasty, use 67950)

21282 Lateral canthopexy

21295 Reduction of masseter muscle and bone (eg, for treatment of benign masseteric hypertrophy); extraoral approach

21296 intraoral approach

Other Procedures

21299 Unlisted craniofacial and maxillofacial procedure

Fracture and/or Dislocation

21300 Closed treatment of skull fracture without operation

(For operative repair, see 62000-62010)

21310 Closed treatment of nasal bone fracture without manipulation

21315 Closed treatment of nasal bone fracture; without stabilization

21320 with stabilization

21325 Open treatment of nasal fracture; uncomplicated

21330 complicated, with internal and/or external skeletal fixation

21335 with concomitant open treatment of fractured septum

21336 Open treatment of nasal septal fracture, with or without stabilization

21337 Closed treatment of nasal septal fracture, with or without stabilization

21338 Open treatment of nasoethmoid fracture; without external fixation

21339 with external fixation

21340 Percutaneous treatment of nasoethmoid complex fracture, with splint, wire or headcap fixation, including repair of canthal ligaments and/or the nasolacrimal apparatus

21343 Open treatment of depressed frontal sinus fracture

21344 Open treatment of complicated (eg, comminuted or involving posterior wall) frontal sinus fracture, via coronal or multiple approaches

21345 Closed treatment of nasomaxillary complex fracture (LeFort II type), with interdental wire fixation or fixation of denture or splint

21346 Open treatment of nasomaxillary complex fracture (LeFort II type); with wiring and/or local fixation

21347 requiring multiple open approaches

21348 with bone grafting (includes obtaining graft)

21355 Percutaneous treatment of fracture of malar area, including zygomatic arch and malar tripod, with manipulation

21356 Open treatment of depressed zygomatic arch fracture (eg, Gillies approach)

21360 Open treatment of depressed malar fracture, including zygomatic arch and malar tripod

21365 Open treatment of complicated (eg, comminuted or involving cranial nerve foramina) fracture(s) of malar area, including zygomatic arch and malar tripod; with internal fixation and multiple surgical approaches

21366 with bone grafting (includes obtaining graft)

21385 Open treatment of orbital floor blowout fracture; transantral approach (Caldwell-Luc type operation)

21386 periorbital approach

21387 combined approach

21390 periorbital approach, with alloplastic or other implant

21395 periorbital approach with bone graft (includes obtaining graft)

21400 Closed treatment of fracture of orbit, except blowout; without manipulation

21401 with manipulation

21406 Open treatment of fracture of orbit, except blowout; without implant

21407 with implant

21408 with bone grafting (includes obtaining graft)

21421 Closed treatment of palatal or maxillary fracture (LeFort I type), with interdental wire fixation or fixation of denture or splint

21422 Open treatment of palatal or maxillary fracture (LeFort I type);

21423 complicated (comminuted or involving cranial nerve foramina), multiple approaches

21431 Closed treatment of craniofacial separation (LeFort III type) using interdental wire fixation of denture or splint

21432 Open treatment of craniofacial separation (LeFort III type); with wiring and/or internal fixation

21433 complicated (eg, comminuted or involving cranial nerve foramina), multiple surgical approaches

21435 complicated, utilizing internal and/or external fixation techniques (eg, head cap, halo device, and/or intermaxillary fixation)

(For removal of internal or external fixation device, use 20670)

21436 complicated, multiple surgical approaches, internal fixation, with bone grafting (includes obtaining graft)

21440 Closed treatment of mandibular or maxillary alveolar ridge fracture (separate procedure)

21445 Open treatment of mandibular or maxillary alveolar ridge fracture (separate procedure)

21450 Closed treatment of mandibular fracture; without manipulation

21451 with manipulation

21452 Percutaneous treatment of mandibular fracture, with external fixation

21453 Closed treatment of mandibular fracture with interdental fixation

21454 Open treatment of mandibular fracture with external fixation

21461 Open treatment of mandibular fracture; without interdental fixation

21462 with interdental fixation

21465 Open treatment of mandibular condylar fracture

21470 Open treatment of complicated mandibular fracture by multiple surgical approaches including internal fixation, interdental fixation, and/or wiring of dentures or splints

21480 Closed treatment of temporomandibular dislocation; initial or subsequent

21485 complicated (eg, recurrent requiring intermaxillary fixation or splinting), initial or subsequent

21490 Open treatment of temporomandibular dislocation

(For interdental wire fixation, use 21497)

21493 Closed treatment of hyoid fracture; without manipulation

21494 with manipulation

21495 Open treatment of hyoid fracture

(For treatment of fracture of larynx, see 31584-31586)

21497 Interdental wiring, for condition other than fracture

Other Procedures

21499 Unlisted musculoskeletal procedure, head

(For unlisted craniofacial or maxillofacial procedure, use 21299)

Neck (Soft Tissues) and Thorax

(For cervical spine and back, see 21920 et seq)

(For injection of fracture site or trigger point, use 20550)

Incision

(For incision and drainage of abscess or hematoma, superficial, see 10060, 10140)

21501 Incision and drainage, deep abscess or hematoma, soft tissues of neck or thorax;

21502 with partial rib ostectomy

21510 Incision, deep, with opening of bone cortex (eg, for osteomyelitis or bone abscess), thorax

Excision

(For bone biopsy, see 20220-20251)

21550 Biopsy, soft tissue of neck or thorax

(For needle biopsy of soft tissue, use 20206)

21555 Excision tumor, soft tissue of neck or thorax; subcutaneous

21556 deep, subfascial, intramuscular

21557 Radical resection of tumor (eg, malignant neoplasm), soft tissue of neck or thorax

21600 Excision of rib, partial

(For radical resection of chest wall and rib cage for tumor, use 19260)

(For radical debridement of chest wall and rib cage for injury, see 11040-11044)

21610 Costotransversectomy (separate procedure)

21615 Excision first and/or cervical rib;

21616 with sympathectomy

21620 Ostectomy of sternum, partial

21627 Sternal debridement

(For debridement and closure, use 21750)

21630 Radical resection of sternum;

21632 with mediastinal lymphadenectomy

Repair, Revision, and/or Reconstruction

(For superficial wound, see **Integumentary System** section under Repair—Simple)

● **21685** Hyoid myotomy and suspension

21700 Division of scalenus anticus; without resection of cervical rib

21705 with resection of cervical rib

Surgery: Musculoskeletal System

21720 Division of sternocleidomastoid for torticollis, open operation; without cast application

(For transection of spinal accessory and cervical nerves, see 63191, 64722)

21725 with cast application

21740 Reconstructive repair of pectus excavatum or carinatum; open

21742 minimally invasive approach (Nuss procedure), without thoracoscopy

21743 minimally invasive approach (Nuss procedure), with thoracoscopy

21750 Closure of median sternotomy separation with or without debridement (separate procedure)

Fracture and/or Dislocation

21800 Closed treatment of rib fracture, uncomplicated, each

21805 Open treatment of rib fracture without fixation, each

21810 Treatment of rib fracture requiring external fixation (flail chest)

21820 Closed treatment of sternum fracture

21825 Open treatment of sternum fracture with or without skeletal fixation

(For sternoclavicular dislocation, see 23520-23532)

Other Procedures

21899 Unlisted procedure, neck or thorax

Back and Flank

Excision

21920 Biopsy, soft tissue of back or flank; superficial

21925 deep

(For needle biopsy of soft tissue, use 20206)

21930 Excision, tumor, soft tissue of back or flank

21935 Radical resection of tumor (eg, malignant neoplasm), soft tissue of back or flank

Spine (Vertebral Column)

Cervical, thoracic, and lumbar spine.

Within the SPINE section, bone grafting procedures are reported separately and in addition to arthrodesis. For bone grafts in other Musculoskeletal sections, see specific code(s) descriptor(s) and/or accompanying guidelines.

To report bone grafts performed after arthrodesis, see codes 20930-20938. Bone graft codes are reported without modifier '-51' (multiple procedure). Do not append modifier '-62' to bone graft codes 20900-20938.

Example:

Posterior arthrodesis of L5-S1 for degenerative disc disease utilizing morselized autogenous iliac bone graft harvested through a separate fascial incision.

Report as 22612 and 20937.

Within the SPINE section, instrumentation is reported separately and in addition to arthrodesis. To report instrumentation procedures performed with definitive vertebral procedure(s), see codes 22840-22855. Instrumentation procedure codes 22840-22848 and 22851 are reported in addition to the definitive procedure(s) without modifier '-51'. The modifier '-62' may not be appended to the definitive or add-on spinal instrumentation procedure code(s) 22840-22848 and 22850-22852.

Example:

Posterior arthrodesis of L4-S1, utilizing morselized autogenous iliac bone graft harvested through separate fascial incision, and pedicle screw fixation.

Report as 22612, 22614, 22842, and 20937.

Vertebral procedures are sometimes followed by arthrodesis and in addition may include bone grafts and instrumentation.

When arthrodesis is performed in addition to another procedure, the arthrodesis should be reported in addition to the original procedure with a modifier '-51' (multiple procedures). Examples are after osteotomy, fracture care, vertebral corpectomy and laminectomy. Since bone grafts and instrumentation are never performed without arthrodesis, modifier '-51' (multiple procedures) is not used.

Arthrodesis, however, may be performed in the absence of other procedures and therefore when it is combined with another definitive procedure, modifier '-51' (multiple procedure) is appropriate.

Example:

Treatment of a burst fracture of L2 by corpectomy followed by arthrodesis of L1-L3, utilizing anterior instrumentation L1-L3 and structural allograft.

Report as 63090, 22558-51, 22585, 22845, and 20931.

When two surgeons work together as primary surgeons performing distinct part(s) of a single reportable procedure, each surgeon should report his/her distinct operative work by appending the modifier '-62' to the single definitive procedure code. If additional procedure(s) (including add-on procedure(s)) are performed during the same surgical session, separate code(s) may be reported by each co-surgeon, with the modifier '-62' appended (see Appendix A).

Example:

A 42-year-old male with a history of posttraumatic degenerative disc disease at L3-4 and L4-5 (internal disc disruption) underwent surgical repair. Surgeon A performed an anterior exposure of the spine with mobilization of the great vessels. Surgeon B performed anterior (minimal) diskectomy and fusion at L3-4 and L4-5 using anterior interbody technique.

Report surgeon A: 22558-62, 22585-62
Report surgeon B: 22558-62, 22585-62, 20931

(Do not append modifier -62 to bone graft code 20931)

(For injection procedure for myelography, use 62284)

(For injection procedure for diskography, see 62290, 62291)

(For injection procedure, chemonucleolysis, single or multiple levels, use 62292)

(For injection procedure for facet joints, see 64470-64476, 64622-64627)

(For needle or trocar biopsy, see 20220-20225)

Excision

For the following codes, when two surgeons work together as primary surgeons performing distinct part(s) of partial vertebral body excision, each surgeon should report his/her distinct operative work by appending the modifier '-62' to the procedure code. In this situation, the modifier '-62' may be appended to the procedure code(s) 22100-22102, 22110-22114 and, as appropriate, to the associated additional vertebral segment add-on code(s) 22103, 22116 as long as both surgeons continue to work together as primary surgeons.

(For bone biopsy, see 20220-20251)

22100 Partial excision of posterior vertebral component (eg, spinous process, lamina or facet) for intrinsic bony lesion, single vertebral segment; cervical

22101 thoracic

22102 lumbar

+ **22103** each additional segment (List separately in addition to code for primary procedure)

(Use 22103 in conjunction with codes 22100, 22101, 22102)

22110 Partial excision of vertebral body, for intrinsic bony lesion, without decompression of spinal cord or nerve root(s), single vertebral segment; cervical

22112 thoracic

22114 lumbar

+ **22116** each additional vertebral segment (List separately in addition to code for primary procedure)

(Use 22116 in conjunction with codes 22110, 22112, 22114)

Osteotomy

To report arthrodesis, see codes 22590-22632. (Report in addition to code(s) for the definitive procedure with modifier '-51'.)

To report instrumentation procedures, see codes 22840-22855. (Report in addition to code(s) for the definitive procedure(s) without modifier '-51'.) Do not append modifier '-62' to spinal instrumentation codes 22840-22848 and 22850-22852.

To report bone graft procedures, see codes 20930-20938. (Report in addition to code(s) for the definitive procedure(s) without modifier '-51'.) Do not append modifier '-62' to bone graft codes 20900-20938.

For the following codes, when two surgeons work together as primary surgeons performing distinct part(s) of an anterior spine osteotomy, each surgeon should report his/her distinct operative work by appending the modifier '-62' to the procedure code. In this situation, the modifier '-62' may be appended to the procedure code(s) 22210-22214, 22220-22224 and, as appropriate, to associated additional segment add-on code(s) 22216, 22226 as long as both surgeons continue to work together as primary surgeons.

22210 Osteotomy of spine, posterior or posterolateral approach, one vertebral segment; cervical

22212 thoracic

22214 lumbar

+ **22216** each additional vertebral segment (List separately in addition to primary procedure)

(Use 22216 in conjunction with codes 22210, 22212, 22214)

22220 Osteotomy of spine, including diskectomy, anterior approach, single vertebral segment; cervical

22222 thoracic

22224 lumbar

+ **22226** each additional vertebral segment (List separately in addition to code for primary procedure)

(Use 22226 in conjunction with codes 22220, 22222, 22224)

Fracture and/or Dislocation

To report arthrodesis, see codes 22590-22632. (Report in addition to code(s) for the definitive procedure with modifier '-51'.)

To report instrumentation procedures, see codes 22840-22855. (Report in addition to code(s) for the definitive procedure(s) without modifier '-51'.) Do not append modifier '-62' to spinal instrumentation codes 22840-22848 and 22850-22852.

To report bone graft procedures, see codes 20930-20938. (Report in addition to code(s) for the definitive procedure(s) without modifier '-51'.) Do not append modifier '-62' to bone graft codes 20900-20938.

For the following codes, when two surgeons work together as primary surgeons performing distinct part(s) of open fracture and/or dislocation procedure(s), each surgeon should report his/her distinct operative work by appending the modifier '-62' to the procedure code. In this situation, the modifier '-62' may be appended to the procedure code(s) 22318-22327 and, as appropriate, the associated additional fracture vertebrae or dislocated segment add-on code 22328 as long as both surgeons continue to work together as primary surgeons.

22305 Closed treatment of vertebral process fracture(s)

22310 Closed treatment of vertebral body fracture(s), without manipulation, requiring and including casting or bracing

22315 Closed treatment of vertebral fracture(s) and/or dislocation(s) requiring casting or bracing, with and including casting and/or bracing, with or without anesthesia, by manipulation or traction

(For spinal subluxation, use 97140)

22318 Open treatment and/or reduction of odontoid fracture(s) and or dislocation(s) (including os odontoideum), anterior approach, including placement of internal fixation; without grafting

22319 with grafting

22325 Open treatment and/or reduction of vertebral fracture(s) and/or dislocation(s), posterior approach, one fractured vertebrae or dislocated segment; lumbar

22326 cervical

22327 thoracic

+ 22328 each additional fractured vertebrae or dislocated segment (List separately in addition to code for primary procedure)

(Use 22328 in conjunction with codes 22325, 22326, 22327)

(For treatment of vertebral fracture by the anterior approach, see corpectomy 63081-63091, and appropriate arthrodesis, bone graft and instrument codes)

Manipulation

22505 Manipulation of spine requiring anesthesia, any region

Vertebral Body, Embolization or Injection

22520 Percutaneous vertebroplasty, one vertebral body, unilateral or bilateral injection; thoracic

22521 lumbar

+ 22522 each additional thoracic or lumbar vertebral body (List separately in addition to code for primary procedure)

(Use 22522 in conjunction with codes 22520, 22521 as appropriate)

(For radiological supervision and interpretation, see 76012, 76013)

►Lateral Extracavitary Approach Technique◄

● 22532 Arthrodesis, lateral extracavitary technique, including minimal diskectomy to prepare interspace (other than for decompression); thoracic

● 22533 lumbar

+ ● 22534 thoracic or lumbar, each additional vertebral segment (List separately in addition to code for primary procedure)

►(Use 22534 in conjunction with 22532 and 22533)◄

Arthrodesis

Arthrodesis may be performed in the absence of other procedures and therefore when it is combined with another definitive procedure (eg, osteotomy, fracture care, vertebral corpectomy or laminectomy), modifier '-51' is appropriate. However, arthrodesis codes 22585, 22614, and 22632 are considered add-on procedure codes and should not be used with modifier '-51'.

To report instrumentation procedures, see codes 22840-22855. (Report in addition to code(s) for the definitive procedure(s) without modifier '-51'.) Do not append modifier '-62' to spinal instrumentation codes 22840-22848 and 22850-22852.

To report bone graft procedures, see codes 20930-20938. (Report in addition to code(s) for the definitive procedure(s) without modifier '-51'.) Do not append modifier '-62' to bone graft codes 20900-20938.

Anterior or Anterolateral Approach Technique

Procedure codes 22554-22558 are for SINGLE interspace; for additional interspaces, use 22585. A vertebral interspace is the non-bony compartment between two adjacent vertebral bodies, which contains the intervertebral disk, and includes the nucleus pulposus, annulus fibrosus, and two cartilagenous endplates.

For the following codes, when two surgeons work together as primary surgeons performing distinct part(s) of an anterior interbody arthrodesis, each surgeon should report his/her distinct operative work by appending the modifier '-62' to the procedure code. In this situation, the modifier '-62' may be appended to the procedure code(s) 22548-22558 and, as appropriate, to the associated additional interspace add-on code 22585 as long as both surgeons continue to work together as primary surgeons.

22548 Arthrodesis, anterior transoral or extraoral technique, clivus-C1-C2 (atlas-axis), with or without excision of odontoid process

22554 Arthrodesis, anterior interbody technique, including minimal diskectomy to prepare interspace (other than for decompression); cervical below C2

22556 thoracic

22558 lumbar

+ 22585 each additional interspace (List separately in addition to code for primary procedure)

(Use 22585 in conjunction with codes 22554, 22556, 22558)

Posterior, Posterolateral or Lateral Transverse Process Technique

To report instrumentation procedures, see codes 22840-22855. (Report in addition to code(s) for the definitive procedure(s) without modifier '-51'.) Do not append modifier '-62' to spinal instrumentation codes 22840-22848 and 22850-22852.

To report bone graft procedures, see codes 20930-20938. (Report in addition to code(s) for the definitive procedure(s) without modifier '-51'.) Do not append modifier '-62' to bone graft codes 20900-20938.

A vertebral segment describes the basic constituent part into which the spine may be divided. It represents a single complete vertebral bone with its associated articular processes and laminae. A vertebral interspace is the non-bony compartment between two adjacent vertebral bodies which contains the intervertebral disk, and includes the nucleus pulposus, annulus fibrosus, and two cartilagenous endplates.

22590 Arthrodesis, posterior technique, craniocervical (occiput-C2)

22595 Arthrodesis, posterior technique, atlas-axis (C1-C2)

22600 Arthrodesis, posterior or posterolateral technique, single level; cervical below C2 segment

22610 thoracic (with or without lateral transverse technique)

22612 lumbar (with or without lateral transverse technique)

+ 22614 each additional vertebral segment (List separately in addition to code for primary procedure)

(Use 22614 in conjunction with codes 22600, 22610, 22612)

22630 Arthrodesis, posterior interbody technique, including laminectomy and/or diskectomy to prepare interspace (other than for decompression), single interspace; lumbar

+ 22632 each additional interspace (List separately in addition to code for primary procedure)

(Use 22632 in conjunction with code 22630)

Spine Deformity (eg, Scoliosis, Kyphosis)

To report instrumentation procedures, see codes 22840-22855. (Report in addition to code(s) for the definitive procedure(s) without modifier '-51'.) Do not append modifier '-62' to spinal instrumentation codes 22840-22848 and 22850-22852.

To report bone graft procedures, see codes 20930-20938. (Report in addition to code(s) for the definitive procedure(s) without modifier '-51'.) Do not append modifier '-62' to bone graft codes 20900-20938.

A vertebral segment describes the basic constituent part into which the spine may be divided. It represents a single complete vertebral bone with its associated articular processes and laminae.

For the following codes, when two surgeons work together as primary surgeons performing distinct part(s) of an arthrodesis for spinal deformity, each surgeon should report his/her distinct operative work by appending the modifier '-62' to the procedure code. In this situation, the modifier '-62' may be appended to the procedure code(s) 22800-22819 as long as both surgeons continue to work together as primary surgeons.

22800 Arthrodesis, posterior, for spinal deformity, with or without cast; up to 6 vertebral segments

22802 7 to 12 vertebral segments

22804 13 or more vertebral segments

22808 Arthrodesis, anterior, for spinal deformity, with or without cast; 2 to 3 vertebral segments

22810 4 to 7 vertebral segments

22812 8 or more vertebral segments

22818 Kyphectomy, circumferential exposure of spine and resection of vertebral segment(s) (including body and posterior elements); single or 2 segments

22819 3 or more segments

(To report arthrodesis, see 22800-22804 and add modifier '-51')

Exploration

22830 Exploration of spinal fusion

Spinal Instrumentation

Segmental instrumentation is defined as fixation at each end of the construct and at least one additional interposed bony attachment.

Non-segmental instrumentation is defined as fixation at each end of the construct and may span several vertebral segments without attachment to the intervening segments.

Insertion of spinal instrumentation is reported separately and in addition to arthrodesis. Instrumentation procedure codes 22840-22848, 22851 are reported in addition to the definitive procedure(s) without modifier '-51'. Do not append modifier '-62' to spinal instrumentation codes 22840-22848 and 22850-22852.

To report bone graft procedures, see codes 20930-20938. (Report in addition to code(s) for definitive procedure(s) without modifier '-51'.) Do not append modifier '-62' to bone graft codes 20900-20938.

A vertebral segment describes the basic constituent part into which the spine may be divided. It represents a single complete vertebral bone with its associated articular processes and laminae. A vertebral interspace is the non-bony compartment between two adjacent vertebral bodies, which contains the intervertebral disk, and includes the nucleus pulposus, annulus fibrosus, and two cartilagenous endplates.

(List codes 22840-22848, 22851 separately, in addition to code for fracture, dislocation, or arthrodesis of the spine, 22325, 22326, 22327, 22548-22812)

⊘ **22840** Posterior non-segmental instrumentation (eg, Harrington rod technique, pedicle fixation across one interspace, atlantoaxial transarticular screw fixation, sublaminar wiring at C1, facet screw fixation)

⊘ **22841** Internal spinal fixation by wiring of spinous processes

⊘ **22842** Posterior segmental instrumentation (eg, pedicle fixation, dual rods with multiple hooks and sublaminar wires); 3 to 6 vertebral segments

⊘ **22843** 7 to 12 vertebral segments

⊘ **22844** 13 or more vertebral segments

⊘ **22845** Anterior instrumentation; 2 to 3 vertebral segments

⊘ **22846** 4 to 7 vertebral segments

⊘ **22847** 8 or more vertebral segments

⊘ **22848** Pelvic fixation (attachment of caudal end of instrumentation to pelvic bony structures) other than sacrum

22849 Reinsertion of spinal fixation device

22850 Removal of posterior nonsegmental instrumentation (eg, Harrington rod)

⊘ **22851** Application of intervertebral biomechanical device(s) (eg, synthetic cage(s), threaded bone dowel(s), methylmethacrylate) to vertebral defect or interspace

22852 Removal of posterior segmental instrumentation

22855 Removal of anterior instrumentation

Other Procedures

22899 Unlisted procedure, spine

Abdomen

Excision

22900 Excision, abdominal wall tumor, subfascial (eg, desmoid)

Other Procedures

22999 Unlisted procedure, abdomen, musculoskeletal system

Shoulder

Clavicle, scapula, humerus head and neck, sterno-clavicular joint, acromioclavicular joint and shoulder joint.

Incision

23000 Removal of subdeltoid calcareous deposits, open

(For arthroscopic removal of bursal deposits, use 29999)

23020 Capsular contracture release (eg, Sever type procedure)

(For incision and drainage procedures, superficial, see 10040-10160)

23030 Incision and drainage, shoulder area; deep abscess or hematoma

23031 infected bursa

23035 Incision, bone cortex (eg, osteomyelitis or bone abscess), shoulder area

23040 Arthrotomy, glenohumeral joint, including exploration, drainage, or removal of foreign body

23044 Arthrotomy, acromioclavicular, sternoclavicular joint, including exploration, drainage, or removal of foreign body

Excision

23065 Biopsy, soft tissue of shoulder area; superficial

23066 deep

(For needle biopsy of soft tissue, use 20206)

23075 Excision, soft tissue tumor, shoulder area; subcutaneous

23076 deep, subfascial, or intramuscular

23077 Radical resection of tumor (eg, malignant neoplasm), soft tissue of shoulder area

23100 Arthrotomy, glenohumeral joint, including biopsy

23101 Arthrotomy, acromioclavicular joint or sternoclavicular joint, including biopsy and/or excision of torn cartilage

23105 Arthrotomy; glenohumeral joint, with synovectomy, with or without biopsy

23106 sternoclavicular joint, with synovectomy, with or without biopsy

23107 Arthrotomy, glenohumeral joint, with joint exploration, with or without removal of loose or foreign body

23120 Claviculectomy; partial

(For arthroscopic procedure, use 29824)

23125 total

23130 Acromioplasty or acromionectomy, partial, with or without coracoacromial ligament release

23140 Excision or curettage of bone cyst or benign tumor of clavicle or scapula;

23145 with autograft (includes obtaining graft)

23146 with allograft

23150 Excision or curettage of bone cyst or benign tumor of proximal humerus;

23155 with autograft (includes obtaining graft)

23156 with allograft

23170 Sequestrectomy (eg, for osteomyelitis or bone abscess), clavicle

23172 Sequestrectomy (eg, for osteomyelitis or bone abscess), scapula

23174 Sequestrectomy (eg, for osteomyelitis or bone abscess), humeral head to surgical neck

23180 Partial excision (craterization, saucerization, or diaphysectomy) bone (eg, osteomyelitis), clavicle

23182 Partial excision (craterization, saucerization, or diaphysectomy) bone (eg, osteomyelitis), scapula

23184 Partial excision (craterization, saucerization, or diaphysectomy) bone (eg, osteomyelitis), proximal humerus

23190 Ostectomy of scapula, partial (eg, superior medial angle)

23195 Resection, humeral head

(For replacement with implant, use 23470)

23200 Radical resection for tumor; clavicle

23210 scapula

23220 Radical resection of bone tumor, proximal humerus;

23221 with autograft (includes obtaining graft)

23222 with prosthetic replacement

Introduction or Removal

(For arthrocentesis or needling of bursa, use 20610)

(For K-wire or pin insertion or removal, see 20650, 20670, 20680)

23330 Removal of foreign body, shoulder; subcutaneous

23331 deep (eg, Neer hemiarthroplasty removal)

23332 complicated (eg, total shoulder)

23350 Injection procedure for shoulder arthrography or enhanced CT/MRI shoulder arthrography

(For radiographic arthrography, radiological supervision and interpretation, use 73040. Fluoroscopy (76003) is inclusive of radiographic arthrography)

(When fluoroscopic guided injection is performed for enhanced CT arthrography, use codes 23350, 76003, and 73201 or 73202)

(When fluoroscopic guided injection is performed for enhanced MR arthrography, use codes 23350, 76003, and 73222 or 73223)

(For enhanced CT or enhanced MRI arthrography, use 76003 and either 73201, 73202, 73222 or 73223)

Repair, Revision, and/or Reconstruction

23395 Muscle transfer, any type, shoulder or upper arm; single

23397 multiple

23400 Scapulopexy (eg, Sprengels deformity or for paralysis)

23405 Tenotomy, shoulder area; single tendon

23406 multiple tendons through same incision

23410 Repair of ruptured musculotendinous cuff (eg, rotator cuff) open; acute

23412 chronic

(For arthroscopic procedure, use 29827)

23415 Coracoacromial ligament release, with or without acromioplasty

(For arthroscopic procedure, use 29826)

23420 Reconstruction of complete shoulder (rotator) cuff avulsion, chronic (includes acromioplasty)

23430 Tenodesis of long tendon of biceps

23440 Resection or transplantation of long tendon of biceps

23450 Capsulorrhaphy, anterior; Putti-Platt procedure or Magnuson type operation

(To report arthroscopic thermal capsulorrhaphy, use 29999)

23455 with labral repair (eg, Bankart procedure)

(For arthroscopic procedure, use ▶29806◀)

23460 Capsulorrhaphy, anterior, any type; with bone block

23462 with coracoid process transfer

(To report open thermal capsulorrhaphy, use 23929)

23465 Capsulorrhaphy, glenohumeral joint, posterior, with or without bone block

(For sternoclavicular and acromioclavicular reconstruction, see 23530, 23550)

23466 Capsulorrhaphy, glenohumeral joint, any type multi-directional instability

23470 Arthroplasty, glenohumeral joint; hemiarthroplasty

23472 total shoulder (glenoid and proximal humeral replacement (eg, total shoulder))

(For removal of total shoulder implants, see 23331, 23332)

(For osteotomy, proximal humerus, use 24400)

23480 Osteotomy, clavicle, with or without internal fixation;

23485 with bone graft for nonunion or malunion (includes obtaining graft and/or necessary fixation)

23490 Prophylactic treatment (nailing, pinning, plating or wiring) with or without methylmethacrylate; clavicle

23491 proximal humerus

Fracture and/or Dislocation

23500 Closed treatment of clavicular fracture; without manipulation

23505 with manipulation

23515 Open treatment of clavicular fracture, with or without internal or external fixation

23520 Closed treatment of sternoclavicular dislocation; without manipulation

23525 with manipulation

23530 Open treatment of sternoclavicular dislocation, acute or chronic;

23532 with fascial graft (includes obtaining graft)

23540 Closed treatment of acromioclavicular dislocation; without manipulation

23545 with manipulation

23550 Open treatment of acromioclavicular dislocation, acute or chronic;

23552 with fascial graft (includes obtaining graft)

23570 Closed treatment of scapular fracture; without manipulation

23575 with manipulation, with or without skeletal traction (with or without shoulder joint involvement)

23585 Open treatment of scapular fracture (body, glenoid or acromion) with or without internal fixation

23600 Closed treatment of proximal humeral (surgical or anatomical neck) fracture; without manipulation

23605 with manipulation, with or without skeletal traction

23615 Open treatment of proximal humeral (surgical or anatomical neck) fracture, with or without internal or external fixation, with or without repair of tuberosity(s);

23616 with proximal humeral prosthetic replacement

23620 Closed treatment of greater humeral tuberosity fracture; without manipulation

23625 with manipulation

23630 Open treatment of greater humeral tuberosity fracture, with or without internal or external fixation

23650 Closed treatment of shoulder dislocation, with manipulation; without anesthesia

23655 requiring anesthesia

23660 Open treatment of acute shoulder dislocation

(Repairs for recurrent dislocations, see 23450-23466)

23665 Closed treatment of shoulder dislocation, with fracture of greater humeral tuberosity, with manipulation

23670 Open treatment of shoulder dislocation, with fracture of greater humeral tuberosity, with or without internal or external fixation

23675 Closed treatment of shoulder dislocation, with surgical or anatomical neck fracture, with manipulation

23680 Open treatment of shoulder dislocation, with surgical or anatomical neck fracture, with or without internal or external fixation

Manipulation

23700 Manipulation under anesthesia, shoulder joint, including application of fixation apparatus (dislocation excluded)

Arthrodesis

23800 Arthrodesis, glenohumeral joint;

23802 with autogenous graft (includes obtaining graft)

Amputation

23900 Interthoracoscapular amputation (forequarter)

23920 Disarticulation of shoulder;

23921 secondary closure or scar revision

Other Procedures

23929 Unlisted procedure, shoulder

Humerus (Upper Arm) and Elbow

Elbow area includes head and neck of radius and olecranon process.

Incision

(For incision and drainage procedures, superficial, see 10040-10160)

23930 Incision and drainage, upper arm or elbow area; deep abscess or hematoma

23931 bursa

23935 Incision, deep, with opening of bone cortex (eg, for osteomyelitis or bone abscess), humerus or elbow

24000 Arthrotomy, elbow, including exploration, drainage, or removal of foreign body

24006 Arthrotomy of the elbow, with capsular excision for capsular release (separate procedure)

Excision

24065 Biopsy, soft tissue of upper arm or elbow area; superficial

24066 deep (subfascial or intramuscular)

(For needle biopsy of soft tissue, use 20206)

24075 Excision, tumor, soft tissue of upper arm or elbow area; subcutaneous

24076 deep (subfascial or intramuscular)

24077 Radical resection of tumor (eg, malignant neoplasm), soft tissue of upper arm or elbow area

24100 Arthrotomy, elbow; with synovial biopsy only

24101 with joint exploration, with or without biopsy, with or without removal of loose or foreign body

24102 with synovectomy

24105 Excision, olecranon bursa

24110 Excision or curettage of bone cyst or benign tumor, humerus;

24115 with autograft (includes obtaining graft)

24116 with allograft

24120 Excision or curettage of bone cyst or benign tumor of head or neck of radius or olecranon process;

24125 with autograft (includes obtaining graft)

24126 with allograft

24130 Excision, radial head

(For replacement with implant, use 24366)

24134 Sequestrectomy (eg, for osteomyelitis or bone abscess), shaft or distal humerus

24136 Sequestrectomy (eg, for osteomyelitis or bone abscess), radial head or neck

24138 Sequestrectomy (eg, for osteomyelitis or bone abscess), olecranon process

24140 Partial excision (craterization, saucerization, or diaphysectomy) bone (eg, osteomyelitis), humerus

24145 Partial excision (craterization, saucerization, or diaphysectomy) bone (eg, osteomyelitis), radial head or neck

24147 Partial excision (craterization, saucerization, or diaphysectomy) bone (eg, osteomyelitis), olecranon process

24149 Radical resection of capsule, soft tissue, and heterotopic bone, elbow, with contracture release (separate procedure)

(For capsular and soft tissue release only, use 24006)

24150 Radical resection for tumor, shaft or distal humerus;

24151 with autograft (includes obtaining graft)

24152 Radical resection for tumor, radial head or neck;

24153 with autograft (includes obtaining graft)

24155 Resection of elbow joint (arthrectomy)

Introduction or Removal

(For K-wire or pin insertion or removal, see 20650, 20670, 20680)

(For arthrocentesis or needling of bursa or joint, use 20605)

24160 Implant removal; elbow joint

24164 radial head

24200 Removal of foreign body, upper arm or elbow area; subcutaneous

24201 deep (subfascial or intramuscular)

24220 Injection procedure for elbow arthrography

(For radiological supervision and interpretation, use 73085. Do not report 76003 in addition to 73085)

(For injection for tennis elbow, use 20550)

Repair, Revision, and/or Reconstruction

24300 Manipulation, elbow, under anesthesia

(For application of external fixation, see 20690 or 20692)

24301 Muscle or tendon transfer, any type, upper arm or elbow, single (excluding 24320-24331)

24305 Tendon lengthening, upper arm or elbow, each tendon

24310 Tenotomy, open, elbow to shoulder, each tendon

24320 Tenoplasty, with muscle transfer, with or without free graft, elbow to shoulder, single (Seddon-Brookes type procedure)

24330 Flexor-plasty, elbow (eg, Steindler type advancement);

24331 with extensor advancement

24332 Tenolysis, triceps

24340 Tenodesis of biceps tendon at elbow (separate procedure)

24341 Repair, tendon or muscle, upper arm or elbow, each tendon or muscle, primary or secondary (excludes rotator cuff)

24342 Reinsertion of ruptured biceps or triceps tendon, distal, with or without tendon graft

24343 Repair lateral collateral ligament, elbow, with local tissue

24344 Reconstruction lateral collateral ligament, elbow, with tendon graft (includes harvesting of graft)

24345 Repair medial collateral ligament, elbow, with local tissue

24346 Reconstruction medial collateral ligament, elbow, with tendon graft (includes harvesting of graft)

24350 Fasciotomy, lateral or medial (eg, tennis elbow or epicondylitis);

24351 with extensor origin detachment

24352 with annular ligament resection

24354 with stripping

24356 with partial ostectomy

24360 Arthroplasty, elbow; with membrane (eg, fascial)

24361 with distal humeral prosthetic replacement

24362 with implant and fascia lata ligament reconstruction

24363 with distal humerus and proximal ulnar prosthetic replacement (eg, total elbow)

24365 Arthroplasty, radial head;

24366 with implant

24400 Osteotomy, humerus, with or without internal fixation

24410 Multiple osteotomies with realignment on intramedullary rod, humeral shaft (Sofield type procedure)

24420 Osteoplasty, humerus (eg, shortening or lengthening) (excluding 64876)

24430 Repair of nonunion or malunion, humerus; without graft (eg, compression technique)

24435 with iliac or other autograft (includes obtaining graft)

(For proximal radius and/or ulna, see 25400-25420)

24470 Hemiepiphyseal arrest (eg, cubitus varus or valgus, distal humerus)

24495 Decompression fasciotomy, forearm, with brachial artery exploration

24498 Prophylactic treatment (nailing, pinning, plating or wiring), with or without methylmethacrylate, humeral shaft

Fracture and/or Dislocation

24500 Closed treatment of humeral shaft fracture; without manipulation

24505 with manipulation, with or without skeletal traction

24515 Open treatment of humeral shaft fracture with plate/screws, with or without cerclage

24516 Treatment of humeral shaft fracture, with insertion of intramedullary implant, with or without cerclage and/or locking screws

24530 Closed treatment of supracondylar or transcondylar humeral fracture, with or without intercondylar extension; without manipulation

24535 with manipulation, with or without skin or skeletal traction

24538 Percutaneous skeletal fixation of supracondylar or transcondylar humeral fracture, with or without intercondylar extension

24545 Open treatment of humeral supracondylar or transcondylar fracture, with or without internal or external fixation; without intercondylar extension

24546 with intercondylar extension

24560 Closed treatment of humeral epicondylar fracture, medial or lateral; without manipulation

24565 with manipulation

24566 Percutaneous skeletal fixation of humeral epicondylar fracture, medial or lateral, with manipulation

24575 Open treatment of humeral epicondylar fracture, medial or lateral, with or without internal or external fixation

24576 Closed treatment of humeral condylar fracture, medial or lateral; without manipulation

24577 with manipulation

24579 Open treatment of humeral condylar fracture, medial or lateral, with or without internal or external fixation

24582 Percutaneous skeletal fixation of humeral condylar fracture, medial or lateral, with manipulation

24586 Open treatment of periarticular fracture and/or dislocation of the elbow (fracture distal humerus and proximal ulna and/or proximal radius);

24587 with implant arthroplasty

(See also 24361)

24600 Treatment of closed elbow dislocation; without anesthesia

24605 requiring anesthesia

24615 Open treatment of acute or chronic elbow dislocation

24620 Closed treatment of Monteggia type of fracture dislocation at elbow (fracture proximal end of ulna with dislocation of radial head), with manipulation

24635 Open treatment of Monteggia type of fracture dislocation at elbow (fracture proximal end of ulna with dislocation of radial head), with or without internal or external fixation

24640 Closed treatment of radial head subluxation in child, nursemaid elbow, with manipulation

24650 Closed treatment of radial head or neck fracture; without manipulation

24655 with manipulation

24665 Open treatment of radial head or neck fracture, with or without internal fixation or radial head excision;

24666 with radial head prosthetic replacement

24670 Closed treatment of ulnar fracture, proximal end (olecranon process); without manipulation

24675 with manipulation

24685 Open treatment of ulnar fracture proximal end (olecranon process), with or without internal or external fixation

Arthrodesis

24800 Arthrodesis, elbow joint; local

24802 with autogenous graft (includes obtaining graft)

Amputation

24900 Amputation, arm through humerus; with primary closure

24920 open, circular (guillotine)

24925 secondary closure or scar revision

24930 re-amputation

24931 with implant

24935 Stump elongation, upper extremity

24940 Cineplasty, upper extremity, complete procedure

Other Procedures

24999 Unlisted procedure, humerus or elbow

Forearm and Wrist

Radius, ulna, carpal bones and joints.

Incision

25000 Incision, extensor tendon sheath, wrist (eg, deQuervains disease)

(For decompression median nerve or for carpal tunnel syndrome, use 64721)

25001 Incision, flexor tendon sheath, wrist (eg, flexor carpi radialis)

25020 Decompression fasciotomy, forearm and/or wrist, flexor OR extensor compartment; without debridement of nonviable muscle and/or nerve

25023 with debridement of nonviable muscle and/or nerve

(For decompression fasciotomy with brachial artery exploration, use 24495)

(For incision and drainage procedures, superficial, see 10060-10160)

(For debridement, see also 11000-11044)

25024 Decompression fasciotomy, forearm and/or wrist, flexor AND extensor compartment; without debridement of nonviable muscle and/or nerve

25025 with debridement of nonviable muscle and/or nerve

25028 Incision and drainage, forearm and/or wrist; deep abscess or hematoma

25031 bursa

25035 Incision, deep, bone cortex, forearm and/or wrist (eg, osteomyelitis or bone abscess)

25040 Arthrotomy, radiocarpal or midcarpal joint, with exploration, drainage, or removal of foreign body

Excision

25065 Biopsy, soft tissue of forearm and/or wrist; superficial

25066 deep (subfascial or intramuscular)

(For needle biopsy of soft tissue, use 20206)

25075 Excision, tumor, soft tissue of forearm and/or wrist area; subcutaneous

25076 deep (subfascial or intramuscular)

25077 Radical resection of tumor (eg, malignant neoplasm), soft tissue of forearm and/or wrist area

25085 Capsulotomy, wrist (eg, contracture)

25100 Arthrotomy, wrist joint; with biopsy

25101 with joint exploration, with or without biopsy, with or without removal of loose or foreign body

25105 with synovectomy

25107 Arthrotomy, distal radioulnar joint including repair of triangular cartilage, complex

25110 Excision, lesion of tendon sheath, forearm and/or wrist

25111 Excision of ganglion, wrist (dorsal or volar); primary

25112 recurrent

(For hand or finger, use 26160)

25115 Radical excision of bursa, synovia of wrist, or forearm tendon sheaths (eg, tenosynovitis, fungus, Tbc, or other granulomas, rheumatoid arthritis); flexors

25116 extensors, with or without transposition of dorsal retinaculum

(For finger synovectomies, use 26145)

25118 Synovectomy, extensor tendon sheath, wrist, single compartment;

25119 with resection of distal ulna

25120 Excision or curettage of bone cyst or benign tumor of radius or ulna (excluding head or neck of radius and olecranon process);

(For head or neck of radius or olecranon process, see 24120-24126)

25125 with autograft (includes obtaining graft)

25126 with allograft

25130 Excision or curettage of bone cyst or benign tumor of carpal bones;

25135 with autograft (includes obtaining graft)

25136 with allograft

25145 Sequestrectomy (eg, for osteomyelitis or bone abscess), forearm and/or wrist

25150 Partial excision (craterization, saucerization, or diaphysectomy) of bone (eg, for osteomyelitis); ulna

25151 radius

(For head or neck of radius or olecranon process, see 24145, 24147)

25170 Radical resection for tumor, radius or ulna

25210 Carpectomy; one bone

(For carpectomy with implant, see 25441-25445)

25215 all bones of proximal row

25230 Radial styloidectomy (separate procedure)

25240 Excision distal ulna partial or complete (eg, Darrach type or matched resection)

(For implant replacement, distal ulna, use 25442)

(For obtaining fascia for interposition, see 20920, 20922)

Introduction or Removal

(For K-wire, pin or rod insertion or removal, see 20650, 20670, 20680)

25246 Injection procedure for wrist arthrography

(For radiological supervision and interpretation, use 73115. Do not report 76003 in addition to 73115)

(For foreign body removal, superficial use 20520)

25248 Exploration with removal of deep foreign body, forearm or wrist

25250 Removal of wrist prosthesis; (separate procedure)

25251 complicated, including total wrist

25259 Manipulation, wrist, under anesthesia

(For application of external fixation, see 20690 or 20692)

Repair, Revision, and/or Reconstruction

25260 Repair, tendon or muscle, flexor, forearm and/or wrist; primary, single, each tendon or muscle

25263 secondary, single, each tendon or muscle

25265 secondary, with free graft (includes obtaining graft), each tendon or muscle

25270 Repair, tendon or muscle, extensor, forearm and/or wrist; primary, single, each tendon or muscle

25272 secondary, single, each tendon or muscle

25274 secondary, with free graft (includes obtaining graft), each tendon or muscle

25275 Repair, tendon sheath, extensor, forearm and/or wrist, with free graft (includes obtaining graft) (eg, for extensor carpi ulnaris subluxation)

25280 Lengthening or shortening of flexor or extensor tendon, forearm and/or wrist, single, each tendon

25290 Tenotomy, open, flexor or extensor tendon, forearm and/or wrist, single, each tendon

25295 Tenolysis, flexor or extensor tendon, forearm and/or wrist, single, each tendon

25300 Tenodesis at wrist; flexors of fingers

25301 extensors of fingers

25310 Tendon transplantation or transfer, flexor or extensor, forearm and/or wrist, single; each tendon

25312 with tendon graft(s) (includes obtaining graft), each tendon

25315 Flexor origin slide (eg, for cerebral palsy, Volkmann contracture), forearm and/or wrist;

25316 with tendon(s) transfer

25320 Capsulorrhaphy or reconstruction, wrist, open (eg, capsulodesis, ligament repair, tendon transfer or graft) (includes synovectomy, capsulotomy and open reduction) for carpal instability

25332 Arthroplasty, wrist, with or without interposition, with or without external or internal fixation

(For obtaining fascia for interposition, see 20920, 20922)

(For prosthetic replacement arthroplasty, see 25441-25446)

25335 Centralization of wrist on ulna (eg, radial club hand)

25337 Reconstruction for stabilization of unstable distal ulna or distal radioulnar joint, secondary by soft tissue stabilization (eg, tendon transfer, tendon graft or weave, or tenodesis) with or without open reduction of distal radioulnar joint

(For harvesting of fascia lata graft, see 20920, 20922)

25350 Osteotomy, radius; distal third

25355 middle or proximal third

25360 Osteotomy; ulna

25365 radius AND ulna

25370 Multiple osteotomies, with realignment on intramedullary rod (Sofield type procedure); radius OR ulna

25375 radius AND ulna

25390 Osteoplasty, radius OR ulna; shortening

25391 lengthening with autograft

25392 Osteoplasty, radius AND ulna; shortening (excluding 64876)

25393 lengthening with autograft

25394 Osteoplasty, carpal bone, shortening

25400 Repair of nonunion or malunion, radius OR ulna; without graft (eg, compression technique)

25405 with autograft (includes obtaining graft)

25415 Repair of nonunion or malunion, radius AND ulna; without graft (eg, compression technique)

25420 with autograft (includes obtaining graft)

25425 Repair of defect with autograft; radius OR ulna

25426 radius AND ulna

25430 Insertion of vascular pedicle into carpal bone (eg, Hori procedure)

25431 Repair of nonunion of carpal bone (excluding carpal scaphoid (navicular)) (includes obtaining graft and necessary fixation), each bone

25440 Repair of nonunion, scaphoid carpal (navicular) bone, with or without radial styloidectomy (includes obtaining graft and necessary fixation)

25441 Arthroplasty with prosthetic replacement; distal radius

25442 distal ulna

25443 scaphoid carpal (navicular)

25444 lunate

25445 trapezium

25446 distal radius and partial or entire carpus (total wrist)

25447 Arthroplasty, interposition, intercarpal or carpometacarpal joints

(For wrist arthroplasty, use 25332)

25449 Revision of arthroplasty, including removal of implant, wrist joint

25450 Epiphyseal arrest by epiphysiodesis or stapling; distal radius OR ulna

25455 distal radius AND ulna

25490 Prophylactic treatment (nailing, pinning, plating or wiring) with or without methylmethacrylate; radius

25491 ulna

25492 radius AND ulna

Fracture and/or Dislocation

25500 Closed treatment of radial shaft fracture; without manipulation

25505 with manipulation

25515 Open treatment of radial shaft fracture, with or without internal or external fixation

25520 Closed treatment of radial shaft fracture and closed treatment of dislocation of distal radioulnar joint (Galeazzi fracture/dislocation)

25525 Open treatment of radial shaft fracture, with internal and/ or external fixation and closed treatment of dislocation of distal radioulnar joint (Galeazzi fracture/dislocation), with or without percutaneous skeletal fixation

25526 Open treatment of radial shaft fracture, with internal and/or external fixation and open treatment, with or without internal or external fixation of distal radioulnar joint (Galeazzi fracture/dislocation), includes repair of triangular fibrocartilage complex

25530 Closed treatment of ulnar shaft fracture; without manipulation

25535 with manipulation

25545 Open treatment of ulnar shaft fracture, with or without internal or external fixation

25560 Closed treatment of radial and ulnar shaft fractures; without manipulation

25565 with manipulation

25574 Open treatment of radial AND ulnar shaft fractures, with internal or external fixation; of radius OR ulna

25575 of radius AND ulna

25600 Closed treatment of distal radial fracture (eg, Colles or Smith type) or epiphyseal separation, with or without fracture of ulnar styloid; without manipulation

25605 with manipulation

25611 Percutaneous skeletal fixation of distal radial fracture (eg, Colles or Smith type) or epiphyseal separation, with or without fracture of ulnar styloid, requiring manipulation, with or without external fixation

25620 Open treatment of distal radial fracture (eg, Colles or Smith type) or epiphyseal separation, with or without fracture of ulnar styloid, with or without internal or external fixation

25622 Closed treatment of carpal scaphoid (navicular) fracture; without manipulation

25624 with manipulation

25628 Open treatment of carpal scaphoid (navicular) fracture, with or without internal or external fixation

25630 Closed treatment of carpal bone fracture (excluding carpal scaphoid (navicular)); without manipulation, each bone

25635 with manipulation, each bone

25645 Open treatment of carpal bone fracture (other than carpal scaphoid (navicular)), each bone

25650 Closed treatment of ulnar styloid fracture

25651 Percutaneous skeletal fixation of ulnar styloid fracture

25652 Open treatment of ulnar styloid fracture

25660 Closed treatment of radiocarpal or intercarpal dislocation, one or more bones, with manipulation

25670 Open treatment of radiocarpal or intercarpal dislocation, one or more bones

25671 Percutaneous skeletal fixation of distal radioulnar dislocation

25675 Closed treatment of distal radioulnar dislocation with manipulation

25676 Open treatment of distal radioulnar dislocation, acute or chronic

25680 Closed treatment of trans-scaphoperilunar type of fracture dislocation, with manipulation

25685 Open treatment of trans-scaphoperilunar type of fracture dislocation

25690 Closed treatment of lunate dislocation, with manipulation

25695 Open treatment of lunate dislocation

Arthrodesis

25800 Arthrodesis, wrist; complete, without bone graft (includes radiocarpal and/or intercarpal and/or carpometacarpal joints)

25805 with sliding graft

25810 with iliac or other autograft (includes obtaining graft)

25820 Arthrodesis, wrist; limited, without bone graft (eg, intercarpal or radiocarpal)

25825 with autograft (includes obtaining graft)

25830 Arthrodesis, distal radioulnar joint with segmental resection of ulna, with or without bone graft (eg, Sauve-Kapandji procedure)

Amputation

25900 Amputation, forearm, through radius and ulna;

25905 open, circular (guillotine)

25907 secondary closure or scar revision

25909 re-amputation

25915 Krukenberg procedure

25920 Disarticulation through wrist;

25922 secondary closure or scar revision

25924 re-amputation

25927 Transmetacarpal amputation;

25929 secondary closure or scar revision

25931 re-amputation

Other Procedures

25999 Unlisted procedure, forearm or wrist

Hand and Fingers

Incision

26010 Drainage of finger abscess; simple

26011 complicated (eg, felon)

26020 Drainage of tendon sheath, digit and/or palm, each

26025 Drainage of palmar bursa; single, bursa

26030 multiple bursa

26034 Incision, bone cortex, hand or finger (eg, osteomyelitis or bone abscess)

26035 Decompression fingers and/or hand, injection injury (eg, grease gun)

26037 Decompressive fasciotomy, hand (excludes 26035)

(For injection injury, use 26035)

26040 Fasciotomy, palmar (eg, Dupuytren's contracture); percutaneous

26045 open, partial

(For fasciectomy, see 26121-26125)

26055 Tendon sheath incision (eg, for trigger finger)

26060 Tenotomy, percutaneous, single, each digit

26070 Arthrotomy, with exploration, drainage, or removal of loose or foreign body; carpometacarpal joint

26075 metacarpophalangeal joint, each

26080 interphalangeal joint, each

Excision

26100 Arthrotomy with biopsy; carpometacarpal joint, each

26105 metacarpophalangeal joint, each

26110 interphalangeal joint, each

26115 Excision, tumor or vascular malformation, soft tissue of hand or finger; subcutaneous

26116 deep (subfascial or intramuscular)

26117 Radical resection of tumor (eg, malignant neoplasm), soft tissue of hand or finger

26121 Fasciectomy, palm only, with or without Z-plasty, other local tissue rearrangement, or skin grafting (includes obtaining graft)

26123 Fasciectomy, partial palmar with release of single digit including proximal interphalangeal joint, with or without Z-plasty, other local tissue rearrangement, or skin grafting (includes obtaining graft);

+ 26125 each additional digit (List separately in addition to code for primary procedure)

(Use 26125 in conjunction with code 26123)

(For fasciotomy, see 26040, 26045)

26130 Synovectomy, carpometacarpal joint

26135 Synovectomy, metacarpophalangeal joint including intrinsic release and extensor hood reconstruction, each digit

26140 Synovectomy, proximal interphalangeal joint, including extensor reconstruction, each interphalangeal joint

26145 Synovectomy, tendon sheath, radical (tenosynovectomy), flexor tendon, palm and/or finger, each tendon

(For tendon sheath synovectomies at wrist, see 25115, 25116)

26160 Excision of lesion of tendon sheath or joint capsule (eg, cyst, mucous cyst, or ganglion), hand or finger

(For wrist ganglion, see 25111, 25112)

(For trigger digit, use 26055)

26170 Excision of tendon, palm, flexor, single (separate procedure), each

26180 Excision of tendon, finger, flexor (separate procedure), each tendon

26185 Sesamoidectomy, thumb or finger (separate procedure)

26200 Excision or curettage of bone cyst or benign tumor of metacarpal;

26205 with autograft (includes obtaining graft)

26210 Excision or curettage of bone cyst or benign tumor of proximal, middle, or distal phalanx of finger;

26215 with autograft (includes obtaining graft)

26230 Partial excision (craterization, saucerization, or diaphysectomy) bone (eg, osteomyelitis); metacarpal

26235 proximal or middle phalanx of finger

26236 distal phalanx of finger

26250 Radical resection, metacarpal (eg, tumor);

26255 with autograft (includes obtaining graft)

26260 Radical resection, proximal or middle phalanx of finger (eg, tumor);

26261 with autograft (includes obtaining graft)

26262 Radical resection, distal phalanx of finger (eg, tumor)

Introduction or Removal

26320 Removal of implant from finger or hand

(For removal of foreign body in hand or finger, see 20520, 20525)

Repair, Revision, and/or Reconstruction

26340 Manipulation, finger joint, under anesthesia, each joint

(For application of external fixation, see 20690 or 20692)

26350 Repair or advancement, flexor tendon, not in zone 2 digital flexor tendon sheath (eg, no man's land); primary or secondary without free graft, each tendon

26352 secondary with free graft (includes obtaining graft), each tendon

▲26356 Repair or advancement, flexor tendon, in zone 2 digital flexor tendon sheath (eg, no man's land); primary, without free graft, each tendon

▲26357 secondary, without free graft, each tendon

26358 secondary, with free graft (includes obtaining graft), each tendon

26370 Repair or advancement of profundus tendon, with intact superficialis tendon; primary, each tendon

26372 secondary with free graft (includes obtaining graft), each tendon

26373 secondary without free graft, each tendon

26390 Excision flexor tendon, with implantation of synthetic rod for delayed tendon graft, hand or finger, each rod

26392 Removal of synthetic rod and insertion of flexor tendon graft, hand or finger (includes obtaining graft), each rod

26410 Repair, extensor tendon, hand, primary or secondary; without free graft, each tendon

26412 with free graft (includes obtaining graft), each tendon

26415 Excision of extensor tendon, with implantation of synthetic rod for delayed tendon graft, hand or finger, each rod

26416 Removal of synthetic rod and insertion of extensor tendon graft (includes obtaining graft), hand or finger, each rod

26418 Repair, extensor tendon, finger, primary or secondary; without free graft, each tendon

26420 with free graft (includes obtaining graft) each tendon

26426 Repair of extensor tendon, central slip, secondary (eg, boutonniere deformity); using local tissue(s), including lateral band(s), each finger

26428 with free graft (includes obtaining graft), each finger

26432 Closed treatment of distal extensor tendon insertion, with or without percutaneous pinning (eg, mallet finger)

26433 Repair of extensor tendon, distal insertion, primary or secondary; without graft (eg, mallet finger)

26434 with free graft (includes obtaining graft)

(For tenovaginotomy for trigger finger, use 26055)

26437 Realignment of extensor tendon, hand, each tendon

26440 Tenolysis, flexor tendon; palm OR finger, each tendon

26442 palm AND finger, each tendon

26445 Tenolysis, extensor tendon, hand OR finger; each tendon

26449 Tenolysis, complex, extensor tendon, finger, including forearm, each tendon

26450 Tenotomy, flexor, palm, open, each tendon

26455 Tenotomy, flexor, finger, open, each tendon

26460 Tenotomy, extensor, hand or finger, open, each tendon

26471 Tenodesis; of proximal interphalangeal joint, each joint

26474 of distal joint, each joint

26476 Lengthening of tendon, extensor, hand or finger, each tendon

26477 Shortening of tendon, extensor, hand or finger, each tendon

26478 Lengthening of tendon, flexor, hand or finger, each tendon

26479 Shortening of tendon, flexor, hand or finger, each tendon

26480 Transfer or transplant of tendon, carpometacarpal area or dorsum of hand; without free graft, each tendon

26483 with free tendon graft (includes obtaining graft), each tendon

26485 Transfer or transplant of tendon, palmar; without free tendon graft, each tendon

26489 with free tendon graft (includes obtaining graft), each tendon

26490 Opponensplasty; superficialis tendon transfer type, each tendon

26492 tendon transfer with graft (includes obtaining graft), each tendon

26494 hypothenar muscle transfer

26496 other methods

(For thumb fusion in opposition, use 26820)

26497 Transfer of tendon to restore intrinsic function; ring and small finger

26498 all four fingers

26499 Correction claw finger, other methods

26500 Reconstruction of tendon pulley, each tendon; with local tissues (separate procedure)

26502 with tendon or fascial graft (includes obtaining graft) (separate procedure)

26504 with tendon prosthesis (separate procedure)

26508 Release of thenar muscle(s) (eg, thumb contracture)

26510 Cross intrinsic transfer, each tendon

26516 Capsulodesis, metacarpophalangeal joint; single digit

26517 two digits

26518 three or four digits

26520 Capsulectomy or capsulotomy; metacarpophalangeal joint, each joint

26525 interphalangeal joint, each joint

26530 Arthroplasty, metacarpophalangeal joint; each joint

26531 with prosthetic implant, each joint

26535 Arthroplasty, interphalangeal joint; each joint

26536 with prosthetic implant, each joint

26540 Repair of collateral ligament, metacarpophalangeal or interphalangeal joint

26541 Reconstruction, collateral ligament, metacarpophalangeal joint, single; with tendon or fascial graft (includes obtaining graft)

26542 with local tissue (eg, adductor advancement)

26545 Reconstruction, collateral ligament, interphalangeal joint, single, including graft, each joint

26546 Repair non-union, metacarpal or phalanx, (includes obtaining bone graft with or without external or internal fixation)

26548 Repair and reconstruction, finger, volar plate, interphalangeal joint

26550 Pollicization of a digit

26551 Transfer, toe-to-hand with microvascular anastomosis; great toe wrap-around with bone graft

(For great toe with web space, use 20973)

26553 other than great toe, single

26554 other than great toe, double

(Do not report code 69990 in addition to codes 26551-26554)

26555 Transfer, finger to another position without microvascular anastomosis

26556 Transfer, free toe joint, with microvascular anastomosis

(Do not report code 69990 in addition to code 26556)

26560 Repair of syndactyly (web finger) each web space; with skin flaps

26561 with skin flaps and grafts

26562 complex (eg, involving bone, nails)

26565 Osteotomy; metacarpal, each

26567 phalanx of finger, each

26568 Osteoplasty, lengthening, metacarpal or phalanx

26580 Repair cleft hand

(26585 has been deleted. To report, use 26587)

26587 Reconstruction of polydactylous digit, soft tissue and bone

(For excision of polydactylous digit, soft tissue only, use 11200)

26590 Repair macrodactylia, each digit

26591 Repair, intrinsic muscles of hand, each muscle

26593 Release, intrinsic muscles of hand, each muscle

26596 Excision of constricting ring of finger, with multiple Z-plasties

(26597 has been deleted. To report, see 11041-11042, 14040-14041, or 15120, 15240)

Fracture and/or Dislocation

26600 Closed treatment of metacarpal fracture, single; without manipulation, each bone

26605 with manipulation, each bone

26607 Closed treatment of metacarpal fracture, with manipulation, with external fixation, each bone

26608 Percutaneous skeletal fixation of metacarpal fracture, each bone

26615 Open treatment of metacarpal fracture, single, with or without internal or external fixation, each bone

26641 Closed treatment of carpometacarpal dislocation, thumb, with manipulation

26645 Closed treatment of carpometacarpal fracture dislocation, thumb (Bennett fracture), with manipulation

26650 Percutaneous skeletal fixation of carpometacarpal fracture dislocation, thumb (Bennett fracture), with manipulation, with or without external fixation

26665 Open treatment of carpometacarpal fracture dislocation, thumb (Bennett fracture), with or without internal or external fixation

26670 Closed treatment of carpometacarpal dislocation, other than thumb, with manipulation, each joint; without anesthesia

26675 requiring anesthesia

26676 Percutaneous skeletal fixation of carpometacarpal dislocation, other than thumb, with manipulation, each joint

26685 Open treatment of carpometacarpal dislocation, other than thumb; with or without internal or external fixation, each joint

26686 complex, multiple or delayed reduction

26700 Closed treatment of metacarpophalangeal dislocation, single, with manipulation; without anesthesia

26705 requiring anesthesia

26706 Percutaneous skeletal fixation of metacarpophalangeal dislocation, single, with manipulation

26715 Open treatment of metacarpophalangeal dislocation, single, with or without internal or external fixation

26720 Closed treatment of phalangeal shaft fracture, proximal or middle phalanx, finger or thumb; without manipulation, each

26725 with manipulation, with or without skin or skeletal traction, each

26727 Percutaneous skeletal fixation of unstable phalangeal shaft fracture, proximal or middle phalanx, finger or thumb, with manipulation, each

26735 Open treatment of phalangeal shaft fracture, proximal or middle phalanx, finger or thumb, with or without internal or external fixation, each

26740 Closed treatment of articular fracture, involving metacarpophalangeal or interphalangeal joint; without manipulation, each

26742 with manipulation, each

26746 Open treatment of articular fracture, involving metacarpophalangeal or interphalangeal joint, with or without internal or external fixation, each

26750 Closed treatment of distal phalangeal fracture, finger or thumb; without manipulation, each

26755 with manipulation, each

26756 Percutaneous skeletal fixation of distal phalangeal fracture, finger or thumb, each

26765 Open treatment of distal phalangeal fracture, finger or thumb, with or without internal or external fixation, each

26770 Closed treatment of interphalangeal joint dislocation, single, with manipulation; without anesthesia

26775 requiring anesthesia

26776 Percutaneous skeletal fixation of interphalangeal joint dislocation, single, with manipulation

26785 Open treatment of interphalangeal joint dislocation, with or without internal or external fixation, single

Arthrodesis

26820 Fusion in opposition, thumb, with autogenous graft (includes obtaining graft)

26841 Arthrodesis, carpometacarpal joint, thumb, with or without internal fixation;

26842 with autograft (includes obtaining graft)

26843 Arthrodesis, carpometacarpal joint, digit, other than thumb, each;

26844 with autograft (includes obtaining graft)

26850 Arthrodesis, metacarpophalangeal joint, with or without internal fixation;

26852 with autograft (includes obtaining graft)

26860 Arthrodesis, interphalangeal joint, with or without internal fixation;

+ 26861 each additional interphalangeal joint (List separately in addition to code for primary procedure)

(Use 26861 in conjunction with code 26860)

26862 with autograft (includes obtaining graft)

+ 26863 with autograft (includes obtaining graft), each additional joint (List separately in addition to code for primary procedure)

(Use 26863 in conjunction with code 26862)

Amputation

(For hand through metacarpal bones, use 25927)

26910 Amputation, metacarpal, with finger or thumb (ray amputation), single, with or without interosseous transfer

(For repositioning, see 26550, 26555)

26951 Amputation, finger or thumb, primary or secondary, any joint or phalanx, single, including neurectomies; with direct closure

26952 with local advancement flaps (V-Y, hood)

(For repair of soft tissue defect requiring split or full thickness graft or other pedicle flaps, see 15050-15758)

Other Procedures

26989 Unlisted procedure, hands or fingers

Pelvis and Hip Joint

Including head and neck of femur.

Incision

(For incision and drainage procedures, superficial, see 10040-10160)

26990 Incision and drainage, pelvis or hip joint area; deep abscess or hematoma

26991 infected bursa

26992 Incision, bone cortex, pelvis and/or hip joint (eg, osteomyelitis or bone abscess)

27000 Tenotomy, adductor of hip, percutaneous (separate procedure)

27001 Tenotomy, adductor of hip, open

27003 Tenotomy, adductor, subcutaneous, open, with obturator neurectomy

27005 Tenotomy, hip flexor(s), open (separate procedure)

27006 Tenotomy, abductors and/or extensor(s) of hip, open (separate procedure)

27025 Fasciotomy, hip or thigh, any type

27030 Arthrotomy, hip, with drainage (eg, infection)

27033 Arthrotomy, hip, including exploration or removal of loose or foreign body

27035 Denervation, hip joint, intrapelvic or extrapelvic intra-articular branches of sciatic, femoral, or obturator nerves

(For obturator neurectomy, see 64763, 64766)

27036 Capsulectomy or capsulotomy, hip, with or without excision of heterotopic bone, with release of hip flexor muscles (ie, gluteus medius, gluteus minimus, tensor fascia latae, rectus femoris, sartorius, iliopsoas)

Excision

27040 Biopsy, soft tissue of pelvis and hip area; superficial

27041 deep, subfascial or intramuscular

(For needle biopsy of soft tissue, use 20206)

27047 Excision, tumor, pelvis and hip area; subcutaneous tissue

27048 deep, subfascial, intramuscular

27049 Radical resection of tumor, soft tissue of pelvis and hip area (eg, malignant neoplasm)

27050 Arthrotomy, with biopsy; sacroiliac joint

27052 hip joint

27054 Arthrotomy with synovectomy, hip joint

27060 Excision; ischial bursa

27062 trochanteric bursa or calcification

(For arthrocentesis or needling of bursa, use 20610)

27065 Excision of bone cyst or benign tumor; superficial (wing of ilium, symphysis pubis, or greater trochanter of femur) with or without autograft

27066 deep, with or without autograft

27067 with autograft requiring separate incision

27070 Partial excision (craterization, saucerization) (eg, osteomyelitis or bone abscess); superficial (eg, wing of ilium, symphysis pubis, or greater trochanter of femur)

27071 deep (subfascial or intramuscular)

27075 Radical resection of tumor or infection; wing of ilium, one pubic or ischial ramus or symphysis pubis

27076 ilium, including acetabulum, both pubic rami, or ischium and acetabulum

27077 innominate bone, total

27078 ischial tuberosity and greater trochanter of femur

27079 ischial tuberosity and greater trochanter of femur, with skin flaps

27080 Coccygectomy, primary

(For pressure (decubitus) ulcer, see 15920, 15922 and 15931-15958)

Introduction or Removal

27086 Removal of foreign body, pelvis or hip; subcutaneous tissue

27087 deep (subfascial or intramuscular)

27090 Removal of hip prosthesis; (separate procedure)

27091 complicated, including total hip prosthesis, methylmethacrylate with or without insertion of spacer

27093 Injection procedure for hip arthrography; without anesthesia

(For radiological supervision and interpretation, use 73525. Do not report 76003 in addition to 73525)

27095 with anesthesia

(For radiological supervision and interpretation, use 73525. Do not report 76003 in addition to 73525)

27096 Injection procedure for sacroiliac joint, arthrography and/or anesthetic/steroid

(27096 is to be used only with imaging confirmation of intra-articular needle positioning)

(For radiological supervision and interpretation of sacroiliac joint arthrography, use 73542)

(For fluoroscopic guidance without formal arthrography, use 76005)

(Code 27096 is a unilateral procedure. For bilateral procedure, use modifier '-50')

Repair, Revision, and/or Reconstruction

27097 Release or recession, hamstring, proximal

27098 Transfer, adductor to ischium

27100 Transfer external oblique muscle to greater trochanter including fascial or tendon extension (graft)

27105 Transfer paraspinal muscle to hip (includes fascial or tendon extension graft)

27110 Transfer iliopsoas; to greater trochanter of femur

27111 to femoral neck

27120 Acetabuloplasty; (eg, Whitman, Colonna, Haygroves, or cup type)

27122 resection, femoral head (eg, Girdlestone procedure)

27125 Hemiarthroplasty, hip, partial (eg, femoral stem prosthesis, bipolar arthroplasty)

(For prosthetic replacement following fracture of the hip, use 27236)

27130 Arthroplasty, acetabular and proximal femoral prosthetic replacement (total hip arthroplasty), with or without autograft or allograft

27132 Conversion of previous hip surgery to total hip arthroplasty, with or without autograft or allograft

27134 Revision of total hip arthroplasty; both components, with or without autograft or allograft

27137 acetabular component only, with or without autograft or allograft

27138 femoral component only, with or without allograft

27140 Osteotomy and transfer of greater trochanter of femur (separate procedure)

27146 Osteotomy, iliac, acetabular or innominate bone;

27147 with open reduction of hip

27151 with femoral osteotomy

27156 with femoral osteotomy and with open reduction of hip

27158 Osteotomy, pelvis, bilateral (eg, congenital malformation)

27161 Osteotomy, femoral neck (separate procedure)

27165 Osteotomy, intertrochanteric or subtrochanteric including internal or external fixation and/or cast

27170 Bone graft, femoral head, neck, intertrochanteric or subtrochanteric area (includes obtaining bone graft)

27175 Treatment of slipped femoral epiphysis; by traction, without reduction

27176 by single or multiple pinning, in situ

27177 Open treatment of slipped femoral epiphysis; single or multiple pinning or bone graft (includes obtaining graft)

27178 closed manipulation with single or multiple pinning

27179 osteoplasty of femoral neck (Heyman type procedure)

27181 osteotomy and internal fixation

27185 Epiphyseal arrest by epiphysiodesis or stapling, greater trochanter of femur

27187 Prophylactic treatment (nailing, pinning, plating or wiring) with or without methylmethacrylate, femoral neck and proximal femur

Fracture and/or Dislocation

27193 Closed treatment of pelvic ring fracture, dislocation, diastasis or subluxation; without manipulation

27194 with manipulation, requiring more than local anesthesia

27200 Closed treatment of coccygeal fracture

27202 Open treatment of coccygeal fracture

27215 Open treatment of iliac spine(s), tuberosity avulsion, or iliac wing fracture(s) (eg, pelvic fracture(s) which do not disrupt the pelvic ring), with internal fixation

27216 Percutaneous skeletal fixation of posterior pelvic ring fracture and/or dislocation (includes ilium, sacroiliac joint and/or sacrum)

27217 Open treatment of anterior ring fracture and/or dislocation with internal fixation (includes pubic symphysis and/or rami)

27218 Open treatment of posterior ring fracture and/or dislocation with internal fixation (includes ilium, sacroiliac joint and/or sacrum)

27220 Closed treatment of acetabulum (hip socket) fracture(s); without manipulation

27222 with manipulation, with or without skeletal traction

27226 Open treatment of posterior or anterior acetabular wall fracture, with internal fixation

27227 Open treatment of acetabular fracture(s) involving anterior or posterior (one) column, or a fracture running transversely across the acetabulum, with internal fixation

27228 Open treatment of acetabular fracture(s) involving anterior and posterior (two) columns, includes T-fracture and both column fracture with complete articular detachment, or single column or transverse fracture with associated acetabular wall fracture, with internal fixation

27230 Closed treatment of femoral fracture, proximal end, neck; without manipulation

27232 with manipulation, with or without skeletal traction

27235 Percutaneous skeletal fixation of femoral fracture, proximal end, neck

27236 Open treatment of femoral fracture, proximal end, neck, internal fixation or prosthetic replacement

27238 Closed treatment of intertrochanteric, pertrochanteric, or subtrochanteric femoral fracture; without manipulation

27240 with manipulation, with or without skin or skeletal traction

27244 Treatment of intertrochanteric, pertrochanteric, or subtrochanteric femoral fracture; with plate/screw type implant, with or without cerclage

27245 with intramedullary implant, with or without interlocking screws and/or cerclage

27246 Closed treatment of greater trochanteric fracture, without manipulation

27248 Open treatment of greater trochanteric fracture, with or without internal or external fixation

27250 Closed treatment of hip dislocation, traumatic; without anesthesia

27252 requiring anesthesia

27253 Open treatment of hip dislocation, traumatic, without internal fixation

27254 Open treatment of hip dislocation, traumatic, with acetabular wall and femoral head fracture, with or without internal or external fixation

27256 Treatment of spontaneous hip dislocation (developmental, including congenital or pathological), by abduction, splint or traction; without anesthesia, without manipulation

27257 with manipulation, requiring anesthesia

27258 Open treatment of spontaneous hip dislocation (developmental, including congenital or pathological), replacement of femoral head in acetabulum (including tenotomy, etc);

27259 with femoral shaft shortening

27265 Closed treatment of post hip arthroplasty dislocation; without anesthesia

27266 requiring regional or general anesthesia

Manipulation

27275 Manipulation, hip joint, requiring general anesthesia

Arthrodesis

27280 Arthrodesis, sacroiliac joint (including obtaining graft)

27282 Arthrodesis, symphysis pubis (including obtaining graft)

27284 Arthrodesis, hip joint (including obtaining graft);

27286 with subtrochanteric osteotomy

Amputation

27290 Interpelviabdominal amputation (hindquarter amputation)

27295 Disarticulation of hip

Other Procedures

27299 Unlisted procedure, pelvis or hip joint

Femur (Thigh Region) and Knee Joint

Including tibial plateaus.

Incision

(For incision and drainage of abscess or hematoma, superficial, see 10040-10160)

27301 Incision and drainage, deep abscess, bursa, or hematoma, thigh or knee region

27303 Incision, deep, with opening of bone cortex, femur or knee (eg, osteomyelitis or bone abscess)

27305 Fasciotomy, iliotibial (tenotomy), open

(For combined Ober-Yount fasciotomy, use 27025)

27306 Tenotomy, percutaneous, adductor or hamstring; single tendon (separate procedure)

27307 multiple tendons

27310 Arthrotomy, knee, with exploration, drainage, or removal of foreign body (eg, infection)

27315 Neurectomy, hamstring muscle

27320 Neurectomy, popliteal (gastrocnemius)

Excision

27323 Biopsy, soft tissue of thigh or knee area; superficial

27324 deep (subfascial or intramuscular)

(For needle biopsy of soft tissue, use 20206)

27327 Excision, tumor, thigh or knee area; subcutaneous

27328 deep, subfascial, or intramuscular

27329 Radical resection of tumor (eg, malignant neoplasm), soft tissue of thigh or knee area

27330 Arthrotomy, knee; with synovial biopsy only

27331 including joint exploration, biopsy, or removal of loose or foreign bodies

27332 Arthrotomy, with excision of semilunar cartilage (meniscectomy) knee; medial OR lateral

27333 medial AND lateral

27334 Arthrotomy, with synovectomy, knee; anterior OR posterior

27335 anterior AND posterior including popliteal area

27340 Excision, prepatellar bursa

27345 Excision of synovial cyst of popliteal space (eg, Baker's cyst)

27347 Excision of lesion of meniscus or capsule (eg, cyst, ganglion), knee

27350 Patellectomy or hemipatellectomy

27355 Excision or curettage of bone cyst or benign tumor of femur;

27356 with allograft

27357 with autograft (includes obtaining graft)

+ 27358 with internal fixation (List in addition to code for primary procedure)

(Use 27358 in conjunction with codes 27355, 27356, or 27357)

27360 Partial excision (craterization, saucerization, or diaphysectomy) bone, femur, proximal tibia and/or fibula (eg, osteomyelitis or bone abscess)

27365 Radical resection of tumor, bone, femur or knee

(For radical resection of tumor, soft tissue, use 27329)

Introduction or Removal

27370 Injection procedure for knee arthrography

(For radiological supervision and interpretation, use 73580. Do not report 76003 in addition to 73580)

27372 Removal of foreign body, deep, thigh region or knee area

(For removal of knee prosthesis including "total knee," use 27488)

Repair, Revision, and/or Reconstruction

27380 Suture of infrapatellar tendon; primary

27381 secondary reconstruction, including fascial or tendon graft

27385 Suture of quadriceps or hamstring muscle rupture; primary

27386 secondary reconstruction, including fascial or tendon graft

27390 Tenotomy, open, hamstring, knee to hip; single tendon

27391 multiple tendons, one leg

27392 multiple tendons, bilateral

27393 Lengthening of hamstring tendon; single tendon

27394 multiple tendons, one leg

27395 multiple tendons, bilateral

27396 Transplant, hamstring tendon to patella; single tendon

27397 multiple tendons

27400 Transfer, tendon or muscle, hamstrings to femur (eg, Egger's type procedure)

27403 Arthrotomy with meniscus repair, knee

(For arthroscopic repair, use 29882)

27405 Repair, primary, torn ligament and/or capsule, knee; collateral

27407 cruciate

27409 collateral and cruciate ligaments

27418 Anterior tibial tubercleplasty (eg, Maquet type procedure)

27420 Reconstruction of dislocating patella; (eg, Hauser type procedure)

27422 with extensor realignment and/or muscle advancement or release (eg, Campbell, Goldwaite type procedure)

27424 with patellectomy

27425 Lateral retinacular release, open

(For arthroscopic lateral release, use 29873)

27427 Ligamentous reconstruction (augmentation), knee; extra-articular

27428 intra-articular (open)

27429 intra-articular (open) and extra-articular

(For primary repair of ligament(s) performed in addition to reconstruction, report 27405, 27407 or 27409 in addition to code 27427, 27428 or 27429)

27430 Quadricepsplasty (eg, Bennett or Thompson type)

27435 Capsulotomy, posterior capsular release, knee

27437 Arthroplasty, patella; without prosthesis

27438 with prosthesis

27440 Arthroplasty, knee, tibial plateau;

27441 with debridement and partial synovectomy

27442 Arthroplasty, femoral condyles or tibial plateau(s), knee;

27443 with debridement and partial synovectomy

27445 Arthroplasty, knee, hinge prosthesis (eg, Walldius type)

27446 Arthroplasty, knee, condyle and plateau; medial OR lateral compartment

27447 medial AND lateral compartments with or without patella resurfacing (total knee arthroplasty)

(For revision of total knee arthroplasty, use 27487)

(For removal of total knee prosthesis, use 27488)

27448 Osteotomy, femur, shaft or supracondylar; without fixation

27450 with fixation

27454 Osteotomy, multiple, with realignment on intramedullary rod, femoral shaft (eg, Sofield type procedure)

27455 Osteotomy, proximal tibia, including fibular excision or osteotomy (includes correction of genu varus (bowleg) or genu valgus (knock-knee)); before epiphyseal closure

27457 after epiphyseal closure

27465 Osteoplasty, femur; shortening (excluding 64876)

27466 lengthening

27468 combined, lengthening and shortening with femoral segment transfer

27470 Repair, nonunion or malunion, femur, distal to head and neck; without graft (eg, compression technique)

27472 with iliac or other autogenous bone graft (includes obtaining graft)

27475 Arrest, epiphyseal, any method (eg, epiphysiodesis); distal femur

27477 tibia and fibula, proximal

27479 combined distal femur, proximal tibia and fibula

27485 Arrest, hemiepiphyseal, distal femur or proximal tibia or fibula (eg, genu varus or valgus)

27486 Revision of total knee arthroplasty, with or without allograft; one component

27487 femoral and entire tibial component

27488 Removal of prosthesis, including total knee prosthesis, methylmethacrylate with or without insertion of spacer, knee

27495 Prophylactic treatment (nailing, pinning, plating or wiring) with or without methylmethacrylate, femur

27496 Decompression fasciotomy, thigh and/or knee, one compartment (flexor or extensor or adductor);

27497 with debridement of nonviable muscle and/or nerve

27498 Decompression fasciotomy, thigh and/or knee, multiple compartments;

27499 with debridement of nonviable muscle and/or nerve

Fracture and/or Dislocation

(For arthroscopic treatment of intercondylar spine(s) and tuberosity fracture(s) of the knee, see 29850, 29851)

(For arthroscopic treatment of tibial fracture, see 29855, 29856)

27500 Closed treatment of femoral shaft fracture, without manipulation

27501 Closed treatment of supracondylar or transcondylar femoral fracture with or without intercondylar extension, without manipulation

27502 Closed treatment of femoral shaft fracture, with manipulation, with or without skin or skeletal traction

27503 Closed treatment of supracondylar or transcondylar femoral fracture with or without intercondylar extension, with manipulation, with or without skin or skeletal traction

27506 Open treatment of femoral shaft fracture, with or without external fixation, with insertion of intramedullary implant, with or without cerclage and/or locking screws

27507 Open treatment of femoral shaft fracture with plate/screws, with or without cerclage

27508 Closed treatment of femoral fracture, distal end, medial or lateral condyle, without manipulation

27509 Percutaneous skeletal fixation of femoral fracture, distal end, medial or lateral condyle, or supracondylar or transcondylar, with or without intercondylar extension, or distal femoral epiphyseal separation

27510 Closed treatment of femoral fracture, distal end, medial or lateral condyle, with manipulation

27511 Open treatment of femoral supracondylar or transcondylar fracture without intercondylar extension, with or without internal or external fixation

27513 Open treatment of femoral supracondylar or transcondylar fracture with intercondylar extension, with or without internal or external fixation

27514 Open treatment of femoral fracture, distal end, medial or lateral condyle, with or without internal or external fixation

27516 Closed treatment of distal femoral epiphyseal separation; without manipulation

27517 with manipulation, with or without skin or skeletal traction

27519 Open treatment of distal femoral epiphyseal separation, with or without internal or external fixation

27520 Closed treatment of patellar fracture, without manipulation

27524 Open treatment of patellar fracture, with internal fixation and/or partial or complete patellectomy and soft tissue repair

27530 Closed treatment of tibial fracture, proximal (plateau); without manipulation

27532 with or without manipulation, with skeletal traction

(For arthroscopic treatment, see 29855, 29856)

27535 Open treatment of tibial fracture, proximal (plateau); unicondylar, with or without internal or external fixation

27536 bicondylar, with or without internal fixation

(For arthroscopic treatment, see 29855, 29856)

27538 Closed treatment of intercondylar spine(s) and/or tuberosity fracture(s) of knee, with or without manipulation

(For arthroscopic treatment, see 29850, 29851)

27540 Open treatment of intercondylar spine(s) and/or tuberosity fracture(s) of the knee, with or without internal or external fixation

27550 Closed treatment of knee dislocation; without anesthesia

27552 requiring anesthesia

27556 Open treatment of knee dislocation, with or without internal or external fixation; without primary ligamentous repair or augmentation/reconstruction

27557 with primary ligamentous repair

27558 with primary ligamentous repair, with augmentation/reconstruction

27560 Closed treatment of patellar dislocation; without anesthesia

(For recurrent dislocation, see 27420-27424)

27562 requiring anesthesia

27566 Open treatment of patellar dislocation, with or without partial or total patellectomy

Manipulation

27570 Manipulation of knee joint under general anesthesia (includes application of traction or other fixation devices)

Arthrodesis

27580 Arthrodesis, knee, any technique

Amputation

27590 Amputation, thigh, through femur, any level;

27591 immediate fitting technique including first cast

27592 open, circular (guillotine)

27594 secondary closure or scar revision

27596 re-amputation

27598 Disarticulation at knee

Other Procedures

27599 Unlisted procedure, femur or knee

Leg (Tibia and Fibula) and Ankle Joint

Incision

27600 Decompression fasciotomy, leg; anterior and/or lateral compartments only

27601 posterior compartment(s) only

27602 anterior and/or lateral, and posterior compartment(s)

(For incision and drainage procedures, superficial, see 10040-10160)

(For decompression fasciotomy with debridement, see 27892-27894)

27603 Incision and drainage, leg or ankle; deep abscess or hematoma

27604 infected bursa

27605 Tenotomy, percutaneous, Achilles tendon (separate procedure); local anesthesia

27606 general anesthesia

27607 Incision (eg, osteomyelitis or bone abscess), leg or ankle

27610 Arthrotomy, ankle, including exploration, drainage, or removal of foreign body

27612 Arthrotomy, posterior capsular release, ankle, with or without Achilles tendon lengthening

(See also 27685)

Excision

27613 Biopsy, soft tissue of leg or ankle area; superficial

27614 deep (subfascial or intramuscular)

(For needle biopsy of soft tissue, use 20206)

27615 Radical resection of tumor (eg, malignant neoplasm), soft tissue of leg or ankle area

27618 Excision, tumor, leg or ankle area; subcutaneous tissue

27619 deep (subfascial or intramuscular)

27620 Arthrotomy, ankle, with joint exploration, with or without biopsy, with or without removal of loose or foreign body

27625 Arthrotomy, with synovectomy, ankle;

27626 including tenosynovectomy

27630 Excision of lesion of tendon sheath or capsule (eg, cyst or ganglion), leg and/or ankle

27635 Excision or curettage of bone cyst or benign tumor, tibia or fibula;

27637 with autograft (includes obtaining graft)

27638 with allograft

27640 Partial excision (craterization, saucerization, or diaphysectomy) bone (eg, osteomyelitis or exostosis); tibia

27641 fibula

27645 Radical resection of tumor, bone; tibia

27646 fibula

27647 talus or calcaneus

Introduction or Removal

27648 Injection procedure for ankle arthrography

(For radiological supervision and interpretation, use 73615. Do not report 76003 in addition to 73615)

(For ankle arthroscopy, see 29894-29898)

Repair, Revision, and/or Reconstruction

27650 Repair, primary, open or percutaneous, ruptured Achilles tendon;

27652 with graft (includes obtaining graft)

27654 Repair, secondary, Achilles tendon, with or without graft

27656 Repair, fascial defect of leg

27658 Repair, flexor tendon, leg; primary, without graft, each tendon

27659 secondary, with or without graft, each tendon

27664 Repair, extensor tendon, leg; primary, without graft, each tendon

27665 secondary, with or without graft, each tendon

27675 Repair, dislocating peroneal tendons; without fibular osteotomy

27676 with fibular osteotomy

27680 Tenolysis, flexor or extensor tendon, leg and/or ankle; single, each tendon

27681 multiple tendons (through separate incision(s))

27685 Lengthening or shortening of tendon, leg or ankle; single tendon (separate procedure)

27686 multiple tendons (through same incision), each

27687 Gastrocnemius recession (eg, Strayer procedure)

(Toe extensors are considered as a group to be a single tendon when transplanted into midfoot)

27690 Transfer or transplant of single tendon (with muscle redirection or rerouting); superficial (eg, anterior tibial extensors into midfoot)

27691 deep (eg, anterior tibial or posterior tibial through interosseous space, flexor digitorum longus, flexor hallucis longus, or peroneal tendon to midfoot or hindfoot)

+ 27692 each additional tendon (List separately in addition to code for primary procedure)

(Use 27692 in conjunction with codes 27690, 27691)

27695 Repair, primary, disrupted ligament, ankle; collateral

27696 both collateral ligaments

27698 Repair, secondary, disrupted ligament, ankle, collateral (eg, Watson-Jones procedure)

27700 Arthroplasty, ankle;

27702 with implant (total ankle)

27703 revision, total ankle

27704 Removal of ankle implant

27705 Osteotomy; tibia

27707 fibula

27709 tibia and fibula

27712 multiple, with realignment on intramedullary rod (eg, Sofield type procedure)

(For osteotomy to correct genu varus (bowleg) or genu valgus (knock-knee), see 27455-27457)

27715 Osteoplasty, tibia and fibula, lengthening or shortening

27720 Repair of nonunion or malunion, tibia; without graft, (eg, compression technique)

27722 with sliding graft

27724 with iliac or other autograft (includes obtaining graft)

27725 by synostosis, with fibula, any method

27727 Repair of congenital pseudarthrosis, tibia

27730 Arrest, epiphyseal (epiphysiodesis), open; distal tibia

27732 distal fibula

27734 distal tibia and fibula

27740 Arrest, epiphyseal (epiphysiodesis), any method, combined, proximal and distal tibia and fibula;

27742 and distal femur

(For epiphyseal arrest of proximal tibia and fibula, use 27477)

27745 Prophylactic treatment (nailing, pinning, plating or wiring) with or without methylmethacrylate, tibia

Fracture and/or Dislocation

27750 Closed treatment of tibial shaft fracture (with or without fibular fracture); without manipulation

27752 with manipulation, with or without skeletal traction

27756 Percutaneous skeletal fixation of tibial shaft fracture (with or without fibular fracture) (eg, pins or screws)

27758 Open treatment of tibial shaft fracture, (with or without fibular fracture) with plate/screws, with or without cerclage

27759 Treatment of tibial shaft fracture (with or without fibular fracture) by intramedullary implant, with or without interlocking screws and/or cerclage

27760 Closed treatment of medial malleolus fracture; without manipulation

27762 with manipulation, with or without skin or skeletal traction

27766 Open treatment of medial malleolus fracture, with or without internal or external fixation

27780 Closed treatment of proximal fibula or shaft fracture; without manipulation

27781 with manipulation

27784 Open treatment of proximal fibula or shaft fracture, with or without internal or external fixation

27786 Closed treatment of distal fibular fracture (lateral malleolus); without manipulation

27788 with manipulation

27792 Open treatment of distal fibular fracture (lateral malleolus), with or without internal or external fixation

27808 Closed treatment of bimalleolar ankle fracture, (including Potts); without manipulation

27810 with manipulation

27814 Open treatment of bimalleolar ankle fracture, with or without internal or external fixation

27816 Closed treatment of trimalleolar ankle fracture; without manipulation

27818 with manipulation

27822 Open treatment of trimalleolar ankle fracture, with or without internal or external fixation, medial and/or lateral malleolus; without fixation of posterior lip

27823 with fixation of posterior lip

27824 Closed treatment of fracture of weight bearing articular portion of distal tibia (eg, pilon or tibial plafond), with or without anesthesia; without manipulation

27825 with skeletal traction and/or requiring manipulation

27826 Open treatment of fracture of weight bearing articular surface/portion of distal tibia (eg, pilon or tibial plafond), with internal or external fixation; of fibula only

27827 of tibia only

27828 of both tibia and fibula

27829 Open treatment of distal tibiofibular joint (syndesmosis) disruption, with or without internal or external fixation

27830 Closed treatment of proximal tibiofibular joint dislocation; without anesthesia

27831 requiring anesthesia

27832 Open treatment of proximal tibiofibular joint dislocation, with or without internal or external fixation, or with excision of proximal fibula

27840 Closed treatment of ankle dislocation; without anesthesia

27842 requiring anesthesia, with or without percutaneous skeletal fixation

27846 Open treatment of ankle dislocation, with or without percutaneous skeletal fixation; without repair or internal fixation

27848 with repair or internal or external fixation

Manipulation

27860 Manipulation of ankle under general anesthesia (includes application of traction or other fixation apparatus)

Arthrodesis

27870 Arthrodesis, ankle, open

(For arthroscopic ankle arthrodesis, use 29899)

27871 Arthrodesis, tibiofibular joint, proximal or distal

Amputation

27880 Amputation, leg, through tibia and fibula;

27881 with immediate fitting technique including application of first cast

27882 open, circular (guillotine)

27884 secondary closure or scar revision

27886 re-amputation

27888 Amputation, ankle, through malleoli of tibia and fibula (eg, Syme, Pirogoff type procedures), with plastic closure and resection of nerves

27889 Ankle disarticulation

Other Procedures

27892 Decompression fasciotomy, leg; anterior and/or lateral compartments only, with debridement of nonviable muscle and/or nerve

(For decompression fasciotomy of the leg without debridement, use 27600)

27893 posterior compartment(s) only, with debridement of nonviable muscle and/or nerve

(For decompression fasciotomy of the leg without debridement, use 27601)

27894 anterior and/or lateral, and posterior compartment(s), with debridement of nonviable muscle and/or nerve

(For decompression fasciotomy of the leg without debridement, use 27602)

27899 Unlisted procedure, leg or ankle

Foot and Toes

Incision

(For incision and drainage procedures, superficial, see 10040-10160)

28001 Incision and drainage, bursa, foot

28002 Incision and drainage below fascia, with or without tendon sheath involvement, foot; single bursal space

28003 multiple areas

28005 Incision, bone cortex (eg, osteomyelitis or bone abscess), foot

28008 Fasciotomy, foot and/or toe

(See also 28060, 28062, 28250)

28010 Tenotomy, percutaneous, toe; single tendon

28011 multiple tendons

(For open tenotomy, see 28230-28234)

28020 Arthrotomy, including exploration, drainage, or removal of loose or foreign body; intertarsal or tarsometatarsal joint

28022 metatarsophalangeal joint

28024 interphalangeal joint

28030 Neurectomy, intrinsic musculature of foot

28035 Release, tarsal tunnel (posterior tibial nerve decompression)

(For other nerve entrapments, see 64704, 64722)

Excision

28043 Excision, tumor, foot; subcutaneous tissue

28045 deep, subfascial, intramuscular

28046 Radical resection of tumor (eg, malignant neoplasm), soft tissue of foot

28050 Arthrotomy with biopsy; intertarsal or tarsometatarsal joint

28052 metatarsophalangeal joint

28054 interphalangeal joint

28060 Fasciectomy, plantar fascia; partial (separate procedure)

28062 radical (separate procedure)

(For plantar fasciotomy, see 28008, 28250)

28070 Synovectomy; intertarsal or tarsometatarsal joint, each

28072 metatarsophalangeal joint, each

28080 Excision, interdigital (Morton) neuroma, single, each

28086 Synovectomy, tendon sheath, foot; flexor

28088 extensor

28090 Excision of lesion, tendon, tendon sheath, or capsule (including synovectomy) (eg, cyst or ganglion); foot

28092 toe(s), each

28100 Excision or curettage of bone cyst or benign tumor, talus or calcaneus;

28102 with iliac or other autograft (includes obtaining graft)

28103 with allograft

28104 Excision or curettage of bone cyst or benign tumor, tarsal or metatarsal, except talus or calcaneus;

28106 with iliac or other autograft (includes obtaining graft)

28107 with allograft

28108 Excision or curettage of bone cyst or benign tumor, phalanges of foot

(For ostectomy, partial (eg, hallux valgus, Silver type procedure), use 28290)

28110 Ostectomy, partial excision, fifth metatarsal head (bunionette) (separate procedure)

28111 Ostectomy, complete excision; first metatarsal head

28112 other metatarsal head (second, third or fourth)

28113 fifth metatarsal head

28114 all metatarsal heads, with partial proximal phalangectomy, excluding first metatarsal (eg, Clayton type procedure)

28116 Ostectomy, excision of tarsal coalition

28118 Ostectomy, calcaneus;

28119 for spur, with or without plantar fascial release

28120 Partial excision (craterization, saucerization, sequestrectomy, or diaphysectomy) bone (eg, osteomyelitis or bossing); talus or calcaneus

28122 tarsal or metatarsal bone, except talus or calcaneus

(For partial excision of talus or calcaneus, use 28120)

(For cheilectomy for hallux rigidus, use 28289)

28124 phalanx of toe

28126 Resection, partial or complete, phalangeal base, each toe

28130 Talectomy (astragalectomy)

28140 Metatarsectomy

28150 Phalangectomy, toe, each toe

28153 Resection, condyle(s), distal end of phalanx, each toe

28160 Hemiphalangectomy or interphalangeal joint excision, toe, proximal end of phalanx, each

28171 Radical resection of tumor, bone; tarsal (except talus or calcaneus)

28173 metatarsal

28175 phalanx of toe

(For talus or calcaneus, use 27647)

Introduction or Removal

28190 Removal of foreign body, foot; subcutaneous

28192 deep

28193 complicated

Repair, Revision, and/or Reconstruction

28200 Repair, tendon, flexor, foot; primary or secondary, without free graft, each tendon

28202 secondary with free graft, each tendon (includes obtaining graft)

28208 Repair, tendon, extensor, foot; primary or secondary, each tendon

28210 secondary with free graft, each tendon (includes obtaining graft)

28220 Tenolysis, flexor, foot; single tendon

28222 multiple tendons

28225 Tenolysis, extensor, foot; single tendon

28226 multiple tendons

28230 Tenotomy, open, tendon flexor; foot, single or multiple tendon(s) (separate procedure)

28232 toe, single tendon (separate procedure)

28234 Tenotomy, open, extensor, foot or toe, each tendon

28238 Reconstruction (advancement), posterior tibial tendon with excision of accessory tarsal navicular bone (eg, Kidner type procedure)

(For subcutaneous tenotomy, see 28010, 28011)

(For transfer or transplant of tendon with muscle redirection or rerouting, see 27690-27692)

(For extensor hallucis longus transfer with great toe IP fusion (Jones procedure), use 28760)

28240 Tenotomy, lengthening, or release, abductor hallucis muscle

28250 Division of plantar fascia and muscle (eg, Steindler stripping) (separate procedure)

28260 Capsulotomy, midfoot; medial release only (separate procedure)

28261 with tendon lengthening

28262 extensive, including posterior talotibial capsulotomy and tendon(s) lengthening (eg, resistant clubfoot deformity)

28264 Capsulotomy, midtarsal (eg, Heyman type procedure)

28270 Capsulotomy; metatarsophalangeal joint, with or without tenorrhaphy, each joint (separate procedure)

28272 interphalangeal joint, each joint (separate procedure)

28280 Syndactylization, toes (eg, webbing or Kelikian type procedure)

28285 Correction, hammertoe (eg, interphalangeal fusion, partial or total phalangectomy)

28286 Correction, cock-up fifth toe, with plastic skin closure (eg, Ruiz-Mora type procedure)

28288 Ostectomy, partial, exostectomy or condylectomy, metatarsal head, each metatarsal head

28289 Hallux rigidus correction with cheilectomy, debridement and capsular release of the first metatarsophalangeal joint

28290 Correction, hallux valgus (bunion), with or without sesamoidectomy; simple exostectomy (eg, Silver type procedure)

28292 Keller, McBride, or Mayo type procedure

28293 resection of joint with implant

28294 with tendon transplants (eg, Joplin type procedure)

28296 with metatarsal osteotomy (eg, Mitchell, Chevron, or concentric type procedures)

28297 Lapidus type procedure

28298 by phalanx osteotomy

28299 by double osteotomy

28300 Osteotomy; calcaneus (eg, Dwyer or Chambers type procedure), with or without internal fixation

28302 talus

28304 Osteotomy, tarsal bones, other than calcaneus or talus;

28305 with autograft (includes obtaining graft) (eg, Fowler type)

28306 Osteotomy, with or without lengthening, shortening or angular correction, metatarsal; first metatarsal

28307 first metatarsal with autograft (other than first toe)

28308 other than first metatarsal, each

28309 multiple (eg, Swanson type cavus foot procedure)

28310 Osteotomy, shortening, angular or rotational correction; proximal phalanx, first toe (separate procedure)

28312 other phalanges, any toe

28313 Reconstruction, angular deformity of toe, soft tissue procedures only (eg, overlapping second toe, fifth toe, curly toes)

28315 Sesamoidectomy, first toe (separate procedure)

28320 Repair, nonunion or malunion; tarsal bones

28322 metatarsal, with or without bone graft (includes obtaining graft)

28340 Reconstruction, toe, macrodactyly; soft tissue resection

28341 requiring bone resection

28344 Reconstruction, toe(s); polydactyly

28345 syndactyly, with or without skin graft(s), each web

28360 Reconstruction, cleft foot

Fracture and/or Dislocation

28400 Closed treatment of calcaneal fracture; without manipulation

28405 with manipulation

28406 Percutaneous skeletal fixation of calcaneal fracture, with manipulation

28415 Open treatment of calcaneal fracture, with or without internal or external fixation;

28420 with primary iliac or other autogenous bone graft (includes obtaining graft)

28430 Closed treatment of talus fracture; without manipulation

28435 with manipulation

28436 Percutaneous skeletal fixation of talus fracture, with manipulation

28445 Open treatment of talus fracture, with or without internal or external fixation

28450 Treatment of tarsal bone fracture (except talus and calcaneus); without manipulation, each

28455 with manipulation, each

28456 Percutaneous skeletal fixation of tarsal bone fracture (except talus and calcaneus), with manipulation, each

28465 Open treatment of tarsal bone fracture (except talus and calcaneus), with or without internal or external fixation, each

28470 Closed treatment of metatarsal fracture; without manipulation, each

28475 with manipulation, each

28476 Percutaneous skeletal fixation of metatarsal fracture, with manipulation, each

28485 Open treatment of metatarsal fracture, with or without internal or external fixation, each

28490 Closed treatment of fracture great toe, phalanx or phalanges; without manipulation

28495 with manipulation

28496 Percutaneous skeletal fixation of fracture great toe, phalanx or phalanges, with manipulation

28505 Open treatment of fracture great toe, phalanx or phalanges, with or without internal or external fixation

28510 Closed treatment of fracture, phalanx or phalanges, other than great toe; without manipulation, each

28515 with manipulation, each

28525 Open treatment of fracture, phalanx or phalanges, other than great toe, with or without internal or external fixation, each

28530 Closed treatment of sesamoid fracture

28531 Open treatment of sesamoid fracture, with or without internal fixation

28540 Closed treatment of tarsal bone dislocation, other than talotarsal; without anesthesia

28545 requiring anesthesia

28546 Percutaneous skeletal fixation of tarsal bone dislocation, other than talotarsal, with manipulation

28555 Open treatment of tarsal bone dislocation, with or without internal or external fixation

28570 Closed treatment of talotarsal joint dislocation; without anesthesia

28575 requiring anesthesia

28576 Percutaneous skeletal fixation of talotarsal joint dislocation, with manipulation

28585 Open treatment of talotarsal joint dislocation, with or without internal or external fixation

28600 Closed treatment of tarsometatarsal joint dislocation; without anesthesia

28605 requiring anesthesia

28606 Percutaneous skeletal fixation of tarsometatarsal joint dislocation, with manipulation

28615 Open treatment of tarsometatarsal joint dislocation, with or without internal or external fixation

28630 Closed treatment of metatarsophalangeal joint dislocation; without anesthesia

28635 requiring anesthesia

28636 Percutaneous skeletal fixation of metatarsophalangeal joint dislocation, with manipulation

28645 Open treatment of metatarsophalangeal joint dislocation, with or without internal or external fixation

28660 Closed treatment of interphalangeal joint dislocation; without anesthesia

28665 requiring anesthesia

28666 Percutaneous skeletal fixation of interphalangeal joint dislocation, with manipulation

28675 Open treatment of interphalangeal joint dislocation, with or without internal or external fixation

Arthrodesis

28705 Arthrodesis; pantalar

28715 triple

28725 subtalar

28730 Arthrodesis, midtarsal or tarsometatarsal, multiple or transverse;

28735 with osteotomy (eg, flatfoot correction)

28737 Arthrodesis, with tendon lengthening and advancement, midtarsal, tarsal navicular-cuneiform (eg, Miller type procedure)

28740 Arthrodesis, midtarsal or tarsometatarsal, single joint

28750 Arthrodesis, great toe; metatarsophalangeal joint

28755 interphalangeal joint

28760 Arthrodesis, with extensor hallucis longus transfer to first metatarsal neck, great toe, interphalangeal joint (eg, Jones type procedure)

(For hammertoe operation or interphalangeal fusion, use 28285)

Amputation

28800 Amputation, foot; midtarsal (eg, Chopart type procedure)

28805 transmetatarsal

28810 Amputation, metatarsal, with toe, single

28820 Amputation, toe; metatarsophalangeal joint

28825 interphalangeal joint

(For amputation of tuft of distal phalanx, use 11752)

Other Procedures

(For extracorporeal shock wave therapy involving musculoskeletal system, or plantar fascia, see Category III codes 0019T, 0020T)

28899 Unlisted procedure, foot or toes

Application of Casts and Strapping

The listed procedures apply when the cast application or strapping is a replacement procedure used during or after the period of follow-up care, or when the cast application or strapping is an initial service performed without a restorative treatment or procedure(s) to stabilize or protect a fracture, injury, or dislocation and/or to afford comfort to a patient. Restorative treatment or procedure(s) rendered by another physician following the application of the initial cast/splint/strap may be reported with a treatment of fracture and/or dislocation code.

A physician who applies the initial cast, strap or splint and also assumes all of the subsequent fracture, dislocation, or injury care cannot use the application of casts and strapping codes as an initial service, since the first cast/splint or strap application is included in the treatment of fracture and/or dislocation codes. (See notes under Musculoskeletal System, page 59). A temporary cast/splint/strap is not considered to be part of the preoperative care, and the use of the modifier '-56' is not applicable. Additional evaluation and management services are reportable only if significant identifiable further services are provided at the time of the cast application or strapping.

If cast application or strapping is provided as an initial service (eg, casting of a sprained ankle or knee) in which no other procedure or treatment (eg, surgical repair, reduction of a fracture or joint dislocation) is performed or is expected to be performed by a physician rendering the initial care only, use the casting, strapping and/or supply code (99070) in addition to an evaluation and management code as appropriate.

Listed procedures include removal of cast or strapping.

(For orthotics fitting and training, use 97504)

Body and Upper Extremity

Casts

29000 Application of halo type body cast (see 20661-20663 for insertion)

29010 Application of Risser jacket, localizer, body; only

29015 including head

29020 Application of turnbuckle jacket, body; only

29025 including head

29035 Application of body cast, shoulder to hips;

29040 including head, Minerva type

29044 including one thigh

29046 including both thighs

29049 Application, cast; figure-of-eight

29055 shoulder spica

29058 plaster Velpeau

29065 shoulder to hand (long arm)

29075 elbow to finger (short arm)

29085 hand and lower forearm (gauntlet)

29086 finger (eg, contracture)

Splints

29105 Application of long arm splint (shoulder to hand)

29125 Application of short arm splint (forearm to hand); static

29126 dynamic

29130 Application of finger splint; static

29131 dynamic

Strapping—Any Age

29200 Strapping; thorax

29220 low back

29240 shoulder (eg, Velpeau)

29260 elbow or wrist

29280 hand or finger

Lower Extremity

Casts

29305 Application of hip spica cast; one leg

29325 one and one-half spica or both legs

(For hip spica (body) cast, including thighs only, use 29046)

29345 Application of long leg cast (thigh to toes);

29355 walker or ambulatory type

29358 Application of long leg cast brace

29365 Application of cylinder cast (thigh to ankle)

29405 Application of short leg cast (below knee to toes);

29425 walking or ambulatory type

29435 Application of patellar tendon bearing (PTB) cast

29440 Adding walker to previously applied cast

29445 Application of rigid total contact leg cast

29450 Application of clubfoot cast with molding or manipulation, long or short leg

Splints

29505 Application of long leg splint (thigh to ankle or toes)

29515 Application of short leg splint (calf to foot)

Strapping—Any Age

29520 Strapping; hip

29530 knee

29540 ankle and/or foot

29550 toes

29580 Unna boot

29590 Denis-Browne splint strapping

Removal or Repair

Codes for cast removals should be employed only for casts applied by another physician.

29700 Removal or bivalving; gauntlet, boot or body cast

29705 full arm or full leg cast

29710 shoulder or hip spica, Minerva, or Risser jacket, etc.

29715 turnbuckle jacket

29720 Repair of spica, body cast or jacket

29730 Windowing of cast

29740 Wedging of cast (except clubfoot casts)

29750 Wedging of clubfoot cast

Other Procedures

29799 Unlisted procedure, casting or strapping

Endoscopy/Arthroscopy

Surgical endoscopy/arthroscopy always includes a diagnostic endoscopy/arthroscopy.

When arthroscopy is performed in conjunction with arthrotomy, add modifier '-51'.

29800 Arthroscopy, temporomandibular joint, diagnostic, with or without synovial biopsy (separate procedure)

29804 Arthroscopy, temporomandibular joint, surgical

(For open procedure, use 21010)

29805 Arthroscopy, shoulder, diagnostic, with or without synovial biopsy (separate procedure)

(For open procedure, see 23065-23066, 23100-23101)

29806 Arthroscopy, shoulder, surgical; capsulorrhaphy

(For open procedure, see 23450-23466)

(To report thermal capsulorrhaphy, use 29999)

29807 repair of SLAP lesion

(29815 has been deleted. To report, use 29805)

29819 with removal of loose body or foreign body

(For open procedure, see 23040-23044, 23107)

29820 synovectomy, partial

(For open procedure, see 23105)

29821 synovectomy, complete

(For open procedure, see 23105)

29822 debridement, limited

(For open procedure, see specific open shoulder procedure performed)

29823 debridement, extensive

(For open procedure, see specific open shoulder procedure performed)

29824 distal claviculectomy including distal articular surface (Mumford procedure)

(For open procedure, use 23120)

29825 with lysis and resection of adhesions, with or without manipulation

(For open procedure, see specific open shoulder procedure performed)

29826 decompression of subacromial space with partial acromioplasty, with or without coracoacromial release

(For open procedure, use 23130 or 23415)

29827 with rotator cuff repair

(For open or mini-open rotator cuff repair, use 23412)

(When arthroscopic subacromial decompression is performed at the same setting, use 29826 and append modifier '-51')

(When arthroscopic distal clavicle resection is performed at the same setting, use 29824 and append modifier '-51')

29830 Arthroscopy, elbow, diagnostic, with or without synovial biopsy (separate procedure)

29834 Arthroscopy, elbow, surgical; with removal of loose body or foreign body

29835 synovectomy, partial

29836 synovectomy, complete

29837 debridement, limited

29838 debridement, extensive

29840 Arthroscopy, wrist, diagnostic, with or without synovial biopsy (separate procedure)

29843 Arthroscopy, wrist, surgical; for infection, lavage and drainage

29844 synovectomy, partial

29845 synovectomy, complete

29846 excision and/or repair of triangular fibrocartilage and/or joint debridement

29847 internal fixation for fracture or instability

29848 Endoscopy, wrist, surgical, with release of transverse carpal ligament

(For open procedure, use 64721)

29850 Arthroscopically aided treatment of intercondylar spine(s) and/or tuberosity fracture(s) of the knee, with or without manipulation; without internal or external fixation (includes arthroscopy)

29851 with internal or external fixation (includes arthroscopy)

(For bone graft, use 20900, 20902)

29855 Arthroscopically aided treatment of tibial fracture, proximal (plateau); unicondylar, with or without internal or external fixation (includes arthroscopy)

29856 bicondylar, with or without internal or external fixation (includes arthroscopy)

(For bone graft, use 20900, 20902)

29860 Arthroscopy, hip, diagnostic with or without synovial biopsy (separate procedure)

29861 Arthroscopy, hip, surgical; with removal of loose body or foreign body

29862 with debridement/shaving of articular cartilage (chondroplasty), abrasion arthroplasty, and/or resection of labrum

29863 with synovectomy

29870 Arthroscopy, knee, diagnostic, with or without synovial biopsy (separate procedure)

(For surgical arthroscopy of the knee with implantation of osteochondral graft for treatment of articular surface defect, see Category III codes 0012T, 0013T)

(For meniscal transplantation, medial or lateral, knee, use Category III code 0014T)

29871 Arthroscopy, knee, surgical; for infection, lavage and drainage

29873 with lateral release

(For open lateral release, use 27425)

29874 for removal of loose body or foreign body (eg, osteochondritis dissecans fragmentation, chondral fragmentation)

29875 synovectomy, limited (eg, plica or shelf resection) (separate procedure)

29876 synovectomy, major, two or more compartments (eg, medial or lateral)

29877 debridement/shaving of articular cartilage (chondroplasty)

29879 abrasion arthroplasty (includes chondroplasty where necessary) or multiple drilling or microfracture

29880 with meniscectomy (medial AND lateral, including any meniscal shaving)

29881 with meniscectomy (medial OR lateral, including any meniscal shaving)

29882 with meniscus repair (medial OR lateral)

29883 with meniscus repair (medial AND lateral)

29884 with lysis of adhesions, with or without manipulation (separate procedure)

29885 drilling for osteochondritis dissecans with bone grafting, with or without internal fixation (including debridement of base of lesion)

29886 drilling for intact osteochondritis dissecans lesion

29887 drilling for intact osteochondritis dissecans lesion with internal fixation

29888 Arthroscopically aided anterior cruciate ligament repair/augmentation or reconstruction

29889 Arthroscopically aided posterior cruciate ligament repair/augmentation or reconstruction

(Procedures 29888 and 29889 should not be used with reconstruction procedures 27427-27429)

29891 Arthroscopy, ankle, surgical; excision of osteochondral defect of talus and/or tibia, including drilling of the defect

29892 Arthroscopically aided repair of large osteochondritis dissecans lesion, talar dome fracture, or tibial plafond fracture, with or without internal fixation (includes arthroscopy)

29893 Endoscopic plantar fasciotomy

29894 Arthroscopy, ankle (tibiotalar and fibulotalar joints), surgical; with removal of loose body or foreign body

29895 synovectomy, partial

29897 debridement, limited

29898 debridement, extensive

29899 with ankle arthrodesis

(For open ankle arthrodesis, use 27870)

29900 Arthroscopy, metacarpophalangeal joint, diagnostic, includes synovial biopsy

(Do not report 29900 with 29901, 29902)

29901 Arthroscopy, metacarpophalangeal joint, surgical; with debridement

29902 with reduction of displaced ulnar collateral ligament (eg, Stenar lesion)

(29909 has been deleted. To report, use 29999)

29999 Unlisted procedure, arthroscopy

Respiratory System

Nose

Incision

30000 Drainage abscess or hematoma, nasal, internal approach

(For external approach, see 10060, 10140)

30020 Drainage abscess or hematoma, nasal septum

(For lateral rhinotomy, see specific application (eg, 30118, 30320))

Excision

30100 Biopsy, intranasal

(For biopsy skin of nose, see 11100, 11101)

30110 Excision, nasal polyp(s), simple

(30110 would normally be completed in an office setting)

30115 Excision, nasal polyp(s), extensive

(30115 would normally require the facilities available in a hospital setting)

30117 Excision or destruction (eg, laser), intranasal lesion; internal approach

30118 external approach (lateral rhinotomy)

30120 Excision or surgical planing of skin of nose for rhinophyma

30124 Excision dermoid cyst, nose; simple, skin, subcutaneous

30125 complex, under bone or cartilage

30130 Excision turbinate, partial or complete, any method

30140 Submucous resection turbinate, partial or complete, any method

(For submucous resection of nasal septum, use 30520)

(For reduction of turbinates, use 30140 with modifier '-52')

30150 Rhinectomy; partial

30160 total

(For closure and/or reconstruction, primary or delayed, see **Integumentary System,** 13150-13160, 14060-14300, 15120, 15121, 15260, 15261, 15760, 20900-20912)

Introduction

30200 Injection into turbinate(s), therapeutic

30210 Displacement therapy (Proetz type)

30220 Insertion, nasal septal prosthesis (button)

Removal of Foreign Body

30300 Removal foreign body, intranasal; office type procedure

30310 requiring general anesthesia

30320 by lateral rhinotomy

Repair

(For obtaining tissues for graft, see 20900-20926, 21210)

30400 Rhinoplasty, primary; lateral and alar cartilages and/or elevation of nasal tip

(For columellar reconstruction, see 13150 et seq)

30410 complete, external parts including bony pyramid, lateral and alar cartilages, and/or elevation of nasal tip

30420 including major septal repair

30430 Rhinoplasty, secondary; minor revision (small amount of nasal tip work)

30435 intermediate revision (bony work with osteotomies)

30450 major revision (nasal tip work and osteotomies)

30460 Rhinoplasty for nasal deformity secondary to congenital cleft lip and/or palate, including columellar lengthening; tip only

30462 tip, septum, osteotomies

30465 Repair of nasal vestibular stenosis (eg, spreader grafting, lateral nasal wall reconstruction)

(30465 excludes obtaining graft. For graft procedure, see 20900-20926, 21210)

(30465 is used to report a bilateral procedure. For unilateral procedure, use modifier '-52')

30520 Septoplasty or submucous resection, with or without cartilage scoring, contouring or replacement with graft

(For submucous resection of turbinates, use 30140)

30540 Repair choanal atresia; intranasal

30545 transpalatine

(Do not report modifier '-63' in conjunction with 30540, 30545)

30560 Lysis intranasal synechia

30580 Repair fistula; oromaxillary (combine with 31030 if antrotomy is included)

30600 oronasal

30620 Septal or other intranasal dermatoplasty (does not include obtaining graft)

30630 Repair nasal septal perforations

Destruction

30801 Cautery and/or ablation, mucosa of turbinates, unilateral or bilateral, any method, (separate procedure); superficial

30802 intramural

Other Procedures

30901 Control nasal hemorrhage, anterior, simple (limited cautery and/or packing) any method

30903 Control nasal hemorrhage, anterior, complex (extensive cautery and/or packing) any method

30905 Control nasal hemorrhage, posterior, with posterior nasal packs and/or cautery, any method; initial

30906 subsequent

30915 Ligation arteries; ethmoidal

30920 internal maxillary artery, transantral

(For ligation external carotid artery, use 37600)

30930 Fracture nasal turbinate(s), therapeutic

30999 Unlisted procedure, nose

Accessory Sinuses

Incision

31000 Lavage by cannulation; maxillary sinus (antrum puncture or natural ostium)

31002 sphenoid sinus

31020 Sinusotomy, maxillary (antrotomy); intranasal

31030 radical (Caldwell-Luc) without removal of antrochoanal polyps

31032 radical (Caldwell-Luc) with removal of antrochoanal polyps

31040 Pterygomaxillary fossa surgery, any approach

(For transantral ligation of internal maxillary artery, use 30920)

31050 Sinusotomy, sphenoid, with or without biopsy;

31051 with mucosal stripping or removal of polyp(s)

31070 Sinusotomy frontal; external, simple (trephine operation)

31075 transorbital, unilateral (for mucocele or osteoma, Lynch type)

31080 obliterative without osteoplastic flap, brow incision (includes ablation)

31081 obliterative, without osteoplastic flap, coronal incision (includes ablation)

31084 obliterative, with osteoplastic flap, brow incision

31085 obliterative, with osteoplastic flap, coronal incision

31086 nonobliterative, with osteoplastic flap, brow incision

31087 nonobliterative, with osteoplastic flap, coronal incision

31090 Sinusotomy, unilateral, three or more paranasal sinuses (frontal, maxillary, ethmoid, sphenoid)

Excision

31200 Ethmoidectomy; intranasal, anterior

31201 intranasal, total

31205 extranasal, total

31225 Maxillectomy; without orbital exenteration

31230 with orbital exenteration (en bloc)

(For orbital exenteration only, see 65110 et seq)

(For skin grafts, see 15120 et seq)

Endoscopy

A surgical sinus endoscopy includes a sinusotomy (when appropriate) and diagnostic endoscopy.

Codes 31231-31294 are used to report unilateral procedures unless otherwise specified.

The codes 31231-31235 for diagnostic evaluation refer to employing a nasal/sinus endoscope to inspect the interior of the nasal cavity and the middle and superior meatus, the turbinates, and the spheno-ethmoid recess. Any time a diagnostic evaluation is performed all these areas would be inspected and a separate code is not reported for each area.

31231 Nasal endoscopy, diagnostic, unilateral or bilateral (separate procedure)

31233 Nasal/sinus endoscopy, diagnostic with maxillary sinusoscopy (via inferior meatus or canine fossa puncture)

31235 Nasal/sinus endoscopy, diagnostic with sphenoid sinusoscopy (via puncture of sphenoidal face or cannulation of ostium)

31237 Nasal/sinus endoscopy, surgical; with biopsy, polypectomy or debridement (separate procedure)

31238 with control of nasal hemorrhage

31239 with dacryocystorhinostomy

31240 with concha bullosa resection

31254 Nasal/sinus endoscopy, surgical; with ethmoidectomy, partial (anterior)

31255 with ethmoidectomy, total (anterior and posterior)

24B - Pla

11 Physician Office
12 Private Residence
21 Inpatient Hospital
22 Outpatient Hospital
23 Hospital Emergency Room
25 Birthing Center
31 Skilled nursing Facility
81 Independent laboratory

4F Medicaid - Leave blank
7F Medicaid - Leave blank
Champus - on duty - duty address
- OVERSEA - APO or FPO adresss

31256 Nasal/sinus endoscopy, surgical, with maxillary antrostomy;

31267 with removal of tissue from maxillary sinus

31276 Nasal/sinus endoscopy, surgical with frontal sinus exploration, with or without removal of tissue from frontal sinus

31287 Nasal/sinus endoscopy, surgical, with sphenoidotomy;

31288 with removal of tissue from the sphenoid sinus

31290 Nasal/sinus endoscopy, surgical, with repair of cerebrospinal fluid leak; ethmoid region

31291 sphenoid region

31292 Nasal/sinus endoscopy, surgical; with medial or inferior orbital wall decompression

31293 with medial orbital wall and inferior orbital wall decompression

31294 with optic nerve decompression

Other Procedures

(For hypophysectomy, transantral or transeptal approach, use 61548)

(For transcranial hypophysectomy, use 61546)

31299 Unlisted procedure, accessory sinuses

Larynx

Excision

31300 Laryngotomy (thyrotomy, laryngofissure); with removal of tumor or laryngocele, cordectomy

31320 diagnostic

31360 Laryngectomy; total, without radical neck dissection

31365 total, with radical neck dissection

31367 subtotal supraglottic, without radical neck dissection

31368 subtotal supraglottic, with radical neck dissection

31370 Partial laryngectomy (hemilaryngectomy); horizontal

31375 laterovertical

31380 anterovertical

31382 antero-latero-vertical

31390 Pharyngolaryngectomy, with radical neck dissection; without reconstruction

31395 with reconstruction

31400 Arytenoidectomy or arytenoidopexy, external approach

(For endoscopic arytenoidectomy, use 31560)

31420 Epiglottidectomy

Introduction

⊘ 31500 Intubation, endotracheal, emergency procedure

(For injection procedure for bronchography, see 31656, 31708, 31710)

31502 Tracheotomy tube change prior to establishment of fistula tract

Endoscopy

For endoscopic procedures, code appropriate endoscopy of each anatomic site examined.

31505 Laryngoscopy, indirect; diagnostic (separate procedure)

31510 with biopsy

31511 with removal of foreign body

31512 with removal of lesion

31513 with vocal cord injection

31515 Laryngoscopy direct, with or without tracheoscopy; for aspiration

31520 diagnostic, newborn

(Do not report modifier '-63' in conjunction with 31520)

31525 diagnostic, except newborn

31526 diagnostic, with operating microscope

(Do not report code 69990 in addition to code 31526)

31527 with insertion of obturator

31528 with dilation, initial

31529 with dilation, subsequent

31530 Laryngoscopy, direct, operative, with foreign body removal;

31531 with operating microscope

(Do not report code 69990 in addition to code 31531)

31535 Laryngoscopy, direct, operative, with biopsy;

31536 with operating microscope

(Do not report code 69990 in addition to code 31536)

31540 Laryngoscopy, direct, operative, with excision of tumor and/or stripping of vocal cords or epiglottis;

31541 with operating microscope

(Do not report code 69990 in addition to code 31541)

31560 Laryngoscopy, direct, operative, with arytenoidectomy;

31561 with operating microscope

(Do not report code 69990 in addition to code 31561)

31570 Laryngoscopy, direct, with injection into vocal cord(s), therapeutic;

31571 with operating microscope

(Do not report code 69990 in addition to code 31571)

31575 Laryngoscopy, flexible fiberoptic; diagnostic

31576 with biopsy

31577 with removal of foreign body

31578 with removal of lesion

(To report flexible fiberoptic endoscopic evaluation of swallowing, see 92612-92613)

(To report flexible fiberoptic endoscopic evaluation with sensory testing, see 92614-92615)

(To report flexible fiberoptic endoscopic evaluation of swallowing with sensory testing, see 92616-92617)

►(For flexible fiberoptic laryngoscopy as part of flexible fiberoptic endoscopic evaluation of swallowing and/or laryngeal sensory testing by cine or video recording, see 92612-92617)◄

31579 Laryngoscopy, flexible or rigid fiberoptic, with stroboscopy

Repair

31580 Laryngoplasty; for laryngeal web, two stage, with keel insertion and removal

31582 for laryngeal stenosis, with graft or core mold, including tracheotomy

31584 with open reduction of fracture

31585 Treatment of closed laryngeal fracture; without manipulation

31586 with closed manipulative reduction

31587 Laryngoplasty, cricoid split

31588 Laryngoplasty, not otherwise specified (eg, for burns, reconstruction after partial laryngectomy)

31590 Laryngeal reinnervation by neuromuscular pedicle

Destruction

31595 Section recurrent laryngeal nerve, therapeutic (separate procedure), unilateral

Other Procedures

31599 Unlisted procedure, larynx

Trachea and Bronchi

Incision

31600 Tracheostomy, planned (separate procedure);

31601 under two years

31603 Tracheostomy, emergency procedure; transtracheal

31605 cricothyroid membrane

31610 Tracheostomy, fenestration procedure with skin flaps

(For endotracheal intubation, use 31500)

(For tracheal aspiration under direct vision, use 31515)

31611 Construction of tracheoesophageal fistula and subsequent insertion of an alaryngeal speech prosthesis (eg, voice button, Blom-Singer prosthesis)

31612 Tracheal puncture, percutaneous with transtracheal aspiration and/or injection

31613 Tracheostoma revision; simple, without flap rotation

31614 complex, with flap rotation

Endoscopy

For endoscopy procedures, code appropriate endoscopy of each anatomic site examined. Surgical bronchoscopy always includes diagnostic bronchoscopy when performed by the same physician. Codes 31622-31646 include fluoroscopic guidance, when performed.

(For tracheoscopy, see laryngoscopy codes 31515-31578)

31615 Tracheobronchoscopy through established tracheostomy incision

▲**31622** Bronchoscopy, rigid or flexible, with or without fluoroscopic guidance; diagnostic, with or without cell washing (separate procedure)

31623 with brushing or protected brushings

31624 with bronchial alveolar lavage

▲**31625** with bronchial or endobronchial biopsy(s), single or multiple sites

▲**31628** with transbronchial lung biopsy(s), single lobe

►(31628 should be reported only once regardless of how many transbronchial lung biopsies are performed in a lobe)◄

►(To report transbronchial lung biopsies performed on additional lobe, use 31632)◄

▲**31629** with transbronchial needle aspiration biopsy(s), trachea, main stem and/or lobar bronchus(i)

►(31629 should be reported only once for upper airway biopsies regardless of how many transbronchial needle aspiration biopsies are performed in the upper airway or in a lobe)◄

►(To report transbronchial needle aspiration biopsies performed on additional lobe(s), use 31633)◄

31630 with tracheal or bronchial dilation or closed reduction of fracture

31631 with tracheal dilation and placement of tracheal stent

+ ●**31632** with transbronchial lung biopsy(s), each additional lobe (List separately in addition to code for primary procedure)

►(Use 31632 in conjunction with 31628)◄

►(31632 should be reported only once regardless of how many transbronchial lung biopsies are performed in a lobe)◄

+ ●**31633** with transbronchial needle aspiration biopsy(s), each additional lobe (List separately in addition to code for primary procedure)

►(Use 31633 in conjunction with 31629)◄

►(31633 should be reported only once regardless of how many transbronchial needle aspiration biopsies are performed in the trachea or the additional lobe)◄

31635 with removal of foreign body

31640 with excision of tumor

31641 Bronchoscopy, (rigid or flexible); with destruction of tumor or relief of stenosis by any method other than excision (eg, laser therapy, cryotherapy)

(For bronchoscopic photodynamic therapy, report 31641 in addition to 96570, 96571 as appropriate)

31643 with placement of catheter(s) for intracavitary radioelement application

(For intracavitary radioelement application, see 77761-77763, 77781-77784)

31645 with therapeutic aspiration of tracheobronchial tree, initial (eg, drainage of lung abscess)

31646 with therapeutic aspiration of tracheobronchial tree, subsequent

(For catheter aspiration of tracheobronchial tree at bedside, use 31725)

31656 with injection of contrast material for segmental bronchography (fiberscope only)

(For radiological supervision and interpretation, see 71040, 71060)

Introduction

(For endotracheal intubation, use 31500)

(For tracheal aspiration under direct vision, see 31515)

31700 Catheterization, transglottic (separate procedure)

31708 Instillation of contrast material for laryngography or bronchography, without catheterization

(For radiological supervision and interpretation, see 70373, 71040, 71060)

31710 Catheterization for bronchography, with or without instillation of contrast material

(For bronchoscopic catheterization for bronchography, fiberscope only, use 31656)

(For radiological supervision and interpretation, see 71040, 71060)

31715 Transtracheal injection for bronchography

(For radiological supervision and interpretation, see 71040, 71060)

(For prolonged services, see 99354-99360)

31717 Catheterization with bronchial brush biopsy

31720 Catheter aspiration (separate procedure); nasotracheal

31725 tracheobronchial with fiberscope, bedside

31730 Transtracheal (percutaneous) introduction of needle wire dilator/stent or indwelling tube for oxygen therapy

Repair

31750 Tracheoplasty; cervical

31755 tracheopharyngeal fistulization, each stage

31760 intrathoracic

31766 Carinal reconstruction

31770 Bronchoplasty; graft repair

31775 excision stenosis and anastomosis

(For lobectomy and bronchoplasty, use 32501)

31780 Excision tracheal stenosis and anastomosis; cervical

31781 cervicothoracic

31785 Excision of tracheal tumor or carcinoma; cervical

31786 thoracic

31800 Suture of tracheal wound or injury; cervical

31805 intrathoracic

31820 Surgical closure tracheostomy or fistula; without plastic repair

31825 with plastic repair

(For repair tracheoesophageal fistula, see 43305, 43312)

31830 Revision of tracheostomy scar

Other Procedures

31899 Unlisted procedure, trachea, bronchi

Lungs and Pleura

Incision

⊘ **32000** Thoracentesis, puncture of pleural cavity for aspiration, initial or subsequent

(If imaging guidance is performed,see 76003, 76360, 76942)

⊘ **32002** Thoracentesis with insertion of tube with or without water seal (eg, for pneumothorax) (separate procedure)

(If imaging guidance is performed, see 76003, 76360, 76942)

32005 Chemical pleurodesis (eg, for recurrent or persistent pneumothorax)

⊘ **32020** Tube thoracostomy with or without water seal (eg, for abscess, hemothorax, empyema) (separate procedure)

(If imaging guidance is performed, use 75989)

32035 Thoracostomy; with rib resection for empyema

32036 with open flap drainage for empyema

32095 Thoracotomy, limited, for biopsy of lung or pleura

(To report wound exploration due to penetrating trauma without thoractomy, use 20102)

32100 Thoracotomy, major; with exploration and biopsy

32110 with control of traumatic hemorrhage and/or repair of lung tear

32120 for postoperative complications

32124 with open intrapleural pneumonolysis

32140 with cyst(s) removal, with or without a pleural procedure

32141 with excision-plication of bullae, with or without any pleural procedure

(For lung volume reduction, use 32491)

32150 with removal of intrapleural foreign body or fibrin deposit

32151 with removal of intrapulmonary foreign body

32160 with cardiac massage

(For segmental or other resections of lung, see 32480-32525)

32200 Pneumonostomy; with open drainage of abscess or cyst

32201 with percutaneous drainage of abscess or cyst

(For radiological supervision and interpretation, use 75989)

32215 Pleural scarification for repeat pneumothorax

32220 Decortication, pulmonary (separate procedure); total

32225 partial

Excision

32310 Pleurectomy, parietal (separate procedure)

32320 Decortication and parietal pleurectomy

32400 Biopsy, pleura; percutaneous needle

(If imaging guidance is performed, see 76003, 76360, 76393, 76942)

(For fine needle aspiration, use 10021 or 10022)

(For evaluation of fine needle aspirate, see 88172, 88173)

32402 open

32405 Biopsy, lung or mediastinum, percutaneous needle

(For radiological supervision and interpretation, see 76003, 76360, 76393, 76942)

(For fine needle aspiration, use 10022)

(For evaluation of fine needle aspirate, see 88172, 88173)

32420 Pneumocentesis, puncture of lung for aspiration

32440 Removal of lung, total pneumonectomy;

32442 with resection of segment of trachea followed by broncho-tracheal anastomosis (sleeve pneumonectomy)

32445 extrapleural

32480 Removal of lung, other than total pneumonectomy; single lobe (lobectomy)

32482 two lobes (bilobectomy)

32484 single segment (segmentectomy)

32486 with circumferential resection of segment of bronchus followed by broncho-bronchial anastomosis (sleeve lobectomy)

32488 all remaining lung following previous removal of a portion of lung (completion pneumonectomy)

32491 excision-plication of emphysematous lung(s) (bullous or non-bullous) for lung volume reduction, sternal split or transthoracic approach, with or without any pleural procedure

32500 wedge resection, single or multiple

✚ **32501** Resection and repair of portion of bronchus (bronchoplasty) when performed at time of lobectomy or segmentectomy (List separately in addition to code for primary procedure)

(Use 32501 in conjunction with codes 32480, 32482, 32484)

(32501 is to be used when a portion of the bronchus to preserved lung is removed and requires plastic closure to preserve function of that preserved lung. It is not to be used for closure for the proximal end of a resected bronchus)

32520 Resection of lung; with resection of chest wall

32522 with reconstruction of chest wall, without prosthesis

32525 with major reconstruction of chest wall, with prosthesis

32540 Extrapleural enucleation of empyema (empyemectomy)

Endoscopy

Surgical thoracoscopy always includes diagnostic thoracoscopy.

For endoscopic procedures, code appropriate endoscopy of each anatomic site examined.

32601 Thoracoscopy, diagnostic (separate procedure); lungs and pleural space, without biopsy

32602 lungs and pleural space, with biopsy

32603 pericardial sac, without biopsy

32604 pericardial sac, with biopsy

32605 mediastinal space, without biopsy

32606 mediastinal space, with biopsy

(Surgical thoracoscopy always includes diagnostic thoracoscopy)

32650 Thoracoscopy, surgical; with pleurodesis (eg, mechanical or chemical)

32651 with partial pulmonary decortication

32652 with total pulmonary decortication, including intrapleural pneumonolysis

32653 with removal of intrapleural foreign body or fibrin deposit

32654 with control of traumatic hemorrhage

32655 with excision-plication of bullae, including any pleural procedure

32656 with parietal pleurectomy

32657 with wedge resection of lung, single or multiple

32658 with removal of clot or foreign body from pericardial sac

32659 with creation of pericardial window or partial resection of pericardial sac for drainage

32660 with total pericardiectomy

32661 with excision of pericardial cyst, tumor, or mass

32662 with excision of mediastinal cyst, tumor, or mass

32663 with lobectomy, total or segmental

32664 with thoracic sympathectomy

32665 with esophagomyotomy (Heller type)

Repair

32800 Repair lung hernia through chest wall

32810 Closure of chest wall following open flap drainage for empyema (Clagett type procedure)

32815 Open closure of major bronchial fistula

32820 Major reconstruction, chest wall (posttraumatic)

Lung Transplantation

32850 Donor pneumonectomy(ies) with preparation and maintenance of allograft (cadaver)

32851 Lung transplant, single; without cardiopulmonary bypass

32852 with cardiopulmonary bypass

32853 Lung transplant, double (bilateral sequential or en bloc); without cardiopulmonary bypass

32854 with cardiopulmonary bypass

Surgical Collapse Therapy; Thoracoplasty

(See also 32520-32525)

32900 Resection of ribs, extrapleural, all stages

32905 Thoracoplasty, Schede type or extrapleural (all stages);

32906 with closure of bronchopleural fistula

(For open closure of major bronchial fistula, use 32815)

(For resection of first rib for thoracic outlet compression, see 21615, 21616)

32940 Pneumonolysis, extraperiosteal, including filling or packing procedures

32960 Pneumothorax, therapeutic, intrapleural injection of air

Other Procedures

32997 Total lung lavage (unilateral)

(For bronchoscopic bronchial alveolar lavage, use 31624)

32999 Unlisted procedure, lungs and pleura

Notes

Cardiovascular System

Selective vascular catheterizations should be coded to include introduction and all lesser order selective catheterizations used in the approach (eg, the description for a selective right middle cerebral artery catheterization includes the introduction and placement catheterization of the right common and internal carotid arteries).

Additional second and/or third order arterial catheterizations within the same family of arteries supplied by a single first order artery should be expressed by 36218 or 36248. Additional first order or higher catheterizations in vascular families supplied by a first order vessel different from a previously selected and coded family should be separately coded using the conventions described above.

(For monitoring, operation of pump and other nonsurgical services, see 99190-99192, 99291, 99292, 99354-99360)

(For other medical or laboratory related services, see appropriate section)

(For radiological supervision and interpretation, see 75600-75978)

Heart and Pericardium

Pericardium

33010 Pericardiocentesis; initial

(For radiological supervision and interpretation, use 76930)

33011 subsequent

(For radiological supervision and interpretation, use 76930)

33015 Tube pericardiostomy

33020 Pericardiotomy for removal of clot or foreign body (primary procedure)

33025 Creation of pericardial window or partial resection for drainage

33030 Pericardiectomy, subtotal or complete; without cardiopulmonary bypass

33031 with cardiopulmonary bypass

33050 Excision of pericardial cyst or tumor

Cardiac Tumor

33120 Excision of intracardiac tumor, resection with cardiopulmonary bypass

33130 Resection of external cardiac tumor

Transmyocardial Revascularization

33140 Transmyocardial laser revascularization, by thoracotomy; (separate procedure)

+ 33141 performed at the time of other open cardiac procedure(s) (List separately in addition to code for primary procedure)

(Use 33141 in conjunction with codes 33400-33496,33510-33536, 33542)

Pacemaker or Pacing Cardioverter-Defibrillator

A pacemaker system includes a pulse generator containing electronics and a battery, and one or more electrodes (leads). Pulse generators are placed in a subcutaneous "pocket" created in either a subclavicular site or underneath the abdominal muscles just below the ribcage. Electrodes may be inserted through a vein (transvenous) or they may be placed on the surface of the heart (epicardial). The epicardial location of electrodes requires a thoracotomy for electrode insertion.

A single chamber pacemaker system includes a pulse generator and one electrode inserted in either the atrium or ventricle. A dual chamber pacemaker system includes a pulse generator and one electrode inserted in the right atrium and one electrode inserted in the right ventricle. In certain circumstances, an additional electrode may be required to achieve pacing of the left ventricle (bi-ventricular pacing). In this event, transvenous (cardiac vein) placement of the electrode should be separately reported using code 33224 or 33225.

Like a pacemaker system, a pacing cardioverter-defibrillator system includes a pulse generator and electrodes, although pacing cardioverter-defibrillators may require multiple leads, even when only a single chamber is being paced. A pacing cardioverter-defibrillator system may be inserted in a single chamber (pacing in the ventricle) or in dual chambers (pacing in atrium and ventricle). These devices use a combination of antitachycardia pacing, low energy cardioversion or defibrillating shocks to treat ventricular tachycardia or ventricular fibrillation.

Pacing cardioverter-defibrillator pulse generators may be implanted in a subcutaneous infraclavicular pocket or in an abdominal pocket. Removal of a pacing cardioverter-defibrillator pulse generator requires opening of the existing subcutaneous pocket and disconnection of the pulse generator from its electrode(s). A thoracotomy (or laparotomy in the case of abdominally placed pulse generators) is not required to remove the pulse generator.

The electrodes (leads) of a pacing cardioverter-defibrillator system are positioned in the heart via the venous system (transvenously), in most circumstances. In certain circumstances, an additional electrode may be required to achieve pacing of the left ventricle (biventricular pacing). In this event, transvenous (cardiac vein) placement of the electrode should be separately reported using code 33224 or 33225.

Electrode positioning on the epicardial surface of the heart requires a thoracotomy (codes 33245-33246). Removal of electrode(s) may first be attempted by transvenous extraction (code 33244). However, if transvenous extraction is unsuccessful, a thoracotomy may be required to remove the electrodes (code 33243).

When the "battery" of a pacemaker or pacing cardioverter-defibrillator is changed, it is actually the pulse generator that is changed. Replacement of a pulse generator should be reported with a code for removal of the pulse generator and another code for insertion of a pulse generator.

Repositioning of a pacemaker electrode, pacing cardioverter-defibrillator electrode(s), or a left ventricular pacing electrode is reported using 33215 or 33226, as appropriate. Replacement of a pacemaker electrode, pacing cardioverter-defibrillator electrode(s), or a left ventricular pacing electrode is reported using 33206-33208, 33210-33213, or 33224, as appropriate.

(For electronic, telephonic analysis of internal pacemaker system, see 93731-93736)

(For radiological supervision and interpretation with insertion of pacemaker, use 71090)

33200 Insertion of permanent pacemaker with epicardial electrode(s); by thoracotomy

33201 by xiphoid approach

33206 Insertion or replacement of permanent pacemaker with transvenous electrode(s); atrial

33207 ventricular

33208 atrial and ventricular

(Codes 33206-33208 include subcutaneous insertion of the pulse generator and transvenous placement of electrode(s))

33210 Insertion or replacement of temporary transvenous single chamber cardiac electrode or pacemaker catheter (separate procedure)

33211 Insertion or replacement of temporary transvenous dual chamber pacing electrodes (separate procedure)

33212 Insertion or replacement of pacemaker pulse generator only; single chamber, atrial or ventricular

33213 dual chamber

33214 Upgrade of implanted pacemaker system, conversion of single chamber system to dual chamber system (includes removal of previously placed pulse generator, testing of existing lead, insertion of new lead, insertion of new pulse generator)

33215 Repositioning of previously implanted transvenous pacemaker or pacing cardioverter-defibrillator (right atrial or right ventricular) electrode

33216 Insertion of a transvenous electrode; single chamber (one electrode) permanent pacemaker or single chamber pacing cardioverter-defibrillator

33217 dual chamber (two electrodes) permanent pacemaker or dual chamber pacing cardioverter-defibrillator

(Do not report 33216-33217 in conjunction with code 33214)

33218 Repair of single transvenous electrode for a single chamber, permanent pacemaker or single chamber pacing cardioverter-defibrillator

33220 Repair of two transvenous electrodes for a dual chamber permanent pacemaker or dual chamber pacing cardioverter-defibrillator

33222 Revision or relocation of skin pocket for pacemaker

33223 Revision of skin pocket for single or dual chamber pacing cardioverter-defibrillator

33224 Insertion of pacing electrode, cardiac venous system, for left ventricular pacing, with attachment to previously placed pacemaker or pacing cardioverter-defibrillator pulse generator (including revision of pocket, removal, insertion and/or replacement of generator)

+ 33225 Insertion of pacing electrode, cardiac venous system, for left ventricular pacing, at time of insertion of pacing cardioverter-defibrillator or pacemaker pulse generator (including upgrade to dual chamber system) (List separately in addition to code for primary procedure)

(Use 33225 in conjunction with 33206, 33207, 33208, 33212, 33213, 33214, 33216, 33217, 33222, 33233, 33234, 33235, 33240, 33249)

33226 Repositioning of previously implanted cardiac venous system (left ventricular) electrode (including removal, insertion and/or replacement of generator)

33233 Removal of permanent pacemaker pulse generator

33234 Removal of transvenous pacemaker electrode(s); single lead system, atrial or ventricular

33235 dual lead system

33236 Removal of permanent epicardial pacemaker and electrodes by thoracotomy; single lead system, atrial or ventricular

33237 dual lead system

33238 Removal of permanent transvenous electrode(s) by thoracotomy

33240 Insertion of single or dual chamber pacing cardioverter-defibrillator pulse generator

33241 Subcutaneous removal of single or dual chamber pacing cardioverter-defibrillator pulse generator

(For removal of electrode(s) by thoracotomy, use 33243 in conjunction with code 33241)

(For removal of electrode(s) by transvenous extraction, use 33244 in conjunction with code 33241)

(For removal and reinsertion of a pacing cardioverter-defibrillator system (pulse generator and electrodes), report 33241 and 33243 or 33244 and 33249)

(33242 has been deleted. To report, see 33218, 33220)

33243 Removal of single or dual chamber pacing cardioverter-defibrillator electrode(s); by thoracotomy

33244 by transvenous extraction

(For subcutaneous removal of the pulse generator, use 33241 in conjunction with code 33243 or 33244)

33245 Insertion of epicardial single or dual chamber pacing cardioverter-defibrillator electrodes by thoracotomy;

33246 with insertion of pulse generator

33249 Insertion or repositioning of electrode lead(s) for single or dual chamber pacing cardioverter-defibrillator and insertion of pulse generator

(For removal and reinsertion of a pacing cardioverter-defibrillator system (pulse generator and electrodes), report 33241 and 33243 or 33244 and 33249)

Electrophysiologic Operative Procedures

33250 Operative ablation of supraventricular arrhythmogenic focus or pathway (eg, Wolff-Parkinson-White, atrioventricular node re-entry), tract(s) and/or focus (foci); without cardiopulmonary bypass

33251 with cardiopulmonary bypass

33253 Operative incisions and reconstruction of atria for treatment of atrial fibrillation or atrial flutter (eg, maze procedure)

33261 Operative ablation of ventricular arrhythmogenic focus with cardiopulmonary bypass

Patient-Activated Event Recorder

33282 Implantation of patient-activated cardiac event recorder

(Initial implantation includes programming. For subsequent electronic analysis and/or reprogramming, use 93727)

33284 Removal of an implantable, patient-activated cardiac event recorder

Wounds of the Heart and Great Vessels

33300 Repair of cardiac wound; without bypass

33305 with cardiopulmonary bypass

▲**33310** Cardiotomy, exploratory (includes removal of foreign body, atrial or ventricular thrombus); without bypass

33315 with cardiopulmonary bypass

►(Do not report removal of thrombus (33310-33315) in conjunction with other cardiac procedures unless a separate incision in the heart is required to remove the atrial or ventricular thrombus)◄

►(If removal of thrombus with coronary bypass (33315) is reported in conjunction with 33120, 33130, 33420-33430, 33460-33468, 33496, 33542, 33545, 33641-33647, 33670, 33681, 33975-33980 which requires a separate heart incision, report 33315 with modifier '-59')◄

33320 Suture repair of aorta or great vessels; without shunt or cardiopulmonary bypass

33321 with shunt bypass

33322 with cardiopulmonary bypass

33330 Insertion of graft, aorta or great vessels; without shunt, or cardiopulmonary bypass

33332 with shunt bypass

33335 with cardiopulmonary bypass

Cardiac Valves

Aortic Valve

33400 Valvuloplasty, aortic valve; open, with cardiopulmonary bypass

33401 open, with inflow occlusion

33403 using transventricular dilation, with cardiopulmonary bypass

(Do not report modifier '-63' in conjunction with 33401, 33403)

33404 Construction of apical-aortic conduit

33405 Replacement, aortic valve, with cardiopulmonary bypass; with prosthetic valve other than homograft or stentless valve

33406 with allograft valve (freehand)

33410 with stentless tissue valve

33411 Replacement, aortic valve; with aortic annulus enlargement, noncoronary cusp

33412 with transventricular aortic annulus enlargement (Konno procedure)

33413 by translocation of autologous pulmonary valve with allograft replacement of pulmonary valve (Ross procedure)

33414 Repair of left ventricular outflow tract obstruction by patch enlargement of the outflow tract

33415 Resection or incision of subvalvular tissue for discrete subvalvular aortic stenosis

33416 Ventriculomyotomy (-myectomy) for idiopathic hypertrophic subaortic stenosis (eg, asymmetric septal hypertrophy)

33417 Aortoplasty (gusset) for supravalvular stenosis

Mitral Valve

33420 Valvotomy, mitral valve; closed heart

33422 open heart, with cardiopulmonary bypass

33425 Valvuloplasty, mitral valve, with cardiopulmonary bypass;

33426 with prosthetic ring

33427 radical reconstruction, with or without ring

33430 Replacement, mitral valve, with cardiopulmonary bypass

Tricuspid Valve

33460 Valvectomy, tricuspid valve, with cardiopulmonary bypass

33463 Valvuloplasty, tricuspid valve; without ring insertion

33464 with ring insertion

33465 Replacement, tricuspid valve, with cardiopulmonary bypass

33468 Tricuspid valve repositioning and plication for Ebstein anomaly

Pulmonary Valve

33470 Valvotomy, pulmonary valve, closed heart; transventricular

(Do not report modifier '-63' in conjunction with 33470)

33471 via pulmonary artery

(To report percutaneous valvuloplasty of pulmonary valve, use 92990)

33472 Valvotomy, pulmonary valve, open heart; with inflow occlusion

(Do not report modifier '-63' in conjunction with 33472)

33474 with cardiopulmonary bypass

33475 Replacement, pulmonary valve

33476 Right ventricular resection for infundibular stenosis, with or without commissurotomy

33478 Outflow tract augmentation (gusset), with or without commissurotomy or infundibular resection

Other Valvular Procedures

33496 Repair of non-structural prosthetic valve dysfunction with cardiopulmonary bypass (separate procedure)

(For reoperation, use 33530 in addition to 33496)

Coronary Artery Anomalies

Basic procedures include endarterectomy or angioplasty.

33500 Repair of coronary arteriovenous or arteriocardiac chamber fistula; with cardiopulmonary bypass

33501 without cardiopulmonary bypass

33502 Repair of anomalous coronary artery; by ligation

33503 by graft, without cardiopulmonary bypass

(Do not report modifier '-63' in conjunction with 33502, 33503)

33504 by graft, with cardiopulmonary bypass

33505 with construction of intrapulmonary artery tunnel (Takeuchi procedure)

33506 by translocation from pulmonary artery to aorta

(Do not report modifier '-63' in conjunction with 33505, 33506)

Endoscopy

Surgical vascular endoscopy always includes diagnostic endoscopy.

+ 33508 Endoscopy, surgical, including video-assisted harvest of vein(s) for coronary artery bypass procedure (List separately in addition to code for primary procedure)

(Use 33508 in conjunction with 33510-33523)

(For open harvest of upper extremity vein procedure, use 35500)

Venous Grafting Only for Coronary Artery Bypass

The following codes are used to report coronary artery bypass procedures using venous grafts only. These codes should NOT be used to report the performance of coronary artery bypass procedures using arterial grafts and venous grafts during the same procedure. See 33517-33523 and 33533-33536 for reporting combined arterial-venous grafts.

Procurement of the saphenous vein graft is included in the description of the work for 33510-33516 and should not be reported as a separate service or co-surgery. To report harvesting of an upper extremity vein, use 35500 in addition to the bypass procedure. To report harvesting of a femoropopliteal vein segment, report 35572 in addition to the bypass procedure. When surgical assistant performs graft procurement, add modifier '-80' to 33510-33516.

33510 Coronary artery bypass, vein only; single coronary venous graft

33511 two coronary venous grafts

33512 three coronary venous grafts

33513 four coronary venous grafts

33514 five coronary venous grafts

33516 six or more coronary venous grafts

Combined Arterial-Venous Grafting for Coronary Bypass

The following codes are used to report coronary artery bypass procedures using venous grafts and arterial grafts during the same procedure. These codes may NOT be used alone.

To report combined arterial-venous grafts it is necessary to report two codes: 1) the appropriate combined arterial-venous graft code (33517-33523); and 2) the appropriate arterial graft code (33533-33536).

Procurement of the saphenous vein graft is included in the description of the work for 33517-33523 and should not be reported as a separate service or co-surgery. Procurement of the artery for grafting is included in the description of the work for 33533-33536 and should not be reported as a separate service or co-surgery, except when an upper extremity artery (eg, radial artery) is procured. To report harvesting of an upper extremity artery, use 35600 in addition to the bypass procedure. To report harvesting of an upper extremity vein, use 35500 in addition to the bypass procedure. To report harvesting of a femoropopliteal vein segment, report 35572 in addition to the bypass procedure. When surgical assistant performs arterial and/or venous graft procurement, add modifier '-80' to 33517-33523, 33533-33536, as appropriate.

⊘ **33517** Coronary artery bypass, using venous graft(s) and arterial graft(s); single vein graft (List separately in addition to code for arterial graft)

⊘ **33518** two venous grafts (List separately in addition to code for arterial graft)

⊘ **33519** three venous grafts (List separately in addition to code for arterial graft)

⊘ **33521** four venous grafts (List separately in addition to code for arterial graft)

⊘ **33522** five venous grafts (List separately in addition to code for arterial graft)

⊘ **33523** six or more venous grafts (List separately in addition to code for arterial graft)

✚ **33530** Reoperation, coronary artery bypass procedure or valve procedure, more than one month after original operation (List separately in addition to code for primary procedure)

(Use 33530 in conjunction with codes 33400-33496; 33510-33536, 33863)

Arterial Grafting for Coronary Artery Bypass

The following codes are used to report coronary artery bypass procedures using either arterial grafts only or a combination of arterial-venous grafts. The codes include the use of the internal mammary artery, gastroepiploic artery, epigastric artery, radial artery, and arterial conduits procured from other sites.

To report combined arterial-venous grafts it is necessary to report two codes: 1) the appropriate arterial graft code (33533-33536); and 2) the appropriate combined arterial-venous graft code (33517-33523).

Procurement of the artery for grafting is included in the description of the work for 33533-33536 and should not be reported as a separate service or co-surgery, except when an upper extremity artery (eg, radial artery) is procured. To report harvesting of an upper extremity artery, use 35600 in addition to the bypass procedure. To report harvesting of an upper extremity vein, use 35500 in addition to the bypass procedure. To report harvesting of a femoropopliteal vein segment, report 35572 in addition to the bypass procedure. When surgical assistant performs arterial and/or venous graft procurement, add modifier '-80' to 33517-33523, 33533-33536, as appropriate.

33533 Coronary artery bypass, using arterial graft(s); single arterial graft

33534 two coronary arterial grafts

33535 three coronary arterial grafts

33536 four or more coronary arterial grafts

33542 Myocardial resection (eg, ventricular aneurysmectomy)

33545 Repair of postinfarction ventricular septal defect, with or without myocardial resection

Coronary Endarterectomy

✚ **33572** Coronary endarterectomy, open, any method, of left anterior descending, circumflex, or right coronary artery performed in conjunction with coronary artery bypass graft procedure, each vessel (List separately in addition to primary procedure)

(Use 33572 in conjunction with 33510-33516, 33533-33536)

Single Ventricle and Other Complex Cardiac Anomalies

33600 Closure of atrioventricular valve (mitral or tricuspid) by suture or patch

33602 Closure of semilunar valve (aortic or pulmonary) by suture or patch

33606 Anastomosis of pulmonary artery to aorta (Damus-Kaye-Stansel procedure)

33608 Repair of complex cardiac anomaly other than pulmonary atresia with ventricular septal defect by construction or replacement of conduit from right or left ventricle to pulmonary artery

(For repair of pulmonary atresia with ventricular septal defect, see 33918, 33919, 33920)

33610 Repair of complex cardiac anomalies (eg, single ventricle with subaortic obstruction) by surgical enlargement of ventricular septal defect

(Do not report modifier '-63' in conjunction with 33610)

33611 Repair of double outlet right ventricle with intraventricular tunnel repair;

(Do not report modifier '-63' in conjunction with 33611)

33612 with repair of right ventricular outflow tract obstruction

33615 Repair of complex cardiac anomalies (eg, tricuspid atresia) by closure of atrial septal defect and anastomosis of atria or vena cava to pulmonary artery (simple Fontan procedure)

33617 Repair of complex cardiac anomalies (eg, single ventricle) by modified Fontan procedure

33619 Repair of single ventricle with aortic outflow obstruction and aortic arch hypoplasia (hypoplastic left heart syndrome) (eg, Norwood procedure)

(Do not report modifier '-63' in conjunction with 33619)

Septal Defect

33641 Repair atrial septal defect, secundum, with cardiopulmonary bypass, with or without patch

33645 Direct or patch closure, sinus venosus, with or without anomalous pulmonary venous drainage

33647 Repair of atrial septal defect and ventricular septal defect, with direct or patch closure

(Do not report modifier '-63' in conjunction with 33647)

33660 Repair of incomplete or partial atrioventricular canal (ostium primum atrial septal defect), with or without atrioventricular valve repair

33665 Repair of intermediate or transitional atrioventricular canal, with or without atrioventricular valve repair

33670 Repair of complete atrioventricular canal, with or without prosthetic valve

(Do not report modifier '-63' in conjunction with 33670)

33681 Closure of ventricular septal defect, with or without patch;

33684 with pulmonary valvotomy or infundibular resection (acyanotic)

33688 with removal of pulmonary artery band, with or without gusset

33690 Banding of pulmonary artery

(Do not report modifier '-63' in conjunction with 33690)

33692 Complete repair tetralogy of Fallot without pulmonary atresia;

33694 with transannular patch

(Do not report modifier '-63' in conjunction with 33694)

33697 Complete repair tetralogy of Fallot with pulmonary atresia including construction of conduit from right ventricle to pulmonary artery and closure of ventricular septal defect

Sinus of Valsalva

33702 Repair sinus of Valsalva fistula, with cardiopulmonary bypass;

33710 with repair of ventricular septal defect

33720 Repair sinus of Valsalva aneurysm, with cardiopulmonary bypass

33722 Closure of aortico-left ventricular tunnel

Total Anomalous Pulmonary Venous Drainage

33730 Complete repair of anomalous venous return (supracardiac, intracardiac, or infracardiac types)

(Do not report modifier '-63' in conjunction with 33730)

(For partial anomalous return, see atrial septal defect)

33732 Repair of cor triatriatum or supravalvular mitral ring by resection of left atrial membrane

(Do not report modifier '-63' in conjunction with 33732)

Shunting Procedures

33735 Atrial septectomy or septostomy; closed heart (Blalock-Hanlon type operation)

33736 open heart with cardiopulmonary bypass

(Do not report modifier '-63' in conjunction with 33735, 33736)

33737 open heart, with inflow occlusion

33750 Shunt; subclavian to pulmonary artery (Blalock-Taussig type operation)

33755 ascending aorta to pulmonary artery (Waterston type operation)

33762 descending aorta to pulmonary artery (Potts-Smith type operation)

(Do not report modifier '-63' in conjunction with 33750, 33755, 33762)

33764 central, with prosthetic graft

33766 superior vena cava to pulmonary artery for flow to one lung (classical Glenn procedure)

33767 superior vena cava to pulmonary artery for flow to both lungs (bidirectional Glenn procedure)

Transposition of the Great Vessels

33770 Repair of transposition of the great arteries with ventricular septal defect and subpulmonary stenosis; without surgical enlargement of ventricular septal defect

33771 with surgical enlargement of ventricular septal defect

33774 Repair of transposition of the great arteries, atrial baffle procedure (eg, Mustard or Senning type) with cardiopulmonary bypass;

33775 with removal of pulmonary band

33776 with closure of ventricular septal defect

33777 with repair of subpulmonic obstruction

33778 Repair of transposition of the great arteries, aortic pulmonary artery reconstruction (eg, Jatene type);

(Do not report modifier '-63' in conjunction with 33778)

33779 with removal of pulmonary band

33780 with closure of ventricular septal defect

33781 with repair of subpulmonic obstruction

Truncus Arteriosus

33786 Total repair, truncus arteriosus (Rastelli type operation)

(Do not report modifier '-63' in conjunction with 33786)

33788 Reimplantation of an anomalous pulmonary artery

(For pulmonary artery band, use 33690)

Aortic Anomalies

33800 Aortic suspension (aortopexy) for tracheal decompression (eg, for tracheomalacia) (separate procedure)

33802 Division of aberrant vessel (vascular ring);

33803 with reanastomosis

33813 Obliteration of aortopulmonary septal defect; without cardiopulmonary bypass

33814 with cardiopulmonary bypass

33820 Repair of patent ductus arteriosus; by ligation

33822 by division, under 18 years

33824 by division, 18 years and older

33840 Excision of coarctation of aorta, with or without associated patent ductus arteriosus; with direct anastomosis

33845 with graft

33851 repair using either left subclavian artery or prosthetic material as gusset for enlargement

33852 Repair of hypoplastic or interrupted aortic arch using autogenous or prosthetic material; without cardiopulmonary bypass

33853 with cardiopulmonary bypass

Thoracic Aortic Aneurysm

33860 Ascending aorta graft, with cardiopulmonary bypass, with or without valve suspension;

33861 with coronary reconstruction

33863 with aortic root replacement using composite prosthesis and coronary reconstruction

33870 Transverse arch graft, with cardiopulmonary bypass

33875 Descending thoracic aorta graft, with or without bypass

33877 Repair of thoracoabdominal aortic aneurysm with graft, with or without cardiopulmonary bypass

Pulmonary Artery

33910 Pulmonary artery embolectomy; with cardiopulmonary bypass

33915 without cardiopulmonary bypass

33916 Pulmonary endarterectomy, with or without embolectomy, with cardiopulmonary bypass

33917 Repair of pulmonary artery stenosis by reconstruction with patch or graft

33918 Repair of pulmonary atresia with ventricular septal defect, by unifocalization of pulmonary arteries; without cardiopulmonary bypass

33919 with cardiopulmonary bypass

(Do not report modifier '-63' in conjunction with 33918, 33919)

33920 Repair of pulmonary atresia with ventricular septal defect, by construction or replacement of conduit from right or left ventricle to pulmonary artery

(For repair of other complex cardiac anomalies by construction or replacement of right or left ventricle to pulmonary artery conduit, use 33608)

33922 Transection of pulmonary artery with cardiopulmonary bypass

(Do not report modifier '-63' in conjunction with 33922)

+ **33924** Ligation and takedown of a systemic-to-pulmonary artery shunt, performed in conjunction with a congenital heart procedure (List separately in addition to code for primary procedure)

(Use 33924 in conjunction with 33470-33475, 33600-33619, 33684-33688, 33692-33697, 33735-33767, 33770-33781, 33786, 33918-33922)

Heart/Lung Transplantation

►(For implantation of a total replacement heart system (artificial heart) with recipient cardiectomy or heart replacement system components, see Category III codes 0051T-0053T)◄

33930 Donor cardiectomy-pneumonectomy, with preparation and maintenance of allograft

33935 Heart-lung transplant with recipient cardiectomy-pneumonectomy

33940 Donor cardiectomy, with preparation and maintenance of allograft

33945 Heart transplant, with or without recipient cardiectomy

Cardiac Assist

►(For percutaneous implantation of extracorporeal ventricular assist device or for removal of percutaneously implanted extracorporeal ventricular assist device, see Category III codes 0048T-0050T)◄

33960 Prolonged extracorporeal circulation for cardiopulmonary insufficiency; initial 24 hours

+ **33961** each additional 24 hours (List separately in addition to code for primary procedure)

(Do not report modifier '-63' in conjunction with 33960, 33961)

(Use 33961 in conjunction with code 33960)

(For insertion of cannula for prolonged extracorporeal circulation, use 36822)

33967 Insertion of intra-aortic balloon assist device, percutaneous

33968 Removal of intra-aortic balloon assist device, percutaneous

33970 Insertion of intra-aortic balloon assist device through the femoral artery, open approach

33971 Removal of intra-aortic balloon assist device including repair of femoral artery, with or without graft

33973 Insertion of intra-aortic balloon assist device through the ascending aorta

33974 Removal of intra-aortic balloon assist device from the ascending aorta, including repair of the ascending aorta, with or without graft

33975 Insertion of ventricular assist device; extracorporeal, single ventricle

33976 extracorporeal, biventricular

33977 Removal of ventricular assist device; extracorporeal, single ventricle

33978 extracorporeal, biventricular

33979 Insertion of ventricular assist device, implantable intracorporeal, single ventricle

33980 Removal of ventricular assist device, implantable intracorporeal, single ventricle

Other Procedures

33999 Unlisted procedure, cardiac surgery

Arteries and Veins

Primary vascular procedure listings include establishing both inflow and outflow by whatever procedures necessary. Also included is that portion of the operative arteriogram performed by the surgeon, as indicated. Sympathectomy, when done, is included in the listed aortic procedures. For unlisted vascular procedure, use 37799.

Embolectomy/Thrombectomy

Arterial, With or Without Catheter

34001 Embolectomy or thrombectomy, with or without catheter; carotid, subclavian or innominate artery, by neck incision

34051 innominate, subclavian artery, by thoracic incision

34101 axillary, brachial, innominate, subclavian artery, by arm incision

34111 radial or ulnar artery, by arm incision

34151 renal, celiac, mesentery, aortoiliac artery, by abdominal incision

34201 femoropopliteal, aortoiliac artery, by leg incision

34203 popliteal-tibio-peroneal artery, by leg incision

Venous, Direct or With Catheter

34401 Thrombectomy, direct or with catheter; vena cava, iliac vein, by abdominal incision

34421 vena cava, iliac, femoropopliteal vein, by leg incision

34451 vena cava, iliac, femoropopliteal vein, by abdominal and leg incision

34471 subclavian vein, by neck incision

34490 axillary and subclavian vein, by arm incision

Venous Reconstruction

34501 Valvuloplasty, femoral vein

34502 Reconstruction of vena cava, any method

34510 Venous valve transposition, any vein donor

34520 Cross-over vein graft to venous system

34530 Saphenopopliteal vein anastomosis

Endovascular Repair of Abdominal Aortic Aneurysm

Codes 34800-34826 represent a family of component procedures to report placement of an endovascular graft for abdominal aortic aneurysm repair. These codes describe open femoral or iliac artery exposure, device manipulation and deployment, and closure of the arteriotomy sites. Balloon angioplasty and/or stent deployment within the target treatment zone for the endoprosthesis, either before or after endograft deployment, are not separately reportable. Introduction of guidewires and catheters should be reported separately (eg, 36200, 36245-36248, 36140). Extensive repair or replacement of an artery should be additionally reported (eg, 35226 or 35286).

For fluoroscopic guidance in conjunction with endovascular aneurysm repair, see code 75952 or 75953, as appropriate. Code 75952 includes angiography of the aorta and its branches for diagnostic imaging prior to deployment of the endovascular device (including all routine components of modular devices), fluoroscopic guidance in the delivery of the endovascular components, and intraprocedural arterial angiography (eg, confirm position, detect endoleak, evaluate runoff). Code 75953 includes the analogous services for placement of additional extension prostheses (not for routine components of modular devices).

Other interventional procedures performed at the time of endovascular abdominal aortic aneurysm repair should be additionally reported (eg, renal transluminal angioplasty, arterial embolization, intravascular ultrasound, balloon angioplasty or stenting of native artery(s) outside the endoprosthesis target zone, when done before or after deployment of graft).

34800 Endovascular repair of infrarenal abdominal aortic aneurysm or dissection; using aorto-aortic tube prosthesis

34802 using modular bifurcated prosthesis (one docking limb)

(For endovascular repair of infrarenal abdominal aortic aneurysm or dissection using a modular bifurcated prosthesis (two docking limbs), use Category III code 0001T)

34804 using unibody bifurcated prosthesis

● **34805** using aorto-uniiliac or aorto-unifemoral prosthesis

✚ **34808** Endovascular placement of iliac artery occlusion device (List separately in addition to code for primary procedure)

(Use 34808 in conjunction with codes 34800, 34813, 34825, 34826)

(For radiological supervision and interpretation, use 75952 in conjunction with 34800, 34802, 34804, 34805, 34808)

(For open arterial exposure, report codes 34812, 34820, 34833, 34834 as appropriate, in addition to codes 34800, 34802, 34804, ►34805◄, 34808)

34812 Open femoral artery exposure for delivery of endovascular prosthesis, by groin incision, unilateral

(For bilateral procedure, use modifier '-50')

✚ **34813** Placement of femoral-femoral prosthetic graft during endovascular aortic aneurysm repair (List separately in addition to code for primary procedure)

(Use 34813 in conjunction with code 34812)

(For femoral artery grafting, see 35521, 35533, 35546, 35551-35558, 35566, 35621, 35646, 35651-35661, 35666, 35700)

34820 Open iliac artery exposure for delivery of endovascular prosthesis or iliac occlusion during endovascular therapy, by abdominal or retroperitoneal incision, unilateral

(For bilateral procedure, use modifier '-50')

34825 Placement of proximal or distal extension prosthesis for endovascular repair of infrarenal abdominal aortic or iliac aneurysm, false aneurysm, or dissection; initial vessel

✚ **34826** each additional vessel (List separately in addition to code for primary procedure)

(Use 34826 in conjunction with code 34825)

(Use 34825, 34826 in addition to codes 34800-34808, 34900 as appropriate)

(For staged procedure, use modifier '-58')

(For radiological supervision and interpretation, use 75953)

34830 Open repair of infrarenal aortic aneurysm or dissection, plus repair of associated arterial trauma, following unsuccessful endovascular repair; tube prosthesis

34831 aorto-bi-iliac prosthesis

34832 aorto-bifemoral prosthesis

34833 Open iliac artery exposure with creation of conduit for delivery of infrarenal aortic or iliac endovascular prosthesis, by abdominal or retroperitoneal incision, unilateral

(For bilateral procedure, use modifier '-50')

(Do not report 34833 in addition to 34820)

34834 Open brachial artery exposure to assist in the deployment of infrarenal aortic or iliac endovascular prosthesis by arm incision, unilateral

(For bilateral procedure, use modifier '-50')

Endovascular Repair of Iliac Aneurysm

Code 34900 represents a procedure to report introduction, positioning, and deployment of an endovascular graft for treatment of aneurysm, pseudoaneurysm, or arteriovenous malformation or trauma of the iliac artery (common, hypogastric, external). All balloon angioplasty and/or stent deployments within the target treatment zone for the endoprosthesis, either before or after endograft deployment, are included in the work of 34900 and are not separately reportable. Open femoral or iliac artery exposure (eg, 34812, 34820), introduction of guidewires and catheters (eg, 36200, 36215-36218), and extensive repair or replacement of an artery (eg, 35206-35286) should be additionally reported.

For fluoroscopic guidance in conjunction with endovascular iliac aneurysm repair, see code 75954. Code 75954 includes angiography of the aorta and iliac arteries for diagnostic imaging prior to deployment of the endovascular device (including all routine components), fluoroscopic guidance in the delivery of the endovascular components, and intraprocedural arterial angiography to confirm appropriate position of the graft, detect endoleaks, and evaluate the status of the runoff vessels (eg, evaluation for dissection, stenosis, thrombosis, distal embolization, or iatrogenic injury).

Other interventional procedures performed at the time of endovascular aortic aneurysm repair should be additionally reported (eg, transluminal angioplasty outside the aneurysm target zone, arterial embolization, intravascular ultrasound).

34900 Endovascular graft placement for repair of iliac artery (eg, aneurysm, pseudoaneurysm, arteriovenous malformation, trauma)

(For radiological supervision and interpretation, use 75954)

(For placement of extension prosthesis during endovascular iliac artery repair, use 34825)

(For bilateral procedure, use modifier '-50')

Direct Repair of Aneurysm or Excision (Partial or Total) and Graft Insertion for Aneurysm, Pseudoaneurysm, Ruptured Aneurysm, and Associated Occlusive Disease

Procedures 35001-35162 include preparation of artery for anastomosis including endarterectomy.

(For direct repairs associated with occlusive disease only, see 35201-35286)

(For intracranial aneurysm, see 61700 et seq)

(For endovascular repair of abdominal aortic aneurysm, see 34800-34826)

(For endovascular repair of iliac artery aneurysm, see 34900)

(For thoracic aortic aneurysm, see 33860-33875)

(For endovascular repair of thoracic aortic aneurysm, see Category III codes 0033T-0034T)

35001 Direct repair of aneurysm, pseudoaneurysm, or excision (partial or total) and graft insertion, with or without patch graft; for aneurysm and associated occlusive disease, carotid, subclavian artery, by neck incision

35002 for ruptured aneurysm, carotid, subclavian artery, by neck incision

35005 for aneurysm, pseudoaneurysm, and associated occlusive disease, vertebral artery

35011 for aneurysm and associated occlusive disease, axillary-brachial artery, by arm incision

35013 for ruptured aneurysm, axillary-brachial artery, by arm incision

35021 for aneurysm, pseudoaneurysm, and associated occlusive disease, innominate, subclavian artery, by thoracic incision

35022 for ruptured aneurysm, innominate, subclavian artery, by thoracic incision

35045 for aneurysm, pseudoaneurysm, and associated occlusive disease, radial or ulnar artery

35081 for aneurysm, pseudoaneurysm, and associated occlusive disease, abdominal aorta

35082 for ruptured aneurysm, abdominal aorta

35091 for aneurysm, pseudoaneurysm, and associated occlusive disease, abdominal aorta involving visceral vessels (mesenteric, celiac, renal)

35092 for ruptured aneurysm, abdominal aorta involving visceral vessels (mesenteric, celiac, renal)

35102 for aneurysm, pseudoaneurysm, and associated occlusive disease, abdominal aorta involving iliac vessels (common, hypogastric, external)

35103 for ruptured aneurysm, abdominal aorta involving iliac vessels (common, hypogastric, external)

35111 for aneurysm, pseudoaneurysm, and associated occlusive disease, splenic artery

35112 for ruptured aneurysm, splenic artery

35121 for aneurysm, pseudoaneurysm, and associated occlusive disease, hepatic, celiac, renal, or mesenteric artery

35122 for ruptured aneurysm, hepatic, celiac, renal, or mesenteric artery

35131 for aneurysm, pseudoaneurysm, and associated occlusive disease, iliac artery (common, hypogastric, external)

35132 for ruptured aneurysm, iliac artery (common, hypogastric, external)

35141 for aneurysm, pseudoaneurysm, and associated occlusive disease, common femoral artery (profunda femoris, superficial femoral)

35142 for ruptured aneurysm, common femoral artery (profunda femoris, superficial femoral)

35151 for aneurysm, pseudoaneurysm, and associated occlusive disease, popliteal artery

35152 for ruptured aneurysm, popliteal artery

35161 for aneurysm, pseudoaneurysm, and associated occlusive disease, other arteries

35162 for ruptured aneurysm, other arteries

Repair Arteriovenous Fistula

35180 Repair, congenital arteriovenous fistula; head and neck

35182 thorax and abdomen

35184 extremities

35188 Repair, acquired or traumatic arteriovenous fistula; head and neck

35189 thorax and abdomen

35190 extremities

Repair Blood Vessel Other Than for Fistula, With or Without Patch Angioplasty

(For AV fistula repair, see 35180-35190)

35201 Repair blood vessel, direct; neck

35206 upper extremity

35207 hand, finger

35211 intrathoracic, with bypass

35216 intrathoracic, without bypass

35221 intra-abdominal

35226 lower extremity

35231 Repair blood vessel with vein graft; neck

35236 upper extremity

35241 intrathoracic, with bypass

35246 intrathoracic, without bypass

35251 intra-abdominal

35256 lower extremity

35261 Repair blood vessel with graft other than vein; neck

35266 upper extremity

35271 intrathoracic, with bypass

35276 intrathoracic, without bypass

35281 intra-abdominal

35286 lower extremity

Thromboendarterectomy

(For coronary artery, see 33510-33536 and 33572)

35301 Thromboendarterectomy, with or without patch graft; carotid, vertebral, subclavian, by neck incision

35311 subclavian, innominate, by thoracic incision

35321 axillary-brachial

35331 abdominal aorta

35341 mesenteric, celiac, or renal

35351 iliac

35355 iliofemoral

35361 combined aortoiliac

35363 combined aortoiliofemoral

35371 common femoral

35372 deep (profunda) femoral

35381 femoral and/or popliteal, and/or tibioperoneal

✚ **35390** Reoperation, carotid, thromboendarterectomy, more than one month after original operation (List separately in addition to code for primary procedure)

(Use 35390 in conjunction with code 35301)

Angioscopy

✚ **35400** Angioscopy (non-coronary vessels or grafts) during therapeutic intervention (List separately in addition to code for primary procedure)

Transluminal Angioplasty

If done as part of another operation, use modifier '-51' or use modifier '-52'.

(For radiological supervision and interpretation, see 75962-75968 and 75978)

Open

35450 Transluminal balloon angioplasty, open; renal or other visceral artery

35452 aortic

35454 iliac

35456 femoral-popliteal

35458 brachiocephalic trunk or branches, each vessel

35459 tibioperoneal trunk and branches

35460 venous

Surgery: Cardiovascular System

Percutaneous

Codes for catheter placement and the radiologic supervision and interpretation should also be reported, in addition to the code(s) for the therapeutic aspect of the procedure.

35470 Transluminal balloon angioplasty, percutaneous; tibioperoneal trunk or branches, each vessel

35471 renal or visceral artery

35472 aortic

35473 iliac

35474 femoral-popliteal

35475 brachiocephalic trunk or branches, each vessel

35476 venous

(For radiological supervision and interpretation, use 75978)

Transluminal Atherectomy

If done as part of another operation, use modifier '-51' or use modifier '-52'.

(For radiological supervision and interpretation, see 75992-75996)

Open

35480 Transluminal peripheral atherectomy, open; renal or other visceral artery

35481 aortic

35482 iliac

35483 femoral-popliteal

35484 brachiocephalic trunk or branches, each vessel

35485 tibioperoneal trunk and branches

Percutaneous

Codes for catheter placement and the radiologic supervision and interpretation should also be reported, in addition to the code(s) for the therapeutic aspect of the procedure.

35490 Transluminal peripheral atherectomy, percutaneous; renal or other visceral artery

35491 aortic

35492 iliac

35493 femoral-popliteal

35494 brachiocephalic trunk or branches, each vessel

35495 tibioperoneal trunk and branches

Bypass Graft

Vein

Procurement of the saphenous vein graft is included in the description of the work for 35501-35587 and should not be reported as a separate service or co-surgery. To report harvesting of an upper extremity vein, use 35500 in addition to the bypass procedure. To report harvesting of a femoropopliteal vein segment, use 35572 in addition to the bypass procedure. To report harvesting and construction of an autogenous composite graft of two segments from two distant locations, report 35682 in addition to the bypass procedure, for autogenous composite of three or more segments from distant sites, report 35683.

✚ 35500 Harvest of upper extremity vein, one segment, for lower extremity or coronary artery bypass procedure (List separately in addition to code for primary procedure)

(Use 35500 in conjunction with codes 33510-33536, 35556, 35566, 35571, 35583-35587)

(For harvest of more than one vein segment, see 35682, 35683)

(For endoscopic procedure, use 33508)

35501 Bypass graft, with vein; carotid

35506 carotid-subclavian

35507 subclavian-carotid

35508 carotid-vertebral

35509 carotid-carotid

● 35510 carotid-brachial

35511 subclavian-subclavian

● 35512 subclavian-brachial

35515 subclavian-vertebral

35516 subclavian-axillary

35518 axillary-axillary

35521 axillary-femoral

(For bypass graft performed with synthetic graft, use 35621)

● 35522 axillary-brachial

● 35525 brachial-brachial

35526 aortosubclavian or carotid

(For bypass graft performed with synthetic graft, use 35626)

35531 aortoceliac or aortomesenteric

35533 axillary-femoral-femoral

(For bypass graft performed with synthetic graft, use 35654)

35536 splenorenal

35541 aortoiliac or bi-iliac

(For bypass graft performed with synthetic graft, use 35641)

35546 aortofemoral or bifemoral

(For bypass graft performed with synthetic graft, use 35646)

35548 aortoiliofemoral, unilateral

(For bypass graft performed with synthetic graft, use 37799)

35549 aortoiliofemoral, bilateral

(For bypass graft performed with synthetic graft, use 37799)

35551 aortofemoral-popliteal

35556 femoral-popliteal

35558 femoral-femoral

35560 aortorenal

35563 ilioiliac

35565 iliofemoral

35566 femoral-anterior tibial, posterior tibial, peroneal artery or other distal vessels

35571 popliteal-tibial, -peroneal artery or other distal vessels

+ 35572 Harvest of femoropopliteal vein, one segment, for vascular reconstruction procedure (eg, aortic, vena caval, coronary, peripheral artery) (List separately in addition to code for primary procedure)

(Use 35572 in conjunction with codes 33510-33516, 33517-33523, 33533- 33536, 34502, 34520, 35001-35002, 35011-35022, 35102-35103, 35121-35152, 35231-35256, 35501-35587, 35901-35907)

►(For bilateral procedure, use modifier '-50')◄

In-Situ Vein

35582 In-situ vein bypass; aortofemoral-popliteal (only femoral-popliteal portion in-situ)

35583 femoral-popliteal

35585 femoral-anterior tibial, posterior tibial, or peroneal artery

35587 popliteal-tibial, peroneal

Other Than Vein

⊘ 35600 Harvest of upper extremity artery, one segment, for coronary artery bypass procedure

35601 Bypass graft, with other than vein; carotid

35606 carotid-subclavian

(For open subclavian to carotid artery transposition performed in conjunction with endovascular thoracic aneurysm repair, use Category III code 0037T)

35612 subclavian-subclavian

35616 subclavian-axillary

35621 axillary-femoral

35623 axillary-popliteal or -tibial

35626 aortosubclavian or carotid

35631 aortoceliac, aortomesenteric, aortorenal

35636 splenorenal (splenic to renal arterial anastomosis)

35641 aortoiliac or bi-iliac

(For open placement of aorto-bi-iliac prosthesis following unsuccessful endovascular repair, use 34831)

35642 carotid-vertebral

35645 subclavian-vertebral

35646 aortobifemoral

(For open placement of aortobifemoral prosthesis following unsuccessful endovascular repair, use 34832)

35647 aortofemoral

35650 axillary-axillary

35651 aortofemoral-popliteal

35654 axillary-femoral-femoral

35656 femoral-popliteal

35661 femoral-femoral

35663 ilioiliac

35665 iliofemoral

35666 femoral-anterior tibial, posterior tibial, or peroneal artery

35671 popliteal-tibial or -peroneal artery

Composite Grafts

Codes 35682-35683 are used to report harvest and anastomosis of multiple vein segments from distant sites for use as arterial bypass graft conduits. These codes are intended for use when the two or more vein segments are harvested from a limb other than that undergoing bypass. Add-on codes 35682 and 35683 may be reported in addition to codes 35556, 35566, 35571, 35583-35587, as appropriate.

+ 35681 Bypass graft; composite, prosthetic and vein (List separately in addition to code for primary procedure)

(Do not report 35681 in addition to 35682, 35683)

+ 35682 autogenous composite, two segments of veins from two locations (List separately in addition to code for primary procedure)

(Do not report 35682 in addition to 35681, 35683)

+ 35683 autogenous composite, three or more segments of vein from two or more locations (List separately in addition to code for primary procedure)

(Do not report 35683 in addition to 35681, 35682)

Adjuvant Techniques

Adjuvant (additional) technique(s) may be required at the time a bypass graft is created to improve patency of the lower extremity autogenous or synthetic bypass graft (eg, femoral-popliteal, femoral-tibial, or popliteal-tibial arteries). Code 35685 should be reported in addition to the primary synthetic bypass graft procedure, when an interposition of venous tissue (vein patch or cuff) is placed at the anastomosis between the synthetic bypass conduit and the involved artery (includes harvest).

Code 35686 should be reported in addition to the primary bypass graft procedure, when autogenous vein is used to create a fistula between the tibial or peroneal artery and vein at or beyond the distal bypass anastomosis site of the involved artery.

(For composite graft(s), see 35681-35683)

+ 35685 Placement of vein patch or cuff at distal anastomosis of bypass graft, synthetic conduit (List separately in addition to code for primary procedure)

(Use 35685 in conjunction with codes 35656, 35666, or 35671)

+ 35686 Creation of distal arteriovenous fistula during lower extremity bypass surgery (non-hemodialysis) (List separately in addition to code for primary procedure)

(Use 35686 in conjunction with codes 35556, 35566, 35571, 35583-35587, 35623, 35656, 35666, 35671)

Arterial Transposition

35691 Transposition and/or reimplantation; vertebral to carotid artery

35693 vertebral to subclavian artery

35694 subclavian to carotid artery

(For open subclavian to carotid artery transposition performed in conjunction with endovascular thoracic aneurysm repair, use Category III code 0037T)

35695 carotid to subclavian artery

+ ● 35697 Reimplantation, visceral artery to infrarenal aortic prosthesis, each artery (List separately in addition to code for primary procedure)

►(Do not report 35697 in conjunction with 33877)◄

Exploration/Revision

+ 35700 Reoperation, femoral-popliteal or femoral (popliteal)-anterior tibial, posterior tibial, peroneal artery or other distal vessels, more than one month after original operation (List separately in addition to code for primary procedure)

(Use 35700 in conjunction with codes 35556, 35566, 35571, 35583, 35585, 35587, 35656, 35666, 35671)

35701 Exploration (not followed by surgical repair), with or without lysis of artery; carotid artery

35721 femoral artery

35741 popliteal artery

35761 other vessels

35800 Exploration for postoperative hemorrhage, thrombosis or infection; neck

35820 chest

35840 abdomen

35860 extremity

35870 Repair of graft-enteric fistula

35875 Thrombectomy of arterial or venous graft (other than hemodialysis graft or fistula);

35876 with revision of arterial or venous graft

(For thrombectomy of hemodialysis graft or fistula, see 36831, 36833)

Codes 35879 and 35881 describe open revision of graft-threatening stenoses of lower extremity arterial bypass graft(s) (previously constructed with autogenous vein conduit) using vein patch angioplasty or segmental vein interposition techniques. For thrombectomy with revision of any non-coronary arterial or venous graft, including those of the lower extremity, (other than hemodialysis graft or fistula), use 35876. For direct repair (other than for fistula) of a lower extremity blood vessel (with or without patch angioplasty), use 35226. For repair (other than for fistula) of a lower extremity blood vessel using a vein graft, use 35256.

35879 Revision, lower extremity arterial bypass, without thrombectomy, open; with vein patch angioplasty

35881 with segmental vein interposition

35901 Excision of infected graft; neck

35903 extremity

35905 thorax

35907 abdomen

Vascular Injection Procedures

Listed services for injection procedures include necessary local anesthesia, introduction of needles or catheter, injection of contrast media with or without automatic power injection, and/or necessary pre- and postinjection care specifically related to the injection procedure.

Catheters, drugs, and contrast media are not included in the listed service for the injection procedures.

Selective vascular catheterization should be coded to include introduction and all lesser order selective catheterization used in the approach (eg, the description for a selective right middle cerebral artery catheterization includes the introduction and placement catheterization of the right common and internal carotid arteries).

Additional second and/or third order arterial catheterization within the same family of arteries or veins supplied by a single first order vessel should be expressed by 36012, 36218 or 36248.

Additional first order or higher catheterization in vascular families supplied by a first order vessel different from a previously selected and coded family should be separately coded using the conventions described above.

(For radiological supervision and interpretation, see **Radiology**)

(For injection procedures in conjunction with cardiac catheterization, see 93541-93545)

(For chemotherapy of malignant disease, see 96400-96549)

Intravenous

An intracatheter is a sheathed combination of needle and short catheter.

36000 Introduction of needle or intracatheter, vein

36002 Injection procedures (eg, thrombin) for percutaneous treatment of extremity pseudoaneurysm

(For imaging guidance, see 76003, 76360, 76393, or 76942)

(For ultrasound guided compression repair of pseudoaneurysms, use 76936)

(Do not report 36002 for vascular sealant of an arteriotomy site)

36005 Injection procedure for extremity venography (including introduction of needle or intracatheter)

(For radiological supervision and interpretation, see 75820, 75822)

36010 Introduction of catheter, superior or inferior vena cava

36011 Selective catheter placement, venous system; first order branch (eg, renal vein, jugular vein)

36012 second order, or more selective, branch (eg, left adrenal vein, petrosal sinus)

36013 Introduction of catheter, right heart or main pulmonary artery

36014 Selective catheter placement, left or right pulmonary artery

36015 Selective catheter placement, segmental or subsegmental pulmonary artery

(For insertion of flow directed catheter (eg, Swan-Ganz), use 93503)

(For venous catheterization for selective organ blood sampling, use 36500)

Intra-Arterial—Intra-Aortic

(For radiological supervision and interpretation, see **Radiology**)

36100 Introduction of needle or intracatheter, carotid or vertebral artery

36120 Introduction of needle or intracatheter; retrograde brachial artery

36140 extremity artery

36145 arteriovenous shunt created for dialysis (cannula, fistula, or graft)

(For insertion of arteriovenous cannula, see 36810-36821)

36160 Introduction of needle or intracatheter, aortic, translumbar

36200 Introduction of catheter, aorta

36215 Selective catheter placement, arterial system; each first order thoracic or brachiocephalic branch, within a vascular family

(For catheter placement for coronary angiography, use 93508)

36216 initial second order thoracic or brachiocephalic branch, within a vascular family

36217 initial third order or more selective thoracic or brachiocephalic branch, within a vascular family

+ 36218 additional second order, third order, and beyond, thoracic or brachiocephalic branch, within a vascular family (List in addition to code for initial second or third order vessel as appropriate)

(Use 36218 in conjunction with codes 36216, 36217)

(For angiography, see 75600-75790)

(For angioplasty, see 35470-35475)

(For transcatheter therapies, see 37200-37208, 61624, 61626)

36245 Selective catheter placement, arterial system; each first order abdominal, pelvic, or lower extremity artery branch, within a vascular family

36246 initial second order abdominal, pelvic, or lower extremity artery branch, within a vascular family

36247 initial third order or more selective abdominal, pelvic, or lower extremity artery branch, within a vascular family

+ 36248 additional second order, third order, and beyond, abdominal, pelvic, or lower extremity artery branch, within a vascular family (List in addition to code for initial second or third order vessel as appropriate)

(Use 36248 in conjunction with codes 36246, 36247)

36260 Insertion of implantable intra-arterial infusion pump (eg, for chemotherapy of liver)

36261 Revision of implanted intra-arterial infusion pump

36262 Removal of implanted intra-arterial infusion pump

36299 Unlisted procedure, vascular injection

Venous

Venipuncture, needle or catheter for diagnostic study or intravenous therapy, percutaneous.

▲36400 Venipuncture, under age 3 years, necessitating physician's skill, not to be used for routine venipuncture; femoral or jugular vein

36405 scalp vein

36406 other vein

▲36410 Venipuncture, age 3 years or older, necessitating physician's skill (separate procedure), for diagnostic or therapeutic purposes (not to be used for routine venipuncture)

36415 Collection of venous blood by venipuncture

(Do not report modifier '-63' in conjunction with 36415)

36416 Collection of capillary blood specimen (eg, finger, heel, ear stick)

36420 Venipuncture, cutdown; under age 1 year

(Do not report modifier '-63' in conjunction with 36420)

36425 age 1 or over

36430 Transfusion, blood or blood components

36440 Push transfusion, blood, 2 years or under

36450 Exchange transfusion, blood; newborn

(Do not report modifier '-63' in conjunction with 36450)

36455 other than newborn

36460 Transfusion, intrauterine, fetal

(Do not report modifier '-63' in conjunction with 36460)

(For radiological supervision and interpretation, use 76941)

36468 Single or multiple injections of sclerosing solutions, spider veins (telangiectasia); limb or trunk

36469 face

36470 Injection of sclerosing solution; single vein

36471 multiple veins, same leg

36481 Percutaneous portal vein catheterization by any method

(For radiological supervision and interpretation, see 75885, 75887)

►(36488-36491 have been deleted. To report, see 36555-36556, 36568-36569, 36580, 36584)◄

►(36493 has been deleted. To report, use 36597)◄

36500 Venous catheterization for selective organ blood sampling

(For catheterization in superior or inferior vena cava, use 36010)

(For radiological supervision and interpretation, use 75893)

36510 Catheterization of umbilical vein for diagnosis or therapy, newborn

(Do not report modifier '-63' in conjunction with 36510)

36511 Therapeutic apheresis; for white blood cells

36512 for red blood cells

36513 for platelets

36514 for plasma pheresis

36515 with extracorporeal immunoadsorption and plasma reinfusion

36516 with extracorporeal selective adsorption or selective filtration and plasma reinfusion

►(For physician evaluation, use modifier '-26')◄

(36520 has been deleted. To report, see 36511-36512)

(36521 has been deleted. To report, use 36516)

36522 Photopheresis, extracorporeal

►(36530 has been deleted. To report, use 36563)◄

►(36531 has been deleted. To report, see 36575-36576, 36578, 36581-36582, 36584-36585)◄

►(36532 has been deleted. To report, use 36590)◄

►(36533 has been deleted. To report, see 36557-36561, 36565-36566, 36570-36571)◄

►(36534 has been deleted. To report, see 36575-36578, 36581-36583, 36585)◄

►(36535 has been deleted. To report, use 36589)◄

►(36536 has been deleted. To report, use 36595)◄

►(36537 have been deleted. To report, use 36596)◄

36540 Collection of blood specimen from a completely implantable venous access device

(Do not report 36540 in conjunction with 36415, 36416)

(For collection of venous blood specimen by venipuncture, use 36415)

(For collection of capillary blood specimen, use 36416)

36550 Declotting by thrombolytic agent of implanted vascular access device or catheter

►Central Venous Access Procedures◄

►To qualify as a central venous access catheter or device, the tip of the catheter/device must terminate in the subclavian, brachiocephalic (innominate) or iliac veins, the superior or inferior vena cava, or the right atrium. The venous access device may be either centrally inserted (jugular, subclavian, femoral vein or inferior vena cava catheter entry site) or peripherally inserted (eg, basilic or cephalic vein). The device may be accessed for use either via exposed catheter (external to the skin), via a subcutaneous port or via a subcutaneous pump.◄

►The procedures involving these types of devices fall into five categories:

►1) ***Insertion*** (placement of catheter through a newly established venous access)◄

►2) ***Repair*** (fixing device without replacement of either catheter or port/pump, other than pharmacologic or mechanical correction of intracatheter or pericatheter occlusion (see 36595 or 36596))◄

►3) ***Partial replacement*** of only the catheter component associated with a port/pump device, but not entire device◄

►4) ***Complete replacement*** of entire device via same venous access site (complete exchange)◄

►5) ***Removal*** of entire device.◄

►There is no coding distinction between venous access achieved percutaneously versus by cutdown or based on catheter size.◄

►For the repair, partial (catheter only) replacement, complete replacement, or removal of both catheters (placed from separate venous access sites) of a multi-catheter device, with or without subcutaneous ports/pumps, use the appropriate code describing the service with a frequency of two.◄

►If an existing central venous access device is removed and a new one placed via a separate venous access site, appropriate codes for both procedures (removal of old, if code exists, and insertion of new device) should be reported.◄

►When imaging is used for these procedures, either for gaining access to the venous entry site or for manipulating the catheter into final central position, use 76937, 75998.◄

(For refilling and maintenance of an implantable pump or reservoir for intravenus or intra-arterial drug delivery, use 96530)

►*Insertion of Central Venous Access Device*◄

●**36555** Insertion of non-tunneled centrally inserted central venous catheter; under 5 years of age

►(For peripherally inserted non-tunneled central venous catheter, under 5 years of age, use 36568)◄

●**36556** age 5 years or older

►(For peripherally inserted non-tunneled central venous catheter, age 5 years or older, use 36569)◄

●**36557** Insertion of tunneled centrally inserted central venous catheter, without subcutaneous port or pump; under 5 years of age

●**36558** age 5 years or older

►(For peripherally inserted central venous catheter with port, 5 years or older, use 36571)◄

●**36560** Insertion of tunneled centrally inserted central venous access device, with subcutaneous port; under 5 years of age

►(For peripherally inserted central venous access device with subcutaneous port, under 5 years of age, use 36570)◄

●**36561** age 5 years or older

►(For peripherally inserted central venous catheter with subcutaneous port, 5 years or older, use 36571)◄

●**36563** Insertion of tunneled centrally inserted central venous access device with subcutaneous pump

●**36565** Insertion of tunneled centrally inserted central venous access device, requiring two catheters via two separate venous access sites; without subcutaneous port or pump (eg, Tesio type catheter)

●**36566** with subcutaneous port(s)

●**36568** Insertion of peripherally inserted central venous catheter (PICC), without subcutaneous port or pump; under 5 years of age

►(For placement of centrally inserted non-tunneled central venous catheter, without subcutaneous port or pump, under 5 years of age, use 36555)◄

●**36569** age 5 years or older

►(For placement of centrally inserted non-tunneled central venous catheter, without subcutaneous port or pump, age 5 years or older, use 36556)◄

● 36570 Insertion of peripherally inserted central venous access device, with subcutaneous port; under 5 years of age

►(For insertion of tunneled centrally inserted central venous access device with subcutaneous port, under 5 years of age, use 36560)◄

● 36571 age 5 years or older

►(For insertion of tunneled centrally inserted central venous access device with subcutaneous port, age 5 years or older, use 36561)◄

►*Repair of Central Venous Access Device*◄

►(For mechanical removal of pericatheter obstructive material, use 36595)◄

►(For mechanical removal of intracatheter obstructive material, use 36596)◄

● 36575 Repair of tunneled or non-tunneled central venous access catheter, without subcutaneous port or pump, central or peripheral insertion site

● 36576 Repair of central venous access device, with subcutaneous port or pump, central or peripheral insertion site

►*Partial Replacement of Central Venous Access Device (Catheter Only)*◄

● 36578 Replacement, catheter only, of central venous access device, with subcutaneous port or pump, central or peripheral insertion site

►(For complete replacement of entire device through same venous access, use 36582 or 36583)◄

►*Complete Replacement of Central Venous Access Device Through Same Venous Access Site*◄

● 36580 Replacement, complete, of a non-tunneled centrally inserted central venous catheter, without subcutaneous port or pump, through same venous access

● 36581 Replacement, complete, of a tunneled centrally inserted central venous catheter, without subcutaneous port or pump, through same venous access

● 36582 Replacement, complete, of a tunneled centrally inserted central venous access device, with subcutaneous port, through same venous access

● 36583 Replacement, complete, of a tunneled centrally inserted central venous access device, with subcutaneous pump, through same venous access

● 36584 Replacement, complete, of a peripherally inserted central venous catheter (PICC), without subcutaneous port or pump, through same venous access

● 36585 Replacement, complete, of a peripherally inserted central venous access device, with subcutaneous port, through same venous access

►*Removal of Central Venous Access Device*◄

● 36589 Removal of tunneled central venous catheter, without subcutaneous port or pump

● 36590 Removal of tunneled central venous access device, with subcutaneous port or pump, central or peripheral insertion

►(Do not report 36589 or 36590 for removal of non-tunneled central venous catheters)◄

►*Mechanical Removal of Obstructive Material*◄

● 36595 Mechanical removal of pericatheter obstructive material (eg, fibrin sheath) from central venous device via separate venous access

►(Do not report 36550 in addition to 36595)◄

►(For venous catheterization, see 36010-36012)◄

►(For radiological supervision and interpretation, use 75901)◄

● 36596 Mechanical removal of intraluminal (intracatheter) obstructive material from central venous device through device lumen

►(Do not report 36550 in addition to 36596)◄

►(For venous catheterization, see 36010-36012)◄

►(For radiological supervision and interpretation, use 75902)◄

►*Other Central Venous Access Procedures*◄

● 36597 Repositioning of previously placed central venous catheter under fluoroscopic guidance

►(For fluoroscopic guidance, use 76000)◄

Arterial

36600 Arterial puncture, withdrawal of blood for diagnosis

⊘ 36620 Arterial catheterization or cannulation for sampling, monitoring or transfusion (separate procedure); percutaneous

36625 cutdown

36640 Arterial catheterization for prolonged infusion therapy (chemotherapy), cutdown

(See also 96420-96425)

(For arterial catheterization for occlusion therapy, see 75894)

Surgery: Cardiovascular System

⊘ **36660** Catheterization, umbilical artery, newborn, for diagnosis or therapy

(Do not report modifier '-63' in conjunction with 36660)

Intraosseous

36680 Placement of needle for intraosseous infusion

Hemodialysis Access, Intervascular Cannulation for Extracorporeal Circulation, or Shunt Insertion

36800 Insertion of cannula for hemodialysis, other purpose (separate procedure); vein to vein

36810 arteriovenous, external (Scribner type)

36815 arteriovenous, external revision, or closure

36819 Arteriovenous anastomosis, open; by upper arm basilic vein transposition

36820 by forearm vein transposition

36821 direct, any site (eg, Cimino type) (separate procedure)

36822 Insertion of cannula(s) for prolonged extracorporeal circulation for cardiopulmonary insufficiency (ECMO) (separate procedure)

(For maintenance of prolonged extracorporeal circulation, see 33960, 33961)

36823 Insertion of arterial and venous cannula(s) for isolated extracorporeal circulation including regional chemotherapy perfusion to an extremity, with or without hyperthermia, with removal of cannula(s) and repair of arteriotomy and venotomy sites

(36823 includes chemotherapy perfusion supported by a membrane oxygenator/perfusion pump. Do not report 96408-96425 in conjunction with 36823)

36825 Creation of arteriovenous fistula by other than direct arteriovenous anastomosis (separate procedure); autogenous graft

(For direct arteriovenous anastomosis, use 36821)

36830 nonautogenous graft (eg, biological collagen, thermoplastic graft)

(For direct arteriovenous anastomosis, use 36821)

36831 Thrombectomy, open, arteriovenous fistula without revision, autogenous or nonautogenous dialysis graft (separate procedure)

36832 Revision, open, arteriovenous fistula; without thrombectomy, autogenous or nonautogenous dialysis graft (separate procedure)

36833 with thrombectomy, autogenous or nonautogenous dialysis graft (separate procedure)

36834 Plastic repair of arteriovenous aneurysm (separate procedure)

36835 Insertion of Thomas shunt (separate procedure)

● **36838** Distal revascularization and interval ligation (DRIL), upper extremity hemodialysis access (steal syndrome)

►(Do not report 36838 in conjunction with 35512, 35522, 36832, 37607, 37618)◄

36860 External cannula declotting (separate procedure); without balloon catheter

36861 with balloon catheter

(If imaging guidance is performed, use 76000)

36870 Thrombectomy, percutaneous, arteriovenous fistula, autogenous or nonautogenous graft (includes mechanical thrombus extraction and intra-graft thrombolysis)

(Do not report 36550 in conjunction with code 36870)

(For catheterization, use 36145)

(For radiological supervision and interpretation, use 75790)

Portal Decompression Procedures

37140 Venous anastomosis, open; portocaval

(For peritoneal-venous shunt, use 49425)

37145 renoportal

37160 caval-mesenteric

37180 splenorenal, proximal

37181 splenorenal, distal (selective decompression of esophagogastric varices, any technique)

(For percutaneous procedure, use 37182)

37182 Insertion of transvenous intrahepatic portosystemic shunt(s) (TIPS) (includes venous access, hepatic and portal vein catheterization, portography with hemodynamic evaluation, intrahepatic tract formation/dilatation, stent placement and all associated imaging guidance and documentation)

(Do not report 75885 or 75887 in conjunction with code 37182)

(For open procedure, use 37140)

37183 Revision of transvenous intrahepatic portosystemic shunt(s) (TIPS) (includes venous access, hepatic and portal vein catheterization, portography with hemodynamic evaluation, intrahepatic tract recanulization/dilatation, stent placement and all associated imaging guidance and documentation)

(Do not report 75885 or 75887 in conjunction with code 37183)

Transcatheter Procedures

Codes for catheter placement and the radiologic supervision and interpretation should also be reported, in addition to the code(s) for the therapeutic aspect of the procedure.

37195 Thrombolysis, cerebral, by intravenous infusion

37200 Transcatheter biopsy

(For radiological supervision and interpretation, use 75970)

37201 Transcatheter therapy, infusion for thrombolysis other than coronary

(For radiological supervision and interpretation, use 75896)

37202 Transcatheter therapy, infusion other than for thrombolysis, any type (eg, spasmolytic, vasoconstrictive)

(For thrombolysis of coronary vessels, see 92975, 92977)

(For radiological supervision and interpretation, use 75896)

37203 Transcatheter retrieval, percutaneous, of intravascular foreign body (eg, fractured venous or arterial catheter)

(For radiological supervision and interpretation, use 75961)

37204 Transcatheter occlusion or embolization (eg, for tumor destruction, to achieve hemostasis, to occlude a vascular malformation), percutaneous, any method, non-central nervous system, non-head or neck

(See also 61624, 61626)

(For radiological supervision and interpretation, use 75894)

37205 Transcatheter placement of an intravascular stent(s), (non-coronary vessel), percutaneous; initial vessel

(For radiological supervision and interpretation, use 75960)

+ 37206 each additional vessel (List separately in addition to code for primary procedure)

(Use 37206 in conjunction with code 37205)

(For transcatheter placement of extracranial cerebrovascular artery stent(s), see Category III codes 0005T, 0006T)

(For radiological supervision and interpretation, use 75960)

37207 Transcatheter placement of an intravascular stent(s), (non-coronary vessel), open; initial vessel

+ 37208 each additional vessel (List separately in addition to code for primary procedure)

(Use 37208 in conjunction with code 37207)

(For radiological supervision and interpretation, use 75960)

(For catheterizations, see 36215-36248)

(For transcatheter placement of intracoronary stent(s), see 92980, 92981)

37209 Exchange of a previously placed arterial catheter during thrombolytic therapy

(For radiological supervision and interpretation, use 75900)

Intravascular Ultrasound Services

Intravascular ultrasound services include all transducer manipulations and repositioning within the specific vessel being examined, both before and after therapeutic intervention (eg, stent placement).

Vascular access for intravascular ultrasound performed during a therapeutic intervention is not reported separately.

+ 37250 Intravascular ultrasound (non-coronary vessel) during diagnostic evaluation and/or therapeutic intervention; initial vessel (List separately in addition to code for primary procedure)

+ 37251 each additional vessel (List separately in addition to code for primary procedure)

(Use 37251 in conjunction with code 37250)

(For catheterizations, see 36215-36248)

(For transcatheter therapies, see 37200-37208, 61624, 61626)

(For radiological supervision and interpretation see 75945, 75946)

Endoscopy

Surgical vascular endoscopy always includes diagnostic endoscopy.

37500 Vascular endoscopy, surgical, with ligation of perforator veins, subfascial (SEPS)

(For open procedure, use 37760)

37501 Unlisted vascular endoscopy procedure

Ligation and Other Procedures

37565 Ligation, internal jugular vein

37600 Ligation; external carotid artery

37605 internal or common carotid artery

37606 internal or common carotid artery, with gradual occlusion, as with Selverstone or Crutchfield clamp

(For transcatheter permanent arterial occlusion or embolization, see 61624-61626)

Surgery: Cardiovascular System

(For endovascular temporary arterial balloon occlusion, use 61623)

(For ligation treatment of intracranial aneurysm, use 61703)

37607 Ligation or banding of angioaccess arteriovenous fistula

37609 Ligation or biopsy, temporal artery

37615 Ligation, major artery (eg, post-traumatic, rupture); neck

37616 chest

37617 abdomen

37618 extremity

37620 Interruption, partial or complete, of inferior vena cava by suture, ligation, plication, clip, extravascular, intravascular (umbrella device)

(For radiological supervision and interpretation, use 75940)

37650 Ligation of femoral vein

37660 Ligation of common iliac vein

37700 Ligation and division of long saphenous vein at saphenofemoral junction, or distal interruptions

37720 Ligation and division and complete stripping of long or short saphenous veins

37730 Ligation and division and complete stripping of long and short saphenous veins

37735 Ligation and division and complete stripping of long or short saphenous veins with radical excision of ulcer and skin graft and/or interruption of communicating veins of lower leg, with excision of deep fascia

37760 Ligation of perforator veins, subfascial, radical (Linton type), with or without skin graft, open

(For endoscopic procedure, use 37500)

●**37765** Stab phlebectomy of varicose veins, one extremity; 10-20 stab incisions

►(For less than 10 incisions, use 37799)◄

►(For more than 20 incisions, use 37766)◄

●**37766** more than 20 incisions

37780 Ligation and division of short saphenous vein at saphenopopliteal junction (separate procedure)

▲**37785** Ligation, division, and/or excision of varicose vein cluster(s), one leg

37788 Penile revascularization, artery, with or without vein graft

37790 Penile venous occlusive procedure

37799 Unlisted procedure, vascular surgery

Hemic and Lymphatic Systems

Spleen

Excision

38100 Splenectomy; total (separate procedure)

38101 partial (separate procedure)

✚ **38102** total, en bloc for extensive disease, in conjunction with other procedure (List in addition to code for primary procedure)

Repair

38115 Repair of ruptured spleen (splenorrhaphy) with or without partial splenectomy

Laparoscopy

Surgical laparoscopy always includes diagnostic laparoscopy. To report a diagnostic laparoscopy (peritoneoscopy) (separate procedure), use 49320.

38120 Laparoscopy, surgical, splenectomy

38129 Unlisted laparoscopy procedure, spleen

Introduction

38200 Injection procedure for splenoportography

(For radiological supervision and interpretation, use 75810)

General

Bone Marrow or Stem Cell Services/Procedures

►Codes 38207-38215 describe various steps used to preserve, prepare and purify bone marrow/stem cells prior to transplantation or reinfusion. Each code may be reported only once per day regardless of the quantity of bone marrow/stem cells manipulated.◄

38204 Management of recipient hematopoietic progenitor cell donor search and cell acquisition

38205 Blood-derived hematopoietic progenitor cell harvesting for transplantation, per collection; allogenic

38206 autologous

38207 Transplant preparation of hematopoietic progenitor cells; cryopreservation and storage

(For diagnostic cryopreservation and storage, see 88240)

▲38208 thawing of previously frozen harvest, without washing

(For diagnostic thawing and expansion of frozen cells, see 88241)

▲38209 thawing of previously frozen harvest, with washing

38210 specific cell depletion within harvest, T-cell depletion

38211 tumor cell depletion

38212 red blood cell removal

38213 platelet depletion

38214 plasma (volume) depletion

38215 cell concentration in plasma, mononuclear, or buffy coat layer

►(Do not report 88180, 88182 in conjunction with 38207-38215)◄

38220 Bone marrow; aspiration only

38221 biopsy, needle or trocar

(For bone marrow biopsy interpretation, use 88305)

38230 Bone marrow harvesting for transplantation

(38231 has been deleted. To report, use 38205-38206)

38240 Bone marrow or blood-derived peripheral stem cell transplantation; allogenic

38241 autologous

38242 allogeneic donor lymphocyte infusions

(For bone marrow aspiration, use 38220)

(For modification, treatment, and processing of bone marrow or blood-derived stem cell specimens for transplantation, use 38210-38213)

(For cryopreservation, freezing and storage of blood-derived stem cells for transplantation, use 88240)

(For thawing and expansion of blood-derived stem cells for transplantation, use 88241)

(For compatibility studies, see 86812-86822)

Lymph Nodes and Lymphatic Channels

Incision

38300 Drainage of lymph node abscess or lymphadenitis; simple

38305 extensive

38308 Lymphangiotomy or other operations on lymphatic channels

38380 Suture and/or ligation of thoracic duct; cervical approach

38381 thoracic approach

38382 abdominal approach

Excision

(For injection for sentinel node identification, use 38792)

38500 Biopsy or excision of lymph node(s); open, superficial

(Do not report 38500 with 38700-38780)

38505 by needle, superficial (eg, cervical, inguinal, axillary)

(If imaging guidance is performed, see 76360, 76393, 76942)

(For fine needle aspiration, use 10021 or 10022)

(For evaluation of fine needle aspirate, see 88172, 88173)

38510 open, deep cervical node(s)

38520 open, deep cervical node(s) with excision scalene fat pad

38525 open, deep axillary node(s)

38530 open, internal mammary node(s)

(Do not report 38530 with 38720-38746)

(For percutaneous needle biopsy, retroperitoneal lymph node or mass, use 49180. For fine needle aspiration, use 10022)

38542 Dissection, deep jugular node(s)

(For radical cervical neck dissection, use 38720)

38550 Excision of cystic hygroma, axillary or cervical; without deep neurovascular dissection

38555 with deep neurovascular dissection

Limited Lymphadenectomy for Staging

38562 Limited lymphadenectomy for staging (separate procedure); pelvic and para-aortic

(When combined with prostatectomy, use 55812 or 55842)

(When combined with insertion of radioactive substance into prostate, use 55862)

38564 retroperitoneal (aortic and/or splenic)

Laparoscopy

Surgical laparoscopy always includes diagnostic laparoscopy. To report a diagnostic laparoscopy (peritoneoscopy) (separate procedure), use 49320.

38570 Laparoscopy, surgical; with retroperitoneal lymph node sampling (biopsy), single or multiple

38571 with bilateral total pelvic lymphadenectomy

38572 with bilateral total pelvic lymphadenectomy and peri-aortic lymph node sampling (biopsy), single or multiple

(For drainage of lymphocele to peritoneal cavity, use 49323)

38589 Unlisted laparoscopy procedure, lymphatic system

Radical Lymphadenectomy (Radical Resection of Lymph Nodes)

(For limited pelvic and retroperitoneal lymphadenectomies, see 38562, 38564)

38700 Suprahyoid lymphadenectomy

38720 Cervical lymphadenectomy (complete)

38724 Cervical lymphadenectomy (modified radical neck dissection)

38740 Axillary lymphadenectomy; superficial

38745 complete

+ 38746 Thoracic lymphadenectomy, regional, including mediastinal and peritracheal nodes (List separately in addition to code for primary procedure)

+ 38747 Abdominal lymphadenectomy, regional, including celiac, gastric, portal, peripancreatic, with or without para-aortic and vena caval nodes (List separately in addition to code for primary procedure)

38760 Inguinofemoral lymphadenectomy, superficial, including Cloquets node (separate procedure)

38765 Inguinofemoral lymphadenectomy, superficial, in continuity with pelvic lymphadenectomy, including external iliac, hypogastric, and obturator nodes (separate procedure)

38770 Pelvic lymphadenectomy, including external iliac, hypogastric, and obturator nodes (separate procedure)

38780 Retroperitoneal transabdominal lymphadenectomy, extensive, including pelvic, aortic, and renal nodes (separate procedure)

(For excision and repair of lymphedematous skin and subcutaneous tissue, see 15000, 15570-15650)

Introduction

38790 Injection procedure; lymphangiography

(For radiological supervision and interpretation, see 75801-75807)

⊘ 38792 for identification of sentinel node

(For excision of sentinel node, see 38500-38542)

(For nuclear medicine lymphatics and lymph gland imaging, use 78195)

38794 Cannulation, thoracic duct

Other Procedures

38999 Unlisted procedure, hemic or lymphatic system

Mediastinum and Diaphragm

Mediastinum

Incision

39000 Mediastinotomy with exploration, drainage, removal of foreign body, or biopsy; cervical approach

39010 transthoracic approach, including either transthoracic or median sternotomy

Excision

39200 Excision of mediastinal cyst

39220 Excision of mediastinal tumor

(For substernal thyroidectomy, use 60270)

(For thymectomy, use 60520)

Endoscopy

39400 Mediastinoscopy, with or without biopsy

Other Procedures

39499 Unlisted procedure, mediastinum

Diaphragm

Repair

39501 Repair, laceration of diaphragm, any approach

39502 Repair, paraesophageal hiatus hernia, transabdominal, with or without fundoplasty, vagotomy, and/or pyloroplasty, except neonatal

39503 Repair, neonatal diaphragmatic hernia, with or without chest tube insertion and with or without creation of ventral hernia

(Do not report modifier '-63' in conjunction with 39503)

39520 Repair, diaphragmatic hernia (esophageal hiatal); transthoracic

39530 combined, thoracoabdominal

39531 combined, thoracoabdominal, with dilation of stricture (with or without gastroplasty)

39540 Repair, diaphragmatic hernia (other than neonatal), traumatic; acute

39541 chronic

39545 Imbrication of diaphragm for eventration, transthoracic or transabdominal, paralytic or nonparalytic

39560 Resection, diaphragm; with simple repair (eg, primary suture)

39561 with complex repair (eg, prosthetic material, local muscle flap)

Other Procedures

39599 Unlisted procedure, diaphragm

Digestive System

Lips

(For procedures on skin of lips, see 10040 et seq)

Excision

40490 Biopsy of lip

40500 Vermilionectomy (lip shave), with mucosal advancement

40510 Excision of lip; transverse wedge excision with primary closure

40520 V-excision with primary direct linear closure

(For excision of mucous lesions, see 40810-40816)

40525 full thickness, reconstruction with local flap (eg, Estlander or fan)

40527 full thickness, reconstruction with cross lip flap (Abbe-Estlander)

40530 Resection of lip, more than one-fourth, without reconstruction

(For reconstruction, see 13131 et seq)

Repair (Cheiloplasty)

40650 Repair lip, full thickness; vermilion only

40652 up to half vertical height

40654 over one-half vertical height, or complex

40700 Plastic repair of cleft lip/nasal deformity; primary, partial or complete, unilateral

40701 primary bilateral, one stage procedure

40702 primary bilateral, one of two stages

40720 secondary, by recreation of defect and reclosure

(To report rhinoplasty only for nasal deformity secondary to congenital cleft lip, see 30460, 30462)

40761 with cross lip pedicle flap (Abbe-Estlander type), including sectioning and inserting of pedicle

(For repair cleft palate, see 42200 et seq)

(For other reconstructive procedures, see 14060, 14061, 15120-15261, 15574, 15576, 15630)

Other Procedures

40799 Unlisted procedure, lips

Vestibule of Mouth

The vestibule is the part of the oral cavity outside the dentoalveolar structures; it includes the mucosal and submucosal tissue of lips and cheeks.

Incision

40800 Drainage of abscess, cyst, hematoma, vestibule of mouth; simple

40801 complicated

40804 Removal of embedded foreign body, vestibule of mouth; simple

40805 complicated

40806 Incision of labial frenum (frenotomy)

Excision, Destruction

40808 Biopsy, vestibule of mouth

40810 Excision of lesion of mucosa and submucosa, vestibule of mouth; without repair

40812 with simple repair

40814 with complex repair

40816 complex, with excision of underlying muscle

40818 Excision of mucosa of vestibule of mouth as donor graft

40819 Excision of frenum, labial or buccal (frenumectomy, frenulectomy, frenectomy)

40820 Destruction of lesion or scar of vestibule of mouth by physical methods (eg, laser, thermal, cryo, chemical)

Repair

40830 Closure of laceration, vestibule of mouth; 2.5 cm or less

40831 over 2.5 cm or complex

40840 Vestibuloplasty; anterior

40842 posterior, unilateral

40843 posterior, bilateral

40844 entire arch

40845 complex (including ridge extension, muscle repositioning)

(For skin grafts, see 15000 et seq)

Other Procedures

40899 Unlisted procedure, vestibule of mouth

Tongue and Floor of Mouth

Incision

41000 Intraoral incision and drainage of abscess, cyst, or hematoma of tongue or floor of mouth; lingual

41005 sublingual, superficial

41006 sublingual, deep, supramylohyoid

41007 submental space

41008 submandibular space

41009 masticator space

41010 Incision of lingual frenum (frenotomy)

41015 Extraoral incision and drainage of abscess, cyst, or hematoma of floor of mouth; sublingual

41016 submental

41017 submandibular

41018 masticator space

(For frenoplasty, use 41520)

Excision

41100 Biopsy of tongue; anterior two-thirds

41105 posterior one-third

41108 Biopsy of floor of mouth

41110 Excision of lesion of tongue without closure

41112 Excision of lesion of tongue with closure; anterior two-thirds

41113 posterior one-third

41114 with local tongue flap

(List 41114 in addition to code 41112 or 41113)

41115 Excision of lingual frenum (frenectomy)

41116 Excision, lesion of floor of mouth

41120 Glossectomy; less than one-half tongue

41130 hemiglossectomy

41135 partial, with unilateral radical neck dissection

41140 complete or total, with or without tracheostomy, without radical neck dissection

41145 complete or total, with or without tracheostomy, with unilateral radical neck dissection

41150 composite procedure with resection floor of mouth and mandibular resection, without radical neck dissection

41153 composite procedure with resection floor of mouth, with suprahyoid neck dissection

41155 composite procedure with resection floor of mouth, mandibular resection, and radical neck dissection (Commando type)

Repair

41250 Repair of laceration 2.5 cm or less; floor of mouth and/or anterior two-thirds of tongue

41251 posterior one-third of tongue

41252 Repair of laceration of tongue, floor of mouth, over 2.6 cm or complex

Other Procedures

41500 Fixation of tongue, mechanical, other than suture (eg, K-wire)

41510 Suture of tongue to lip for micrognathia (Douglas type procedure)

41520 Frenoplasty (surgical revision of frenum, eg, with Z-plasty)

(For frenotomy, see 40806, 41010)

41599 Unlisted procedure, tongue, floor of mouth

Dentoalveolar Structures

Incision

41800 Drainage of abscess, cyst, hematoma from dentoalveolar structures

41805 Removal of embedded foreign body from dentoalveolar structures; soft tissues

41806 bone

Excision, Destruction

41820 Gingivectomy, excision gingiva, each quadrant

41821 Operculectomy, excision pericoronal tissues

41822 Excision of fibrous tuberosities, dentoalveolar structures

41823 Excision of osseous tuberosities, dentoalveolar structures

41825 Excision of lesion or tumor (except listed above), dentoalveolar structures; without repair

41826 with simple repair

41827 with complex repair

(For nonexcisional destruction, use 41850)

41828 Excision of hyperplastic alveolar mucosa, each quadrant (specify)

41830 Alveolectomy, including curettage of osteitis or sequestrectomy

41850 Destruction of lesion (except excision), dentoalveolar structures

Other Procedures

41870 Periodontal mucosal grafting

41872 Gingivoplasty, each quadrant (specify)

41874 Alveoloplasty, each quadrant (specify)

(For closure of lacerations, see 40830, 40831)

(For segmental osteotomy, use 21206)

(For reduction of fractures, see 21421-21490)

41899 Unlisted procedure, dentoalveolar structures

Palate and Uvula

Incision

42000 Drainage of abscess of palate, uvula

Excision, Destruction

42100 Biopsy of palate, uvula

42104 Excision, lesion of palate, uvula; without closure

42106 with simple primary closure

42107 with local flap closure

(For skin graft, see 14040-14300)

(For mucosal graft, use 40818)

42120 Resection of palate or extensive resection of lesion

(For reconstruction of palate with extraoral tissue, see 14040-14300, 15050, 15120, 15240, 15576)

42140 Uvulectomy, excision of uvula

42145 Palatopharyngoplasty (eg, uvulopalatopharyngoplasty, uvulopharyngoplasty)

42160 Destruction of lesion, palate or uvula (thermal, cryo or chemical)

Repair

42180 Repair, laceration of palate; up to 2 cm

42182 over 2 cm or complex

42200 Palatoplasty for cleft palate, soft and/or hard palate only

42205 Palatoplasty for cleft palate, with closure of alveolar ridge; soft tissue only

42210 with bone graft to alveolar ridge (includes obtaining graft)

42215 Palatoplasty for cleft palate; major revision

42220 secondary lengthening procedure

42225 attachment pharyngeal flap

42226 Lengthening of palate, and pharyngeal flap

42227 Lengthening of palate, with island flap

42235 Repair of anterior palate, including vomer flap

42260 Repair of nasolabial fistula

(For repair of cleft lip, see 40700 et seq)

42280 Maxillary impression for palatal prosthesis

42281 Insertion of pin-retained palatal prosthesis

Other Procedures

42299 Unlisted procedure, palate, uvula

Salivary Gland and Ducts

Incision

42300 Drainage of abscess; parotid, simple

42305 parotid, complicated

42310 Drainage of abscess; submaxillary or sublingual, intraoral

42320 submaxillary, external

42325 Fistulization of sublingual salivary cyst (ranula);

42326 with prosthesis

42330 Sialolithotomy; submandibular (submaxillary), sublingual or parotid, uncomplicated, intraoral

42335 submandibular (submaxillary), complicated, intraoral

42340 parotid, extraoral or complicated intraoral

Excision

42400 Biopsy of salivary gland; needle

(For fine needle aspiration, see 10021, 10022)

(For evaluation of fine needle aspirate, see 88172, 88173)

(If imaging guidance is performed, see 76003, 76360, 76393, 76942)

42405 incisional

(If imaging guidance is performed, see 76003, 76360, 76393, 76942)

42408 Excision of sublingual salivary cyst (ranula)

42409 Marsupialization of sublingual salivary cyst (ranula)

(For fistulization of sublingual salivary cyst, use 42325)

42410 Excision of parotid tumor or parotid gland; lateral lobe, without nerve dissection

42415 lateral lobe, with dissection and preservation of facial nerve

42420 total, with dissection and preservation of facial nerve

42425 total, en bloc removal with sacrifice of facial nerve

42426 total, with unilateral radical neck dissection

(For suture or grafting of facial nerve, see 64864, 64865, 69740, 69745)

42440 Excision of submandibular (submaxillary) gland

42450 Excision of sublingual gland

Repair

42500 Plastic repair of salivary duct, sialodochoplasty; primary or simple

42505 secondary or complicated

42507 Parotid duct diversion, bilateral (Wilke type procedure);

42508 with excision of one submandibular gland

42509 with excision of both submandibular glands

42510 with ligation of both submandibular (Wharton's) ducts

Other Procedures

42550 Injection procedure for sialography

(For radiological supervision and interpretation, use 70390)

42600 Closure salivary fistula

42650 Dilation salivary duct

42660 Dilation and catheterization of salivary duct, with or without injection

42665 Ligation salivary duct, intraoral

42699 Unlisted procedure, salivary glands or ducts

Pharynx, Adenoids, and Tonsils

Incision

42700 Incision and drainage abscess; peritonsillar

42720 retropharyngeal or parapharyngeal, intraoral approach

42725 retropharyngeal or parapharyngeal, external approach

Excision, Destruction

42800 Biopsy; oropharynx

42802 hypopharynx

42804 nasopharynx, visible lesion, simple

42806 nasopharynx, survey for unknown primary lesion

(For laryngoscopic biopsy, see 31510, 31535, 31536)

42808 Excision or destruction of lesion of pharynx, any method

42809 Removal of foreign body from pharynx

42810 Excision branchial cleft cyst or vestige, confined to skin and subcutaneous tissues

42815 Excision branchial cleft cyst, vestige, or fistula, extending beneath subcutaneous tissues and/or into pharynx

42820 Tonsillectomy and adenoidectomy; under age 12

42821 age 12 or over

42825 Tonsillectomy, primary or secondary; under age 12

42826 age 12 or over

42830 Adenoidectomy, primary; under age 12

42831 age 12 or over

42835 Adenoidectomy, secondary; under age 12

42836 age 12 or over

42842 Radical resection of tonsil, tonsillar pillars, and/or retromolar trigone; without closure

42844 closure with local flap (eg, tongue, buccal)

42845 closure with other flap

(For closure with other flap(s), use appropriate number for flap(s))

(When combined with radical neck dissection, use also 38720)

42860 Excision of tonsil tags

42870 Excision or destruction lingual tonsil, any method (separate procedure)

42890 Limited pharyngectomy

42892 Resection of lateral pharyngeal wall or pyriform sinus, direct closure by advancement of lateral and posterior pharyngeal walls

(When combined with radical neck dissection, use also 38720)

42894 Resection of pharyngeal wall requiring closure with myocutaneous flap

(When combined with radical neck dissection, use also 38720)

Repair

42900 Suture pharynx for wound or injury

42950 Pharyngoplasty (plastic or reconstructive operation on pharynx)

(For pharyngeal flap, use 42225)

42953 Pharyngoesophageal repair

(For closure with myocutaneous or other flap, use appropriate number in addition)

Other Procedures

42955 Pharyngostomy (fistulization of pharynx, external for feeding)

42960 Control oropharyngeal hemorrhage, primary or secondary (eg, post-tonsillectomy); simple

42961 complicated, requiring hospitalization

42962 with secondary surgical intervention

42970 Control of nasopharyngeal hemorrhage, primary or secondary (eg, postadenoidectomy); simple, with posterior nasal packs, with or without anterior packs and/or cautery

42971 complicated, requiring hospitalization

42972 with secondary surgical intervention

42999 Unlisted procedure, pharynx, adenoids, or tonsils

Esophagus

Incision

(For esophageal intubation with laparotomy, use 43510)

43020 Esophagotomy, cervical approach, with removal of foreign body

43030 Cricopharyngeal myotomy

43045 Esophagotomy, thoracic approach, with removal of foreign body

Excision

(For gastrointestinal reconstruction for previous esophagectomy, see 43360, 43361)

43100 Excision of lesion, esophagus, with primary repair; cervical approach

43101 thoracic or abdominal approach

43107 Total or near total esophagectomy, without thoracotomy; with pharyngogastrostomy or cervical esophagogastrostomy, with or without pyloroplasty (transhiatal)

43108 with colon interposition or small intestine reconstruction, including intestine mobilization, preparation and anastomosis(es)

43112 Total or near total esophagectomy, with thoracotomy; with pharyngogastrostomy or cervical esophagogastrostomy, with or without pyloroplasty

43113 with colon interposition or small intestine reconstruction, including intestine mobilization, preparation, and anastomosis(es)

43116 Partial esophagectomy, cervical, with free intestinal graft, including microvascular anastomosis, obtaining the graft and intestinal reconstruction

(Do not report code 69990 in addition to code 43116)

(Report 43116 with the modifier '-52' appended if intestinal or free jejunal graft with microvascular anastomosis is performed by another physician)

(For free jejunal graft with microvascular anastomosis performed by another physician, use 43496)

43117 Partial esophagectomy, distal two-thirds, with thoracotomy and separate abdominal incision, with or without proximal gastrectomy; with thoracic esophagogastrostomy, with or without pyloroplasty (Ivor Lewis)

43118 with colon interposition or small intestine reconstruction, including intestine mobilization, preparation, and anastomosis(es)

43121 Partial esophagectomy, distal two-thirds, with thoracotomy only, with or without proximal gastrectomy, with thoracic esophagogastrostomy, with or without pyloroplasty

43122 Partial esophagectomy, thoracoabdominal or abdominal approach, with or without proximal gastrectomy; with esophagogastrostomy, with or without pyloroplasty

43123 with colon interposition or small intestine reconstruction, including intestine mobilization, preparation, and anastomosis(es)

43124 Total or partial esophagectomy, without reconstruction (any approach), with cervical esophagostomy

43130 Diverticulectomy of hypopharynx or esophagus, with or without myotomy; cervical approach

43135 thoracic approach

Endoscopy

For endoscopic procedures, code appropriate endoscopy of each anatomic site examined.

Surgical endoscopy always includes diagnostic endoscopy.

►(To report endoscopic delivery of thermal energy to the muscle of lower esophageal sphincter and/or gastric cardia, use Category III code 0057T)◄

►(For upper gastrointestinal endoscopy with suturing of the esophagogastric junction, use Category III code 0008T)◄

43200 Esophagoscopy, rigid or flexible; diagnostic, with or without collection of specimen(s) by brushing or washing (separate procedure)

43201 with directed submucosal injection(s), any substance

(For injection sclerosis of esophageal varices, use 43204)

43202 with biopsy, single or multiple

43204 with injection sclerosis of esophageal varices

43205 with band ligation of esophageal varices

43215 with removal of foreign body

(For radiological supervision and interpretation, use 74235)

43216 with removal of tumor(s), polyp(s), or other lesion(s) by hot biopsy forceps or bipolar cautery

43217 with removal of tumor(s), polyp(s), or other lesion(s) by snare technique

43219 with insertion of plastic tube or stent

43220 with balloon dilation (less than 30 mm diameter)

(If imaging guidance is performed, use 74360)

(For endoscopic dilation with balloon 30 mm diameter or larger, use 43458)

(For dilation without visualization, use 43450-43453)

43226 with insertion of guide wire followed by dilation over guide wire

(For radiological supervision and interpretation, use 74360)

43227 with control of bleeding (eg, injection, bipolar cautery, unipolar cautery, laser, heater probe, stapler, plasma coagulator)

43228 with ablation of tumor(s), polyp(s), or other lesion(s), not amenable to removal by hot biopsy forceps, bipolar cautery or snare technique

(For esophagoscopic photodynamic therapy, report 43228 in addition to 96570, 96571 as appropriate)

43231 with endoscopic ultrasound examination

43232 with transendoscopic ultrasound-guided intramural or transmural fine needle aspiration/biopsy(s)

►(Do not report 43232 in conjunction with 76942)◄

(For interpretation of specimen, see 88172-88173)

43234 Upper gastrointestinal endoscopy, simple primary examination (eg, with small diameter flexible endoscope) (separate procedure)

43235 Upper gastrointestinal endoscopy including esophagus, stomach, and either the duodenum and/or jejunum as appropriate; diagnostic, with or without collection of specimen(s) by brushing or washing (separate procedure)

43236 with directed submucosal injection(s), any substance

(For injection sclerosis of esophageal and/or gastric varices, use 43243)

● **43237** with endoscopic ultrasound examination limited to the esophagus

►(Do not report 43237 in conjunction with 76975)◄

● **43238** with transendoscopic ultrasound-guided intramural or transmural fine needle aspiration/biopsy(s), esophagus (includes endoscopic ultrasound examination limited to the esophagus)

►(Do not report 43238 in conjunction with 76942 or 76975)◄

43239 with biopsy, single or multiple

(For upper gastrointestinal endoscopy with suturing of the esophagogastric junction, use Category III code 0008T)

43240 with transmural drainage of pseudocyst

43241 with transendoscopic intraluminal tube or catheter placement

▲ **43242** with transendoscopic ultrasound-guided intramural or transmural fine needle aspiration/biopsy(s) (includes endoscopic ultrasound examination of the esophagus, stomach, and either the duodenum and/or jejunum as appropriate)

►(Do not report 43242 in conjunction with 76942 or 76975)◄

►(For transendoscopic fine needle aspiration/biopsy limited to esophagus, use 43238)◄

(For interpretation of specimen, see 88172-88173)

43243 with injection sclerosis of esophageal and/or gastric varices

43244 with band ligation of esophageal and/or gastric varices

43245 with dilation of gastric outlet for obstruction (eg, balloon, guide wire, bougie)

(Do not report 43245 in conjunction with 43256)

43246 with directed placement of percutaneous gastrostomy tube

(For radiological supervision and interpretation, use 74350)

43247 with removal of foreign body

(For radiological supervision and interpretation, use 74235)

43248 with insertion of guide wire followed by dilation of esophagus over guide wire

43249 with balloon dilation of esophagus (less than 30 mm diameter)

43250 with removal of tumor(s), polyp(s), or other lesion(s) by hot biopsy forceps or bipolar cautery

43251 with removal of tumor(s), polyp(s), or other lesion(s) by snare technique

43255 with control of bleeding, any method

43256 with transendoscopic stent placement (includes predilation)

43258 with ablation of tumor(s), polyp(s), or other lesion(s) not amenable to removal by hot biopsy forceps, bipolar cautery or snare technique

(For injection sclerosis of esophageal varices, use 43204 or 43243)

▲ **43259** with endoscopic ultrasound examination, including the esophagus, stomach, and either the duodenum and/or jejunum as appropriate

►(Do not report 43259 in conjunction with 76975)◄

43260 Endoscopic retrograde cholangiopancreatography (ERCP); diagnostic, with or without collection of specimen(s) by brushing or washing (separate procedure)

(For radiological supervision and interpretation, see 74328, 74329, 74330)

43261 with biopsy, single or multiple

(For radiological supervision and interpretation, see 74328, 74329, 74330)

43262 with sphincterotomy/papillotomy

(For radiological supervision and interpretation, see 74328, 74329, 74330)

43263 with pressure measurement of sphincter of Oddi (pancreatic duct or common bile duct)

(For radiological supervision and interpretation, see 74328, 74329, 74330)

43264 with endoscopic retrograde removal of calculus/calculi from biliary and/or pancreatic ducts

(When done with sphincterotomy, also use 43262)

(For radiological supervision and interpretation, see 74328, 74329, 74330)

43265 with endoscopic retrograde destruction, lithotripsy of calculus/calculi, any method

(When done with sphincterotomy, also use 43262)

(For radiological supervision and interpretation, see 74328, 74329, 74330)

43267 with endoscopic retrograde insertion of nasobiliary or nasopancreatic drainage tube

(When done with sphincterotomy, also use 43262)

(For radiological supervision and interpretation, see 74328, 74329, 74330)

43268 with endoscopic retrograde insertion of tube or stent into bile or pancreatic duct

(When done with sphincterotomy, also use 43262)

(For radiological supervision and interpretation, see 74328, 74329, 74330)

43269 with endoscopic retrograde removal of foreign body and/or change of tube or stent

(When done with sphincterotomy, also use 43262)

(For radiological supervision and interpretation, see 74328, 74329, 74330)

43271 with endoscopic retrograde balloon dilation of ampulla, biliary and/or pancreatic duct(s)

(When done with sphincterotomy, also use 43262)

(For radiological supervision and interpretation, see 74328, 74329, 74330)

43272 with ablation of tumor(s), polyp(s), or other lesion(s) not amenable to removal by hot biopsy forceps, bipolar cautery or snare technique

(For radiological supervision and interpretation, see 74328, 74329, 74330)

Laparoscopy

Surgical laparoscopy always includes diagnostic laparoscopy. To report a diagnostic laparoscopy (peritoneoscopy) (separate procedure), use 49320.

43280 Laparoscopy, surgical, esophagogastric fundoplasty (eg, Nissen, Toupet procedures)

(For open approach, use 43324)

43289 Unlisted laparoscopy procedure, esophagus

Repair

43300 Esophagoplasty (plastic repair or reconstruction), cervical approach; without repair of tracheoesophageal fistula

43305 with repair of tracheoesophageal fistula

43310 Esophagoplasty (plastic repair or reconstruction), thoracic approach; without repair of tracheoesophageal fistula

43312 with repair of tracheoesophageal fistula

43313 Esophagoplasty for congenital defect (plastic repair or reconstruction), thoracic approach; without repair of congenital tracheoesophageal fistula

43314 with repair of congenital tracheoesophageal fistula

(Do not report modifier '-63' in conjunction with 43313, 43314)

43320 Esophagogastrostomy (cardioplasty), with or without vagotomy and pyloroplasty, transabdominal or transthoracic approach

43324 Esophagogastric fundoplasty (eg, Nissen, Belsey IV, Hill procedures)

(For laparoscopic procedure, use 43280)

43325 Esophagogastric fundoplasty; with fundic patch (Thal-Nissen procedure)

(For cricopharyngeal myotomy, use 43030)

43326 with gastroplasty (eg, Collis)

43330 Esophagomyotomy (Heller type); abdominal approach

43331 thoracic approach

(For thoracoscopic esophagomyotomy, use 32665)

43340 Esophagojejunostomy (without total gastrectomy); abdominal approach

43341 thoracic approach

43350 Esophagostomy, fistulization of esophagus, external; abdominal approach

43351 thoracic approach

43352 cervical approach

43360 Gastrointestinal reconstruction for previous esophagectomy, for obstructing esophageal lesion or fistula, or for previous esophageal exclusion; with stomach, with or without pyloroplasty

43361 with colon interposition or small intestine reconstruction, including intestine mobilization, preparation, and anastomosis(es)

43400 Ligation, direct, esophageal varices

43401 Transection of esophagus with repair, for esophageal varices

43405 Ligation or stapling at gastroesophageal junction for pre-existing esophageal perforation

43410 Suture of esophageal wound or injury; cervical approach

43415 transthoracic or transabdominal approach

43420 Closure of esophagostomy or fistula; cervical approach

43425 transthoracic or transabdominal approach

(For repair of esophageal hiatal hernia, see 39520 et seq)

Manipulation

(For associated esophagogram, use 74220)

43450 Dilation of esophagus, by unguided sound or bougie, single or multiple passes

43453 Dilation of esophagus, over guide wire

(For dilation with direct visualization, use 43220)

43456 Dilation of esophagus, by balloon or dilator, retrograde

43458 Dilation of esophagus with balloon (30 mm diameter or larger) for achalasia

(For dilation with balloon less than 30 mm diameter, use 43220)

(For radiological supervision and interpretation, use 74360)

43460 Esophagogastric tamponade, with balloon (Sengstaaken type)

(For removal of esophageal foreign body by balloon catheter, see 43215, 43247, 74235)

Other Procedures

43496 Free jejunum transfer with microvascular anastomosis

(Do not report code 69990 in addition to code 43496)

43499 Unlisted procedure, esophagus

Stomach

Incision

43500 Gastrotomy; with exploration or foreign body removal

43501 with suture repair of bleeding ulcer

43502 with suture repair of pre-existing esophagogastric laceration (eg, Mallory-Weiss)

43510 with esophageal dilation and insertion of permanent intraluminal tube (eg, Celestin or Mousseaux-Barbin)

43520 Pyloromyotomy, cutting of pyloric muscle (Fredet-Ramstedt type operation)

(Do not report modifier '-63' in conjunction with 43520)

Excision

43600 Biopsy of stomach; by capsule, tube, peroral (one or more specimens)

43605 by laparotomy

43610 Excision, local; ulcer or benign tumor of stomach

43611 malignant tumor of stomach

43620 Gastrectomy, total; with esophagoenterostomy

43621 with Roux-en-Y reconstruction

43622 with formation of intestinal pouch, any type

43631 Gastrectomy, partial, distal; with gastroduodenostomy

43632 with gastrojejunostomy

43633 with Roux-en-Y reconstruction

43634 with formation of intestinal pouch

✚ **43635** Vagotomy when performed with partial distal gastrectomy (List separately in addition to code(s) for primary procedure)

(Use 43635 in conjunction with codes 43631, 43632, 43633, 43634)

43638 Gastrectomy, partial, proximal, thoracic or abdominal approach including esophagogastrostomy, with vagotomy;

43639 with pyloroplasty or pyloromyotomy

(For regional thoracic lymphadenectomy, use 38746)

(For regional abdominal lymphadenectomy, use 38747)

43640 Vagotomy including pyloroplasty, with or without gastrostomy; truncal or selective

(For pyloroplasty, use 43800)

(For vagotomy, see 64752-64760)

43641 parietal cell (highly selective)

(For upper gastrointestinal endoscopy, see 43234-43259)

Laparoscopy

Surgical laparoscopy always includes diagnostic laparoscopy. To report a diagnostic laparoscopy (peritoneoscopy) (separate procedure), use 49320.

43651 Laparoscopy, surgical; transection of vagus nerves, truncal

43652 transection of vagus nerves, selective or highly selective

43653 gastrostomy, without construction of gastric tube (eg, Stamm procedure) (separate procedure)

43659 Unlisted laparoscopy procedure, stomach

Introduction

43750 Percutaneous placement of gastrostomy tube

(For radiological supervision and interpretation, use 74350)

▲**43752** Naso- or oro-gastric tube placement, requiring physician's skill and fluoroscopic guidance (includes fluoroscopy, image documentation and report)

(For enteric tube placement, see 44500, 74340)

(Do not report 43752 in conjunction with critical care codes 99291-99292, neonatal ►critical care codes 99295-99296, pediatric critical care codes 99293-99294 or low birth weight intensive care service codes 99298-99299)◄

43760 Change of gastrostomy tube

(For endoscopic placement of gastrostomy tube, use 43246)

(For radiological supervision and interpretation, use 75984)

43761 Repositioning of the gastric feeding tube, any method, through the duodenum for enteric nutrition

(If imaging guidance is performed, use 75984)

Other Procedures

43800 Pyloroplasty

(For pyloroplasty and vagotomy, use 43640)

43810 Gastroduodenostomy

43820 Gastrojejunostomy; without vagotomy

43825 with vagotomy, any type

43830 Gastrostomy, open; without construction of gastric tube (eg, Stamm procedure) (separate procedure)

43831 neonatal, for feeding

(For change of gastrostomy tube, use 43760)

(Do not report modifier '-63' in conjunction with 43831)

43832 with construction of gastric tube (eg, Janeway procedure)

43840 Gastrorrhaphy, suture of perforated duodenal or gastric ulcer, wound, or injury

43842 Gastric restrictive procedure, without gastric bypass, for morbid obesity; vertical-banded gastroplasty

43843 other than vertical-banded gastroplasty

43846 Gastric restrictive procedure, with gastric bypass for morbid obesity; with short limb (less than 100 cm) Roux-en-Y gastroenterostomy

43847 with small intestine reconstruction to limit absorption

43848 Revision of gastric restrictive procedure for morbid obesity (separate procedure)

43850 Revision of gastroduodenal anastomosis (gastroduodenostomy) with reconstruction; without vagotomy

43855 with vagotomy

43860 Revision of gastrojejunal anastomosis (gastrojejunostomy) with reconstruction, with or without partial gastrectomy or intestine resection; without vagotomy

43865 with vagotomy

43870 Closure of gastrostomy, surgical

43880 Closure of gastrocolic fistula

43999 Unlisted procedure, stomach

Intestines (Except Rectum)

Incision

44005 Enterolysis (freeing of intestinal adhesion) (separate procedure)

(Do not report 44005 in addition to 45136)

(For laparoscopic approach, use 44200)

44010 Duodenotomy, for exploration, biopsy(s), or foreign body removal

+ **44015** Tube or needle catheter jejunostomy for enteral alimentation, intraoperative, any method (List separately in addition to primary procedure)

44020 Enterotomy, small intestine, other than duodenum; for exploration, biopsy(s), or foreign body removal

44021 for decompression (eg, Baker tube)

44025 Colotomy, for exploration, biopsy(s), or foreign body removal

44050 Reduction of volvulus, intussusception, internal hernia, by laparotomy

44055 Correction of malrotation by lysis of duodenal bands and/or reduction of midgut volvulus (eg, Ladd procedure)

(Do not report modifier '-63' in conjunction with 44055)

Excision

44100 Biopsy of intestine by capsule, tube, peroral (one or more specimens)

44110 Excision of one or more lesions of small or large intestine not requiring anastomosis, exteriorization, or fistulization; single enterotomy

44111 multiple enterotomies

44120 Enterectomy, resection of small intestine; single resection and anastomosis

(Do not report 44120 in addition to 45136)

+ 44121 each additional resection and anastomosis (List separately in addition to code for primary procedure)

(Use 44121 in conjunction with code 44120)

44125 with enterostomy

44126 Enterectomy, resection of small intestine for congenital atresia, single resection and anastomosis of proximal segment of intestine; without tapering

44127 with tapering

+ 44128 each additional resection and anastomosis (List separately in addition to code for primary procedure)

(Use 44128 in conjunction with codes 44126, 44127)

(Do not report modifier '-63' in conjunction with 44126, 44127, 44128)

44130 Enteroenterostomy, anastomosis of intestine, with or without cutaneous enterostomy (separate procedure)

44132 Donor enterectomy, open, with preparation and maintenance of allograft; from cadaver donor

44133 partial, from living donor

44135 Intestinal allotransplantation; from cadaver donor

44136 from living donor

+ 44139 Mobilization (take-down) of splenic flexure performed in conjunction with partial colectomy (List separately in addition to primary procedure)

(Use 44139 in conjunction with codes 44140-44147)

44140 Colectomy, partial; with anastomosis

(For laparoscopic procedure, use 44204)

44141 with skin level cecostomy or colostomy

44143 with end colostomy and closure of distal segment (Hartmann type procedure)

(For laparoscopic procedure, use 44206)

44144 with resection, with colostomy or ileostomy and creation of mucofistula

44145 with coloproctostomy (low pelvic anastomosis)

(For laparoscopic procedure, use 44207)

44146 with coloproctostomy (low pelvic anastomosis), with colostomy

(For laparoscopic procedure, use 44208)

44147 abdominal and transanal approach

44150 Colectomy, total, abdominal, without proctectomy; with ileostomy or ileoproctostomy

(For laparoscopic procedure, use 44210)

44151 with continent ileostomy

44152 with rectal mucosectomy, ileoanal anastomosis, with or without loop ileostomy

(For laparoscopic procedure, use 44211)

44153 with rectal mucosectomy, ileoanal anastomosis, creation of ileal reservoir (S or J), with or without loop ileostomy

(For laparoscopic procedure, use 44211)

44155 Colectomy, total, abdominal, with proctectomy; with ileostomy

(For laparoscopic procedure, use 44212)

44156 with continent ileostomy

44160 Colectomy, partial, with removal of terminal ileum with ileocolostomy

(For laparoscopic procedure, use 44205)

Laparoscopy

Surgical laparoscopy always includes diagnostic laparoscopy. To report a diagnostic laparoscopy (peritoneoscopy) (separate procedure), use 49320.

44200 Laparoscopy, surgical; enterolysis (freeing of intestinal adhesion) (separate procedure)

(For laparoscopy with salpingolysis, ovariolysis, use 58660)

44201 jejunostomy (eg, for decompression or feeding)

44202 enterectomy, resection of small intestine, single resection and anastomosis

+ 44203 each additional small intestine resection and anastomosis (List separately in addition to code for primary procedure)

(Use 44203 in conjunction with code 44202)

(For open procedure, see 44120, 44121)

44204 colectomy, partial, with anastomosis

(For open procedure, use 44140)

44205 colectomy, partial, with removal of terminal ileum with ileocolostomy

(For open procedure, use 44160)

44206 colectomy, partial, with end colostomy and closure of distal segment (Hartmann type procedure)

(For open procedure, use 44143)

44207 colectomy, partial, with anastomosis, with coloproctostomy (low pelvic anastomosis)

(For open procedure, use 44145)

44208 colectomy, partial, with anastomosis, with coloproctostomy (low pelvic anastomosis) with colostomy

(For open procedure, use 44146)

(44209 has been deleted. To report, use 44238)

44210 colectomy, total, abdominal, without proctectomy, with ileostomy or ileoproctostomy

(For open procedure, use 44150)

44211 colectomy, total, abdominal, with proctectomy, with ileoanal anastomosis, creation of ileal reservoir (S or J), with loop ileostomy, with or without rectal mucosectomy

(For open procedure, see 44152, 44153)

44212 colectomy, total, abdominal, with proctectomy, with ileostomy

(For open procedure, use 44155)

44238 Unlisted laparoscopy procedure, intestine (except rectum)

44239 Unlisted laparoscopy procedure, rectum

Enterostomy—External Fistulization of Intestines

44300 Enterostomy or cecostomy, tube (eg, for decompression or feeding) (separate procedure)

44310 Ileostomy or jejunostomy, non-tube (separate procedure)

(Do not report 44310 in addition to 45136)

44312 Revision of ileostomy; simple (release of superficial scar) (separate procedure)

44314 complicated (reconstruction in-depth) (separate procedure)

44316 Continent ileostomy (Kock procedure) (separate procedure)

(For fiberoptic evaluation, use 44385)

44320 Colostomy or skin level cecostomy; (separate procedure)

44322 with multiple biopsies (eg, for congenital megacolon) (separate procedure)

44340 Revision of colostomy; simple (release of superficial scar) (separate procedure)

44345 complicated (reconstruction in-depth) (separate procedure)

44346 with repair of paracolostomy hernia (separate procedure)

Endoscopy, Small Intestine and Stomal

Surgical endoscopy always includes diagnostic endoscopy.

(For upper gastrointestinal endoscopy, see 43234-43258)

44360 Small intestinal endoscopy, enteroscopy beyond second portion of duodenum, not including ileum; diagnostic, with or without collection of specimen(s) by brushing or washing (separate procedure)

44361 with biopsy, single or multiple

44363 with removal of foreign body

44364 with removal of tumor(s), polyp(s), or other lesion(s) by snare technique

44365 with removal of tumor(s), polyp(s), or other lesion(s) by hot biopsy forceps or bipolar cautery

44366 with control of bleeding (eg, injection, bipolar cautery, unipolar cautery, laser, heater probe, stapler, plasma coagulator)

44369 with ablation of tumor(s), polyp(s), or other lesion(s) not amenable to removal by hot biopsy forceps, bipolar cautery or snare technique

44370 with transendoscopic stent placement (includes predilation)

44372 with placement of percutaneous jejunostomy tube

44373 with conversion of percutaneous gastrostomy tube to percutaneous jejunostomy tube

44376 Small intestinal endoscopy, enteroscopy beyond second portion of duodenum, including ileum; diagnostic, with or without collection of specimen(s) by brushing or washing (separate procedure)

44377 with biopsy, single or multiple

44378 with control of bleeding (eg, injection, bipolar cautery, unipolar cautery, laser, heater probe, stapler, plasma coagulator)

44379 with transendoscopic stent placement (includes predilation)

44380 Ileoscopy, through stoma; diagnostic, with or without collection of specimen(s) by brushing or washing (separate procedure)

44382 with biopsy, single or multiple

44383 with transendoscopic stent placement (includes predilation)

44385 Endoscopic evaluation of small intestinal (abdominal or pelvic) pouch; diagnostic, with or without collection of specimen(s) by brushing or washing (separate procedure)

44386 with biopsy, single or multiple

44388 Colonoscopy through stoma; diagnostic, with or without collection of specimen(s) by brushing or washing (separate procedure)

44389 with biopsy, single or multiple

44390 with removal of foreign body

44391 with control of bleeding (eg, injection, bipolar cautery, unipolar cautery, laser, heater probe, stapler, plasma coagulator)

44392 with removal of tumor(s), polyp(s), or other lesion(s) by hot biopsy forceps or bipolar cautery

44393 with ablation of tumor(s), polyp(s), or other lesion(s) not amenable to removal by hot biopsy forceps, bipolar cautery or snare technique

44394 with removal of tumor(s), polyp(s), or other lesion(s) by snare technique

(For colonoscopy per rectum, see 45330-45385)

44397 with transendoscopic stent placement (includes predilation)

Introduction

⊘ **44500** Introduction of long gastrointestinal tube (eg, Miller-Abbott) (separate procedure)

(For radiological supervision and interpretation, use 74340)

(For naso- or oro-gastric tube placement, use 43752)

Repair

44602 Suture of small intestine (enterorrhaphy) for perforated ulcer, diverticulum, wound, injury or rupture; single perforation

44603 multiple perforations

44604 Suture of large intestine (colorrhaphy) for perforated ulcer, diverticulum, wound, injury or rupture (single or multiple perforations); without colostomy

44605 with colostomy

44615 Intestinal stricturoplasty (enterotomy and enterorrhaphy) with or without dilation, for intestinal obstruction

44620 Closure of enterostomy, large or small intestine;

44625 with resection and anastomosis other than colorectal

44626 with resection and colorectal anastomosis (eg, closure of Hartmann type procedure)

44640 Closure of intestinal cutaneous fistula

44650 Closure of enteroenteric or enterocolic fistula

44660 Closure of enterovesical fistula; without intestinal or bladder resection

44661 with intestine and/or bladder resection

(For closure of renocolic fistula, see 50525, 50526)

(For closure of gastrocolic fistula, use 43880)

(For closure of rectovesical fistula, see 45800, 45805)

44680 Intestinal plication (separate procedure)

Other Procedures

44700 Exclusion of small intestine from pelvis by mesh or other prosthesis, or native tissue (eg, bladder or omentum)

(For therapeutic radiation clinical treatment, see **Radiation Oncology** section)

✚ **44701** Intraoperative colonic lavage (List separately in addition to code for primary procedure)

(Use 44701 in conjunction with codes 44140, 44145, 44150, or 44604 as appropriate)

(Do not report 44701 in conjunction with 44300, 44950-44960)

44799 Unlisted procedure, intestine

(For unlisted laparoscopic procedure, intestine except rectum, use 44238)

Meckel's Diverticulum and the Mesentery

Excision

44800 Excision of Meckel's diverticulum (diverticulectomy) or omphalomesenteric duct

44820 Excision of lesion of mesentery (separate procedure)

(With intestine resection, see 44120 or 44140 et seq)

Suture

44850 Suture of mesentery (separate procedure)

(For reduction and repair of internal hernia, use 44050)

Other Procedures

44899 Unlisted procedure, Meckel's diverticulum and the mesentery

Appendix

Incision

44900 Incision and drainage of appendiceal abscess; open

44901 percutaneous

(For radiological supervision and interpretation, use 75989)

Excision

44950 Appendectomy;

(Incidental appendectomy during intra-abdominal surgery does not usually warrant a separate identification. If necessary to report, add modifier '-52')

+ 44955 when done for indicated purpose at time of other major procedure (not as separate procedure) (List separately in addition to code for primary procedure)

44960 for ruptured appendix with abscess or generalized peritonitis

Laparoscopy

Surgical laparoscopy always includes diagnostic laparoscopy. To report a diagnostic laparoscopy (peritoneoscopy) (separate procedure), use 49320.

44970 Laparoscopy, surgical, appendectomy

44979 Unlisted laparoscopy procedure, appendix

Rectum

Incision

45000 Transrectal drainage of pelvic abscess

45005 Incision and drainage of submucosal abscess, rectum

45020 Incision and drainage of deep supralevator, pelvirectal, or retrorectal abscess

(See also 46050, 46060)

Excision

45100 Biopsy of anorectal wall, anal approach (eg, congenital megacolon)

(For endoscopic biopsy, use 45305)

45108 Anorectal myomectomy

45110 Proctectomy; complete, combined abdominoperineal, with colostomy

45111 partial resection of rectum, transabdominal approach

45112 Proctectomy, combined abdominoperineal, pull-through procedure (eg, colo-anal anastomosis)

(For colo-anal anastomosis with colonic reservoir or pouch, use 45119)

45113 Proctectomy, partial, with rectal mucosectomy, ileoanal anastomosis, creation of ileal reservoir (S or J), with or without loop ileostomy

45114 Proctectomy, partial, with anastomosis; abdominal and transsacral approach

45116 transsacral approach only (Kraske type)

45119 Proctectomy, combined abdominoperineal pull-through procedure (eg, colo-anal anastomosis), with creation of colonic reservoir (eg, J-pouch), with or without proximal diverting ostomy

45120 Proctectomy, complete (for congenital megacolon), abdominal and perineal approach; with pull-through procedure and anastomosis (eg, Swenson, Duhamel, or Soave type operation)

45121 with subtotal or total colectomy, with multiple biopsies

45123 Proctectomy, partial, without anastomosis, perineal approach

45126 Pelvic exenteration for colorectal malignancy, with proctectomy (with or without colostomy), with removal of bladder and ureteral transplantations, and/or hysterectomy, or cervicectomy, with or without removal of tube(s), with or without removal of ovary(s), or any combination thereof

45130 Excision of rectal procidentia, with anastomosis; perineal approach

45135 abdominal and perineal approach

45136 Excision of ileoanal reservoir with ileostomy

(Do not report 45136 in addition to 44005, 44120, 44310)

45150 Division of stricture of rectum

45160 Excision of rectal tumor by proctotomy, transsacral or transcoccygeal approach

45170 Excision of rectal tumor, transanal approach

Destruction

45190 Destruction of rectal tumor (eg, electrodessication, electrosurgery, laser ablation, laser resection, cryosurgery) transanal approach

Endoscopy

Definitions

Proctosigmoidoscopy is the examination of the rectum and sigmoid colon.

Sigmoidoscopy is the examination of the entire rectum, sigmoid colon and may include examination of a portion of the descending colon.

Colonoscopy is the examination of the entire colon, from the rectum to the cecum, and may include the examination of the terminal ileum.

For an incomplete colonoscopy, with full preparation for a colonoscopy, use a colonoscopy code with the modifier '-52' and provide documentation.

Surgical endoscopy always includes diagnostic endoscopy.

45300 Proctosigmoidoscopy, rigid; diagnostic, with or without collection of specimen(s) by brushing or washing (separate procedure)

45303 with dilation (eg, balloon, guide wire, bougie)

(For radiological supervision and interpretation, use 74360)

45305 with biopsy, single or multiple

45307 with removal of foreign body

45308 with removal of single tumor, polyp, or other lesion by hot biopsy forceps or bipolar cautery

45309 with removal of single tumor, polyp, or other lesion by snare technique

45315 with removal of multiple tumors, polyps, or other lesions by hot biopsy forceps, bipolar cautery or snare technique

45317 with control of bleeding (eg, injection, bipolar cautery, unipolar cautery, laser, heater probe, stapler, plasma coagulator)

45320 with ablation of tumor(s), polyp(s), or other lesion(s) not amenable to removal by hot biopsy forceps, bipolar cautery or snare technique (eg, laser)

45321 with decompression of volvulus

(45325 colonoscopy has been renumbered 45355 without change in terminology)

45327 with transendoscopic stent placement (includes predilation)

45330 Sigmoidoscopy, flexible; diagnostic, with or without collection of specimen(s) by brushing or washing (separate procedure)

45331 with biopsy, single or multiple

45332 with removal of foreign body

45333 with removal of tumor(s), polyp(s), or other lesion(s) by hot biopsy forceps or bipolar cautery

45334 with control of bleeding (eg, injection, bipolar cautery, unipolar cautery, laser, heater probe, stapler, plasma coagulator)

45335 with directed submucosal injection(s), any substance

45337 with decompression of volvulus, any method

45338 with removal of tumor(s), polyp(s), or other lesion(s) by snare technique

45339 with ablation of tumor(s), polyp(s), or other lesion(s) not amenable to removal by hot biopsy forceps, bipolar cautery or snare technique

45340 with dilation by balloon, 1 or more strictures

(Do not report 45340 in conjunction with 45345)

45341 with endoscopic ultrasound examination

45342 with transendoscopic ultrasound guided intramural or transmural fine needle aspiration/biopsy(s)

►(Do not report 76942 in conjunction with 45341, 45342)◄

(Do not report 76975 in conjunction with 45341, 45342)

(For interpretation of specimen, see 88172-88173)

(For transrectal ultrasound utilizing rigid probe device, use 76872)

45345 with transendoscopic stent placement (includes predilation)

45355 Colonoscopy, rigid or flexible, transabdominal via colotomy, single or multiple

45378 Colonoscopy, flexible, proximal to splenic flexure; diagnostic, with or without collection of specimen(s) by brushing or washing, with or without colon decompression (separate procedure)

45379 with removal of foreign body

45380 with biopsy, single or multiple

45381 with directed submucosal injection(s), any substance

45382 with control of bleeding (eg, injection, bipolar cautery, unipolar cautery, laser, heater probe, stapler, plasma coagulator)

45383 with ablation of tumor(s), polyp(s), or other lesion(s) not amenable to removal by hot biopsy forceps, bipolar cautery or snare technique

45384 with removal of tumor(s), polyp(s), or other lesion(s) by hot biopsy forceps or bipolar cautery

45385 with removal of tumor(s), polyp(s), or other lesion(s) by snare technique

(For small intestine and stomal endoscopy, see 44360-44393)

45386 with dilation by balloon, 1 or more strictures

(Do not report 45386 in conjunction with 45387)

45387 with transendoscopic stent placement (includes predilation)

Repair

45500 Proctoplasty; for stenosis

45505 for prolapse of mucous membrane

45520 Perirectal injection of sclerosing solution for prolapse

45540 Proctopexy for prolapse; abdominal approach

45541 perineal approach

45550 Proctopexy combined with sigmoid resection, abdominal approach

45560 Repair of rectocele (separate procedure)

(For repair of rectocele with posterior colporrhaphy, use 57250)

45562 Exploration, repair, and presacral drainage for rectal injury;

45563 with colostomy

45800 Closure of rectovesical fistula;

45805 with colostomy

45820 Closure of rectourethral fistula;

45825 with colostomy

(For rectovaginal fistula closure, see 57300-57308)

Manipulation

45900 Reduction of procidentia (separate procedure) under anesthesia

45905 Dilation of anal sphincter (separate procedure) under anesthesia other than local

45910 Dilation of rectal stricture (separate procedure) under anesthesia other than local

45915 Removal of fecal impaction or foreign body (separate procedure) under anesthesia

Other Procedures

45999 Unlisted procedure, rectum

(For unlisted laparoscopic procedure, rectum, use 44239)

Anus

Incision

46020 Placement of seton

(Do not report 46020 in addition to 46060, 46280, 46600)

46030 Removal of anal seton, other marker

46040 Incision and drainage of ischiorectal and/or perirectal abscess (separate procedure)

46045 Incision and drainage of intramural, intramuscular, or submucosal abscess, transanal, under anesthesia

46050 Incision and drainage, perianal abscess, superficial

(See also 45020, 46060)

46060 Incision and drainage of ischiorectal or intramural abscess, with fistulectomy or fistulotomy, submuscular, with or without placement of seton

(Do not report 46060 in addition to 46020)

(See also 45020)

46070 Incision, anal septum (infant)

(For anoplasty, see 46700-46705)

(Do not report modifier '-63' in conjunction with 46070)

46080 Sphincterotomy, anal, division of sphincter (separate procedure)

46083 Incision of thrombosed hemorrhoid, external

Excision

46200 Fissurectomy, with or without sphincterotomy

46210 Cryptectomy; single

46211 multiple (separate procedure)

46220 Papillectomy or excision of single tag, anus (separate procedure)

46221 Hemorrhoidectomy, by simple ligature (eg, rubber band)

46230 Excision of external hemorrhoid tags and/or multiple papillae

46250 Hemorrhoidectomy, external, complete

46255 Hemorrhoidectomy, internal and external, simple;

46257 with fissurectomy

46258 with fistulectomy, with or without fissurectomy

46260 Hemorrhoidectomy, internal and external, complex or extensive;

46261 with fissurectomy

46262 with fistulectomy, with or without fissurectomy

46270 Surgical treatment of anal fistula (fistulectomy/fistulotomy); subcutaneous

46275 submuscular

46280 complex or multiple, with or without placement of seton

(Do not report 46280 in addition to 46020)

(46281 has been renumbered to 46288 without change in terminology)

46285 second stage

46288 Closure of anal fistula with rectal advancement flap

46320 Enucleation or excision of external thrombotic hemorrhoid

Introduction

46500 Injection of sclerosing solution, hemorrhoids

Endoscopy

Surgical endoscopy always includes diagnostic endoscopy.

46600 Anoscopy; diagnostic, with or without collection of specimen(s) by brushing or washing (separate procedure)

(Do not report 46600 in addition to 46020)

46604 with dilation (eg, balloon, guide wire, bougie)

46606 with biopsy, single or multiple

46608 with removal of foreign body

46610 with removal of single tumor, polyp, or other lesion by hot biopsy forceps or bipolar cautery

46611 with removal of single tumor, polyp, or other lesion by snare technique

46612 with removal of multiple tumors, polyps, or other lesions by hot biopsy forceps, bipolar cautery or snare technique

46614 with control of bleeding (eg, injection, bipolar cautery, unipolar cautery, laser, heater probe, stapler, plasma coagulator)

46615 with ablation of tumor(s), polyp(s), or other lesion(s) not amenable to removal by hot biopsy forceps, bipolar cautery or snare technique

Repair

46700 Anoplasty, plastic operation for stricture; adult

46705 infant

(For simple incision of anal septum, use 46070)

(Do not report modifier '-63' in conjunction with 46705)

46706 Repair of anal fistula with fibrin glue

46715 Repair of low imperforate anus; with anoperineal fistula (cut-back procedure)

46716 with transposition of anoperineal or anovestibular fistula

(Do not report modifier '-63' in conjunction with 46715, 46716)

46730 Repair of high imperforate anus without fistula; perineal or sacroperineal approach

46735 combined transabdominal and sacroperineal approaches

(Do not report modifier '-63' in conjunction with 46730, 46735)

46740 Repair of high imperforate anus with rectourethral or rectovaginal fistula; perineal or sacroperineal approach

46742 combined transabdominal and sacroperineal approaches

(Do not report modifier '-63' in conjunction with 46740, 46742)

46744 Repair of cloacal anomaly by anorectovaginoplasty and urethroplasty, sacroperineal approach

(Do not report modifier '-63' in conjunction with 46744)

46746 Repair of cloacal anomaly by anorectovaginoplasty and urethroplasty, combined abdominal and sacroperineal approach;

46748 with vaginal lengthening by intestinal graft or pedicle flaps

46750 Sphincteroplasty, anal, for incontinence or prolapse; adult

46751 child

46753 Graft (Thiersch operation) for rectal incontinence and/or prolapse

46754 Removal of Thiersch wire or suture, anal canal

46760 Sphincteroplasty, anal, for incontinence, adult; muscle transplant

46761 levator muscle imbrication (Park posterior anal repair)

46762 implantation artificial sphincter

Destruction

46900 Destruction of lesion(s), anus (eg, condyloma, papilloma, molluscum contagiosum, herpetic vesicle), simple; chemical

46910 electrodesiccation

46916 cryosurgery

46917 laser surgery

46922 surgical excision

46924 Destruction of lesion(s), anus (eg, condyloma, papilloma, molluscum contagiosum, herpetic vesicle), extensive (eg, laser surgery, electrosurgery, cryosurgery, chemosurgery)

46934 Destruction of hemorrhoids, any method; internal

46935 external

46936 internal and external

46937 Cryosurgery of rectal tumor; benign

46938 malignant

46940 Curettage or cautery of anal fissure, including dilation of anal sphincter (separate procedure); initial

46942 subsequent

Suture

46945 Ligation of internal hemorrhoids; single procedure

46946 multiple procedures

Other Procedures

46999 Unlisted procedure, anus

Liver

Incision

47000 Biopsy of liver, needle; percutaneous

(If imaging guidance is performed, see 76003, 76360, 76393, 76942)

+ 47001 when done for indicated purpose at time of other major procedure (List separately in addition to code for primary procedure)

(If imaging guidance is performed, see 76003, 76942)

(For fine needle aspiration in conjunction with 47000, 47001, see 10021, 10022)

(For evaluation of fine needle aspirate in conjunction with 47000, 47001, see 88172, 88173)

47010 Hepatotomy; for open drainage of abscess or cyst, one or two stages

47011 for percutaneous drainage of abscess or cyst, one or two stages

(For radiological supervision and interpretation, use 75989)

47015 Laparotomy, with aspiration and/or injection of hepatic parasitic (eg, amoebic or echinococcal) cyst(s) or abscess(es)

Excision

47100 Biopsy of liver, wedge

47120 Hepatectomy, resection of liver; partial lobectomy

47122 trisegmentectomy

47125 total left lobectomy

47130 total right lobectomy

47133 Donor hepatectomy, with preparation and maintenance of allograft, from cadaver donor

►(47134 has been deleted. To report, use 47140)◄

47135 Liver allotransplantation; orthotopic, partial or whole, from cadaver or living donor, any age

47136 heterotopic, partial or whole, from cadaver or living donor, any age

● 47140 Donor hepatectomy, with preparation and maintenance of allograft, from living donor; left lateral segment only (segments II and III)

● 47141 total left lobectomy (segments II, III and IV)

● 47142 total right lobectomy (segments V, VI, VII and VIII)

Repair

47300 Marsupialization of cyst or abscess of liver

47350 Management of liver hemorrhage; simple suture of liver wound or injury

47360 complex suture of liver wound or injury, with or without hepatic artery ligation

47361 exploration of hepatic wound, extensive debridement, coagulation and/or suture, with or without packing of liver

47362 re-exploration of hepatic wound for removal of packing

Laparoscopy

Surgical laparoscopy always includes diagnostic laparoscopy. To report a diagnostic laparoscopy (peritoneoscopy) (separate procedure), use 49320

47370 Laparoscopy, surgical, ablation of one or more liver tumor(s); radiofrequency

(For imaging guidance, use 76940)

47371 cryosurgical

(For imaging guidance, use 76940)

47379 Unlisted laparoscopic procedure, liver

Other Procedures

47380 Ablation, open, of one or more liver tumor(s); radiofrequency

(For imaging guidance, use 76940)

47381 cryosurgical

(For imaging guidance, use 76940)

47382 Ablation, one or more liver tumor(s), percutaneous, radiofrequency

(For imaging guidance and monitoring, see code 76362, 76394, or 76940)

47399 Unlisted procedure, liver

Biliary Tract

Incision

47400 Hepaticotomy or hepaticostomy with exploration, drainage, or removal of calculus

47420 Choledochotomy or choledochostomy with exploration, drainage, or removal of calculus, with or without cholecystotomy; without transduodenal sphincterotomy or sphincteroplasty

47425 with transduodenal sphincterotomy or sphincteroplasty

47460 Transduodenal sphincterotomy or sphincteroplasty, with or without transduodenal extraction of calculus (separate procedure)

47480 Cholecystotomy or cholecystostomy with exploration, drainage, or removal of calculus (separate procedure)

47490 Percutaneous cholecystostomy

(For radiological supervision and interpretation, use 75989)

Introduction

47500 Injection procedure for percutaneous transhepatic cholangiography

(For radiological supervision and interpretation, use 74320)

47505 Injection procedure for cholangiography through an existing catheter (eg, percutaneous transhepatic or T-tube)

(For radiological supervision and interpretation, use 74305)

47510 Introduction of percutaneous transhepatic catheter for biliary drainage

(For radiological supervision and interpretation, use 75980)

47511 Introduction of percutaneous transhepatic stent for internal and external biliary drainage

(For radiological supervision and interpretation, use 75982)

47525 Change of percutaneous biliary drainage catheter

(For radiological supervision and interpretation, use 75984)

47530 Revision and/or reinsertion of transhepatic tube

(For radiological supervision and interpretation, use 75984)

Endoscopy

Surgical endoscopy always includes diagnostic endoscopy.

✚ **47550** Biliary endoscopy, intraoperative (choledochoscopy) (List separately in addition to code for primary procedure)

47552 Biliary endoscopy, percutaneous via T-tube or other tract; diagnostic, with or without collection of specimen(s) by brushing and/or washing (separate procedure)

47553 with biopsy, single or multiple

47554 with removal of calculus/calculi

47555 with dilation of biliary duct stricture(s) without stent

(For ERCP, see 43260-43272, 74363)

(If imaging guidance is performed, see 74363, 75982)

47556 with dilation of biliary duct stricture(s) with stent

(If imaging guidance is performed, see 74363, 75982)

Laparoscopy

Surgical laparoscopy always includes diagnostic laparoscopy. To report a diagnostic laparoscopy (peritoneoscopy) (separate procedure), use 49320.

47560 Laparoscopy, surgical; with guided transhepatic cholangiography, without biopsy

47561 with guided transhepatic cholangiography with biopsy

47562 cholecystectomy

47563 cholecystectomy with cholangiography

47564 cholecystectomy with exploration of common duct

47570 cholecystoenterostomy

47579 Unlisted laparoscopy procedure, biliary tract

Excision

47600 Cholecystectomy;

47605 with cholangiography

(For laparoscopic approach, see 47562-47564)

47610 Cholecystectomy with exploration of common duct;

47612 with choledochoenterostomy

47620 with transduodenal sphincterotomy or sphincteroplasty, with or without cholangiography

47630 Biliary duct stone extraction, percutaneous via T-tube tract, basket, or snare (eg, Burhenne technique)

(For radiological supervision and interpretation, use 74327)

47700 Exploration for congenital atresia of bile ducts, without repair, with or without liver biopsy, with or without cholangiography

(Do not report modifier '-63' in conjunction with 47700)

47701 Portoenterostomy (eg, Kasai procedure)

(Do not report modifier '-63' in conjunction with 47701)

47711 Excision of bile duct tumor, with or without primary repair of bile duct; extrahepatic

47712 intrahepatic

(For anastomosis, see 47760-47800)

47715 Excision of choledochal cyst

47716 Anastomosis, choledochal cyst, without excision

Repair

47720 Cholecystoenterostomy; direct

(For laparoscopic approach, use 47570)

47721 with gastroenterostomy

47740 Roux-en-Y

47741 Roux-en-Y with gastroenterostomy

47760 Anastomosis, of extrahepatic biliary ducts and gastrointestinal tract

47765 Anastomosis, of intrahepatic ducts and gastrointestinal tract

47780 Anastomosis, Roux-en-Y, of extrahepatic biliary ducts and gastrointestinal tract

47785 Anastomosis, Roux-en-Y, of intrahepatic biliary ducts and gastrointestinal tract

47800 Reconstruction, plastic, of extrahepatic biliary ducts with end-to-end anastomosis

47801 Placement of choledochal stent

47802 U-tube hepaticoenterostomy

47900 Suture of extrahepatic biliary duct for pre-existing injury (separate procedure)

Other Procedures

47999 Unlisted procedure, biliary tract

Pancreas

(For peroral pancreatic endoscopic procedures, see 43260-43272)

Incision

48000 Placement of drains, peripancreatic, for acute pancreatitis;

48001 with cholecystostomy, gastrostomy, and jejunostomy

48005 Resection or debridement of pancreas and peripancreatic tissue for acute necrotizing pancreatitis

48020 Removal of pancreatic calculus

Excision

48100 Biopsy of pancreas, open (eg, fine needle aspiration, needle core biopsy, wedge biopsy)

48102 Biopsy of pancreas, percutaneous needle

(For radiological supervision and interpretation, see 76003, 76360, 76393, 76942)

(For fine needle aspiration, use 10022)

(For evaluation of fine needle aspirate, see 88172, 88173)

48120 Excision of lesion of pancreas (eg, cyst, adenoma)

48140 Pancreatectomy, distal subtotal, with or without splenectomy; without pancreaticojejunostomy

48145 with pancreaticojejunostomy

48146 Pancreatectomy, distal, near-total with preservation of duodenum (Child-type procedure)

48148 Excision of ampulla of Vater

48150 Pancreatectomy, proximal subtotal with total duodenectomy, partial gastrectomy, choledochoenterostomy and gastrojejunostomy (Whipple-type procedure); with pancreatojejunostomy

48152 without pancreatojejunostomy

48153 Pancreatectomy, proximal subtotal with near-total duodenectomy, choledochoenterostomy and duodenojejunostomy (pylorus-sparing, Whipple-type procedure); with pancreatojejunostomy

48154 without pancreatojejunostomy

48155 Pancreatectomy, total

48160 Pancreatectomy, total or subtotal, with autologous transplantation of pancreas or pancreatic islet cells

48180 Pancreaticojejunostomy, side-to-side anastomosis (Puestow-type operation)

Introduction

+ **48400** Injection procedure for intraoperative pancreatography (List separately in addition to code for primary procedure)

(For radiological supervision and interpretation, see 74300-74305)

Repair

48500 Marsupialization of pancreatic cyst

48510 External drainage, pseudocyst of pancreas; open

48511 percutaneous

(For radiological supervision and interpretation, use 75989)

48520 Internal anastomosis of pancreatic cyst to gastrointestinal tract; direct

48540 Roux-en-Y

48545 Pancreatorrhaphy for injury

48547 Duodenal exclusion with gastrojejunostomy for pancreatic injury

Pancreas Transplantation

48550 Donor pancreatectomy, with preparation and maintenance of allograft from cadaver donor, with or without duodenal segment for transplantation

48554 Transplantation of pancreatic allograft

48556 Removal of transplanted pancreatic allograft

Other Procedures

48999 Unlisted procedure, pancreas

Abdomen, Peritoneum, and Omentum

Incision

49000 Exploratory laparotomy, exploratory celiotomy with or without biopsy(s) (separate procedure)

(To report wound exploration due to penetrating trauma without laparotomy, use 20102)

49002 Reopening of recent laparotomy

(To report re-exploration of hepatic wound for removal of packing, use 47362)

49010 Exploration, retroperitoneal area with or without biopsy(s) (separate procedure)

(To report wound exploration due to penetrating trauma without laparotomy, use 20102)

49020 Drainage of peritoneal abscess or localized peritonitis, exclusive of appendiceal abscess; open

(For appendiceal abscess, use 44900)

49021 percutaneous

(For radiological supervision and interpretation, use 75989)

49040 Drainage of subdiaphragmatic or subphrenic abscess; open

49041 percutaneous

(For radiological supervision and interpretation, use 75989)

49060 Drainage of retroperitoneal abscess; open

49061 percutaneous

(For laparoscopic drainage, use 49323)

(For radiological supervision and interpretation, use 75989)

49062 Drainage of extraperitoneal lymphocele to peritoneal cavity, open

49080 Peritoneocentesis, abdominal paracentesis, or peritoneal lavage (diagnostic or therapeutic); initial

49081 subsequent

(If imaging guidance is performed, see 76360, 76942)

49085 Removal of peritoneal foreign body from peritoneal cavity

(For lysis of intestinal adhesions, use 44005)

Excision, Destruction

49180 Biopsy, abdominal or retroperitoneal mass, percutaneous needle

(If imaging guidance is performed, see 76003, 76360, 76393, 76942)

(For fine needle aspiration, use 10021 or 10022)

(For evaluation of fine needle aspirate, see 88172, 88173)

49200 Excision or destruction, open, intra-abdominal or retroperitoneal tumors or cysts or endometriomas;

49201 extensive

49215 Excision of presacral or sacrococcygeal tumor

(Do not report modifier '-63' in conjunction with 49215)

49220 Staging laparotomy for Hodgkins disease or lymphoma (includes splenectomy, needle or open biopsies of both liver lobes, possibly also removal of abdominal nodes, abdominal node and/or bone marrow biopsies, ovarian repositioning)

49250 Umbilectomy, omphalectomy, excision of umbilicus (separate procedure)

49255 Omentectomy, epiploectomy, resection of omentum (separate procedure)

Laparoscopy

Surgical laparoscopy always includes diagnostic laparoscopy. To report a diagnostic laparoscopy (peritoneoscopy), (separate procedure), use 49320.

For laparoscopic fulguration or excision of lesions of the ovary, pelvic viscera, or peritoneal surface use 58662.

49320 Laparoscopy, abdomen, peritoneum, and omentum, diagnostic, with or without collection of specimen(s) by brushing or washing (separate procedure)

49321 Laparoscopy, surgical; with biopsy (single or multiple)

49322 with aspiration of cavity or cyst (eg, ovarian cyst) (single or multiple)

49323 with drainage of lymphocele to peritoneal cavity

(For percutaneous or open drainage, see 49060, 49061)

49329 Unlisted laparoscopy procedure, abdomen, peritoneum and omentum

Introduction, Revision, and/or Removal

49400 Injection of air or contrast into peritoneal cavity (separate procedure)

(For radiological supervision and interpretation, use 74190)

49419 Insertion of intraperitoneal cannula or catheter, with subcutaneous reservoir, permanent (ie, totally implantable)

(For removal, use 49422)

49420 Insertion of intraperitoneal cannula or catheter for drainage or dialysis; temporary

49421 permanent

49422 Removal of permanent intraperitoneal cannula or catheter

(For removal of a temporary catheter/cannula, use appropriate E/M code)

49423 Exchange of previously placed abscess or cyst drainage catheter under radiological guidance (separate procedure)

(For radiological supervision and interpretation, use 75984)

49424 Contrast injection for assessment of abscess or cyst via previously placed drainage catheter or tube (separate procedure)

(For radiological supervision and interpretation, use 76080)

49425 Insertion of peritoneal-venous shunt

49426 Revision of peritoneal-venous shunt

(For shunt patency test, use 78291)

49427 Injection procedure (eg, contrast media) for evaluation of previously placed peritoneal-venous shunt

(For radiological supervision and interpretation, see 75809, 78291)

49428 Ligation of peritoneal-venous shunt

49429 Removal of peritoneal-venous shunt

Repair

Hernioplasty, Herniorrhaphy, Herniotomy

The hernia repair codes in this section are categorized primarily by the type of hernia (inguinal, femoral, incisional, etc.).

Some types of hernias are further categorized as "initial" or "recurrent" based on whether or not the hernia has required previous repair(s).

Additional variables accounted for by some of the codes include patient age and clinical presentation (reducible vs. incarcerated or strangulated).

With the exception of the incisional hernia repairs (see 49560-49566) the use of mesh or other prostheses is not separately reported.

The excision/repair of strangulated organs or structures such as testicle(s), intestine, ovaries are reported by using the appropriate code for the excision/repair (eg, 44120, 54520, and 58940) in addition to the appropriate code for the repair of the strangulated hernia.

(For reduction and repair of intra-abdominal hernia, use 44050)

(For debridement of abdominal wall, see 11042, 11043)

49491 Repair, initial inguinal hernia, preterm infant (less than 37 weeks gestation at birth), performed from birth up to 50 weeks postconception age, with or without hydrocelectomy; reducible

49492 incarcerated or strangulated

(Do not report modifier '-63' in conjunction with 49491, 49492)

(Postconception age equals gestational age at birth plus age of infant in weeks at the time of the hernia repair. Initial inguinal hernia repairs that are performed on preterm infants who are over 50 weeks postconception age and under age 6 months at the time of surgery, should be reported using codes 49495, 49496)

49495 Repair, initial inguinal hernia, full term infant under age 6 months, or preterm infant over 50 weeks postconception age and under age 6 months at the time of surgery, with or without hydrocelectomy; reducible

49496 incarcerated or strangulated

(Do not report modifier '-63' in conjunction with 49495, 49496)

(Postconception age equals gestational age at birth plus age in weeks at the time of the hernia repair. Initial inguinal hernia repairs that are performed on preterm infants who are under or up to 50 weeks postconception age but under 6 months of age since birth, should be reported using codes 49491, 49492. Inguinal hernia repairs on infants age 6 months to under 5 years should be reported using codes 49500-49501)

49500 Repair initial inguinal hernia, age 6 months to under 5 years, with or without hydrocelectomy; reducible

49501 incarcerated or strangulated

49505 Repair initial inguinal hernia, age 5 years or over; reducible

49507 incarcerated or strangulated

49520 Repair recurrent inguinal hernia, any age; reducible

49521 incarcerated or strangulated

49525 Repair inguinal hernia, sliding, any age

49540 Repair lumbar hernia

49550 Repair initial femoral hernia, any age; reducible

49553 incarcerated or strangulated

49555 Repair recurrent femoral hernia; reducible

49557 incarcerated or strangulated

49560 Repair initial incisional or ventral hernia; reducible

49561 incarcerated or strangulated

49565 Repair recurrent incisional or ventral hernia; reducible

49566 incarcerated or strangulated

+ **49568** Implantation of mesh or other prosthesis for incisional or ventral hernia repair (List separately in addition to code for the incisional or ventral hernia repair)

49570 Repair epigastric hernia (eg, preperitoneal fat); reducible (separate procedure)

49572 incarcerated or strangulated

49580 Repair umbilical hernia, under age 5 years; reducible

49582 incarcerated or strangulated

49585 Repair umbilical hernia, age 5 years or over; reducible

49587 incarcerated or strangulated

49590 Repair spigelian hernia

49600 Repair of small omphalocele, with primary closure

(Do not report modifier '-63' in conjunction with 49600)

49605 Repair of large omphalocele or gastroschisis; with or without prosthesis

49606 with removal of prosthesis, final reduction and closure, in operating room

(Do not report modifier '-63' in conjunction with 49605, 49606)

49610 Repair of omphalocele (Gross type operation); first stage

49611 second stage

(Do not report modifier '-63' in conjunction with 49610, 49611)

(For diaphragmatic or hiatal hernia repair, see 39502-39541)

Laparoscopy

Surgical laparoscopy always includes diagnostic laparoscopy. To report a diagnostic laparoscopy (peritoneoscopy) (separate procedure), use 49320.

49650 Laparoscopy, surgical; repair initial inguinal hernia

49651 repair recurrent inguinal hernia

49659 Unlisted laparoscopy procedure, hernioplasty, herniorrhaphy, herniotomy

Suture

49900 Suture, secondary, of abdominal wall for evisceration or dehiscence

(For suture of ruptured diaphragm, see 39540, 39541)

(For debridement of abdominal wall, see 11042, 11043)

Other Procedures

49904 Omental flap, extra-abdominal (eg, for reconstruction of sternal and chest wall defects)

(Code 49904 includes harvest and transfer. If a second surgeon harvests the omental flap, then the two surgeons should code 49904 as co-surgeons, using modifier '-62')

+ **49905** Omental flap, intra-abdominal (List separately in addition to code for primary procedure)

(Do not report 49905 in conjunction with 44700)

49906 Free omental flap with microvascular anastomosis

(Do not report code 69990 in addition to 49906)

49999 Unlisted procedure, abdomen, peritoneum and omentum

Urinary System

(For provision of chemotherapeutic agents, use 96545 in addition to code for primary procedure)

Kidney

Incision

(For retroperitoneal exploration, abscess, tumor, or cyst, see 49010, 49060, 49200, 49201)

50010 Renal exploration, not necessitating other specific procedures

(For laparoscopic ablation of renal mass lesion(s), use 50542)

50020 Drainage of perirenal or renal abscess; open

50021 percutaneous

(For radiological supervision and interpretation, use 75989)

50040 Nephrostomy, nephrotomy with drainage

50045 Nephrotomy, with exploration

(For renal endoscopy performed in conjunction with this procedure, see 50570-50580)

50060 Nephrolithotomy; removal of calculus

50065 secondary surgical operation for calculus

50070 complicated by congenital kidney abnormality

50075 removal of large staghorn calculus filling renal pelvis and calyces (including anatrophic pyelolithotomy)

50080 Percutaneous nephrostolithotomy or pyelostolithotomy, with or without dilation, endoscopy, lithotripsy, stenting, or basket extraction; up to 2 cm

50081 over 2 cm

(For establishment of nephrostomy without nephrostolithotomy, see 50040, 50395, 52334)

(For fluoroscopic guidance, see 76000, 76001)

50100 Transection or repositioning of aberrant renal vessels (separate procedure)

50120 Pyelotomy; with exploration

(For renal endoscopy performed in conjunction with this procedure, see 50570-50580)

50125 with drainage, pyelostomy

50130 with removal of calculus (pyelolithotomy, pelviolithotomy, including coagulum pyelolithotomy)

50135 complicated (eg, secondary operation, congenital kidney abnormality)

(For supply of anticarcinogenic agents, use 99070 in addition to code for primary procedure)

Excision

(For excision of retroperitoneal tumor or cyst, see 49200, 49201)

(For laparoscopic ablation of renal mass lesion(s), use 50542)

50200 Renal biopsy; percutaneous, by trocar or needle

(For radiological supervision and interpretation, see 76003, 76360, 76393, 76942)

(For fine needle aspiration, use 10022)

(For evaluation of fine needle aspirate, see 88172, 88173)

50205 by surgical exposure of kidney

50220 Nephrectomy, including partial ureterectomy, any open approach including rib resection;

50225 complicated because of previous surgery on same kidney

50230 radical, with regional lymphadenectomy and/or vena caval thrombectomy

(When vena caval resection with reconstruction is necessary, use 37799)

50234 Nephrectomy with total ureterectomy and bladder cuff; through same incision

50236 through separate incision

50240 Nephrectomy, partial

(For laparoscopic partial nephrectomy, use 50543)

50280 Excision or unroofing of cyst(s) of kidney

(For laparoscopic ablation of renal cysts, use 50541)

50290 Excision of perinephric cyst

Renal Transplantation

(For dialysis, see 90935-90999)

(For laparoscopic donor nephrectomy, use 50547)

(For laparoscopic drainage of lymphocele to peritoneal cavity, use 49323)

50300 Donor nephrectomy, with preparation and maintenance of allograft, from cadaver donor, unilateral or bilateral

50320 Donor nephrectomy, open from living donor (excluding preparation and maintenance of allograft)

50340 Recipient nephrectomy (separate procedure)

50360 Renal allotransplantation, implantation of graft; excluding donor and recipient nephrectomy

50365 with recipient nephrectomy

50370 Removal of transplanted renal allograft

50380 Renal autotransplantation, reimplantation of kidney

(For extra-corporeal "bench" surgery, use autotransplantation as the primary procedure and add the secondary procedure (eg, partial nephrectomy, nephrolithotomy), and use the modifier '-51')

Introduction

50390 Aspiration and/or injection of renal cyst or pelvis by needle, percutaneous

(For radiological supervision and interpretation, see 74425, 74470, 76003, 76360, 76393, 76942)

(For evaluation of fine needle aspirate, see 88172, 88173)

50392 Introduction of intracatheter or catheter into renal pelvis for drainage and/or injection, percutaneous

(For radiological supervision and interpretation, see 74475, 76360, 76942)

50393 Introduction of ureteral catheter or stent into ureter through renal pelvis for drainage and/or injection, percutaneous

(For radiological supervision and interpretation, see 74480, 76003, 76360, 76942)

50394 Injection procedure for pyelography (as nephrostogram, pyelostogram, antegrade pyeloureterograms) through nephrostomy or pyelostomy tube, or indwelling ureteral catheter

(For radiological supervision and interpretation, use 74425)

50395 Introduction of guide into renal pelvis and/or ureter with dilation to establish nephrostomy tract, percutaneous

(For radiological supervision and interpretation, see 74475, 74480, 74485)

(For nephrostolithotomy, see 50080, 50081)

(For retrograde percutaneous nephrostomy, use 52334)

(For endoscopic surgery, see 50551-50561)

50396 Manometric studies through nephrostomy or pyelostomy tube, or indwelling ureteral catheter

(For radiological supervision and interpretation, see 74425, 74475, 74480)

50398 Change of nephrostomy or pyelostomy tube

(For radiological supervision and interpretation, use 75984)

Repair

50400 Pyeloplasty (Foley Y-pyeloplasty), plastic operation on renal pelvis, with or without plastic operation on ureter, nephropexy, nephrostomy, pyelostomy, or ureteral splinting; simple

50405 complicated (congenital kidney abnormality, secondary pyeloplasty, solitary kidney, calycoplasty)

(For laparoscopic approach, use 50544)

50500 Nephrorrhaphy, suture of kidney wound or injury

50520 Closure of nephrocutaneous or pyelocutaneous fistula

50525 Closure of nephrovisceral fistula (eg, renocolic), including visceral repair; abdominal approach

50526 thoracic approach

50540 Symphysiotomy for horseshoe kidney with or without pyeloplasty and/or other plastic procedure, unilateral or bilateral (one operation)

Laparoscopy

Surgical laparoscopy always includes diagnostic laparoscopy. To report a diagnostic laparoscopy (peritoneoscopy) (separate procedure), use 49320.

50541 Laparoscopy, surgical; ablation of renal cysts

50542 ablation of renal mass lesion(s)

(For open procedure, see 50220-50240)

50543 partial nephrectomy

(For open procedure, use 50240)

50544 pyeloplasty

50545 radical nephrectomy (includes removal of Gerota's fascia and surrounding fatty tissue, removal of regional lymph nodes, and adrenalectomy)

(For open procedure, use 50230)

50546 nephrectomy, including partial ureterectomy

50547 donor nephrectomy from living donor (excluding preparation and maintenance of allograft)

(For open procedure, use 50320)

50548 nephrectomy with total ureterectomy

(For open procedure, see 50234, 50236)

50549 Unlisted laparoscopy procedure, renal

(For laparoscopic drainage of lymphocele to peritoneal cavity, use 49323)

Endoscopy

(For supplies and materials, use 99070)

50551 Renal endoscopy through established nephrostomy or pyelostomy, with or without irrigation, instillation, or ureteropyelography, exclusive of radiologic service;

50553 with ureteral catheterization, with or without dilation of ureter

50555 with biopsy

50557 with fulguration and/or incision, with or without biopsy

50559 with insertion of radioactive substance with or without biopsy and/or fulguration

50561 with removal of foreign body or calculus

50562 with resection of tumor

(When procedures 50570-50580 provide a significant identifiable service, they may be added to 50045 and 50120)

50570 Renal endoscopy through nephrotomy or pyelotomy, with or without irrigation, instillation, or ureteropyelography, exclusive of radiologic service;

(For nephrotomy, use 50045)

(For pyelotomy, use 50120)

50572 with ureteral catheterization, with or without dilation of ureter

50574 with biopsy

50575 with endopyelotomy (includes cystoscopy, ureteroscopy, dilation of ureter and ureteral pelvic junction, incision of ureteral pelvic junction and insertion of endopyelotomy stent)

50576 with fulguration and/or incision, with or without biopsy

50578 with insertion of radioactive substance, with or without biopsy and/or fulguration

50580 with removal of foreign body or calculus

Other Procedures

50590 Lithotripsy, extracorporeal shock wave

Ureter

Incision

50600 Ureterotomy with exploration or drainage (separate procedure)

(For ureteral endoscopy performed in conjunction with this procedure, see 50970-50980)

50605 Ureterotomy for insertion of indwelling stent, all types

50610 Ureterolithotomy; upper one-third of ureter

50620 middle one-third of ureter

50630 lower one-third of ureter

(For laparoscopic approach, use 50945)

(For transvesical ureterolithotomy, use 51060)

(For cystotomy with stone basket extraction of ureteral calculus, use 51065)

(For endoscopic extraction or manipulation of ureteral calculus, see 50080, 50081, 50561, 50961, 50980, 52320-52330, 52352, 52353)

Excision

(For ureterocele, see 51535, 52300)

50650 Ureterectomy, with bladder cuff (separate procedure)

50660 Ureterectomy, total, ectopic ureter, combination abdominal, vaginal and/or perineal approach

Introduction

50684 Injection procedure for ureterography or ureteropyelography through ureterostomy or indwelling ureteral catheter

(For radiological supervision and interpretation, use 74425)

50686 Manometric studies through ureterostomy or indwelling ureteral catheter

50688 Change of ureterostomy tube

(If imaging guidance is performed, use 75984)

50690 Injection procedure for visualization of ileal conduit and/or ureteropyelography, exclusive of radiologic service

(For radiological supervision and interpretation, use 74425)

Repair

50700 Ureteroplasty, plastic operation on ureter (eg, stricture)

50715 Ureterolysis, with or without repositioning of ureter for retroperitoneal fibrosis

50722 Ureterolysis for ovarian vein syndrome

50725 Ureterolysis for retrocaval ureter, with reanastomosis of upper urinary tract or vena cava

50727 Revision of urinary-cutaneous anastomosis (any type urostomy);

50728 with repair of fascial defect and hernia

50740 Ureteropyelostomy, anastomosis of ureter and renal pelvis

50750 Ureterocalycostomy, anastomosis of ureter to renal calyx

50760 Ureteroureterostomy

50770 Transureteroureterostomy, anastomosis of ureter to contralateral ureter

(Codes 50780-50785 include minor procedures to prevent vesicoureteral reflux)

50780 Ureteroneocystostomy; anastomosis of single ureter to bladder

(When combined with cystourethroplasty or vesical neck revision, use 51820)

50782 anastomosis of duplicated ureter to bladder

50783 with extensive ureteral tailoring

50785 with vesico-psoas hitch or bladder flap

50800 Ureteroenterostomy, direct anastomosis of ureter to intestine

50810 Ureterosigmoidostomy, with creation of sigmoid bladder and establishment of abdominal or perineal colostomy, including intestine anastomosis

50815 Ureterocolon conduit, including intestine anastomosis

50820 Ureteroileal conduit (ileal bladder), including intestine anastomosis (Bricker operation)

(For combination of 50800-50820 with cystectomy, see 51580-51595)

50825 Continent diversion, including intestine anastomosis using any segment of small and/or large intestine (Kock pouch or Camey enterocystoplasty)

50830 Urinary undiversion (eg, taking down of ureteroileal conduit, ureterosigmoidostomy or ureteroenterostomy with ureteroureterostomy or ureteroneocystostomy)

50840 Replacement of all or part of ureter by intestine segment, including intestine anastomosis

50845 Cutaneous appendico-vesicostomy

50860 Ureterostomy, transplantation of ureter to skin

50900 Ureterorrhaphy, suture of ureter (separate procedure)

50920 Closure of ureterocutaneous fistula

50930 Closure of ureterovisceral fistula (including visceral repair)

50940 Deligation of ureter

(For ureteroplasty, ureterolysis, see 50700-50860)

Laparoscopy

Surgical laparoscopy always includes diagnostic laparoscopy. To report a diagnostic laparoscopy (peritoneoscopy) (separate procedure), use 49320.

50945 Laparoscopy, surgical; ureterolithotomy

50947 ureteroneocystostomy with cystoscopy and ureteral stent placement

50948 ureteroneocystostomy without cystoscopy and ureteral stent placement

(For open ureteroneocystostomy, see 50780-50785)

50949 Unlisted laparoscopy procedure, ureter

Endoscopy

50951 Ureteral endoscopy through established ureterostomy, with or without irrigation, instillation, or ureteropyelography, exclusive of radiologic service;

50953 with ureteral catheterization, with or without dilation of ureter

50955 with biopsy

50957 with fulguration and/or incision, with or without biopsy

50959 with insertion of radioactive substance, with or without biopsy and/or fulguration (not including provision of material)

50961 with removal of foreign body or calculus

(When procedures 50970-50980 provide a significant identifiable service, they may be added to 50600)

50970 Ureteral endoscopy through ureterotomy, with or without irrigation, instillation, or ureteropyelography, exclusive of radiologic service;

(For ureterotomy, use 50600)

50972 with ureteral catheterization, with or without dilation of ureter

50974 with biopsy

50976 with fulguration and/or incision, with or without biopsy

50978 with insertion of radioactive substance, with or without biopsy and/or fulguration (not including provision of material)

50980 with removal of foreign body or calculus

Bladder

Incision

51000 Aspiration of bladder by needle

51005 Aspiration of bladder; by trocar or intracatheter

51010 with insertion of suprapubic catheter

(If imaging guidance is performed, see 76003, 76360, 76942)

51020 Cystotomy or cystostomy; with fulguration and/or insertion of radioactive material

51030 with cryosurgical destruction of intravesical lesion

51040 Cystostomy, cystotomy with drainage

51045 Cystotomy, with insertion of ureteral catheter or stent (separate procedure)

51050 Cystolithotomy, cystotomy with removal of calculus, without vesical neck resection

51060 Transvesical ureterolithotomy

51065 Cystotomy, with calculus basket extraction and/or ultrasonic or electrohydraulic fragmentation of ureteral calculus

51080 Drainage of perivesical or prevesical space abscess

Excision

51500 Excision of urachal cyst or sinus, with or without umbilical hernia repair

51520 Cystotomy; for simple excision of vesical neck (separate procedure)

51525 for excision of bladder diverticulum, single or multiple (separate procedure)

51530 for excision of bladder tumor

(For transurethral resection, see 52234-52240, 52305)

51535 Cystotomy for excision, incision, or repair of ureterocele

(For transurethral excision, use 52300)

51550 Cystectomy, partial; simple

51555 complicated (eg, postradiation, previous surgery, difficult location)

51565 Cystectomy, partial, with reimplantation of ureter(s) into bladder (ureteroneocystostomy)

51570 Cystectomy, complete; (separate procedure)

51575 with bilateral pelvic lymphadenectomy, including external iliac, hypogastric, and obturator nodes

51580 Cystectomy, complete, with ureterosigmoidostomy or ureterocutaneous transplantations;

51585 with bilateral pelvic lymphadenectomy, including external iliac, hypogastric, and obturator nodes

51590 Cystectomy, complete, with ureteroileal conduit or sigmoid bladder, including intestine anastomosis;

51595 with bilateral pelvic lymphadenectomy, including external iliac, hypogastric, and obturator nodes

51596 Cystectomy, complete, with continent diversion, any open technique, using any segment of small and/or large intestine to construct neobladder

51597 Pelvic exenteration, complete, for vesical, prostatic or urethral malignancy, with removal of bladder and ureteral transplantations, with or without hysterectomy and/or abdominoperineal resection of rectum and colon and colostomy, or any combination thereof

(For pelvic exenteration for gynecologic malignancy, use 58240)

Introduction

51600 Injection procedure for cystography or voiding urethrocystography

(For radiological supervision and interpretation, see 74430, 74455)

51605 Injection procedure and placement of chain for contrast and/or chain urethrocystography

(For radiological supervision and interpretation, use 74430)

51610 Injection procedure for retrograde urethrocystography

(For radiological supervision and interpretation, use 74450)

51700 Bladder irrigation, simple, lavage and/or instillation

(Codes 51701-51702 are reported only when performed independently. Do not report 51701-51702 when catheter insertion is an inclusive component of another procedure.)

51701 Insertion of non-indwelling bladder catheter (eg, straight catheterization for residual urine)

51702 Insertion of temporary indwelling bladder catheter; simple (eg, Foley)

51703 complicated (eg, altered anatomy, fractured catheter/balloon)

51705 Change of cystostomy tube; simple

51710 complicated

(If imaging guidance is performed, use 75984)

51715 Endoscopic injection of implant material into the submucosal tissues of the urethra and/or bladder neck

51720 Bladder instillation of anticarcinogenic agent (including detention time)

Urodynamics

The following section (51725-51797) lists procedures that may be used separately or in many and varied combinations.

When multiple procedures are performed in the same investigative session, modifier '-51' should be employed.

All procedures in this section imply that these services are performed by, or are under the direct supervision of, a physician and that all instruments, equipment, fluids, gases, probes, catheters, technician's fees, medications, gloves, trays, tubing and other sterile supplies be provided by the physician. When the physician only interprets the results and/or operates the equipment, a professional component, modifier '-26', should be used to identify physicians' services.

51725 Simple cystometrogram (CMG) (eg, spinal manometer)

51726 Complex cystometrogram (eg, calibrated electronic equipment)

51736 Simple uroflowmetry (UFR) (eg, stop-watch flow rate, mechanical uroflowmeter)

51741 Complex uroflowmetry (eg, calibrated electronic equipment)

51772 Urethral pressure profile studies (UPP) (urethral closure pressure profile), any technique

51784 Electromyography studies (EMG) of anal or urethral sphincter, other than needle, any technique

51785 Needle electromyography studies (EMG) of anal or urethral sphincter, any technique

51792 Stimulus evoked response (eg, measurement of bulbocavernosus reflex latency time)

51795 Voiding pressure studies (VP); bladder voiding pressure, any technique

51797 intra-abdominal voiding pressure (AP) (rectal, gastric, intraperitoneal)

51798 Measurement of post-voiding residual urine and/or bladder capacity by ultrasound, non-imaging

Repair

51800 Cystoplasty or cystourethroplasty, plastic operation on bladder and/or vesical neck (anterior Y-plasty, vesical fundus resection), any procedure, with or without wedge resection of posterior vesical neck

51820 Cystourethroplasty with unilateral or bilateral ureteroneocystostomy

51840 Anterior vesicourethropexy, or urethropexy (eg, Marshall-Marchetti-Krantz, Burch); simple

51841 complicated (eg, secondary repair)

(For urethropexy (Pereyra type), use 57289)

51845 Abdomino-vaginal vesical neck suspension, with or without endoscopic control (eg, Stamey, Raz, modified Pereyra)

51860 Cystorrhaphy, suture of bladder wound, injury or rupture; simple

51865 complicated

51880 Closure of cystostomy (separate procedure)

51900 Closure of vesicovaginal fistula, abdominal approach

(For vaginal approach, see 57320-57330)

51920 Closure of vesicouterine fistula;

51925 with hysterectomy

(For closure of vesicoenteric fistula, see 44660, 44661)

(For closure of rectovesical fistula, see 45800-45805)

51940 Closure, exstrophy of bladder

(See also 54390)

51960 Enterocystoplasty, including intestinal anastomosis

51980 Cutaneous vesicostomy

Laparoscopy

Surgical laparoscopy always includes diagnostic laparoscopy. To report a diagnostic laparoscopy (peritoneoscopy) (separate procedure), use 49320.

51990 Laparoscopy, surgical; urethral suspension for stress incontinence

51992 sling operation for stress incontinence (eg, fascia or synthetic)

(For open sling operation for stress incontinence, use 57288)

(For reversal or removal of sling operation for stress incontinence, use 57287)

Endoscopy—Cystoscopy, Urethroscopy, Cystourethroscopy

Endoscopic descriptions are listed so that the main procedure can be identified without having to list all the minor related functions performed at the same time. For example: meatotomy, urethral calibration and/or dilation, urethro-scopy, and cystoscopy prior to a transurethral resection of prostate; ureteral catheterization following extraction of ureteral calculus; internal urethrotomy and bladder neck fulguration when performing a cystourethroscopy for the female urethral syndrome. When the secondary procedure requires significant additional time and effort, it may be identified by the addition of modifier '-22'.

For example: urethrotomy performed for a documented pre-existing stricture or bladder neck contracture.

52000 Cystourethroscopy (separate procedure)

52001 Cystourethroscopy with irrigation and evacuation of multiple obstructing clots

(Do not report 52001 in addition to 52000)

52005 Cystourethroscopy, with ureteral catheterization, with or without irrigation, instillation, or ureteropyelography, exclusive of radiologic service;

52007 with brush biopsy of ureter and/or renal pelvis

52010 Cystourethroscopy, with ejaculatory duct catheterization, with or without irrigation, instillation, or duct radiography, exclusive of radiologic service

(For radiological supervision and interpretation, use 74440)

Transurethral Surgery

Urethra and Bladder

52204 Cystourethroscopy, with biopsy

52214 Cystourethroscopy, with fulguration (including cryosurgery or laser surgery) of trigone, bladder neck, prostatic fossa, urethra, or periurethral glands

52224 Cystourethroscopy, with fulguration (including cryosurgery or laser surgery) or treatment of MINOR (less than 0.5 cm) lesion(s) with or without biopsy

52234 Cystourethroscopy, with fulguration (including cryosurgery or laser surgery) and/or resection of; SMALL bladder tumor(s) (0.5 to 2.0 cm)

52235 MEDIUM bladder tumor(s) (2.0 to 5.0 cm)

52240 LARGE bladder tumor(s)

52250 Cystourethroscopy with insertion of radioactive substance, with or without biopsy or fulguration

52260 Cystourethroscopy, with dilation of bladder for interstitial cystitis; general or conduction (spinal) anesthesia

52265 local anesthesia

52270 Cystourethroscopy, with internal urethrotomy; female

52275 male

52276 Cystourethroscopy with direct vision internal urethrotomy

52277 Cystourethroscopy, with resection of external sphincter (sphincterotomy)

52281 Cystourethroscopy, with calibration and/or dilation of urethral stricture or stenosis, with or without meatotomy, with or without injection procedure for cystography, male or female

52282 Cystourethroscopy, with insertion of urethral stent

52283 Cystourethroscopy, with steroid injection into stricture

52285 Cystourethroscopy for treatment of the female urethral syndrome with any or all of the following: urethral meatotomy, urethral dilation, internal urethrotomy, lysis of urethrovaginal septal fibrosis, lateral incisions of the bladder neck, and fulguration of polyp(s) of urethra, bladder neck, and/or trigone

52290 Cystourethroscopy; with ureteral meatotomy, unilateral or bilateral

52300 with resection or fulguration of orthotopic ureterocele(s), unilateral or bilateral

52301 with resection or fulguration of ectopic ureterocele(s), unilateral or bilateral

52305 with incision or resection of orifice of bladder diverticulum, single or multiple

52310 Cystourethroscopy, with removal of foreign body, calculus, or ureteral stent from urethra or bladder (separate procedure); simple

52315 complicated

52317 Litholapaxy: crushing or fragmentation of calculus by any means in bladder and removal of fragments; simple or small (less than 2.5 cm)

52318 complicated or large (over 2.5 cm)

Ureter and Pelvis

Surgical cystourethroscopy always includes diagnostic cystourethroscopy. To report a diagnostic cystourethroscopy, use 52351.

Do not report 52351 in conjunction with 52341-52346, 52352-52355.

The insertion and removal of a temporary stent during diagnostic or therapeutic cystourethroscopic intervention(s) is included in 52320-52355 and should not be reported separately.

To report insertion of a self-retaining, indwelling stent performed during cystourethroscopic diagnostic or therapeutic intervention(s), use code 52332, in addition to primary procedure(s) performed, and append the modifier '-51'. Code 52332 is used to report a unilateral procedure unless otherwise specified.

For bilateral insertion of self-retaining, indwelling ureteral stents, use code 52332, and append the modifier '-50'.

To report cystourethroscopic removal of a self-retaining, indwelling ureteral stent, see codes 52310, 52315, and append the modifier '-58'.

52320 Cystourethroscopy (including ureteral catheterization); with removal of ureteral calculus

52325 with fragmentation of ureteral calculus (eg, ultrasonic or electro-hydraulic technique)

52327 with subureteric injection of implant material

52330 with manipulation, without removal of ureteral calculus

52332 Cystourethroscopy, with insertion of indwelling ureteral stent (eg, Gibbons or double-J type)

52334 Cystourethroscopy with insertion of ureteral guide wire through kidney to establish a percutaneous nephrostomy, retrograde

(For percutaneous nephrostolithotomy, see 50080, 50081; for establishment of nephrostomy tract only, use 50395)

52341 Cystourethroscopy; with treatment of ureteral stricture (eg, balloon dilation, laser, electrocautery, and incision)

52342 with treatment of ureteropelvic junction stricture (eg, balloon dilation, laser, electrocautery, and incision)

52343 with treatment of intra-renal stricture (eg, balloon dilation, laser, electrocautery, and incision)

52344 Cystourethroscopy with ureteroscopy; with treatment of ureteral stricture (eg, balloon dilation, laser, electrocautery, and incision)

52345 with treatment of ureteropelvic junction stricture (eg, balloon dilation, laser, electrocautery, and incision)

52346 with treatment of intra-renal stricture (eg, balloon dilation, laser, electrocautery, and incision)

52347 Cystourethroscopy with transurethral resection or incision of ejaculatory ducts

52351 Cystourethroscopy, with ureteroscopy and/or pyeloscopy; diagnostic

(For radiological supervision and interpretation, use 74485)

(Do not report 52351 in conjunction with 52341-52346, 52352-52355)

52352 with removal or manipulation of calculus (ureteral catheterization is included)

52353 with lithotripsy (ureteral catheterization is included)

52354 with biopsy and/or fulguration of ureteral or renal pelvic lesion

52355 with resection of ureteral or renal pelvic tumor

Vesical Neck and Prostate

52400 Cystourethroscopy with incision, fulguration, or resection of congenital posterior urethral valves, or congenital obstructive hypertrophic mucosal folds

52450 Transurethral incision of prostate

52500 Transurethral resection of bladder neck (separate procedure)

52510 Transurethral balloon dilation of the prostatic urethra

52601 Transurethral electrosurgical resection of prostate, including control of postoperative bleeding, complete (vasectomy, meatotomy, cystourethroscopy, urethral calibration and/or dilation, and internal urethrotomy are included)

(For other approaches, see 55801-55845)

52606 Transurethral fulguration for postoperative bleeding occurring after the usual follow-up time

52612 Transurethral resection of prostate; first stage of two-stage resection (partial resection)

52614 second stage of two-stage resection (resection completed)

52620 Transurethral resection; of residual obstructive tissue after 90 days postoperative

52630 of regrowth of obstructive tissue longer than one year postoperative

52640 of postoperative bladder neck contracture

52647 Non-contact laser coagulation of prostate, including control of postoperative bleeding, complete (vasectomy, meatotomy, cystourethroscopy, urethral calibration and/or dilation, and internal urethrotomy are included)

52648 Contact laser vaporization with or without transurethral resection of prostate, including control of postoperative bleeding, complete (vasectomy, meatotomy, cystourethroscopy, urethral calibration and/or dilation, and internal urethrotomy are included)

52700 Transurethral drainage of prostatic abscess

Urethra

(For endoscopy, see cystoscopy, urethroscopy, cystourethroscopy, 52000-52700)

(For injection procedure for urethrocystography, see 51600-51610)

Incision

53000 Urethrotomy or urethrostomy, external (separate procedure); pendulous urethra

53010 perineal urethra, external

53020 Meatotomy, cutting of meatus (separate procedure); except infant

53025 infant

(Do not report modifier '-63' in conjunction with 53025)

53040 Drainage of deep periurethral abscess

(For subcutaneous abscess, see 10060, 10061)

53060 Drainage of Skene's gland abscess or cyst

53080 Drainage of perineal urinary extravasation; uncomplicated (separate procedure)

53085 complicated

Excision

53200 Biopsy of urethra

53210 Urethrectomy, total, including cystostomy; female

53215 male

53220 Excision or fulguration of carcinoma of urethra

53230 Excision of urethral diverticulum (separate procedure); female

53235 male

53240 Marsupialization of urethral diverticulum, male or female

53250 Excision of bulbourethral gland (Cowper's gland)

53260 Excision or fulguration; urethral polyp(s), distal urethra

(For endoscopic approach, see 52214, 52224)

53265 urethral caruncle

53270 Skene's glands

53275 urethral prolapse

Repair

(For hypospadias, see 54300-54352)

53400 Urethroplasty; first stage, for fistula, diverticulum, or stricture (eg, Johannsen type)

53405 second stage (formation of urethra), including urinary diversion

53410 Urethroplasty, one-stage reconstruction of male anterior urethra

53415 Urethroplasty, transpubic or perineal, one stage, for reconstruction or repair of prostatic or membranous urethra

53420 Urethroplasty, two-stage reconstruction or repair of prostatic or membranous urethra; first stage

53425 second stage

53430 Urethroplasty, reconstruction of female urethra

53431 Urethroplasty with tubularization of posterior urethra and/or lower bladder for incontinence (eg, Tenago, Leadbetter procedure)

53440 Sling operation for correction of male urinary incontinence (eg, fascia or synthetic)

53442 Removal or revision of sling for male urinary incontinence (eg, fascia or synthetic)

(53443 has been deleted. To report, use 53431)

53444 Insertion of tandem cuff (dual cuff)

53445 Insertion of inflatable urethral/bladder neck sphincter, including placement of pump, reservoir, and cuff

53446 Removal of inflatable urethral/bladder neck sphincter, including pump, reservoir, and cuff

53447 Removal and replacement of inflatable urethral/bladder neck sphincter including pump, reservoir, and cuff at the same operative session

53448 Removal and replacement of inflatable urethral/bladder neck sphincter including pump, reservoir, and cuff through an infected field at the same operative session including irrigation and debridement of infected tissue

(Do not report 11040-11043 in addition to 53448)

53449 Repair of inflatable urethral/bladder neck sphincter, including pump, reservoir, and cuff

53450 Urethromeatoplasty, with mucosal advancement

(For meatotomy, see 53020, 53025)

53460 Urethromeatoplasty, with partial excision of distal urethral segment (Richardson type procedure)

● **53500** Urethrolysis, transvaginal, secondary, open, including cystourethroscopy (eg, postsurgical obstruction, scarring)

►(For urethrolysis by retropubic approach, use 53899)◄

►(Do not report 53500 in conjunction with 52000)◄

53502 Urethrorrhaphy, suture of urethral wound or injury, female

53505 Urethrorrhaphy, suture of urethral wound or injury; penile

53510 perineal

53515 prostatomembranous

53520 Closure of urethrostomy or urethrocutaneous fistula, male (separate procedure)

(For closure of urethrovaginal fistula, use 57310)

(For closure of urethrorectal fistula, see 45820, 45825)

Manipulation

(For radiological supervision and interpretation, use 74485)

53600 Dilation of urethral stricture by passage of sound or urethral dilator, male; initial

53601 subsequent

53605 Dilation of urethral stricture or vesical neck by passage of sound or urethral dilator, male, general or conduction (spinal) anesthesia

53620 Dilation of urethral stricture by passage of filiform and follower, male; initial

53621 subsequent

53660 Dilation of female urethra including suppository and/or instillation; initial

53661 subsequent

53665 Dilation of female urethra, general or conduction (spinal) anesthesia

(53670 has been deleted. To report, see 51701, 51702)

(53675 has been deleted. To report, use 51703)

Other Procedures

53850 Transurethral destruction of prostate tissue; by microwave thermotherapy

53852 by radiofrequency thermotherapy

53853 by water-induced thermotherapy

53899 Unlisted procedure, urinary system

Notes

Male Genital System

Penis

Incision

54000 Slitting of prepuce, dorsal or lateral (separate procedure); newborn

(Do not report modifier '-63' in conjunction with 54000)

54001 except newborn

54015 Incision and drainage of penis, deep

(For skin and subcutaneous abscess, see 10060-10160)

Destruction

54050 Destruction of lesion(s), penis (eg, condyloma, papilloma, molluscum contagiosum, herpetic vesicle), simple; chemical

54055 electrodesiccation

54056 cryosurgery

54057 laser surgery

54060 surgical excision

54065 Destruction of lesion(s), penis (eg, condyloma, papilloma, molluscum contagiosum, herpetic vesicle), extensive (eg, laser surgery, electrosurgery, cryosurgery, chemosurgery)

(For destruction or excision of other lesions, see **Integumentary System**)

Excision

54100 Biopsy of penis; (separate procedure)

54105 deep structures

54110 Excision of penile plaque (Peyronie disease);

54111 with graft to 5 cm in length

54112 with graft greater than 5 cm in length

54115 Removal foreign body from deep penile tissue (eg, plastic implant)

54120 Amputation of penis; partial

54125 complete

54130 Amputation of penis, radical; with bilateral inguinofemoral lymphadenectomy

54135 in continuity with bilateral pelvic lymphadenectomy, including external iliac, hypogastric and obturator nodes

(For lymphadenectomy (separate procedure), see 38760-38770)

54150 Circumcision, using clamp or other device; newborn

(Do not report modifier '-63' in conjunction with 54150)

54152 except newborn

54160 Circumcision, surgical excision other than clamp, device or dorsal slit; newborn

(Do not report modifier '-63' in conjunction with 54160)

54161 except newborn

54162 Lysis or excision of penile post-circumcision adhesions

54163 Repair incomplete circumcision

54164 Frenulotomy of penis

(Do not report 54164 with circumcision codes 54150-54161, 54162, 54163)

Introduction

54200 Injection procedure for Peyronie disease;

54205 with surgical exposure of plaque

54220 Irrigation of corpora cavernosa for priapism

54230 Injection procedure for corpora cavernosography

(For radiological supervision and interpretation, use 74445)

54231 Dynamic cavernosometry, including intracavernosal injection of vasoactive drugs (eg, papaverine, phentolamine)

54235 Injection of corpora cavernosa with pharmacologic agent(s) (eg, papaverine, phentolamine)

54240 Penile plethysmography

54250 Nocturnal penile tumescence and/or rigidity test

Repair

(For other urethroplasties, see 53400-53430)

(For penile revascularization, use 37788)

54300 Plastic operation of penis for straightening of chordee (eg, hypospadias), with or without mobilization of urethra

54304 Plastic operation on penis for correction of chordee or for first stage hypospadias repair with or without transplantation of prepuce and/or skin flaps

54308 Urethroplasty for second stage hypospadias repair (including urinary diversion); less than 3 cm

54312 greater than 3 cm

54316 Urethroplasty for second stage hypospadias repair (including urinary diversion) with free skin graft obtained from site other than genitalia

54318 Urethroplasty for third stage hypospadias repair to release penis from scrotum (eg, third stage Cecil repair)

54322 One stage distal hypospadias repair (with or without chordee or circumcision); with simple meatal advancement (eg, Magpi, V-flap)

54324 with urethroplasty by local skin flaps (eg, flip-flap, prepucial flap)

54326 with urethroplasty by local skin flaps and mobilization of urethra

54328 with extensive dissection to correct chordee and urethroplasty with local skin flaps, skin graft patch, and/or island flap

54332 One stage proximal penile or penoscrotal hypospadias repair requiring extensive dissection to correct chordee and urethroplasty by use of skin graft tube and/or island flap

54336 One stage perineal hypospadias repair requiring extensive dissection to correct chordee and urethroplasty by use of skin graft tube and/or island flap

54340 Repair of hypospadias complications (ie, fistula, stricture, diverticula); by closure, incision, or excision, simple

54344 requiring mobilization of skin flaps and urethroplasty with flap or patch graft

54348 requiring extensive dissection and urethroplasty with flap, patch or tubed graft (includes urinary diversion)

54352 Repair of hypospadias cripple requiring extensive dissection and excision of previously constructed structures including re-release of chordee and reconstruction of urethra and penis by use of local skin as grafts and island flaps and skin brought in as flaps or grafts

54360 Plastic operation on penis to correct angulation

54380 Plastic operation on penis for epispadias distal to external sphincter;

54385 with incontinence

54390 with exstrophy of bladder

54400 Insertion of penile prosthesis; non-inflatable (semi-rigid)

54401 inflatable (self-contained)

(54402 has been deleted. To report, see 54415, 54416)

54405 Insertion of multi-component, inflatable penile prosthesis, including placement of pump, cylinders, and reservoir

(For reduced services, report 54405 with modifier '-52')

54406 Removal of all components of a multi-component, inflatable penile prosthesis without replacement of prosthesis

(For reduced services, report 54406 with modifier '-52')

(54407 has been deleted. To report, see 54406, 54408, 54410)

54408 Repair of component(s) of a multi-component, inflatable penile prosthesis

(54409 has been deleted. To report, use 54408)

54410 Removal and replacement of all component(s) of a multi-component, inflatable penile prosthesis at the same operative session

54411 Removal and replacement of all components of a multi-component inflatable penile prosthesis through an infected field at the same operative session, including irrigation and debridement of infected tissue

(For reduced services, report 54411 with modifier '-52')

(Do not report 11040-11043 in addition to 54411)

54415 Removal of non-inflatable (semi-rigid) or inflatable (self-contained) penile prosthesis, without replacement of prosthesis

54416 Removal and replacement of non-inflatable (semi-rigid) or inflatable (self-contained) penile prosthesis at the same operative session

54417 Removal and replacement of non-inflatable (semi-rigid) or inflatable (self-contained) penile prosthesis through an infected field at the same operative session, including irrigation and debridement of infected tissue

(Do not report 11040-11043 in addition to 54417)

54420 Corpora cavernosa-saphenous vein shunt (priapism operation), unilateral or bilateral

54430 Corpora cavernosa-corpus spongiosum shunt (priapism operation), unilateral or bilateral

54435 Corpora cavernosa-glans penis fistulization (eg, biopsy needle, Winter procedure, rongeur, or punch) for priapism

54440 Plastic operation of penis for injury

Manipulation

54450 Foreskin manipulation including lysis of preputial adhesions and stretching

Testis

Excision

54500 Biopsy of testis, needle (separate procedure)

(For fine needle aspiration, see 10021, 10022)

(For evaluation of fine needle aspirate, see 88172, 88173)

54505 Biopsy of testis, incisional (separate procedure)

(When combined with vasogram, seminal vesiculogram, or epididymogram, use 55300)

(54510 has been deleted. To report, use 54512)

54512 Excision of extraparenchymal lesion of testis

54520 Orchiectomy, simple (including subcapsular), with or without testicular prosthesis, scrotal or inguinal approach

54522 Orchiectomy, partial

54530 Orchiectomy, radical, for tumor; inguinal approach

54535 with abdominal exploration

(For orchiectomy with repair of hernia, see 49505 or 49507 and 54520)

(For radical retroperitoneal lymphadenectomy, use 38780)

54550 Exploration for undescended testis (inguinal or scrotal area)

54560 Exploration for undescended testis with abdominal exploration

Repair

54600 Reduction of torsion of testis, surgical, with or without fixation of contralateral testis

54620 Fixation of contralateral testis (separate procedure)

54640 Orchiopexy, inguinal approach, with or without hernia repair

(For inguinal hernia repair performed in conjunction with inguinal orchiopexy, see 49495-49525)

54650 Orchiopexy, abdominal approach, for intra-abdominal testis (eg, Fowler-Stephens)

(For laparoscopic approach, use 54692)

54660 Insertion of testicular prosthesis (separate procedure)

54670 Suture or repair of testicular injury

54680 Transplantation of testis(es) to thigh (because of scrotal destruction)

Laparoscopy

Surgical laparoscopy always includes diagnostic laparoscopy. To report a diagnostic laparoscopy (peritoneoscopy) (separate procedure), use 49320.

54690 Laparoscopy, surgical; orchiectomy

54692 orchiopexy for intra-abdominal testis

54699 Unlisted laparoscopy procedure, testis

Epididymis

Incision

54700 Incision and drainage of epididymis, testis and/or scrotal space (eg, abscess or hematoma)

Excision

54800 Biopsy of epididymis, needle

(For fine needle aspiration, see 10021, 10022)

(For evaluation of fine needle aspirate, see 88172, 88173)

54820 Exploration of epididymis, with or without biopsy

54830 Excision of local lesion of epididymis

54840 Excision of spermatocele, with or without epididymectomy

54860 Epididymectomy; unilateral

54861 bilateral

Repair

54900 Epididymovasostomy, anastomosis of epididymis to vas deferens; unilateral

54901 bilateral

(For operating microscope, use 69990)

Tunica Vaginalis

Incision

55000 Puncture aspiration of hydrocele, tunica vaginalis, with or without injection of medication

Excision

55040 Excision of hydrocele; unilateral

55041 bilateral

(With hernia repair, see 49495-49501)

Repair

55060 Repair of tunica vaginalis hydrocele (Bottle type)

Scrotum

Incision

55100 Drainage of scrotal wall abscess

(See also 54700)

55110 Scrotal exploration

55120 Removal of foreign body in scrotum

Excision

(For excision of local lesion of skin of scrotum, see **Integumentary System**)

55150 Resection of scrotum

Repair

55175 Scrotoplasty; simple

55180 complicated

Vas Deferens

Incision

55200 Vasotomy, cannulization with or without incision of vas, unilateral or bilateral (separate procedure)

Excision

55250 Vasectomy, unilateral or bilateral (separate procedure), including postoperative semen examination(s)

Introduction

55300 Vasotomy for vasograms, seminal vesiculograms, or epididymograms, unilateral or bilateral

(For radiological supervision and interpretation, use 74440)

(When combined with biopsy of testis, see 54505 and use modifier '-51')

Repair

55400 Vasovasostomy, vasovasorrhaphy

(For operating microscope, use 69990)

Suture

55450 Ligation (percutaneous) of vas deferens, unilateral or bilateral (separate procedure)

Spermatic Cord

Excision

55500 Excision of hydrocele of spermatic cord, unilateral (separate procedure)

55520 Excision of lesion of spermatic cord (separate procedure)

55530 Excision of varicocele or ligation of spermatic veins for varicocele; (separate procedure)

55535 abdominal approach

55540 with hernia repair

Laparoscopy

Surgical laparoscopy always includes diagnostic laparoscopy. To report a diagnostic laparoscopy (peritoneoscopy) (separate procedure), use 49320.

55550 Laparoscopy, surgical, with ligation of spermatic veins for varicocele

55559 Unlisted laparoscopy procedure, spermatic cord

Seminal Vesicles

Incision

55600 Vesiculotomy;

55605 complicated

Excision

55650 Vesiculectomy, any approach

55680 Excision of Mullerian duct cyst

(For injection procedure, see 52010, 55300)

Prostate

Incision

55700 Biopsy, prostate; needle or punch, single or multiple, any approach

(If imaging guidance is performed, use 76942)

(For fine needle aspiration, see 10021, 10022)

(For evaluation of fine needle aspirate, see 88172, 88173)

55705 incisional, any approach

55720 Prostatotomy, external drainage of prostatic abscess, any approach; simple

55725 complicated

(For transurethral drainage, use 52700)

Excision

(For transurethral removal of prostate, see 52601-52640)

(For transurethral destruction of prostate, see 53850-53852)

(For limited pelvic lymphadenectomy for staging (separate procedure), use 38562)

(For independent node dissection, see 38770-38780)

55801 Prostatectomy, perineal, subtotal (including control of postoperative bleeding, vasectomy, meatotomy, urethral calibration and/or dilation, and internal urethrotomy)

55810 Prostatectomy, perineal radical;

55812 with lymph node biopsy(s) (limited pelvic lymphadenectomy)

55815 with bilateral pelvic lymphadenectomy, including external iliac, hypogastric and obturator nodes

(If 55815 is carried out on separate days, use 38770 with modifier '-50' and 55810)

55821 Prostatectomy (including control of postoperative bleeding, vasectomy, meatotomy, urethral calibration and/or dilation, and internal urethrotomy); suprapubic, subtotal, one or two stages

55831 retropubic, subtotal

55840 Prostatectomy, retropubic radical, with or without nerve sparing;

55842 with lymph node biopsy(s) (limited pelvic lymphadenectomy)

55845 with bilateral pelvic lymphadenectomy, including external iliac, hypogastric, and obturator nodes

(If 55845 is carried out on separate days, use 38770 with modifier '-50' and 55840)

(For laparoscopic retropubic radical prostatectomy, use 55866)

55859 Transperineal placement of needles or catheters into prostate for interstitial radioelement application, with or without cystoscopy

(For interstitial radioelement application, see 77776-77778)

(For ultrasonic guidance for interstitial radioelement application, use 76965)

55860 Exposure of prostate, any approach, for insertion of radioactive substance;

(For application of interstitial radioelement, see 77776-77778)

55862 with lymph node biopsy(s) (limited pelvic lymphadenectomy)

55865 with bilateral pelvic lymphadenectomy, including external iliac, hypogastric and obturator nodes

Laparoscopy

Surgical laparoscopy always includes diagnostic laparoscopy. To report a diagnostic laparoscopy (peritoneoscopy) (separate procedure), use 49320.

55866 Laparoscopy, surgical prostatectomy, retropubic radical, including nerve sparing

(For open procedure, use 55840)

Other Procedures

(For artificial insemination, see 58321, 58322)

55870 Electroejaculation

55873 Cryosurgical ablation of the prostate (includes ultrasonic guidance for interstitial cryosurgical probe placement)

55899 Unlisted procedure, male genital system

Intersex Surgery

55970 Intersex surgery; male to female

55980 female to male

Notes

Female Genital System

(For pelvic laparotomy, use 49000)

(For excision or destruction of endometriomas, open method, see 49200, 49201)

(For paracentesis, see 49080, 49081)

(For secondary closure of abdominal wall evisceration or disruption, use 49900)

(For fulguration or excision of lesions, laparoscopic approach, use 58662)

(For chemotherapy, see 96400-96549)

Vulva, Perineum and Introitus

Definitions

The following definitions apply to the vulvectomy codes (56620-56640).

A ***simple*** procedure is the removal of skin and superficial subcutaneous tissues.

A ***radical*** procedure is the removal of skin and deep subcutaneous tissue.

A ***partial*** procedure is the removal of less than 80% of the vulvar area.

A ***complete*** procedure is the removal of greater than 80% of the vulvar area.

Incision

(For incision and drainage of sebaceous cyst, furuncle, or abscess, see 10040, 10060, 10061)

56405 Incision and drainage of vulva or perineal abscess

56420 Incision and drainage of Bartholin's gland abscess

(For incision and drainage of Skene's gland abscess or cyst, use 53060)

56440 Marsupialization of Bartholin's gland cyst

56441 Lysis of labial adhesions

Destruction

56501 Destruction of lesion(s), vulva; simple (eg, laser surgery, electrosurgery, cryosurgery, chemosurgery)

56515 extensive (eg, laser surgery, electrosurgery, cryosurgery, chemosurgery)

(For destruction of Skene's gland cyst or abscess, use 53270)

(For cautery destruction of urethral caruncle, use 53265)

Excision

56605 Biopsy of vulva or perineum (separate procedure); one lesion

+ 56606 each separate additional lesion (List separately in addition to code for primary procedure)

(Use 56606 in conjunction with code 56605)

(For excision of local lesion, see 11420-11426, 11620-11626)

56620 Vulvectomy simple; partial

56625 complete

(For skin graft, see 15000 et seq)

56630 Vulvectomy, radical, partial;

(For skin graft, if used, see 15000, 15120, 15121, 15240, 15241)

56631 with unilateral inguinofemoral lymphadenectomy

56632 with bilateral inguinofemoral lymphadenectomy

56633 Vulvectomy, radical, complete;

56634 with unilateral inguinofemoral lymphadenectomy

56637 with bilateral inguinofemoral lymphadenectomy

56640 Vulvectomy, radical, complete, with inguinofemoral, iliac, and pelvic lymphadenectomy

(For lymphadenectomy, see 38760-38780)

56700 Partial hymenectomy or revision of hymenal ring

56720 Hymenotomy, simple incision

56740 Excision of Bartholin's gland or cyst

(For excision of Skene's gland, use 53270)

(For excision of urethral caruncle, use 53265)

(For excision or fulguration of urethral carcinoma, use 53220)

(For excision or marsupialization of urethral diverticulum, see 53230, 53240)

Repair

(For repair of urethra for mucosal prolapse, use 53275)

56800 Plastic repair of introitus

56805 Clitoroplasty for intersex state

56810 Perineoplasty, repair of perineum, nonobstetrical (separate procedure)

(See also 56800)

(For repair of wounds to genitalia, see 12001-12007, 12041-12047, 13131-13133)

(For repair of recent injury of vagina and perineum, nonobstetrical, use 57210)

(For anal sphincteroplasty, see 46750, 46751)

(For episiorrhaphy, episioperineorrhaphy for recent injury of vulva and/or perineum, nonobstetrical, use 57210)

Endoscopy

56820 Colposcopy of the vulva;

56821 with biopsy(s)

(For colposcopic examinations/procedures involving the vagina, see 57420, 57421; cervix, see 57452-57461)

Vagina

Incision

57000 Colpotomy; with exploration

57010 with drainage of pelvic abscess

57020 Colpocentesis (separate procedure)

57022 Incision and drainage of vaginal hematoma; obstetrical/postpartum

57023 non-obstetrical (eg, post-trauma, spontaneous bleeding)

Destruction

57061 Destruction of vaginal lesion(s); simple (eg, laser surgery, electrosurgery, cryosurgery, chemosurgery)

57065 extensive (eg, laser surgery, electrosurgery, cryosurgery, chemosurgery)

Excision

57100 Biopsy of vaginal mucosa; simple (separate procedure)

57105 extensive, requiring suture (including cysts)

57106 Vaginectomy, partial removal of vaginal wall;

57107 with removal of paravaginal tissue (radical vaginectomy)

57109 with removal of paravaginal tissue (radical vaginectomy) with bilateral total pelvic lymphadenectomy and para-aortic lymph node sampling (biopsy)

57110 Vaginectomy, complete removal of vaginal wall;

57111 with removal of paravaginal tissue (radical vaginectomy)

57112 with removal of paravaginal tissue (radical vaginectomy) with bilateral total pelvic lymphadenectomy and para-aortic lymph node sampling (biopsy)

57120 Colpocleisis (Le Fort type)

57130 Excision of vaginal septum

57135 Excision of vaginal cyst or tumor

Introduction

57150 Irrigation of vagina and/or application of medicament for treatment of bacterial, parasitic, or fungoid disease

57155 Insertion of uterine tandems and/or vaginal ovoids for clinical brachytherapy

(For insertion of radioelement sources or ribbons, see 77761-77763, 77781-77784)

57160 Fitting and insertion of pessary or other intravaginal support device

57170 Diaphragm or cervical cap fitting with instructions

57180 Introduction of any hemostatic agent or pack for spontaneous or traumatic nonobstetrical vaginal hemorrhage (separate procedure)

Repair

(For urethral suspension, Marshall-Marchetti-Krantz type, abdominal approach, see 51840, 51841)

(For laparoscopic suspension, use 51990)

57200 Colporrhaphy, suture of injury of vagina (nonobstetrical)

57210 Colpoperineorrhaphy, suture of injury of vagina and/or perineum (nonobstetrical)

57220 Plastic operation on urethral sphincter, vaginal approach (eg, Kelly urethral plication)

57230 Plastic repair of urethrocele

57240 Anterior colporrhaphy, repair of cystocele with or without repair of urethrocele

57250 Posterior colporrhaphy, repair of rectocele with or without perineorrhaphy

(For repair of rectocele (separate procedure) without posterior colporrhaphy, use 45560)

57260 Combined anteroposterior colporrhaphy;

57265 with enterocele repair

57268 Repair of enterocele, vaginal approach (separate procedure)

57270 Repair of enterocele, abdominal approach (separate procedure)

57280 Colpopexy, abdominal approach

57282 Sacrospinous ligament fixation for prolapse of vagina

57284 Paravaginal defect repair (including repair of cystocele, stress urinary incontinence, and/or incomplete vaginal prolapse)

57287 Removal or revision of sling for stress incontinence (eg, fascia or synthetic)

57288 Sling operation for stress incontinence (eg, fascia or synthetic)

(For laparoscopic approach, use 51992)

57289 Pereyra procedure, including anterior colporrhaphy

57291 Construction of artificial vagina; without graft

57292 with graft

57300 Closure of rectovaginal fistula; vaginal or transanal approach

57305 abdominal approach

57307 abdominal approach, with concomitant colostomy

57308 transperineal approach, with perineal body reconstruction, with or without levator plication

57310 Closure of urethrovaginal fistula;

57311 with bulbocavernosus transplant

57320 Closure of vesicovaginal fistula; vaginal approach

(For concomitant cystostomy, see 51005-51040)

57330 transvesical and vaginal approach

(For abdominal approach, use 51900)

57335 Vaginoplasty for intersex state

Manipulation

57400 Dilation of vagina under anesthesia

57410 Pelvic examination under anesthesia

57415 Removal of impacted vaginal foreign body (separate procedure) under anesthesia

(For removal without anesthesia of an impacted vaginal foreign body, use the appropriate E/M code)

Endoscopy

(For speculoscopy, see Category III codes 0031T, 0032T)

57420 Colposcopy of the entire vagina, with cervix if present;

57421 with biopsy(s)

(For colposcopic visualization of cervix and adjacent upper vagina, use 57452)

(When reporting colposcopies of multiple sites, use modifier '-51' as appropriate. For colposcopic examinations/procedures involving the vulva, see 56820, 56821; cervix, see 57452-57461)

(57450, 57451 have been deleted)

● **57425** Laparoscopy, surgical, colpopexy (suspension of vaginal apex)

Cervix Uteri

(For cervicography, see Category III code 0003T)

Endoscopy

(For colposcopic examinations/procedures involving the vulva, see 56820, 56821; vagina, see 57420, 57421)

57452 Colposcopy of the cervix including upper/adjacent vagina;

(Do not report 57452 in addition to 57454-57461)

57454 with biopsy(s) of the cervix and endocervical curettage

57455 with biopsy(s) of the cervix

57456 with endocervical curettage

57460 with loop electrode biopsy(s) of the cervix

57461 with loop electrode conization of the cervix

(Do not report 57456 in addition to 57461)

Excision

(For radical surgical procedures, see 58200-58240)

57500 Biopsy, single or multiple, or local excision of lesion, with or without fulguration (separate procedure)

57505 Endocervical curettage (not done as part of a dilation and curettage)

57510 Cautery of cervix; electro or thermal

57511 cryocautery, initial or repeat

57513 laser ablation

57520 Conization of cervix, with or without fulguration, with or without dilation and curettage, with or without repair; cold knife or laser

(See also 58120)

57522 loop electrode excision

57530 Trachelectomy (cervicectomy), amputation of cervix (separate procedure)

57531 Radical trachelectomy, with bilateral total pelvic lymphadenectomy and para-aortic lymph node sampling biopsy, with or without removal of tube(s), with or without removal of ovary(s)

(For radical abdominal hysterectomy, use 58210)

57540 Excision of cervical stump, abdominal approach;

57545 with pelvic floor repair

57550 Excision of cervical stump, vaginal approach;

57555 with anterior and/or posterior repair

57556 with repair of enterocele

(For insertion of intrauterine device, use 58300)

Repair

57700 Cerclage of uterine cervix, nonobstetrical

57720 Trachelorrhaphy, plastic repair of uterine cervix, vaginal approach

Manipulation

57800 Dilation of cervical canal, instrumental (separate procedure)

57820 Dilation and curettage of cervical stump

Corpus Uteri

Excision

58100 Endometrial sampling (biopsy) with or without endocervical sampling (biopsy), without cervical dilation, any method (separate procedure)

(For endocervical curettage only, use 57505)

58120 Dilation and curettage, diagnostic and/or therapeutic (nonobstetrical)

(For postpartum hemorrhage, use 59160)

58140 Myomectomy, excision of fibroid tumor(s) of uterus, 1 to 4 intramural myoma(s) with total weight of 250 grams or less and/or removal of surface myomas; abdominal approach

58145 vaginal approach

58146 Myomectomy, excision of fibroid tumor(s) of uterus, 5 or more intramural myomas and/or intramural myomas with total weight greater than 250 grams, abdominal approach

(Do not report 58146 in addition to 58140-58145, 58150-58240)

58150 Total abdominal hysterectomy (corpus and cervix), with or without removal of tube(s), with or without removal of ovary(s);

58152 with colpo-urethrocystopexy (eg, Marshall-Marchetti-Krantz, Burch)

(For urethrocystopexy without hysterectomy, see 51840, 51841)

58180 Supracervical abdominal hysterectomy (subtotal hysterectomy), with or without removal of tube(s), with or without removal of ovary(s)

58200 Total abdominal hysterectomy, including partial vaginectomy, with para-aortic and pelvic lymph node sampling, with or without removal of tube(s), with or without removal of ovary(s)

58210 Radical abdominal hysterectomy, with bilateral total pelvic lymphadenectomy and para-aortic lymph node sampling (biopsy), with or without removal of tube(s), with or without removal of ovary(s)

(For radical hysterectomy with ovarian transposition, use also 58825)

58240 Pelvic exenteration for gynecologic malignancy, with total abdominal hysterectomy or cervicectomy, with or without removal of tube(s), with or without removal of ovary(s), with removal of bladder and ureteral transplantations, and/or abdominoperineal resection of rectum and colon and colostomy, or any combination thereof

(For pelvic exenteration for lower urinary tract or male genital malignancy, use 51597)

58260 Vaginal hysterectomy, for uterus 250 grams or less;

58262 with removal of tube(s), and/or ovary(s)

58263 with removal of tube(s), and/or ovary(s), with repair of enterocele

58267 with colpo-urethrocystopexy (Marshall-Marchetti-Krantz type, Pereyra type) with or without endoscopic control

58270 with repair of enterocele

(For repair of enterocele with removal of tubes and/or ovaries, use 58263)

58275 Vaginal hysterectomy, with total or partial vaginectomy;

58280 with repair of enterocele

58285 Vaginal hysterectomy, radical (Schauta type operation)

58290 Vaginal hysterectomy, for uterus greater than 250 grams;

58291 with removal of tube(s) and/or ovary(s)

58292 with removal of tube(s) and/or ovary(s), with repair of enterocele

58293 with colpo-urethrocystopexy (Marshall-Marchetti-Krantz type, Pereyra type) with or without endoscopic control

58294 with repair of enterocele

Introduction

(For insertion/removal of implantable contraceptive capsules, see 11975, 11976, 11977)

58300 Insertion of intrauterine device (IUD)

58301 Removal of intrauterine device (IUD)

58321 Artificial insemination; intra-cervical

58322 intra-uterine

58323 Sperm washing for artificial insemination

▲ **58340** Catheterization and introduction of saline or contrast material for saline infusion sonohysterography (SIS) or hysterosalpingography

(For radiological supervision and interpretation of ►saline infusion sonohysterography,◄ use 76831)

(For radiological supervision and interpretation of hysterosalpingography, use 74740)

(For endometrial cryoablation with ultrasonic guidance, use Category III code 0009T)

Surgery: Male/Female Genital System

58345 Transcervical introduction of fallopian tube catheter for diagnosis and/or re-establishing patency (any method), with or without hysterosalpingography

(For radiological supervision and interpretation, use 74742)

58346 Insertion of Heyman capsules for clinical brachytherapy

(For insertion of radioelement sources or ribbons, see 77761-77763, 77781-77784)

58350 Chromotubation of oviduct, including materials

(For materials supplied by physician, use 99070)

58353 Endometrial ablation, thermal, without hysteroscopic guidance

(For hysteroscopic procedure, use 58563)

Repair

58400 Uterine suspension, with or without shortening of round ligaments, with or without shortening of sacrouterine ligaments; (separate procedure)

58410 with presacral sympathectomy

58520 Hysterorrhaphy, repair of ruptured uterus (nonobstetrical)

58540 Hysteroplasty, repair of uterine anomaly (Strassman type)

(For closure of vesicouterine fistula, use 51920)

Laparoscopy/Hysteroscopy

Surgical laparoscopy always includes diagnostic laparoscopy. To report a diagnostic laparoscopy (peritoneoscopy) (separate procedure), use 49320. To report a diagnostic hysteroscopy (separate procedure), use 58555.

58545 Laparoscopy, surgical, myomectomy, excision; 1 to 4 intramural myomas with total weight of 250 grams or less and/or removal of surface myomas

58546 5 or more intramural myomas and/or intramural myomas with total weight greater than 250 grams

58550 Laparoscopy surgical, with vaginal hysterectomy, for uterus 250 grams or less;

(58551 has been deleted. To report see 58545, 58546)

58552 with removal of tube(s) and/or ovary(s)

58553 Laparoscopy, surgical, with vaginal hysterectomy, for uterus greater than 250 grams;

58554 with removal of tube(s) and/or ovary(s)

58555 Hysteroscopy, diagnostic (separate procedure)

58558 Hysteroscopy, surgical; with sampling (biopsy) of endometrium and/or polypectomy, with or without D & C

58559 with lysis of intrauterine adhesions (any method)

58560 with division or resection of intrauterine septum (any method)

58561 with removal of leiomyomata

58562 with removal of impacted foreign body

58563 with endometrial ablation (eg, endometrial resection, electrosurgical ablation, thermoablation)

58578 Unlisted laparoscopy procedure, uterus

58579 Unlisted hysteroscopy procedure, uterus

Oviduct/Ovary

Incision

58600 Ligation or transection of fallopian tube(s), abdominal or vaginal approach, unilateral or bilateral

58605 Ligation or transection of fallopian tube(s), abdominal or vaginal approach, postpartum, unilateral or bilateral, during same hospitalization (separate procedure)

(For laparoscopic procedures, use 58670, 58671)

+ **58611** Ligation or transection of fallopian tube(s) when done at the time of cesarean delivery or intra-abdominal surgery (not a separate procedure) (List separately in addition to code for primary procedure)

58615 Occlusion of fallopian tube(s) by device (eg, band, clip, Falope ring) vaginal or suprapubic approach

(For laparoscopic approach, use 58671)

Laparoscopy

Surgical laparoscopy always includes diagnostic laparoscopy. To report a diagnostic laparoscopy (peritoneoscopy) (separate procedure), use 49320.

(For laparoscopic biopsy of the ovary or fallopian tube, use 49321)

58660 Laparoscopy, surgical; with lysis of adhesions (salpingolysis, ovariolysis) (separate procedure)

58661 with removal of adnexal structures (partial or total oophorectomy and/or salpingectomy)

58662 with fulguration or excision of lesions of the ovary, pelvic viscera, or peritoneal surface by any method

58670 with fulguration of oviducts (with or without transection)

58671 with occlusion of oviducts by device (eg, band, clip, or Falope ring)

58672 with fimbrioplasty

58673 with salpingostomy (salpingoneostomy)

(Codes 58672 and 58673 are used to report unilateral procedures. For bilateral procedure, use modifier '-50')

58679 Unlisted laparoscopy procedure, oviduct, ovary

Excision

58700 Salpingectomy, complete or partial, unilateral or bilateral (separate procedure)

58720 Salpingo-oophorectomy, complete or partial, unilateral or bilateral (separate procedure)

Repair

58740 Lysis of adhesions (salpingolysis, ovariolysis)

(For laparoscopic approach, use 58660)

(For excision or destruction of endometriomas, open method, see 49200, 49201)

(For fulguration or excision of lesions, laparoscopic approach, use 58662)

58750 Tubotubal anastomosis

58752 Tubouterine implantation

58760 Fimbrioplasty

(For laparoscopic approach, use 58672)

58770 Salpingostomy (salpingoneostomy)

(For laparoscopic approach, use 58673)

Ovary

Incision

58800 Drainage of ovarian cyst(s), unilateral or bilateral, (separate procedure); vaginal approach

58805 abdominal approach

58820 Drainage of ovarian abscess; vaginal approach, open

58822 abdominal approach

58823 Drainage of pelvic abscess, transvaginal or transrectal approach, percutaneous (eg, ovarian, pericolic)

(For radiological supervision and interpretation, use 75989)

58825 Transposition, ovary(s)

Excision

58900 Biopsy of ovary, unilateral or bilateral (separate procedure)

(For laparoscopic biopsy of the ovary or fallopian tube, use 49321)

58920 Wedge resection or bisection of ovary, unilateral or bilateral

58925 Ovarian cystectomy, unilateral or bilateral

58940 Oophorectomy, partial or total, unilateral or bilateral;

58943 for ovarian, tubal or primary peritoneal malignancy, with para-aortic and pelvic lymph node biopsies, peritoneal washings, peritoneal biopsies, diaphragmatic assessments, with or without salpingectomy(s), with or without omentectomy

58950 Resection of ovarian, tubal or primary peritoneal malignancy with bilateral salpingo-oophorectomy and omentectomy;

58951 with total abdominal hysterectomy, pelvic and limited para-aortic lymphadenectomy

58952 with radical dissection for debulking (ie, radical excision or destruction, intra-abdominal or retroperitoneal tumors)

58953 Bilateral salpingo-oophorectomy with omentectomy, total abdominal hysterectomy and radical dissection for debulking;

58954 with pelvic lymphadenectomy and limited para-aortic lymphadenectomy

58960 Laparotomy, for staging or restaging of ovarian, tubal or primary peritoneal malignancy (second look), with or without omentectomy, peritoneal washing, biopsy of abdominal and pelvic peritoneum, diaphragmatic assessment with pelvic and limited para-aortic lymphadenectomy

In Vitro Fertilization

58970 Follicle puncture for oocyte retrieval, any method

(For radiological supervision and interpretation, use 76948)

58974 Embryo transfer, intrauterine

58976 Gamete, zygote, or embryo intrafallopian transfer, any method

Other Procedures

58999 Unlisted procedure, female genital system (nonobstetrical)

Maternity Care and Delivery

The services normally provided in uncomplicated maternity cases include antepartum care, delivery, and postpartum care.

Antepartum care includes the initial and subsequent history, physical examinations, recording of weight, blood pressures, fetal heart tones, routine chemical urinalysis, and monthly visits up to 28 weeks gestation, biweekly visits to 36 weeks gestation, and weekly visits until delivery. Any other visits or services within this time period should be coded separately.

Delivery services include admission to the hospital, the admission history and physical examination, management of uncomplicated labor, vaginal delivery (with or without episiotomy, with or without forceps), or cesarean delivery. Medical problems complicating labor and delivery management may require additional resources and should be identified by utilizing the codes in the **Medicine** and **Evaluation and Management Services** section in addition to codes for maternity care.

Postpartum care includes hospital and office visits following vaginal or cesarean section delivery.

For medical complications of pregnancy (eg, cardiac problems, neurological problems, diabetes, hypertension, toxemia, hyperemesis, pre-term labor, premature rupture of membranes), see services in the **Medicine** and **Evaluation and Management Services** section.

For surgical complications of pregnancy (eg, appendectomy, hernia, ovarian cyst, Bartholin cyst), see services in the **Surgery** section.

If a physician provides all or part of the antepartum and/or postpartum patient care but does not perform delivery due to termination of pregnancy by abortion or referral to another physician for delivery, see the antepartum and postpartum care codes 59425-59426 and 59430.

(For circumcision of newborn, see 54150, 54160)

Antepartum Services

(For insertion of transcervical or transvaginal fetal oximetry sensor, use Category III code 0021T)

59000 Amniocentesis; diagnostic

(For radiological supervision and interpretation, use 76946)

59001 therapeutic amniotic fluid reduction (includes ultrasound guidance)

59012 Cordocentesis (intrauterine), any method

(For radiological supervision and interpretation, use 76941)

59015 Chorionic villus sampling, any method

(For radiological supervision and interpretation, use 76945)

59020 Fetal contraction stress test

59025 Fetal non-stress test

59030 Fetal scalp blood sampling

59050 Fetal monitoring during labor by consulting physician (ie, non-attending physician) with written report; supervision and interpretation

59051 interpretation only

● **59070** Transabdominal amnioinfusion, including ultrasound guidance

● **59072** Fetal umbilical cord occlusion, including ultrasound guidance

● **59074** Fetal fluid drainage (eg, vesicocentesis, thoracocentesis, paracentesis), including ultrasound guidance

● **59076** Fetal shunt placement, including ultrasound guidance

►(For unlisted fetal invasive procedure, use 59897)◄

Excision

59100 Hysterotomy, abdominal (eg, for hydatidiform mole, abortion)

(When tubal ligation is performed at the same time as hysterotomy, use 58611 in addition to 59100)

59120 Surgical treatment of ectopic pregnancy; tubal or ovarian, requiring salpingectomy and/or oophorectomy, abdominal or vaginal approach

59121 tubal or ovarian, without salpingectomy and/or oophorectomy

59130 abdominal pregnancy

59135 interstitial, uterine pregnancy requiring total hysterectomy

59136 interstitial, uterine pregnancy with partial resection of uterus

59140 cervical, with evacuation

59150 Laparoscopic treatment of ectopic pregnancy; without salpingectomy and/or oophorectomy

59151 with salpingectomy and/or oophorectomy

59160 Curettage, postpartum

Introduction

(For intrauterine fetal transfusion, use 36460)

(For introduction of hypertonic solution and/or prostaglandins to initiate labor, see 59850-59857)

59200 Insertion of cervical dilator (eg, laminaria, prostaglandin) (separate procedure)

Repair

(For tracheloplasty, use 57700)

59300 Episiotomy or vaginal repair, by other than attending physician

59320 Cerclage of cervix, during pregnancy; vaginal

59325 abdominal

59350 Hysterorrhaphy of ruptured uterus

Vaginal Delivery, Antepartum and Postpartum Care

(For insertion of transcervical or transvaginal fetal oximetry sensor, use Category III code 0021T)

59400 Routine obstetric care including antepartum care, vaginal delivery (with or without episiotomy, and/or forceps) and postpartum care

59409 Vaginal delivery only (with or without episiotomy and/or forceps);

59410 including postpartum care

59412 External cephalic version, with or without tocolysis

(Use 59412 in addition to code(s) for delivery)

59414 Delivery of placenta (separate procedure)

(For 1-3 antepartum care visits, see appropriate E/M code(s))

59425 Antepartum care only; 4-6 visits

59426 7 or more visits

59430 Postpartum care only (separate procedure)

Cesarean Delivery

(For standby attendance for infant, use 99360)

(For insertion of transcervical or transvaginal fetal oximetry sensor, use Category III code 0021T)

59510 Routine obstetric care including antepartum care, cesarean delivery, and postpartum care

59514 Cesarean delivery only;

59515 including postpartum care

✚ **59525** Subtotal or total hysterectomy after cesarean delivery (List separately in addition to code for primary procedure)

(Use 59525 in conjunction with codes 59510, 59514, 59515, 59618, 59620, 59622)

Delivery After Previous Cesarean Delivery

Patients who have had a previous cesarean delivery and now present with the expectation of a vaginal delivery are coded using codes 59610-59622. If the patient has a successful vaginal delivery after a previous cesarean delivery (VBAC), use codes 59610-59614. If the attempt is unsuccessful and another cesarean delivery is carried out, use codes 59618-59622. To report elective cesarean deliveries use code 59510, 59514 or 59515.

(For insertion of transcervical or transvaginal fetal oximetry sensor, use Category III code 0021T)

59610 Routine obstetric care including antepartum care, vaginal delivery (with or without episiotomy, and/or forceps) and postpartum care, after previous cesarean delivery

59612 Vaginal delivery only, after previous cesarean delivery (with or without episiotomy and/or forceps);

59614 including postpartum care

59618 Routine obstetric care including antepartum care, cesarean delivery, and postpartum care, following attempted vaginal delivery after previous cesarean delivery

59620 Cesarean delivery only, following attempted vaginal delivery after previous cesarean delivery;

59622 including postpartum care

Abortion

(For medical treatment of spontaneous complete abortion, any trimester, use E/M codes 99201-99233)

59812 Treatment of incomplete abortion, any trimester, completed surgically

59820 Treatment of missed abortion, completed surgically; first trimester

59821 second trimester

59830 Treatment of septic abortion, completed surgically

59840 Induced abortion, by dilation and curettage

59841 Induced abortion, by dilation and evacuation

59850 Induced abortion, by one or more intra-amniotic injections (amniocentesis-injections), including hospital admission and visits, delivery of fetus and secundines;

59851 with dilation and curettage and/or evacuation

59852 with hysterotomy (failed intra-amniotic injection)

(For insertion of cervical dilator, use 59200)

59855 Induced abortion, by one or more vaginal suppositories (eg, prostaglandin) with or without cervical dilation (eg, laminaria), including hospital admission and visits, delivery of fetus and secundines;

59856 with dilation and curettage and/or evacuation

59857 with hysterotomy (failed medical evacuation)

Other Procedures

59866 Multifetal pregnancy reduction(s) (MPR)

59870 Uterine evacuation and curettage for hydatidiform mole

59871 Removal of cerclage suture under anesthesia (other than local)

● **59897** Unlisted fetal invasive procedure, including ultrasound guidance

59898 Unlisted laparoscopy procedure, maternity care and delivery

59899 Unlisted procedure, maternity care and delivery

Endocrine System

(For pituitary and pineal surgery, see **Nervous System**)

Thyroid Gland

Incision

60000 Incision and drainage of thyroglossal duct cyst, infected

Excision

60001 Aspiration and/or injection, thyroid cyst

(For fine needle aspiration, see 10021, 10022)

(If imaging guidance is performed, see 76360, 76942)

60100 Biopsy thyroid, percutaneous core needle

(If imaging guidance is performed, see 76003, 76360, 76393, 76942)

(For fine needle aspiration, use 10021 or 10022)

(For evaluation of fine needle aspirate, see 88172, 88173)

60200 Excision of cyst or adenoma of thyroid, or transection of isthmus

60210 Partial thyroid lobectomy, unilateral; with or without isthmusectomy

60212 with contralateral subtotal lobectomy, including isthmusectomy

60220 Total thyroid lobectomy, unilateral; with or without isthmusectomy

60225 with contralateral subtotal lobectomy, including isthmusectomy

60240 Thyroidectomy, total or complete

60252 Thyroidectomy, total or subtotal for malignancy; with limited neck dissection

60254 with radical neck dissection

60260 Thyroidectomy, removal of all remaining thyroid tissue following previous removal of a portion of thyroid

60270 Thyroidectomy, including substernal thyroid; sternal split or transthoracic approach

60271 cervical approach

60280 Excision of thyroglossal duct cyst or sinus;

60281 recurrent

(For thyroid ultrasonography, use 76536)

Parathyroid, Thymus, Adrenal Glands, ▸Pancreas◂, and Carotid Body

Excision

(For pituitary and pineal surgery, see **Nervous System**)

60500 Parathyroidectomy or exploration of parathyroid(s);

60502 re-exploration

60505 with mediastinal exploration, sternal split or transthoracic approach

✚ **60512** Parathyroid autotransplantation (List separately in addition to code for primary procedure)

(Use 60512 in conjunction with codes 60500, 60502, 60505, 60212, 60225, 60240, 60252, 60254, 60260, 60270, 60271)

60520 Thymectomy, partial or total; transcervical approach (separate procedure)

60521 sternal split or transthoracic approach, without radical mediastinal dissection (separate procedure)

60522 sternal split or transthoracic approach, with radical mediastinal dissection (separate procedure)

60540 Adrenalectomy, partial or complete, or exploration of adrenal gland with or without biopsy, transabdominal, lumbar or dorsal (separate procedure);

60545 with excision of adjacent retroperitoneal tumor

(For excision of remote or disseminated pheochromocytoma, see 49200, 49201)

(For laparoscopic approach, use 60650)

60600 Excision of carotid body tumor; without excision of carotid artery

60605 with excision of carotid artery

Laparoscopy

Surgical laparoscopy always includes diagnostic laparoscopy. To report a diagnostic laparoscopy (peritoneoscopy) (separate procedure), use 49320.

60650 Laparoscopy, surgical, with adrenalectomy, partial or complete, or exploration of adrenal gland with or without biopsy, transabdominal, lumbar or dorsal

60659 Unlisted laparoscopy procedure, endocrine system

Other Procedures

60699 Unlisted procedure, endocrine system

Notes

Nervous System

Skull, Meninges, and Brain

(For injection procedure for cerebral angiography, see 36100-36218)

(For injection procedure for ventriculography, see 61026, 61120)

(For injection procedure for pneumoencephalography, use 61055)

Injection, Drainage, or Aspiration

61000 Subdural tap through fontanelle, or suture, infant, unilateral or bilateral; initial

61001 subsequent taps

61020 Ventricular puncture through previous burr hole, fontanelle, suture, or implanted ventricular catheter/reservoir; without injection

61026 with injection of medication or other substance for diagnosis or treatment

61050 Cisternal or lateral cervical (C1-C2) puncture; without injection (separate procedure)

61055 with injection of medication or other substance for diagnosis or treatment (eg, C1-C2)

(For radiological supervision and interpretation, see **Radiology**)

61070 Puncture of shunt tubing or reservoir for aspiration or injection procedure

(For radiological supervision and interpretation, use 75809)

Twist Drill, Burr Hole(s), or Trephine

61105 Twist drill hole for subdural or ventricular puncture;

⃠ **61107** for implanting ventricular catheter or pressure recording device

(For intracranial neuroendoscopic ventricular catheter placement, use 62160)

61108 for evacuation and/or drainage of subdural hematoma

61120 Burr hole(s) for ventricular puncture (including injection of gas, contrast media, dye, or radioactive material)

61140 Burr hole(s) or trephine; with biopsy of brain or intracranial lesion

61150 with drainage of brain abscess or cyst

61151 with subsequent tapping (aspiration) of intracranial abscess or cyst

61154 Burr hole(s) with evacuation and/or drainage of hematoma, extradural or subdural

61156 Burr hole(s); with aspiration of hematoma or cyst, intracerebral

⃠ **61210** for implanting ventricular catheter, reservoir, EEG electrode(s) or pressure recording device (separate procedure)

(For intracranial neuroendoscopic ventricular catheter placement, use 62160)

61215 Insertion of subcutaneous reservoir, pump or continuous infusion system for connection to ventricular catheter

(For refilling and maintenance of an implantable infusion pump for spinal or brain drug therapy, use 95990)

(For chemotherapy, use 96450)

61250 Burr hole(s) or trephine, supratentorial, exploratory, not followed by other surgery

61253 Burr hole(s) or trephine, infratentorial, unilateral or bilateral

(If burr hole(s) or trephine are followed by craniotomy at same operative session, use 61304-61321; do not use 61250 or 61253)

Craniectomy or Craniotomy

61304 Craniectomy or craniotomy, exploratory; supratentorial

61305 infratentorial (posterior fossa)

61312 Craniectomy or craniotomy for evacuation of hematoma, supratentorial; extradural or subdural

61313 intracerebral

61314 Craniectomy or craniotomy for evacuation of hematoma, infratentorial; extradural or subdural

61315 intracerebellar

✚ **61316** Incision and subcutaneous placement of cranial bone graft (List separately in addition to code for primary procedure)

(Use 61316 in conjunction with codes 61304, 61312, 61313, 61322, 61323, 61340, 61570, 61571, 61680-61705)

61320 Craniectomy or craniotomy, drainage of intracranial abscess; supratentorial

61321 infratentorial

61322 Craniectomy or craniotomy, decompressive, with or without duraplasty, for treatment of intracranial hypertension, without evacuation of associated intraparenchymal hematoma; without lobectomy

(Do not report 61313 in addition to 61322)

(For subtemporal decompression, use 61340)

61323 with lobectomy

(Do not report 61313 in addition to 61323)

(For subtemporal decompression, use 61340)

61330 Decompression of orbit only, transcranial approach

61332 Exploration of orbit (transcranial approach); with biopsy

61333 with removal of lesion

61334 with removal of foreign body

61340 Subtemporal cranial decompression (pseudotumor cerebri, slit ventricle syndrome)

(For decompressive craniotomy or craniectomy for intracranial hypertension, without hematoma evacuation, see 61322, 61323)

61343 Craniectomy, suboccipital with cervical laminectomy for decompression of medulla and spinal cord, with or without dural graft (eg, Arnold-Chiari malformation)

61345 Other cranial decompression, posterior fossa

(For orbital decompression by lateral wall approach, Kroenlein type, use 67445)

61440 Craniotomy for section of tentorium cerebelli (separate procedure)

61450 Craniectomy, subtemporal, for section, compression, or decompression of sensory root of gasserian ganglion

61458 Craniectomy, suboccipital; for exploration or decompression of cranial nerves

61460 for section of one or more cranial nerves

61470 for medullary tractotomy

61480 for mesencephalic tractotomy or pedunculotomy

61490 Craniotomy for lobotomy, including cingulotomy

61500 Craniectomy; with excision of tumor or other bone lesion of skull

61501 for osteomyelitis

61510 Craniectomy, trephination, bone flap craniotomy; for excision of brain tumor, supratentorial, except meningioma

61512 for excision of meningioma, supratentorial

61514 for excision of brain abscess, supratentorial

61516 for excision or fenestration of cyst, supratentorial

(For excision of pituitary tumor or craniopharyngioma, see 61545, 61546, 61548)

+ 61517 Implantation of brain intracavitary chemotherapy agent (List separately in addition to code for primary procedure)

(Use 61517 only in conjunction with codes 61510 or 61518)

(Do not report 61517 for brachytherapy insertion. For intracavitary insertion of radioelement sources or ribbons, see 77781-77784)

61518 Craniectomy for excision of brain tumor, infratentorial or posterior fossa; except meningioma, cerebellopontine angle tumor, or midline tumor at base of skull

61519 meningioma

61520 cerebellopontine angle tumor

61521 midline tumor at base of skull

61522 Craniectomy, infratentorial or posterior fossa; for excision of brain abscess

61524 for excision or fenestration of cyst

61526 Craniectomy, bone flap craniotomy, transtemporal (mastoid) for excision of cerebellopontine angle tumor;

61530 combined with middle/posterior fossa craniotomy/craniectomy

61531 Subdural implantation of strip electrodes through one or more burr or trephine hole(s) for long term seizure monitoring

(For stereotactic implantation of electrodes, use 61760)

61533 Craniotomy with elevation of bone flap; for subdural implantation of an electrode array, for long term seizure monitoring

(For continuous EEG monitoring, see 95950-95954)

61534 for excision of epileptogenic focus without electrocorticography during surgery

61535 for removal of epidural or subdural electrode array, without excision of cerebral tissue (separate procedure)

61536 for excision of cerebral epileptogenic focus, with electrocorticography during surgery (includes removal of electrode array)

● 61537 for lobectomy, temporal lobe, without electrocorticography during surgery

▲ 61538 for lobectomy, temporal lobe, with electrocorticography during surgery

▲ 61539 for lobectomy, other than temporal lobe, partial or total, with electrocorticography during surgery

● 61540 for lobectomy, other than temporal lobe, partial or total, without electrocorticography during surgery

61541 for transection of corpus callosum

61542 for total hemispherectomy

▲ 61543 for partial or subtotal (functional) hemispherectomy

61544 for excision or coagulation of choroid plexus

61545 for excision of craniopharyngioma

►(For craniotomy for selective amygdalohippocampectomy, use 61566)◄

►(For craniotomy for multiple subpial transections during surgery, use 61567)◄

61546 Craniotomy for hypophysectomy or excision of pituitary tumor, intracranial approach

61548 Hypophysectomy or excision of pituitary tumor, transnasal or transseptal approach, nonstereotactic

(Do not report code 69990 in addition to code 61548)

61550 Craniectomy for craniosynostosis; single cranial suture

61552 multiple cranial sutures

(For cranial reconstruction for orbital hypertelorism, see 21260-21263)

61556 Craniotomy for craniosynostosis; frontal or parietal bone flap

61557 bifrontal bone flap

61558 Extensive craniectomy for multiple cranial suture craniosynostosis (eg, cloverleaf skull); not requiring bone grafts

61559 recontouring with multiple osteotomies and bone autografts (eg, barrel-stave procedure) (includes obtaining grafts)

61563 Excision, intra and extracranial, benign tumor of cranial bone (eg, fibrous dysplasia); without optic nerve decompression

61564 with optic nerve decompression

(For reconstruction, see 21181-21183)

●**61566** Craniotomy with elevation of bone flap; for selective amygdalohippocampectomy

●**61567** for multiple subpial transections, with electrocorticography during surgery

61570 Craniectomy or craniotomy; with excision of foreign body from brain

61571 with treatment of penetrating wound of brain

(For sequestrectomy for osteomyelitis, use 61501)

61575 Transoral approach to skull base, brain stem or upper spinal cord for biopsy, decompression or excision of lesion;

61576 requiring splitting of tongue and/or mandible (including tracheostomy)

(For arthrodesis, use 22548)

Surgery of Skull Base

The surgical management of lesions involving the skull base (base of anterior, middle, and posterior cranial fossae) often requires the skills of several surgeons of different surgical specialties working together or in tandem during the operative session. These operations are usually not staged because of the need for definitive closure of dura, subcutaneous tissues, and skin to avoid serious infections such as osteomyelitis and/or meningitis.

The procedures are categorized according to: 1) ***approach procedure*** necessary to obtain adequate exposure to the lesion (pathologic entity), 2) ***definitive procedure(s)*** necessary to biopsy, excise or otherwise treat the lesion, and 3) ***repair/reconstruction*** of the defect present following the definitive procedure(s).

The ***approach procedure*** is described according to anatomical area involved, ie, anterior cranial fossa, middle cranial fossa, posterior cranial fossa, and brain stem or upper spinal cord.

The ***definitive procedure(s)*** describes the repair, biopsy, resection, or excision of various lesions of the skull base and, when appropriate, primary closure of the dura, mucous membranes, and skin.

The ***repair/reconstruction procedure(s)*** is reported separately if extensive dural grafting, cranioplasty, local or regional myocutaneous pedicle flaps, or extensive skin grafts are required.

For primary closure, see the appropriate codes, ie, 15732, 15756-15758.

When one surgeon performs the approach procedure, another surgeon performs the definitive procedure, and another surgeon performs the repair/reconstruction procedure, each surgeon reports only the code for the specific procedure performed.

If one surgeon performs more than one procedure (ie, approach procedure and definitive procedure), then both codes are reported, adding modifier '-51' to the secondary, additional procedure(s).

Approach Procedures

Anterior Cranial Fossa

61580 Craniofacial approach to anterior cranial fossa; extradural, including lateral rhinotomy, ethmoidectomy, sphenoidectomy, without maxillectomy or orbital exenteration

61581 extradural, including lateral rhinotomy, orbital exenteration, ethmoidectomy, sphenoidectomy and/or maxillectomy

61582 extradural, including unilateral or bifrontal craniotomy, elevation of frontal lobe(s), osteotomy of base of anterior cranial fossa

61583 intradural, including unilateral or bifrontal craniotomy, elevation or resection of frontal lobe, osteotomy of base of anterior cranial fossa

61584 Orbitocranial approach to anterior cranial fossa, extradural, including supraorbital ridge osteotomy and elevation of frontal and/or temporal lobe(s); without orbital exenteration

61585 with orbital exenteration

61586 Bicoronal, transzygomatic and/or LeFort I osteotomy approach to anterior cranial fossa with or without internal fixation, without bone graft

Middle Cranial Fossa

61590 Infratemporal pre-auricular approach to middle cranial fossa (parapharyngeal space, infratemporal and midline skull base, nasopharynx), with or without disarticulation of the mandible, including parotidectomy, craniotomy, decompression and/or mobilization of the facial nerve and/or petrous carotid artery

61591 Infratemporal post-auricular approach to middle cranial fossa (internal auditory meatus, petrous apex, tentorium, cavernous sinus, parasellar area, infratemporal fossa) including mastoidectomy, resection of sigmoid sinus, with or without decompression and/or mobilization of contents of auditory canal or petrous carotid artery

61592 Orbitocranial zygomatic approach to middle cranial fossa (cavernous sinus and carotid artery, clivus, basilar artery or petrous apex) including osteotomy of zygoma, craniotomy, extra- or intradural elevation of temporal lobe

Posterior Cranial Fossa

61595 Transtemporal approach to posterior cranial fossa, jugular foramen or midline skull base, including mastoidectomy, decompression of sigmoid sinus and/or facial nerve, with or without mobilization

61596 Transcochlear approach to posterior cranial fossa, jugular foramen or midline skull base, including labyrinthectomy, decompression, with or without mobilization of facial nerve and/or petrous carotid artery

61597 Transcondylar (far lateral) approach to posterior cranial fossa, jugular foramen or midline skull base, including occipital condylectomy, mastoidectomy, resection of C1-C3 vertebral body(s), decompression of vertebral artery, with or without mobilization

61598 Transpetrosal approach to posterior cranial fossa, clivus or foramen magnum, including ligation of superior petrosal sinus and/or sigmoid sinus

Definitive Procedures

Base of Anterior Cranial Fossa

61600 Resection or excision of neoplastic, vascular or infectious lesion of base of anterior cranial fossa; extradural

61601 intradural, including dural repair, with or without graft

Base of Middle Cranial Fossa

61605 Resection or excision of neoplastic, vascular or infectious lesion of infratemporal fossa, parapharyngeal space, petrous apex; extradural

61606 intradural, including dural repair, with or without graft

61607 Resection or excision of neoplastic, vascular or infectious lesion of parasellar area, cavernous sinus, clivus or midline skull base; extradural

61608 intradural, including dural repair, with or without graft

Codes 61609-61612 are reported in addition to code(s) for primary procedure(s) 61605-61608. Report only one transection or ligation of carotid artery code per operative session.

+ 61609 Transection or ligation, carotid artery in cavernous sinus; without repair (List separately in addition to code for primary procedure)

+ 61610 with repair by anastomosis or graft (List separately in addition to code for primary procedure)

+ 61611 Transection or ligation, carotid artery in petrous canal; without repair (List separately in addition to code for primary procedure)

+ 61612 with repair by anastomosis or graft (List separately in addition to code for primary procedure)

61613 Obliteration of carotid aneurysm, arteriovenous malformation, or carotid-cavernous fistula by dissection within cavernous sinus

Base of Posterior Cranial Fossa

61615 Resection or excision of neoplastic, vascular or infectious lesion of base of posterior cranial fossa, jugular foramen, foramen magnum, or C1-C3 vertebral bodies; extradural

61616 intradural, including dural repair, with or without graft

Repair and/or Reconstruction of Surgical Defects of Skull Base

61618 Secondary repair of dura for cerebrospinal fluid leak, anterior, middle or posterior cranial fossa following surgery of the skull base; by free tissue graft (eg, pericranium, fascia, tensor fascia lata, adipose tissue, homologous or synthetic grafts)

61619 by local or regionalized vascularized pedicle flap or myocutaneous flap (including galea, temporalis, frontalis or occipitalis muscle)

Endovascular Therapy

61623 Endovascular temporary balloon arterial occlusion, head or neck (extracranial/intracranial) including selective catheterization of vessel to be occluded, positioning and inflation of occlusion balloon, concomitant neurological monitoring, and radiologic supervision and interpretation of all angiography required for balloon occlusion and to exclude vascular injury post occlusion

(If selective catheterization and angiography of arteries other than artery to be occluded is performed, use appropriate catheterization and radiologic supervision and interpretation codes)

(If complete diagnostic angiography of the artery to be occluded is performed immediately prior to temporary occlusion, use appropriate radiologic supervision and interpretation codes only)

61624 Transcatheter permanent occlusion or embolization (eg, for tumor destruction, to achieve hemostasis, to occlude a vascular malformation), percutaneous, any method; central nervous system (intracranial, spinal cord)

(See also 37204)

(For radiological supervision and interpretation, use 75894)

61626 non-central nervous system, head or neck (extracranial, brachiocephalic branch)

(See also 37204)

(For radiological supervision and interpretation, use 75894)

Surgery for Aneurysm, Arteriovenous Malformation or Vascular Disease

Includes craniotomy when appropriate for procedure.

61680 Surgery of intracranial arteriovenous malformation; supratentorial, simple

61682 supratentorial, complex

61684 infratentorial, simple

61686 infratentorial, complex

61690 dural, simple

61692 dural, complex

61697 Surgery of complex intracranial aneurysm, intracranial approach; carotid circulation

61698 vertebrobasilar circulation

(61697, 61698 involve aneurysms that are larger than 15 mm or with calcification of the aneurysm neck, or with incorporation of normal vessels into the aneurysm neck, or a procedure requiring temporary vessel occlusion, trapping or cardiopulmonary bypass to successfully treat the aneurysm)

61700 Surgery of simple intracranial aneurysm, intracranial approach; carotid circulation

61702 vertebrobasilar circulation

61703 Surgery of intracranial aneurysm, cervical approach by application of occluding clamp to cervical carotid artery (Selverstone-Crutchfield type)

(For cervical approach for direct ligation of carotid artery, see 37600-37606)

61705 Surgery of aneurysm, vascular malformation or carotid-cavernous fistula; by intracranial and cervical occlusion of carotid artery

61708 by intracranial electrothrombosis

(For ligation or gradual occlusion of internal/common carotid artery, see 37605, 37606)

61710 by intra-arterial embolization, injection procedure, or balloon catheter

61711 Anastomosis, arterial, extracranial-intracranial (eg, middle cerebral/cortical) arteries

(For carotid or vertebral thromboendarterectomy, use 35301)

Stereotaxis

61720 Creation of lesion by stereotactic method, including burr hole(s) and localizing and recording techniques, single or multiple stages; globus pallidus or thalamus

61735 subcortical structure(s) other than globus pallidus or thalamus

61750 Stereotactic biopsy, aspiration, or excision, including burr hole(s), for intracranial lesion;

61751 with computed tomography and/or magnetic resonance guidance

(For radiological supervision and interpretation of computerized tomography, see 70450, 70460, or 70470 as appropriate)

(For radiological supervision and interpretation of magnetic resonance imaging, see 70551, 70552, or 70553 as appropriate)

61760 Stereotactic implantation of depth electrodes into the cerebrum for long term seizure monitoring

61770 Stereotactic localization, including burr hole(s), with insertion of catheter(s) or probe(s) for placement of radiation source

61790 Creation of lesion by stereotactic method, percutaneous, by neurolytic agent (eg, alcohol, thermal, electrical, radiofrequency); gasserian ganglion

61791 trigeminal medullary tract

61793 Stereotactic radiosurgery (particle beam, gamma ray or linear accelerator), one or more sessions

(For intensity modulated beam delivery plan and treatment, see 77301, 77418)

+ 61795 Stereotactic computer assisted volumetric (navigational) procedure, intracranial, extracranial, or spinal (List separately in addition to code for primary procedure)

Neurostimulators (Intracranial)

Codes 61850-61888 apply to both simple and complex neurostimulators. For initial or subsequent electronic analysis and programming of neurostimulator pulse generators, see codes 95970-95975.

►Microelectrode recording, when performed by the operating surgeon in association with implantation of neurostimulator electrode arrays, is an inclusive service and should not be reported separately. If another physician participates in neurophysiological mapping during a deep brain stimulator implantation procedure, this service may be reported by the other physician with codes 95961-95962.◄

61850 Twist drill or burr hole(s) for implantation of neurostimulator electrodes, cortical

61860 Craniectomy or craniotomy for implantation of neurostimulator electrodes, cerebral, cortical

►(61862 has been deleted. To report, see 61867, 61868)◄

●**61863** Twist drill, burr hole, craniotomy, or craniectomy with stereotactic implantation of neurostimulator electrode array in subcortical site (eg, thalamus, globus pallidus, subthalamic nucleus, periventricular, periaqueductal gray), without use of intraoperative microelectrode recording; first array

+●**61864** each additional array (List separately in addition to primary procedure)

►(Use 61864 in conjunction with 61863)◄

(61865 has been deleted. To report, use 61867, 61868)

●**61867** Twist drill, burr hole, craniotomy, or craniectomy with stereotactic implantation of neurostimulator electrode array in subcortical site (eg, thalamus, globus pallidus, subthalamic nucleus, periventricular, periaqueductal gray), with use of intraoperative microelectrode recording; first array

+●**61868** each additional array (List separately in addition to primary procedure)

►(Use 61868 in conjunction with 61867)◄

61870 Craniectomy for implantation of neurostimulator electrodes, cerebellar; cortical

61875 subcortical

61880 Revision or removal of intracranial neurostimulator electrodes

61885 Incision and subcutaneous placement of cranial neurostimulator pulse generator or receiver, direct or inductive coupling; with connection to a single electrode array

61886 with connection to two or more electrode arrays

(For open placement of cranial nerve (eg, vagal, trigeminal) neurostimulator electrode(s), use 64573)

(For percutaneous placement of cranial nerve (eg, vagal, trigeminal) neurostimulator electrode(s), use 64553)

(For revision or removal of cranial nerve (eg, vagal, trigeminal) neurostimulator electrode(s), use 64585)

61888 Revision or removal of cranial neurostimulator pulse generator or receiver

Repair

62000 Elevation of depressed skull fracture; simple, extradural

62005 compound or comminuted, extradural

62010 with repair of dura and/or debridement of brain

62100 Craniotomy for repair of dural/cerebrospinal fluid leak, including surgery for rhinorrhea/otorrhea

(For repair of spinal dural/CSF leak, see 63707, 63709)

62115 Reduction of craniomegalic skull (eg, treated hydrocephalus); not requiring bone grafts or cranioplasty

62116 with simple cranioplasty

62117 requiring craniotomy and reconstruction with or without bone graft (includes obtaining grafts)

62120 Repair of encephalocele, skull vault, including cranioplasty

62121 Craniotomy for repair of encephalocele, skull base

62140 Cranioplasty for skull defect; up to 5 cm diameter

62141 larger than 5 cm diameter

62142 Removal of bone flap or prosthetic plate of skull

62143 Replacement of bone flap or prosthetic plate of skull

62145 Cranioplasty for skull defect with reparative brain surgery

62146 Cranioplasty with autograft (includes obtaining bone grafts); up to 5 cm diameter

62147 larger than 5 cm diameter

+ **62148** Incision and retrieval of subcutaneous cranial bone graft for cranioplasty (List separately in addition to code for primary procedure)

(Use 62148 in conjunction with codes 62140-62147)

Neuroendoscopy

Surgical endoscopy always includes diagnostic endoscopy.

+ **62160** Neuroendoscopy, intracranial, for placement or replacement of ventricular catheter and attachment to shunt system or external drainage (List separately in addition to code for primary procedure)

(Use 62160 only in conjunction with codes 61107, 61210, 62220, 62223, 62225, or 62230)

62161 Neuroendoscopy, intracranial; with dissection of adhesions, fenestration of septum pellucidum or intraventricular cysts (including placement, replacement, or removal of ventricular catheter)

62162 with fenestration or excision of colloid cyst, including placement of external ventricular catheter for drainage

62163 with retrieval of foreign body

62164 with excision of brain tumor, including placement of external ventricular catheter for drainage

62165 with excision of pituitary tumor, transnasal or trans-sphenoidal approach

Cerebrospinal Fluid (CSF) Shunt

62180 Ventriculocisternostomy (Torkildsen type operation)

62190 Creation of shunt; subarachnoid/subdural-atrial, -jugular, -auricular

62192 subarachnoid/subdural-peritoneal, -pleural, other terminus

62194 Replacement or irrigation, subarachnoid/subdural catheter

62200 Ventriculocisternostomy, third ventricle;

62201 stereotactic, neuroendoscopic method

(For intracranial neuroendoscopic procedures, see 62161-62165)

62220 Creation of shunt; ventriculo-atrial, -jugular, -auricular

(For intracranial neuroendoscopic ventricular catheter placement, use 62160)

62223 ventriculo-peritoneal, -pleural, other terminus

(For intracranial neuroendoscopic ventricular catheter placement, use 62160)

62225 Replacement or irrigation, ventricular catheter

(For intracranial neuroendoscopic ventricular catheter placement, use 62160)

62230 Replacement or revision of cerebrospinal fluid shunt, obstructed valve, or distal catheter in shunt system

(For intracranial neuroendoscopic ventricular catheter placement, use 62160)

62252 Reprogramming of programmable cerebrospinal shunt

62256 Removal of complete cerebrospinal fluid shunt system; without replacement

62258 with replacement by similar or other shunt at same operation

(For percutaneous irrigation or aspiration of shunt reservoir, use 61070)

(For reprogramming of programmable CSF shunt, use 62252)

Spine and Spinal Cord

(For application of caliper or tongs, use 20660)

(For treatment of fracture or dislocation of spine, see 22305-22327)

Injection, Drainage, or Aspiration

Injection of contrast during fluoroscopic guidance and localization is an inclusive component of codes 62263, 62270-62273, 62280-62282, 62310-62319, 0027T. Fluoroscopic guidance and localization is reported by code 76005, unless a formal contrast study (myelography, epidurography, or arthrography) is performed, in which case the use of fluoroscopy is included in the supervision and interpretation codes.

For radiologic supervision and interpretation of epidurography, use 72275. Code 72275 is only to be used when an epidurogram is performed, ►images documented,◄ and a formal radiologic report is issued.

Code 62263 describes a catheter-based treatment involving targeted injection of various substances (eg, hypertonic saline, steroid, anesthetic) via an indwelling epidural catheter. Code 62263 includes percutaneous insertion and removal of an epidural catheter (remaining in place over a several-day period), for the administration of multiple injections of a neurolytic agent(s) performed during serial treatment sessions (ie, spanning two or more treatment days). If required, adhesions or scarring may also be lysed by mechanical means. Code 62263 is NOT reported for each adhesiolysis treatment, but should be reported ONCE to describe the entire series of injections/infusions spanning two or more treatment days. For endoscopic lysis of adhesions, use 0027T.

Code 62264 describes multiple adhesiolysis treatment sessions performed on the same day. Adhesions or scarring may be lysed by injections of neurolytic agent(s). If required, adhesions or scarring may also be lysed mechanically using a percutaneously-deployed catheter.

Codes 62263 and 62264 include the procedure of injections of contrast for epidurography (72275) and fluoroscopic guidance and localization (76005) during initial or subsequent sessions.

►(Report 01996 for daily hospital management of continuous epidural or subarachnoid drug administration performed in conjunction with 62318-62319)◄

(For endoscopic lysis of epidural adhesions, use Category III code 0027T)

62263 Percutaneous lysis of epidural adhesions using solution injection (eg, hypertonic saline, enzyme) or mechanical means (eg, catheter) including radiologic localization (includes contrast when administered), multiple adhesiolysis sessions; 2 or more days

(62263 includes codes 76005 and 72275)

62264 1 day

(Do not report 62264 with 62263)

(62264 includes codes 76005 and 72275)

62268 Percutaneous aspiration, spinal cord cyst or syrinx

(For radiological supervision and interpretation, see 76003, 76360, 76942)

62269 Biopsy of spinal cord, percutaneous needle

(For radiological supervision and interpretation, see 76003, 76360, 76942)

(For fine needle aspiration, see 10021, 10022)

(For evaluation of fine needle aspirate, see 88172, 88173)

62270 Spinal puncture, lumbar, diagnostic

62272 Spinal puncture, therapeutic, for drainage of cerebrospinal fluid (by needle or catheter)

62273 Injection, epidural, of blood or clot patch

62280 Injection/infusion of neurolytic substance (eg, alcohol, phenol, iced saline solutions), with or without other therapeutic substance; subarachnoid

62281 epidural, cervical or thoracic

62282 epidural, lumbar, sacral (caudal)

⊘ **62284** Injection procedure for myelography and/or computed tomography, spinal (other than C1-C2 and posterior fossa)

(For injection procedure at C1-C2, use 61055)

(For radiological supervision and interpretation, see **Radiology**)

62287 Aspiration or decompression procedure, percutaneous, of nucleus pulposus of intervertebral disk, any method, single or multiple levels, lumbar (eg, manual or automated percutaneous diskectomy, percutaneous laser diskectomy)

(For fluoroscopic guidance, use 76003)

62290 Injection procedure for diskography, each level; lumbar

62291 cervical or thoracic

(For radiological supervision and interpretation, see 72285, 72295)

62292 Injection procedure for chemonucleolysis, including diskography, intervertebral disk, single or multiple levels, lumbar

62294 Injection procedure, arterial, for occlusion of arteriovenous malformation, spinal

62310 Injection, single (not via indwelling catheter), not including neurolytic substances, with or without contrast (for either localization or epidurography), of diagnostic or therapeutic substance(s) (including anesthetic, antispasmodic, opioid, steroid, other solution), epidural or subarachnoid; cervical or thoracic

62311 lumbar, sacral (caudal)

62318 Injection, including catheter placement, continuous infusion or intermittent bolus, not including neurolytic substances, with or without contrast (for either localization or epidurography), of diagnostic or therapeutic substance(s) (including anesthetic, antispasmodic, opioid, steroid, other solution), epidural or subarachnoid; cervical or thoracic

62319 lumbar, sacral (caudal)

(For transforaminal epidural injection, see 64479-64484)

►(Report 01996 for daily hospital management of continuous epidural or subarachnoid drug administration performed in conjunction with codes 62318-62319)◄

Catheter Implantation

(For percutaneous placement of intrathecal or epidural catheter, see codes 62270-62273, 62280-62284, 62310-62319)

62350 Implantation, revision or repositioning of tunneled intrathecal or epidural catheter, for long-term medication administration via an external pump or implantable reservoir/infusion pump; without laminectomy

62351 with laminectomy

(For refilling and maintenance of an implantable infusion pump for spinal or brain drug therapy, use 95990)

62355 Removal of previously implanted intrathecal or epidural catheter

Reservoir/Pump Implantation

62360 Implantation or replacement of device for intrathecal or epidural drug infusion; subcutaneous reservoir

62361 non-programmable pump

62362 programmable pump, including preparation of pump, with or without programming

62365 Removal of subcutaneous reservoir or pump, previously implanted for intrathecal or epidural infusion

62367 Electronic analysis of programmable, implanted pump for intrathecal or epidural drug infusion (includes evaluation of reservoir status, alarm status, drug prescription status); without reprogramming

62368 with reprogramming

(For refilling and maintenance of an implantable infusion pump for spinal or brain drug therapy, use 95990)

Posterior Extradural Laminotomy or Laminectomy for Exploration/Decompression of Neural Elements or Excision of Herniated Intervertebral Disks

(When 63001-63048 are followed by arthrodesis, see 22590-22614)

63001 Laminectomy with exploration and/or decompression of spinal cord and/or cauda equina, without facetectomy, foraminotomy or diskectomy, (eg, spinal stenosis), one or two vertebral segments; cervical

63003 thoracic

63005 lumbar, except for spondylolisthesis

63011 sacral

63012 Laminectomy with removal of abnormal facets and/or pars inter-articularis with decompression of cauda equina and nerve roots for spondylolisthesis, lumbar (Gill type procedure)

63015 Laminectomy with exploration and/or decompression of spinal cord and/or cauda equina, without facetectomy, foraminotomy or diskectomy, (eg, spinal stenosis), more than 2 vertebral segments; cervical

63016 thoracic

63017 lumbar

63020 Laminotomy (hemilaminectomy), with decompression of nerve root(s), including partial facetectomy, foraminotomy and/or excision of herniated intervertebral disk; one interspace, cervical

63030 one interspace, lumbar (including open or endoscopically-assisted approach)

+ 63035 each additional interspace, cervical or lumbar (List separately in addition to code for primary procedure)

(Use 63035 in conjunction with codes 63020-63030)

►(63020, 63030, 63035 are unilateral procedures. For bilateral procedures, use modifier '-50')◄

63040 Laminotomy (hemilaminectomy), with decompression of nerve root(s), including partial facetectomy, foraminotomy and/or excision of herniated intervertebral disk, reexploration, single interspace; cervical

63042 lumbar

(Codes 63040-63044 are unilateral procedures. For bilateral procedures, use modifier '-50')

+ 63043 each additional cervical interspace (List separately in addition to code for primary procedure)

(Use 63043 in conjunction with code 63040)

+ 63044 each additional lumbar interspace (List separately in addition to code for primary procedure)

(Use 63044 in conjunction with code 63042)

63045 Laminectomy, facetectomy and foraminotomy (unilateral or bilateral with decompression of spinal cord, cauda equina and/or nerve root(s), (eg, spinal or lateral recess stenosis)), single vertebral segment; cervical

63046 thoracic

63047 lumbar

+ 63048 each additional segment, cervical, thoracic, or lumbar (List separately in addition to code for primary procedure)

(Use 63048 in conjunction with codes 63045-63047)

Transpedicular or Costovertebral Approach for Posterolateral Extradural Exploration/Decompression

63055 Transpedicular approach with decompression of spinal cord, equina and/or nerve root(s) (eg, herniated intervertebral disk), single segment; thoracic

63056 lumbar (including transfacet, or lateral extraforaminal approach) (eg, far lateral herniated intervertebral disk)

+ 63057 each additional segment, thoracic or lumbar (List separately in addition to code for primary procedure)

(Use 63057 in conjunction with codes 63055, 63056)

63064 Costovertebral approach with decompression of spinal cord or nerve root(s), (eg, herniated intervertebral disk), thoracic; single segment

+ 63066 each additional segment (List separately in addition to code for primary procedure)

(Use 63066 in conjunction with code 63064)

(For excision of thoracic intraspinal lesions by laminectomy, see 63266, 63271, 63276, 63281, 63286)

Anterior or Anterolateral Approach for Extradural Exploration/Decompression

For the following codes, when two surgeons work together as primary surgeons performing distinct part(s) of spinal cord exploration/decompression operation, each surgeon should report his/her distinct operative work by appending the modifier '-62' to the procedure code (and any associated add-on codes for that procedure code as long as both surgeons continue to work together as primary surgeons). In this situation, the modifier '-62' may be appended to the definitive procedure code(s) 63075, 63077, 63081, 63085, 63087, 63090 and, as appropriate, to associated additional interspace add-on code(s) 63076, 63078 or additional segment add-on code(s) 63082, 63086, 63088, 63091 as long as both surgeons continue to work together as primary surgeons.

63075 Diskectomy, anterior, with decompression of spinal cord and/or nerve root(s), including osteophytectomy; cervical, single interspace

+ 63076 cervical, each additional interspace (List separately in addition to code for primary procedure)

(Use 63076 in conjunction with code 63075)

63077 thoracic, single interspace

+ 63078 thoracic, each additional interspace (List separately in addition to code for primary procedure)

(Use 63078 in conjunction with code 63077)

(Do not report code 69990 in addition to codes 63075-63078)

63081 Vertebral corpectomy (vertebral body resection), partial or complete, anterior approach with decompression of spinal cord and/or nerve root(s); cervical, single segment

+ 63082 cervical, each additional segment (List separately in addition to code for primary procedure)

(Use 63082 in conjunction with code 63081)

(For transoral approach, see 61575, 61576)

63085 Vertebral corpectomy (vertebral body resection), partial or complete, transthoracic approach with decompression of spinal cord and/or nerve root(s); thoracic, single segment

+ 63086 thoracic, each additional segment (List separately in addition to code for primary procedure)

(Use 63086 in conjunction with code 63085)

63087 Vertebral corpectomy (vertebral body resection), partial or complete, combined thoracolumbar approach with decompression of spinal cord, cauda equina or nerve root(s), lower thoracic or lumbar; single segment

+ 63088 each additional segment (List separately in addition to code for primary procedure)

(Use 63088 in conjunction with code 63087)

63090 Vertebral corpectomy (vertebral body resection), partial or complete, transperitoneal or retroperitoneal approach with decompression of spinal cord, cauda equina or nerve root(s), lower thoracic, lumbar, or sacral; single segment

+ 63091 each additional segment (List separately in addition to code for primary procedure)

(Use 63091 in conjunction with code 63090)

(Procedures 63081-63091 include diskectomy above and/or below vertebral segment)

(If followed by arthrodesis, see 22548-22812)

(For reconstruction of spine, use appropriate vertebral corpectomy codes 63081-63091, bone graft codes 20930-20938, arthrodesis codes 22548-22812, and spinal instrumentation codes 22840-22855)

►Lateral Extracavitary Approach for Extradural Exploration/Decompression◄

● 63101 Vertebral corpectomy (vertebral body resection), partial or complete, lateral extracavitary approach with decompression of spinal cord and/or nerve root(s) (eg, for tumor or retropulsed bone fragments); thoracic, single segment

● 63102 lumbar, single segment

+ ● 63103 thoracic or lumbar, each additional segment (List separately in addition to code for primary procedure)

►(Use 63103 in conjunction with 63101 and 63102)◄

Incision

63170 Laminectomy with myelotomy (eg, Bischof or DREZ type), cervical, thoracic, or thoracolumbar

63172 Laminectomy with drainage of intramedullary cyst/syrinx; to subarachnoid space

▲ 63173 to peritoneal or pleural space

63180 Laminectomy and section of dentate ligaments, with or without dural graft, cervical; one or two segments

63182 more than two segments

63185 Laminectomy with rhizotomy; one or two segments

63190 more than two segments

63191 Laminectomy with section of spinal accessory nerve

(For resection of sternocleidomastoid muscle, use 21720)

63194 Laminectomy with cordotomy, with section of one spinothalamic tract, one stage; cervical

63195 thoracic

63196 Laminectomy with cordotomy, with section of both spinothalamic tracts, one stage; cervical

63197 thoracic

63198 Laminectomy with cordotomy with section of both spinothalamic tracts, two stages within 14 days; cervical

63199 thoracic

63200 Laminectomy, with release of tethered spinal cord, lumbar

Excision by Laminectomy of Lesion Other Than Herniated Disk

63250 Laminectomy for excision or occlusion of arteriovenous malformation of spinal cord; cervical

63251 thoracic

63252 thoracolumbar

63265 Laminectomy for excision or evacuation of intraspinal lesion other than neoplasm, extradural; cervical

63266 thoracic

63267 lumbar

63268 sacral

63270 Laminectomy for excision of intraspinal lesion other than neoplasm, intradural; cervical

63271 thoracic

63272 lumbar

63273 sacral

63275 Laminectomy for biopsy/excision of intraspinal neoplasm; extradural, cervical

63276 extradural, thoracic

63277 extradural, lumbar

63278 extradural, sacral

63280 intradural, extramedullary, cervical

63281 intradural, extramedullary, thoracic

63282 intradural, extramedullary, lumbar

63283 intradural, sacral

63285 intradural, intramedullary, cervical

63286 intradural, intramedullary, thoracic

63287 intradural, intramedullary, thoracolumbar

63290 combined extradural-intradural lesion, any level

(For drainage of intramedullary cyst/syrinx, use 63172, 63173)

Excision, Anterior or Anterolateral Approach, Intraspinal Lesion

For the following codes, when two surgeons work together as primary surgeons performing distinct part(s) of an anterior approach for an intraspinal excision, each surgeon should report his/her distinct operative work by appending the modifier '-62' to the single definitive procedure code. In this situation, the modifier '-62' may be appended to the definitive procedure code(s) 63300-63307 and, as appropriate, to the associated additional segment add-on code 63308 as long as both surgeons continue to work together as primary surgeons.

(For arthrodesis, see 22548-22585)

(For reconstruction of spine, see 20930-20938)

63300 Vertebral corpectomy (vertebral body resection), partial or complete, for excision of intraspinal lesion, single segment; extradural, cervical

63301 extradural, thoracic by transthoracic approach

63302 extradural, thoracic by thoracolumbar approach

63303 extradural, lumbar or sacral by transperitoneal or retroperitoneal approach

63304 intradural, cervical

63305 intradural, thoracic by transthoracic approach

63306 intradural, thoracic by thoracolumbar approach

63307 intradural, lumbar or sacral by transperitoneal or retroperitoneal approach

+ 63308 each additional segment (List separately in addition to codes for single segment)

(Use 63308 in conjunction with codes 63300-63307)

Stereotaxis

63600 Creation of lesion of spinal cord by stereotactic method, percutaneous, any modality (including stimulation and/or recording)

63610 Stereotactic stimulation of spinal cord, percutaneous, separate procedure not followed by other surgery

63615 Stereotactic biopsy, aspiration, or excision of lesion, spinal cord

Neurostimulators (Spinal)

Codes 63650-63688 apply to both simple and complex neurostimulators. For initial or subsequent electronic analysis and programming of neurostimulator pulse generators, see codes 95970-95975.

Codes 63650, 63655, and 63660 describe the operative placement, revision, or removal of the spinal neurostimulator system components to provide spinal electrical stimulation. A neurostimulator system includes an implanted neurostimulator, external controller, extension, and collection of contacts. Multiple contacts or electrodes (4 or more) provide the actual electrical stimulation in the epidural space.

For percutaneously placed neurostimulator systems (63650, 63660), the contacts are on a catheter-like lead. An array defines the collection of contacts that are on one catheter.

For systems placed via an open surgical exposure (63655, 63660), the contacts are on a plate or paddle-shaped surface.

63650 Percutaneous implantation of neurostimulator electrode array, epidural

63655 Laminectomy for implantation of neurostimulator electrodes, plate/paddle, epidural

63660 Revision or removal of spinal neurostimulator electrode percutaneous array(s) or plate/paddle(s)

63685 Incision and subcutaneous placement of spinal neurostimulator pulse generator or receiver, direct or inductive coupling

63688 Revision or removal of implanted spinal neurostimulator pulse generator or receiver

Repair

63700 Repair of meningocele; less than 5 cm diameter

63702 larger than 5 cm diameter

(Do not use modifier '-63' in conjunction with 63700, 63702)

63704 Repair of myelomeningocele; less than 5 cm diameter

63706 larger than 5 cm diameter

(Do not use modifier '-63' in conjunction with 63704, 63706)

(For complex skin closure, see **Integumentary System**)

63707 Repair of dural/cerebrospinal fluid leak, not requiring laminectomy

63709 Repair of dural/cerebrospinal fluid leak or pseudomeningocele, with laminectomy

63710 Dural graft, spinal

(For laminectomy and section of dentate ligaments, with or without dural graft, cervical, see 63180, 63182)

Shunt, Spinal CSF

63740 Creation of shunt, lumbar, subarachnoid-peritoneal, -pleural, or other; including laminectomy

63741 percutaneous, not requiring laminectomy

63744 Replacement, irrigation or revision of lumbosubarachnoid shunt

63746 Removal of entire lumbosubarachnoid shunt system without replacement

Extracranial Nerves, Peripheral Nerves, and Autonomic Nervous System

(For intracranial surgery on cranial nerves, see 61450, 61460, 61790)

Introduction/Injection of Anesthetic Agent (Nerve Block), Diagnostic or Therapeutic

Somatic Nerves

64400 Injection, anesthetic agent; trigeminal nerve, any division or branch

64402 facial nerve

64405 greater occipital nerve

64408 vagus nerve

64410 phrenic nerve

64412 spinal accessory nerve

64413 cervical plexus

64415 brachial plexus, single

64416 brachial plexus, continuous infusion by catheter (including catheter placement) including daily management for anesthetic agent administration

(Do not report 01996 in addition to 64416)

64417 axillary nerve

64418 suprascapular nerve

64420 intercostal nerve, single

64421 intercostal nerves, multiple, regional block

64425 ilioinguinal, iliohypogastric nerves

64430 pudendal nerve

64435 paracervical (uterine) nerve

64445 sciatic nerve, single

64446 sciatic nerve, continuous infusion by catheter, (including catheter placement) including daily management for anesthetic agent administration

(Do not report 01996 in addition to 64446)

64447 femoral nerve, single

(Do not report 01996 in addition to 64447)

64448 femoral nerve, continuous infusion by catheter (including catheter placement) including daily management for anesthetic agent administration

(Do not report 01996 in addition to 64448)

●**64449** lumbar plexus, posterior approach, continuous infusion by catheter (including catheter placement) including daily management for anesthetic agent administration

►(Do not report 01996 in conjunction with 64449)◄

64450 other peripheral nerve or branch

(For phenol destruction, see 64622-64627)

(For subarachnoid or subdural injection, see 62280, 62310-62319)

(For epidural or caudal injection, see 62273, 62281-62282, 62310-62319)

(Codes 64470-64484 are unilateral procedures. For bilateral procedures, use modifier '-50')

(For fluoroscopic guidance and localization for needle placement and injection in conjunction with codes 64470-64484, use code 76005)

64470 Injection, anesthetic agent and/or steroid, paravertebral facet joint or facet joint nerve; cervical or thoracic, single level

✚ **64472** cervical or thoracic, each additional level (List separately in addition to code for primary procedure)

(Use code 64472 in conjunction with code 64470)

64475 lumbar or sacral, single level

✚ **64476** lumbar or sacral, each additional level (List separately in addition to code for primary procedure)

(Use code 64476 in conjunction with code 64475)

64479 Injection, anesthetic agent and/or steroid, transforaminal epidural; cervical or thoracic, single level

✚ **64480** cervical or thoracic, each additional level (List separately in addition to code for primary procedure)

(Use code 64480 in conjunction with code 64479)

64483 lumbar or sacral, single level

✚ **64484** lumbar or sacral, each additional level (List separately in addition to code for primary procedure)

(Use code 64484 in conjunction with code 64483)

Sympathetic Nerves

64505 Injection, anesthetic agent; sphenopalatine ganglion

64508 carotid sinus (separate procedure)

64510 stellate ganglion (cervical sympathetic)

● **64517** superior hypogastric plexus

64520 lumbar or thoracic (paravertebral sympathetic)

64530 celiac plexus, with or without radiologic monitoring

Neurostimulators (Peripheral Nerve)

Codes 64553-64595 apply to both simple and complex neurostimulators. For initial or subsequent electronic analysis and programming of neurostimulator pulse generators, see codes 95970-95975.

64550 Application of surface (transcutaneous) neurostimulator

64553 Percutaneous implantation of neurostimulator electrodes; cranial nerve

(For open placement of cranial nerve (eg, vagal, trigeminal) neurostimulator pulse generator or receiver, see 61885, 61886, as appropriate)

64555 peripheral nerve (excludes sacral nerve)

64560 autonomic nerve

64561 sacral nerve (transforaminal placement)

64565 neuromuscular

64573 Incision for implantation of neurostimulator electrodes; cranial nerve

(For open placement of cranial nerve (eg, vagal, trigeminal) neurostimulator pulse generator or receiver, see 61885, 61886, as appropriate)

(For revision or removal of cranial nerve (eg, vagal, trigeminal) neurostimulator pulse generator or receiver, use 61888)

64575 peripheral nerve (excludes sacral nerve)

64577 autonomic nerve

64580 neuromuscular

64581 sacral nerve (transforaminal placement)

64585 Revision or removal of peripheral neurostimulator electrodes

64590 Incision and subcutaneous placement of peripheral neurostimulator pulse generator or receiver, direct or inductive coupling

64595 Revision or removal of peripheral neurostimulator pulse generator or receiver

Destruction by Neurolytic Agent (eg, Chemical, Thermal, Electrical ►or◄ Radiofrequency)

►(Codes 64600-64681 include the injection of other therapeutic agents (eg, corticosteroids).◄

Somatic Nerves

64600 Destruction by neurolytic agent, trigeminal nerve; supraorbital, infraorbital, mental, or inferior alveolar branch

64605 second and third division branches at foramen ovale

64610 second and third division branches at foramen ovale under radiologic monitoring

64612 Chemodenervation of muscle(s); muscle(s) innervated by facial nerve (eg, for blepharospasm, hemifacial spasm)

64613 cervical spinal muscle(s) (eg, for spasmodic torticollis)

64614 extremity(s) and/or trunk muscle(s) (eg, for dystonia, cerebral palsy, multiple sclerosis)

(For chemodenervation for strabismus involving the extraocular muscles, use 67345)

64620 Destruction by neurolytic agent, intercostal nerve

(Codes 64622-64627 are unilateral procedures. For bilateral procedures, use modifier '-50')

(For fluoroscopic guidance and localization for needle placement and neurolysis in conjunction with codes 64622-64627, use 76005)

64622 Destruction by neurolytic agent, paravertebral facet joint nerve; lumbar or sacral, single level

✚ **64623** lumbar or sacral, each additional level (List separately in addition to code for primary procedure)

(Use 64623 in conjunction with code 64622)

64626 cervical or thoracic, single level

✚ **64627** cervical or thoracic, each additional level (List separately in addition to code for primary procedure)

(Use 64627 in conjunction with code 64626)

64630 Destruction by neurolytic agent; pudendal nerve

64640 other peripheral nerve or branch

Sympathetic Nerves

▲ **64680** Destruction by neurolytic agent, with or without radiologic monitoring; celiac plexus

● **64681** superior hypogastric plexus

Neuroplasty (Exploration, Neurolysis or Nerve Decompression)

Neuroplasty is the decompression or freeing of intact nerve from scar tissue, including external neurolysis and/or transposition.

(For internal neurolysis requiring use of operating microscope, use 64727)

(For facial nerve decompression, use 69720)

64702 Neuroplasty; digital, one or both, same digit

64704 nerve of hand or foot

64708 Neuroplasty, major peripheral nerve, arm or leg; other than specified

64712 sciatic nerve

64713 brachial plexus

64714 lumbar plexus

64716 Neuroplasty and/or transposition; cranial nerve (specify)

64718 ulnar nerve at elbow

64719 ulnar nerve at wrist

64721 median nerve at carpal tunnel

(For arthroscopic procedure, use 29848)

64722 Decompression; unspecified nerve(s) (specify)

64726 plantar digital nerve

+ 64727 Internal neurolysis, requiring use of operating microscope (List separately in addition to code for neuroplasty) (Neuroplasty includes external neurolysis)

(Do not report code 69990 in addition to code 64727)

Transection or Avulsion

(For stereotactic lesion of gasserian ganglion, use 61790)

64732 Transection or avulsion of; supraorbital nerve

64734 infraorbital nerve

64736 mental nerve

64738 inferior alveolar nerve by osteotomy

64740 lingual nerve

64742 facial nerve, differential or complete

64744 greater occipital nerve

64746 phrenic nerve

(For section of recurrent laryngeal nerve, use 31595)

64752 vagus nerve (vagotomy), transthoracic

64755 vagus nerves limited to proximal stomach (selective proximal vagotomy, proximal gastric vagotomy, parietal cell vagotomy, supra- or highly selective vagotomy)

(For laparoscopic approach, use 43652)

64760 vagus nerve (vagotomy), abdominal

(For laparoscopic approach, use 43651)

64761 pudendal nerve

64763 Transection or avulsion of obturator nerve, extrapelvic, with or without adductor tenotomy

64766 Transection or avulsion of obturator nerve, intrapelvic, with or without adductor tenotomy

64771 Transection or avulsion of other cranial nerve, extradural

64772 Transection or avulsion of other spinal nerve, extradural

(For excision of tender scar, skin and subcutaneous tissue, with or without tiny neuroma, see 11400-11446, 13100-13153)

Excision

Somatic Nerves

(For Morton neurectomy, use 28080)

64774 Excision of neuroma; cutaneous nerve, surgically identifiable

64776 digital nerve, one or both, same digit

+ 64778 digital nerve, each additional digit (List separately in addition to code for primary procedure)

(Use 64778 in conjunction with code 64776)

64782 hand or foot, except digital nerve

+ 64783 hand or foot, each additional nerve, except same digit (List separately in addition to code for primary procedure)

(Use 64783 in conjunction with code 64782)

64784 major peripheral nerve, except sciatic

64786 sciatic nerve

+ 64787 Implantation of nerve end into bone or muscle (List separately in addition to neuroma excision)

(Use 64787 in conjunction with codes 64774-64786)

64788 Excision of neurofibroma or neurolemmoma; cutaneous nerve

64790 major peripheral nerve

64792 extensive (including malignant type)

64795 Biopsy of nerve

Sympathetic Nerves

64802 Sympathectomy, cervical

64804 Sympathectomy, cervicothoracic

64809 Sympathectomy, thoracolumbar

64818 Sympathectomy, lumbar

64820 Sympathectomy; digital arteries, each digit

(Do not report 69990 in addition to code 64820)

64821 radial artery

(Do not report 69990 in addition to code 64821)

64822 ulnar artery

(Do not report 69990 in addition to code 64822)

64823 superficial palmar arch

(Do not report 69990 in addition to code 64823)

Neurorrhaphy

64831 Suture of digital nerve, hand or foot; one nerve

+ 64832 each additional digital nerve (List separately in addition to code for primary procedure)

(Use 64832 in conjunction with code 64831)

64834 Suture of one nerve, hand or foot; common sensory nerve

64835 median motor thenar

64836 ulnar motor

+ 64837 Suture of each additional nerve, hand or foot (List separately in addition to code for primary procedure)

(Use 64837 in conjunction with codes 64834-64836)

64840 Suture of posterior tibial nerve

64856 Suture of major peripheral nerve, arm or leg, except sciatic; including transposition

64857 without transposition

64858 Suture of sciatic nerve

+ 64859 Suture of each additional major peripheral nerve (List separately in addition to code for primary procedure)

(Use 64859 in conjunction with codes 64856, 64857)

64861 Suture of; brachial plexus

64862 lumbar plexus

64864 Suture of facial nerve; extracranial

64865 infratemporal, with or without grafting

64866 Anastomosis; facial-spinal accessory

64868 facial-hypoglossal

64870 facial-phrenic

+ 64872 Suture of nerve; requiring secondary or delayed suture (List separately in addition to code for primary neurorrhaphy)

(Use 64872 in conjunction with codes 64831-64865)

+ 64874 requiring extensive mobilization, or transposition of nerve (List separately in addition to code for nerve suture)

(Use 64874 in conjunction with codes 64831-64865)

+ 64876 requiring shortening of bone of extremity (List separately in addition to code for nerve suture)

(Use 64876 in conjunction with codes 64831-64865)

Neurorrhaphy With Nerve Graft

64885 Nerve graft (includes obtaining graft), head or neck; up to 4 cm in length

64886 more than 4 cm length

64890 Nerve graft (includes obtaining graft), single strand, hand or foot; up to 4 cm length

64891 more than 4 cm length

64892 Nerve graft (includes obtaining graft), single strand, arm or leg; up to 4 cm length

64893 more than 4 cm length

64895 Nerve graft (includes obtaining graft), multiple strands (cable), hand or foot; up to 4 cm length

64896 more than 4 cm length

64897 Nerve graft (includes obtaining graft), multiple strands (cable), arm or leg; up to 4 cm length

64898 more than 4 cm length

+ 64901 Nerve graft, each additional nerve; single strand (List separately in addition to code for primary procedure)

(Use 64901 in conjunction with codes 64885-64893)

+ 64902 multiple strands (cable) (List separately in addition to code for primary procedure)

(Use 64902 in conjunction with codes 64885, 64886, 64895-64898)

64905 Nerve pedicle transfer; first stage

64907 second stage

Other Procedures

64999 Unlisted procedure, nervous system

Notes

Eye and Ocular Adnexa

(For diagnostic and treatment ophthalmological services, see **Medicine, Ophthalmology,** and 92002 et seq)

(Do not report code 69990 in addition to codes 65091-68850)

Eyeball

Removal of Eye

65091 Evisceration of ocular contents; without implant

65093 with implant

65101 Enucleation of eye; without implant

65103 with implant, muscles not attached to implant

65105 with implant, muscles attached to implant

(For conjunctivoplasty after enucleation, see 68320 et seq)

65110 Exenteration of orbit (does not include skin graft), removal of orbital contents; only

65112 with therapeutic removal of bone

65114 with muscle or myocutaneous flap

(For skin graft to orbit (split skin), see 15120, 15121; free, full thickness, see 15260, 15261)

(For eyelid repair involving more than skin, see 67930 et seq)

Secondary Implant(s) Procedures

An ocular implant is an implant inside muscular cone; an orbital implant is an implant outside muscular cone.

65125 Modification of ocular implant with placement or replacement of pegs (eg, drilling receptacle for prosthesis appendage) (separate procedure)

65130 Insertion of ocular implant secondary; after evisceration, in scleral shell

65135 after enucleation, muscles not attached to implant

65140 after enucleation, muscles attached to implant

65150 Reinsertion of ocular implant; with or without conjunctival graft

65155 with use of foreign material for reinforcement and/or attachment of muscles to implant

65175 Removal of ocular implant

(For orbital implant (implant outside muscle cone) insertion, use 67550; removal, use 67560)

Removal of Foreign Body

(For removal of implanted material: ocular implant, use 65175; anterior segment implant, use 65920; posterior segment implant, use 67120; orbital implant, use 67560)

(For diagnostic x-ray for foreign body, use 70030)

(For diagnostic echography for foreign body, use 76529)

(For removal of foreign body from orbit: frontal approach, use 67413; lateral approach, use 67430; transcranial approach, use 61334)

(For removal of foreign body from eyelid, embedded, use 67938)

(For removal of foreign body from lacrimal system, use 68530)

65205 Removal of foreign body, external eye; conjunctival superficial

65210 conjunctival embedded (includes concretions), subconjunctival, or scleral nonperforating

65220 corneal, without slit lamp

65222 corneal, with slit lamp

(For repair of corneal laceration with foreign body, use 65275)

65235 Removal of foreign body, intraocular; from anterior chamber of eye or lens

(For removal of implanted material from anterior segment, use 65920)

65260 from posterior segment, magnetic extraction, anterior or posterior route

65265 from posterior segment, nonmagnetic extraction

(For removal of implanted material from posterior segment, use 67120)

Repair of Laceration

(For fracture of orbit, see 21385 et seq)

(For repair of wound of eyelid, skin, linear, simple, see 12011-12018; intermediate, layered closure, see 12051-12057; linear, complex, see 13150-13160; other, see 67930, 67935)

(For repair of wound of lacrimal system, use 68700)

(For repair of operative wound, use 66250)

65270 Repair of laceration; conjunctiva, with or without nonperforating laceration sclera, direct closure

65272 conjunctiva, by mobilization and rearrangement, without hospitalization

65273 conjunctiva, by mobilization and rearrangement, with hospitalization

65275 cornea, nonperforating, with or without removal foreign body

65280 cornea and/or sclera, perforating, not involving uveal tissue

65285 cornea and/or sclera, perforating, with reposition or resection of uveal tissue

65286 application of tissue glue, wounds of cornea and/or sclera

(Repair of laceration includes use of conjunctival flap and restoration of anterior chamber, by air or saline injection when indicated)

(For repair of iris or ciliary body, use 66680)

65290 Repair of wound, extraocular muscle, tendon and/or Tenon's capsule

Anterior Segment

Cornea

Excision

65400 Excision of lesion, cornea (keratectomy, lamellar, partial), except pterygium

65410 Biopsy of cornea

65420 Excision or transposition of pterygium; without graft

65426 with graft

Removal or Destruction

65430 Scraping of cornea, diagnostic, for smear and/or culture

65435 Removal of corneal epithelium; with or without chemocauterization (abrasion, curettage)

65436 with application of chelating agent (eg, EDTA)

65450 Destruction of lesion of cornea by cryotherapy, photocoagulation or thermocauterization

65600 Multiple punctures of anterior cornea (eg, for corneal erosion, tattoo)

Keratoplasty

Corneal transplant includes use of fresh or preserved grafts, and preparation of donor material.

(Keratoplasty excludes refractive keratoplasty procedures, 65760, 65765, and 65767)

65710 Keratoplasty (corneal transplant); lamellar

65730 penetrating (except in aphakia)

65750 penetrating (in aphakia)

65755 penetrating (in pseudophakia)

Other Procedures

65760 Keratomileusis

65765 Keratophakia

65767 Epikeratoplasty

65770 Keratoprosthesis

65771 Radial keratotomy

65772 Corneal relaxing incision for correction of surgically induced astigmatism

65775 Corneal wedge resection for correction of surgically induced astigmatism

(For fitting of contact lens for treatment of disease, use 92070)

(For unlisted procedures on cornea, use 66999)

● 65780 Ocular surface reconstruction; amniotic membrane transplantation

● 65781 limbal stem cell allograft (eg, cadaveric or living donor)

● 65782 limbal conjunctival autograft (includes obtaining graft)

►(For harvesting conjunctival allograft, living donor, use 68371)◄

Anterior Chamber

Incision

65800 Paracentesis of anterior chamber of eye (separate procedure); with diagnostic aspiration of aqueous

65805 with therapeutic release of aqueous

65810 with removal of vitreous and/or discission of anterior hyaloid membrane, with or without air injection

65815 with removal of blood, with or without irrigation and/or air injection

(For injection, see 66020-66030)

(For removal of blood clot, use 65930)

65820 Goniotomy

(Do not report modifier '-63' in conjunction with 65820)

65850 Trabeculotomy ab externo

65855 Trabeculoplasty by laser surgery, one or more sessions (defined treatment series)

(If re-treatment is necessary after several months because of disease progression, a new treatment or treatment series should be reported with a modifier, if necessary, to indicate lesser or greater complexity)

(For trabeculectomy, use 66170)

65860 Severing adhesions of anterior segment, laser technique (separate procedure)

Other Procedures

65865 Severing adhesions of anterior segment of eye, incisional technique (with or without injection of air or liquid) (separate procedure); goniosynechiae

(For trabeculoplasty by laser surgery, use 65855)

65870 anterior synechiae, except goniosynechiae

65875 posterior synechiae

65880 corneovitreal adhesions

(For laser surgery, use 66821)

65900 Removal of epithelial downgrowth, anterior chamber of eye

65920 Removal of implanted material, anterior segment of eye

65930 Removal of blood clot, anterior segment of eye

66020 Injection, anterior chamber of eye (separate procedure); air or liquid

66030 medication

(For unlisted procedures on anterior segment, use 66999)

Anterior Sclera

Excision

(For removal of intraocular foreign body, use 65235)

(For operations on posterior sclera, use 67250, 67255)

66130 Excision of lesion, sclera

66150 Fistulization of sclera for glaucoma; trephination with iridectomy

66155 thermocauterization with iridectomy

66160 sclerectomy with punch or scissors, with iridectomy

66165 iridencleisis or iridotasis

66170 trabeculectomy ab externo in absence of previous surgery

(For trabeculotomy ab externo, use 65850)

(For repair of operative wound, use 66250)

66172 trabeculectomy ab externo with scarring from previous ocular surgery or trauma (includes injection of antifibrotic agents)

66180 Aqueous shunt to extraocular reservoir (eg, Molteno, Schocket, Denver-Krupin)

66185 Revision of aqueous shunt to extraocular reservoir

(For removal of implanted shunt, use 67120)

Repair or Revision

(For scleral procedures in retinal surgery, see 67101 et seq)

66220 Repair of scleral staphyloma; without graft

66225 with graft

(For scleral reinforcement, see 67250, 67255)

66250 Revision or repair of operative wound of anterior segment, any type, early or late, major or minor procedure

(For unlisted procedures on anterior sclera, use 66999)

Iris, Ciliary Body

Incision

66500 Iridotomy by stab incision (separate procedure); except transfixion

66505 with transfixion as for iris bombe

(For iridotomy by photocoagulation, use 66761)

Excision

66600 Iridectomy, with corneoscleral or corneal section; for removal of lesion

66605 with cyclectomy

66625 peripheral for glaucoma (separate procedure)

66630 sector for glaucoma (separate procedure)

66635 optical (separate procedure)

(For coreoplasty by photocoagulation, use 66762)

Repair

66680 Repair of iris, ciliary body (as for iridodialysis)

(For reposition or resection of uveal tissue with perforating wound of cornea or sclera, use 65285)

66682 Suture of iris, ciliary body (separate procedure) with retrieval of suture through small incision (eg, McCannel suture)

Destruction

66700 Ciliary body destruction; diathermy

66710 cyclophotocoagulation

66720 cryotherapy

66740 cyclodialysis

66761 Iridotomy/iridectomy by laser surgery (eg, for glaucoma) (one or more sessions)

66762 Iridoplasty by photocoagulation (one or more sessions) (eg, for improvement of vision, for widening of anterior chamber angle)

66770 Destruction of cyst or lesion iris or ciliary body (nonexcisional procedure)

(For excision lesion iris, ciliary body, see 66600, 66605; for removal of epithelial downgrowth, use 65900)

(For unlisted procedures on iris, ciliary body, use 66999)

Lens

Incision

66820 Discission of secondary membranous cataract (opacified posterior lens capsule and/or anterior hyaloid); stab incision technique (Ziegler or Wheeler knife)

66821 laser surgery (eg, YAG laser) (one or more stages)

66825 Repositioning of intraocular lens prosthesis, requiring an incision (separate procedure)

Removal Cataract

Lateral canthotomy, iridectomy, iridotomy, anterior capsulotomy, posterior capsulotomy, the use of viscoelastic agents, enzymatic zonulysis, use of other pharmacologic agents, and subconjunctival or sub-tenon injections are included as part of the code for the extraction of lens.

66830 Removal of secondary membranous cataract (opacified posterior lens capsule and/or anterior hyaloid) with corneo-scleral section, with or without iridectomy (iridocapsulotomy, iridocapsulectomy)

66840 Removal of lens material; aspiration technique, one or more stages

66850 phacofragmentation technique (mechanical or ultrasonic) (eg, phacoemulsification), with aspiration

66852 pars plana approach, with or without vitrectomy

66920 intracapsular

66930 intracapsular, for dislocated lens

66940 extracapsular (other than 66840, 66850, 66852)

(For removal of intralenticular foreign body without lens extraction, use 65235)

(For repair of operative wound, use 66250)

66982 Extracapsular cataract removal with insertion of intraocular lens prosthesis (one stage procedure), manual or mechanical technique (eg, irrigation and aspiration or phacoemulsification), complex, requiring devices or techniques not generally used in routine cataract surgery (eg, iris expansion device, suture support for intraocular lens, or primary posterior capsulorrhexis) or performed on patients in the amblyogenic developmental stage

66983 Intracapsular cataract extraction with insertion of intraocular lens prosthesis (one stage procedure)

66984 Extracapsular cataract removal with insertion of intraocular lens prosthesis (one stage procedure), manual or mechanical technique (eg, irrigation and aspiration or phacoemulsification)

(For complex extracapsular cataract removal, use 66982)

66985 Insertion of intraocular lens prosthesis (secondary implant), not associated with concurrent cataract removal

(To code implant at time of concurrent cataract surgery, see 66982, 66983, 66984)

(For intraocular lens prosthesis supplied by physician, use 99070)

(For ultrasonic determination of intraocular lens power, use 76519)

(For removal of implanted material from anterior segment, use 65920)

(For secondary fixation (separate procedure), use 66682)

66986 Exchange of intraocular lens

+ 66990 Use of ophthalmic endoscope (List separately in addition to code for primary procedure)

(66990 may be used only with codes 65820, 65875, 65920, 66985, 66986, 67038, 67039, 67040)

Other Procedures

66999 Unlisted procedure, anterior segment of eye

Posterior Segment

Vitreous

67005 Removal of vitreous, anterior approach (open sky technique or limbal incision); partial removal

67010 subtotal removal with mechanical vitrectomy

(For removal of vitreous by paracentesis of anterior chamber, use 65810)

(For removal of corneovitreal adhesions, use 65880)

67015 Aspiration or release of vitreous, subretinal or choroidal fluid, pars plana approach (posterior sclerotomy)

67025 Injection of vitreous substitute, pars plana or limbal approach, (fluid-gas exchange), with or without aspiration (separate procedure)

67027 Implantation of intravitreal drug delivery system (eg, ganciclovir implant), includes concomitant removal of vitreous

(For removal, use 67121)

67028 Intravitreal injection of a pharmacologic agent (separate procedure)

67030 Discission of vitreous strands (without removal), pars plana approach

67031 Severing of vitreous strands, vitreous face adhesions, sheets, membranes or opacities, laser surgery (one or more stages)

67036 Vitrectomy, mechanical, pars plana approach;

67038 with epiretinal membrane stripping

67039 with focal endolaser photocoagulation

67040 with endolaser panretinal photocoagulation

(For use of ophthalmic endoscope with 67038, 67039, 67040, use 66990)

(For associated lensectomy, use 66850)

(For use of vitrectomy in retinal detachment surgery, use 67108)

(For associated removal of foreign body, see 65260, 65265)

(For unlisted procedures on vitreous, use 67299)

Retina or Choroid

Repair

(If diathermy, cryotherapy and/or photocoagulation are combined, report under principal modality used)

67101 Repair of retinal detachment, one or more sessions; cryotherapy or diathermy, with or without drainage of subretinal fluid

67105 photocoagulation, with or without drainage of subretinal fluid

67107 Repair of retinal detachment; scleral buckling (such as lamellar scleral dissection, imbrication or encircling procedure), with or without implant, with or without cryotherapy, photocoagulation, and drainage of subretinal fluid

67108 with vitrectomy, any method, with or without air or gas tamponade, focal endolaser photocoagulation, cryotherapy, drainage of subretinal fluid, scleral buckling, and/or removal of lens by same technique

67110 by injection of air or other gas (eg, pneumatic retinopexy)

67112 by scleral buckling or vitrectomy, on patient having previous ipsilateral retinal detachment repair(s) using scleral buckling or vitrectomy techniques

(For aspiration or drainage of subretinal or subchoroidal fluid, use 67015)

67115 Release of encircling material (posterior segment)

67120 Removal of implanted material, posterior segment; extraocular

67121 intraocular

(For removal from anterior segment, use 65920)

(For removal of foreign body, see 65260, 65265)

Prophylaxis

Repetitive services. The services listed below are often performed in multiple sessions or groups of sessions. The methods of reporting vary.

The following descriptors are intended to include all sessions in a defined treatment period.

67141 Prophylaxis of retinal detachment (eg, retinal break, lattice degeneration) without drainage, one or more sessions; cryotherapy, diathermy

67145 photocoagulation (laser or xenon arc)

Destruction

67208 Destruction of localized lesion of retina (eg, macular edema, tumors), one or more sessions; cryotherapy, diathermy

67210 photocoagulation

67218 radiation by implantation of source (includes removal of source)

67220 Destruction of localized lesion of choroid (eg, choroidal neovascularization); photocoagulation (eg, laser), one or more sessions

(For destruction of macular drusen, photocoagulation, use Category III code 0017T)

(For destruction of localized lesion of choroid by transpupillary thermotherapy, use Category III code 0016T)

67221 photodynamic therapy (includes intravenous infusion)

+ 67225 photodynamic therapy, second eye, at single session (List separately in addition to code for primary eye treatment)

(Use 67225 in conjunction with code 67221)

67227 Destruction of extensive or progressive retinopathy (eg, diabetic retinopathy), one or more sessions; cryotherapy, diathermy

67228 photocoagulation (laser or xenon arc)

(For unlisted procedures on retina, use 67299)

Sclera

Repair

(For excision lesion sclera, use 66130)

67250 Scleral reinforcement (separate procedure); without graft

67255 with graft

(For repair scleral staphyloma, see 66220, 66225)

Other Procedures

67299 Unlisted procedure, posterior segment

Ocular Adnexa

Extraocular Muscles

67311 Strabismus surgery, recession or resection procedure; one horizontal muscle

67312 two horizontal muscles

67314 one vertical muscle (excluding superior oblique)

67316 two or more vertical muscles (excluding superior oblique)

(For adjustable sutures, use 67335 in addition to codes 67311-67334 for primary procedure reflecting number of muscles operated on)

67318 Strabismus surgery, any procedure, superior oblique muscle

+ 67320 Transposition procedure (eg, for paretic extraocular muscle), any extraocular muscle (specify) (List separately in addition to code for primary procedure)

(Use 67320 in conjunction with codes 67311-67318)

+ 67331 Strabismus surgery on patient with previous eye surgery or injury that did not involve the extraocular muscles (List separately in addition to code for primary procedure)

(Use 67331 in conjunction with codes 67311-67318)

+ 67332 Strabismus surgery on patient with scarring of extraocular muscles (eg, prior ocular injury, strabismus or retinal detachment surgery) or restrictive myopathy (eg, dysthyroid ophthalmopathy) (List separately in addition to code for primary procedure)

(Use 67332 in conjunction with codes 67311-67318)

+ 67334 Strabismus surgery by posterior fixation suture technique, with or without muscle recession (List separately in addition to code for primary procedure)

(Use 67334 in conjunction with codes 67311-67318)

+ 67335 Placement of adjustable suture(s) during strabismus surgery, including postoperative adjustment(s) of suture(s) (List separately in addition to code for specific strabismus surgery)

(Use 67335 in conjunction with codes 67311-67334)

+ 67340 Strabismus surgery involving exploration and/or repair of detached extraocular muscle(s) (List separately in addition to code for primary procedure)

(Use 67340 in conjunction with codes 67311-67334)

67343 Release of extensive scar tissue without detaching extraocular muscle (separate procedure)

(Use 67343 in conjunction with codes 67311-67340, when such procedures are performed other than on the affected muscle)

67345 Chemodenervation of extraocular muscle

(For chemodenervation for blepharospasm and other neurological disorders, see 64612 and 64613)

Other Procedures

67350 Biopsy of extraocular muscle

(For repair of wound, extraocular muscle, tendon or Tenon's capsule, use 65290)

67399 Unlisted procedure, ocular muscle

Orbit

Exploration, Excision, Decompression

67400 Orbitotomy without bone flap (frontal or transconjunctival approach); for exploration, with or without biopsy

67405 with drainage only

67412 with removal of lesion

67413 with removal of foreign body

67414 with removal of bone for decompression

67415 Fine needle aspiration of orbital contents

(For exenteration, enucleation, and repair, see 65101 et seq; for optic nerve decompression, use 67570)

67420 Orbitotomy with bone flap or window, lateral approach (eg, Kroenlein); with removal of lesion

67430 with removal of foreign body

67440 with drainage

67445 with removal of bone for decompression

(For optic nerve sheath decompression, use 67570)

67450 for exploration, with or without biopsy

(For orbitotomy, transcranial approach, see 61330-61334)

(For orbital implant, see 67550, 67560)

(For removal of eyeball or for repair after removal, see 65091-65175)

Other Procedures

67500 Retrobulbar injection; medication (separate procedure, does not include supply of medication)

67505 alcohol

67515 Injection of medication or other substance into Tenon's capsule

(For subconjunctival injection, use 68200)

67550 Orbital implant (implant outside muscle cone); insertion

67560 removal or revision

(For ocular implant (implant inside muscle cone), see 65093-65105, 65130-65175)

(For treatment of fractures of malar area, orbit, see 21355 et seq)

67570 Optic nerve decompression (eg, incision or fenestration of optic nerve sheath)

67599 Unlisted procedure, orbit

Eyelids

Incision

67700 Blepharotomy, drainage of abscess, eyelid

67710 Severing of tarsorrhaphy

67715 Canthotomy (separate procedure)

(For canthoplasty, use 67950)

(For division of symblepharon, use 68340)

Excision

Codes for removal of lesion include more than skin (ie, involving lid margin, tarsus, and/or palpebral conjunctiva).

(For removal of lesion, involving mainly skin of eyelid, see 11310-11313; 11440-11446, 11640-11646; 17000-17004)

(For repair of wounds, blepharoplasty, grafts, reconstructive surgery, see 67930-67975)

67800 Excision of chalazion; single

67801 multiple, same lid

67805 multiple, different lids

67808 under general anesthesia and/or requiring hospitalization, single or multiple

67810 Biopsy of eyelid

67820 Correction of trichiasis; epilation, by forceps only

67825 epilation by other than forceps (eg, by electrosurgery, cryotherapy, laser surgery)

67830 incision of lid margin

67835 incision of lid margin, with free mucous membrane graft

67840 Excision of lesion of eyelid (except chalazion) without closure or with simple direct closure

(For excision and repair of eyelid by reconstructive surgery, see 67961, 67966)

67850 Destruction of lesion of lid margin (up to 1 cm)

(For Mohs micrographic surgery, see 17304-17310)

(For initiation or follow-up care of topical chemotherapy (eg, 5-FU or similar agents), see appropriate office visits)

Tarsorrhaphy

67875 Temporary closure of eyelids by suture (eg, Frost suture)

67880 Construction of intermarginal adhesions, median tarsorrhaphy, or canthorrhaphy;

67882 with transposition of tarsal plate

(For severing of tarsorrhaphy, use 67710)

(For canthoplasty, reconstruction canthus, use 67950)

(For canthotomy, use 67715)

Repair (Brow Ptosis, Blepharoptosis, Lid Retraction, Ectropion, Entropion)

67900 Repair of brow ptosis (supraciliary, mid-forehead or coronal approach)

(For forehead rhytidectomy, use 15824)

67901 Repair of blepharoptosis; frontalis muscle technique with suture or other material

67902 frontalis muscle technique with fascial sling (includes obtaining fascia)

67903 (tarso) levator resection or advancement, internal approach

67904 (tarso) levator resection or advancement, external approach

67906 superior rectus technique with fascial sling (includes obtaining fascia)

67908 conjunctivo-tarso-Muller's muscle-levator resection (eg, Fasanella-Servat type)

67909 Reduction of overcorrection of ptosis

67911 Correction of lid retraction

(For obtaining autogenous graft materials, see 20920, 20922 or 20926)

(For correction of trichiasis by mucous membrane graft, use 67835)

●**67912** Correction of lagophthalmos, with implantation of upper eyelid lid load (eg, gold weight)

67914 Repair of ectropion; suture

67915 thermocauterization

▲**67916** excision tarsal wedge

▲**67917** extensive (eg, tarsal strip operations)

(For correction of everted punctum, use 68705)

67921 Repair of entropion; suture

67922 thermocauterization

▲**67923** excision tarsal wedge

▲**67924** extensive (eg, tarsal strip or capsulopalpebral fascia repairs operation)

(For repair of cicatricial ectropion or entropion requiring scar excision or skin graft, see also 67961 et seq)

Reconstruction

Codes for blepharoplasty involve more than skin (ie, involving lid margin, tarsus, and/or palpebral conjunctiva).

67930 Suture of recent wound, eyelid, involving lid margin, tarsus, and/or palpebral conjunctiva direct closure; partial thickness

67935 full thickness

67938 Removal of embedded foreign body, eyelid

(For repair of skin of eyelid, see 12011-12018; 12051-12057; 13150-13153)

(For tarsorrhaphy, canthorrhaphy, see 67880, 67882)

(For repair of blepharoptosis and lid retraction, see 67901-67911)

(For blepharoplasty for entropion, ectropion, see 67916, 67917, 67923, 67924)

(For correction of blepharochalasis (blepharorhytidectomy), see 15820-15823)

(For repair of skin of eyelid, adjacent tissue transfer, see 14060, 14061; preparation for graft, use 15000; free graft, see 15120, 15121, 15260, 15261)

(For excision of lesion of eyelid, use 67800 et seq)

(For repair of lacrimal canaliculi, use 68700)

67950 Canthoplasty (reconstruction of canthus)

67961 Excision and repair of eyelid, involving lid margin, tarsus, conjunctiva, canthus, or full thickness, may include preparation for skin graft or pedicle flap with adjacent tissue transfer or rearrangement; up to one-fourth of lid margin

67966 over one-fourth of lid margin

(For canthoplasty, use 67950)

(For free skin grafts, see 15120, 15121, 15260, 15261)

(For tubed pedicle flap preparation, use 15576; for delay, use 15630; for attachment, use 15650)

67971 Reconstruction of eyelid, full thickness by transfer of tarsoconjunctival flap from opposing eyelid; up to two-thirds of eyelid, one stage or first stage

67973 total eyelid, lower, one stage or first stage

67974 total eyelid, upper, one stage or first stage

67975 second stage

Other Procedures

67999 Unlisted procedure, eyelids

Conjunctiva

(For removal of foreign body, see 65205 et seq)

Incision and Drainage

68020 Incision of conjunctiva, drainage of cyst

68040 Expression of conjunctival follicles (eg, for trachoma)

Excision and/or Destruction

68100 Biopsy of conjunctiva

68110 Excision of lesion, conjunctiva; up to 1 cm

68115 over 1 cm

68130 with adjacent sclera

68135 Destruction of lesion, conjunctiva

Injection

(For injection into Tenon's capsule or retrobulbar injection, see 67500-67515)

68200 Subconjunctival injection

Conjunctivoplasty

(For wound repair, see 65270-65273)

68320 Conjunctivoplasty; with conjunctival graft or extensive rearrangement

68325 with buccal mucous membrane graft (includes obtaining graft)

68326 Conjunctivoplasty, reconstruction cul-de-sac; with conjunctival graft or extensive rearrangement

68328 with buccal mucous membrane graft (includes obtaining graft)

68330 Repair of symblepharon; conjunctivoplasty, without graft

68335 with free graft conjunctiva or buccal mucous membrane (includes obtaining graft)

68340 division of symblepharon, with or without insertion of conformer or contact lens

Other Procedures

68360 Conjunctival flap; bridge or partial (separate procedure)

68362 total (such as Gunderson thin flap or purse string flap)

(For conjunctival flap for perforating injury, see 65280, 65285)

(For repair of operative wound, use 66250)

(For removal of conjunctival foreign body, see 65205, 65210)

●**68371** Harvesting conjunctival allograft, living donor

68399 Unlisted procedure, conjunctiva

Lacrimal System

Incision

68400 Incision, drainage of lacrimal gland

68420 Incision, drainage of lacrimal sac (dacryocystotomy or dacryocystostomy)

68440 Snip incision of lacrimal punctum

Excision

68500 Excision of lacrimal gland (dacryoadenectomy), except for tumor; total

68505 partial

68510 Biopsy of lacrimal gland

68520 Excision of lacrimal sac (dacryocystectomy)

68525 Biopsy of lacrimal sac

68530 Removal of foreign body or dacryolith, lacrimal passages

68540 Excision of lacrimal gland tumor; frontal approach

68550 involving osteotomy

Repair

68700 Plastic repair of canaliculi

68705 Correction of everted punctum, cautery

68720 Dacryocystorhinostomy (fistulization of lacrimal sac to nasal cavity)

68745 Conjunctivorhinostomy (fistulization of conjunctiva to nasal cavity); without tube

68750 with insertion of tube or stent

68760 Closure of the lacrimal punctum; by thermocauterization, ligation, or laser surgery

68761 by plug, each

68770 Closure of lacrimal fistula (separate procedure)

Probing and/or Related Procedures

68801 Dilation of lacrimal punctum, with or without irrigation

(To report a bilateral procedure, use 68801 with modifier '-50')

68810 Probing of nasolacrimal duct, with or without irrigation;

68811 requiring general anesthesia

68815 with insertion of tube or stent

(See also 92018)

(To report a bilateral procedure, use 68810, 68811, or 68815 with modifier '-50')

68840 Probing of lacrimal canaliculi, with or without irrigation

68850 Injection of contrast medium for dacryocystography

(For radiological supervision and interpretation, see 70170, 78660)

Other Procedures

68899 Unlisted procedure, lacrimal system

Notes

Auditory System

(For diagnostic services (eg, audiometry, vestibular tests), see 92502 et seq)

External Ear

Incision

69000 Drainage external ear, abscess or hematoma; simple

69005 complicated

69020 Drainage external auditory canal, abscess

69090 Ear piercing

Excision

69100 Biopsy external ear

69105 Biopsy external auditory canal

69110 Excision external ear; partial, simple repair

69120 complete amputation

(For reconstruction of ear, see 15120 et seq)

69140 Excision exostosis(es), external auditory canal

69145 Excision soft tissue lesion, external auditory canal

69150 Radical excision external auditory canal lesion; without neck dissection

69155 with neck dissection

(For resection of temporal bone, use 69535)

(For skin grafting, see 15000-15261)

Removal of Foreign Body

69200 Removal foreign body from external auditory canal; without general anesthesia

69205 with general anesthesia

69210 Removal impacted cerumen (separate procedure), one or both ears

69220 Debridement, mastoidectomy cavity, simple (eg, routine cleaning)

69222 Debridement, mastoidectomy cavity, complex (eg, with anesthesia or more than routine cleaning)

Repair

(For suture of wound or injury of external ear, see 12011-14300)

69300 Otoplasty, protruding ear, with or without size reduction

69310 Reconstruction of external auditory canal (meatoplasty) (eg, for stenosis due to injury, infection) (separate procedure)

69320 Reconstruction external auditory canal for congenital atresia, single stage

(For combination with middle ear reconstruction, see 69631, 69641)

(For other reconstructive procedures with grafts (eg, skin, cartilage, bone), see 13150-15760, 21230-21235)

Other Procedures

(For otoscopy under general anesthesia, use 92502)

69399 Unlisted procedure, external ear

Middle Ear

Introduction

69400 Eustachian tube inflation, transnasal; with catheterization

69401 without catheterization

69405 Eustachian tube catheterization, transtympanic

69410 Focal application of phase control substance, middle ear (baffle technique)

Incision

69420 Myringotomy including aspiration and/or eustachian tube inflation

69421 Myringotomy including aspiration and/or eustachian tube inflation requiring general anesthesia

69424 Ventilating tube removal requiring general anesthesia

(69424 is a unilateral procedure. To report a bilateral procedure, use 69424 with modifier '-50')

(Do not report code 69424 in conjunction with codes 69205, 69210, 69420, 69421, 69433-69676, 69710-69745, 69801-69930)

69433 Tympanostomy (requiring insertion of ventilating tube), local or topical anesthesia

69436 Tympanostomy (requiring insertion of ventilating tube), general anesthesia

69440 Middle ear exploration through postauricular or ear canal incision

(For atticotomy, see 69601 et seq)

69450 Tympanolysis, transcanal

Excision

69501 Transmastoid antrotomy (simple mastoidectomy)

69502 Mastoidectomy; complete

69505 modified radical

69511 radical

(For skin graft, see 15000 et seq)

(For mastoidectomy cavity debridement, see 69220, 69222)

69530 Petrous apicectomy including radical mastoidectomy

69535 Resection temporal bone, external approach

(For middle fossa approach, see 69950-69970)

69540 Excision aural polyp

69550 Excision aural glomus tumor; transcanal

69552 transmastoid

69554 extended (extratemporal)

Repair

69601 Revision mastoidectomy; resulting in complete mastoidectomy

69602 resulting in modified radical mastoidectomy

69603 resulting in radical mastoidectomy

69604 resulting in tympanoplasty

(For planned secondary tympanoplasty after mastoidectomy, see 69631, 69632)

69605 with apicectomy

(For skin graft, see 15120, 15121, 15260, 15261)

69610 Tympanic membrane repair, with or without site preparation of perforation for closure, with or without patch

69620 Myringoplasty (surgery confined to drumhead and donor area)

69631 Tympanoplasty without mastoidectomy (including canalplasty, atticotomy and/or middle ear surgery), initial or revision; without ossicular chain reconstruction

69632 with ossicular chain reconstruction (eg, postfenestration)

69633 with ossicular chain reconstruction and synthetic prosthesis (eg, partial ossicular replacement prosthesis (PORP), total ossicular replacement prosthesis (TORP))

69635 Tympanoplasty with antrotomy or mastoidotomy (including canalplasty, atticotomy, middle ear surgery, and/or tympanic membrane repair); without ossicular chain reconstruction

69636 with ossicular chain reconstruction

69637 with ossicular chain reconstruction and synthetic prosthesis (eg, partial ossicular replacement prosthesis (PORP), total ossicular replacement prosthesis (TORP))

69641 Tympanoplasty with mastoidectomy (including canalplasty, middle ear surgery, tympanic membrane repair); without ossicular chain reconstruction

69642 with ossicular chain reconstruction

69643 with intact or reconstructed wall, without ossicular chain reconstruction

69644 with intact or reconstructed canal wall, with ossicular chain reconstruction

69645 radical or complete, without ossicular chain reconstruction

69646 radical or complete, with ossicular chain reconstruction

69650 Stapes mobilization

69660 Stapedectomy or stapedotomy with reestablishment of ossicular continuity, with or without use of foreign material;

69661 with footplate drill out

69662 Revision of stapedectomy or stapedotomy

69666 Repair oval window fistula

69667 Repair round window fistula

69670 Mastoid obliteration (separate procedure)

69676 Tympanic neurectomy

Other Procedures

69700 Closure postauricular fistula, mastoid (separate procedure)

69710 Implantation or replacement of electromagnetic bone conduction hearing device in temporal bone

(Replacement procedure includes removal of old device)

69711 Removal or repair of electromagnetic bone conduction hearing device in temporal bone

69714 Implantation, osseointegrated implant, temporal bone, with percutaneous attachment to external speech processor/cochlear stimulator; without mastoidectomy

69715 with mastoidectomy

69717 Replacement (including removal of existing device), osseointegrated implant, temporal bone, with percutaneous attachment to external speech processor/cochlear stimulator; without mastoidectomy

69718 with mastoidectomy

69720 Decompression facial nerve, intratemporal; lateral to geniculate ganglion

69725 including medial to geniculate ganglion

69740 Suture facial nerve, intratemporal, with or without graft or decompression; lateral to geniculate ganglion

69745 including medial to geniculate ganglion

(For extracranial suture of facial nerve, use 64864)

69799 Unlisted procedure, middle ear

Inner Ear

Incision and/or Destruction

69801 Labyrinthotomy, with or without cryosurgery including other nonexcisional destructive procedures or perfusion of vestibuloactive drugs (single or multiple perfusions); transcanal

(69801 includes all required infusions performed on initial and subsequent days of treatment)

69802 with mastoidectomy

69805 Endolymphatic sac operation; without shunt

69806 with shunt

69820 Fenestration semicircular canal

69840 Revision fenestration operation

Excision

69905 Labyrinthectomy; transcanal

69910 with mastoidectomy

69915 Vestibular nerve section, translabyrinthine approach

(For transcranial approach, use 69950)

Introduction

69930 Cochlear device implantation, with or without mastoidectomy

Other Procedures

69949 Unlisted procedure, inner ear

Temporal Bone, Middle Fossa Approach

(For external approach, use 69535)

69950 Vestibular nerve section, transcranial approach

69955 Total facial nerve decompression and/or repair (may include graft)

69960 Decompression internal auditory canal

69970 Removal of tumor, temporal bone

Other Procedures

69979 Unlisted procedure, temporal bone, middle fossa approach

Operating Microscope

The surgical microscope is employed when the surgical services are performed using the techniques of microsurgery. Code 69990 should be reported (without the modifier '-51' appended) in addition to the code for the primary procedure performed. Do not use 69990 for visualization with magnifying loupes or corrected vision. Do not report code 69990 in addition to procedures where use of the operating microscope is an inclusive component (15756-15758, 15842, 19364, 19368, 20955-20962, 20969-20973, 26551-26554, 26556, 31526, 31531, 31536, 31541, 31561, 31571, 43116, 43496, 49906, 61548, 63075-63078, 64727, 64820–64823, 65091-68850).

+ 69990 Microsurgical techniques, requiring use of operating microscope (List separately in addition to code for primary procedure)

Notes

Surgery: Ocular/Auditory System

Radiology Guidelines (Including Nuclear Medicine and Diagnostic Ultrasound)

Items used by all physicians in reporting their services are presented in the **Introduction.** Some of the commonalities are repeated here for the convenience of those physicians referring to this section on **Radiology (Including Nuclear Medicine and Diagnostic Ultrasound).** Other definitions and items unique to Radiology are also listed.

Subject Listings

Subject listings apply when radiological services are performed by or under the responsible supervision of a physician.

Separate Procedures

Some of the procedures or services listed in *CPT* that are commonly carried out as an integral component of a total service or procedure have been identified by the inclusion of the term "separate procedure." The codes designated as "separate procedure" should not be reported in addition to the code for the total procedure or service of which it is considered an integral component.

However, when a procedure or service that is designated as a "separate procedure" is carried out independently or considered to be unrelated or distinct from other procedures/services provided at that time, it may be reported by itself, or in addition to other procedures/services by appending the modifier '-59' to the specific "separate procedure" code to indicate that the procedure is not considered to be a component of another procedure, but is a distinct, independent procedure. This may represent a different session or patient encounter, different procedure or surgery, different site or organ system, separate incision/excision, separate lesion, or separate injury (or area of injury in extensive injuries).

Subsection Information

Several of the subheadings or subsections have special needs or instructions unique to that section. Where these are indicated (eg, "Radiation Oncology") special **"Notes"** will be presented preceding those procedural terminology listings, referring to that subsection specifically. If there is an "Unlisted Procedure" code number (see section below) for the individual subsection, it will be shown. Those subsections with **"Notes"** are as follows:

Diagnostic Radiology (Diagnostic Imaging) 70010-76499
Aorta and Arteries 75600-75790
Diagnostic Ultrasound 76506-76999
Radiation Oncology 77261-77799
Clinical Treatment Planning 77261-77299
Radiation Treatment Management 77427-77499
Proton Beam Treatment Delivery 77520-77525
Hyperthermia 77600-77620
Clinical Brachytherapy 77750-77799
Nuclear Medicine 78000-78299
Musculoskeletal System 78300-78399
Cardiovascular System 78414-78499

Unlisted Service or Procedure

A service or procedure may be provided that is not listed in this edition of *CPT*. When reporting such a service, the appropriate "Unlisted Procedure" code may be used to indicate the service, identifying it by "Special Report" as discussed below. The "Unlisted Procedures" and accompanying codes for **Radiology (Including Nuclear Medicine and Diagnostic Ultrasound)** are as follows:

76496 Unlisted fluoroscopic procedure (eg, diagnostic, interventional)

76497 Unlisted computed tomography procedure (eg, diagnostic, interventional)

76498 Unlisted magnetic resonance procedure (eg, diagnostic, interventional)

76499 Unlisted diagnostic radiographic procedure

76999 Unlisted ultrasound procedure (eg, diagnostic, interventional)

77299	Unlisted procedure, therapeutic radiology clinical treatment planning
77399	Unlisted procedure, medical radiation physics, dosimetry, and treatment devices, and special services
77499	Unlisted procedure, therapeutic radiology treatment management
77799	Unlisted procedure, clinical brachytherapy
78099	Unlisted endocrine procedure, diagnostic nuclear medicine
78199	Unlisted hematopoietic, reticuloendothelial and lymphatic procedure, diagnostic nuclear medicine
78299	Unlisted gastrointestinal procedure, diagnostic nuclear medicine
78399	Unlisted musculoskeletal procedure, diagnostic nuclear medicine
78499	Unlisted cardiovascular procedure, diagnostic nuclear medicine
78599	Unlisted respiratory procedure, diagnostic nuclear medicine
78699	Unlisted nervous system procedure, diagnostic nuclear medicine
78799	Unlisted genitourinary procedure, diagnostic nuclear medicine
78999	Unlisted miscellaneous procedure, diagnostic nuclear medicine
79999	Unlisted radiopharmaceutical therapeutic procedure

Special Report

A service that is rarely provided, unusual, variable, or new may require a special report in determining medical appropriateness of the service. Pertinent information should include an adequate definition or description of the nature, extent, and need for the procedure; and the time, effort, and equipment necessary to provide the service. Additional items which may be included are:

- complexity of symptoms;
- final diagnosis;
- pertinent physical findings;
- diagnostic and therapeutic procedures;
- concurrent problems;
- follow-up care.

Supervision and Interpretation

When a procedure is performed by two physicians, the radiologic portion of the procedure is designated as "radiological supervision and interpretation." When a physician performs both the procedure and provides imaging supervision and interpretation, a combination of procedure codes outside the 70000 series and imaging supervision and interpretation codes are to be used.

(The Radiological Supervision and Interpretation codes are not applicable to the Radiation Oncology subsection.)

Administration of Contrast Material(s)

The phrase "with contrast" used in the codes for procedures performed using contrast for imaging enhancement represents contrast material administered intravascularly, intra-articularly or intrathecally.

For intra-articular injection, use the appropriate joint injection code. If radiographic arthrography is performed, also use the arthrography supervision and interpretation code for the appropriate joint (which includes fluoroscopy). If CT or MR arthrography are performed without radiographic arthrography, use the appropriate joint injection code, the appropriate CT or MR code ("with contrast" or "without followed by contrast"), and the appropriate imaging guidance code for needle placement for contrast injection.

For spine examinations using computed tomography, magnetic resonance imaging, magnetic resonance angiography, "with contrast" includes intrathecal or intravascular injection. For intrathecal injection, use also 61055 or 62284.

Injection of intravascular contrast material is part of the "with contrast" CT, CTA, MRI, MRA procedure.

Oral and/or rectal contrast administration alone does not qualify as a study "with contrast."

Written Report(s)

A written report, signed by the interpreting physician, should be considered an integral part of a radiologic procedure or interpretation.

Radiology

Diagnostic Radiology (Diagnostic Imaging)

Head and Neck

(70002, 70003 have been deleted. To report, use 76499)

70010 Myelography, posterior fossa, radiological supervision and interpretation

70015 Cisternography, positive contrast, radiological supervision and interpretation

70030 Radiologic examination, eye, for detection of foreign body

70100 Radiologic examination, mandible; partial, less than four views

70110 complete, minimum of four views

70120 Radiologic examination, mastoids; less than three views per side

70130 complete, minimum of three views per side

70134 Radiologic examination, internal auditory meati, complete

70140 Radiologic examination, facial bones; less than three views

70150 complete, minimum of three views

70160 Radiologic examination, nasal bones, complete, minimum of three views

70170 Dacryocystography, nasolacrimal duct, radiological supervision and interpretation

70190 Radiologic examination; optic foramina

70200 orbits, complete, minimum of four views

70210 Radiologic examination, sinuses, paranasal, less than three views

70220 Radiologic examination, sinuses, paranasal, complete, minimum of three views

70240 Radiologic examination, sella turcica

▲**70250** Radiologic examination, skull; less than four views

▲**70260** complete, minimum of four views

70300 Radiologic examination, teeth; single view

70310 partial examination, less than full mouth

70320 complete, full mouth

70328 Radiologic examination, temporomandibular joint, open and closed mouth; unilateral

70330 bilateral

70332 Temporomandibular joint arthrography, radiological supervision and interpretation

(Do not report 76003 in addition to 70332)

70336 Magnetic resonance (eg, proton) imaging, temporomandibular joint(s)

70350 Cephalogram, orthodontic

70355 Orthopantogram

70360 Radiologic examination; neck, soft tissue

70370 pharynx or larynx, including fluoroscopy and/or magnification technique

70371 Complex dynamic pharyngeal and speech evaluation by cine or video recording

70373 Laryngography, contrast, radiological supervision and interpretation

70380 Radiologic examination, salivary gland for calculus

70390 Sialography, radiological supervision and interpretation

70450 Computed tomography, head or brain; without contrast material

70460 with contrast material(s)

70470 without contrast material, followed by contrast material(s) and further sections

(For coronal, sagittal, and/or oblique sections, use 76375)

70480 Computed tomography, orbit, sella, or posterior fossa or outer, middle, or inner ear; without contrast material

70481 with contrast material(s)

70482 without contrast material, followed by contrast material(s) and further sections

(For coronal, sagittal, and/or oblique sections, use 76375)

70486 Computed tomography, maxillofacial area; without contrast material

70487 with contrast material(s)

70488 without contrast material, followed by contrast material(s) and further sections

(For coronal, sagittal, and/or oblique sections, use 76375)

70490 Computed tomography, soft tissue neck; without contrast material

70491 with contrast material(s)

70492 without contrast material followed by contrast material(s) and further sections

(For coronal, sagittal, and/or oblique sections, use 76375)

(For cervical spine, see 72125, 72126)

70496 Computed tomographic angiography, head, without contrast material(s), followed by contrast material(s) and further sections, including image post-processing

70498 Computed tomographic angiography, neck, without contrast material(s), followed by contrast material(s) and further sections, including image post-processing

70540 Magnetic resonance (eg, proton) imaging, orbit, face, and neck; without contrast material(s)

70542 with contrast material(s)

70543 without contrast material(s), followed by contrast material(s) and further sequences

70544 Magnetic resonance angiography, head; without contrast material(s)

70545 with contrast material(s)

70546 without contrast material(s), followed by contrast material(s) and further sequences

70547 Magnetic resonance angiography, neck; without contrast material(s)

70548 with contrast material(s)

70549 without contrast material(s), followed by contrast material(s) and further sequences

70551 Magnetic resonance (eg, proton) imaging, brain (including brain stem); without contrast material

70552 with contrast material(s)

70553 without contrast material, followed by contrast material(s) and further sequences

(For magnetic spectroscopy, use 76390)

● **70557** Magnetic resonance (eg, proton) imaging, brain (including brain stem and skull base), during open intracranial procedure (eg, to assess for residual tumor or residual vascular malformation); without contrast material

● **70558** with contrast material(s)

● **70559** without contrast material(s), followed by contrast material(s) and further sequences

►(For stereotactic biopsy of intracranial lesion with magnetic resonance guidance, use 61751. 70557, 70558 or 70559 may be reported only if a separate report is generated. Report only one of the above codes once per operative session. Do not use these codes in conjunction with 61751, 76393, 76394)◄

Chest

(71000 has been deleted)

71010 Radiologic examination, chest; single view, frontal

71015 stereo, frontal

71020 Radiologic examination, chest, two views, frontal and lateral;

71021 with apical lordotic procedure

71022 with oblique projections

71023 with fluoroscopy

71030 Radiologic examination, chest, complete, minimum of four views;

71034 with fluoroscopy

(For separate chest fluoroscopy, use 76000)

71035 Radiologic examination, chest, special views (eg, lateral decubitus, Bucky studies)

71040 Bronchography, unilateral, radiological supervision and interpretation

71060 Bronchography, bilateral, radiological supervision and interpretation

71090 Insertion pacemaker, fluoroscopy and radiography, radiological supervision and interpretation

(For procedure, see appropriate organ or site)

71100 Radiologic examination, ribs, unilateral; two views

71101 including posteroanterior chest, minimum of three views

71110 Radiologic examination, ribs, bilateral; three views

71111 including posteroanterior chest, minimum of four views

71120 Radiologic examination; sternum, minimum of two views

71130 sternoclavicular joint or joints, minimum of three views

71250 Computed tomography, thorax; without contrast material

71260 with contrast material(s)

71270 without contrast material, followed by contrast material(s) and further sections

(For coronal, sagittal, and/or oblique sections, use 76375)

71275 Computed tomographic angiography, chest, without contrast material(s), followed by contrast material(s) and further sections, including image post-processing

71550 Magnetic resonance (eg, proton) imaging, chest (eg, for evaluation of hilar and mediastinal lymphadenopathy); without contrast material(s)

71551 with contrast material(s)

71552 without contrast material(s), followed by contrast material(s) and further sequences

(For breast MRI, see 76093 and 76094)

71555 Magnetic resonance angiography, chest (excluding myocardium), with or without contrast material(s)

Spine and Pelvis

72010 Radiologic examination, spine, entire, survey study, anteroposterior and lateral

72020 Radiologic examination, spine, single view, specify level

72040 Radiologic examination, spine, cervical; two or three views

72050 minimum of four views

72052 complete, including oblique and flexion and/or extension studies

72069 Radiologic examination, spine, thoracolumbar, standing (scoliosis)

72070 Radiologic examination, spine; thoracic, two views

72072 thoracic, three views

72074 thoracic, minimum of four views

72080 thoracolumbar, two views

72090 scoliosis study, including supine and erect studies

72100 Radiologic examination, spine, lumbosacral; two or three views

72110 minimum of four views

72114 complete, including bending views

72120 Radiologic examination, spine, lumbosacral, bending views only, minimum of four views

(Contrast material in CT of spine is either by intrathecal or intravenous injection. For intrathecal injection, use also 61055 or 62284. IV injection of contrast material is part of the CT procedure)

72125 Computed tomography, cervical spine; without contrast material

72126 with contrast material

72127 without contrast material, followed by contrast material(s) and further sections

(For intrathecal injection procedure, see 61055, 62284)

72128 Computed tomography, thoracic spine; without contrast material

72129 with contrast material

(For intrathecal injection procedure, see 61055, 62284)

72130 without contrast material, followed by contrast material(s) and further sections

(For intrathecal injection procedure, see 61055, 62284)

72131 Computed tomography, lumbar spine; without contrast material

72132 with contrast material

72133 without contrast material, followed by contrast material(s) and further sections

(For intrathecal injection procedure, see 61055, 62284)

(For coronal, sagittal, and/or oblique sections, use 76375)

72141 Magnetic resonance (eg, proton) imaging, spinal canal and contents, cervical; without contrast material

72142 with contrast material(s)

(For cervical spinal canal imaging without contrast material followed by contrast material, use 72156)

72146 Magnetic resonance (eg, proton) imaging, spinal canal and contents, thoracic; without contrast material

72147 with contrast material(s)

(For thoracic spinal canal imaging without contrast material followed by contrast material, use 72157)

72148 Magnetic resonance (eg, proton) imaging, spinal canal and contents, lumbar; without contrast material

72149 with contrast material(s)

(For lumbar spinal canal imaging without contrast material followed by contrast material, use 72158)

72156 Magnetic resonance (eg, proton) imaging, spinal canal and contents, without contrast material, followed by contrast material(s) and further sequences; cervical

72157 thoracic

72158 lumbar

72159 Magnetic resonance angiography, spinal canal and contents, with or without contrast material(s)

72170 Radiologic examination, pelvis; one or two views

72190 complete, minimum of three views

(For pelvimetry, use 74710)

72191 Computed tomographic angiography, pelvis, without contrast material(s), followed by contrast material(s) and further sections, including image post-processing

(For CTA aorto-iliofemoral runoff, use 75635)

72192 Computed tomography, pelvis; without contrast material

72193 with contrast material(s)

72194 without contrast material, followed by contrast material(s) and further sections

(For coronal, sagittal, and/or oblique sections, use 76375)

72195 Magnetic resonance (eg, proton) imaging, pelvis; without contrast material(s)

72196 with contrast material(s)

72197 without contrast material(s), followed by contrast material(s) and further sequences

72198 Magnetic resonance angiography, pelvis, with or without contrast material(s)

72200 Radiologic examination, sacroiliac joints; less than three views

72202 three or more views

72220 Radiologic examination, sacrum and coccyx, minimum of two views

72240 Myelography, cervical, radiological supervision and interpretation

72255 Myelography, thoracic, radiological supervision and interpretation

72265 Myelography, lumbosacral, radiological supervision and interpretation

▲72270 Myelography, two or more regions (eg, lumbar/thoracic, cervical/thoracic, lumbar/cervical, lumbar/thoracic/cervical), radiological supervision and interpretation

72275 Epidurography, radiological supervision and interpretation

(72275 includes 76005)

(For injection procedure, see 62280-62282, 62310-62319, 64479-64484, ►0027T◄)

►(Use 72275 only when an epidurogram is performed, images documented, and a formal radiologic report is issued)◄

72285 Diskography, cervical or thoracic, radiological supervision and interpretation

72295 Diskography, lumbar, radiological supervision and interpretation

Upper Extremities

(For stress views, any joint, use 76006)

73000 Radiologic examination; clavicle, complete

73010 scapula, complete

73020 Radiologic examination, shoulder; one view

73030 complete, minimum of two views

73040 Radiologic examination, shoulder, arthrography, radiological supervision and interpretation

(Do not report 76003 in addition to 73040)

73050 Radiologic examination; acromioclavicular joints, bilateral, with or without weighted distraction

73060 humerus, minimum of two views

73070 Radiologic examination, elbow; two views

73080 complete, minimum of three views

73085 Radiologic examination, elbow, arthrography, radiological supervision and interpretation

(Do not report 76003 in addition to 73085)

73090 Radiologic examination; forearm, two views

73092 upper extremity, infant, minimum of two views

73100 Radiologic examination, wrist; two views

73110 complete, minimum of three views

73115 Radiologic examination, wrist, arthrography, radiological supervision and interpretation

(Do not report 76003 in addition to 73115)

73120 Radiologic examination, hand; two views

73130 minimum of three views

73140 Radiologic examination, finger(s), minimum of two views

73200 Computed tomography, upper extremity; without contrast material

73201 with contrast material(s)

73202 without contrast material, followed by contrast material(s) and further sections

(For coronal, sagittal, and/or oblique sections, use 76375)

73206 Computed tomographic angiography, upper extremity, without contrast material(s), followed by contrast material(s) and further sections, including image post-processing

73218 Magnetic resonance (eg, proton) imaging, upper extremity, other than joint; without contrast material(s)

73219 with contrast material(s)

73220 without contrast material(s), followed by contrast material(s) and further sequences

73221 Magnetic resonance (eg, proton) imaging, any joint of upper extremity; without contrast material(s)

73222 with contrast material(s)

73223 without contrast material(s), followed by contrast material(s) and further sequences

73225 Magnetic resonance angiography, upper extremity, with or without contrast material(s)

Lower Extremities

(For stress views, any joint, use 76006)

73500 Radiologic examination, hip, unilateral; one view

73510 complete, minimum of two views

73520 Radiologic examination, hips, bilateral, minimum of two views of each hip, including anteroposterior view of pelvis

73525 Radiologic examination, hip, arthrography, radiological supervision and interpretation

(Do not report 76003 in addition to 73525)

73530 Radiologic examination, hip, during operative procedure

73540 Radiologic examination, pelvis and hips, infant or child, minimum of two views

73542 Radiological examination, sacroiliac joint arthrography, radiological supervision and interpretation

(Do not report 76003 in addition to 73542)

(For procedure, use 27096. If formal arthrography is not performed, recorded, and a formal radiologic report is not issued, use 76005 for fluoroscopic guidance for sacroiliac joint injections)

73550 Radiologic examination, femur, two views

73560 Radiologic examination, knee; one or two views

73562 three views

73564 complete, four or more views

73565 both knees, standing, anteroposterior

73580 Radiologic examination, knee, arthrography, radiological supervision and interpretation

(Do not report 76003 in addition to 73580)

73590 Radiologic examination; tibia and fibula, two views

73592 lower extremity, infant, minimum of two views

73600 Radiologic examination, ankle; two views

73610 complete, minimum of three views

73615 Radiologic examination, ankle, arthrography, radiological supervision and interpretation

(Do not report 76003 in addition to 73615)

73620 Radiologic examination, foot; two views

73630 complete, minimum of three views

73650 Radiologic examination; calcaneus, minimum of two views

73660 toe(s), minimum of two views

73700 Computed tomography, lower extremity; without contrast material

73701 with contrast material(s)

73702 without contrast material, followed by contrast material(s) and further sections

(For coronal, sagittal, and/or oblique sections, use 76375)

73706 Computed tomographic angiography, lower extremity, without contrast material(s), followed by contrast material(s) and further sections, including image post-processing

(For CTA aorto-iliofemoral runoff, use 75635)

73718 Magnetic resonance (eg, proton) imaging, lower extremity other than joint; without contrast material(s)

73719 with contrast material(s)

73720 without contrast material(s), followed by contrast material(s) and further sequences

73721 Magnetic resonance (eg, proton) imaging, any joint of lower extremity; without contrast material

73722 with contrast material(s)

73723 without contrast material(s), followed by contrast material(s) and further sequences

73725 Magnetic resonance angiography, lower extremity, with or without contrast material(s)

Abdomen

74000 Radiologic examination, abdomen; single anteroposterior view

74010 anteroposterior and additional oblique and cone views

74020 complete, including decubitus and/or erect views

74022 complete acute abdomen series, including supine, erect, and/or decubitus views, single view chest

74150 Computed tomography, abdomen; without contrast material

74160 with contrast material(s)

74170 without contrast material, followed by contrast material(s) and further sections

(For coronal, sagittal, and/or oblique sections, use 76375)

74175 Computed tomographic angiography, abdomen, without contrast material(s), followed by contrast material(s) and further sections, including image post-processing

(For CTA aorto-iliofemoral runoff, use 75635)

74181 Magnetic resonance (eg, proton) imaging, abdomen; without contrast material(s)

74182 with contrast material(s)

74183 without contrast material(s), followed by with contrast material(s) and further sequences

74185 Magnetic resonance angiography, abdomen, with or without contrast material(s)

74190 Peritoneogram (eg, after injection of air or contrast), radiological supervision and interpretation

(For procedure, use 49400)

(For computed tomography, see 72192 or 74150)

Gastrointestinal Tract

(For percutaneous placement of gastrostomy tube, use 43750)

74210 Radiologic examination; pharynx and/or cervical esophagus

74220 esophagus

74230 Swallowing function, with cineradiography/videoradiography

74235 Removal of foreign body(s), esophageal, with use of balloon catheter, radiological supervision and interpretation

(For procedure, see 43215, 43247)

74240 Radiologic examination, gastrointestinal tract, upper; with or without delayed films, without KUB

74241 with or without delayed films, with KUB

74245 with small intestine, includes multiple serial films

74246 Radiological examination, gastrointestinal tract, upper, air contrast, with specific high density barium, effervescent agent, with or without glucagon; with or without delayed films, without KUB

74247 with or without delayed films, with KUB

74249 with small intestine follow-through

74250 Radiologic examination, small intestine, includes multiple serial films;

74251 via enteroclysis tube

74260 Duodenography, hypotonic

74270 Radiologic examination, colon; barium enema, with or without KUB

74280 air contrast with specific high density barium, with or without glucagon

74283 Therapeutic enema, contrast or air, for reduction of intussusception or other intraluminal obstruction (eg, meconium ileus)

74290 Cholecystography, oral contrast;

74291 additional or repeat examination or multiple day examination

74300 Cholangiography and/or pancreatography; intraoperative, radiological supervision and interpretation

+ 74301 additional set intraoperative, radiological supervision and interpretation (List separately in addition to code for primary procedure)

(Use 74301 in conjunction with code 74300)

74305 through existing catheter, radiological supervision and interpretation

(For procedure, see 47505, 48400, 47560-47561, 47563)

(For biliary duct stone extraction, percutaneous, see 47630, 74327)

74320 Cholangiography, percutaneous, transhepatic, radiological supervision and interpretation

74327 Postoperative biliary duct calculus removal, percutaneous via T-tube tract, basket, or snare (eg, Burhenne technique), radiological supervision and interpretation

(For procedure, use 47630)

74328 Endoscopic catheterization of the biliary ductal system, radiological supervision and interpretation

(For procedure, see 43260-43272 as appropriate)

74329 Endoscopic catheterization of the pancreatic ductal system, radiological supervision and interpretation

(For procedure, see 43260-43272 as appropriate)

74330 Combined endoscopic catheterization of the biliary and pancreatic ductal systems, radiological supervision and interpretation

(For procedure, see 43260-43272 as appropriate)

74340 Introduction of long gastrointestinal tube (eg, Miller-Abbott), including multiple fluoroscopies and films, radiological supervision and interpretation

(For tube placement, use 44500)

74350 Percutaneous placement of gastrostomy tube, radiological supervision and interpretation

74355 Percutaneous placement of enteroclysis tube, radiological supervision and interpretation

74360 Intraluminal dilation of strictures and/or obstructions (eg, esophagus), radiological supervision and interpretation

74363 Percutaneous transhepatic dilation of biliary duct stricture with or without placement of stent, radiological supervision and interpretation

(For procedure, see 47510, 47511, 47555, 47556)

Urinary Tract

74400 Urography (pyelography), intravenous, with or without KUB, with or without tomography

74410 Urography, infusion, drip technique and/or bolus technique;

74415 with nephrotomography

74420 Urography, retrograde, with or without KUB

74425 Urography, antegrade, (pyelostogram, nephrostogram, loopogram), radiological supervision and interpretation

74430 Cystography, minimum of three views, radiological supervision and interpretation

74440 Vasography, vesiculography, or epididymography, radiological supervision and interpretation

74445 Corpora cavernosography, radiological supervision and interpretation

74450 Urethrocystography, retrograde, radiological supervision and interpretation

74455 Urethrocystography, voiding, radiological supervision and interpretation

74470 Radiologic examination, renal cyst study, translumbar, contrast visualization, radiological supervision and interpretation

74475 Introduction of intracatheter or catheter into renal pelvis for drainage and/or injection, percutaneous, radiological supervision and interpretation

74480 Introduction of ureteral catheter or stent into ureter through renal pelvis for drainage and/or injection, percutaneous, radiological supervision and interpretation

(For transurethral surgery (ureter and pelvis), see 52320-52355)

74485 Dilation of nephrostomy, ureters, or urethra, radiological supervision and interpretation

(For dilation of ureter without radiologic guidance, use 52341, 52344)

(For change of nephrostomy or pyelostomy tube, use 50398)

Gynecological and Obstetrical

(For abdomen and pelvis, see 72170-72190, 74000-74170)

74710 Pelvimetry, with or without placental localization

74740 Hysterosalpingography, radiological supervision and interpretation

(For introduction of saline or contrast for hysterosalpingography, see 58340)

74742 Transcervical catheterization of fallopian tube, radiological supervision and interpretation

(For procedure, use 58345)

74775 Perineogram (eg, vaginogram, for sex determination or extent of anomalies)

Heart

(For separate injection procedures for vascular radiology, see **Surgery** section, 36000-36299)

(For cardiac catheterization procedures, see 93501-93556)

75552 Cardiac magnetic resonance imaging for morphology; without contrast material

75553 with contrast material

75554 Cardiac magnetic resonance imaging for function, with or without morphology; complete study

75555 limited study

75556 Cardiac magnetic resonance imaging for velocity flow mapping

Aorta and Arteries

Selective vascular catheterizations should be coded to include introduction and all lesser order selective catheterizations used in the approach (eg, the description for a selective right middle cerebral artery catheterization includes the introduction and placement catheterization of the right common and internal carotid arteries).

Additional second and/or third order arterial catheterizations within the same family of arteries supplied by a single first order artery should be expressed by 36218 or 36248. Additional first order or higher catheterizations in vascular families supplied by a first order vessel different from a previously selected and coded family should be separately coded using the conventions described above.

(For intravenous procedure, see 36000-36013, 36400-36425 and 36100-36248 for intra-arterial procedure)

(For radiological supervision and interpretation, see 75600-75978)

75600 Aortography, thoracic, without serialography, radiological supervision and interpretation

(For injection procedure, use 93544)

75605 Aortography, thoracic, by serialography, radiological supervision and interpretation

(For injection procedure, use 93544)

(75620, 75621, 75622, 75623 have been deleted. To report, use 76499)

75625 Aortography, abdominal, by serialography, radiological supervision and interpretation

(For injection procedure, use 93544)

75630 Aortography, abdominal plus bilateral iliofemoral lower extremity, catheter, by serialography, radiological supervision and interpretation

75635 Computed tomographic angiography, abdominal aorta and bilateral iliofemoral lower extremity runoff, radiological supervision and interpretation, without contrast material(s), followed by contrast material(s) and further sections, including image post-processing

75650 Angiography, cervicocerebral, catheter, including vessel origin, radiological supervision and interpretation

75658 Angiography, brachial, retrograde, radiological supervision and interpretation

75660 Angiography, external carotid, unilateral, selective, radiological supervision and interpretation

75662 Angiography, external carotid, bilateral, selective, radiological supervision and interpretation

75665 Angiography, carotid, cerebral, unilateral, radiological supervision and interpretation

75671 Angiography, carotid, cerebral, bilateral, radiological supervision and interpretation

75676 Angiography, carotid, cervical, unilateral, radiological supervision and interpretation

75680 Angiography, carotid, cervical, bilateral, radiological supervision and interpretation

75685 Angiography, vertebral, cervical, and/or intracranial, radiological supervision and interpretation

75705 Angiography, spinal, selective, radiological supervision and interpretation

75710 Angiography, extremity, unilateral, radiological supervision and interpretation

75716 Angiography, extremity, bilateral, radiological supervision and interpretation

75722 Angiography, renal, unilateral, selective (including flush aortogram), radiological supervision and interpretation

75724 Angiography, renal, bilateral, selective (including flush aortogram), radiological supervision and interpretation

75726 Angiography, visceral, selective or supraselective, (with or without flush aortogram), radiological supervision and interpretation

(For selective angiography, each additional visceral vessel studied after basic examination, use 75774)

75731 Angiography, adrenal, unilateral, selective, radiological supervision and interpretation

75733 Angiography, adrenal, bilateral, selective, radiological supervision and interpretation

75736 Angiography, pelvic, selective or supraselective, radiological supervision and interpretation

75741 Angiography, pulmonary, unilateral, selective, radiological supervision and interpretation

(For injection procedure, use 93541)

75743 Angiography, pulmonary, bilateral, selective, radiological supervision and interpretation

(For injection procedure, use 93541)

75746 Angiography, pulmonary, by nonselective catheter or venous injection, radiological supervision and interpretation

(For injection procedure, use 93541)

(For introduction of catheter, injection procedure, see 93501-93533, 93539, 93540, 93545, 93556)

(For introduction of catheter, injection procedure, see 93501-93533, 93545, 93556)

(For introduction of catheter, injection procedure, see 93501-93533, 93539, 93540, 93545, 93556)

75756 Angiography, internal mammary, radiological supervision and interpretation

(For introduction of catheter, injection procedure, see 93501-93533, 93545, 93556)

+ 75774 Angiography, selective, each additional vessel studied after basic examination, radiological supervision and interpretation (List separately in addition to code for primary procedure)

(Use 75774 in addition to code for specific initial vessel studied)

(For angiography, see codes 75600-75790)

(For catheterizations, see codes 36215-36248)

(For introduction of catheter, injection procedure, see 93501-93533, 93545, 93555, 93556)

75790 Angiography, arteriovenous shunt (eg, dialysis patient), radiological supervision and interpretation

(For introduction of catheter, use 36140, 36145, 36215-36217, 36245-36247)

Veins and Lymphatics

(For injection procedure for venous system, see 36000-36015, 36400-36510)

(For injection procedure for lymphatic system, use 38790)

75801 Lymphangiography, extremity only, unilateral, radiological supervision and interpretation

75803 Lymphangiography, extremity only, bilateral, radiological supervision and interpretation

75805 Lymphangiography, pelvic/abdominal, unilateral, radiological supervision and interpretation

75807 Lymphangiography, pelvic/abdominal, bilateral, radiological supervision and interpretation

75809 Shuntogram for investigation of previously placed indwelling nonvascular shunt (eg, LeVeen shunt, ventriculoperitoneal shunt, indwelling infusion pump), radiological supervision and interpretation

(For procedure, see 49427 or 61070)

75810 Splenoportography, radiological supervision and interpretation

75820 Venography, extremity, unilateral, radiological supervision and interpretation

75822 Venography, extremity, bilateral, radiological supervision and interpretation

75825 Venography, caval, inferior, with serialography, radiological supervision and interpretation

75827 Venography, caval, superior, with serialography, radiological supervision and interpretation

75831 Venography, renal, unilateral, selective, radiological supervision and interpretation

75833 Venography, renal, bilateral, selective, radiological supervision and interpretation

75840 Venography, adrenal, unilateral, selective, radiological supervision and interpretation

75842 Venography, adrenal, bilateral, selective, radiological supervision and interpretation

▲ 75860 Venography, venous sinus (eg, petrosal and inferior sagittal) or jugular, catheter, radiological supervision and interpretation

75870 Venography, superior sagittal sinus, radiological supervision and interpretation

75872 Venography, epidural, radiological supervision and interpretation

75880 Venography, orbital, radiological supervision and interpretation

75885 Percutaneous transhepatic portography with hemodynamic evaluation, radiological supervision and interpretation

75887 Percutaneous transhepatic portography without hemodynamic evaluation, radiological supervision and interpretation

75889 Hepatic venography, wedged or free, with hemodynamic evaluation, radiological supervision and interpretation

75891 Hepatic venography, wedged or free, without hemodynamic evaluation, radiological supervision and interpretation

75893 Venous sampling through catheter, with or without angiography (eg, for parathyroid hormone, renin), radiological supervision and interpretation

(For procedure, use 36500)

Transcatheter Procedures

75894 Transcatheter therapy, embolization, any method, radiological supervision and interpretation

75896 Transcatheter therapy, infusion, any method (eg, thrombolysis other than coronary), radiological supervision and interpretation

(For infusion for coronary disease, see 92975, 92977)

75898 Angiography through existing catheter for follow-up study for transcatheter therapy, embolization or infusion

75900 Exchange of a previously placed arterial catheter during thrombolytic therapy with contrast monitoring, radiological supervision and interpretation

(For procedure, use 37209)

75901 Mechanical removal of pericatheter obstructive material (eg, fibrin sheath) from central venous device via separate venous access, radiologic supervision and interpretation

(For procedure, use ►36595◄)

(For venous catheterization, see 36010-36012)

75902 Mechanical removal of intraluminal (intracatheter) obstructive material from central venous device through device lumen, radiologic supervision and interpretation

(For procedure, use ►36596◄)

(For venous catheterization, see 36010-36012)

75940 Percutaneous placement of IVC filter, radiological supervision and interpretation

75945 Intravascular ultrasound (non-coronary vessel), radiological supervision and interpretation; initial vessel

+ 75946 each additional non-coronary vessel (List separately in addition to code for primary procedure)

(Use 75946 in conjunction with code 75945)

(For catheterizations, see codes 36215-36248)

(For transcatheter therapies, see codes 37200-37208, 61624, 61626)

(For procedure, see 37250, 37251)

75952 Endovascular repair of infrarenal abdominal aortic aneurysm or dissection, radiological supervision and interpretation

(For implantation of endovascular grafts, see 34800-34808)

75953 Placement of proximal or distal extension prosthesis for endovascular repair of infrarenal aortic or iliac artery aneurysm, pseudoaneurysm, or dissection, radiological supervision and interpretation

(For implantation of endovascular extension prostheses, see 34825, 34826)

75954 Endovascular repair of iliac artery aneurysm, pseudoaneurysm, arteriovenous malformation, or trauma, radiological supervision and interpretation

(For implantation of endovascular graft, see 34900)

75960 Transcatheter introduction of intravascular stent(s), (non-coronary vessel), percutaneous and/or open, radiological supervision and interpretation, each vessel

(For procedure, see 37205-37208)

(For radiologic supervision and interpretation for transcatheter placement of extracranial cerebrovascular artery stent(s), use Category III code 0007T)

75961 Transcatheter retrieval, percutaneous, of intravascular foreign body (eg, fractured venous or arterial catheter), radiological supervision and interpretation

(For procedure, use 37203)

75962 Transluminal balloon angioplasty, peripheral artery, radiological supervision and interpretation

+ 75964 Transluminal balloon angioplasty, each additional peripheral artery, radiological supervision and interpretation (List separately in addition to code for primary procedure)

(Use 75964 in conjunction with code 75962)

75966 Transluminal balloon angioplasty, renal or other visceral artery, radiological supervision and interpretation

+ 75968 Transluminal balloon angioplasty, each additional visceral artery, radiological supervision and interpretation (List separately in addition to code for primary procedure)

(Use 75968 in conjunction with code 75966)

(For percutaneous transluminal coronary angioplasty, see 92982-92984)

75970 Transcatheter biopsy, radiological supervision and interpretation

(For injection procedure only for transcatheter therapy or biopsy, see 36100-36299)

(For transcatheter renal and ureteral biopsy, use 52007)

(For percutaneous needle biopsy of pancreas, use 48102; of retroperitoneal lymph node or mass, use 49180)

75978 Transluminal balloon angioplasty, venous (eg, subclavian stenosis), radiological supervision and interpretation

75980 Percutaneous transhepatic biliary drainage with contrast monitoring, radiological supervision and interpretation

75982 Percutaneous placement of drainage catheter for combined internal and external biliary drainage or of a drainage stent for internal biliary drainage in patients with an inoperable mechanical biliary obstruction, radiological supervision and interpretation

75984 Change of percutaneous tube or drainage catheter with contrast monitoring (eg, gastrointestinal system, genitourinary system, abscess), radiological supervision and interpretation

(For change of nephrostomy or pyelostomy tube only, use 50398)

(For introduction procedure only for percutaneous biliary drainage, see 47510, 47511)

(For percutaneous cholecystostomy, use 47490)

(For change of percutaneous biliary drainage catheter only, use 47525)

(For percutaneous nephrostolithotomy or pyelostolithotomy, see 50080, 50081)

75989 Radiological guidance (ie, fluoroscopy, ultrasound, or computed tomography), for percutaneous drainage (eg, abscess, specimen collection), with placement of catheter, radiological supervision and interpretation

Transluminal Atherectomy

75992 Transluminal atherectomy, peripheral artery, radiological supervision and interpretation

(For procedure, see 35481-35485, 35491-35495)

+ 75993 Transluminal atherectomy, each additional peripheral artery, radiological supervision and interpretation (List separately in addition to code for primary procedure)

(Use 75993 in conjunction with code 75992)

(For procedure, see 35481-35485, 35491-35495)

75994 Transluminal atherectomy, renal, radiological supervision and interpretation

(For procedure, see 35480, 35490)

75995 Transluminal atherectomy, visceral, radiological supervision and interpretation

(For procedure, see 35480, 35490)

+ 75996 Transluminal atherectomy, each additional visceral artery, radiological supervision and interpretation (List separately in addition to code for primary procedure)

(Use 75996 in conjunction with code 75995)

(For procedure, see 35480, 35490)

Other Procedures

(For computed tomography cerebral perfusion analysis, see Category III code 0042T)

(For arthrography of shoulder, use 73040; elbow, use 73085; wrist, use 73115; hip, use 73525; knee, use 73580; ankle, use 73615)

+ ● 75998 Fluoroscopic guidance for central venous access device placement, replacement (catheter only or complete), or removal (includes fluoroscopic guidance for vascular access and catheter manipulation, any necessary contrast injections through access site or catheter with related venography radiologic supervision and interpretation, and radiographic documentation of final catheter position) (List separately in addition to code for primary procedure)

►(Do not use 76003 in conjunction with 75998)◄

►(If formal extremity venography is performed from separate venous access and separately interpreted, use 36005 and 75820, 75822, 75825 or 75827)◄

76000 Fluoroscopy (separate procedure), up to one hour physician time, other than 71023 or 71034 (eg, cardiac fluoroscopy)

76001 Fluoroscopy, physician time more than one hour, assisting a non-radiologic physician (eg, nephrostolithotomy, ERCP, bronchoscopy, transbronchial biopsy)

76003 Fluoroscopic guidance for needle placement (eg, biopsy, aspiration, injection, localization device)

(See appropriate surgical code for procedure and anatomic location)

(Fluoroscopy 76003 is considered inclusive of all radiographic arthrography with the exception of supervision and interpretation for CT and MR arthrography)

(Do not report 76003 in addition to 70332, 73040, 73085, 73115, 73525, 73580, 73615)

(Fluoroscopy 76003 is considered inclusive of organ/anatomic specific radiological supervision and interpretation procedures 74320, 74350, 74355, 74445, 74470, 74475, 75809, 75810, 75885, 75887, 75980, 75982, 75989)

76005 Fluoroscopic guidance and localization of needle or catheter tip for spine or paraspinous diagnostic or therapeutic injection procedures (epidural, transforaminal epidural, subarachnoid, paravertebral facet joint, paravertebral facet joint nerve or sacroiliac joint), including neurolytic agent destruction

(Injection of contrast during fluoroscopic guidance and localization is an inclusive component of codes 62263, 62264, 62270-62273, 62280-62282, 62310-62319, 0027T)

(Fluoroscopic guidance for subarachnoid puncture for diagnostic radiographic myelography is included in supervision and interpretation codes 72240, 72255, 72265, 72270)

(For epidural or subarachnoid needle or catheter placement and injection, see codes 62270-62273, 62280-62282, 62310-62319)

(For sacroiliac joint arthrography, see 27096, 73542. If formal arthrography is not performed, recorded, and a formal radiographic report is not issued, use 76005 for fluoroscopic guidance for sacroiliac joint injections)

(For paravertebral facet joint injection, see 64470-64476. For transforaminal epidural needle placement and injection, see 64479-64484)

(For destruction by neurolytic agent, see 64600-64680)

(For percutaneous or endoscopic lysis of epidural adhesions, codes 62263, 62264, 0027T include fluoroscopic guidance and localization)

76006 Manual application of stress performed by physician for joint radiography, including contralateral joint if indicated

(For radiographic interpretation of stressed images, see appropriate anatomic site and number of views)

76010 Radiologic examination from nose to rectum for foreign body, single view, child

76012 Radiological supervision and interpretation, percutaneous vertebroplasty, per vertebral body; under fluoroscopic guidance

76013 under CT guidance

(For procedure, see 22520-22522)

76020 Bone age studies

76040 Bone length studies (orthoroentgenogram, scanogram)

76061 Radiologic examination, osseous survey; limited (eg, for metastases)

76062 complete (axial and appendicular skeleton)

76065 Radiologic examination, osseous survey, infant

76066 Joint survey, single view, two or more joints (specify)

76070 Computed tomography, bone mineral density study, one or more sites; axial skeleton (eg, hips, pelvis, spine)

76071 appendicular skeleton (peripheral) (eg, radius, wrist, heel)

76075 Dual energy x-ray absorptiometry (DEXA), bone density study, one or more sites; axial skeleton (eg, hips, pelvis, spine)

76076 appendicular skeleton (peripheral) (eg, radius, wrist, heel)

(To report dual energy x-ray absorptiometry (DEXA) body composition study, one or more sites, use Category III code 0028T)

76078 Radiographic absorptiometry (eg, photodensitometry, radiogrammetry), one or more sites

76080 Radiologic examination, abscess, fistula or sinus tract study, radiological supervision and interpretation

+ ● 76082 Computer aided detection (computer algorithm analysis of digital image data for lesion detection) with further physician review for interpretation, with or without digitization of film radiographic images; diagnostic mammography (List separately in addition to code for primary procedure)

►(Use 76082 in conjunction with 76090 or 76091)◄

+ ● 76083 screening mammography (List separately in addition to code for primary procedure)

►(Use 76083 in conjunction with 76092)◄

(76085 has been deleted. To report, see 76082, 76083)

76086 Mammary ductogram or galactogram, single duct, radiological supervision and interpretation

76088 Mammary ductogram or galactogram, multiple ducts, radiological supervision and interpretation

76090 Mammography; unilateral

76091 bilateral

►(Use 76082 in conjunction with 76090 or 76091 for computer aided detection applied to a diagnostic mammogram)◄

76092 Screening mammography, bilateral (two view film study of each breast)

►(Use 76083 in conjunction with 76092 for computer aided detection applied to a screening mammogram)◄

►(To report electrical impedance scan of the breast, bilateral, use Category III code 0060T)◄

76093 Magnetic resonance imaging, breast, without and/or with contrast material(s); unilateral

76094 bilateral

76095 Stereotactic localization guidance for breast biopsy or needle placement (eg, for wire localization or for injection), each lesion, radiological supervision and interpretation

(For procedure, see 10022, 19000, 19001, 19102, 19103, 19290, 19291)

(For injection for sentinel node localization without lymphoscintigraphy, use 38792)

76096 Mammographic guidance for needle placement, breast (eg, for wire localization or for injection), each lesion, radiological supervision and interpretation

(For procedure, see 10022, 19000, 19102, 19103, 19290, 19291)

(For injection for sentinel node localization without lymphoscintigraphy, use 38792)

76098 Radiological examination, surgical specimen

76100 Radiologic examination, single plane body section (eg, tomography), other than with urography

76101 Radiologic examination, complex motion (ie, hypercycloidal) body section (eg, mastoid polytomography), other than with urography; unilateral

76102 bilateral

(For nephrotomography, use 74415)

76120 Cineradiography/videoradiography, except where specifically included

+ 76125 Cineradiography/videoradiography to complement routine examination (List separately in addition to code for primary procedure)

76140 Consultation on x-ray examination made elsewhere, written report

76150 Xeroradiography

(76150 is to be used for non-mammographic studies only)

76350 Subtraction in conjunction with contrast studies

76355 Computed tomography guidance for stereotactic localization

76360 Computed tomography guidance for needle placement (eg, biopsy, aspiration, injection, localization device), radiological supervision and interpretation

▲76362 Computed tomography guidance for, and monitoring of, visceral tissue ablation

(For percutaneous radiofrequency ablation, use 47382)

76370 Computed tomography guidance for placement of radiation therapy fields

76375 Coronal, sagittal, multiplanar, oblique, 3-dimensional and/or holographic reconstruction of computed tomography, magnetic resonance imaging, or other tomographic modality

(Use 76375 in addition to code for imaging procedure)

76380 Computed tomography, limited or localized follow-up study

76390 Magnetic resonance spectroscopy

(For magnetic resonance imaging, use appropriate MRI body site code)

76393 Magnetic resonance guidance for needle placement (eg, for biopsy, needle aspiration, injection, or placement of localization device) radiological supervision and interpretation

(For procedure see appropriate organ or site)

▲76394 Magnetic resonance guidance for, and monitoring of, visceral tissue ablation

(For percutaneous radiofrequency ablation, use 47382)

76400 Magnetic resonance (eg, proton) imaging, bone marrow blood supply

►(76490 has been deleted. To report, use 76940)◄

76496 Unlisted fluoroscopic procedure (eg, diagnostic, interventional)

76497 Unlisted computed tomography procedure (eg, diagnostic, interventional)

76498 Unlisted magnetic resonance procedure (eg, diagnostic, interventional)

76499 Unlisted diagnostic radiographic procedure

Diagnostic Ultrasound

Definitions

A-mode implies a one-dimensional ultrasonic measurement procedure.

M-mode implies a one-dimensional ultrasonic measurement procedure with movement of the trace to record amplitude and velocity of moving echo-producing structures.

B-scan implies a two-dimensional ultrasonic scanning procedure with a two-dimensional display.

Real-time scan implies a two-dimensional ultrasonic scanning procedure with display of both two-dimensional structure and motion with time.

►(To report diagnostic vascular ultrasound studies, see 93875-93990)◄

Head and Neck

76506 Echoencephalography, B-scan and/or real time with image documentation (gray scale) (for determination of ventricular size, delineation of cerebral contents and detection of fluid masses or other intracranial abnormalities), including A-mode encephalography as secondary component where indicated

76511 Ophthalmic ultrasound, echography, diagnostic; A-scan only, with amplitude quantification

76512 contact B-scan (with or without simultaneous A-scan)

76513 anterior segment ultrasound, immersion (water bath) B-scan or high resolution biomicroscopy

● 76514 corneal pachymetry, unilateral or bilateral (determination of corneal thickness)

76516 Ophthalmic biometry by ultrasound echography, A-scan;

76519 with intraocular lens power calculation

(For partial coherence interferometry, use 92136)

76529 Ophthalmic ultrasonic foreign body localization

76536 Ultrasound, soft tissues of head and neck (eg, thyroid, parathyroid, parotid), B-scan and/or real time with image documentation

Chest

76604 Ultrasound, chest, B-scan (includes mediastinum) and/or real time with image documentation

76645 Ultrasound, breast(s) (unilateral or bilateral), B-scan and/or real time with image documentation

Abdomen and Retroperitoneum

76700 Ultrasound, abdominal, B-scan and/or real time with image documentation; complete

76705 limited (eg, single organ, quadrant, follow-up)

76770 Ultrasound, retroperitoneal (eg, renal, aorta, nodes), B-scan and/or real time with image documentation; complete

76775 limited

76778 Ultrasound, transplanted kidney, B-scan and/or real time with image documentation, with or without duplex Doppler study

Spinal Canal

76800 Ultrasound, spinal canal and contents

Pelvis

Obstetrical

Codes 76801 and 76802 include determination of the number of gestational sacs and fetuses, gestational sac/fetal measurements appropriate for gestation (<14 weeks 0 days), survey of visible fetal and placental anatomic structure, qualitative assessment of amniotic fluid volume/gestational sac shape and examination of the maternal uterus and adnexa.

Codes 76805 and 76810 include determination of number of fetuses and amniotic/chorionic sacs, measurements appropriate for gestational age (> or = 14 weeks 0 days), survey of intracranial/spinal/abdominal anatomy, 4 chambered heart, umbilical cord insertion site, placenta location and amniotic fluid assessment and, when visible, examination of maternal adnexa.

Codes 76811 and 76812 include all elements of codes 76805 and 76810 plus detailed anatomic evaluation of the fetal brain/ventricles, face, heart/outflow tracts and chest anatomy, abdominal organ specific anatomy, number/length/architecture of limbs and detailed evaluation of the umbilical cord and placenta and other fetal anatomy as clinically indicated.

Report should document the results of the evaluation of each element described above or the reason for non-visualization.

Code 76815 represents a focused "quick look" exam limited to the assessment of one or more of the elements listed in code 76815.

Code 76816 describes an examination designed to reassess fetal size and interval growth or reevaluate one or more anatomic abnormalities of a fetus previously demonstrated on ultrasound, and should be coded once for each fetus requiring reevaluation using modifier '-59' for each fetus after the first.

Code 76817 describes a transvaginal obstetric ultrasound performed separately or in addition to one of the transabdominal examinations described above. For transvaginal examinations performed for non-obstetrical purposes, use code 76830.

76801 Ultrasound, pregnant uterus, real time with image documentation, fetal and maternal evaluation, first trimester (<14 weeks 0 days), transabdominal approach; single or first gestation

+ 76802 each additional gestation (List separately in addition to code for primary procedure)

(Use 76802 in conjunction with code 76801)

76805 Ultrasound, pregnant uterus, real time with image documentation, fetal and maternal evaluation, after first trimester (> or = 14 weeks 0 days), transabdominal approach; single or first gestation

+ 76810 each additional gestation (List separately in addition to code for primary procedure)

(Use 76810 in conjunction with code 76805)

76811 Ultrasound, pregnant uterus, real time with image documentation, fetal and maternal evaluation plus detailed fetal anatomic examination, transabdominal approach; single or first gestation

+ 76812 each additional gestation (List separately in addition to code for primary procedure)

(Use 76812 in conjunction with code 76811)

76815 Ultrasound, pregnant uterus, real time with image documentation, limited (eg, fetal heart beat, placental location, fetal position and/or qualitative amniotic fluid volume), one or more fetuses

(Use 76815 only once per exam and not per element)

76816 Ultrasound, pregnant uterus, real time with image documentation, follow-up (eg, re-evaluation of fetal size by measuring standard growth parameters and amniotic fluid volume, re-evaluation of organ system(s) suspected or confirmed to be abnormal on a previous scan), transabdominal approach, per fetus

(Report 76816 with modifier '-59' for each additional fetus examined in a multiple pregnancy)

76817 Ultrasound, pregnant uterus, real time with image documentation, transvaginal

(For non-obstetrical transvaginal ultrasound, use 76830)

(If transvaginal examination is done in addition to transabdominal obstetrical ultrasound exam, use 76817 in addition to appropriate transabdominal exam code)

76818 Fetal biophysical profile; with non-stress testing

76819 without non-stress testing

(Fetal biophysical profile assessments for the second and any additional fetuses, should be reported separately by code 76818 or 76819 with the modifier '-59' appended)

(For amniotic fluid index without non-stress test, use 76815)

76825 Echocardiography, fetal, cardiovascular system, real time with image documentation (2D), with or without M-mode recording;

76826 follow-up or repeat study

76827 Doppler echocardiography, fetal, cardiovascular system, pulsed wave and/or continuous wave with spectral display; complete

76828 follow-up or repeat study

(To report the use of color mapping, use 93325)

Non-Obstetrical

76830 Ultrasound, transvaginal

(For obstetrical transvaginal ultrasound, use 76817)

(If transvaginal examination is done in addition to transabdominal non-obstetrical ultrasound exam, use 76830 in addition to appropriate transabdominal exam code)

▲76831 Saline infusion sonohysterography (SIS), including color flow Doppler, when performed

(For introduction of saline for ►saline infusion sonohysterography,◄ use 58340)

76856 Ultrasound, pelvic (nonobstetric), B-scan and/or real time with image documentation; complete

76857 limited or follow-up (eg, for follicles)

Genitalia

76870 Ultrasound, scrotum and contents

▲76872 Ultrasound, transrectal

76873 prostate volume study for brachytherapy treatment planning (separate procedure)

Extremities

76880 Ultrasound, extremity, non-vascular, B-scan and/or real time with image documentation

76885 Ultrasound, infant hips, real time with imaging documentation; dynamic (requiring physician manipulation)

76886 limited, static (not requiring physician manipulation)

Ultrasonic Guidance Procedures

76930 Ultrasonic guidance for pericardiocentesis, imaging supervision and interpretation

76932 Ultrasonic guidance for endomyocardial biopsy, imaging supervision and interpretation

76936 Ultrasound guided compression repair of arterial pseudoaneurysm or arteriovenous fistulae (includes diagnostic ultrasound evaluation, compression of lesion and imaging)

+●76937 Ultrasound guidance for vascular access requiring ultrasound evaluation of potential access sites, documentation of selected vessel patency, concurrent realtime ultrasound visualization of vascular needle entry, with permanent recording and reporting (List separately in addition to code for primary procedure)

►(Do not use 76937 in conjunction with 76942)◄

►(If extremity venous non-invasive vascular diagnostic study is performed separate from venous access guidance, use 93965, 93970 or 93971)◄

●76940 Ultrasound guidance for, and monitoring of, visceral tissue ablation

►(Do not report 76940 in conjunction with 76986)◄

►(For ablation, see 47370-47382)◄

76941 Ultrasonic guidance for intrauterine fetal transfusion or cordocentesis, imaging supervision and interpretation

(For procedure, see 36460, 59012)

76942 Ultrasonic guidance for needle placement (eg, biopsy, aspiration, injection, localization device), imaging supervision and interpretation

►(Do not report 76942 in conjunction with 43232, 43237, 43242, 45341, 45342, or 76975)◄

►(For microwave thermotherapy of the breast, use Category III code 0061T)◄

76945 Ultrasonic guidance for chorionic villus sampling, imaging supervision and interpretation

(For procedure, use 59015)

76946 Ultrasonic guidance for amniocentesis, imaging supervision and interpretation

76948 Ultrasonic guidance for aspiration of ova, imaging supervision and interpretation

76950 Ultrasonic guidance for placement of radiation therapy fields

76965 Ultrasonic guidance for interstitial radioelement application

Other Procedures

76970 Ultrasound study follow-up (specify)

76975 Gastrointestinal endoscopic ultrasound, supervision and interpretation

(Do not report 76975 in conjunction with 43231, 43232, ►43237, 43238, 43242, 43259, 45341, 45342, or 76942◄)

76977 Ultrasound bone density measurement and interpretation, peripheral site(s), any method

76986 Ultrasonic guidance, intraoperative

(Do not report 76986 in addition to 47370-47382)

(For ultrasound guidance for open and laparoscopic radiofrequency tissue ablation, use 76940)

76999 Unlisted ultrasound procedure (eg, diagnostic, interventional)

Radiation Oncology

Listings for Radiation Oncology provide for teletherapy and brachytherapy to include initial consultation, clinical treatment planning, simulation, medical radiation physics, dosimetry, treatment devices, special services, and clinical treatment management procedures. They include normal follow-up care during course of treatment and for three months following its completion.

When a service or procedure is provided that is not listed in this edition of *CPT* it should be identified by a Special Report (see page 208) and one of the unlisted procedure codes listed below:

77299 Unlisted procedure, therapeutic radiology clinical treatment planning

77399 Unlisted procedure, medical radiation physics, dosimetry and treatment devices, and special services

77499 Unlisted procedure, therapeutic radiology treatment management

77799 Unlisted procedure, clinical brachytherapy

For treatment by injectable or ingestible isotopes, see subsection **Nuclear Medicine**.

Consultation: Clinical Management

Preliminary consultation, evaluation of patient prior to decision to treat, or full medical care (in addition to treatment management) when provided by the therapeutic radiologist may be identified by the appropriate procedure codes from **Evaluation and Management, Medicine,** or **Surgery** sections.

Clinical Treatment Planning (External and Internal Sources)

The clinical treatment planning process is a complex service including interpretation of special testing, tumor localization, treatment volume determination, treatment time/dosage determination, choice of treatment modality, determination of number and size of treatment ports, selection of appropriate treatment devices, and other procedures.

Definitions

Simple planning requires a single treatment area of interest encompassed in a single port or simple parallel opposed ports with simple or no blocking.

Intermediate planning requires three or more converging ports, two separate treatment areas, multiple blocks, or special time dose constraints.

Complex planning requires highly complex blocking, custom shielding blocks, tangential ports, special wedges or compensators, three or more separate treatment areas, rotational or special beam considerations, combination of therapeutic modalities.

(77260, 77265, 77270, 77275 have been deleted. To report, see 77261-77263)

77261 Therapeutic radiology treatment planning; simple

77262 intermediate

77263 complex

Definitions

Simple simulation of a single treatment area with either a single port or parallel opposed ports. Simple or no blocking.

Intermediate simulation of three or more converging ports, two separate treatment areas, multiple blocks.

Complex simulation of tangential portals, three or more treatment areas, rotation or arc therapy, complex blocking, custom shielding blocks, brachytherapy source verification, hyperthermia probe verification, any use of contrast materials.

Three-dimensional computer-generated three dimensional reconstruction of tumor volume and surrounding critical normal tissue structures from direct CT scans and/or MRI data in preparation for non-coplanar or coplanar therapy. The simulation utilizes documented three-dimensional beam's eye view volume-dose displays of multiple or moving beams. Documentation with three-dimensional volume reconstruction and dose distribution is required.

Simulation may be carried out on a dedicated simulator, a radiation therapy treatment unit, or diagnostic x-ray machine.

77280 Therapeutic radiology simulation-aided field setting; simple

77285 intermediate

77290 complex

77295 three-dimensional

77299 Unlisted procedure, therapeutic radiology clinical treatment planning

Medical Radiation Physics, Dosimetry, Treatment Devices, and Special Services

77300 Basic radiation dosimetry calculation, central axis depth dose calculation, TDF, NSD, gap calculation, off axis factor, tissue inhomogeneity factors, calculation of non-ionizing radiation surface and depth dose, as required during course of treatment, only when prescribed by the treating physician

77301 Intensity modulated radiotherapy plan, including dose-volume histograms for target and critical structure partial tolerance specifications

(Dose plan is optimized using inverse or forward planning technique for modulated beam delivery (eg, binary, dynamic MLC) to create highly conformal dose distribution. Computer plan distribution must be verified for positional accuracy based on dosimetric verification of the intensity map with verification of treatment set-up and interpretation of verification methodology)

77305 Teletherapy, isodose plan (whether hand or computer calculated); simple (one or two parallel opposed unmodified ports directed to a single area of interest)

77310 intermediate (three or more treatment ports directed to a single area of interest)

77315 complex (mantle or inverted Y, tangential ports, the use of wedges, compensators, complex blocking, rotational beam, or special beam considerations)

(Only one teletherapy isodose plan may be reported for a given course of therapy to a specific treatment area)

77321 Special teletherapy port plan, particles, hemibody, total body

77326 Brachytherapy isodose plan; simple (calculation made from single plane, one to four sources/ribbon application, remote afterloading brachytherapy, 1 to 8 sources)

(For definition of source/ribbon, see page 225)

77327 intermediate (multiplane dosage calculations, application involving 5 to 10 sources/ribbons, remote afterloading brachytherapy, 9 to 12 sources)

77328 complex (multiplane isodose plan, volume implant calculations, over 10 sources/ribbons used, special spatial reconstruction, remote afterloading brachytherapy, over 12 sources)

77331 Special dosimetry (eg, TLD, microdosimetry) (specify), only when prescribed by the treating physician

77332 Treatment devices, design and construction; simple (simple block, simple bolus)

77333 intermediate (multiple blocks, stents, bite blocks, special bolus)

77334 complex (irregular blocks, special shields, compensators, wedges, molds or casts)

77336 Continuing medical physics consultation, including assessment of treatment parameters, quality assurance of dose delivery, and review of patient treatment documentation in support of the radiation oncologist, reported per week of therapy

77370 Special medical radiation physics consultation

77399 Unlisted procedure, medical radiation physics, dosimetry and treatment devices, and special services

Radiation Treatment Delivery

(Radiation treatment delivery (77401-77416) recognizes the technical component and the various energy levels.)

(77400 has been deleted)

77401 Radiation treatment delivery, superficial and/or ortho voltage

77402 Radiation treatment delivery, single treatment area, single port or parallel opposed ports, simple blocks or no blocks; up to 5 MeV

77403 6-10 MeV

77404 11-19 MeV

77406 20 MeV or greater

77407 Radiation treatment delivery, two separate treatment areas, three or more ports on a single treatment area, use of multiple blocks; up to 5 MeV

77408 6-10 MeV

77409 11-19 MeV

77411 20 MeV or greater

77412 Radiation treatment delivery, three or more separate treatment areas, custom blocking, tangential ports, wedges, rotational beam, compensators, special particle beam (eg, electron or neutrons); up to 5 MeV

77413 6-10 MeV

77414 11-19 MeV

77416 20 MeV or greater

77417 Therapeutic radiology port film(s)

77418 Intensity modulated treatment delivery, single or multiple fields/arcs, via narrow spatially and temporally modulated beams (eg, binary, dynamic MLC), per treatment session

(For intensity modulated treatment planning, use 77301)

Radiation Treatment Management

Radiation treatment management is reported in units of five fractions or treatment sessions, regardless of the actual time period in which the services are furnished. The services need not be furnished on consecutive days. Multiple fractions representing two or more treatment sessions furnished on the same day may be counted separately as long as there has been a distinct break in therapy sessions, and the fractions are of the character usually furnished on different days. Code 77427 is also reported if there are three or four fractions beyond a multiple of five at the end of a course of treatment; one or two fractions beyond a multiple of five at the end of a course of treatment are not reported separately. The professional services furnished during treatment management typically consists of:

- Review of port films;
- Review of dosimetry, dose delivery, and treatment parameters;
- Review of patient treatment set-up;
- Examination of patient for medical evaluation and management (eg, assessment of the patient's response to treatment, coordination of care and treatment, review of imaging and/or lab test results).

77427 Radiation treatment management, five treatments

77431 Radiation therapy management with complete course of therapy consisting of one or two fractions only

(77431 is not to be used to fill in the last week of a long course of therapy)

77432 Stereotactic radiation treatment management of cerebral lesion(s) (complete course of treatment consisting of one session)

77470 Special treatment procedure (eg, total body irradiation, hemibody radiation, per oral, endocavitary or intraoperative cone irradiation)

(77470 assumes that the procedure is performed one or more times during the course of therapy, in addition to daily or weekly patient management)

77499 Unlisted procedure, therapeutic radiology treatment management

Proton Beam Treatment Delivery

Definitions

Simple proton treatment delivery to a single treatment area utilizing a single non-tangential/oblique port, custom block with compensation (77522) and without compensation (77520).

Intermediate proton treatment delivery to one or more treatment areas utilizing two or more ports or one or more tangential/oblique ports, with custom blocks and compensators.

Complex proton treatment delivery to one or more treatment areas utilizing two or more ports per treatment area with matching or patching fields and/or multiple isocenters, with custom blocks and compensators.

77520 Proton treatment delivery; simple, without compensation

77522 simple, with compensation

77523 intermediate

77525 complex

Hyperthermia

Hyperthermia treatments as listed in this section include external (superficial and deep), interstitial, and intracavitary.

Radiation therapy when given concurrently is listed separately.

Hyperthermia is used only as an adjunct to radiation therapy or chemotherapy. It may be induced by a variety of sources (eg, microwave, ultrasound, low energy radio-frequency conduction, or by probes).

The listed treatments include management during the course of therapy and follow-up care for three months after completion.

Preliminary consultation is not included (see **Medicine** 99241-99263).

Physics planning and interstitial insertion of temperature sensors, and use of external or interstitial heat generating sources are included.

The following descriptors are included in the treatment schedule:

77600 Hyperthermia, externally generated; superficial (ie, heating to a depth of 4 cm or less)

77605 deep (ie, heating to depths greater than 4 cm)

77610 Hyperthermia generated by interstitial probe(s); 5 or fewer interstitial applicators

77615 more than 5 interstitial applicators

Clinical Intracavitary Hyperthermia

77620 Hyperthermia generated by intracavitary probe(s)

Clinical Brachytherapy

Clinical brachytherapy requires the use of either natural or man-made radioelements applied into or around a treatment field of interest. The supervision of radioelements and dose interpretation are performed solely by the therapeutic radiologist.

Services 77750-77799 include admission to the hospital and daily visits.

For insertion of ovoids and tandems, use 57155.

For insertion of Heyman capsules, use 58346.

Definitions

(Sources refer to intracavitary placement or permanent interstitial placement; ribbons refer to temporary interstitial placement)

A simple application has one to four sources/ribbons.

An intermediate application has five to ten sources/ribbons.

A complex application has greater than ten sources/ribbons.

(77700-77749 have been deleted. To report, see 77761-77799)

77750 Infusion or instillation of radioelement solution

►(For administration of radiolabeled monoclonal antibodies see 79403)◄

77761 Intracavitary radiation source application; simple

77762 intermediate

77763 complex

77776 Interstitial radiation source application; simple

77777 intermediate

77778 complex

77781 Remote afterloading high intensity brachytherapy; 1-4 source positions or catheters

77782 5-8 source positions or catheters

77783 9-12 source positions or catheters

77784 over 12 source positions or catheters

Radiology

77789 Surface application of radiation source

77790 Supervision, handling, loading of radiation source

77799 Unlisted procedure, clinical brachytherapy

Nuclear Medicine

Listed procedures may be performed independently or in the course of overall medical care. If the physician providing these services is also responsible for diagnostic work-up and/or follow-up care of patient, see appropriate sections also.

Radioimmunoassay tests are found in the **Clinical Pathology** section (codes 82000-84999). These codes can be appropriately used by any specialist performing such tests in a laboratory licensed and/or certified for radioimmunoassays. The reporting of these tests is not confined to clinical pathology laboratories alone.

The services listed do not include the provision of radium or other radioelements. Those materials supplied by the physician should be listed separately and identified by the code 78990 for diagnostic radiopharmaceutical and 79900 for therapeutic radiopharmaceutical.

Diagnostic

Endocrine System

78000 Thyroid uptake; single determination

78001 multiple determinations

78003 stimulation, suppression or discharge (not including initial uptake studies)

78006 Thyroid imaging, with uptake; single determination

78007 multiple determinations

78010 Thyroid imaging; only

78011 with vascular flow

78015 Thyroid carcinoma metastases imaging; limited area (eg, neck and chest only)

78016 with additional studies (eg, urinary recovery)

78018 whole body

+ **78020** Thyroid carcinoma metastases uptake (List separately in addition to code for primary procedure)

(Use 78020 in conjunction with code 78018 only)

78070 Parathyroid imaging

78075 Adrenal imaging, cortex and/or medulla

78099 Unlisted endocrine procedure, diagnostic nuclear medicine

(For chemical analysis, see **Chemistry** section)

Hematopoietic, Reticuloendothelial and Lymphatic System

78102 Bone marrow imaging; limited area

78103 multiple areas

78104 whole body

78110 Plasma volume, radiopharmaceutical volume-dilution technique (separate procedure); single sampling

78111 multiple samplings

78120 Red cell volume determination (separate procedure); single sampling

78121 multiple samplings

78122 Whole blood volume determination, including separate measurement of plasma volume and red cell volume (radiopharmaceutical volume-dilution technique)

78130 Red cell survival study;

78135 differential organ/tissue kinetics, (eg, splenic and/or hepatic sequestration)

78140 Labeled red cell sequestration, differential organ/tissue, (eg, splenic and/or hepatic)

78160 Plasma radioiron disappearance (turnover) rate

78162 Radioiron oral absorption

78170 Radioiron red cell utilization

78172 Chelatable iron for estimation of total body iron

78185 Spleen imaging only, with or without vascular flow

(If combined with liver study, use procedures 78215 and 78216)

78190 Kinetics, study of platelet survival, with or without differential organ/tissue localization

78191 Platelet survival study

78195 Lymphatics and lymph nodes imaging

(For sentinel node identification without scintigraphy imaging, use 38792)

(For sentinal node excision, see 38500-38542)

78199 Unlisted hematopoietic, reticuloendothelial and lymphatic procedure, diagnostic nuclear medicine

(For chemical analysis, see **Chemistry** section)

Gastrointestinal System

78201 Liver imaging; static only

78202 with vascular flow

(For spleen imaging only, use 78185)

78205 Liver imaging (SPECT);

78206 with vascular flow

Radiology

78215 Liver and spleen imaging; static only

78216 with vascular flow

78220 Liver function study with hepatobiliary agents, with serial images

78223 Hepatobiliary ductal system imaging, including gallbladder, with or without pharmacologic intervention, with or without quantitative measurement of gallbladder function

78230 Salivary gland imaging;

78231 with serial images

78232 Salivary gland function study

78258 Esophageal motility

78261 Gastric mucosa imaging

78262 Gastroesophageal reflux study

78264 Gastric emptying study

78267 Urea breath test, C-14; acquisition for analysis

78268 analysis

78270 Vitamin B-12 absorption study (eg, Schilling test); without intrinsic factor

78271 with intrinsic factor

78272 Vitamin B-12 absorption studies combined, with and without intrinsic factor

78278 Acute gastrointestinal blood loss imaging

78282 Gastrointestinal protein loss

78290 Intestine imaging (eg, ectopic gastric mucosa, Meckel's localization, volvulus)

78291 Peritoneal-venous shunt patency test (eg, for LeVeen, Denver shunt)

(For injection procedure, use 49427)

78299 Unlisted gastrointestinal procedure, diagnostic nuclear medicine

Musculoskeletal System

Bone and joint imaging can be used in the diagnosis of a variety of inflammatory processes (eg, osteomyelitis), as well as for localization of primary and/or metastatic neoplasms.

78300 Bone and/or joint imaging; limited area

78305 multiple areas

78306 whole body

78315 three phase study

78320 tomographic (SPECT)

78350 Bone density (bone mineral content) study, one or more sites; single photon absorptiometry

78351 dual photon absorptiometry, one or more sites

(For radiographic bone density (photodensitometry), use 76078)

78399 Unlisted musculoskeletal procedure, diagnostic nuclear medicine

Cardiovascular System

Myocardial perfusion and cardiac blood pool imaging studies may be performed at rest and/or during stress. When performed during exercise and/or pharmacologic stress, the appropriate stress testing code from the 93015-93018 series should be reported in addition to code(s) 78460-78465, 78472, 78473, 78478, 78480, 78481, 78483, 78491, and 78492.

(78401-78412 have been deleted. To report, see 78472-78483)

78414 Determination of central c-v hemodynamics (non-imaging) (eg, ejection fraction with probe technique) with or without pharmacologic intervention or exercise, single or multiple determinations

78428 Cardiac shunt detection

78445 Non-cardiac vascular flow imaging (ie, angiography, venography)

78455 Venous thrombosis study (eg, radioactive fibrinogen)

78456 Acute venous thrombosis imaging, peptide

78457 Venous thrombosis imaging, venogram; unilateral

78458 bilateral

78459 Myocardial imaging, positron emission tomography (PET), metabolic evaluation

(For myocardial perfusion study, see 78491-78492)

78460 Myocardial perfusion imaging; (planar) single study, at rest or stress (exercise and/or pharmacologic), with or without quantification

78461 multiple studies, (planar) at rest and/or stress (exercise and/or pharmacologic), and redistribution and/or rest injection, with or without quantification

78464 tomographic (SPECT), single study at rest or stress (exercise and/or pharmacologic), with or without quantification

78465 tomographic (SPECT), multiple studies, at rest and/or stress (exercise and/or pharmacologic) and redistribution and/or rest injection, with or without quantification

78466 Myocardial imaging, infarct avid, planar; qualitative or quantitative

78468 with ejection fraction by first pass technique

78469 tomographic SPECT with or without quantification

78472 Cardiac blood pool imaging, gated equilibrium; planar, single study at rest or stress (exercise and/or pharmacologic), wall motion study plus ejection fraction, with or without additional quantitative processing

(For assessment of cardiac function by first pass technique, use 78496)

78473 multiple studies, wall motion study plus ejection fraction, at rest and stress (exercise and/or pharmacologic), with or without additional quantification

+ 78478 Myocardial perfusion study with wall motion, qualitative or quantitative study (List separately in addition to code for primary procedure)

(Use 78478 in conjunction with codes 78460, 78461, 78464, 78465)

+ 78480 Myocardial perfusion study with ejection fraction (List separately in addition to code for primary procedure)

(Use 78480 in conjunction with codes 78460, 78461, 78464, 78465)

78481 Cardiac blood pool imaging, (planar), first pass technique; single study, at rest or with stress (exercise and/or pharmacologic), wall motion study plus ejection fraction, with or without quantification

78483 multiple studies, at rest and with stress (exercise and/ or pharmacologic), wall motion study plus ejection fraction, with or without quantification

(For cerebral blood flow study, use 78615)

78491 Myocardial imaging, positron emission tomography (PET), perfusion; single study at rest or stress

78492 multiple studies at rest and/or stress

78494 Cardiac blood pool imaging, gated equilibrium, SPECT, at rest, wall motion study plus ejection fraction, with or without quantitative processing

+ 78496 Cardiac blood pool imaging, gated equilibrium, single study, at rest, with right ventricular ejection fraction by first pass technique (List separately in addition to code for primary procedure)

(Use 78496 in conjunction with code 78472)

78499 Unlisted cardiovascular procedure, diagnostic nuclear medicine

Respiratory System

78580 Pulmonary perfusion imaging, particulate

78584 Pulmonary perfusion imaging, particulate, with ventilation; single breath

78585 rebreathing and washout, with or without single breath

78586 Pulmonary ventilation imaging, aerosol; single projection

78587 multiple projections (eg, anterior, posterior, lateral views)

78588 Pulmonary perfusion imaging, particulate, with ventilation imaging, aerosol, one or multiple projections

78591 Pulmonary ventilation imaging, gaseous, single breath, single projection

78593 Pulmonary ventilation imaging, gaseous, with rebreathing and washout with or without single breath; single projection

78594 multiple projections (eg, anterior, posterior, lateral views)

78596 Pulmonary quantitative differential function (ventilation/perfusion) study

78599 Unlisted respiratory procedure, diagnostic nuclear medicine

Nervous System

78600 Brain imaging, limited procedure; static

78601 with vascular flow

78605 Brain imaging, complete study; static

78606 with vascular flow

78607 tomographic (SPECT)

78608 Brain imaging, positron emission tomography (PET); metabolic evaluation

78609 perfusion evaluation

78610 Brain imaging, vascular flow only

78615 Cerebral vascular flow

78630 Cerebrospinal fluid flow, imaging (not including introduction of material); cisternography

(For injection procedure, see 61000-61070, 62270-62319)

78635 ventriculography

(For injection procedure, see 61000-61070, 62270-62294)

78645 shunt evaluation

(For injection procedure, see 61000-61070, 62270-62294)

78647 tomographic (SPECT)

78650 Cerebrospinal fluid leakage detection and localization

(For injection procedure, see 61000-61070, 62270-62294)

78660 Radiopharmaceutical dacryocystography

78699 Unlisted nervous system procedure, diagnostic nuclear medicine

Genitourinary System

78700 Kidney imaging; static only

78701 with vascular flow

78704 with function study (ie, imaging renogram)

78707 Kidney imaging with vascular flow and function; single study without pharmacological intervention

78708 single study, with pharmacological intervention (eg, angiotensin converting enzyme inhibitor and/or diuretic)

78709 multiple studies, with and without pharmacological intervention (eg, angiotensin converting enzyme inhibitor and/or diuretic)

(For introduction of radioactive substance in association with renal endoscopy, see 50559, 50578)

78710 Kidney imaging, tomographic (SPECT)

78715 Kidney vascular flow only

78725 Kidney function study, non-imaging radioisotopic study

78730 Urinary bladder residual study

(For introduction of radioactive substance in association with cystotomy or cystostomy, use 51020; in association with cystourethroscopy, use 52250)

78740 Ureteral reflux study (radiopharmaceutical voiding cystogram)

(For catheterization, see 51701, 51702, 51703)

78760 Testicular imaging;

78761 with vascular flow

(For introduction of radioactive substance in association with ureteral endoscopy, see 50959, 50978)

78799 Unlisted genitourinary procedure, diagnostic nuclear medicine

(For chemical analysis, see **Chemistry** section)

Other Procedures

(For specific organ, see appropriate heading)

(For radiophosphorus tumor identification, ocular, see 78800)

▲**78800** Radiopharmaceutical localization of tumor or distribution of radiopharmaceutical agent(s); limited area

(For specific organ, see appropriate heading)

78801 multiple areas

▲**78802** whole body, single day imaging

78803 tomographic (SPECT)

●**78804** whole body, requiring two or more days imaging

78805 Radiopharmaceutical localization of inflammatory process; limited area

78806 whole body

78807 tomographic (SPECT)

(For imaging bone infectious or inflammatory disease with a bone imaging radiopharmaceutical, see 78300, 78305, 78306)

78810 Tumor imaging, positron emission tomography (PET), metabolic evaluation

78890 Generation of automated data: interactive process involving nuclear physician and/or allied health professional personnel; simple manipulations and interpretation, not to exceed 30 minutes

78891 complex manipulations and interpretation, exceeding 30 minutes

(Use 78890 or 78891 in addition to primary procedure)

78990 Provision of diagnostic radiopharmaceutical(s)

78999 Unlisted miscellaneous procedure, diagnostic nuclear medicine

Therapeutic

79000 Radiopharmaceutical therapy, hyper-thyroidism; initial, including evaluation of patient

79001 subsequent, each therapy

(For follow-up visit, see 99211-99215)

79020 Radiopharmaceutical therapy, thyroid suppression (euthyroid cardiac disease), including evaluation of patient

79030 Radiopharmaceutical ablation of gland for thyroid carcinoma

79035 Radiopharmaceutical therapy for metastases of thyroid carcinoma

▲**79100** Radiopharmaceutical therapy, polycythemia vera, chronic leukemia, each treatment by intravenous injection

►(For monoclonal antibody therapy, use 79403)◄

79200 Intracavitary radioactive colloid therapy

79300 Interstitial radioactive colloid therapy

▲**79400** Radiopharmaceutical therapy, nonthyroid, nonhematologic by intravenous injection

►(Do not report 79400 in conjunction with 79403)◄

►(For monoclonal antibody therapy, use 79403)◄

●**79403** Radiopharmaceutical therapy, radiolabeled monoclonal antibody by intravenous infusion

► (For pre-treatment imaging, see 78802, 78804)◄

► (Do not report 79403 in conjunction with 79400)◄

79420 Intravascular radiopharmaceutical therapy, particulate

79440 Intra-articular radiopharmaceutical therapy

79900 Provision of therapeutic radiopharmaceutical(s)

79999 Unlisted radiopharmaceutical therapeutic procedure

Notes

Pathology and Laboratory Guidelines

Items used by all physicians in reporting their services are presented in the **Introduction.** Some of the commonalities are repeated here for the convenience of those physicians referring to this section on **Pathology and Laboratory.** Other definitions and items unique to Pathology and Laboratory are also listed.

Services in Pathology and Laboratory

Services in Pathology and Laboratory are provided by a physician or by technologists under responsible supervision of a physician.

Separate or Multiple Procedures

It is appropriate to designate multiple procedures that are rendered on the same date by separate entries.

Subsection Information

Several of the subheadings or subsections have special needs or instructions unique to that section. Where these are indicated, (eg, "Panel Tests"), special **"Notes"** will be presented preceding those procedural terminology listings referring to that subsection specifically. If there is an "Unlisted Procedure" code number (see section below) for the individual subsection, it will be shown. Those subsections with **"Notes"** are as follows:

Organ or Disease Panels 80048-80076
Drug Testing.................... 80100-80103
Therapeutic Drug Assays 80150-80299
Evocative/Suppression Testing 80400-80440
Consultations
  (Clinical Pathology) 80500-80502
Urinalysis 81000-81099
Chemistry...................... 82000-84999
Molecular Diagnostics 83890-83912
  Infectious Agent Detection 87470-87999
Infectious Agent Antibodies........ 86602-86804
Microbiology 87001-87254
  Infectious Agent Detection 87260-87999
Anatomic Pathology............. 88000-88099
Cytopathology 88104-88199
Surgical Pathology 88300-88399

Unlisted Service or Procedure

A service or procedure may be provided that is not listed in this edition of *CPT.* When reporting such a service, the appropriate "Unlisted Procedure" code may be used to indicate the service, identifying it by "Special Report" as discussed below. The "Unlisted Procedures" and accompanying codes for **Pathology and Laboratory** are as follows:

81099	Unlisted urinalysis procedure
84999	Unlisted chemistry procedure
85999	Unlisted hematology and coagulation procedure
86586	Unlisted antigen, each
86849	Unlisted immunology procedure
86999	Unlisted transfusion medicine procedure
87999	Unlisted microbiology procedure
88099	Unlisted necropsy (autopsy) procedure
88199	Unlisted cytopathology procedure
88299	Unlisted cytogenetic study
88399	Unlisted surgical pathology procedure
89240	Unlisted miscellaneous pathology test

Special Report

A service that is rarely provided, unusual, variable, or new may require a special report in determining medical appropriateness of the service. Pertinent information should include an adequate definition or description of the nature, extent, and need for the procedure; and the time, effort, and equipment necessary to provide the service. Additional items which may be included are:

- complexity of symptoms;
- final diagnosis;
- pertinent physical findings;
- diagnostic and therapeutic procedures;
- concurrent problems;
- follow-up care.

Notes

Pathology and Laboratory

Organ or Disease Oriented Panels

These panels were developed for coding purposes only and should not be interpreted as clinical parameters. The tests listed with each panel identify the defined components of that panel.

These panel components are not intended to limit the performance of other tests. If one performs tests in addition to those specifically indicated for a particular panel, those tests should be reported separately in addition to the panel code.

80048 Basic metabolic panel

This panel must include the following:

Calcium (82310)

Carbon dioxide (82374)

Chloride (82435)

Creatinine (82565)

Glucose (82947)

Potassium (84132)

Sodium (84295)

Urea nitrogen (BUN) (84520)

(Do not use 80048 in addition to 80053)

▲**80050** General health panel

This panel must include the following:

Comprehensive metabolic panel (80053)

Blood count, complete (CBC), automated and automated differential WBC count (85025 or 85027 and 85004)

OR

Blood count, complete (CBC), automated (85027) and appropriate manual differential WBC count (85007 or 85009)

Thyroid stimulating hormone (TSH) (84443)

80051 Electrolyte panel

This panel must include the following:

Carbon dioxide (82374)

Chloride (82435)

Potassium (84132)

Sodium (84295)

80053 Comprehensive metabolic panel

This panel must include the following:

Albumin (82040)

Bilirubin, total (82247)

Calcium (82310)

Carbon dioxide (bicarbonate) (82374)

Chloride (82435)

Creatinine (82565)

Glucose (82947)

Phosphatase, alkaline (84075)

Potassium (84132)

Protein, total (84155)

Sodium (84295)

Transferase, alanine amino (ALT) (SGPT) (84460)

Transferase, aspartate amino (AST) (SGOT) (84450)

Urea nitrogen (BUN) (84520)

(Do not use 80053 in addition to 80048, 80076)

▲**80055** Obstetric panel

This panel must include the following:

Blood count, complete (CBC), automated and automated differential WBC count (85025 or 85027 and 85004)

OR

Blood count, complete (CBC), automated (85027) and appropriate manual differential WBC count (85007 or 85009)

Hepatitis B surface antigen (HBsAg) (87340)

Antibody, rubella (86762)

Syphilis test, qualitative (eg, VDRL, RPR, ART) (86592)

Antibody screen, RBC, each serum technique (86850)

Blood typing, ABO (86900) AND

Blood typing, Rh (D) (86901)

80061 Lipid panel

This panel must include the following:

Cholesterol, serum, total (82465)

Lipoprotein, direct measurement, high density cholesterol (HDL cholesterol) (83718)

Triglycerides (84478)

80069 Renal function panel

This panel must include the following:

Albumin (82040)

Calcium (82310)

Carbon dioxide (bicarbonate) (82374)

Chloride (82435)

Creatinine (82565)

Glucose (82947)

Phosphorus inorganic (phosphate) (84100)

Potassium (84132)

Sodium (84295)

Urea nitrogen (BUN) (84520)

(80073 has been deleted. To report, see codes for specific tests)

80074 Acute hepatitis panel

This panel must include the following:

Hepatitis A antibody (HAAb), IgM antibody (86709)

Hepatitis B core antibody (HBcAb), IgM antibody (86705)

Hepatitis B surface antigen (HBsAg) (87340)

Hepatitis C antibody (86803)

80076 Hepatic function panel

This panel must include the following:

Albumin (82040)

Bilirubin, total (82247)

Bilirubin, direct (82248)

Phosphatase, alkaline (84075)

Protein, total (84155)

Transferase, alanine amino (ALT) (SGPT) (84460)

Transferase, aspartate amino (AST) (SGOT) (84450)

(Do not use 80076 in addition to 80053)

(80090 has been deleted. To report, see codes for specific tests)

Drug Testing

The following list contains examples of drugs or classes of drugs that are commonly assayed by qualitative screen, followed by confirmation with a second method.

Alcohols

Amphetamines

Barbiturates

Benzodiazepines

Cocaine and Metabolites

Methadones

Methaqualones

Opiates

Phencyclidines

Phenothiazines

Propoxyphenes

Tetrahydrocannabinoids

Tricyclic Antidepressants

Confirmed drugs may also be quantitated.

Use 80100 for each multiple drug class chromatographic procedure. Use 80102 for each procedure necessary for confirmation. For chromatography, each combination of stationary and mobile phase is to be counted as one procedure. For example, if detection of three drugs by chromatography requires one stationary phase with three mobile phases, use 80100 three (3) times. However, if multiple drugs can be detected using a single analysis (eg, one stationary phase with one mobile phase), use 80100 only once.

For quantitation of drugs screened, use appropriate code in **Chemistry** section (82000-84999) or **Therapeutic Drug Assay** section (80150-80299).

80100 Drug screen, qualitative; multiple drug classes chromatographic method, each procedure

80101 single drug class method (eg, immunoassay, enzyme assay), each drug class

80102 Drug confirmation, each procedure

80103 Tissue preparation for drug analysis

Therapeutic Drug Assays

The material for examination may be from any source. Examination is quantitative. For nonquantitative testing, see Drug Testing (80100-80103).

80150 Amikacin

80152 Amitriptyline

80154 Benzodiazepines

80156 Carbamazepine; total

80157 free

80158 Cyclosporine

80160 Desipramine

80162 Digoxin

80164 Dipropylacetic acid (valproic acid)

80166 Doxepin

80168 Ethosuximide

80170 Gentamicin

80172 Gold

80173 Haloperidol

80174 Imipramine

80176 Lidocaine

80178 Lithium

80182 Nortriptyline

80184 Phenobarbital

80185 Phenytoin; total

80186 free

80188 Primidone

80190 Procainamide;

80192 with metabolites (eg, n-acetyl procainamide)

80194 Quinidine

80196 Salicylate

80197 Tacrolimus

80198 Theophylline

80200 Tobramycin

80201 Topiramate

80202 Vancomycin

80299 Quantitation of drug, not elsewhere specified

Evocative/Suppression Testing

The following test panels involve the administration of evocative or suppressive agents, and the baseline and subsequent measurement of their effects on chemical constituents. These codes are to be used for the reporting of the laboratory component of the overall testing protocol. For the physician's administration of the evocative or suppressive agents, see 90780-90784; for the supplies and drugs, see 99070. To report physician attendance and monitoring during the testing, use the appropriate evaluation and management code, including the prolonged physician care codes if required. Prolonged physician care codes are not separately reported when evocative/suppression testing involves prolonged infusions reported with 90780 and 90781. In the code descriptors where reference is made to a particular analyte (eg, Cortisol (82533 x 2)) the "x 2" refers to the number of times the test for that particular analyte is performed.

80400 ACTH stimulation panel; for adrenal insufficiency

This panel must include the following:

Cortisol (82533 x 2)

80402 for 21 hydroxylase deficiency

This panel must include the following:

Cortisol (82533 x 2)

17 hydroxyprogesterone (83498 x 2)

80406 for 3 beta-hydroxydehydrogenase deficiency

This panel must include the following:

Cortisol (82533 x 2)

17 hydroxypregnenolone (84143 x 2)

80408 Aldosterone suppression evaluation panel (eg, saline infusion)

This panel must include the following:

Aldosterone (82088 x 2)

Renin (84244 x 2)

80410 Calcitonin stimulation panel (eg, calcium, pentagastrin)

This panel must include the following:

Calcitonin (82308 x 3)

80412 Corticotropic releasing hormone (CRH) stimulation panel

This panel must include the following:

Cortisol (82533 x 6)

Adrenocorticotropic hormone (ACTH) (82024 x 6)

80414 Chorionic gonadotropin stimulation panel; testosterone response

This panel must include the following:

Testosterone (84403 x 2 on three pooled blood samples)

80415 estradiol response

This panel must include the following:

Estradiol (82670 x 2 on three pooled blood samples)

80416 Renal vein renin stimulation panel (eg, captopril)

This panel must include the following:

Renin (84244 x 6)

80417 Peripheral vein renin stimulation panel (eg, captopril)

This panel must include the following:

Renin (84244 x 2)

80418 Combined rapid anterior pituitary evaluation panel

This panel must include the following:

Adrenocorticotropic hormone (ACTH) (82024 x 4)

Luteinizing hormone (LH) (83002 x 4)

Follicle stimulating hormone (FSH) (83001 x 4)

Prolactin (84146 x 4)

Human growth hormone (HGH) (83003 x 4)

Cortisol (82533 x 4)

Thyroid stimulating hormone (TSH) (84443 x 4)

80420 Dexamethasone suppression panel, 48 hour

This panel must include the following:

Free cortisol, urine (82530 x 2)

Cortisol (82533 x 2)

Volume measurement for timed collection (81050 x 2)

(For single dose dexamethasone, use 82533)

80422 Glucagon tolerance panel; for insulinoma

This panel must include the following:

Glucose (82947 x 3)

Insulin (83525 x 3)

80424 for pheochromocytoma

This panel must include the following:

Catecholamines, fractionated (82384 x 2)

80426 Gonadotropin releasing hormone stimulation panel

This panel must include the following:

Follicle stimulating hormone (FSH) (83001 x 4)

Luteinizing hormone (LH) (83002 x 4)

80428 Growth hormone stimulation panel (eg, arginine infusion, l-dopa administration)

This panel must include the following:

Human growth hormone (HGH) (83003 x 4)

80430 Growth hormone suppression panel (glucose administration)

This panel must include the following:

Glucose (82947 x 3)

Human growth hormone (HGH) (83003 x 4)

80432 Insulin-induced C-peptide suppression panel

This panel must include the following:

Insulin (83525)

C-peptide (84681 x 5)

Glucose (82947 x 5)

80434 Insulin tolerance panel; for ACTH insufficiency

This panel must include the following:

Cortisol (82533 x 5)

Glucose (82947 x 5)

80435 for growth hormone deficiency

This panel must include the following:

Glucose (82947 x 5)

Human growth hormone (HGH) (83003 x 5)

80436 Metyrapone panel

This panel must include the following:

Cortisol (82533 x 2)

11 deoxycortisol (82634 x 2)

80438 Thyrotropin releasing hormone (TRH) stimulation panel; one hour

This panel must include the following:

Thyroid stimulating hormone (TSH) (84443 x 3)

80439 two hour

This panel must include the following:

Thyroid stimulating hormone (TSH) (84443 x 4)

80440 for hyperprolactinemia

This panel must include the following:

Prolactin (84146 x 3)

Consultations (Clinical Pathology)

A clinical pathology consultation is a service, including a written report, rendered by the pathologist in response to a request from an attending physician in relation to a test result(s) requiring additional medical interpretive judgment.

Reporting of a test result(s) without medical interpretive judgment is not considered a clinical pathology consultation.

80500 Clinical pathology consultation; limited, without review of patient's history and medical records

80502 comprehensive, for a complex diagnostic problem, with review of patient's history and medical records

(These codes may also be used for pharmacokinetic consultations)

(For consultations involving the examination and evaluation of the patient, see 99241-99275)

Urinalysis

For specific analyses, see appropriate section.

(For urinalysis, infectious agent detection, semi-quantitative analysis of volatile compounds, use Category III code 0041T)

81000 Urinalysis, by dip stick or tablet reagent for bilirubin, glucose, hemoglobin, ketones, leukocytes, nitrite, pH, protein, specific gravity, urobilinogen, any number of these constituents; non-automated, with microscopy

81001 automated, with microscopy

81002 non-automated, without microscopy

81003 automated, without microscopy

81005 Urinalysis; qualitative or semiquantitative, except immunoassays

(For non-immunoassay reagent strip urinalysis, see 81000, 81002)

(For immunoassay, qualitative or semiquantitative, use 83518)

(For microalbumin, see 82043, 82044)

81007 bacteriuria screen, except by culture or dipstick

(For culture, see 87086-87088)

(For dipstick, use 81000 or 81002)

81015 microscopic only

81020 two or three glass test

81025 Urine pregnancy test, by visual color comparison methods

81050 Volume measurement for timed collection, each

81099 Unlisted urinalysis procedure

Chemistry

The material for examination may be from any source unless otherwise specified in the code descriptor. When an analyte is measured in multiple specimens from different sources, or in specimens that are obtained at different times, the analyte is reported separately for each source and for each specimen. The examination is quantitative unless specified. To report an organ or disease oriented panel, see codes 80048-80076.

When a code describes a method where measurement of multiple analytes may require one or several procedures, each procedure is coded separately (eg, 82491-82492, 82541-82544). For example, if two (2) analytes are measured using column chromatography using a single stationary or mobile phase, use 82492. If the same two analytes are measured using different stationary or mobile phase conditions, 82491 would be used twice. If a total of four (4) analytes are measured where two (2) analytes are measured with a single stationary and mobile phase, and the other two (2) analytes are measured using a different stationary and mobile phase, use 82492 twice. If a total of three (3) analytes are measured where two (2) analytes are measured using a single stationary or mobile phase condition, and the third analyte is measured separately using a different stationary or mobile phase procedure, use 82492 once for the (2) analytes measured under the same condition, and use 82491 once for the third analyte measured separately.

Clinical information derived from the results of laboratory data that is mathematically calculated (eg, free thyroxine index (T7)) is considered part of the test procedure and therefore is not a separately reportable service.

82000 Acetaldehyde, blood

82003 Acetaminophen

82009 Acetone or other ketone bodies, serum; qualitative

82010 quantitative

82013 Acetylcholinesterase

(Acid, gastric, see gastric acid, 82926, 82928)

(Acid phosphatase, see 84060-84066)

82016 Acylcarnitines; qualitative, each specimen

82017 quantitative, each specimen

(For carnitine, use 82379)

82024 Adrenocorticotropic hormone (ACTH)

82030 Adenosine, 5-monophosphate, cyclic (cyclic AMP)

82040 Albumin; serum

82042 urine or other source, quantitative, each specimen

82043 urine, microalbumin, quantitative

82044 urine, microalbumin, semiquantitative (eg, reagent strip assay)

(For prealbumin, use 84134)

82055 Alcohol (ethanol); any specimen except breath

(For other volatiles, alcohol, use 84600)

82075 breath

82085 Aldolase

82088 Aldosterone

(Alkaline phosphatase, see 84075, 84080)

82101 Alkaloids, urine, quantitative

(Alphaketoglutarate, see 82009, 82010)

(Alpha tocopherol (Vitamin E), use 84446)

82103 Alpha-1-antitrypsin; total

82104 phenotype

82105 Alpha-fetoprotein; serum

82106 amniotic fluid

82108 Aluminum

82120 Amines, vaginal fluid, qualitative

(For combined pH and amines test for vaginitis, use 82120 and 83986)

82127 Amino acids; single, qualitative, each specimen

82128 multiple, qualitative, each specimen

82131 single, quantitative, each specimen

82135 Aminolevulinic acid, delta (ALA)

82136 Amino acids, 2 to 5 amino acids, quantitative, each specimen

82139 Amino acids, 6 or more amino acids, quantitative, each specimen

82140 Ammonia

82143 Amniotic fluid scan (spectrophotometric)

(For L/S ratio, use 83661)

(Amobarbital, see 80100-80103 for qualitative analysis, 82205 for quantitative analysis)

82145 Amphetamine or methamphetamine

(For qualitative analysis, see 80100-80103)

82150 Amylase

82154 Androstanediol glucuronide

82157 Androstenedione

82160 Androsterone

82163 Angiotensin II

82164 Angiotensin I - converting enzyme (ACE)

(Antidiuretic hormone (ADH), use 84588)

(Antimony, use 83015)

(Antitrypsin, alpha-1-, see 82103, 82104)

82172 Apolipoprotein, each

82175 Arsenic

(For heavy metal screening, use 83015)

82180 Ascorbic acid (Vitamin C), blood

(Aspirin, see acetylsalicylic acid, 80196)

(Atherogenic index, blood, ultracentrifugation, quantitative, use 83716)

82190 Atomic absorption spectroscopy, each analyte

82205 Barbiturates, not elsewhere specified

(For qualitative analysis, see 80100-80103)

(For B-Natriuretic peptide, use 83880)

82232 Beta-2 microglobulin

(Bicarbonate, use 82374)

82239 Bile acids; total

82240 cholylglycine

(For bile pigments, urine, see 81000-81005)

82247 Bilirubin; total

82248 direct

82252 feces, qualitative

82261 Biotinidase, each specimen

82270 Blood, occult, by peroxidase activity (eg, guaiac), qualitative; feces, 1-3 simultaneous determinations

82273 other sources

(Blood urea nitrogen (BUN), see 84520, 84525)

82274 Blood, occult, by fecal hemoglobin determination by immunoassay, qualitative, feces, 1-3 simultaneous determinations

82286 Bradykinin

82300 Cadmium

82306 Calcifediol (25-OH Vitamin D-3)

82307 Calciferol (Vitamin D)

(For 1,25-Dihydroxyvitamin D, use 82652)

82308 Calcitonin

82310 Calcium; total

82330 ionized

82331 after calcium infusion test

82340 urine quantitative, timed specimen

82355 Calculus; qualitative analysis

82360 quantitative analysis, chemical

82365 infrared spectroscopy

82370 x-ray diffraction

(Carbamates, see individual listings)

82373 Carbohydrate deficient transferrin

82374 Carbon dioxide (bicarbonate)

(See also 82803)

82375 Carbon monoxide, (carboxyhemoglobin); quantitative

82376 qualitative

(To report end-tidal carbon monoxide, use Category III code 0043T)

82378 Carcinoembryonic antigen (CEA)

82379 Carnitine (total and free), quantitative, each specimen

(For acylcarnitine, see 82016, 82017)

82380 Carotene

82382 Catecholamines; total urine

82383 blood

82384 fractionated

(For urine metabolites, see 83835, 84585)

82387 Cathepsin-D

82390 Ceruloplasmin

82397 Chemiluminescent assay

82415 Chloramphenicol

82435 Chloride; blood

82436 urine

82438 other source

(For sweat collection by iontophoresis, use 89230)

82441 Chlorinated hydrocarbons, screen

(Chlorpromazine, use 84022)

(Cholecalciferol (Vitamin D), use 82307)

82465 Cholesterol, serum or whole blood, total

(For high density lipoprotein (HDL), use 83718)

82480 Cholinesterase; serum

82482 RBC

82485 Chondroitin B sulfate, quantitative

(Chorionic gonadotropin, see gonadotropin, 84702, 84703)

82486 Chromatography, qualitative; column (eg, gas liquid or HPLC), analyte not elsewhere specified

82487 paper, 1-dimensional, analyte not elsewhere specified

82488 paper, 2-dimensional, analyte not elsewhere specified

82489 thin layer, analyte not elsewhere specified

82491 Chromatography, quantitative, column (eg, gas liquid or HPLC); single analyte not elsewhere specified, single stationary and mobile phase

82492 multiple analytes, single stationary and mobile phase

82495 Chromium

82507 Citrate

82520 Cocaine or metabolite

(Cocaine, qualitative analysis, see 80100-80103)

(Codeine, qualitative analysis, see 80100-80103)

(Codeine, quantitative analysis, see 82101)

(Complement, see 86160-86162)

82523 Collagen cross links, any method

82525 Copper

(Coproporphyrin, see 84119, 84120)

(Corticosteroids, use 83491)

82528 Corticosterone

82530 Cortisol; free

82533 total

(C-peptide, use 84681)

82540 Creatine

82541 Column chromatography/mass spectrometry (eg, GC/MS, or HPLC/MS), analyte not elsewhere specified; qualitative, single stationary and mobile phase

82542 quantitative, single stationary and mobile phase

82543 stable isotope dilution, single analyte, quantitative, single stationary and mobile phase

82544 stable isotope dilution, multiple analytes, quantitative, single stationary and mobile phase

82550 Creatine kinase (CK), (CPK); total

82552 isoenzymes

82553 MB fraction only

82554 isoforms

82565 Creatinine; blood

82570 other source

82575 clearance

82585 Cryofibrinogen

82595 Cryoglobulin, qualitative or semi-quantitative (eg, cryocrit)

(For quantitative, cryoglobulin, see 82784, 82785)

(Crystals, pyrophosphate vs. urate, use 89060)

82600 Cyanide

82607 Cyanocobalamin (Vitamin B-12);

82608 unsaturated binding capacity

(Cyclic AMP, use 82030)

(Cyclic GMP, use 83008)

(Cyclosporine, use 80158)

82615 Cystine and homocystine, urine, qualitative

82626 Dehydroepiandrosterone (DHEA)

82627 Dehydroepiandrosterone-sulfate (DHEA-S)

(Delta-aminolevulinic acid (ALA), use 82135)

82633 Desoxycorticosterone, 11-

82634 Deoxycortisol, 11-

(Dexamethasone suppression test, use 80420)

(Diastase, urine, use 82150)

82638 Dibucaine number

(Dichloroethane, use 84600)

(Dichloromethane, use 84600)

(Diethylether, use 84600)

82646 Dihydrocodeinone

(For qualitative analysis, see 80100-80103)

82649 Dihydromorphinone

(For qualitative analysis, see 80100-80103)

82651 Dihydrotestosterone (DHT)

82652 Dihydroxyvitamin D, 1,25-

82654 Dimethadione

(For qualitative analysis, see 80100-80103)

(Diphenylhydantoin, use 80185)

(Dipropylacetic acid, use 80164)

(Dopamine, see 82382-82384)

(Duodenal contents, see individual enzymes; for intubation and collection, use 89100)

82657 Enzyme activity in blood cells, cultured cells, or tissue, not elsewhere specified; nonradioactive substrate, each specimen

82658 radioactive substrate, each specimen

82664 Electrophoretic technique, not elsewhere specified

(Endocrine receptor assays, see 84233-84235)

82666 Epiandrosterone

(Epinephrine, see 82382-82384)

82668 Erythropoietin

82670 Estradiol

82671 Estrogens; fractionated

82672 total

(Estrogen receptor assay, use 84233)

82677 Estriol

82679 Estrone

(Ethanol, see 82055 and 82075)

82690 Ethchlorvynol

(Ethyl alcohol, see 82055 and 82075)

82693 Ethylene glycol

82696 Etiocholanolone

(For fractionation of ketosteroids, use 83593)

82705 Fat or lipids, feces; qualitative

82710 quantitative

82715 Fat differential, feces, quantitative

82725 Fatty acids, nonesterified

82726 Very long chain fatty acids

82728 Ferritin

(Fetal hemoglobin, see hemoglobin 83030, 83033, and 85460)

(Fetoprotein, alpha-1, see 82105, 82106)

82731 Fetal fibronectin, cervicovaginal secretions, semi-quantitative

82735 Fluoride

82742 Flurazepam

(For qualitative analysis, see 80100-80103)

(Foam stability test, use 83662)

82746 Folic acid; serum

82747 RBC

(Follicle stimulating hormone (FSH), use 83001)

82757 Fructose, semen

(Fructosamine, use 82985)

(Fructose, TLC screen, use 84375)

82759 Galactokinase, RBC

82760 Galactose

82775 Galactose-1-phosphate uridyl transferase; quantitative

82776 screen

82784 Gammaglobulin; IgA, IgD, IgG, IgM, each

82785 IgE

(For allergen specific IgE, see 86003, 86005)

82787 immunoglobulin subclasses, (IgG1, 2, 3, or 4), each

(Gamma-glutamyltransferase (GGT), use 82977)

82800 Gases, blood, pH only

82803 Gases, blood, any combination of pH, pCO_2, pO_2, CO_2, HCO_3 (including calculated O_2 saturation);

(Use 82803 for two or more of the above listed analytes)

82805 with O_2 saturation, by direct measurement, except pulse oximetry

82810 Gases, blood, O_2 saturation only, by direct measurement, except pulse oximetry

(For pulse oximetry, use 94760)

82820 Hemoglobin-oxygen affinity (pO_2 for 50% hemoglobin saturation with oxygen)

82926 Gastric acid, free and total, each specimen

82928 Gastric acid, free or total; each specimen

82938 Gastrin after secretin stimulation

82941 Gastrin

(Gentamicin, use 80170)

(GGT, use 82977)

(GLC, gas liquid chromatography, use 82486)

82943 Glucagon

82945 Glucose, body fluid, other than blood

82946 Glucagon tolerance test

82947 Glucose; quantitative, blood (except reagent strip)

82948 blood, reagent strip

82950 post glucose dose (includes glucose)

82951 tolerance test (GTT), three specimens (includes glucose)

82952 tolerance test, each additional beyond three specimens

82953 tolbutamide tolerance test

(For insulin tolerance test, see 80434, 80435)

(For leucine tolerance test, use 80428)

(For semiquantitative urine glucose, see 81000, 81002, 81005, 81099)

82955 Glucose-6-phosphate dehydrogenase (G6PD); quantitative

82960 screen

(For glucose tolerance test with medication, use 90784 in addition)

82962 Glucose, blood by glucose monitoring device(s) cleared by the FDA specifically for home use

82963 Glucosidase, beta

82965 Glutamate dehydrogenase

82975 Glutamine (glutamic acid amide)

82977 Glutamyltransferase, gamma (GGT)

82978 Glutathione

82979 Glutathione reductase, RBC

82980 Glutethimide

(Glycohemoglobin, use 83036)

82985 Glycated protein

(Gonadotropin, chorionic, see 84702, 84703)

83001 Gonadotropin; follicle stimulating hormone (FSH)

83002 luteinizing hormone (LH)

(For luteinizing releasing factor (LRH), use 83727)

83003 Growth hormone, human (HGH) (somatotropin)

(For antibody to human growth hormone, use 86277)

83008 Guanosine monophosphate (GMP), cyclic

83010 Haptoglobin; quantitative

83012 phenotypes

83013 Helicobacter pylori; analysis for urease activity, non-radioactive isotope

83014 drug administration and sample collection

(For H. pylori, stool, use 87338. For H. pylori, liquid scintillation counter, see 78267, 78268. For H. pylori, enzyme immunoassay, use 87339)

83015 Heavy metal (eg, arsenic, barium, beryllium, bismuth, antimony, mercury); screen

83018 quantitative, each

83020 Hemoglobin fractionation and quantitation; electrophoresis (eg, A2, S, C, and/or F)

83021 chromatography (eg, A2, S, C, and/or F)

83026 Hemoglobin; by copper sulfate method, non-automated

83030 F (fetal), chemical

83033 F (fetal), qualitative

83036 glycated

(For fecal hemoglobin detection by immunoassay, use 82274)

83045 methemoglobin, qualitative

83050 methemoglobin, quantitative

83051 plasma

83055 sulfhemoglobin, qualitative

83060 sulfhemoglobin, quantitative

83065 thermolabile

83068 unstable, screen

83069 urine

83070 Hemosiderin; qualitative

83071 quantitative

(Heroin, see 80100-80103)

(HIAA, use 83497)

(High performance liquid chromatography (HPLC), use 82486)

83080 b-Hexosaminidase, each assay

83088 Histamine

(Hollander test, use 91052)

83090 Homocystine

83150 Homovanillic acid (HVA)

(Hormones, see individual alphabetic listings in **Chemistry** section)

(Hydrogen breath test, use 91065)

83491 Hydroxycorticosteroids, 17- (17-OHCS)

(For cortisol, see 82530, 82533. For deoxycortisol, use 82634)

83497 Hydroxyindolacetic acid, 5-(HIAA)

(For urine qualitative test, use 81005)

(5-Hydroxytryptamine, use 84260)

83498 Hydroxyprogesterone, 17-d

83499 Hydroxyprogesterone, 20-

83500 Hydroxyproline; free

83505 total

83516 Immunoassay for analyte other than infectious agent antibody or infectious agent antigen, qualitative or semiquantitative; multiple step method

83518 single step method (eg, reagent strip)

83519 Immunoassay, analyte, quantitative; by radiopharmaceutical technique (eg, RIA)

83520 not otherwise specified

(For immunoassays for antibodies to infectious agent antigens, see analyte and method specific codes in the **Immunology** section)

(For immunoassay of tumor antigen not elsewhere specified, use 86316)

(Immunoglobulins, see 82784, 82785)

83525 Insulin; total

(For proinsulin, use 84206)

83527 free

83528 Intrinsic factor

(For intrinsic factor antibodies, use 86340)

83540 Iron

83550 Iron binding capacity

83570 Isocitric dehydrogenase (IDH)

(Isonicotinic acid hydrazide, INH, see code for specific method)

(Isopropyl alcohol, use 84600)

83582 Ketogenic steroids, fractionation

(Ketone bodies, for serum, see 82009, 82010; for urine, see 81000-81003)

83586 Ketosteroids, 17- (17-KS); total

83593 fractionation

83605 Lactate (lactic acid)

83615 Lactate dehydrogenase (LD), (LDH);

83625 isoenzymes, separation and quantitation

83632 Lactogen, human placental (HPL) human chorionic somatomammotropin

83633 Lactose, urine; qualitative

83634 quantitative

(For tolerance, see 82951, 82952)

(For breath hydrogen test for lactase deficiency, use 91065)

83655 Lead

83661 Fetal lung maturity assessment; lecithin sphingomyelin (L/S) ratio

83662 foam stability test

83663 fluorescence polarization

83664 lamellar body density

(For phosphatidylglycerol, use 84081)

83670 Leucine aminopeptidase (LAP)

83690 Lipase

83715 Lipoprotein, blood; electrophoretic separation and quantitation

▲**83716** high resolution fractionation and quantitation of lipoproteins including lipoprotein subclasses when performed (eg, electrophoresis, nuclear magnetic resonance, ultracentrifugation)

83718 Lipoprotein, direct measurement; high density cholesterol (HDL cholesterol)

83719 direct measurement, VLDL cholesterol

83721 direct measurement, LDL cholesterol

(For fractionation by nuclear magnetic resonance or high resolution electrophoresis, use 83716)

(To report direct measurement, intermediate density lipoproteins (remnant lipoproteins), use Category III code 0026T)

(Luteinizing hormone (LH), use 83002)

83727 Luteinizing releasing factor (LRH)

(For qualitative analysis, see 80100-80103)

(Macroglobulins, alpha-2, use 86329)

83735 Magnesium

83775 Malate dehydrogenase

(Maltose tolerance, see 82951, 82952)

(Mammotropin, use 84146)

83785 Manganese

(Marijuana, see 80100-80103)

83788 Mass spectrometry and tandem mass spectrometry (MS, MS/MS), analyte not elsewhere specified; qualitative, each specimen

83789 quantitative, each specimen

83805 Meprobamate

(For qualitative analysis, see 80100-80103)

83825 Mercury, quantitative

(Mercury screen, use 83015)

83835 Metanephrines

(For catecholamines, see 82382-82384)

83840 Methadone

(For methadone qualitative analysis, see 80100-80103)

(Methamphetamine, see 80100-80103, 82145)

(Methanol, use 84600)

83857 Methemalbumin

(Methemoglobin, see hemoglobin 83045, 83050)

83858 Methsuximide

(Methyl alcohol, use 84600)

(Microalbumin, see 82043 for quantitative, see 82044 for semiquantitative)

(Microglobulin, beta-2, use 82232)

83864 Mucopolysaccharides, acid; quantitative

83866 screen

83872 Mucin, synovial fluid (Ropes test)

83873 Myelin basic protein, cerebrospinal fluid

(For oligoclonal bands, use 83916)

83874 Myoglobin

(Nalorphine, use 83925)

83880 Natriuretic peptide

83883 Nephelometry, each analyte not elsewhere specified

83885 Nickel

83887 Nicotine

Codes 83890-83912 are intended for use with molecular diagnostic techniques for analysis of nucleic acids.

Codes 83890-83912 are coded by procedure rather than analyte.

Code separately for each procedure used in an analysis. For example, a procedure requiring isolation of DNA, restriction endonuclease digestion, electrophoresis, and nucleic acid probe amplification would be coded 83890, 83892, 83894, and 83898.

(For microbial identification, see 87797, 87798)

83890 Molecular diagnostics; molecular isolation or extraction

83891 isolation or extraction of highly purified nucleic acid

83892 enzymatic digestion

83893 dot/slot blot production

83894 separation by gel electrophoresis (eg, agarose, polyacrylamide)

83896 nucleic acid probe, each

83897 nucleic acid transfer (eg, Southern, Northern)

83898 amplification of patient nucleic acid (eg, PCR, LCR), single primer pair, each primer pair

83901 amplification of patient nucleic acid, multiplex, each multiplex reaction

83902 reverse transcription

83903 mutation scanning, by physical properties (eg, single strand conformational polymorphisms (SSCP), heteroduplex, denaturing gradient gel electrophoresis (DGGE), RNA'ase A), single segment, each

83904 mutation identification by sequencing, single segment, each segment

83905 mutation identification by allele specific transcription, single segment, each segment

83906 mutation identification by allele specific translation, single segment, each segment

83912 interpretation and report

83915 Nucleotidase 5-

83916 Oligoclonal immune (oligoclonal bands)

83918 Organic acids; total, quantitative, each specimen

83919 qualitative, each specimen

83921 Organic acid, single, quantitative

83925 Opiates, (eg, morphine, meperidine)

83930 Osmolality; blood

83935 urine

83937 Osteocalcin (bone g1a protein)

83945 Oxalate

83950 Oncoprotein, HER-2/neu

(For tissue, see 88342, 88365)

83970 Parathormone (parathyroid hormone)

(Pesticide, quantitative, see code for specific method. For screen for chlorinated hydrocarbons, use 82441)

83986 pH, body fluid, except blood

(For blood pH, see 82800, 82803)

83992 Phencyclidine (PCP)

(For qualitative analysis, see 80100-80103)

(Phenobarbital, use 80184)

84022 Phenothiazine

(For qualitative analysis, see 80100, 80101)

84030 Phenylalanine (PKU), blood

(Phenylalanine-tyrosine ratio, see 84030, 84510)

84035 Phenylketones, qualitative

84060 Phosphatase, acid; total

84061 forensic examination

84066 prostatic

84075 Phosphatase, alkaline;

84078 heat stable (total not included)

84080 isoenzymes

84081 Phosphatidylglycerol

(Phosphates inorganic, use 84100)

(Phosphates, organic, see code for specific method. For cholinesterase, see 82480, 82482)

84085 Phosphogluconate, 6-, dehydrogenase, RBC

84087 Phosphohexose isomerase

84100 Phosphorus inorganic (phosphate);

84105 urine

(Pituitary gonadotropins, see 83001-83002)

(PKU, see 84030, 84035)

84106 Porphobilinogen, urine; qualitative

84110 quantitative

84119 Porphyrins, urine; qualitative

84120 quantitation and fractionation

84126 Porphyrins, feces; quantitative

84127 qualitative

(Porphyrin precursors, see 82135, 84106, 84110)

(For protoporphyrin, RBC, see 84202, 84203)

84132 Potassium; serum

84133 urine

84134 Prealbumin

(For microalbumin, see 82043, 82044)

84135 Pregnanediol

84138 Pregnanetriol

84140 Pregnenolone

84143 17-hydroxypregnenolone

84144 Progesterone

(Progesterone receptor assay, use 84234)

(For proinsulin, use 84206)

84146 Prolactin

84150 Prostaglandin, each

84152 Prostate specific antigen (PSA); complexed (direct measurement)

84153 total

84154 free

▲**84155** Protein, total, except by refractometry; serum

●**84156** urine

●**84157** other source (eg, synovial fluid, cerebrospinal fluid)

▲**84160** Protein, total, by refractometry, any source

►(For urine total protein by dipstick method, use 81000-81003)◄

▲**84165** Protein, electrophoretic fractionation and quantitation

84181 Western Blot, with interpretation and report, blood or other body fluid

84182 Western Blot, with interpretation and report, blood or other body fluid, immunological probe for band identification, each

(For Western Blot tissue analysis, use 88371)

84202 Protoporphyrin, RBC; quantitative

84203 screen

84206 Proinsulin

(Pseudocholinesterase, use 82480)

84207 Pyridoxal phosphate (Vitamin B-6)

84210 Pyruvate

84220 Pyruvate kinase

84228 Quinine

84233 Receptor assay; estrogen

84234 progesterone

84235 endocrine, other than estrogen or progesterone (specify hormone)

84238 non-endocrine (eg, acetylcholine) (specify receptor)

84244 Renin

84252 Riboflavin (Vitamin B-2)

(Salicylates, use 80196)

(Secretin test, see 99070, 89100 and appropriate analyses)

84255 Selenium

84260 Serotonin

(For urine metabolites (HIAA), use 83497)

84270 Sex hormone binding globulin (SHBG)

84275 Sialic acid

(Sickle hemoglobin, use 85660)

84285 Silica

84295 Sodium; serum

84300 urine

84302 other source

(Somatomammotropin, use 83632)

(Somatotropin, use 83003)

84305 Somatomedin

84307 Somatostatin

84311 Spectrophotometry, analyte not elsewhere specified

84315 Specific gravity (except urine)

(For specific gravity, urine, see 81000-81003)

(Stone analysis, see 82355-82370)

84375 Sugars, chromatographic, TLC or paper chromatography

84376 Sugars (mono-, di-, and oligosaccharides); single qualitative, each specimen

84377 multiple qualitative, each specimen

84378 single quantitative, each specimen

84379 multiple quantitative, each specimen

84392 Sulfate, urine

(Sulfhemoglobin, see hemoglobin, 83055, 83060)

(T-3, see 84479-84481)

(T-4, see 84436-84439)

84402 Testosterone; free

84403 total

84425 Thiamine (Vitamin B-1)

84430 Thiocyanate

84432 Thyroglobulin

(Thyroglobulin, antibody, use 86800)

(Thyrotropin releasing hormone (TRH) test, see 80438, 80439)

84436 Thyroxine; total

84437 requiring elution (eg, neonatal)

84439 free

84442 Thyroxine binding globulin (TBG)

84443 Thyroid stimulating hormone (TSH)

84445 Thyroid stimulating immune globulins (TSI)

(Tobramycin, use 80200)

84446 Tocopherol alpha (Vitamin E)

(Tolbutamide tolerance, use 82953)

84449 Transcortin (cortisol binding globulin)

84450 Transferase; aspartate amino (AST) (SGOT)

84460 alanine amino (ALT) (SGPT)

84466 Transferrin

(Iron binding capacity, use 83550)

84478 Triglycerides

84479 Thyroid hormone (T3 or T4) uptake or thyroid hormone binding ratio (THBR)

84480 Triiodothyronine T3; total (TT-3)

84481 free

84482 reverse

84484 Troponin, quantitative

(For troponin, qualitative assay, use 84512)

84485 Trypsin; duodenal fluid

84488 feces, qualitative

84490 feces, quantitative, 24-hour collection

84510 Tyrosine

(Urate crystal identification, use 89060)

84512 Troponin, qualitative

(For troponin, quantitative assay, use 84484)

84520 Urea nitrogen; quantitative

84525 semiquantitative (eg, reagent strip test)

84540 Urea nitrogen, urine

84545 Urea nitrogen, clearance

84550 Uric acid; blood

84560 other source

84577 Urobilinogen, feces, quantitative

84578 Urobilinogen, urine; qualitative

84580 quantitative, timed specimen

84583 semiquantitative

(Uroporphyrins, use 84120)

(Valproic acid (dipropylacetic acid), use 80164)

84585 Vanillylmandelic acid (VMA), urine

84586 Vasoactive intestinal peptide (VIP)

84588 Vasopressin (antidiuretic hormone, ADH)

84590 Vitamin A

(Vitamin B-1, use 84425)

(Vitamin B-2, use 84252)

(Vitamin B-6, use 84207)

(Vitamin B-12, use 82607)

(Vitamin B-12, absorption (Schilling), see 78270, 78271)

(Vitamin C, use 82180)

(Vitamin D, see 82306, 82307, 82652)

(Vitamin E, use 84446)

84591 Vitamin, not otherwise specified

84597 Vitamin K

(VMA, use 84585)

84600 Volatiles (eg, acetic anhydride, carbon tetrachloride, dichloroethane, dichloromethane, diethylether, isopropyl alcohol, methanol)

(For acetaldehyde, use 82000)

(Volume, blood, RISA or Cr-51, see 78110, 78111)

84620 Xylose absorption test, blood and/or urine

(For administration, use 99070)

84630 Zinc

84681 C-peptide

84702 Gonadotropin, chorionic (hCG); quantitative

84703 qualitative

(For urine pregnancy test by visual color comparison, use 81025)

84830 Ovulation tests, by visual color comparison methods for human luteinizing hormone

84999 Unlisted chemistry procedure

Hematology and Coagulation

(For blood banking procedures, see **Transfusion Medicine**)

(Agglutinins, see **Immunology**)

(Antiplasmin, use 85410)

(Antithrombin III, see 85300, 85301)

85002 Bleeding time

85004 Blood count; automated differential WBC count

85007 blood smear, microscopic examination with manual differential WBC count

85008 blood smear, microscopic examination without manual differential WBC count

(For other fluids (eg, CSF), see 89050, 89051)

85009 manual differential WBC count, buffy coat

(Eosinophils, nasal smear, use 89190)

85013 spun microhematocrit

85014 hematocrit (Hct)

85018 hemoglobin (Hgb)

(For other hemoglobin determination, see 83020-83069)

(For immunoassay, hemoglobin, fecal, use 82274)

(85021 has been deleted)

(85022 has been deleted)

(85023 has been deleted. To report, use 85007 and 85027)

(85024 has been deleted. To report, use 85025)

85025 complete (CBC), automated (Hgb, Hct, RBC, WBC and platelet count) and automated differential WBC count

85027 complete (CBC), automated (Hgb, Hct, RBC, WBC and platelet count)

(85031 has been deleted. To report, use 85014, 85018 and 85032)

85032 manual cell count (erythrocyte, leukocyte, or platelet) each

85041 red blood cell (RBC), automated

(Do not report code 85041 in conjunction with 85025 or 85027)

85044 reticulocyte, manual

85045 reticulocyte, automated

85046 reticulocytes, hemoglobin concentration

85048 leukocyte (WBC), automated

85049 platelet, automated

● 85055 Reticulated platelet assay

85060 Blood smear, peripheral, interpretation by physician with written report

(85095 has been deleted. To report, use 38220)

85097 Bone marrow, smear interpretation

(For special stains, see 85540, 88312, 88313)

(85102 has been deleted. To report, use 38221)

(For bone biopsy, see 20220, 20225, 20240, 20245, 20250, 20251)

85130 Chromogenic substrate assay

(Circulating anti-coagulant screen (mixing studies), see 85611, 85732)

85170 Clot retraction

85175 Clot lysis time, whole blood dilution

(Clotting factor I (fibrinogen), see 85384, 85385)

85210 Clotting; factor II, prothrombin, specific

(See also 85610-85613)

85220 factor V (AcG or proaccelerin), labile factor

85230 factor VII (proconvertin, stable factor)

85240 factor VIII (AHG), one stage

85244 factor VIII related antigen

85245 factor VIII, VW factor, ristocetin cofactor

85246 factor VIII, VW factor antigen

85247 factor VIII, von Willebrand factor, multimetric analysis

85250 factor IX (PTC or Christmas)

85260 factor X (Stuart-Prower)

85270 factor XI (PTA)

85280 factor XII (Hageman)

85290 factor XIII (fibrin stabilizing)

85291 factor XIII (fibrin stabilizing), screen solubility

85292 prekallikrein assay (Fletcher factor assay)

85293 high molecular weight kininogen assay (Fitzgerald factor assay)

85300 Clotting inhibitors or anticoagulants; antithrombin III, activity

85301 antithrombin III, antigen assay

85302 protein C, antigen

85303 protein C, activity

85305 protein S, total

85306 protein S, free

85307 Activated Protein C (APC) resistance assay

85335 Factor inhibitor test

85337 Thrombomodulin

(For mixing studies for inhibitors, use 85732)

85345 Coagulation time; Lee and White

85347 activated

85348 other methods

(Differential count, see 85007 et seq)

(Duke bleeding time, use 85002)

(Eosinophils, nasal smear, use 89190)

85360 Euglobulin lysis

(Fetal hemoglobin, see 83030, 83033, 85460)

85362 Fibrin(ogen) degradation (split) products (FDP)(FSP); agglutination slide, semiquantitative

(Immunoelectrophoresis, use 86320)

85366 paracoagulation

85370 quantitative

85378 Fibrin degradation products, D-dimer; qualitative or semiquantitative

85379 quantitative

►(For ultrasensitive and standard sensitivity quantitative D-dimer, use 85379)◄

85380 ultrasensitive (eg, for evaluation for venous thromboembolism), qualitative or semiquantitative

85384 Fibrinogen; activity

85385 antigen

85390 Fibrinolysins or coagulopathy screen, interpretation and report

● **85396** Coagulation/fibrinolysis assay, whole blood (eg, viscoelastic clot assessment), including use of any pharmacologic additive(s), as indicated, including interpretation and written report, per day

85400 Fibrinolytic factors and inhibitors; plasmin

85410 alpha-2 antiplasmin

85415 plasminogen activator

85420 plasminogen, except antigenic assay

85421 plasminogen, antigenic assay

(Fragility, red blood cell, see 85547, 85555-85557)

85441 Heinz bodies; direct

85445 induced, acetyl phenylhydrazine

(Hematocrit (PCV), see 85014, 85025, 85027)

(Hemoglobin, see 83020-83068, 85018, 85025, 85027)

85460 Hemoglobin or RBCs, fetal, for fetomaternal hemorrhage; differential lysis (Kleihauer-Betke)

(See also 83030, 83033)

(Hemolysins, see 86940, 86941)

85461 rosette

85475 Hemolysin, acid

(See also 86940, 86941)

85520 Heparin assay

85525 Heparin neutralization

85530 Heparin-protamine tolerance test

85536 Iron stain, peripheral blood

(For iron stains on bone marrow or other tissues with physician evaluation, use 88313)

85540 Leukocyte alkaline phosphatase with count

85547 Mechanical fragility, RBC

85549 Muramidase

(Nitroblue tetrazolium dye test, use 86384)

85555 Osmotic fragility, RBC; unincubated

85557 incubated

(Packed cell volume, use 85013)

(Partial thromboplastin time, see 85730, 85732)

(Parasites, blood (eg, malaria smears), use 87207)

(Plasmin, use 85400)

(Plasminogen, use 85420)

(Plasminogen activator, use 85415)

85576 Platelet, aggregation (in vitro), each agent

(85585 has been deleted. To report, use 85008)

(85590 has been deleted. To report, use 85032)

(85595 has been deleted. To report, use 85049)

85597 Platelet neutralization

85610 Prothrombin time;

85611 substitution, plasma fractions, each

85612 Russell viper venom time (includes venom); undiluted

85613 diluted

(Red blood cell count, see 85025, 85027, 85041)

85635 Reptilase test

(Reticulocyte count, see 85044, 85045)

85651 Sedimentation rate, erythrocyte; non-automated

85652 automated

85660 Sickling of RBC, reduction

(Hemoglobin electrophoresis, use 83020)

(Smears (eg, for parasites, malaria), use 87207)

85670 Thrombin time; plasma

85675 titer

85705 Thromboplastin inhibition; tissue

(For individual clotting factors, see 85245-85247)

85730 Thromboplastin time, partial (PTT); plasma or whole blood

85732 substitution, plasma fractions, each

85810 Viscosity

(von Willebrand factor assay, see 85245-85247)

(WBC count, see 85025, 85027, 85048, 89050)

85999 Unlisted hematology and coagulation procedure

Immunology

(Acetylcholine receptor antibody, see 86255, 86256)

(Actinomyces, antibodies to, use 86602)

(Adrenal cortex antibodies, see 86255, 86256)

(For tuberculosis test, cell mediated immunity measurement of gamma interferon antigen response, use Category III code 0010T)

86000 Agglutinins, febrile (eg, Brucella, Francisella, Murine typhus, Q fever, Rocky Mountain spotted fever, scrub typhus), each antigen

(For antibodies to infectious agents, see 86602-86804)

86001 Allergen specific IgG quantitative or semiquantitative, each allergen

(Agglutinins and autohemolysins, see 86940, 86941)

86003 Allergen specific IgE; quantitative or semiquantitative, each allergen

(For total quantitative IgE, use 82785)

86005 qualitative, multiallergen screen (dipstick, paddle or disk)

(For total qualitative IgE, use 83518)

(Alpha-1 antitrypsin, see 82103, 82104)

(Alpha-1 feto-protein, see 82105, 82106)

(Anti-AChR (acetylcholine receptor) antibody titer, see 86255, 86256)

(Anticardiolipin antibody, use 86147)

(Anti-DNA, use 86225)

(Anti-deoxyribonuclease titer, use 86215)

86021 Antibody identification; leukocyte antibodies

86022 platelet antibodies

86023 platelet associated immunoglobulin assay

86038 Antinuclear antibodies (ANA);

86039 titer

(Antistreptococcal antibody, ie, anti-DNAse, use 86215)

(Antistreptokinase titer, use 86590)

86060 Antistreptolysin O; titer

(For antibodies to infectious agents, see 86602-86804)

86063 screen

(For antibodies to infectious agents, see 86602-86804)

(Blastomyces, antibodies to, use 86612)

86077 Blood bank physician services; difficult cross match and/or evaluation of irregular antibody(s), interpretation and written report

86078 investigation of transfusion reaction including suspicion of transmissible disease, interpretation and written report

86079 authorization for deviation from standard blood banking procedures (eg, use of outdated blood, transfusion of Rh incompatible units), with written report

(Brucella, antibodies to, use 86622)

(Candida, antibodies to, use 86628. For skin testing, use 86485)

86140 C-reactive protein;

(Candidiasis, use 86628)

86141 high sensitivity (hsCRP)

86146 Beta 2 Glycoprotein I antibody, each

86147 Cardiolipin (phospholipid) antibody, each Ig class

86148 Anti-phosphatidylserine (phospholipid) antibody

(To report antiprothrombin (phospholipid cofactor) antibody, use Category III code 0030T)

86155 Chemotaxis assay, specify method

(Clostridium difficile toxin, use 87230)

(Coccidioides, antibodies to, see 86635. For skin testing, use 86490)

86156 Cold agglutinin; screen

86157 titer

86160 Complement; antigen, each component

86161 functional activity, each component

86162 total hemolytic (CH50)

86171 Complement fixation tests, each antigen

(Coombs test, see 86880-86886)

86185 Counterimmunoelectrophoresis, each antigen

(Cryptococcus, antibodies to, use 86641)

86215 Deoxyribonuclease, antibody

86225 Deoxyribonucleic acid (DNA) antibody; native or double stranded

(Echinococcus, antibodies to, see code for specific method)

(For HIV antibody tests, see 86701-86703)

86226 single stranded

(Anti D.S., DNA, IFA, eg, using C.Lucilae, see 86255 and 86256)

86235 Extractable nuclear antigen, antibody to, any method (eg, nRNP, SS-A, SS-B, Sm, RNP, Sc170, J01), each antibody

86243 Fc receptor

(Filaria, antibodies to, see code for specific method)

86255 Fluorescent noninfectious agent antibody; screen, each antibody

86256 titer, each antibody

(Fluorescent technique for antigen identification in tissue, use 88346; for indirect fluorescence, use 88347)

(FTA, see 86781)

(Gel (agar) diffusion tests, use 86331)

86277 Growth hormone, human (HGH), antibody

86280 Hemagglutination inhibition test (HAI)

(For rubella, use 86762)

(For antibodies to infectious agents, see 86602-86804)

86294 Immunoassay for tumor antigen, qualitative or semiquantitative (eg, bladder tumor antigen)

86300 Immunoassay for tumor antigen, quantitative; CA 15-3 (27.29)

86301 CA 19-9

86304 CA 125

(For measurement of serum HER-2/neu oncoprotein, see 83950)

(For hepatitis delta agent, antibody, use 86692)

86308 Heterophile antibodies; screening

(For antibodies to infectious agents, see 86602-86804)

86309 titer

(For antibodies to infectious agents, see 86602-86804)

86310 titers after absorption with beef cells and guinea pig kidney

(Histoplasma, antibodies to, use 86698. For skin testing, use 86510)

(For antibodies to infectious agents, see 86602-86804)

(Human growth hormone antibody, use 86277)

86316 Immunoassay for tumor antigen; other antigen, quantitative (eg, CA 50, 72-4, 549), each

86317 Immunoassay for infectious agent antibody, quantitative, not otherwise specified

(For immunoassay techniques for antigens, see 83516, 83518, 83519, 83520, 87301-87450, 87810-87899)

(For particle agglutination procedures, use 86403)

86318 Immunoassay for infectious agent antibody, qualitative or semiquantitative, single step method (eg, reagent strip)

86320 Immunoelectrophoresis; serum

86325 other fluids (eg, urine, cerebrospinal fluid) with concentration

86327 crossed (2-dimensional assay)

86329 Immunodiffusion; not elsewhere specified

86331 gel diffusion, qualitative (Ouchterlony), each antigen or antibody

86332 Immune complex assay

86334 Immunofixation electrophoresis

86336 Inhibin A

86337 Insulin antibodies

86340 Intrinsic factor antibodies

(Leptospira, antibodies to, use 86720)

(Leukoagglutinins, use 86021)

86341 Islet cell antibody

86343 Leukocyte histamine release test (LHR)

86344 Leukocyte phagocytosis

86353 Lymphocyte transformation, mitogen (phytomitogen) or antigen induced blastogenesis

(Lymphocytes immunophenotyping, use 88180 for cytometry; see 88342, 88346 for microscopic techniques)

(Malaria antibodies, use 86750)

86359 T cells; total count

86360 absolute CD4 and CD8 count, including ratio

86361 absolute CD4 count

86376 Microsomal antibodies (eg, thyroid or liver-kidney), each

86378 Migration inhibitory factor test (MIF)

(Mitochondrial antibody, liver, see 86255, 86256)

(Mononucleosis, see 86308-86310)

86382 Neutralization test, viral

86384 Nitroblue tetrazolium dye test (NTD)

(Ouchterlony diffusion, use 86331)

(Platelet antibodies, see 86022, 86023)

86403 Particle agglutination; screen, each antibody

86406 titer, each antibody

(Pregnancy test, see 84702, 84703)

(Rapid plasma reagin test (RPR), see 86592, 86593)

86430 Rheumatoid factor; qualitative

86431 quantitative

(Serologic test for syphilis, see 86592, 86593)

86485 Skin test; candida

(For antibody, candida, use 86628)

86490 coccidioidomycosis

86510 histoplasmosis

(For histoplasma, antibody, use 86698)

86580 tuberculosis, intradermal

86585 tuberculosis, tine test

(For tuberculosis test, cell mediated immunity measurement of gamma interferon antigen response, use Category III code 0010T)

(For skin tests for allergy, see 95010-95199)

(Smooth muscle antibody, see 86255, 86256)

(Sporothrix, antibodies to, see code for specific method)

86586 unlisted antigen, each

86590 Streptokinase, antibody

(For antibodies to infectious agents, see 86602-86804)

(Streptolysin O antibody, see antistreptolysin O, 86060, 86063)

86592 Syphilis test; qualitative (eg, VDRL, RPR, ART)

(For antibodies to infectious agents, see 86602-86804)

86593 quantitative

(For antibodies to infectious agents, see 86602-86804)

(Tetanus antibody, use 86774)

(Thyroglobulin antibody, use 86800)

(Thyroglobulin, use 84432)

(Thyroid microsomal antibody, use 86376)

(For toxoplasma antibody, see 86777-86778)

The following codes (86602-86804) are qualitative or semiquantitative immunoassays performed by multiple step methods for the detection of antibodies to infectious agents. For immunoassays by single step method (eg, reagent strips), use code 86318. Procedures for the identification of antibodies should be coded as precisely as possible. For example, an antibody to a virus could be coded with increasing specificity for virus, family, genus, species, or type. In some cases, further precision may be added to codes by specifying the class of immunoglobulin being detected. When multiple tests are done to detect antibodies to organisms classified more precisely than the specificity allowed by available codes, it is appropriate to code each as a separate service. For example, a test for antibody to an enterovirus is coded as 86658. Coxsackie viruses are enteroviruses, but there are no codes for the individual species of enterovirus. If assays are performed for antibodies to coxsackie A and B species, each assay should be separately coded. Similarly, if multiple assays are performed for antibodies of different immunoglobulin classes, each assay should be coded separately.

(For the detection of antibodies other than those to infectious agents, see specific antibody (eg, 86021, 86022, 86023, 86376, 86800, 86850-86870) or specific method (eg, 83516, 86255, 86256)).

(For infectious agent/antigen detection, see 87260-87899)

86602 Antibody; actinomyces

86603 adenovirus

86606 Aspergillus

86609 bacterium, not elsewhere specified

86611 Bartonella

86612 Blastomyces

86615 Bordetella

86617 Borrelia burgdorferi (Lyme disease) confirmatory test (eg, Western Blot or immunoblot)

86618 Borrelia burgdorferi (Lyme disease)

86619 Borrelia (relapsing fever)

86622 Brucella

86625 Campylobacter

86628 Candida

(For skin test, candida, use 86485)

86631 Chlamydia

86632 Chlamydia, IgM

(For chlamydia antigen, see 87270, 87320. For fluorescent antibody technique, see 86255, 86256)

86635 Coccidioides

86638 Coxiella burnetii (Q fever)

86641 Cryptococcus

86644 cytomegalovirus (CMV)

86645 cytomegalovirus (CMV), IgM

86648 Diphtheria

86651 encephalitis, California (La Crosse)

86652 encephalitis, Eastern equine

86653 encephalitis, St. Louis

86654 encephalitis, Western equine

86658 enterovirus (eg, coxsackie, echo, polio)

(Trichinella, antibodies to, use 86784)

(Trypanosoma, antibodies to, see code for specific method)

(Tuberculosis, use 86580 for skin testing)

(Viral antibodies, see code for specific method)

86663 Epstein-Barr (EB) virus, early antigen (EA)

86664 Epstein-Barr (EB) virus, nuclear antigen (EBNA)

86665 Epstein-Barr (EB) virus, viral capsid (VCA)

86666 Ehrlichia

86668 Francisella tularensis

86671 fungus, not elsewhere specified

86674 Giardia lamblia

86677 Helicobacter pylori

86682 helminth, not elsewhere specified

(86683 has been deleted. To report, use 82274)

86684 Haemophilus influenza

86687 HTLV-I

86688 HTLV-II

86689 HTLV or HIV antibody, confirmatory test (eg, Western Blot)

86692 hepatitis, delta agent

(For hepatitis delta agent, antigen, use 87380)

86694 herpes simplex, non-specific type test

86695 herpes simplex, type 1

86696 herpes simplex, type 2

86698 histoplasma

86701 HIV-1

86702 HIV-2

86703 HIV-1 and HIV-2, single assay

(For HIV-1 antigen, use 87390)

(For HIV-2 antigen, use 87391)

(For confirmatory test for HIV antibody (eg, Western Blot), use 86689)

86704 Hepatitis B core antibody (HBcAb); total

86705 IgM antibody

86706 Hepatitis B surface antibody (HBsAb)

86707 Hepatitis Be antibody (HBeAb)

86708 Hepatitis A antibody (HAAb); total

86709 IgM antibody

86710 Antibody; influenza virus

86713 Legionella

86717 Leishmania

86720 Leptospira

86723 Listeria monocytogenes

86727 lymphocytic choriomeningitis

86729 lymphogranuloma venereum

86732 mucormycosis

86735 mumps

86738 mycoplasma

86741 Neisseria meningitidis

86744 Nocardia

86747 parvovirus

86750 Plasmodium (malaria)

86753 protozoa, not elsewhere specified

86756 respiratory syncytial virus

86757 Rickettsia

86759 rotavirus

86762 rubella

86765 rubeola

86768 Salmonella

86771 Shigella

86774 tetanus

86777 Toxoplasma

86778 Toxoplasma, IgM

86781 Treponema pallidum, confirmatory test (eg, FTA-abs)

86784 Trichinella

86787 varicella-zoster

86790 virus, not elsewhere specified

86793 Yersinia

86800 Thyroglobulin antibody

(For thyroglobulin, use 84432)

86803 Hepatitis C antibody;

86804 confirmatory test (eg, immunoblot)

Tissue Typing

(For pretransplant cross-match, see appropriate code or codes)

86805 Lymphocytotoxicity assay, visual crossmatch; with titration

86806 without titration

86807 Serum screening for cytotoxic percent reactive antibody (PRA); standard method

86808 quick method

86812 HLA typing; A, B, or C (eg, A10, B7, B27), single antigen

86813 A, B, or C, multiple antigens

86816 DR/DQ, single antigen

86817 DR/DQ, multiple antigens

86821 lymphocyte culture, mixed (MLC)

86822 lymphocyte culture, primed (PLC)

86849 Unlisted immunology procedure

Transfusion Medicine

(For apheresis, use 36511, 36512)

(For therapeutic phlebotomy, use 99195)

86850 Antibody screen, RBC, each serum technique

86860 Antibody elution (RBC), each elution

86870 Antibody identification, RBC antibodies, each panel for each serum technique

86880 Antihuman globulin test (Coombs test); direct, each antiserum

86885 indirect, qualitative, each antiserum

86886 indirect, titer, each antiserum

86890 Autologous blood or component, collection processing and storage; predeposited

86891 intra- or postoperative salvage

(For physician services to autologous donors, see 99201-99204)

86900 Blood typing; ABO

86901 Rh (D)

86903 antigen screening for compatible blood unit using reagent serum, per unit screened

86904 antigen screening for compatible unit using patient serum, per unit screened

86905 RBC antigens, other than ABO or Rh (D), each

86906 Rh phenotyping, complete

86910 Blood typing, for paternity testing, per individual; ABO, Rh and MN

86911 each additional antigen system

(86915 has been deleted. To report, see 38210-38213)

86920 Compatibility test each unit; immediate spin technique

86921 incubation technique

86922 antiglobulin technique

86927 Fresh frozen plasma, thawing, each unit

86930 Frozen blood, each unit; freezing (includes preparation)

86931 thawing

86932 freezing (includes preparation) and thawing

86940 Hemolysins and agglutinins; auto, screen, each

86941 incubated

86945 Irradiation of blood product, each unit

86950 Leukocyte transfusion

(For leukapheresis, use 36511)

86965 Pooling of platelets or other blood products

86970 Pretreatment of RBCs for use in RBC antibody detection, identification, and/or compatibility testing; incubation with chemical agents or drugs, each

86971 incubation with enzymes, each

86972 by density gradient separation

86975 Pretreatment of serum for use in RBC antibody identification; incubation with drugs, each

86976 by dilution

86977 incubation with inhibitors, each

86978 by differential red cell absorption using patient RBCs or RBCs of known phenotype, each absorption

86985 Splitting of blood or blood products, each unit

86999 Unlisted transfusion medicine procedure

Microbiology

Includes bacteriology, mycology, parasitology, and virology.

Presumptive identification of microorganisms is defined as identification by colony morphology, growth on selective media, Gram stains, or up to three tests (eg, catalase, oxidase, indole, urease). Definitive identification of microorganisms is defined as an identification to the genus or species level that requires additional tests (eg, biochemical panels, slide cultures). If additional studies involve molecular probes, chromatography, or immunologic techniques, these should be separately coded in addition to definitive identification codes (87140-87158). For multiple specimens/sites use modifier '-59'. For repeat laboratory tests performed on the same day, use modifier '-91'.

87001 Animal inoculation, small animal; with observation

87003 with observation and dissection

87015 Concentration (any type), for infectious agents

(Do not report 87015 in conjunction with 87177)

▲**87040** Culture, bacterial; blood, aerobic, with isolation and presumptive identification of isolates (includes anaerobic culture, if appropriate)

▲**87045** stool, aerobic, with isolation and preliminary examination (eg, KIA, LIA), Salmonella and Shigella species

▲**87046** stool, aerobic, additional pathogens, isolation and presumptive identification of isolates

▲**87070** any other source except urine, blood or stool, aerobic, with isolation and presumptive identification of isolates

(For urine, use 87088)

87071 quantitative, aerobic with isolation and presumptive identification of isolates, any source except urine, blood or stool

(For urine, use 87088)

87073 quantitative, anaerobic with isolation and presumptive identification of isolates, any source except urine, blood or stool

(For definitive identification of isolates, use 87076 or 87077. For typing of isolates see 87140-87158)

▲**87075** any source, except blood, anaerobic with isolation and presumptive identification of isolates

87076 anaerobic isolate, additional methods required for definitive identification, each isolate

(For gas liquid chromatography (GLC) or high pressure liquid chromatography (HPLC), use 87143)

87077 aerobic isolate, additional methods required for definitive identification, each isolate

(For gas liquid chromatography (GLC) or high pressure liquid chromatography (HPLC), use 87143)

87081 Culture, presumptive, pathogenic organisms, screening only;

87084 with colony estimation from density chart

87086 Culture, bacterial; quantitative colony count, urine

87088 with isolation and presumptive identification of isolates, urine

87101 Culture, fungi (mold or yeast) isolation, with presumptive identification of isolates; skin, hair, or nail

87102 other source (except blood)

87103 blood

87106 Culture, fungi, definitive identification, each organism; yeast

(Use 87106 in addition to codes 87101, 87102, or 87103 when appropriate)

87107 mold

87109 Culture, mycoplasma, any source

87110 Culture, chlamydia, any source

(For immunofluorescence staining of shell vials, use 87140)

87116 Culture, tubercle or other acid-fast bacilli (eg, TB, AFB, mycobacteria) any source, with isolation and presumptive identification of isolates

87118 Culture, mycobacterial, definitive identification, each isolate

(For nucleic acid probe identification, use 87149)

(For GLC or HPLC identification, use 87143)

87140 Culture, typing; immunofluorescent method, each antiserum

87143 gas liquid chromatography (GLC) or high pressure liquid chromatography (HPLC) method

87147 immunologic method, other than immunofluoresence (eg, agglutination grouping), per antiserum

87149 identification by nucleic acid probe

87152 identification by pulse field gel typing

87158 other methods

87164 Dark field examination, any source (eg, penile, vaginal, oral, skin); includes specimen collection

87166 without collection

87168 Macroscopic examination; arthropod

87169 parasite

87172 Pinworm exam (eg, cellophane tape prep)

87176 Homogenization, tissue, for culture

87177 Ova and parasites, direct smears, concentration and identification

(Do not report 87177 in conjunction with 87015)

(For direct smears from a primary source, use 87207)

(For coccidia or microsporidia exam, use 87207)

(For trichrome, iron hemotoxylin and other special stains, use 88313)

(For nucleic acid probes in cytologic material, use 88365)

(For molecular diagnostics, see 83890-83898, 87470-87799)

87181 Susceptibility studies, antimicrobial agent; agar dilution method, per agent (eg, antibiotic gradient strip)

87184 disk method, per plate (12 or fewer agents)

87185 enzyme detection (eg, beta lactamase), per enzyme

87186 microdilution or agar dilution (minimum inhibitory concentration (MIC) or breakpoint), each multi-antimicrobial, per plate

✚ **87187** microdilution or agar dilution, minimum lethal concentration (MLC), each plate (List separately in addition to code for primary procedure)

(Use 87187 in conjunction with 87186 or 87188)

87188 macrobroth dilution method, each agent

87190 mycobacteria, proportion method, each agent

(For other mycobacterial susceptibility studies, see 87181, 87184, 87186, or 87188)

87197 Serum bactericidal titer (Schlicter test)

87205 Smear, primary source with interpretation; Gram or Giemsa stain for bacteria, fungi, or cell types

87206 fluorescent and/or acid fast stain for bacteria, fungi, parasites, viruses or cell types

87207 special stain for inclusion bodies or parasites (eg, malaria, coccidia, microsporidia, trypanosomes, herpes viruses

(For direct smears with concentration and identification, use 87177)

(For thick smear preparation, use 87015)

(For complex special stains, see 88312, 88313)

(For fat, meat, fibers, nasal eosinophils, and starch, see miscellaneous section)

87210 wet mount for infectious agents (eg, saline, India ink, KOH preps)

(For KOH examination of skin, hair or nails, see 87220)

87220 Tissue examination by KOH slide of samples from skin, hair, or nails for fungi or ectoparasite ova or mites (eg, scabies)

87230 Toxin or antitoxin assay, tissue culture (eg, Clostridium difficile toxin)

87250 Virus isolation; inoculation of embryonated eggs, or small animal, includes observation and dissection

87252 tissue culture inoculation, observation, and presumptive identification by cytopathic effect

87253 tissue culture, additional studies or definitive identification (eg, hemabsorption, neutralization, immunofluoresence stain), each isolate

(Electron microscopy, use 88348)

(Inclusion bodies in tissue sections, see 88304-88309; in smears, see 87207-87210; in fluids, use 88106)

87254 centrifuge enhanced (shell vial) technique, includes identification with immunofluorescence stain, each virus

(Report 87254 in addition to 87252 as appropriate)

87255 including identification by non-immunologic method, other than by cytopathic effect (eg, virus specific enzymatic activity)

These codes are intended for primary source only. For similar studies on culture material, refer to codes 87140-87158. Infectious agents by antigen detection, immunofluorescence microscopy, or nucleic acid probe techniques should be reported as precisely as possible. The most specific code possible should be reported. If there is no specific agent code, the general methodology code (eg, 87299, 87449, 87450, 87797, 87798, 87799, 87899) should be used. For identification of antibodies to many of the listed infectious agents, see 86602-86804. When separate assays are performed for different species or strain(s) of organisms, each assay should be reported separately.

87260 Infectious agent antigen detection by immunofluorescent technique; adenovirus

87265 Bordetella pertussis/parapertussis

87267 Enterovirus, direct fluorescent antibody (DFA)

● 87269 giardia

87270 Chlamydia trachomatis

87271 Cytomegalovirus, direct fluorescent antibody (DFA)

▲ 87272 cryptosporidium

87273 Herpes simplex virus type 2

87274 Herpes simplex virus type 1

87275 influenza B virus

87276 influenza A virus

87277 Legionella micdadei

87278 Legionella pneumophila

87279 Parainfluenza virus, each type

87280 respiratory syncytial virus

87281 Pneumocystis carinii

87283 Rubeola

87285 Treponema pallidum

87290 Varicella zoster virus

87299 not otherwise specified, each organism

87300 Infectious agent antigen detection by immunofluorescent technique, polyvalent for multiple organisms, each polyvalent antiserum

(For physician evaluation of infectious disease agents by immunofluorescence, use 88346)

87301 Infectious agent antigen detection by enzyme immunoassay technique, qualitative or semiquantitative, multiple step method; adenovirus enteric types 40/41

87320 Chlamydia trachomatis

87324 Clostridium difficile toxin(s)

87327 Cryptococcus neoformans

(For Cryptococcus latex agglutination, use 86403)

▲ 87328 cryptosporidium

● 87329 giardia

87332 cytomegalovirus

87335 Escherichia coli 0157

(For giardia antigen, use 87328)

87336 Entamoeba histolytica dispar group

87337 Entamoeba histolytica group

87338 Helicobacter pylori, stool

87339 Helicobacter pylori

(For H. pylori, stool, use 87338. For H. pylori, breath and blood by mass spectrometry, see 83013, 83014. For H. pylori, liquid scintillation counter, see 78267, 78268)

87340 hepatitis B surface antigen (HBsAg)

87341 hepatitis B surface antigen (HBsAg) neutralization

87350 hepatitis Be antigen (HBeAg)

87380 hepatitis, delta agent

87385 Histoplasma capsulatum

87390 HIV-1

87391 HIV-2

87400 Influenza, A or B, each

87420 respiratory syncytial virus

87425 rotavirus

87427 Shiga-like toxin

87430 Streptococcus, group A

87449 Infectious agent antigen detection by enzyme immunoassay technique qualitative or semiquantitative; multiple step method, not otherwise specified, each organism

87450 single step method, not otherwise specified, each organism

87451 multiple step method, polyvalent for multiple organisms, each polyvalent antiserum

87470 Infectious agent detection by nucleic acid (DNA or RNA); Bartonella henselae and Bartonella quintana, direct probe technique

87471 Bartonella henselae and Bartonella quintana, amplified probe technique

87472 Bartonella henselae and Bartonella quintana, quantification

87475 Borrelia burgdorferi, direct probe technique

87476 Borrelia burgdorferi, amplified probe technique

87477 Borrelia burgdorferi, quantification

87480 Candida species, direct probe technique

87481 Candida species, amplified probe technique

87482 Candida species, quantification

87485 Chlamydia pneumoniae, direct probe technique

87486 Chlamydia pneumoniae, amplified probe technique

87487 Chlamydia pneumoniae, quantification

87490 Chlamydia trachomatis, direct probe technique

87491 Chlamydia trachomatis, amplified probe technique

87492 Chlamydia trachomatis, quantification

87495 cytomegalovirus, direct probe technique

87496 cytomegalovirus, amplified probe technique

87497 cytomegalovirus, quantification

87510 Gardnerella vaginalis, direct probe technique

87511 Gardnerella vaginalis, amplified probe technique

87512 Gardnerella vaginalis, quantification

87515 hepatitis B virus, direct probe technique

87516 hepatitis B virus, amplified probe technique

87517 hepatitis B virus, quantification

87520 hepatitis C, direct probe technique

87521 hepatitis C, amplified probe technique

87522 hepatitis C, quantification

87525 hepatitis G, direct probe technique

87526 hepatitis G, amplified probe technique

87527 hepatitis G, quantification

87528 Herpes simplex virus, direct probe technique

87529 Herpes simplex virus, amplified probe technique

87530 Herpes simplex virus, quantification

87531 Herpes virus-6, direct probe technique

87532 Herpes virus-6, amplified probe technique

87533 Herpes virus-6, quantification

87534 HIV-1, direct probe technique

87535 HIV-1, amplified probe technique

87536 HIV-1, quantification

87537 HIV-2, direct probe technique

87538 HIV-2, amplified probe technique

87539 HIV-2, quantification

87540 Legionella pneumophila, direct probe technique

87541 Legionella pneumophila, amplified probe technique

87542 Legionella pneumophila, quantification

87550 Mycobacteria species, direct probe technique

87551 Mycobacteria species, amplified probe technique

87552 Mycobacteria species, quantification

87555 Mycobacteria tuberculosis, direct probe technique

87556 Mycobacteria tuberculosis, amplified probe technique

87557 Mycobacteria tuberculosis, quantification

87560 Mycobacteria avium-intracellulare, direct probe technique

87561 Mycobacteria avium-intracellulare, amplified probe technique

87562 Mycobacteria avium-intracellulare, quantification

87580 Mycoplasma pneumoniae, direct probe technique

87581 Mycoplasma pneumoniae, amplified probe technique

87582 Mycoplasma pneumoniae, quantification

87590 Neisseria gonorrhoeae, direct probe technique

87591 Neisseria gonorrhoeae, amplified probe technique

87592 Neisseria gonorrhoeae, quantification

87620 papillomavirus, human, direct probe technique

87621 papillomavirus, human, amplified probe technique

87622 papillomavirus, human, quantification

87650 Streptococcus, group A, direct probe technique

87651 Streptococcus, group A, amplified probe technique

87652 Streptococcus, group A, quantification

● **87660** Trichomonas vaginalis, direct probe technique

87797 Infectious agent detection by nucleic acid (DNA or RNA), not otherwise specified; direct probe technique, each organism

87798 amplified probe technique, each organism

87799 quantification, each organism

87800 Infectious agent detection by nucleic acid (DNA or RNA), multiple organisms; direct probe(s) technique

87801 amplified probe(s) technique

87802 Infectious agent antigen detection by immunoassay with direct optical observation; Streptococcus, group B

87803 Clostridium difficile toxin A

87804 Influenza

87810 Infectious agent detection by immunoassay with direct optical observation; Chlamydia trachomatis

87850 Neisseria gonorrhoeae

87880 Streptococcus, group A

87899 not otherwise specified

87901 Infectious agent genotype analysis by nucleic acid (DNA or RNA); HIV 1, reverse transcriptase and protease

(For infectious agent drug susceptibility phenotype prediction for HIV-1, use Category III code 0023T)

87902 Hepatitis C virus

87903 Infectious agent phenotype analysis by nucleic acid (DNA or RNA) with drug resistance tissue culture analysis, HIV 1; first through 10 drugs tested

✚ **87904** each additional 1 through 5 drugs tested (List separately in addition to code for primary procedure)

(Use 87904 in conjunction with code 87903)

87999 Unlisted microbiology procedure

Anatomic Pathology

Postmortem Examination

Procedures 88000 through 88099 represent physician services only. Use modifier '-90' or 09990 for outside laboratory services.

88000 Necropsy (autopsy), gross examination only; without CNS

88005 with brain

88007 with brain and spinal cord

88012 infant with brain

88014 stillborn or newborn with brain

88016 macerated stillborn

88020 Necropsy (autopsy), gross and microscopic; without CNS

88025 with brain

88027 with brain and spinal cord

88028 infant with brain

88029 stillborn or newborn with brain

88036 Necropsy (autopsy), limited, gross and/or microscopic; regional

88037 single organ

88040 Necropsy (autopsy); forensic examination

88045 coroner's call

88099 Unlisted necropsy (autopsy) procedure

Cytopathology

(For cervicography, see Category III code 0003T)

(For collection of cytology specimens via mammary duct catheter lavage, report 0045T-0046T)

88104 Cytopathology, fluids, washings or brushings, except cervical or vaginal; smears with interpretation

88106 filter method only with interpretation

88107 smears and filter preparation with interpretation

88108 Cytopathology, concentration technique, smears and interpretation (eg, Saccomanno technique)

(For cervical or vaginal smears, see 88150-88155)

(For gastric intubation with lavage, see 89130-89141, 91055)

(For x-ray localization, use 74340)

● **88112** Cytopathology, selective cellular enhancement technique with interpretation (eg, liquid based slide preparation method), except cervical or vaginal

►(Do not report 88112 with 88108)◄

88125 Cytopathology, forensic (eg, sperm)

88130 Sex chromatin identification; Barr bodies

88140 peripheral blood smear, polymorphonuclear drumsticks

(For Guard stain, use 88313)

Codes 88141-88155, 88164-88167, ►88174-88175◄ are used to report cervical or vaginal screening by various methods and to report physician interpretation services. Use codes 88150-88154 to report Pap smears that are examined using non-Bethesda reporting. Use codes 88164-88167 to report Pap smears that are examined using the Bethesda System of reporting. Use codes 88142-88143 to report specimens collected in fluid medium with automated thin layer preparation that are examined using any system of reporting (Bethesda or non-Bethesda). ►Use codes 88174-88175 to report automated screening of specimens collected in fluid medium with automated thin layer preparation that are examined using any system of reporting (Bethesda or non-Bethesda)◄. Within each of these three code families choose the one code that describes the screening method(s) used. Codes 88141 and 88155 should be reported in addition to the screening code chosen when the additional services are provided.

+ **88141** Cytopathology, cervical or vaginal (any reporting system); requiring interpretation by physician (List separately in addition to code for technical service)

(Use 88141 in conjunction with codes 88142-88154, 88164-88167, 88174-88175)

88142 Cytopathology, cervical or vaginal (any reporting system), collected in preservative fluid, automated thin layer preparation; manual screening under physician supervision

88143 with manual screening and rescreening under physician supervision

(88144 has been deleted)

(88145 has been deleted)

(For automated screening of automated thin layer preparation, see 88174, 88175)

88147 Cytopathology smears, cervical or vaginal; screening by automated system under physician supervision

88148 screening by automated system with manual rescreening under physician supervision

88150 Cytopathology, slides, cervical or vaginal; manual screening under physician supervision

88152 with manual screening and computer-assisted rescreening under physician supervision

88153 with manual screening and rescreening under physician supervision

88154 with manual screening and computer-assisted rescreening using cell selection and review under physician supervision

+ **88155** Cytopathology, slides, cervical or vaginal, definitive hormonal evaluation (eg, maturation index, karyopyknotic index, estrogenic index) (List separately in addition to code(s) for other technical and interpretation services)

(Use 88155 in conjunction with 88142-88154, 88164-88167, 88174-88175)

88160 Cytopathology, smears, any other source; screening and interpretation

88161 preparation, screening and interpretation

88162 extended study involving over 5 slides and/or multiple stains

(For obtaining specimen, see percutaneous needle biopsy under individual organ in **Surgery**)

(For aerosol collection of sputum, use 89220)

(For special stains, see 88312-88314)

88164 Cytopathology, slides, cervical or vaginal (the Bethesda System); manual screening under physician supervision

88165 with manual screening and rescreening under physician supervision

88166 with manual screening and computer-assisted rescreening under physician supervision

88167 with manual screening and computer-assisted rescreening using cell selection and review under physician supervision

(88170 has been deleted. To report, see 10021, 10022)

(88171 has been deleted. To report, see 10021, 10022)

88172 Cytopathology, evaluation of fine needle aspirate; immediate cytohistologic study to determine adequacy of specimen(s)

88173 interpretation and report

88174 Cytopathology, cervical or vaginal (any reporting system), collected in preservative fluid, automated thin layer preparation; screening by automated system, under physician supervision

88175 with screening by automated system and manual rescreening, under physician supervision

(For manual screening, see 88142, 88143)

88180 Flow cytometry; each cell surface, cytoplasmic or nuclear marker

88182 cell cycle or DNA analysis

(For tumor morphometry and DNA and ploidy analysis by imaging techniques, use 88358)

88199 Unlisted cytopathology procedure

(For electron microscopy, see 88348, 88349)

Cytogenetic Studies

(For acetylcholinesterase, use 82013)

(For alpha-fetoprotein, serum or amniotic fluid, see 82105, 82106)

(For laser microdissection of cells from tissue sample, see 88380)

88230 Tissue culture for non-neoplastic disorders; lymphocyte

88233 skin or other solid tissue biopsy

88235 amniotic fluid or chorionic villus cells

88237 Tissue culture for neoplastic disorders; bone marrow, blood cells

88239 solid tumor

88240 Cryopreservation, freezing and storage of cells, each cell line

(For therapeutic cryopreservation and storage, use 38207)

88241 Thawing and expansion of frozen cells, each aliquot

(For therapeutic thawing of previous harvest, use 38208)

88245 Chromosome analysis for breakage syndromes; baseline Sister Chromatid Exchange (SCE), 20-25 cells

88248 baseline breakage, score 50-100 cells, count 20 cells, 2 karyotypes (eg, for ataxia telangiectasia, Fanconi anemia, fragile X)

88249 score 100 cells, clastogen stress (eg, diepoxybutane, mitomycin C, ionizing radiation, UV radiation)

88261 Chromosome analysis; count 5 cells, 1 karyotype, with banding

88262 count 15-20 cells, 2 karyotypes, with banding

88263 count 45 cells for mosaicism, 2 karyotypes, with banding

88264 analyze 20-25 cells

88267 Chromosome analysis, amniotic fluid or chorionic villus, count 15 cells, 1 karyotype, with banding

88269 Chromosome analysis, in situ for amniotic fluid cells, count cells from 6-12 colonies, 1 karyotype, with banding

88271 Molecular cytogenetics; DNA probe, each (eg, FISH)

88272 chromosomal in situ hybridization, analyze 3-5 cells (eg, for derivatives and markers)

88273 chromosomal in situ hybridization, analyze 10-30 cells (eg, for microdeletions)

88274 interphase in situ hybridization, analyze 25-99 cells

88275 interphase in situ hybridization, analyze 100-300 cells

88280 Chromosome analysis; additional karyotypes, each study

88283 additional specialized banding technique (eg, NOR, C-banding)

88285 additional cells counted, each study

88289 additional high resolution study

88291 Cytogenetics and molecular cytogenetics, interpretation and report

88299 Unlisted cytogenetic study

Surgical Pathology

Services 88300 through 88309 include accession, examination, and reporting. They do not include the services designated in codes 88311 through 88365 and 88399, which are coded in addition when provided.

The unit of service for codes 88300 through 88309 is the specimen.

A specimen is defined as tissue or tissues that is (are) submitted for individual and separate attention, requiring individual examination and pathologic diagnosis. Two or more such specimens from the same patient (eg, separately identified endoscopic biopsies, skin lesions, etc.) are each appropriately assigned an individual code reflective of its proper level of service.

Service code 88300 is used for any specimen that in the opinion of the examining pathologist can be accurately diagnosed without microscopic examination. Service code 88302 is used when gross and microscopic examination is performed on a specimen to confirm identification and the absence of disease. Service codes 88304 through 88309 describe all other specimens requiring gross and microscopic examination, and represent additional ascending levels of physician work. Levels 88302 through 88309 are specifically defined by the assigned specimens.

Any unlisted specimen should be assigned to the code which most closely reflects the physician work involved when compared to other specimens assigned to that code.

88300 **Level I** - Surgical pathology, gross examination only

88302 **Level II** - Surgical pathology, gross and microscopic examination

Appendix, Incidental

Fallopian Tube, Sterilization

Fingers/Toes, Amputation, Traumatic

Foreskin, Newborn

Hernia Sac, Any Location

Hydrocele Sac

Nerve

Skin, Plastic Repair

Sympathetic Ganglion

Testis, Castration

Vaginal Mucosa, Incidental

Vas Deferens, Sterilization

88304 **Level III** - Surgical pathology, gross and microscopic examination

Abortion, Induced

Abscess

Aneurysm - Arterial/Ventricular

Anus, Tag

Appendix, Other than Incidental

Artery, Atheromatous Plaque

Bartholin's Gland Cyst

Bone Fragment(s), Other than Pathologic Fracture

Bursa/Synovial Cyst

Carpal Tunnel Tissue

Cartilage, Shavings

Cholesteatoma

Colon, Colostomy Stoma

Conjunctiva - Biopsy/Pterygium

Cornea

Diverticulum - Esophagus/Small Intestine

Dupuytren's Contracture Tissue

Femoral Head, Other than Fracture

Fissure/Fistula

Foreskin, Other than Newborn

Gallbladder

Ganglion Cyst

Hematoma

Hemorrhoids

Hydatid of Morgagni

Intervertebral Disc

Joint, Loose Body

Meniscus

Mucocele, Salivary

Neuroma - Morton's/Traumatic

Pilonidal Cyst/Sinus

Polyps, Inflammatory - Nasal/Sinusoidal

Skin - Cyst/Tag/Debridement

Soft Tissue, Debridement

Soft Tissue, Lipoma

Spermatocele

Tendon/Tendon Sheath

Testicular Appendage

Thrombus or Embolus

Tonsil and/or Adenoids

Varicocele

Vas Deferens, Other than Sterilization

Vein, Varicosity

88305 **Level IV** - Surgical pathology, gross and microscopic examination

Abortion - Spontaneous/Missed

Artery, Biopsy

Bone Marrow, Biopsy

Bone Exostosis

Brain/Meninges, Other than for Tumor Resection

Breast, Biopsy, Not Requiring Microscopic Evaluation of Surgical Margins

Breast, Reduction Mammoplasty

Bronchus, Biopsy

Cell Block, Any Source

Cervix, Biopsy

Colon, Biopsy

Duodenum, Biopsy

Endocervix, Curettings/Biopsy

Endometrium, Curettings/Biopsy

Esophagus, Biopsy

Extremity, Amputation, Traumatic

Fallopian Tube, Biopsy

Fallopian Tube, Ectopic Pregnancy

Femoral Head, Fracture

Fingers/Toes, Amputation, Non-traumatic

Gingiva/Oral Mucosa, Biopsy

Heart Valve

Joint, Resection

Kidney, Biopsy

Larynx, Biopsy

Leiomyoma(s), Uterine Myomectomy - without Uterus

Lip, Biopsy/Wedge Resection

Lung, Transbronchial Biopsy

Lymph Node, Biopsy

Muscle, Biopsy

Nasal Mucosa, Biopsy

Nasopharynx/Oropharynx, Biopsy

Nerve, Biopsy

Odontogenic/Dental Cyst

Omentum, Biopsy

Ovary with or without Tube, Non-neoplastic

Ovary, Biopsy/Wedge Resection

Parathyroid Gland

Peritoneum, Biopsy

Pituitary Tumor

Placenta, Other than Third Trimester

Pleura/Pericardium - Biopsy/Tissue

Polyp, Cervical/Endometrial

Polyp, Colorectal

Polyp, Stomach/Small Intestine

Prostate, Needle Biopsy

Prostate, TUR

Salivary Gland, Biopsy

Sinus, Paranasal Biopsy

Skin, Other than Cyst/Tag/Debridement/Plastic Repair

Small Intestine, Biopsy

Soft Tissue, Other than Tumor/Mass/Lipoma/Debridement

Spleen

Stomach, Biopsy

Synovium

Testis, Other than Tumor/Biopsy/Castration

Thyroglossal Duct/Brachial Cleft Cyst

Tongue, Biopsy

Tonsil, Biopsy

Trachea, Biopsy

Ureter, Biopsy

Urethra, Biopsy

Urinary Bladder, Biopsy

Uterus, with or without Tubes and Ovaries, for Prolapse

Vagina, Biopsy

Vulva/Labia, Biopsy

88307 **Level V** - Surgical pathology, gross and microscopic examination

Adrenal, Resection

Bone - Biopsy/Curettings

Bone Fragment(s), Pathologic Fracture

Brain, Biopsy

Brain/Meninges, Tumor Resection

Breast, Excision of Lesion, Requiring Microscopic Evaluation of Surgical Margins

Breast, Mastectomy - Partial/Simple

Cervix, Conization

Colon, Segmental Resection, Other than for Tumor

Extremity, Amputation, Non-traumatic

Eye, Enucleation

Kidney, Partial/Total Nephrectomy

Larynx, Partial/Total Resection

Liver, Biopsy - Needle/Wedge

Liver, Partial Resection

Lung, Wedge Biopsy

Lymph Nodes, Regional Resection

Mediastinum, Mass

Myocardium, Biopsy

Odontogenic Tumor

Ovary with or without Tube, Neoplastic

Pancreas, Biopsy

Placenta, Third Trimester

Prostate, Except Radical Resection

Salivary Gland

Sentinel Lymph Node

Small Intestine, Resection, Other than for Tumor

Soft Tissue Mass (except Lipoma) - Biopsy/Simple Excision

Stomach - Subtotal/Total Resection, Other than for Tumor

Testis, Biopsy

Thymus, Tumor

Thyroid, Total/Lobe

Ureter, Resection

Urinary Bladder, TUR

Uterus, with or without Tubes and Ovaries, Other than Neoplastic/Prolapse

88309 **Level VI** - Surgical pathology, gross and microscopic examination

Bone Resection

Breast, Mastectomy - with Regional Lymph Nodes

Colon, Segmental Resection for Tumor

Colon, Total Resection

Esophagus, Partial/Total Resection

Extremity, Disarticulation

Fetus, with Dissection

Larynx, Partial/Total Resection - with Regional Lymph Nodes

Lung - Total/Lobe/Segment Resection

Pancreas, Total/Subtotal Resection

Prostate, Radical Resection

Small Intestine, Resection for Tumor

Soft Tissue Tumor, Extensive Resection

Stomach - Subtotal/Total Resection for Tumor

Testis, Tumor

Tongue/Tonsil - Resection for Tumor

Urinary Bladder, Partial/Total Resection

Uterus, with or without Tubes and Ovaries, Neoplastic

Vulva, Total/Subtotal Resection

(For fine needle aspiration, see 10021, 10022)

(For evaluation of fine needle aspirate, see 88172-88173)

+ 88311 Decalcification procedure (List separately in addition to code for surgical pathology examination)

+▲88312 Special stains (List separately in addition to code for primary service); Group I for microorganisms (eg, Gridley, acid fast, methenamine silver), each

+ 88313 Group II, all other, (eg, iron, trichrome), except immunocytochemistry and immunoperoxidase stains, each

(For immunocytochemistry and immunoperoxidase tissue studies, use 88342)

+ 88314 histochemical staining with frozen section(s)

88318 Determinative histochemistry to identify chemical components (eg, copper, zinc)

88319 Determinative histochemistry or cytochemistry to identify enzyme constituents, each

88321 Consultation and report on referred slides prepared elsewhere

88323 Consultation and report on referred material requiring preparation of slides

88325 Consultation, comprehensive, with review of records and specimens, with report on referred material

88329 Pathology consultation during surgery;

88331 first tissue block, with frozen section(s), single specimen

88332 each additional tissue block with frozen section(s)

▲88342 Immunohistochemistry (including tissue immunoperoxidase), each antibody

►(For quantitative or semiquantitative immunohistochemistry, use 88361)◄

88346 Immunofluorescent study, each antibody; direct method

88347 indirect method

88348 Electron microscopy; diagnostic

88349 scanning

88355 Morphometric analysis; skeletal muscle

88356 nerve

▲88358 tumor (eg, DNA ploidy)

►(Do not report 88358 with 88313 unless each procedure is for a different special stain)◄

●88361 tumor immunohistochemistry (eg, Her-2/neu, estrogen receptor/progesterone receptor), quantitative or semiquantitative

►(Do not report 88361 with 88342 unless each procedure is for a different antibody)◄

(When semi-thin plastic-embedded sections are performed in conjunction with morphometric analysis, only the morphometric analysis should be reported; if performed as an independent procedure, see codes 88300-88309 for surgical pathology.)

88362 Nerve teasing preparations

88365 Tissue in situ hybridization, interpretation and report

88371 Protein analysis of tissue by Western Blot, with interpretation and report;

88372 immunological probe for band identification, each

88380 Microdissection (eg, mechanical, laser capture)

88399 Unlisted surgical pathology procedure

Transcutaneous Procedures

88400 Bilirubin, total, transcutaneous

Other Procedures

(Basal metabolic rate has been deleted. If necessary to report, use 89240)

89050 Cell count, miscellaneous body fluids (eg, cerebrospinal fluid, joint fluid), except blood;

89051 with differential count

▲89055 Leukocyte assessment, fecal, qualitative or semiquantitative

89060 Crystal identification by light microscopy with or without polarizing lens analysis, any body fluid (except urine)

89100 Duodenal intubation and aspiration; single specimen (eg, simple bile study or afferent loop culture) plus appropriate test procedure

89105 collection of multiple fractional specimens with pancreatic or gallbladder stimulation, single or double lumen tube

(For radiological localization, use 74340)

(For chemical analyses, see **Chemistry,** this section)

(Electrocardiogram, see 93000-93268)

(Esophagus acid perfusion test (Bernstein), see 91030)

89125 Fat stain, feces, urine, or respiratory secretions

89130 Gastric intubation and aspiration, diagnostic, each specimen, for chemical analyses or cytopathology;

89132 after stimulation

89135 Gastric intubation, aspiration, and fractional collections (eg, gastric secretory study); one hour

89136 two hours

89140 two hours including gastric stimulation (eg, histalog, pentagastrin)

89141 three hours, including gastric stimulation

(For gastric lavage, therapeutic, use 91105)

(For radiologic localization of gastric tube, use 74340)

(For chemical analyses, see 82926, 82928)

(Joint fluid chemistry, see **Chemistry,** this section)

89160 Meat fibers, feces

89190 Nasal smear for eosinophils

(Occult blood, feces, use 82270)

(Paternity tests, use 86910)

● 89220 Sputum, obtaining specimen, aerosol induced technique (separate procedure)

● 89225 Starch granules, feces

● 89230 Sweat collection by iontophoresis

● 89235 Water load test

● 89240 Unlisted miscellaneous pathology test

▸Reproductive Medicine Procedures◂

▲ 89250 Culture of oocyte(s)/embryo(s), less than 4 days;

▲ 89251 with co-culture of oocyte(s)/embryos

►(For extended culture of oocyte(s)/embryo(s), see 89272)◄

►(89252 has been deleted. To report, use 89280-89281)◄

89253 Assisted embryo hatching, microtechniques (any method)

89254 Oocyte identification from follicular fluid

89255 Preparation of embryo for transfer (any method)

►(89256 has been deleted. To report, use 89352)◄

89257 Sperm identification from aspiration (other than seminal fluid)

(For semen analysis, see 89300-89320)

(For sperm identification from testis tissue, use 89264)

▲ 89258 Cryopreservation; embryo(s)

89259 sperm

►(For cryopreservation of reproductive tissue, testicular, use 89335)◄

►(For cryopreservation of reproductive tissue, ovarian, use Category III code 0058T)◄

►(For cryopreservation of oocyte(s), use Category III code 0059T)◄

89260 Sperm isolation; simple prep (eg, sperm wash and swim-up) for insemination or diagnosis with semen analysis

89261 complex prep (eg, Percoll gradient, albumin gradient) for insemination or diagnosis with semen analysis

(For semen analysis without sperm wash or swim-up, use 89320)

89264 Sperm identification from testis tissue, fresh or cryopreserved

(For biopsy of testis, see 54500, 54505)

(For sperm identification from aspiration, use 89257)

(For semen analysis, see 89300-89320)

● 89268 Insemination of oocytes

● 89272 Extended culture of oocyte(s)/embryo(s), 4-7 days

● 89280 Assisted oocyte fertilization, microtechnique; less than or equal to 10 oocytes

● 89281 greater than 10 oocytes

● 89290 Biopsy, oocyte polar body or embryo blastomere, microtechnique (for pre-implantation genetic diagnosis); less than or equal to 5 embryos

● 89291 greater than 5 embryos

89300 Semen analysis; presence and/or motility of sperm including Huhner test (post coital)

89310 motility and count (not including Huhner test)

89320 complete (volume, count, motility, and differential)

(Skin tests, see 86485-86585 and 95010-95199)

89321 Semen analysis, presence and/or motility of sperm

89325 Sperm antibodies

(For medicolegal identification of sperm, use 88125)

89329 Sperm evaluation; hamster penetration test

89330 cervical mucus penetration test, with or without spinnbarkeit test

● 89335 Cryopreservation, reproductive tissue, testicular

►(For cryopreservation of embryo(s), use 89258. For cryopreservation of sperm, use 89259)◄

►(For cryopreservation of reproductive tissue, ovarian, use Category III code 0058T)◄

►(For cryopreservation of oocyte, use Category III code 0059T)◄

● 89342 Storage, (per year); embryo(s)

● 89343 sperm/semen

● 89344 reproductive tissue, testicular/ovarian

● 89346 oocyte

►(89350 has been deleted. To report, use 89220)◄

● 89352 Thawing of cryopreserved; embryo(s)

● 89353 sperm/semen, each aliquot

● 89354 reproductive tissue, testicular/ovarian

►(89355 has been deleted. To report, use 89225)◄

● 89356 oocytes, each aliquot

►(89360 has been deleted. To report, use 89230)◄

►(89365 has been deleted. To report, use 89235)◄

►(89399 has been deleted. To report, use 89240)◄

Medicine Guidelines

In addition to the definitions and commonly used terms presented in the **Introduction**, several other items unique to this section on **Medicine** are defined or identified here.

Multiple Procedures

It is appropriate to designate multiple procedures that are rendered on the same date by separate entries. For example: If individual medical psychotherapy (90829) is rendered in addition to subsequent hospital care (eg, 99231), the psychotherapy would be reported separately from the hospital visit. In this instance, both 99231 and 90829 would be reported.

Add-on Codes

Some of the listed procedures are commonly carried out in addition to the primary procedure performed. All add-on codes found in *CPT* are exempt from the multiple procedure concept. They are exempt from the use of the modifier '-51', as these procedures are not reported as stand-alone codes. These additional or supplemental procedures are designated as "add-on" codes. Add-on codes in *CPT* can be readily identified by specific descriptor nomenclature which includes phrases such as "each additional" or "(List separately in addition to primary procedure)."

Separate Procedures

Some of the procedures or services listed in *CPT* that are commonly carried out as an integral component of a total service or procedure have been identified by the inclusion of the term "separate procedure." The codes designated as "separate procedure" should not be reported in addition to the code for the total procedure or service of which it is considered an integral component.

However, when a procedure or service that is designated as a "separate procedure" is carried out independently or considered to be unrelated or distinct from other procedures/services provided at that time, it may be reported by itself, or in addition to other procedures/services by appending the modifier '-59' to the specific "separate procedure" code to indicate that the procedure is not considered to be a component of another procedure, but is a distinct, independent procedure. This may represent a different session or patient encounter, different procedure or surgery, different site or organ system, separate incision/excision, separate lesion, or separate injury (or area of injury in extensive injuries).

Subsection Information

Several of the subheadings or subsections have special instructions unique to that section. These special instructions will be presented preceding those procedural terminology listings, referring to that subsection specifically. If there is an "Unlisted Procedure" code number (see section below) for the individual subsection, it will also be shown. Those subsections within the **Medicine** section that have special instructions are as follows:

Immune Globulins 90281-90399
Immunization Administration for Vaccines/Toxoids 90471-90474
Vaccines, Toxoids 90476-90749
Therapeutic or Diagnostic Infusions 90780-90781
Psychiatry 90801-90899
Dialysis 90918-90999
Gastroenterology 91000-91299
Ophthalmology 92002-92499
Otorhinolaryngology 92502-92700
Echocardiography 93303-93350
Cardiac Catheterization 93501-93556
Intracardiac Electrophysiological Procedures/Studies 93600-93662
Peripheral Arterial Disease Rehabilitation 93668
Non-Invasive Vascular Diagnostic Studies 93875-93990
Pulmonary 94010-94799
Allergy and Clinical Immunology ...95004-95199
Neurology and Neuromuscular 95805-95999
Neurostimulators, Analysis-Programming 95970-95975
Motion Analysis 96000-96004
Central Nervous System Assessments/Tests 96100-96117
Health and Behavior Assessment/Intervention 96150-96155
Chemotherapy Administration 96400-96549
Dermatological Procedures 96900-96999
Physical Medicine and Rehabilitation
- **Modalities** 97010-97028
- **Constant Attendance** 97032-97039
- **Therapeutic Procedures** 97110-97546
- **Active Wound Care Management** 97601-97602

Medicine Guidelines

Unlisted Service or Procedure

A service or procedure may be provided that is not listed in this edition of *CPT*. When reporting such a service, the appropriate "Unlisted Procedure" code may be used to indicate the service, identifying it by "Special Report" as discussed on this page. The "Unlisted Procedures" and accompanying codes for **Medicine** are as follows:

90399 Unlisted immune globulin
90749 Unlisted vaccine/toxoid
90799 Unlisted therapeutic, prophylactic or diagnostic injection
90899 Unlisted psychiatric service or procedure
90999 Unlisted dialysis procedure, inpatient or outpatient
91299 Unlisted diagnostic gastroenterology procedure
92499 Unlisted ophthalmological service or procedure
92700 Unlisted otorhinolaryngological service or procedure
93799 Unlisted cardiovascular service or procedure
94799 Unlisted pulmonary service or procedure
95199 Unlisted allergy/clinical immunologic service or procedure
95999 Unlisted neurological or neuromuscular diagnostic procedure
96549 Unlisted chemotherapy procedure
96999 Unlisted special dermatological service or procedure
97039 Unlisted modality (specify type and time if constant attendance)
97139 Unlisted therapeutic procedure (specify)
97799 Unlisted physical medicine/rehabilitation service or procedure
99199 Unlisted special service, procedure or report
99600 Unlisted home visit service or procedure

Special Report

A service that is rarely provided, unusual, variable, or new may require a special report in determining medical appropriateness of the service. Pertinent information should include an adequate definition or description of the nature, extent, and need for the procedure; and the time, effort, and equipment necessary to provide the service. Additional items which may be included are:

- complexity of symptoms;
- final diagnosis;
- pertinent physical findings;
- diagnostic and therapeutic procedures;
- concurrent problems;
- follow-up care.

Materials Supplied by Physician

Supplies and materials provided by the physician (eg, sterile trays/drugs), over and above those usually included with the procedure(s) rendered are reported separately. List drugs, trays, supplies, and materials provided. Identify as 99070 or specific supply code.

Medicine

Immune Globulins

Codes 90281-90399 identify the immune globulin product only and must be reported in addition to the administration codes 90780-90784 as appropriate. Immune globulin products listed here include broad-spectrum and anti-infective immune globulins, antitoxins, and various isoantibodies.

⊘ **90281** Immune globulin (Ig), human, for intramuscular use

⊘ **90283** Immune globulin (IgIV), human, for intravenous use

⊘ **90287** Botulinum antitoxin, equine, any route

⊘ **90288** Botulism immune globulin, human, for intravenous use

⊘ **90291** Cytomegalovirus immune globulin (CMV-IgIV), human, for intravenous use

⊘ **90296** Diphtheria antitoxin, equine, any route

⊘ **90371** Hepatitis B immune globulin (HBIg), human, for intramuscular use

⊘ **90375** Rabies immune globulin (RIg), human, for intramuscular and/or subcutaneous use

⊘ **90376** Rabies immune globulin, heat-treated (RIg-HT), human, for intramuscular and/or subcutaneous use

⊘ **90378** Respiratory syncytial virus immune globulin (RSV-IgIM), for intramuscular use, 50 mg, each

⊘ **90379** Respiratory syncytial virus immune globulin (RSV-IgIV), human, for intravenous use

⊘ **90384** Rho(D) immune globulin (RhIg), human, full-dose, for intramuscular use

⊘ **90385** Rho(D) immune globulin (RhIg), human, mini-dose, for intramuscular use

⊘ **90386** Rho(D) immune globulin (RhIgIV), human, for intravenous use

⊘ **90389** Tetanus immune globulin (TIg), human, for intramuscular use

⊘ **90393** Vaccinia immune globulin, human, for intramuscular use

⊘ **90396** Varicella-zoster immune globulin, human, for intramuscular use

⊘ **90399** Unlisted immune globulin

Immunization Administration for Vaccines/Toxoids

Codes 90471-90474 must be reported in addition to the vaccine and toxoid code(s) 90476-90749.

If a significant separately identifiable Evaluation and Management service (eg, office or other outpatient services, preventive medicine services) is performed, the appropriate E/M service code should be reported in addition to the vaccine and toxoid administration codes.

(For allergy testing, see 95004 et seq)

(For skin testing of bacterial, viral, fungal extracts, see 86485-86586)

(For therapeutic or diagnostic injections, see 90782-90799)

90471 Immunization administration (includes percutaneous, intradermal, subcutaneous, intramuscular and jet injections); one vaccine (single or combination vaccine/toxoid)

✚ **90472** each additional vaccine (single or combination vaccine/toxoid) (List separately in addition to code for primary procedure)

(Use 90472 in conjunction with code 90471)

(For administration of immune globulins, use 90780-90784, and see 90281-90399)

(For intravesical administration of BCG vaccine, use 51720, and see 90586)

90473 Immunization administration by intranasal or oral route; one vaccine (single or combination vaccine/toxoid)

✚ **90474** each additional vaccine (single or combination vaccine/toxoid) (List separately in addition to code for primary procedure)

(Use 90474 in conjunction with code 90473)

Vaccines, Toxoids

Codes 90476-90748 identify the vaccine product **only.** To report the administration of a vaccine/toxoid, the vaccine/toxoid product codes 90476-90749 must be used in addition to an immunization administration code(s) 90471, 90472. Do not append the modifier '-51' to the vaccine/toxoid product codes 90476-90749.

If a significantly separately identifiable Evaluation and Management service (eg, office or other outpatient services, preventive medicine services) is performed, the appropriate E/M service code should be reported in addition to the vaccine and toxoid administration codes.

To meet the reporting requirements of immunization registries, vaccine distribution programs, and reporting systems (eg, Vaccine Adverse Event Reporting System) the exact vaccine product administered needs to be reported. Multiple codes for a particular vaccine are provided in *CPT* when the schedule (number of doses or timing) differs for two or more products of the same vaccine type (eg, hepatitis A, Hib) or the vaccine product is available in more than one chemical formulation, dosage, or route of administration.

Separate codes are available for combination vaccines (eg, DTP-Hib, DtaP-Hib, HepB-Hib). It is inappropriate to code each component of a combination vaccine separately. If a specific vaccine code is not available, the unlisted procedure code should be reported, until a new code becomes available.

(For immune globulins, see codes 90281-90399, and 90780-90784 for administration of immune globulins)

⊘ **90476** Adenovirus vaccine, type 4, live, for oral use

⊘ **90477** Adenovirus vaccine, type 7, live, for oral use

⊘ **90581** Anthrax vaccine, for subcutaneous use

⊘ **90585** Bacillus Calmette-Guerin vaccine (BCG) for tuberculosis, live, for percutaneous use

⊘ **90586** Bacillus Calmette-Guerin vaccine (BCG) for bladder cancer, live, for intravesical use

⊘ **90632** Hepatitis A vaccine, adult dosage, for intramuscular use

⊘ **90633** Hepatitis A vaccine, pediatric/adolescent dosage-2 dose schedule, for intramuscular use

⊘ **90634** Hepatitis A vaccine, pediatric/adolescent dosage-3 dose schedule, for intramuscular use

⊘ **90636** Hepatitis A and hepatitis B vaccine (HepA-HepB), adult dosage, for intramuscular use

⊘ **90645** Hemophilus influenza b vaccine (Hib), HbOC conjugate (4 dose schedule), for intramuscular use

⊘ **90646** Hemophilus influenza b vaccine (Hib), PRP-D conjugate, for booster use only, intramuscular use

⊘ **90647** Hemophilus influenza b vaccine (Hib), PRP-OMP conjugate (3 dose schedule), for intramuscular use

⊘ **90648** Hemophilus influenza b vaccine (Hib), PRP-T conjugate (4 dose schedule), for intramuscular use

⊘ ● **90655** Influenza virus vaccine, split virus, preservative free, for children 6-35 months of age, for intramuscular use

⊘ ▲ **90657** Influenza virus vaccine, split virus, for children 6-35 months of age, for intramuscular use

⊘ ▲ **90658** Influenza virus vaccine, split virus, for use in individuals 3 years of age and above, for intramuscular use

►(90659 has been deleted. To report influenza virus vaccine, split virus, see 90657 or 90658)◄

⊘ **90660** Influenza virus vaccine, live, for intranasal use

⊘ **90665** Lyme disease vaccine, adult dosage, for intramuscular use

⊘ **90669** Pneumococcal conjugate vaccine, polyvalent, for children under five years, for intramuscular use

⊘ **90675** Rabies vaccine, for intramuscular use

⊘ **90676** Rabies vaccine, for intradermal use

⊘ **90680** Rotavirus vaccine, tetravalent, live, for oral use

⊘ **90690** Typhoid vaccine, live, oral

⊘ **90691** Typhoid vaccine, Vi capsular polysaccharide (ViCPs), for intramuscular use

⊘ **90692** Typhoid vaccine, heat- and phenol-inactivated (H-P), for subcutaneous or intradermal use

⊘ ▲ **90693** Typhoid vaccine, acetone-killed, dried (AKD), for subcutaneous use (U.S. military)

⊘ ● **90698** Diphtheria, tetanus toxoids, acellular pertussis vaccine, haemophilus influenza Type B, and poliovirus vaccine, inactivated (DTaP – Hib – IPV), for intramuscular use

⊘ **90700** Diphtheria, tetanus toxoids, and acellular pertussis vaccine (DTaP), for intramuscular use

⊘ **90701** Diphtheria, tetanus toxoids, and whole cell pertussis vaccine (DTP), for intramuscular use

⊘ **90702** Diphtheria and tetanus toxoids (DT) adsorbed for use in individuals younger than seven years, for intramuscular use

⊘ ▲ **90703** Tetanus toxoid adsorbed, for intramuscular use

⊘ ▲ **90704** Mumps virus vaccine, live, for subcutaneous use

⊘ ▲ **90705** Measles virus vaccine, live, for subcutaneous use

⊘ ▲ **90706** Rubella virus vaccine, live, for subcutaneous use

⊘ ▲ **90707** Measles, mumps and rubella virus vaccine (MMR), live, for subcutaneous use

⊘ ▲ **90708** Measles and rubella virus vaccine, live, for subcutaneous use

(90709 has been deleted)

⊘ **90710** Measles, mumps, rubella, and varicella vaccine (MMRV), live, for subcutaneous use

⊘ **90712** Poliovirus vaccine, (any type(s)) (OPV), live, for oral use

⊘ **90713** Poliovirus vaccine, inactivated, (IPV), for subcutaneous use

⊘ ● **90715** Tetanus, diphtheria toxoids and acellular pertussis vaccine (TdaP), for use in individuals seven years or older, for intramuscular use

⊘ **90716** Varicella virus vaccine, live, for subcutaneous use

⊘ 90717 Yellow fever vaccine, live, for subcutaneous use

⊘ ▲ 90718 Tetanus and diphtheria toxoids (Td) adsorbed for use in individuals seven years or older, for intramuscular use

⊘ 90719 Diphtheria toxoid, for intramuscular use

⊘ 90720 Diphtheria, tetanus toxoids, and whole cell pertussis vaccine and Hemophilus influenza B vaccine (DTP-Hib), for intramuscular use

⊘ 90721 Diphtheria, tetanus toxoids, and acellular pertussis vaccine and Hemophilus influenza B vaccine (DtaP-Hib), for intramuscular use

⊘ 90723 Diphtheria, tetanus toxoids, acellular pertussis vaccine, Hepatitis B, and poliovirus vaccine, inactivated (DtaP-HepB-IPV), for intramuscular use

⊘ 90725 Cholera vaccine for injectable use

⊘ ▲ 90727 Plague vaccine, for intramuscular use

⊘ 90732 Pneumococcal polysaccharide vaccine, 23-valent, adult or immunosuppressed patient dosage, for use in individuals 2 years or older, for subcutaneous or intramuscular use

⊘ ▲ 90733 Meningococcal polysaccharide vaccine (any group(s)), for subcutaneous use

⊘ ● 90734 Meningococcal conjugate vaccine, serogroups A, C, Y and W-135 (tetravalent), for intramuscular use

⊘ 90735 Japanese encephalitis virus vaccine, for subcutaneous use

⊘ 90740 Hepatitis B vaccine, dialysis or immunosuppressed patient dosage (3 dose schedule), for intramuscular use

⊘ 90743 Hepatitis B vaccine, adolescent (2 dose schedule), for intramuscular use

⊘ 90744 Hepatitis B vaccine, pediatric/adolescent dosage (3 dose schedule), for intramuscular use

⊘ 90746 Hepatitis B vaccine, adult dosage, for intramuscular use

⊘ 90747 Hepatitis B vaccine, dialysis or immunosuppressed patient dosage (4 dose schedule), for intramuscular use

⊘ 90748 Hepatitis B and Hemophilus influenza b vaccine (HepB-Hib), for intramuscular use

⊘ 90749 Unlisted vaccine/toxoid

Therapeutic or Diagnostic Infusions (Excludes Chemotherapy)

These procedures encompass prolonged intravenous injections.

These codes require the presence of the physician during the infusion. These codes are not to be used for intradermal, subcutaneous or intramuscular or routine IV drug injections. For these services, see 90782-90788.

These codes may not be used in addition to prolonged services codes.

90780 Intravenous infusion for therapy/diagnosis, administered by physician or under direct supervision of physician; up to one hour

✚ 90781 each additional hour, up to eight (8) hours (List separately in addition to code for primary procedure)

(Use 90781 in conjunction with code 90780)

Therapeutic, Prophylactic or Diagnostic Injections

90782 Therapeutic, prophylactic or diagnostic injection (specify material injected); subcutaneous or intramuscular

(For administration of vaccines/toxoids, see 90471-90472)

90783 intra-arterial

90784 intravenous

(90782-90784 do not include injections for allergen immunotherapy. For allergen immunotherapy injections, see 95115-95117)

90788 Intramuscular injection of antibiotic (specify)

(90790-90796 have been deleted. To report, see 95990, 96408-96414, 96420-96425, 96440, 96450, 96530, 96545, 96549)

90799 Unlisted therapeutic, prophylactic or diagnostic injection

(For allergy immunizations, see 95004 et seq)

Psychiatry

(For repetitive transcranial magnetic stimulation for treatment of clinical depression, use Category III code 0018T)

Hospital care by the attending physician in treating a psychiatric inpatient or partial hospitalization may be initial or subsequent in nature (see 99221-99233) and may include exchanges with nursing and ancillary personnel. Hospital care services involve a variety of responsibilities unique to the medical management of inpatients, such as physician hospital orders, interpretation of laboratory or other medical diagnostic studies and observations.

Some patients receive hospital evaluation and management services only and others receive evaluation and management services and other procedures. If other procedures such as electroconvulsive therapy or psychotherapy are rendered in addition to hospital evaluation and management services, these should be listed separately (ie, hospital care service plus electroconvulsive therapy or when psychotherapy is done, an appropriate code defining psychotherapy with medical evaluation and management services). The modifier '-22' may be used to indicate a more extensive service. The modifier '-52' may be used to signify a service that is reduced or less extensive than the usual procedure.

Other evaluation and management services, such as office medical service or other patient encounters, may be described as listed in the section on **Evaluation and Management,** if appropriate.

The evaluation and management services should not be reported separately, when reporting codes 90805, 90807, 90809, 90811, 90813, 90815, 90817, 90819, 90822, 90824, 90827, 90829.

Consultation for psychiatric evaluation of a patient includes examination of a patient and exchange of information with the primary physician and other informants such as nurses or family members, and preparation of a report. These consultation services (99241-99263) are limited to initial or follow-up evaluation and do not involve psychiatric treatment.

Psychiatric Diagnostic or Evaluative Interview Procedures

Psychiatric diagnostic interview examination includes a history, mental status, and a disposition, and may include communication with family or other sources, ordering and medical interpretation of laboratory or other medical diagnostic studies. In certain circumstances other informants will be seen in lieu of the patient.

Interactive psychiatric diagnostic interview examination is typically furnished to children. It involves the use of physical aids and non-verbal communication to overcome barriers to therapeutic interaction between the clinician and a patient who has not yet developed, or has lost, either the expressive language communication skills to explain his/her symptoms and response to treatment, or the receptive communication skills to understand the clinician if he/she were to use ordinary adult language for communication.

90801 Psychiatric diagnostic interview examination

90802 Interactive psychiatric diagnostic interview examination using play equipment, physical devices, language interpreter, or other mechanisms of communication

Psychiatric Therapeutic Procedures

Psychotherapy is the treatment for mental illness and behavioral disturbances in which the clinician establishes a professional contract with the patient and, through definitive therapeutic communication, attempts to alleviate the emotional disturbances, reverse or change maladaptive patterns of behavior, and encourage personality growth and development. The codes for reporting psychotherapy are divided into two broad categories: Interactive Psychotherapy; and Insight Oriented, Behavior Modifying and/or Supportive Psychotherapy.

Interactive psychotherapy is typically furnished to children. It involves the use of physical aids and non-verbal communication to overcome barriers to therapeutic interaction between the clinician and a patient who has not yet developed, or has lost, either the expressive language communication skills to explain his/her symptoms and response to treatment, or the receptive communication skills to understand the clinician if he/she were to use ordinary adult language for communication.

Insight oriented, behavior modifying and/or supportive psychotherapy refers to the development of insight or affective understanding, the use of behavior modification techniques, the use of supportive interactions, the use of cognitive discussion of reality, or any combination of the above to provide therapeutic change.

Some patients receive psychotherapy only and others receive psychotherapy and medical evaluation and management services. These evaluation and management services involve a variety of responsibilities unique to the medical management of psychiatric patients, such as medical diagnostic evaluation (eg, evaluation of comorbid medical conditions, drug interactions, and physical examinations), drug management when indicated, physician orders, interpretation of laboratory or other medical diagnostic studies and observations.

In reporting psychotherapy, the appropriate code is chosen on the basis of the type of psychotherapy (interactive using non-verbal techniques versus insight oriented, behavior modifying and/or supportive using verbal techniques), the place of service (office versus inpatient), the face-to-face time spent with the patient during psychotherapy, and whether evaluation and management services are furnished on the same date of service as psychotherapy.

To report medical evaluation and management services furnished on a day when psychotherapy is not provided, select the appropriate code from the **Evaluation and Management Services Guidelines.**

Office or Other Outpatient Facility

Insight Oriented, Behavior Modifying and/or Supportive Psychotherapy

90804 Individual psychotherapy, insight oriented, behavior modifying and/or supportive, in an office or outpatient facility, approximately 20 to 30 minutes face-to-face with the patient;

90805 with medical evaluation and management services

90806 Individual psychotherapy, insight oriented, behavior modifying and/or supportive, in an office or outpatient facility, approximately 45 to 50 minutes face-to-face with the patient;

90807 with medical evaluation and management services

90808 Individual psychotherapy, insight oriented, behavior modifying and/or supportive, in an office or outpatient facility, approximately 75 to 80 minutes face-to-face with the patient;

90809 with medical evaluation and management services

Interactive Psychotherapy

90810 Individual psychotherapy, interactive, using play equipment, physical devices, language interpreter, or other mechanisms of non-verbal communication, in an office or outpatient facility, approximately 20 to 30 minutes face-to-face with the patient;

90811 with medical evaluation and management services

90812 Individual psychotherapy, interactive, using play equipment, physical devices, language interpreter, or other mechanisms of non-verbal communication, in an office or outpatient facility, approximately 45 to 50 minutes face-to-face with the patient;

90813 with medical evaluation and management services

90814 Individual psychotherapy, interactive, using play equipment, physical devices, language interpreter, or other mechanisms of non-verbal communication, in an office or outpatient facility, approximately 75 to 80 minutes face-to-face with the patient;

90815 with medical evaluation and management services

Inpatient Hospital, Partial Hospital or Residential Care Facility

Insight Oriented, Behavior Modifying and/or Supportive Psychotherapy

90816 Individual psychotherapy, insight oriented, behavior modifying and/or supportive, in an inpatient hospital, partial hospital or residential care setting, approximately 20 to 30 minutes face-to-face with the patient;

90817 with medical evaluation and management services

90818 Individual psychotherapy, insight oriented, behavior modifying and/or supportive, in an inpatient hospital, partial hospital or residential care setting, approximately 45 to 50 minutes face-to-face with the patient;

90819 with medical evaluation and management services

90821 Individual psychotherapy, insight oriented, behavior modifying and/or supportive, in an inpatient hospital, partial hospital or residential care setting, approximately 75 to 80 minutes face-to-face with the patient;

90822 with medical evaluation and management services

Interactive Psychotherapy

90823 Individual psychotherapy, interactive, using play equipment, physical devices, language interpreter, or other mechanisms of non-verbal communication, in an inpatient hospital, partial hospital or residential care setting, approximately 20 to 30 minutes face-to-face with the patient;

90824 with medical evaluation and management services

90826 Individual psychotherapy, interactive, using play equipment, physical devices, language interpreter, or other mechanisms of non-verbal communication, in an inpatient hospital, partial hospital or residential care setting, approximately 45 to 50 minutes face-to-face with the patient;

90827 with medical evaluation and management services

90828 Individual psychotherapy, interactive, using play equipment, physical devices, language interpreter, or other mechanisms of non-verbal communication, in an inpatient hospital, partial hospital or residential care setting, approximately 75 to 80 minutes face-to-face with the patient;

90829 with medical evaluation and management services

Other Psychotherapy

90845 Psychoanalysis

90846 Family psychotherapy (without the patient present)

90847 Family psychotherapy (conjoint psychotherapy) (with patient present)

90849 Multiple-family group psychotherapy

90853 Group psychotherapy (other than of a multiple-family group)

90857 Interactive group psychotherapy

Other Psychiatric Services or Procedures

90862 Pharmacologic management, including prescription, use, and review of medication with no more than minimal medical psychotherapy

90865 Narcosynthesis for psychiatric diagnostic and therapeutic purposes (eg, sodium amobarbital (Amytal) interview)

90870 Electroconvulsive therapy (includes necessary monitoring); single seizure

90871 multiple seizures, per day

90875 Individual psychophysiological therapy incorporating biofeedback training by any modality (face-to-face with the patient), with psychotherapy (eg, insight oriented, behavior modifying or supportive psychotherapy); approximately 20-30 minutes

90876 approximately 45-50 minutes

90880 Hypnotherapy

90882 Environmental intervention for medical management purposes on a psychiatric patient's behalf with agencies, employers, or institutions

90885 Psychiatric evaluation of hospital records, other psychiatric reports, psychometric and/or projective tests, and other accumulated data for medical diagnostic purposes

90887 Interpretation or explanation of results of psychiatric, other medical examinations and procedures, or other accumulated data to family or other responsible persons, or advising them how to assist patient

90889 Preparation of report of patient's psychiatric status, history, treatment, or progress (other than for legal or consultative purposes) for other physicians, agencies, or insurance carriers

90899 Unlisted psychiatric service or procedure

Biofeedback

(For psychophysiological therapy incorporating biofeedback training, see 90875, 90876)

90901 Biofeedback training by any modality

90911 Biofeedback training, perineal muscles, anorectal or urethral sphincter, including EMG and/or manometry

(For incontinence treatment by pulsed magnetic neuromodulation, use Category III code 0029T)

Dialysis

Codes 90918-90921 are reported ONCE per month to distinguish age-specific services related to the patient's end-stage renal disease (ESRD) performed in an outpatient setting. ESRD-related physician services include establishment of a dialyzing cycle, outpatient evaluation and management of the dialysis visits, telephone calls, and patient management during the dialysis, provided during a full month. ►These codes are not used if the physician also submits hospitalization codes during the month.◄

►Codes 90918-90921 describe a full month of ESRD-related services provided in an outpatient setting. For ESRD and non-ESRD dialysis services performed in an inpatient setting, and for non-ESRD dialysis services performed in an outpatient setting, see 90935-90937 and 90945-90947.◄

Evaluation and management services unrelated to ESRD services that cannot be performed during the dialysis session may be reported separately.

Codes 90922-90925 are reported when outpatient ESRD-related services are not performed consecutively during an entire full month ►(eg, when the patient spends part of the month as a hospital inpatient, or when the outpatient ESRD-related services are initiated after the first of the month). The appropriate age-related code from this series (90922-90925) is reported daily less the days of hospitalization. For reporting purposes, each month is considered 30 days.◄

Example:

►Outpatient ESRD-related services are initiated on July 1 for a 57-year-old male. On July 11, he is admitted to the hospital as an inpatient and is discharged on July 27.◄

►In this example, code 90925 should be reported for each day outside of the inpatient hospitalization (30 days/month less 17 days/hospitalization = 13 days). Report inpatient E/M services as appropriate. Dialysis procedures rendered during the hospitalization (July 11-27) should be reported as appropriate (90935-90937, 90945-90947).◄

End Stage Renal Disease Services

90918 End stage renal disease (ESRD) related services per full month; for patients under two years of age to include monitoring for the adequacy of nutrition, assessment of growth and development, and counseling of parents

90919 for patients between two and eleven years of age to include monitoring for the adequacy of nutrition, assessment of growth and development, and counseling of parents

90920 for patients between twelve and nineteen years of age to include monitoring for the adequacy of nutrition, assessment of growth and development, and counseling of parents

90921 for patients twenty years of age and over

90922 End stage renal disease (ESRD) related services (less than full month), per day; for patients under two years of age

90923 for patients between two and eleven years of age

90924 for patients between twelve and nineteen years of age

90925 for patients twenty years of age and over

Hemodialysis

Codes 90935, 90937 are reported to describe the hemodialysis procedure with all evaluation and management services related to the patient's renal disease on the day of the hemodialysis procedure. These codes are used for inpatient ESRD and non-ESRD procedures or for outpatient non-ESRD dialysis services. Code 90935 is reported if only one evaluation of the patient is required related to that hemodialysis procedure. Code 90937 is reported when patient re-evaluation(s) is required during a hemodialysis procedure. Utilize the modifier '-25' with Evaluation and Management codes for separately identifiable services unrelated to the dialysis procedure or renal failure which cannot be rendered during the dialysis session.

(For home visit hemodialysis services performed by a non-physician health care professional, use 99512)

(For cannula declotting, see 36831, 36833, 36860, 36861)

(For declotting of implanted vascular access device or catheter by thrombolytic agent, use 36550)

(For collection of blood specimen from a partially or completely implantable venous access device, use 36540)

(For prolonged physician attendance, see 99354-99360)

90935 Hemodialysis procedure with single physician evaluation

90937 Hemodialysis procedure requiring repeated evaluation(s) with or without substantial revision of dialysis prescription

90939 Hemodialysis access flow study to determine blood flow in grafts and arteriovenous fistulae by an indicator dilution method, hook-up; transcutaneous measurement and disconnection

90940 measurement and disconnection

(For duplex scan of hemodialysis access, use 93990)

Miscellaneous Dialysis Procedures

Codes 90945, 90947 describe dialysis procedures other than hemodialysis (eg, peritoneal dialysis, hemofiltration or continuous renal replacement therapies), and all evaluation and management services related to the patient's renal disease on the day of the procedure. Code 90945 is reported if only one evaluation of the patient is required related to that procedure. Code 90947 is reported when patient re-evaluation(s) is required during a procedure. Utilize the modifier '-25' with Evaluation and Management codes for separately identifiable services unrelated to the procedure or the renal failure which cannot be rendered during the dialysis session.

(For insertion of intraperitoneal cannula or catheter, see 49420, 49421)

(For prolonged physician attendance, see 99354-99360)

90945 Dialysis procedure other than hemodialysis (eg, peritoneal dialysis, hemofiltration, or other continuous renal replacement therapies), with single physician evaluation

(For home infusion of peritoneal dialysis, use 99601, 99602)

90947 Dialysis procedure other than hemodialysis (eg, peritoneal dialysis, hemofiltration, or other continuous renal replacement therapies) requiring repeated physician evaluations, with or without substantial revision of dialysis prescription

90989 Dialysis training, patient, including helper where applicable, any mode, completed course

90993 Dialysis training, patient, including helper where applicable, any mode, course not completed, per training session

90997 Hemoperfusion (eg, with activated charcoal or resin)

90999 Unlisted dialysis procedure, inpatient or outpatient

Gastroenterology

(For duodenal intubation and aspiration, see 89100-89105)

(For gastrointestinal radiologic procedures, see 74210-74363)

(For esophagoscopy procedures, see 43200-43228; upper GI endoscopy 43234-43259; endoscopy, small intestine and stomal 44360-44393; proctosigmoidoscopy 45300-45321; sigmoidoscopy 45330-45339; colonoscopy 45355-45385; anoscopy 46600-46615)

91000 Esophageal intubation and collection of washings for cytology, including preparation of specimens (separate procedure)

91010 Esophageal motility (manometric study of the esophagus and/or gastroesophageal junction) study;

91011 with mecholyl or similar stimulant

91012 with acid perfusion studies

91020 Gastric motility (manometric) studies

91030 Esophagus, acid perfusion (Bernstein) test for esophagitis

91032 Esophagus, acid reflux test, with intraluminal pH electrode for detection of gastroesophageal reflux;

91033 prolonged recording

91052 Gastric analysis test with injection of stimulant of gastric secretion (eg, histamine, insulin, pentagastrin, calcium and secretin)

(For gastric biopsy by capsule, peroral, via tube, one or more specimens, use 43600)

(For gastric laboratory procedures, see also 89130-89141)

91055 Gastric intubation, washings, and preparing slides for cytology (separate procedure)

(For gastric lavage, therapeutic, use 91105)

91060 Gastric saline load test

(For biopsy by capsule, small intestine, per oral, via tube (one or more specimens), use 44100)

91065 Breath hydrogen test (eg, for detection of lactase deficiency)

91100 Intestinal bleeding tube, passage, positioning and monitoring

91105 Gastric intubation, and aspiration or lavage for treatment (eg, for ingested poisons)

(For cholangiography, see 47500, 74320)

(For abdominal paracentesis, see 49080, 49081; with instillation of medication, see 96440, 96445)

(For peritoneoscopy, use 49320; with biopsy, use 49321)

(For peritoneoscopy and guided transhepatic cholangiography, use 47560; with biopsy, use 47561)

(For splenoportography, see 38200, 75810)

●**91110** Gastrointestinal tract imaging, intraluminal (eg, capsule endoscopy), esophagus through ileum, with physician interpretation and report

►(Visualization of the colon is not reported separately)◄

►(Append modifier '-52' if the ileum is not visualized)◄

91122 Anorectal manometry

91123 Pulsed irrigation of fecal impaction

Gastric Physiology

91132 Electrogastrography, diagnostic, transcutaneous;

91133 with provocative testing

Other Procedures

91299 Unlisted diagnostic gastroenterology procedure

Ophthalmology

(For surgical procedures, see **Surgery,** Eye and Ocular Adnexa, 65091 et seq)

Definitions

Intermediate ophthalmological services describes an evaluation of a new or existing condition complicated with a new diagnostic or management problem not necessarily relating to the primary diagnosis, including history, general medical observation, external ocular and adnexal examination and other diagnostic procedures as indicated; may include the use of mydriasis for ophthalmoscopy.

For example:

a. Review of history, external examination, ophthalmoscopy, biomicroscopy for an acute complicated condition (eg, iritis) not requiring comprehensive ophthalmological services.

b. Review of interval history, external examination, ophthalmoscopy, biomicroscopy and tonometry in established patient with known cataract not requiring comprehensive ophthalmological services.

Comprehensive ophthalmological services describes a general evaluation of the complete visual system. The comprehensive services constitute a single service entity but need not be performed at one session. The service includes history, general medical observation, external and ophthalmoscopic examinations, gross visual fields and basic sensorimotor examination. It often includes, as indicated: biomicroscopy, examination with cycloplegia or mydriasis and tonometry. It always includes initiation of diagnostic and treatment programs.

Intermediate and comprehensive ophthalmological services constitute integrated services in which medical decision making cannot be separated from the examining techniques used. Itemization of service components, such as slit lamp examination, keratometry, routine ophthalmoscopy, retinoscopy, tonometry, or motor evaluation is not applicable.

For example:

The comprehensive services required for diagnosis and treatment of a patient with symptoms indicating possible disease of the visual system, such as glaucoma, cataract or retinal disease, or to rule out disease of the visual system, new or established patient.

Initiation of diagnostic and treatment program includes the prescription of medication, and arranging for special ophthalmological diagnostic or treatment services, consultations, laboratory procedures and radiological services.

Special ophthalmological services describes services in which a special evaluation of part of the visual system is made, which goes beyond the services included under general ophthalmological services, or in which special treatment is given. Special ophthalmological services may be reported in addition to the general ophthalmological services or evaluation and management services.

For example:

Fluorescein angioscopy, quantitative visual field examination, refraction or extended color vision examination (such as Nagel's anomaloscope) should be separately reported.

Prescription of lenses, when required, is included in 92015 Determination of refractive state. It includes specification of lens type (monofocal, bifocal, other), lens power, axis, prism, absorptive factor, impact resistance, and other factors.

Interpretation and report by the physician is an integral part of special ophthalmological services where indicated. Technical procedures (which may or may not be performed by the physician personally) are often part of the service, but should not be mistaken to constitute the service itself.

General Ophthalmological Services

New Patient

Solely for the purposes of distinguishing between new and established patients, **professional services** are those face-to-face services rendered by a physician and reported by a specific CPT code(s). A new patient is one who has not received any professional services from the physician or another physician of the same specialty who belongs to the same group practice within the past three years.

92002 Ophthalmological services: medical examination and evaluation with initiation of diagnostic and treatment program; intermediate, new patient

92004 comprehensive, new patient, one or more visits

Established Patient

Solely for the purposes of distinguishing between new and established patients, **professional services** are those face-to-face services rendered by a physician and reported by a specific CPT code(s). An established patient is one who has received professional services from the physician or another physician of the same specialty who belongs to the same group practice within the past three years.

92012 Ophthalmological services: medical examination and evaluation, with initiation or continuation of diagnostic and treatment program; intermediate, established patient

92014 comprehensive, established patient, one or more visits

(For surgical procedures, see **Surgery,** Eye and Ocular Adnexa, 65091 et seq)

Special Ophthalmological Services

92015 Determination of refractive state

92018 Ophthalmological examination and evaluation, under general anesthesia, with or without manipulation of globe for passive range of motion or other manipulation to facilitate diagnostic examination; complete

92019 limited

92020 Gonioscopy (separate procedure)

(For gonioscopy under general anesthesia, use 92018)

92060 Sensorimotor examination with multiple measurements of ocular deviation (eg, restrictive or paretic muscle with diplopia) with interpretation and report (separate procedure)

92065 Orthoptic and/or pleoptic training, with continuing medical direction and evaluation

92070 Fitting of contact lens for treatment of disease, including supply of lens

92081 Visual field examination, unilateral or bilateral, with interpretation and report; limited examination (eg, tangent screen, Autoplot, arc perimeter, or single stimulus level automated test, such as Octopus 3 or 7 equivalent)

92082 intermediate examination (eg, at least 2 isopters on Goldmann perimeter, or semiquantitative, automated suprathreshold screening program, Humphrey suprathreshold automatic diagnostic test, Octopus program 33)

92083 extended examination (eg, Goldmann visual fields with at least 3 isopters plotted and static determination within the central 30°, or quantitative, automated threshold perimetry, Octopus program G-1, 32 or 42, Humphrey visual field analyzer full threshold programs 30-2, 24-2, or 30/60-2)

(Gross visual field testing (eg, confrontation testing) is a part of general ophthalmological services and is not reported separately)

92100 Serial tonometry (separate procedure) with multiple measurements of intraocular pressure over an extended time period with interpretation and report, same day (eg, diurnal curve or medical treatment of acute elevation of intraocular pressure)

92120 Tonography with interpretation and report, recording indentation tonometer method or perilimbal suction method

92130 Tonography with water provocation

92135 Scanning computerized ophthalmic diagnostic imaging (eg, scanning laser) with interpretation and report, unilateral

92136 Ophthalmic biometry by partial coherence interferometry with intraocular lens power calculation

92140 Provocative tests for glaucoma, with interpretation and report, without tonography

Ophthalmoscopy

Routine ophthalmoscopy is part of general and special ophthalmologic services whenever indicated. It is a non-itemized service and is not reported separately.

92225 Ophthalmoscopy, extended, with retinal drawing (eg, for retinal detachment, melanoma), with interpretation and report; initial

92226 subsequent

92230 Fluorescein angioscopy with interpretation and report

92235 Fluorescein angiography (includes multiframe imaging) with interpretation and report

92240 Indocyanine-green angiography (includes multiframe imaging) with interpretation and report

92250 Fundus photography with interpretation and report

92260 Ophthalmodynamometry

(For ophthalmoscopy under general anesthesia, use 92018)

Other Specialized Services

92265 Needle oculoelectromyography, one or more extraocular muscles, one or both eyes, with interpretation and report

92270 Electro-oculography with interpretation and report

92275 Electroretinography with interpretation and report

(For electronystagmography for vestibular function studies, see 92541 et seq)

(For ophthalmic echography (diagnostic ultrasound), see 76511-76529)

92283 Color vision examination, extended, eg, anomaloscope or equivalent

(Color vision testing with pseudoisochromatic plates (such as HRR or Ishihara) is not reported separately. It is included in the appropriate general or ophthalmological service, or 99172)

92284 Dark adaptation examination with interpretation and report

92285 External ocular photography with interpretation and report for documentation of medical progress (eg, close-up photography, slit lamp photography, goniophotography, stereo-photography)

92286 Special anterior segment photography with interpretation and report; with specular endothelial microscopy and cell count

92287 with fluorescein angiography

Contact Lens Services

The prescription of contact lens includes specification of optical and physical characteristics (such as power, size, curvature, flexibility, gas-permeability). It is NOT a part of the general ophthalmological services.

The fitting of contact lens includes instruction and training of the wearer and incidental revision of the lens during the training period.

Follow-up of successfully fitted extended wear lenses is reported as part of a general ophthalmological service (92012 et seq).

The supply of contact lenses may be reported as part of the service of fitting. It may also be reported separately by using 92391 or 92396 and modifier '-26' for the service of fitting without supply.

(For therapeutic or surgical use of contact lens, see 68340, 92070)

92310 Prescription of optical and physical characteristics of and fitting of contact lens, with medical supervision of adaptation; corneal lens, both eyes, except for aphakia

(For prescription and fitting of one eye, add modifier '-52')

92311 corneal lens for aphakia, one eye

92312 corneal lens for aphakia, both eyes

92313 corneoscleral lens

92314 Prescription of optical and physical characteristics of contact lens, with medical supervision of adaptation and direction of fitting by independent technician; corneal lens, both eyes except for aphakia

(For prescription and fitting of one eye, add modifier '-52')

92315 corneal lens for aphakia, one eye

92316 corneal lens for aphakia, both eyes

92317 corneoscleral lens

92325 Modification of contact lens (separate procedure), with medical supervision of adaptation

92326 Replacement of contact lens

Ocular Prosthetics, Artificial Eye

92330 Prescription, fitting, and supply of ocular prosthesis (artificial eye), with medical supervision of adaptation

(If supply is not included, use modifier '-26'; to report supply separately, use 92393)

92335 Prescription of ocular prosthesis (artificial eye) and direction of fitting and supply by independent technician, with medical supervision of adaptation

Spectacle Services (Including Prosthesis for Aphakia)

Prescription of lenses, when required, is included in 92015 Determination of refractive state. It includes specification of lens type (monofocal, bifocal, other), lens power, axis, prism, absorptive factor, impact resistance, and other factors.

Fitting of spectacles is a separate service; when provided by the physician, it is reported as indicated by 92340-92371.

Fitting includes measurement of anatomical facial characteristics, the writing of laboratory specifications, and the final adjustment of the spectacles to the visual axes and anatomical topography. Presence of physician is not required.

Supply of materials is a separate service component; it is not part of the service of fitting spectacles.

92340 Fitting of spectacles, except for aphakia; monofocal

92341 bifocal

92342 multifocal, other than bifocal

92352 Fitting of spectacle prosthesis for aphakia; monofocal

92353 multifocal

92354 Fitting of spectacle mounted low vision aid; single element system

92355 telescopic or other compound lens system

92358 Prosthesis service for aphakia, temporary (disposable or loan, including materials)

92370 Repair and refitting spectacles; except for aphakia

92371 spectacle prosthesis for aphakia

Supply of Materials

92390 Supply of spectacles, except prosthesis for aphakia and low vision aids

92391 Supply of contact lenses, except prosthesis for aphakia

(For supply of contact lenses reported as part of the service of fitting, see 92310-92313)

(For replacement of contact lens, use 92326)

92392 Supply of low vision aids (A low vision aid is any lens or device used to aid or improve visual function in a person whose vision cannot be normalized by conventional spectacle correction. Includes reading additions up to 4D.)

92393 Supply of ocular prosthesis (artificial eye)

(For supply reported as part of the service of fitting, use 92330)

92395 Supply of permanent prosthesis for aphakia; spectacles

(For temporary spectacle correction, use 92358)

92396 contact lenses

(For supply reported as part of the service of fitting, see 92311, 92312)

(Use 99070 for the supply of other materials, drugs, trays, etc.)

Other Procedures

92499 Unlisted ophthalmological service or procedure

Special Otorhinolaryngologic Services

Diagnostic or treatment procedures usually included in a comprehensive otorhinolaryngologic evaluation or office visit, are reported as an integrated medical service, using appropriate descriptors from the 99201 series. Itemization of component procedures (eg, otoscopy, rhinoscopy, tuning fork test) does not apply.

Special otorhinolaryngologic services are those diagnostic and treatment services not usually included in a comprehensive otorhinolaryngologic evaluation or office visit. These services are reported separately, using codes 92502-92700.

All services include medical diagnostic evaluation. Technical procedures (which may or may not be performed by the physician personally) are often part of the service, but should not be mistaken to constitute the service itself.

(For laryngoscopy with stroboscopy, use 31579)

92502 Otolaryngologic examination under general anesthesia

92504 Binocular microscopy (separate diagnostic procedure)

92506 Evaluation of speech, language, voice, communication, auditory processing, and/or aural rehabilitation status

92507 Treatment of speech, language, voice, communication, and/or auditory processing disorder (includes aural rehabilitation); individual

92508 group, two or more individuals

92510 Aural rehabilitation following cochlear implant (includes evaluation of aural rehabilitation status and hearing, therapeutic services) with or without speech processor programming

92511 Nasopharyngoscopy with endoscope (separate procedure)

92512 Nasal function studies (eg, rhinomanometry)

92516 Facial nerve function studies (eg, electroneuronography)

92520 Laryngeal function studies

(92525 has been deleted. To report, see 92610-92611 for specific evaluation)

92526 Treatment of swallowing dysfunction and/or oral function for feeding

Vestibular Function Tests, With Observation and Evaluation by Physician, Without Electrical Recording

92531 Spontaneous nystagmus, including gaze

92532 Positional nystagmus test

92533 Caloric vestibular test, each irrigation (binaural, bithermal stimulation constitutes four tests)

92534 Optokinetic nystagmus test

Vestibular Function Tests, With Recording (eg, ENG, PENG), and Medical Diagnostic Evaluation

92541 Spontaneous nystagmus test, including gaze and fixation nystagmus, with recording

92542 Positional nystagmus test, minimum of 4 positions, with recording

92543 Caloric vestibular test, each irrigation (binaural, bithermal stimulation constitutes four tests), with recording

92544 Optokinetic nystagmus test, bidirectional, foveal or peripheral stimulation, with recording

92545 Oscillating tracking test, with recording

92546 Sinusoidal vertical axis rotational testing

✚ **92547** Use of vertical electrodes (List separately in addition to code for primary procedure)

(Use 92547 in conjunction with codes 92541-92546)

(For unlisted vestibular tests, use 92700)

92548 Computerized dynamic posturography

Audiologic Function Tests With Medical Diagnostic Evaluation

The audiometric tests listed below imply the use of calibrated electronic equipment. Other hearing tests (such as whispered voice, tuning fork) are considered part of the general otorhinolaryngologic services and are not reported separately. All descriptors refer to testing both ears. Use the modifier '-52' if a test is applied to one ear instead of to two ears. All descriptors (except 92559) apply to testing of individuals; for testing of groups, use 92559 and specify test(s) used.

(For evaluation of speech, language and/or hearing problems through observation and assessment of performance, use 92506)

92551 Screening test, pure tone, air only

92552 Pure tone audiometry (threshold); air only

92553 air and bone

92555 Speech audiometry threshold;

92556 with speech recognition

92557 Comprehensive audiometry threshold evaluation and speech recognition (92553 and 92556 combined)

(For hearing aid evaluation and selection, see 92590-92595)

92559 Audiometric testing of groups

92560 Bekesy audiometry; screening

92561 diagnostic

92562 Loudness balance test, alternate binaural or monaural

92563 Tone decay test

92564 Short increment sensitivity index (SISI)

92565 Stenger test, pure tone

92567 Tympanometry (impedance testing)

92568 Acoustic reflex testing

92569 Acoustic reflex decay test

92571 Filtered speech test

92572 Staggered spondaic word test

92573 Lombard test

92575 Sensorineural acuity level test

92576 Synthetic sentence identification test

92577 Stenger test, speech

92579 Visual reinforcement audiometry (VRA)

92582 Conditioning play audiometry

92583 Select picture audiometry

92584 Electrocochleography

92585 Auditory evoked potentials for evoked response audiometry and/or testing of the central nervous system; comprehensive

92586 limited

92587 Evoked otoacoustic emissions; limited (single stimulus level, either transient or distortion products)

92588 comprehensive or diagnostic evaluation (comparison of transient and/or distortion product otoacoustic emissions at multiple levels and frequencies)

92589 Central auditory function test(s) (specify)

92590 Hearing aid examination and selection; monaural

92591 binaural

92592 Hearing aid check; monaural

92593 binaural

92594 Electroacoustic evaluation for hearing aid; monaural

92595 binaural

92596 Ear protector attenuation measurements

92597 Evaluation for use and/or fitting of voice prosthetic device to supplement oral speech

(To report augmentative and alternative communication device services, see 92605, 92607, 92608)

(92598 has been deleted)

(92599 has been deleted. To report use 92700)

Evaluative and Therapeutic Services

Codes 92601 and 92603 describe post-operative analysis and fitting of previously placed external devices, connection to the cochlear implant, and programming of the stimulator. Codes 92602 and 92604 describe subsequent sessions for measurements and adjustment of

Medicine

the external transmitter and re-programming of the internal stimulator.

(For placement of cochlear implant, use 69930)

92601 Diagnostic analysis of cochlear implant, patient under 7 years of age; with programming

92602 subsequent reprogramming

(Do not report 92602 in addition to 92601)

(For aural rehabilitation services following cochlear implant, including evaluation of rehabilitation status, use 92510)

92603 Diagnostic analysis of cochlear implant, age 7 years or older; with programming

92604 subsequent reprogramming

(Do not report 92604 in addition to 92603)

92605 Evaluation for prescription of non-speech-generating augmentative and alternative communication device

92606 Therapeutic service(s) for the use of non-speech-generating device, including programming and modification

92607 Evaluation for prescription for speech-generating augmentative and alternative communication device, face-to-face with the patient; first hour

(For evaluation for prescription of a non-speech-generating device, use 92605)

✚ **92608** each additional 30 minutes (List separately in addition to code for primary procedure)

(Use 92608 in conjunction with 92607)

92609 Therapeutic services for the use of speech-generating device, including programming and modification

(For therapeutic service(s) for the use of a non-speech-generating device, use 92606)

92610 Evaluation of oral and pharyngeal swallowing function

(For motion fluoroscopic evaluation of swallowing function, use 92611)

(For flexible endoscopic examination, use 92612-92617)

92611 Motion fluoroscopic evaluation of swallowing function by cine or video recording

(For radiological supervision and interpretation, use 74230)

(For evaluation of oral and pharyngeal swallowing function, use 92610)

►(For flexible fiberoptic diagnostic laryngoscopy, use 31575. Do not report 31575 in conjunction with 92612-92617)◄

92612 Flexible fiberoptic endoscopic evaluation of swallowing by cine or video recording;

(If flexible fiberoptic or endoscopic evaluation of swallowing is performed without cine or video recording, use 92700)

92613 physician interpretation and report only

(To report an evaluation of oral and pharyngeal swallowing function, use 92610)

(To report motion fluoroscopic evaluation of swallowing function, use 92611)

92614 Flexible fiberoptic endoscopic evaluation, laryngeal sensory testing by cine or video recording;

►(If flexible fiberoptic or endoscopic evaluation of swallowing is performed without cine or video recording, use 92700)◄

92615 physician interpretation and report only

92616 Flexible fiberoptic endoscopic evaluation of swallowing and laryngeal sensory testing by cine or video recording;

►(If flexible fiberoptic or endoscopic evaluation of swallowing is performed without cine or video recording, use 92700)◄

92617 physician interpretation and report only

Other Procedures

92700 Unlisted otorhinolaryngological service or procedure

Cardiovascular

Therapeutic Services

(For non-surgical septal reduction therapy (eg, alcohol ablation), use Category III code 0024T)

92950 Cardiopulmonary resuscitation (eg, in cardiac arrest)

(See also critical care services, 99291, 99292)

92953 Temporary transcutaneous pacing

(For physician direction of ambulance or rescue personnel outside the hospital, use 99288)

92960 Cardioversion, elective, electrical conversion of arrhythmia; external

92961 internal (separate procedure)

(Do not report 92961 in addition to codes 93662, 93618-93624, 93631, 93640-93642, 93650-93652, 93741-93744)

92970 Cardioassist-method of circulatory assist; internal

92971 external

(For balloon atrial-septostomy, use 92992)

(For placement of catheters for use in circulatory assist devices such as intra-aortic balloon pump, use 33970)

+ **92973** Percutaneous transluminal coronary thrombectomy (List separately in addition to code for primary procedure)

(Use 92973 in conjunction with codes 92980, 92982)

+ **92974** Transcatheter placement of radiation delivery device for subsequent coronary intravascular brachytherapy (List separately in addition to code for primary procedure)

(Use 92974 in conjunction with codes 92980, 92982, ►92995,◄ 93508)

(For intravascular radioelement application, see 77781-77784)

92975 Thrombolysis, coronary; by intracoronary infusion, including selective coronary angiography

92977 by intravenous infusion

(For thrombolysis of vessels other than coronary, see 37201, 75896)

(For cerebral thrombolysis, use 37195)

+ **92978** Intravascular ultrasound (coronary vessel or graft) during diagnostic evaluation and/or therapeutic intervention including imaging supervision, interpretation and report; initial vessel (List separately in addition to code for primary procedure)

+ **92979** each additional vessel (List separately in addition to code for primary procedure)

(Use 92979 in conjunction with code 92978)

(Intravascular ultrasound services include all transducer manipulations and repositioning within the specific vessel being examined, both before and after therapeutic intervention (eg, stent placement))

92980 Transcatheter placement of an intracoronary stent(s), percutaneous, with or without other therapeutic intervention, any method; single vessel

+ **92981** each additional vessel (List separately in addition to code for primary procedure)

(Use 92981 in conjunction with code 92980)

(To report additional vessels treated by angioplasty or atherectomy only during the same session, see 92984, 92996)

(To report transcatheter placement of radiation delivery device for coronary intravascular brachytherapy, use 92974)

(For intravascular radioelement application, see 77781-77784)

92982 Percutaneous transluminal coronary balloon angioplasty; single vessel

+ **92984** each additional vessel (List separately in addition to code for primary procedure)

(Use 92984 in conjunction with codes 92980, 92982, 92995)

(For stent placement following completion of angioplasty or atherectomy, see 92980, 92981)

(To report transcatheter placement of radiation delivery device for coronary intravascular brachytherapy, use 92974)

(For intravascular radioelement application, see 77781-77784)

92986 Percutaneous balloon valvuloplasty; aortic valve

92987 mitral valve

92990 pulmonary valve

92992 Atrial septectomy or septostomy; transvenous method, balloon (eg, Rashkind type) (includes cardiac catheterization)

92993 blade method (Park septostomy) (includes cardiac catheterization)

92995 Percutaneous transluminal coronary atherectomy, by mechanical or other method, with or without balloon angioplasty; single vessel

+ **92996** each additional vessel (List separately in addition to code for primary procedure)

(Use 92996 in conjunction with code(s) 92980, 92982, 92995)

(For stent placement following completion of angioplasty or atherectomy, see 92980, 92981)

(To report additional vessels treated by angioplasty only during the same session, use 92984)

92997 Percutaneous transluminal pulmonary artery balloon angioplasty; single vessel

+ **92998** each additional vessel (List separately in addition to code for primary procedure)

(Use 92998 in conjunction with code 92997)

Cardiography

(For echocardiography, see 93303-93350)

93000 Electrocardiogram, routine ECG with at least 12 leads; with interpretation and report

93005 tracing only, without interpretation and report

93010 interpretation and report only

(For ECG monitoring, see 99354-99360)

93012 Telephonic transmission of post-symptom electrocardiogram rhythm strip(s), 24-hour attended monitoring, per 30 day period of time; tracing only

93014 physician review with interpretation and report only

93015 Cardiovascular stress test using maximal or submaximal treadmill or bicycle exercise, continuous electrocardiographic monitoring, and/or pharmacological stress; with physician supervision, with interpretation and report

93016 physician supervision only, without interpretation and report

Medicine

93017 tracing only, without interpretation and report

93018 interpretation and report only

93024 Ergonovine provocation test

93025 Microvolt T-wave alternans for assessment of ventricular arrhythmias

93040 Rhythm ECG, one to three leads; with interpretation and report

93041 tracing only without interpretation and report

93042 interpretation and report only

93224 Electrocardiographic monitoring for 24 hours by continuous original ECG waveform recording and storage, with visual superimposition scanning; includes recording, scanning analysis with report, physician review and interpretation

93225 recording (includes hook-up, recording, and disconnection)

93226 scanning analysis with report

93227 physician review and interpretation

93230 Electrocardiographic monitoring for 24 hours by continuous original ECG waveform recording and storage without superimposition scanning utilizing a device capable of producing a full miniaturized printout; includes recording, microprocessor-based analysis with report, physician review and interpretation

93231 recording (includes hook-up, recording, and disconnection)

93232 microprocessor-based analysis with report

93233 physician review and interpretation

93235 Electrocardiographic monitoring for 24 hours by continuous computerized monitoring and non-continuous recording, and real-time data analysis utilizing a device capable of producing intermittent full-sized waveform tracings, possibly patient activated; includes monitoring and real-time data analysis with report, physician review and interpretation

93236 monitoring and real-time data analysis with report

93237 physician review and interpretation

93268 Patient demand single or multiple event recording with presymptom memory loop, 24-hour attended monitoring, per 30 day period of time; includes transmission, physician review and interpretation

93270 recording (includes hook-up, recording, and disconnection)

93271 monitoring, receipt of transmissions, and analysis

93272 physician review and interpretation only

(For postsymptom recording, see 93012, 93014)

(For implanted patient activated cardiac event recording, see 33282, 93727)

93278 Signal-averaged electrocardiography (SAECG), with or without ECG

(For interpretation and report only, use 93278 with modifier '-26')

(For unlisted cardiographic procedure, use 93799)

Echocardiography

Echocardiography includes obtaining ultrasonic signals from the heart and great arteries, with two-dimensional image and/or Doppler ultrasonic signal documentation, and interpretation and report. When interpretation is performed separately use modifier '-26'.

(For fetal echocardiography, see 76825-76828)

93303 Transthoracic echocardiography for congenital cardiac anomalies; complete

93304 follow-up or limited study

93307 Echocardiography, transthoracic, real-time with image documentation (2D) with or without M-mode recording; complete

93308 follow-up or limited study

93312 Echocardiography, transesophageal, real time with image documentation (2D) (with or without M-mode recording); including probe placement, image acquisition, interpretation and report

93313 placement of transesophageal probe only

93314 image acquisition, interpretation and report only

93315 Transesophageal echocardiography for congenital cardiac anomalies; including probe placement, image acquisition, interpretation and report

93316 placement of transesophageal probe only

93317 image acquisition, interpretation and report only

93318 Echocardiography, transesophageal (TEE) for monitoring purposes, including probe placement, real time 2-dimensional image acquisition and interpretation leading to ongoing (continuous) assessment of (dynamically changing) cardiac pumping function and to therapeutic measures on an immediate time basis

+ 93320 Doppler echocardiography, pulsed wave and/or continuous wave with spectral display (List separately in addition to codes for echocardiographic imaging); complete

(Use 93320 in conjunction with codes 93303, 93304, 93307, 93308, 93312, 93314, 93315, 93317, 93350)

+ 93321 follow-up or limited study (List separately in addition to codes for echocardiographic imaging)

(Use 93321 in conjunction with codes 93303, 93304, 93307, 93308, 93312, 93314, 93315, 93317, 93350)

+ **93325** Doppler echocardiography color flow velocity mapping (List separately in addition to codes for echocardiography)

(Use 93325 in conjunction with codes 76825, 76826, 76827, 76828, 93303, 93304, 93307, 93308, 93312, 93314, 93315, 93317, 93320, 93321, 93350)

93350 Echocardiography, transthoracic, real-time with image documentation (2D), with or without M-mode recording, during rest and cardiovascular stress test using treadmill, bicycle exercise and/or pharmacologically induced stress, with interpretation and report

(The appropriate stress testing code from the 93015-93018 series should be reported in addition to 93350 to capture the exercise stress portion of the study)

Cardiac Catheterization

Cardiac catheterization is a diagnostic medical procedure which includes introduction, positioning and repositioning of catheter(s), when necessary, recording of intracardiac and intravascular pressure, obtaining blood samples for measurement of blood gases or dilution curves and cardiac output measurements (Fick or other method, with or without rest and exercise and/or studies) with or without electrode catheter placement, final evaluation and report of procedure. When selective injection procedures are performed without a preceding cardiac catheterization, these services should be reported using codes in the Vascular Injection Procedures section, 36011-36015 and 36215-36218.

When coronary artery, arterial coronary conduit or venous bypass graft angiography is performed without concomitant left heart cardiac catheterization, use 93508. Injection procedures 93539, 93540, 93544, and 93545 represent separate identifiable services and may be coded in conjunction with one another in addition to code 93508, as appropriate. To report imaging supervision, interpretation and report in conjunction with code 93508, use code 93556.

Modifier '-51' should not be appended to codes 93501-93533, 93539-93556

⊘ **93501** Right heart catheterization

(For bundle of His recording, use 93600)

⊘ **93503** Insertion and placement of flow directed catheter (eg, Swan-Ganz) for monitoring purposes

(For subsequent monitoring, see 99356-99357)

⊘ **93505** Endomyocardial biopsy

⊘ **93508** Catheter placement in coronary artery(s), arterial coronary conduit(s), and/or venous coronary bypass graft(s) for coronary angiography without concomitant left heart catheterization

(93508 is to be used only when left heart catheterization 93510, 93511, 93524, 93526 is not performed)

(93508 is to be used only once per procedure)

(To report transcatheter placement of radiation delivery device for coronary intravascular brachytherapy, use 92974)

(For intravascular radioelement application, see 77781-77784)

⊘ **93510** Left heart catheterization, retrograde, from the brachial artery, axillary artery or femoral artery; percutaneous

⊘ **93511** by cutdown

⊘ **93514** Left heart catheterization by left ventricular puncture

⊘ **93524** Combined transseptal and retrograde left heart catheterization

⊘ **93526** Combined right heart catheterization and retrograde left heart catheterization

⊘ **93527** Combined right heart catheterization and transseptal left heart catheterization through intact septum (with or without retrograde left heart catheterization)

⊘ **93528** Combined right heart catheterization with left ventricular puncture (with or without retrograde left heart catheterization)

⊘ **93529** Combined right heart catheterization and left heart catheterization through existing septal opening (with or without retrograde left heart catheterization)

⊘ **93530** Right heart catheterization, for congenital cardiac anomalies

⊘ **93531** Combined right heart catheterization and retrograde left heart catheterization, for congenital cardiac anomalies

⊘ **93532** Combined right heart catheterization and transseptal left heart catheterization through intact septum with or without retrograde left heart catheterization, for congenital cardiac anomalies

⊘ **93533** Combined right heart catheterization and transseptal left heart catheterization through existing septal opening, with or without retrograde left heart catheterization, for congenital cardiac anomalies

(93535 has been deleted. To report, see 33971)

(93536 has been deleted. To report, use 33967)

(When injection procedures are performed in conjunction with cardiac catheterization, these services do not include introduction of catheters but do include repositioning of catheters when necessary and use of automatic power injectors. Injection procedures 93539-93545 represent separate identifiable services and may be coded in conjunction with one another when appropriate. The technical details of angiography, supervision of filming and processing, interpretation and report are not included. To report imaging supervision, interpretation and report, use 93555 and/or 93556. Modifier '-51' should not be appended to 93539-93556.)

⊘ **93539** Injection procedure during cardiac catheterization; for selective opacification of arterial conduits (eg, internal mammary), whether native or used for bypass

⊘ **93540** for selective opacification of aortocoronary venous bypass grafts, one or more coronary arteries

⊘ 93541 for pulmonary angiography

⊘ 93542 for selective right ventricular or right atrial angiography

⊘ 93543 for selective left ventricular or left atrial angiography

⊘ 93544 for aortography

⊘ 93545 for selective coronary angiography (injection of radiopaque material may be by hand)

(To report imaging supervision and interpretation, use 93555)

⊘ 93555 Imaging supervision, interpretation and report for injection procedure(s) during cardiac catheterization; ventricular and/or atrial angiography

⊘ 93556 pulmonary angiography, aortography, and/or selective coronary angiography including venous bypass grafts and arterial conduits (whether native or used in bypass)

(Codes 93561 and 93562 are not to be used with cardiac catheterization codes)

93561 Indicator dilution studies such as dye or thermal dilution, including arterial and/or venous catheterization; with cardiac output measurement (separate procedure)

93562 subsequent measurement of cardiac output

(For radioisotope method of cardiac output, see 78472, 78473, or 78481)

+ 93571 Intravascular Doppler velocity and/or pressure derived coronary flow reserve measurement (coronary vessel or graft) during coronary angiography including pharmacologically induced stress; initial vessel (List separately in addition to code for primary procedure)

+ 93572 each additional vessel (List separately in addition to code for primary procedure)

(Intravascular distal coronary blood flow velocity measurements include all Doppler transducer manipulations and repositioning within the specific vessel being examined, during coronary angiography or therapeutic intervention (eg, angioplasty))

(For unlisted cardiac catheterization procedure, use 93799)

Repair of Septal Defect

93580 Percutaneous transcatheter closure of congenital interatrial communication (ie, Fontan fenestration, atrial septal defect) with implant

(Percutaneous transcatheter closure of atrial septal defect includes a right heart catheterization procedure. Code 93580 includes injection of contrast for atrial and ventricular angiograms. Codes 93501, 93529-93533, 93539, 93543, 93555 should not be reported separately in addition to code 93580)

93581 Percutaneous transcatheter closure of a congenital ventricular septal defect with implant

(Percutaneous transcatheter closure of ventricular septal defect includes a right heart catheterization procedure. Code 93581 includes injection of contrast for atrial and ventricular angiograms. Codes 93501, 93529-93533, 93539, 93543, 93555 should not be reported separately in addition to code 93581)

(For echocardiographic services performed in addition to 93580, 93581, see 93303-93317, 93662 as appropriate)

Intracardiac Electrophysiological Procedures/Studies

Intracardiac electrophysiologic studies (EPS) are an invasive diagnostic medical procedure which include the insertion and repositioning of electrode catheters, recording of electrograms before and during pacing or programmed stimulation of multiple locations in the heart, analysis of recorded information, and report of the procedure. Electrophysiologic studies are most often performed with two or more electrode catheters. In many circumstances, patients with arrhythmias are evaluated and treated at the same encounter. In this situation, a diagnostic *electrophysiologic study* is performed, induced tachycardia(s) are *mapped*, and on the basis of the diagnostic and mapping information, the tissue is *ablated*. Electrophysiologic study(ies), mapping, and ablation represent distinctly different procedures, requiring individual reporting whether performed on the same or subsequent dates.

Definitions

***Arrhythmia Induction*:** In most electrophysiologic studies, an attempt is made to induce arrhythmia(s) from single or multiple sites within the heart. Arrhythmia induction is achieved by performing pacing at different rates, programmed stimulation (introduction of critically timed electrical impulses), and other techniques. Because arrhythmia induction occurs via the same catheter(s) inserted for the electrophysiologic study(ies), catheter insertion and temporary pacemaker codes are not additionally reported. Codes 93600-93603, 93610-93612 and 93618 are used to describe unusual situations where there may be recording, pacing or an attempt at arrhythmia induction from only one site in the heart. Code 93619 describes only evaluation of the sinus node, atrioventricular node and His-Purkinje conduction system, without arrhythmia induction. Codes 93620-93624 and 93640-93642 all include recording, pacing and attempted arrhythmia induction from one or more site(s) in the heart.

***Mapping*:** Mapping is a distinct procedure performed in addition to a diagnostic electrophysiologic procedure and should be separately reported using code 93609 or 93613. Do not report standard mapping (93609) in addition to 3-D mapping (93613). When a tachycardia is induced, the site of tachycardia origination or its electrical

Medicine

path through the heart is often defined by mapping. Mapping creates a multidimensional depiction of a tachycardia by recording multiple electrograms obtained sequentially or simultaneously from multiple catheter sites in the heart. Depending upon the technique, certain types of mapping catheters may be repositioned from point-to-point within the heart, allowing sequential recording from the various sites to construct maps. Other types of mapping catheters allow mapping without a point-to-point technique by allowing simultaneous recording from many electrodes on the same catheter and computer-assisted three dimensional reconstruction of the tachycardia activation sequence.

***Ablation*:** Once the part of the heart involved in the tachycardia is localized, the tachycardia may be treated by ablation (the delivery of a radiofrequency energy to the area to selectively destroy cardiac tissue). Ablation procedures (93651-93652) may be performed: independently on a date subsequent to a diagnostic electrophysiologic study and mapping; or, at the time a diagnostic electrophysiologic study, tachycardia(s) induction and mapping is performed. When an electrophysiologic study, mapping, and ablation are performed on the same date, each procedure should be separately reported. In reporting catheter ablation, code 93651 and/or 93652 should be reported once to describe ablation of cardiac arrhythmias, regardless of the number of arrhythmias ablated.

Modifier '-51' should not be appended to 93600-93660.

⊘ **93600** Bundle of His recording

⊘ **93602** Intra-atrial recording

⊘ **93603** Right ventricular recording

(93604, 93606 have been deleted. To report, see 93603, 93609, and 93622 as appropriate)

(93607 has been deleted. To report, use 93622)

✚ **93609** Intraventricular and/or intra-atrial mapping of tachycardia site(s) with catheter manipulation to record from multiple sites to identify origin of tachycardia (List separately in addition to code for primary procedure)

(Use 93609 in conjunction with codes 93620, 93651, 93652)

(Do not report 93609 in addition to 93613)

⊘ **93610** Intra-atrial pacing

⊘ **93612** Intraventricular pacing

(Do not report 93612 in conjunction with codes 93620-93622)

✚ **93613** Intracardiac electrophysiologic 3-dimensional mapping (List separately in addition to code for primary procedure)

(Use 93613 in conjunction with codes 93620, 93651, 93652)

(Do not report 93613 in addition to 93609)

⊘ **93615** Esophageal recording of atrial electrogram with or without ventricular electrogram(s);

⊘ **93616** with pacing

⊘ **93618** Induction of arrhythmia by electrical pacing

(For intracardiac phonocardiogram, use 93799)

⊘ **93619** Comprehensive electrophysiologic evaluation with right atrial pacing and recording, right ventricular pacing and recording, His bundle recording, including insertion and repositioning of multiple electrode catheters, without induction or attempted induction of arrhythmia

(Do not report 93619 in conjunction with codes 93600, 93602, 93610, 93612, 93618, or 93620-93622)

⊘ **93620** Comprehensive electrophysiologic evaluation including insertion and repositioning of multiple electrode catheters with induction or attempted induction of arrhythmia; with right atrial pacing and recording, right ventricular pacing and recording, His bundle recording

(Do not report 93620 in conjunction with codes 93600, 93602, 93610, 93612, 93618 or 93619)

✚ **93621** with left atrial pacing and recording from coronary sinus or left atrium (List separately in addition to code for primary procedure)

(Use 93621 in conjunction with code 93620)

✚ **93622** with left ventricular pacing and recording (List separately in addition to code for primary procedure)

(Use 93622 in conjunction with code 93620)

✚ **93623** Programmed stimulation and pacing after intravenous drug infusion (List separately in addition to code for primary procedure)

(Use 93623 in conjunction with codes 93619, 93620)

⊘ **93624** Electrophysiologic follow-up study with pacing and recording to test effectiveness of therapy, including induction or attempted induction of arrhythmia

⊘ **93631** Intra-operative epicardial and endocardial pacing and mapping to localize the site of tachycardia or zone of slow conduction for surgical correction

⊘ **93640** Electrophysiologic evaluation of single or dual chamber pacing cardioverter-defibrillator leads including defibrillation threshold evaluation (induction of arrhythmia, evaluation of sensing and pacing for arrhythmia termination) at time of initial implantation or replacement;

⊘ **93641** with testing of single or dual chamber pacing cardioverter-defibrillator pulse generator

(For subsequent or periodic electronic analysis and/or reprogramming of single or dual chamber pacing cardioverter-defibrillators, see 93642, 93741-93744)

⊘ **93642** Electrophysiologic evaluation of single or dual chamber pacing cardioverter-defibrillator (includes defibrillation threshold evaluation, induction of arrhythmia, evaluation of sensing and pacing for arrhythmia termination, and programming or reprogramming of sensing or therapeutic parameters)

⊘ **93650** Intracardiac catheter ablation of atrioventricular node function, atrioventricular conduction for creation of complete heart block, with or without temporary pacemaker placement

⊘ **93651** Intracardiac catheter ablation of arrhythmogenic focus; for treatment of supraventricular tachycardia by ablation of fast or slow atrioventricular pathways, accessory atrioventricular connections or other atrial foci, singly or in combination

⊘ **93652** for treatment of ventricular tachycardia

⊘ **93660** Evaluation of cardiovascular function with tilt table evaluation, with continuous ECG monitoring and intermittent blood pressure monitoring, with or without pharmacological intervention

(For testing of autonomic nervous system function, see 95921-95923)

✚ **93662** Intracardiac echocardiography during therapeutic/diagnostic intervention, including imaging supervision and interpretation (List separately in addition to code for primary procedure)

(Use 93662 in conjunction with 93580, 93581, 93621, 93622, 93651, or 93652, as appropriate)

(Do not report 92961 in addition to 93662)

Peripheral Arterial Disease Rehabilitation

Peripheral arterial disease (PAD) rehabilitative physical exercise consists of a series of sessions, lasting 45-60 minutes per session, involving use of either a motorized treadmill or a track to permit each patient to achieve symptom-limited claudication. Each session is supervised by an exercise physiologist or nurse. The supervising provider monitors the individual patient's claudication threshold and other cardiovascular limitations for adjustment of workload. During this supervised rehabilitation program, the development of new arrhythmias, symptoms that might suggest angina or the continued inability of the patient to progress to an adequate level of exercise may require physician review and examination of the patient. These physician services would be separately reported with an appropriate level E/M service code.

93668 Peripheral arterial disease (PAD) rehabilitation, per session

Other Vascular Studies

(For arterial cannulization and recording of direct arterial pressure, use 36620)

(For radiographic injection procedures, see 36000-36299)

(For vascular cannulization for hemodialysis, see 36800-36821)

(For chemotherapy for malignant disease, see 96408-96549)

(For penile plethysmography, use 54240)

93701 Bioimpedance, thoracic, electrical

93720 Plethysmography, total body; with interpretation and report

93721 tracing only, without interpretation and report

93722 interpretation and report only

(For regional plethysmography, see 93875-93931)

93724 Electronic analysis of antitachycardia pacemaker system (includes electrocardiographic recording, programming of device, induction and termination of tachycardia via implanted pacemaker, and interpretation of recordings)

93727 Electronic analysis of implantable loop recorder (ILR) system (includes retrieval of recorded and stored ECG data, physician review and interpretation of retrieved ECG data and reprogramming)

93731 Electronic analysis of dual-chamber pacemaker system (includes evaluation of programmable parameters at rest and during activity where applicable, using electrocardiographic recording and interpretation of recordings at rest and during exercise, analysis of event markers and device response); without reprogramming

93732 with reprogramming

93733 Electronic analysis of dual chamber internal pacemaker system (may include rate, pulse amplitude and duration, configuration of wave form, and/or testing of sensory function of pacemaker), telephonic analysis

93734 Electronic analysis of single chamber pacemaker system (includes evaluation of programmable parameters at rest and during activity where applicable, using electrocardiographic recording and interpretation of recordings at rest and during exercise, analysis of event markers and device response); without reprogramming

93735 with reprogramming

93736 Electronic analysis of single chamber internal pacemaker system (may include rate, pulse amplitude and duration, configuration of wave form, and/or testing of sensory function of pacemaker), telephonic analysis

(93737 has been deleted. To report, use 93741 or 93743)

(93738 has been deleted. To report, use 93742 or 93744)

93740 Temperature gradient studies

93741 Electronic analysis of pacing cardioverter-defibrillator (includes interrogation, evaluation of pulse generator status, evaluation of programmable parameters at rest and during activity where applicable, using electrocardiographic recording and interpretation of recordings at rest and during exercise, analysis of event markers and device response); single chamber, without reprogramming

93742 single chamber, with reprogramming

93743 dual chamber, without reprogramming

93744 dual chamber, with reprogramming

93760 Thermogram; cephalic

93762 peripheral

93770 Determination of venous pressure

(For central venous cannulization see ►36555-36556,◄ 36500)

93784 Ambulatory blood pressure monitoring, utilizing a system such as magnetic tape and/or computer disk, for 24 hours or longer; including recording, scanning analysis, interpretation and report

93786 recording only

93788 scanning analysis with report

93790 physician review with interpretation and report

Other Procedures

93797 Physician services for outpatient cardiac rehabilitation; without continuous ECG monitoring (per session)

93798 with continuous ECG monitoring (per session)

93799 Unlisted cardiovascular service or procedure

Non-Invasive Vascular Diagnostic Studies

Vascular studies include patient care required to perform the studies, supervision of the studies and interpretation of study results with copies for patient records of hard copy output with analysis of all data, including bidirectional vascular flow or imaging when provided.

The use of a simple hand-held or other Doppler device that does not produce hard copy output, or that produces a record that does not permit analysis of bidirectional vascular flow, is considered to be part of the physical examination of the vascular system and is not separately reported.

Duplex scan (eg, 93880, 93882) describes an ultrasonic scanning procedure for characterizing the pattern and direction of blood flow in arteries or veins with the production of real time images integrating B-mode two-dimensional vascular structure with spectral and/or color flow Doppler mapping or imaging.

Non-invasive physiologic studies are performed using equipment separate and distinct from the duplex scanner. Codes 93875, 93965, 93922, 93923, and 93924 describe the evaluation of non-imaging physiologic recordings of pressures, Doppler analysis of bi-directional blood flow, plethysmography, and/or oxygen tension measurements appropriate for the anatomic area studied.

Cerebrovascular Arterial Studies

93875 Non-invasive physiologic studies of extracranial arteries, complete bilateral study (eg, periorbital flow direction with arterial compression, ocular pneumoplethysmography, Doppler ultrasound spectral analysis)

93880 Duplex scan of extracranial arteries; complete bilateral study

93882 unilateral or limited study

93886 Transcranial Doppler study of the intracranial arteries; complete study

93888 limited study

Extremity Arterial Studies (Including Digits)

93922 Non-invasive physiologic studies of upper or lower extremity arteries, single level, bilateral (eg, ankle/brachial indices, Doppler waveform analysis, volume plethysmography, transcutaneous oxygen tension measurement)

93923 Non-invasive physiologic studies of upper or lower extremity arteries, multiple levels or with provocative functional maneuvers, complete bilateral study (eg, segmental blood pressure measurements, segmental Doppler waveform analysis, segmental volume plethysmography, segmental transcutaneous oxygen tension measurements, measurements with postural provocative tests, measurements with reactive hyperemia)

93924 Non-invasive physiologic studies of lower extremity arteries, at rest and following treadmill stress testing, complete bilateral study

93925 Duplex scan of lower extremity arteries or arterial bypass grafts; complete bilateral study

93926 unilateral or limited study

93930 Duplex scan of upper extremity arteries or arterial bypass grafts; complete bilateral study

93931 unilateral or limited study

Extremity Venous Studies (Including Digits)

93965 Non-invasive physiologic studies of extremity veins, complete bilateral study (eg, Doppler waveform analysis with responses to compression and other maneuvers, phleborheography, impedance plethysmography)

93970 Duplex scan of extremity veins including responses to compression and other maneuvers; complete bilateral study

93971 unilateral or limited study

Visceral and Penile Vascular Studies

93975 Duplex scan of arterial inflow and venous outflow of abdominal, pelvic, scrotal contents and/or retroperitoneal organs; complete study

93976 limited study

93978 Duplex scan of aorta, inferior vena cava, iliac vasculature, or bypass grafts; complete study

93979 unilateral or limited study

93980 Duplex scan of arterial inflow and venous outflow of penile vessels; complete study

93981 follow-up or limited study

Extremity Arterial-Venous Studies

93990 Duplex scan of hemodialysis access (including arterial inflow, body of access and venous outflow)

(For measurement of hemodialysis access flow using indicator dilution methods, use 90940)

Pulmonary

Items 94010-94799 include laboratory procedure(s) and interpretation of test results. If a separate identifiable Evaluation and Management service is performed, the appropriate E/M service code should be reported in addition to 94010-94799.

94010 Spirometry, including graphic record, total and timed vital capacity, expiratory flow rate measurement(s), with or without maximal voluntary ventilation

94014 Patient-initiated spirometric recording per 30-day period of time; includes reinforced education, transmission of spirometric tracing, data capture, analysis of transmitted data, periodic recalibration and physician review and interpretation

94015 recording (includes hook-up, reinforced education, data transmission, data capture, trend analysis, and periodic recalibration)

94016 physician review and interpretation only

94060 Bronchospasm evaluation: spirometry as in 94010, before and after bronchodilator (aerosol or parenteral)

(For prolonged exercise test for bronchospasm with pre- and post-spirometry, use 94620)

94070 Prolonged postexposure evaluation of bronchospasm with multiple spirometric determinations after antigen, cold air, methacholine or other chemical agent, with subsequent spirometrics

94150 Vital capacity, total (separate procedure)

94200 Maximum breathing capacity, maximal voluntary ventilation

94240 Functional residual capacity or residual volume: helium method, nitrogen open circuit method, or other method

94250 Expired gas collection, quantitative, single procedure (separate procedure)

94260 Thoracic gas volume

(For plethysmography, see 93720-93722)

94350 Determination of maldistribution of inspired gas: multiple breath nitrogen washout curve including alveolar nitrogen or helium equilibration time

94360 Determination of resistance to airflow, oscillatory or plethysmographic methods

94370 Determination of airway closing volume, single breath tests

94375 Respiratory flow volume loop

94400 Breathing response to CO_2 (CO_2 response curve)

94450 Breathing response to hypoxia (hypoxia response curve)

94620 Pulmonary stress testing; simple (eg, prolonged exercise test for bronchospasm with pre- and post-spirometry)

94621 complex (including measurements of CO_2 production, O_2 uptake, and electrocardiographic recordings)

94640 Pressurized or nonpressurized inhalation treatment for acute airway obstruction or for sputum induction for diagnostic purposes (eg, with an aerosol generator, nebulizer, metered dose inhaler or intermittent positive pressure breathing (IPPB) device)

(For more than one inhalation treatment performed on the same date, append modifier '-76')

94642 Aerosol inhalation of pentamidine for pneumocystis carinii pneumonia treatment or prophylaxis

(94650, 94651, 94652 have been deleted)

94656 Ventilation assist and management, initiation of pressure or volume preset ventilators for assisted or controlled breathing; first day

94657 subsequent days

94660 Continuous positive airway pressure ventilation (CPAP), initiation and management

94662 Continuous negative pressure ventilation (CNP), initiation and management

94664 Demonstration and/or evaluation of patient utilization of an aerosol generator, nebulizer, metered dose inhaler or IPPB device

(94664 can be reported one time only per day of service)

(94665 has been deleted)

94667 Manipulation chest wall, such as cupping, percussing, and vibration to facilitate lung function; initial demonstration and/or evaluation

94668 subsequent

94680 Oxygen uptake, expired gas analysis; rest and exercise, direct, simple

94681 including CO_2 output, percentage oxygen extracted

94690 rest, indirect (separate procedure)

(For single arterial puncture, use 36600)

94720 Carbon monoxide diffusing capacity (eg, single breath, steady state)

94725 Membrane diffusion capacity

94750 Pulmonary compliance study (eg, plethysmography, volume and pressure measurements)

94760 Noninvasive ear or pulse oximetry for oxygen saturation; single determination

(For blood gases, see 82803-82810)

94761 multiple determinations (eg, during exercise)

94762 by continuous overnight monitoring (separate procedure)

94770 Carbon dioxide, expired gas determination by infrared analyzer

(For bronchoscopy, see 31622-31656)

(For placement of flow directed catheter, use 93503)

(For venipuncture, use 36410)

(For central venous catheter placement, see 36555-36556)

(For arterial puncture, use 36600)

(For arterial catheterization, use 36620)

(For thoracentesis, use 32000)

(For phlebotomy, therapeutic, use 99195)

(For lung biopsy, needle, use 32405)

(For intubation, orotracheal or nasotracheal, use 31500)

94772 Circadian respiratory pattern recording (pediatric pneumogram), 12 to 24 hour continuous recording, infant

(Separate procedure codes for electromyograms, EEG, ECG, and recordings of respiration are excluded when 94772 is reported)

94799 Unlisted pulmonary service or procedure

Allergy and Clinical Immunology

Definitions

Allergy sensitivity tests describe the performance and evaluation of selective cutaneous and mucous membrane tests in correlation with the history, physical examination, and other observations of the patient. The number of tests performed should be judicious and dependent upon the history, physical findings, and clinical judgment. All patients should not necessarily receive the same tests nor the same number of sensitivity tests.

Immunotherapy (desensitization, hyposensitization) is the parenteral administration of allergenic extracts as antigens at periodic intervals, usually on an increasing dosage scale to a dosage which is maintained as maintenance therapy. Indications for immunotherapy are determined by appropriate diagnostic procedures coordinated with clinical judgment and knowledge of the natural history of allergic diseases.

Other therapy: for medical conferences on the use of mechanical and electronic devices (precipitators, air conditioners, air filters, humidifiers, dehumidifiers), climatotherapy, physical therapy, occupational and recreational therapy, see **Evaluation and Management** section.

Allergy Testing

95004 Percutaneous tests (scratch, puncture, prick) with allergenic extracts, immediate type reaction, specify number of tests

95010 Percutaneous tests (scratch, puncture, prick) sequential and incremental, with drugs, biologicals or venoms, immediate type reaction, specify number of tests

95015 Intracutaneous (intradermal) tests, sequential and incremental, with drugs, biologicals, or venoms, immediate type reaction, specify number of tests

95024 Intracutaneous (intradermal) tests with allergenic extracts, immediate type reaction, specify number of tests

95027 Intracutaneous (intradermal) tests, sequential and incremental, with allergenic extracts for airborne allergens, immediate type reaction, specify number of tests

95028 Intracutaneous (intradermal) tests with allergenic extracts, delayed type reaction, including reading, specify number of tests

95044 Patch or application test(s) (specify number of tests)

95052 Photo patch test(s) (specify number of tests)

95056 Photo tests

95060 Ophthalmic mucous membrane tests

95065 Direct nasal mucous membrane test

95070 Inhalation bronchial challenge testing (not including necessary pulmonary function tests); with histamine, methacholine, or similar compounds

95071 with antigens or gases, specify

(For pulmonary function tests, see 94060, 94070)

95075 Ingestion challenge test (sequential and incremental ingestion of test items, eg, food, drug or other substance such as metabisulfite)

95078 Provocative testing (eg, Rinkel test)

(For allergy laboratory tests, see 86000-86999)

(For intravenous therapy for severe or intractable allergic disease, see 90780, 90781, 90784)

Allergen Immunotherapy

Codes 95115-95199 include the professional services necessary for allergen immunotherapy. Office visit codes may be used in addition to allergen immunotherapy if other identifiable services are provided at that time.

95115 Professional services for allergen immunotherapy not including provision of allergenic extracts; single injection

95117 two or more injections

95120 Professional services for allergen immunotherapy in prescribing physicians office or institution, including provision of allergenic extract; single injection

95125 two or more injections

95130 single stinging insect venom

95131 two stinging insect venoms

95132 three stinging insect venoms

95133 four stinging insect venoms

95134 five stinging insect venoms

95144 Professional services for the supervision of preparation and provision of antigens for allergen immunotherapy; single dose vial(s) (specify number of vials)

(A single dose vial contains a single dose of antigen administered in one injection)

95145 Professional services for the supervision of preparation and provision of antigens for allergen immunotherapy (specify number of doses); single stinging insect venom

95146 two single stinging insect venoms

95147 three single stinging insect venoms

95148 four single stinging insect venoms

95149 five single stinging insect venoms

95165 Professional services for the supervision of preparation and provision of antigens for allergen immunotherapy; single or multiple antigens (specify number of doses)

95170 whole body extract of biting insect or other arthropod (specify number of doses)

(For allergy immunotherapy reporting, a dose is the amount of antigen(s) administered in a single injection from a multiple dose vial)

95180 Rapid desensitization procedure, each hour (eg, insulin, penicillin, equine serum)

95199 Unlisted allergy/clinical immunologic service or procedure

(For skin testing of bacterial, viral, fungal extracts, see 95028, 86485-86586)

(For special reports on allergy patients, use 99080)

(For testing procedures such as radioallergosorbent testing (RAST), rat mast cell technique (RMCT), mast cell degranulation test (MCDT), lymphocytic transformation test (LTT), leukocyte histamine release (LHR), migration inhibitory factor test (MIF), transfer factor test (TFT), nitroblue tetrazolium dye test (NTD), see Immunology section in **Pathology** or use 95199)

Endocrinology

95250 Glucose monitoring for up to 72 hours by continuous recording and storage of glucose values from interstitial tissue fluid via a subcutaneous sensor (includes hook-up, calibration, patient initiation and training, recording, disconnection, downloading with printout of data)

(Do not report 95250 in conjunction with 99091)

(To report physician review, interpretation and written report associated with code 95250, see **Evaluation and Management** services codes)

Neurology and Neuromuscular Procedures

Neurologic services are typically consultative, and any of the levels of consultation (99241-99263) may be appropriate.

In addition, services and skills outlined under **Evaluation and Management** levels of service appropriate to neurologic illnesses should be coded similarly.

The EEG, autonomic function, and evoked potential services (95812-95829, 95920-95930 and 95950-95962) include recording, interpretation by a physician, and report. For interpretation only, use modifier '-26'.

(For repetitive transcranial magnetic stimulation for treatment of clinical depression, use Category III code 0018T)

(Do not report codes 95860-95875 in addition to 96000-96004)

Sleep Testing

Sleep studies and polysomnography refer to the continuous and simultaneous monitoring and recording of various physiological and pathophysiological parameters of sleep for 6 or more hours with physician review, interpretation and report. The studies are performed to diagnose a variety of sleep disorders and to evaluate a patient's response to therapies such as nasal continuous positive airway pressure (NCPAP).

Polysomnography is distinguished from sleep studies by the inclusion of sleep staging which is defined to include a 1-4 lead electroencephalogram (EEG), an electro-oculogram (EOG), and a submental electromyogram (EMG). Additional parameters of sleep include: 1) ECG; 2) airflow; 3) ventilation and respiratory effort; 4) gas exchange by oximetry, transcutaneous monitoring, or end tidal gas analysis; 5) extremity muscle activity, motor activity-movement; 6) extended EEG monitoring; 7) penile tumescence; 8) gastroesophageal reflux; 9) continuous blood pressure monitoring; 10) snoring; 11) body positions; etc.

The sleep services (95805-95811) include recording, interpretation and report. For interpretation only, use modifier '-26'.

For a study to be reported as polysomnography, sleep must be recorded and staged.

(Report with a '-52' modifier if less than 6 hours of recording or in other cases of reduced services as appropriate)

(For unattended sleep study, use 95806)

95805 Multiple sleep latency or maintenance of wakefulness testing, recording, analysis and interpretation of physiological measurements of sleep during multiple trials to assess sleepiness

95806 Sleep study, simultaneous recording of ventilation, respiratory effort, ECG or heart rate, and oxygen saturation, unattended by a technologist

95807 Sleep study, simultaneous recording of ventilation, respiratory effort, ECG or heart rate, and oxygen saturation, attended by a technologist

95808 Polysomnography; sleep staging with 1-3 additional parameters of sleep, attended by a technologist

95810 sleep staging with 4 or more additional parameters of sleep, attended by a technologist

95811 sleep staging with 4 or more additional parameters of sleep, with initiation of continuous positive airway pressure therapy or bilevel ventilation, attended by a technologist

Routine Electroencephalography (EEG)

EEG codes 95812-95822 include hyperventilation and/or photic stimulation when appropriate. Routine EEG codes 95816-95822 include 20 to 40 minutes of recording. Extended EEG codes 95812-95813 include reporting times longer than 40 minutes.

95812 Electroencephalogram (EEG) extended monitoring; 41-60 minutes

95813 greater than one hour

95816 Electroencephalogram (EEG); including recording awake and drowsy

95819 including recording awake and asleep

95822 recording in coma or sleep only

95824 cerebral death evaluation only

95827 all night recording

(For 24-hour EEG monitoring, see 95950-95953 or 95956)

(For EEG during nonintracranial surgery, use 95955)

(For Wada test, use 95958)

(For digital analysis of EEG, use 95957)

95829 Electrocorticogram at surgery (separate procedure)

95830 Insertion by physician of sphenoidal electrodes for electroencephalographic (EEG) recording

Muscle and Range of Motion Testing

95831 Muscle testing, manual (separate procedure) with report; extremity (excluding hand) or trunk

95832 hand, with or without comparison with normal side

95833 total evaluation of body, excluding hands

95834 total evaluation of body, including hands

95851 Range of motion measurements and report (separate procedure); each extremity (excluding hand) or each trunk section (spine)

95852 hand, with or without comparison with normal side

95857 Tensilon test for myasthenia gravis;

95858 with electromyographic recording

Electromyography and Nerve Conduction Tests

95860 Needle electromyography; one extremity with or without related paraspinal areas

95861 two extremities with or without related paraspinal areas

(For dynamic electromyography performed during motion analysis studies, see 96002-96003)

95863 three extremities with or without related paraspinal areas

95864 four extremities with or without related paraspinal areas

95867 cranial nerve supplied muscle(s), unilateral

95868 cranial nerve supplied muscles, bilateral

95869 thoracic paraspinal muscles (excluding T1 or T12)

95870 limited study of muscles in one extremity or non-limb (axial) muscles (unilateral or bilateral), other than thoracic paraspinal, cranial nerve supplied muscles, or sphincters

(To report a complete study of the extremities, see 95860-95864)

(For anal or urethral sphincter, detrusor, urethra, perineum musculature, see 51785-51792)

(For eye muscles, use 92265)

95872 Needle electromyography using single fiber electrode, with quantitative measurement of jitter, blocking and/or fiber density, any/all sites of each muscle studied

95875 Ischemic limb exercise test with serial specimen(s) acquisition for muscle(s) metabolite(s)

⊘ **95900** Nerve conduction, amplitude and latency/velocity study, each nerve; motor, without F-wave study

⊘ **95903** motor, with F-wave study

⊘ **95904** sensory

(Report 95900, 95903, and/or 95904 only once when multiple sites on the same nerve are stimulated or recorded)

Intraoperative Neurophysiology

✚ **95920** Intraoperative neurophysiology testing, per hour (List separately in addition to code for primary procedure)

(Use code 95920 in conjunction with the study performed, 92585, 95822, 95860, 95861, 95867, 95868, 95900, 95904, 95925, 95926, 95927, 95930, 95933, 95934, 95936, 95937)

(Code 95920 describes ongoing electrophysiologic testing and monitoring performed during surgical procedures. Code 95920 is reported per hour of service, and includes only the ongoing electrophysiologic monitoring time distinct from performance of specific type(s) of baseline electrophysiologic study(ies) (95860, 95861, 95867, 95868, 95900, 95904, 95933, 95934, 95936, 95937) or interpretation of specific type(s) of baseline electrophysiologic study(ies) (92585, 95822, 95925, 95926, 95927, 95930). The time spent performing or interpreting the baseline electrophysiologic study(ies) should not be counted as intraoperative monitoring, but represents separately reportable procedures. Code 95920 should be used once per hour even if multiple electrophysiologic studies are performed. The baseline electrophysiologic study(ies) should be used once per operative session.)

(For electrocorticography, use 95829)

(For intraoperative EEG during nonintracranial surgery, use 95955)

(For intraoperative functional cortical or subcortical mapping, see 95961-95962)

(For intraoperative neurostimulator programming and analysis, see 95970-95975)

Autonomic Function Tests

95921 Testing of autonomic nervous system function; cardiovagal innervation (parasympathetic function), including two or more of the following: heart rate response to deep breathing with recorded R-R interval, Valsalva ratio, and 30:15 ratio

95922 vasomotor adrenergic innervation (sympathetic adrenergic function), including beat-to-beat blood pressure and R-R interval changes during Valsalva maneuver and at least five minutes of passive tilt

95923 sudomotor, including one or more of the following: quantitative sudomotor axon reflex test (QSART), silastic sweat imprint, thermoregulatory sweat test, and changes in sympathetic skin potential

Evoked Potentials and Reflex Tests

95925 Short-latency somatosensory evoked potential study, stimulation of any/all peripheral nerves or skin sites, recording from the central nervous system; in upper limbs

95926 in lower limbs

95927 in the trunk or head

(To report a unilateral study, use modifier '-52')

(For auditory evoked potentials, use 92585)

95930 Visual evoked potential (VEP) testing central nervous system, checkerboard or flash

95933 Orbicularis oculi (blink) reflex, by electrodiagnostic testing

95934 H-reflex, amplitude and latency study; record gastrocnemius/soleus muscle

95936 record muscle other than gastrocnemius/soleus muscle

(To report a bilateral study, use modifier '-50')

95937 Neuromuscular junction testing (repetitive stimulation, paired stimuli), each nerve, any one method

Special EEG Tests

95950 Monitoring for identification and lateralization of cerebral seizure focus, electroencephalographic (eg, 8 channel EEG) recording and interpretation, each 24 hours

95951 Monitoring for localization of cerebral seizure focus by cable or radio, 16 or more channel telemetry, combined electroencephalographic (EEG) and video recording and interpretation (eg, for presurgical localization), each 24 hours

95953 Monitoring for localization of cerebral seizure focus by computerized portable 16 or more channel EEG, electroencephalographic (EEG) recording and interpretation, each 24 hours

95954 Pharmacological or physical activation requiring physician attendance during EEG recording of activation phase (eg, thiopental activation test)

95955 Electroencephalogram (EEG) during nonintracranial surgery (eg, carotid surgery)

95956 Monitoring for localization of cerebral seizure focus by cable or radio, 16 or more channel telemetry, electroencephalographic (EEG) recording and interpretation, each 24 hours

95957 Digital analysis of electroencephalogram (EEG) (eg, for epileptic spike analysis)

95958 Wada activation test for hemispheric function, including electroencephalographic (EEG) monitoring

95961 Functional cortical and subcortical mapping by stimulation and/or recording of electrodes on brain surface, or of depth electrodes, to provoke seizures or identify vital brain structures; initial hour of physician attendance

+ 95962 each additional hour of physician attendance (List separately in addition to code for primary procedure)

(Use 95962 in conjunction with code 95961)

95965 Magnetoencephalography (MEG), recording and analysis; for spontaneous brain magnetic activity (eg, epileptic cerebral cortex localization)

95966 for evoked magnetic fields, single modality (eg, sensory, motor, language, or visual cortex localization)

+ 95967 for evoked magnetic fields, each additional modality (eg, sensory, motor, language, or visual cortex localization) (List separately in addition to code for primary procedure)

(Use 95967 in conjunction with code 95966)

(For electroencephalography performed in addition to magnetoencephalography, see 95812-95827)

(For somatosensory evoked potentials, auditory evoked potentials, and visual evoked potentials performed in addition to magnetic evoked field responses, see 92585, 95925, 95926, and/or 95930)

(For computerized tomography performed in addition to magnetoencephalography, see 70450-70470, 70496)

(For magnetic resonance imaging performed in addition to magnetoencephalography, see 70551-70553)

Neurostimulators, Analysis-Programming

A simple neurostimulator pulse generator/transmitter (95970, 95971) is one capable of affecting 3 or fewer of the following: pulse amplitude, pulse duration, pulse frequency, 8 or more electrode contacts, cycling, stimulation train duration, train spacing, number of programs, number of channels, alternating electrode polarities, dose time (stimulation parameters changing in time periods of minutes including dose lockout times), more than 1 clinical feature (eg, rigidity, dyskinesia, tremor). A complex neurostimulator pulse generator/transmitter (95970, 95972, 95973, 95974, 95975) is one capable of affecting more than 3 of the above.

Code 95970 describes subsequent electronic analysis of a previously-implanted simple or complex brain, spinal cord, or peripheral neurostimulator pulse generator system, without reprogramming. Code 95971 describes intraoperative or subsequent electronic analysis of an implanted simple brain, spinal cord, or peripheral (ie, peripheral nerve, autonomic nerve, neuromuscular) neurostimulator pulse generator system, with programming. Codes 95972 and 95973 describe intraoperative (at initial insertion/revision) or subsequent electronic analysis of an implanted complex brain, spinal cord or peripheral (except cranial nerve) neurostimulator pulse generator system, with programming. Codes 95974 and 95975 describe intraoperative (at initial insertion/revision) or subsequent electronic analysis of an implanted complex cranial nerve neurostimulator pulse generator system, with programming.

(For insertion of neurostimulator pulse generator, see 61885, 63685, 63688, 64590)

(For revision or removal of neurostimulator pulse generator or receiver, see 61888, 63688, 64595)

(For implantation of neurostimulator electrodes, see 61850-61875, 63650-63655, 64553-64580. For revision or removal of neurostimulator electrodes, see 61880, 63660, 64585)

95970 Electronic analysis of implanted neurostimulator pulse generator system (eg, rate, pulse amplitude and duration, configuration of wave form, battery status, electrode selectability, output modulation, cycling, impedance and patient compliance measurements); simple or complex brain, spinal cord, or peripheral (ie, cranial nerve, peripheral nerve, autonomic nerve, neuromuscular) neurostimulator pulse generator/transmitter, without reprogramming

95971 simple brain, spinal cord, or peripheral (ie, peripheral nerve, autonomic nerve, neuromuscular) neurostimulator pulse generator/transmitter, with intraoperative or subsequent programming

95972 complex brain, spinal cord, or peripheral (except cranial nerve) neurostimulator pulse generator/transmitter, with intraoperative or subsequent programming, first hour

+ 95973 complex brain, spinal cord, or peripheral (except cranial nerve) neurostimulator pulse generator/transmitter, with intraoperative or subsequent programming, each additional 30 minutes after first hour (List separately in addition to code for primary procedure)

(Use 95973 in conjunction with code 95972)

95974 complex cranial nerve neurostimulator pulse generator/transmitter, with intraoperative or subsequent programming, with or without nerve interface testing, first hour

+ 95975 complex cranial nerve neurostimulator pulse generator/transmitter, with intraoperative or subsequent programming, each additional 30 minutes after first hour (List separately in addition to code for primary procedure)

(Use 95975 in conjunction with code 95974)

Other Procedures

95990 Refilling and maintenance of implantable pump or reservoir for drug delivery, spinal (intrathecal, epidural) or brain (intraventricular);

(For analysis and/or reprogramming of implantable infusion pump, see 62367-62368)

(For refill and maintenance of implanted infusion pump or reservoir for systemic drug therapy (eg, chemotherapy or insulin, use 96530)

● 95991 administered by physician

95999 Unlisted neurological or neuromuscular diagnostic procedure

Motion Analysis

Codes 96000-96004 describe services performed as part of a major therapeutic or diagnostic decision making process. Motion analysis is performed in a dedicated motion analysis laboratory (ie, a facility capable of performing videotaping from the front, back and both sides, computerized 3-D kinematics, 3-D kinetics, and dynamic electromyography). Code 96000 may include 3-D kinetics and stride characteristics. Codes 96002-96003 describe dynamic electromyography. Do not report codes 95860-95875 in addition to the motion analysis codes.

Code 96004 should only be reported once regardless of the number of study(ies) reviewed/interpreted.

(For performance of needle electromyography procedures, see 95860-95875)

(For gait training, use 97116)

96000 Comprehensive computer-based motion analysis by video-taping and 3-D kinematics;

96001 with dynamic plantar pressure measurements during walking

96002 Dynamic surface electromyography, during walking or other functional activities, 1-12 muscles

96003 Dynamic fine wire electromyography, during walking or other functional activities, 1 muscle

(Do not report codes 95860-95875 in addition to 96002, 96003)

96004 Physician review and interpretation of comprehensive computer based motion analysis, dynamic plantar pressure measurements, dynamic surface electromyography during walking or other functional activities, and dynamic fine wire electromyography, with written report

Central Nervous System Assessments/Tests (eg, Neuro-Cognitive, Mental Status, Speech Testing)

The following codes are used to report the services provided during testing of the cognitive function of the central nervous system. The testing of cognitive processes, visual motor responses, and abstractive abilities is accomplished by the combination of several types of testing procedures. It is expected that the administration of these tests will generate material that will be formulated into a report.

(For development of cognitive skills, see 97532, 97533)

96100 Psychological testing (includes psychodiagnostic assessment of personality, psychopathology, emotionality, intellectual abilities, eg, WAIS-R, Rorschach, MMPI) with interpretation and report, per hour

96105 Assessment of aphasia (includes assessment of expressive and receptive speech and language function, language comprehension, speech production ability, reading, spelling, writing, eg, by Boston Diagnostic Aphasia Examination) with interpretation and report, per hour

96110 Developmental testing; limited (eg, Developmental Screening Test II, Early Language Milestone Screen), with interpretation and report

96111 extended (includes assessment of motor, language, social, adaptive and/or cognitive functioning by standardized developmental instruments, eg, Bayley Scales of Infant Development) with interpretation and report, per hour

96115 Neurobehavioral status exam (clinical assessment of thinking, reasoning and judgment, eg, acquired knowledge, attention, memory, visual spatial abilities, language functions, planning) with interpretation and report, per hour

(For mini-mental status examination performed by a physician, see **Evaluation and Management** services codes)

96117 Neuropsychological testing battery (eg, Halstead-Reitan, Luria, WAIS-R) with interpretation and report, per hour

Health and Behavior Assessment/Intervention

Health and behavior assessment procedures are used to identify the psychological, behavioral, emotional, cognitive, and social factors important to the prevention, treatment, or management of physical health problems.

The focus of the assessment is not on mental health but on the biopsychosocial factors important to physical health problems and treatments. The focus of the intervention is to improve the patient's health and well-being utilizing cognitive, behavioral, social, and/or psychophysiological procedures designed to ameliorate specific disease-related problems.

Codes 96150-96155 describe services offered to patients who present with established illnesses or symptoms, who are not diagnosed with mental illness, and may benefit from evaluations that focus on the biopsychosocial factors related to the patient's physical health status. These services do not represent preventive medicine counseling and risk factor reduction interventions.

For patients that require psychiatric services (90801-90899) as well as health and behavior assessment/intervention (96150-96155), report the predominant service performed. Do not report codes 96150-96155 in addition to codes 90801-90899 on the same date.

Evaluation and Management services codes (including **Preventive Medicine, Individual Counseling** codes 99401-99404, and **Preventive Medicine, Group Counseling** codes 99411-99412), should not be reported on the same day.

(For health and behavior assessment and/or intervention performed by a physician, see **Evaluation and Management** or **Preventive Medicine** services codes)

96150 Health and behavior assessment (eg, health-focused clinical interview, behavioral observations, psychophysiological monitoring, health-oriented questionnaires), each 15 minutes face-to-face with the patient; initial assessment

96151 re-assessment

96152 Health and behavior intervention, each 15 minutes, face-to-face; individual

96153 group (2 or more patients)

96154 family (with the patient present)

96155 family (without the patient present)

Chemotherapy Administration

Procedures 96400-96549 are independent of the patient's visit.

If a significant separately identifiable Evaluation and Management service is performed, the appropriate E/M service code should be reported in addition to 96400-96549.

Either may occur independently on any date of service, or they may occur sequentially on the same day.

Preparation of chemotherapy agent(s) is included in the service for administration of the agent.

Regional (isolation) chemotherapy perfusion should be reported using the codes for arterial infusion (96420-96425). Placement of the intra-arterial catheter should be reported using the appropriate code from the **Cardiovascular Surgery** section. Placement of arterial and venous cannula(s) for extracorporeal circulation via a membrane oxygenator perfusion pump should be reported using code 36823. Code 36823 includes dose calculation and administration of the chemotherapy agent by injection into the perfusate. Do not report code(s) 96408-96425 in conjunction with code 36823.

Report separate codes for each parenteral method of administration employed when chemotherapy is administered by different techniques. Medications (eg, antibiotics, steroidal agents, antiemetics, narcotics, analgesics, biological agents) administered independently or sequentially as supportive management of chemotherapy administration, should be separately reported using 90780-90788, as appropriate.

96400 Chemotherapy administration, subcutaneous or intramuscular, with or without local anesthesia

96405 Chemotherapy administration, intralesional; up to and including 7 lesions

96406 more than 7 lesions

96408 Chemotherapy administration, intravenous; push technique

96410 infusion technique, up to one hour

+ 96412 infusion technique, one to 8 hours, each additional hour (List separately in addition to code for primary procedure)

(Use 96412 in conjunction with code 96410)

96414 infusion technique, initiation of prolonged infusion (more than 8 hours), requiring the use of a portable or implantable pump

(For refilling and maintenance of a portable pump or an implantable infusion pump or reservoir for drug delivery, see 96520, 96530)

96420 Chemotherapy administration, intra-arterial; push technique

96422 infusion technique, up to one hour

+ 96423 infusion technique, one to 8 hours, each additional hour (List separately in addition to code for primary procedure)

(Use 96423 in conjunction with code 96422)

(For regional chemotherapy perfusion via membrane oxygenator perfusion pump to an extremity, use 36823)

96425 infusion technique, initiation of prolonged infusion (more than 8 hours), requiring the use of a portable or implantable pump

(For refilling and maintenance of a portable pump or an implantable infusion pump or reservoir for drug delivery, see 96520, 96530)

96440 Chemotherapy administration into pleural cavity, requiring and including thoracentesis

96445 Chemotherapy administration into peritoneal cavity, requiring and including peritoneocentesis

96450 Chemotherapy administration, into CNS (eg, intrathecal), requiring and including spinal puncture

(For intravesical (bladder) chemotherapy administration, use 51720)

(For insertion of subarachnoid catheter and reservoir for infusion of drug, see 62350, 62351, 62360, 62361, 62362; for insertion of intraventricular catheter and reservoir, see 61210, 61215)

96520 Refilling and maintenance of portable pump

96530 Refilling and maintenance of implantable pump or reservoir for drug delivery, systemic (eg, intravenous, intra-arterial)

(For refilling and maintenance of an implantable infusion pump for spinal or brain drug infusion, use 95990)

(For collection of blood specimen from a completely implantable venous access device, use 36540)

96542 Chemotherapy injection, subarachnoid or intraventricular via subcutaneous reservoir, single or multiple agents

96545 Provision of chemotherapy agent

(For radioactive isotope therapy, see 79000-79999)

96549 Unlisted chemotherapy procedure

Photodynamic Therapy

(To report ocular photodynamic therapy, use 67221)

96567 Photodynamic therapy by external application of light to destroy premalignant and/or malignant lesions of the skin and adjacent mucosa (eg, lip) by activation of photosensitive drug(s), each phototherapy exposure session

+ 96570 Photodynamic therapy by endoscopic application of light to ablate abnormal tissue via activation of photosensitive drug(s); first 30 minutes (List separately in addition to code for endoscopy or bronchoscopy procedures of lung and esophagus)

+ 96571 each additional 15 minutes (List separately in addition to code for endoscopy or bronchoscopy procedures of lung and esophagus)

(96570, 96571 are to be used in addition to bronchoscopy, endoscopy codes)

(Use 96570, 96571 in conjunction with codes 31641, 43228 as appropriate)

Special Dermatological Procedures

Dermatologic services are typically consultative, and any of the five levels of consultation (99241-99263) may be appropriate.

In addition, services and skills outlined under **Evaluation and Management** levels of service appropriate to dermatologic illnesses should be coded similarly.

(For whole body photography, see Category III code 0044T, 0045T)

(For intralesional injections, see 11900, 11901)

(For Tzanck smear, use 87207)

96900 Actinotherapy (ultraviolet light)

96902 Microscopic examination of hairs plucked or clipped by the examiner (excluding hair collected by the patient) to determine telogen and anagen counts, or structural hair shaft abnormality

96910 Photochemotherapy; tar and ultraviolet B (Goeckerman treatment) or petrolatum and ultraviolet B

96912 psoralens and ultraviolet A (PUVA)

96913 Photochemotherapy (Goeckerman and/or PUVA) for severe photoresponsive dermatoses requiring at least four to eight hours of care under direct supervision of the physician (includes application of medication and dressings)

96920 Laser treatment for inflammatory skin disease (psoriasis); total area less than 250 sq cm

96921 250 sq cm to 500 sq cm

96922 over 500 sq cm

96999 Unlisted special dermatological service or procedure

Physical Medicine and Rehabilitation

(For muscle testing, range of joint motion, electromyography, see 95831 et seq)

(For biofeedback training by EMG, use 90901)

(For transcutaneous nerve stimulation (TNS), use 64550)

97001 Physical therapy evaluation

97002 Physical therapy re-evaluation

97003 Occupational therapy evaluation

97004 Occupational therapy re-evaluation

97005 Athletic training evaluation

97006 Athletic training re-evaluation

Modalities

Any physical agent applied to produce therapeutic changes to biologic tissue; includes but not limited to thermal, acoustic, light, mechanical, or electric energy.

Supervised

The application of a modality that does not require direct (one-on-one) patient contact by the provider.

97010 Application of a modality to one or more areas; hot or cold packs

97012 traction, mechanical

97014 electrical stimulation (unattended)

(For acupuncture with electrical stimulation, use 97781)

97016 vasopneumatic devices

97018 paraffin bath

97020 microwave

97022 whirlpool

97024 diathermy

97026 infrared

97028 ultraviolet

Constant Attendance

The application of a modality that requires direct (one-on-one) patient contact by the provider.

97032 Application of a modality to one or more areas; electrical stimulation (manual), each 15 minutes

97033 iontophoresis, each 15 minutes

97034 contrast baths, each 15 minutes

97035 ultrasound, each 15 minutes

97036 Hubbard tank, each 15 minutes

97039 Unlisted modality (specify type and time if constant attendance)

Therapeutic Procedures

A manner of effecting change through the application of clinical skills and/or services that attempt to improve function.

Physician or therapist required to have direct (one-on-one) patient contact.

97110 Therapeutic procedure, one or more areas, each 15 minutes; therapeutic exercises to develop strength and endurance, range of motion and flexibility

97112 neuromuscular reeducation of movement, balance, coordination, kinesthetic sense, posture, and/or proprioception for sitting and/or standing activities

97113 aquatic therapy with therapeutic exercises

97116 gait training (includes stair climbing)

(Use 96000-96003 to report comprehensive gait and motion analysis procedures)

97124 massage, including effleurage, petrissage and/or tapotement (stroking, compression, percussion)

(For myofascial release, use 97140)

97139 Unlisted therapeutic procedure (specify)

97140 Manual therapy techniques (eg, mobilization/manipulation, manual lymphatic drainage, manual traction), one or more regions, each 15 minutes

97150 Therapeutic procedure(s), group (2 or more individuals)

(Report 97150 for each member of group)

(Group therapy procedures involve constant attendance of the physician or therapist, but by definition do not require one-on-one patient contact by the physician or therapist)

(For manipulation under general anesthesia, see appropriate anatomic section in **Musculoskeletal System**)

(For osteopathic manipulative treatment (OMT), see 98925-98929)

97504 Orthotic(s) fitting and training, upper extremity(ies), lower extremity(ies), and/or trunk, each 15 minutes

(Code 97504 should not be reported with 97116)

(For casting and strapping of fracture, injury or dislocation, see 29000, 29590)

97520 Prosthetic training, upper and/or lower extremities, each 15 minutes

97530 Therapeutic activities, direct (one-on-one) patient contact by the provider (use of dynamic activities to improve functional performance), each 15 minutes

97532 Development of cognitive skills to improve attention, memory, problem solving, (includes compensatory training), direct (one-on-one) patient contact by the provider, each 15 minutes

97533 Sensory integrative techniques to enhance sensory processing and promote adaptive responses to environmental demands, direct (one-on-one) patient contact by the provider, each 15 minutes

97535 Self-care/home management training (eg, activities of daily living (ADL) and compensatory training, meal preparation, safety procedures, and instructions in use of assistive technology devices/adaptive equipment) direct one-on-one contact by provider, each 15 minutes

▲97537 Community/work reintegration training (eg, shopping, transportation, money management, avocational activities and/or work environment/modification analysis, work task analysis, use of assistive technology device/adaptive equipment), direct one-on-one contact by provider, each 15 minutes

(For wheelchair management/propulsion training, use 97542)

97542 Wheelchair management/propulsion training, each 15 minutes

97545 Work hardening/conditioning; initial 2 hours

+ 97546 each additional hour (List separately in addition to code for primary procedure)

(Use 97546 in conjunction with code 97545)

Active Wound Care Management

Active wound care procedures are performed to promote healing, and involve selective and non-selective debridement techniques.

(Do not report 97601, 97602 in addition to 11040-11044)

97601 Removal of devitalized tissue from wound(s); selective debridement, without anesthesia (eg, high pressure waterjet, sharp selective debridement with scissors, scalpel and tweezers), including topical application(s), wound assessment, and instruction(s) for ongoing care, per session

97602 non-selective debridement, without anesthesia (eg, wet-to-moist dressings, enzymatic, abrasion), including topical application(s), wound assessment, and instruction(s) for ongoing care, per session

Tests and Measurements

►Requires direct one-on-one patient contact.◄

(For muscle testing, manual or electrical, joint range of motion, electromyography or nerve velocity determination, see 95831-95904)

97703 Checkout for orthotic/prosthetic use, established patient, each 15 minutes

97750 Physical performance test or measurement (eg, musculoskeletal, functional capacity), with written report, each 15 minutes

●97755 Assistive technology assessment (eg, to restore, augment or compensate for existing function, optimize functional tasks and/or maximize environmental accessibility), direct one-on-one contact by provider, with written report, each 15 minutes

►(To report augmentative and alternative communication devices, use 92605 or 92607)◄

Other Procedures

(For extracorporeal shock wave musculoskeletal therapy, use Category III code 0019T)

97780 Acupuncture, one or more needles; without electrical stimulation

97781 with electrical stimulation

97799 Unlisted physical medicine/rehabilitation service or procedure

Medical Nutrition Therapy

97802 Medical nutrition therapy; initial assessment and intervention, individual, face-to-face with the patient, each 15 minutes

97803 re-assessment and intervention, individual, face-to-face with the patient, each 15 minutes

97804 group (2 or more individual(s)), each 30 minutes

(For medical nutrition therapy assessment and/or intervention performed by a physician, see **Evaluation and Management** or **Preventive Medicine** service codes)

Osteopathic Manipulative Treatment

Osteopathic manipulative treatment is a form of manual treatment applied by a physician to eliminate or alleviate somatic dysfunction and related disorders. This treatment may be accomplished by a variety of techniques.

Evaluation and Management services may be reported separately if, using the modifier '-25,' the patient's condition requires a significant separately identifiable E/M service, above and beyond the usual preservice and postservice work associated with the procedure. The E/M service may be caused or prompted by the same symptoms or condition for which the OMT service was provided. As such, different diagnoses are not required for the reporting of the OMT and E/M service on the same date.

Body regions referred to are: head region; cervical region; thoracic region; lumbar region; sacral region; pelvic region; lower extremities; upper extremities; rib cage region; abdomen and viscera region.

98925 Osteopathic manipulative treatment (OMT); one to two body regions involved

98926 three to four body regions involved

98927 five to six body regions involved

98928 seven to eight body regions involved

98929 nine to ten body regions involved

Chiropractic Manipulative Treatment

Chiropractic manipulative treatment (CMT) is a form of manual treatment to influence joint and neurophysiological function. This treatment may be accomplished using a variety of techniques.

The chiropractic manipulative treatment codes include a pre-manipulation patient assessment. Additional Evaluation and Management services may be reported separately using the modifier '-25', if the patient's condition requires a significant separately identifiable E/M service, above and beyond the usual preservice and postservice work associated with the procedure. The E/M service may be caused or prompted by the same symptoms or condition for which the CMT service was provided. As such, different diagnoses are not required for the reporting of the CMT and E/M service on the same date.

For purposes of CMT, the five spinal regions referred to are: cervical region (includes atlanto-occipital joint); thoracic region (includes costovertebral and costotransverse joints); lumbar region; sacral region; and pelvic (sacro-iliac joint) region. The five extraspinal regions referred to are: head (including temporomandibular joint, excluding atlanto-occipital) region; lower extremities; upper extremities; rib cage (excluding costotransverse and costovertebral joints) and abdomen.

98940 Chiropractic manipulative treatment (CMT); spinal, one to two regions

98941 spinal, three to four regions

98942 spinal, five regions

98943 extraspinal, one or more regions

Special Services, Procedures and Reports

The procedures with code numbers 99000 through 99091 provide the reporting physician ►or other qualified healthcare professional◄ with the means of identifying the completion of special reports and services that are an adjunct to the basic services rendered. The specific number assigned indicates the special circumstances under which a basic procedure is performed.

Code 99091 should be reported no more than once in a 30-day period to include the physician or health care provider time involved with data accession, review and interpretation, modification of care plan as necessary (including communication to patient and/or caregiver), and associated documentation.

If the services described by code 99091 are provided on the same day the patient presents for an E/M service, these services should be considered part of the E/M service and not separately reported.

Do not report 99091 if it occurs within 30 days of care plan oversight services 99374-99380. Do not report 99091 if other more specific CPT codes exist (eg, 93014, 93227, 93233, 93272 for cardiographic services; 95250 for continuous glucose monitoring). Do not report 99091 for transfer and interpretation of data from hospital or clinical laboratory computers.

Miscellaneous Services

99000 Handling and/or conveyance of specimen for transfer from the physician's office to a laboratory

99001 Handling and/or conveyance of specimen for transfer from the patient in other than a physician's office to a laboratory (distance may be indicated)

99002 Handling, conveyance, and/or any other service in connection with the implementation of an order involving devices (eg, designing, fitting, packaging, handling, delivery or mailing) when devices such as orthotics, protectives, prosthetics are fabricated by an outside laboratory or shop but which items have been designed, and are to be fitted and adjusted by the attending physician

(For routine collection of venous blood, use 36415)

▲**99024** Postoperative follow-up visit, normally included in the surgical package, to indicate that an evaluation and management service was performed during a postoperative period for a reason(s) related to the original procedure

(As a component of a surgical "package," see **Surgery Guidelines**)

►(99025 has been deleted)◄

99026 Hospital mandated on call service; in-hospital, each hour

99027 out-of-hospital, each hour

(For physician standby services requiring prolonged physician attendance, use 99360, as appropriate. Time spent performing separately reportable procedure(s) or service(s) should not be included in the time reported as mandated on call service)

▲**99050** Services requested after posted office hours in addition to basic service

99052 Services requested between 10:00 PM and 8:00 AM in addition to basic service

99054 Services requested on Sundays and holidays in addition to basic service

99056 Services provided at request of patient in a location other than physician's office which are normally provided in the office

99058 Office services provided on an emergency basis

99070 Supplies and materials (except spectacles), provided by the physician over and above those usually included with the office visit or other services rendered (list drugs, trays, supplies, or materials provided)

(For spectacles, see 92390-92395)

99071 Educational supplies, such as books, tapes, and pamphlets, provided by the physician for the patient's education at cost to physician

99075 Medical testimony

99078 Physician educational services rendered to patients in a group setting (eg, prenatal, obesity, or diabetic instructions)

99080 Special reports such as insurance forms, more than the information conveyed in the usual medical communications or standard reporting form

►(Do not report 99080 in conjunction with 99455, 99456 for the completion of Workmen's Compensation forms)◄

99082 Unusual travel (eg, transportation and escort of patient)

99090 Analysis of clinical data stored in computers (eg, ECGs, blood pressures, hematologic data)

(For physician/health care professional collection and interpretation of physiologic data stored/transmitted by patient/caregiver, see 99091)

(Do not report 99090 if other more specific CPT codes exist, eg, 93014, 93227, 93233, 93272 for cardiographic services; 95250 for continuous glucose monitoring, 97750 for musculoskeletal function testing)

99091 Collection and interpretation of physiologic data (eg, ECG, blood pressure, glucose monitoring) digitally stored and/or transmitted by the patient and/or caregiver to the physician or other qualified health care professional, requiring a minimum of 30 minutes of time

Qualifying Circumstances for Anesthesia

(For explanation of these services, see **Anesthesia Guidelines**)

+ **99100** Anesthesia for patient of extreme age, under 1 year and over 70 (List separately in addition to code for primary anesthesia procedure)

(For procedure performed on infants less than 1 year of age at time of surgery, see 00326, 00834, 00836)

+ **99116** Anesthesia complicated by utilization of total body hypothermia (List separately in addition to code for primary anesthesia procedure)

+ **99135** Anesthesia complicated by utilization of controlled hypotension (List separately in addition to code for primary anesthesia procedure)

+ **99140** Anesthesia complicated by emergency conditions (specify) (List separately in addition to code for primary anesthesia procedure)

(An emergency is defined as existing when delay in treatment of the patient would lead to a significant increase in the threat to life or body part.)

Sedation With or Without Analgesia (Conscious Sedation)

Sedation with or without analgesia (conscious sedation) is used to achieve a medically controlled state of depressed consciousness while maintaining the patient's airway, protective reflexes and ability to respond to stimulation or verbal commands. Conscious sedation includes performance and documentation of pre- and post-sedation evaluations of the patient, administration of the sedation and/or analgesic agent(s), and monitoring of cardiorespiratory function (ie, pulse oximetry, cardiorespiratory monitor, and blood pressure). The use of these codes requires the presence of an independent trained observer to assist the physician in monitoring the patient's level of consciousness and physiological status.

(If the sedation with or without analgesia (conscious sedation) is administered in support of a procedure provided by another physician, see **Anesthesia** section)

⊘ **99141** Sedation with or without analgesia (conscious sedation); intravenous, intramuscular or inhalation

(94760-94762 may not be reported in addition to 99141)

⊘ **99142** oral, rectal and/or intranasal

(94760-94762 may not be reported in addition to 99142)

Other Services and Procedures

99170 Anogenital examination with colposcopic magnification in childhood for suspected trauma

(For conscious sedation, use 99141, 99142)

99172 Visual function screening, automated or semi-automated bilateral quantitative determination of visual acuity, ocular alignment, color vision by pseudoisochromatic plates, and field of vision (may include all or some screening of the determination(s) for contrast sensitivity, vision under glare)

(This service must employ graduated visual acuity stimuli that allow a quantitative determination of visual acuity (eg, Snellen chart). This service may not be used in addition to a general ophthalmological service or an E/M service)

(Do not report 99172 in conjunction with code 99173)

99173 Screening test of visual acuity, quantitative, bilateral

(The screening test used must employ graduated visual acuity stimuli that allow a quantitative estimate of visual acuity (eg, Snellen chart). Other identifiable services unrelated to this screening test provided at the same time may be reported separately (eg, preventive medicine services). When acuity is measured as part of a general ophthalmological service or of an E/M service of the eye, it is a diagnostic examination and not a screening test.)

(Do not report 99173 in conjunction with code 99172)

99175 Ipecac or similar administration for individual emesis and continued observation until stomach adequately emptied of poison

(For diagnostic intubation, see 82926-82928, 89130-89141)

(For gastric lavage for diagnostic purposes, see 91055)

99183 Physician attendance and supervision of hyperbaric oxygen therapy, per session

(Evaluation and Management services and/or procedures (eg, wound debridement) provided in a hyperbaric oxygen treatment facility in conjunction with a hyperbaric oxygen therapy session should be reported separately)

99185 Hypothermia; regional

99186 total body

99190 Assembly and operation of pump with oxygenator or heat exchanger (with or without ECG and/or pressure monitoring); each hour

99191 3/4 hour

99192 1/2 hour

99195 Phlebotomy, therapeutic (separate procedure)

99199 Unlisted special service, procedure or report

Home Health Procedures/Services

These codes are used by non-physician health care professionals. Physicians should utilize the home visit codes 99341-99350, and utilize CPT codes other than 99500-99600 for any additional procedure/service provided to a patient living in a residence.

The following codes are used to report services provided in a patient's residence (including assisted living apartments, group homes, non-traditional private homes, custodial care facilities, or schools).

Health care professionals who are authorized to use Evaluation and Management Home Visit codes (99341-99350) may report codes 99500-99600 in addition to codes 99341-99350 if both services are performed. Evaluation and Management services may be reported separately, using the modifier '-25', if the patient's condition requires a significant separately identifiable E/M service, above and beyond the home health service(s)/procedure(s) codes 99500-99600.

99500 Home visit for prenatal monitoring and assessment to include fetal heart rate, non-stress test, uterine monitoring, and gestational diabetes monitoring

99501 Home visit for postnatal assessment and follow-up care

99502 Home visit for newborn care and assessment

99503 Home visit for respiratory therapy care (eg, bronchodilator, oxygen therapy, respiratory assessment, apnea evaluation)

99504 Home visit for mechanical ventilation care

99505 Home visit for stoma care and maintenance including colostomy and cystostomy

99506 Home visit for intramuscular injections

99507 Home visit for care and maintenance of catheter(s) (eg, urinary, drainage, and enteral)

(99508 has been deleted. To report see 95806-95811)

99509 Home visit for assistance with activities of daily living and personal care

(To report self-care/home management training, see 97535)

(To report home medical nutrition assessment and intervention services, see 97802-97804)

(To report home speech therapy services, see 92507-92508)

99510 Home visit for individual, family, or marriage counseling

99511 Home visit for fecal impaction management and enema administration

▲**99512** Home visit for hemodialysis

(For home infusion of peritoneal dialysis, use ►99601, 99602◄)

(99539 has been deleted. To report, use 99600)

►(99551-99569 have been deleted. To report, see 99601-99602)◄

99600 Unlisted home visit service or procedure

Home Infusion Procedures/Services

●**99601** Home infusion/specialty drug administration, per visit (up to 2 hours)

+●**99602** each additional hour (List separately in addition to code for primary procedure)

►(Use 99602 in conjunction with 99601)◄

Medicine

Notes

Category II Codes

The following section of *Current Procedural Terminology* (*CPT*) contains a set of supplemental tracking codes that can be used for performance measurement. The use of tracking codes for performance measurement will decrease the need for record abstraction and chart review, and thereby minimize administrative burden on physicians and other health care professionals. These codes are intended to facilitate data collection about quality of care by coding certain services and/or test results that support performance measures and that have been agreed upon as contributing to good patient care. Some codes in this section may relate to compliance by the health care professional with state or federal law.

The use of these codes is optional. The codes are not required for correct coding and may not be used as a substitute for Category I codes.

Services/procedures or test results described in this section make use of alpha characters as the 5th character in the string (ie, 4 digits followed by an alpha character). These digits are not intended to reflect the placement of the code in the regular (Category I) part of the *CPT* Code Set. Also, these codes describe components that are typically included in an evaluation and management service or test results that are part of the laboratory test/procedure. Consequently, they do not have a relative value associated with them.

Tracking codes for performance measurement are released annually as part of the general *CPT* Code Set. Tracking codes are reviewed by the Performance Measures Advisory Group (PMAG), an advisory body to the CPT Editorial Panel and the CPT/HCPAC Advisory Committee. The PMAG is comprised of performance measurement experts representing the Agency for Healthcare Research and Quality (AHRQ), the American Medical Association (AMA), the Centers for Medicare and Medicaid Services (CMS), the Joint Commission on Accreditation of Healthcare Organizations (JCAHO), the National Committee for Quality Assurance (NCQA), and the Physician Consortium for Performance Improvement. The PMAG may seek additional expertise and/or input from other national health care organizations, as necessary, for the development of tracking codes. These may include national medical specialty societies, other national health care professional associations, accrediting bodies, and federal regulatory agencies.

The Category II Codes are published twice a year: January 1 and July 1. Go to www.ama-assn.org/go/cpt for the most current listing.

●**0001F** Blood pressure, measured

●**0002F** Tobacco use, smoking, assessed

●**0003F** Tobacco use, non-smoking, assessed

●**0004F** Tobacco use cessation intervention, counseling

●**0005F** Tobacco use cessation intervention, pharmacologic therapy

●**0006F** Statin therapy, prescribed

●**0007F** Beta-blocker therapy, prescribed

●**0008F** ACE inhibitor therapy, prescribed

●**0009F** Anginal symptoms and level of activity, assessed

●**0010F** Anginal symptoms and level of activity, assessed using a standardized instrument (eg, Canadian Cardiovascular Society Classification-CCSC-System, Seattle Angina Questionnaire-SAQ)

●**0011F** Oral antiplatelet therapy; prescribed (eg, aspirin, clopidogrel/ Plavix, or combination of aspirin and dipyridamole/Aggrenox)

Notes

Category III Codes

The following section contains a set of temporary codes for emerging technology, services, and procedures. Category III codes will allow data collection for these services/procedures. Use of unlisted codes does not offer the opportunity for the collection of specific data. If a Category III code is available, this code must be reported instead of a Category I unlisted code. This is an activity that is critically important in the evaluation of health care delivery and the formation of public and private policy. The use of the codes in this section will allow physicians and other qualified health care professionals, insurers, health services researchers, and health policy experts to identify emerging technology, services, and procedures for clinical efficacy, utilization and outcomes.

The inclusion of a service or procedure in this section neither implies nor endorses clinical efficacy, safety or the applicability to clinical practice. The codes in this section do not conform to the usual requirements for CPT Category I codes established by the Editorial Panel. For Category I codes, the Panel requires that the service/procedure be performed by many health care professionals in clinical practice in multiple locations and that FDA approval, as appropriate, has already been received. The nature of emerging technology, services, and procedures is such that these requirements may not be met. For these reasons, temporary codes for emerging technology, services, and procedures have been placed in a separate section of the *CPT* book and the codes are differentiated from Category I CPT codes by the use of alphanumeric characters.

Services/procedures described in this section make use of alphanumeric characters. These codes have an alpha character as the 5th character in the string, preceded by four digits. The digits are not intended to reflect the placement of the code in the Category I section of CPT nomenclature. Codes in this section may or may not eventually receive a Category I CPT code. In either case, a given Category III code will be archived after five years of its inception unless it is demonstrated that a temporary code is still needed. New codes in this section are released semi-annually via the AMA/CPT internet site, to expedite dissemination for reporting. The full set of temporary codes for emerging technology, services, and procedures are published annually in the *CPT* book.

0001T Endovascular repair of infrarenal abdominal aortic aneurysm or dissection, modular bifurcated prosthesis (two docking limbs)

(For radiological supervision and interpretation, use 75952 in conjunction with ►0001T◄)

►(0002T has been deleted. To report, use 34805)◄

0003T Cervicography

(0004T has been deleted. To report, use 88380)

0005T Transcatheter placement of extracranial cerebrovascular artery stent(s), percutaneous; initial vessel

+ 0006T each additional vessel (List separately in addition to code for primary procedure

(Use 0006T in conjunction with code 0005T)

(For radiological supervision and interpretation, use 0007T)

0007T Transcatheter placement of extracranial cerebrovascular artery stent(s), percutaneous, radiological supervision and interpretation, each vessel

(For procedure, see 0005T, 0006T)

0008T Upper gastrointestinal endoscopy including esophagus, stomach, and either the duodenum and/or jejunum as appropriate; with suturing of the esophagogastric junction

0009T Endometrial cryoablation with ultrasonic guidance

0010T Tuberculosis test, cell mediated immunity measurement of gamma interferon antigen response

0012T Arthroscopy, knee, surgical, implantation of osteochondral graft(s) for treatment of articular surface defect; autografts

0013T allografts

0014T Meniscal transplantation, medial or lateral, knee (any method)

0016T Destruction of localized lesion of choroid (eg, choroidal neovascularization), transpupillary thermotherapy

0017T Destruction of macular drusen, photocoagulation

0018T Delivery of high power, focal magnetic pulses for direct stimulation to cortical neurons

0019T Extracorporeal shock wave therapy; involving musculoskeletal system

0020T involving plantar fascia

0021T Insertion of transcervical or transvaginal fetal oximetry sensor

0023T Infectious agent drug susceptibility phenotype prediction using genotypic comparison to known genotypic/phenotypic database, HIV 1

0024T Non-surgical septal reduction therapy (eg, alcohol ablation), for hypertrophic obstructive cardiomyopathy; with coronary arteriograms, with or without temporary pacemaker

►(0025T has been deleted. To report, use 76514)◄

0026T Lipoprotein, direct measurement, intermediate density lipoproteins (IDL) (remnant lipoproteins)

0027T Endoscopic lysis of epidural adhesions with direct visualization using mechanical means (eg, spinal endoscopic catheter system) or solution injection (eg, normal saline) including radiologic localization and epidurography

(For diagnostic epidurography, use 64999)

0028T Dual energy x-ray absorptiometry (DEXA) body composition study, one or more sites

0029T Treatment(s) for incontinence, pulsed magnetic neuromodulation, per day

0030T Antiprothrombin (phospholipid cofactor) antibody, each Ig class

0031T Speculoscopy;

0032T with directed sampling

0033T Endovascular repair of descending thoracic aortic aneurysm, pseudoaneurysm or dissection; involving coverage of left subclavian artery origin, initial endoprosthesis

(For radiological supervision and interpretation, use 0038T)

0034T not involving coverage of left subclavian artery origin, initial endoprosthesis

(For radiological supervision and interpretation, use 0039T)

0035T Placement of proximal or distal extension prosthesis for endovascular repair of descending thoracic aortic aneurysm, pseudoaneurysm or dissection; initial extension

(For radiological supervision and interpretation, use 0040T)

(Do not report 0034T and 0035T when placement of extension converts repair to cover left subclavian origin, use only 0033T)

+ 0036T each additional extension (List separately in addition to code for primary procedure)

(Use 0036T in conjunction with code 0035T)

(For radiological supervision and interpretation, use 0040T)

0037T Open subclavian to carotid artery transposition performed in conjunction with endovascular thoracic aneurysm repair, by neck incision, unilateral

(For bilateral procedure, use modifier '-50')

(Do not report 0037T in addition to 35694)

0038T Endovascular repair of descending thoracic aortic aneurysm, pseudoaneurysm or dissection involving coverage of left subclavian artery origin, initial endoprosthesis, radiological supervision and interpretation

(For implantation of endovascular graft, use 0033T)

0039T Endovascular repair of descending thoracic aortic aneurysm, pseudoaneurysm or dissection not involving coverage of left subclavian artery origin, initial endoprosthesis, radiological supervision and interpretation

(For implantation of endovascular graft, use 0034T)

0040T Placement of proximal or distal extension prosthesis for endovascular repair of descending thoracic aortic aneurysm, pseudoaneurysm or dissection, each extension, radiological supervision and interpretation

(For implantation of endovascular graft extensions, see 0035T, 0036T)

0041T Urinalysis infectious agent detection, semi-quantitative analysis of volatile compounds

0042T Cerebral perfusion analysis using computed tomography with contrast administration, including post-processing of parametric maps with determination of cerebral blood flow, cerebral blood volume, and mean transit time

0043T Carbon monoxide, expired gas analysis (eg, $ETCO_c$/hemolysis breath test)

0044T Whole body integumentary photography, at request of a physician, for monitoring of high-risk patients; with dysplastic nevus syndrome or familial melanoma

● **0045T** with history of dysplastic nevi or personal history of melanoma

● **0046T** Catheter lavage of a mammary duct(s) for collection of cytology specimen(s), in high risk individuals (GAIL risk scoring or prior personal history of breast cancer), each breast; single duct

● **0047T** each additional duct

● **0048T** Implantation of a ventricular assist device, extracorporeal, percutaneous transseptal access, single or dual cannulation

+ ● **0049T** Prolonged extracorporeal percutaneous transseptal ventricular assist device, greater than 24 hours, each subsequent 24 hour period (List separately in addition to code for primary procedure)

►(Use 0049T in conjunction with 0048T)◄

● **0050T** Removal of a ventricular assist device, extracorporeal, percutaneous transseptal access, single or dual cannulation

● **0051T** Implantation of a total replacement heart system (artificial heart) with recipient cardiectomy

►(For implantation of heart assist or ventricular assist device, see 33975, 33976)◄

● **0052T** Replacement or repair of thoracic unit of a total replacement heart system (artificial heart)

►(For replacement or repair of other implantable components in a total replacement heart system (artificial heart), use 0053T)◄

Category III Codes

● **0053T** Replacement or repair of implantable component or components of total replacement heart system (artificial heart), excluding thoracic unit

►(For replacement or repair of a thoracic unit of a total replacement heart system (artificial heart), use 0052T)◄

+ ● **0054T** Computer assisted musculoskeletal surgical navigational orthopedic procedure, with image-guidance based on fluoroscopic images (List separately in addition to code for primary procedure)

+ ● **0055T** Computer assisted musculoskeletal surgical navigational orthopedic procedure, with image-guidance based on CT and MRI images (List separately in addition to code for primary procedure)

+ ● **0056T** Computer assisted musculoskeletal surgical navigational orthopedic procedure, image-less (List separately in addition to code for primary procedure)

● **0057T** Upper gastrointestinal endoscopy, including esophagus, stomach, and either the duodenum and/or jejunum as appropriate, with delivery of thermal energy to the muscle of the lower esophageal sphincter and/or gastric cardia, for treatment of gastroesophageal reflux disease

● **0058T** Cryopreservation; reproductive tissue, ovarian

● **0059T** oocyte(s)

►(For cryopreservation of embryo(s), sperm and testicular reproductive tissue, see 89258, 89259, 89335)◄

● **0060T** Electrical impedance scan of the breast, bilateral (risk assessment device for breast cancer)

● **0061T** Destruction/reduction of malignant breast tumor including breast carcinoma cells in the margins, microwave phased array thermotherapy, disposable catheter with combined temperature monitoring probe and microwave sensor, externally applied microwave energy, including interstitial placement of sensor

►(For imaging guidance performed in conjunction with 0061T, see 76942, 76986)◄

Notes

Appendix A

Modifiers

This list includes all of the modifiers applicable to *CPT* 2004 codes.

21 Prolonged Evaluation and Management Services: When the face-to-face or floor/unit service(s) provided is prolonged or otherwise greater than that usually required for the highest level of evaluation and management service within a given category, it may be identified by adding modifier '21' to the evaluation and management code number. A report may also be appropriate.

22 Unusual Procedural Services: When the service(s) provided is greater than that usually required for the listed procedure, it may be identified by adding modifier '22' to the usual procedure number. A report may also be appropriate.

23 Unusual Anesthesia: Occasionally, a procedure, which usually requires either no anesthesia or local anesthesia, because of unusual circumstances must be done under general anesthesia. This circumstance may be reported by adding the modifier '23' to the procedure code of the basic service.

24 Unrelated Evaluation and Management Service by the Same Physician During a Postoperative Period: The physician may need to indicate that an evaluation and management service was performed during a postoperative period for a reason(s) unrelated to the original procedure. This circumstance may be reported by adding the modifier '24' to the appropriate level of E/M service.

25 Significant, Separately Identifiable Evaluation and Management Service by the Same Physician on the Same Day of the Procedure or Other Service: The physician may need to indicate that on the day a procedure or service identified by a CPT code was performed, the patient's condition required a significant, separately identifiable E/M service above and beyond the other service provided or beyond the usual preoperative and postoperative care associated with the procedure that was performed. The E/M service may be prompted by the symptom or condition for which the procedure and/or service was provided. As such, different diagnoses are not required for reporting of the E/M services on the same date. This circumstance may be reported by adding the modifier '25' to the appropriate level of E/M service. **Note:** This modifier is not used to report an E/M service that resulted in a decision to perform surgery. See modifier '57.'

26 Professional Component: Certain procedures are a combination of a physician component and a technical component. When the physician component is reported separately, the service may be identified by adding the modifier '26' to the usual procedure number.

32 Mandated Services: Services related to *mandated* consultation and/or related services (eg, PRO, third party payer, governmental, legislative or regulatory requirement) may be identified by adding the modifier '32' to the basic procedure.

47 Anesthesia by Surgeon: Regional or general anesthesia provided by the surgeon may be reported by adding the modifier '47' to the basic service. (This does not include local anesthesia.) **Note:** Modifier '47' would not be used as a modifier for the anesthesia procedures.

50 Bilateral Procedure: Unless otherwise identified in the listings, bilateral procedures that are performed at the same operative session, should be identified by adding the modifier '50' to the appropriate five digit code.

51 Multiple Procedures: When multiple procedures, other than E/M services, are performed at the same session by the same provider, the primary procedure or service may be reported as listed. The additional procedure(s) or service(s) may be identified by appending the modifier '51' to the additional procedure or service code(s). **Note:** This modifier should not be appended to designated "add-on" codes (see Appendix D).

52 Reduced Services: Under certain circumstances a service or procedure is partially reduced or eliminated at the physician's discretion. Under these circumstances the service provided can be identified by its usual procedure number and the addition of the modifier '52', signifying that the service is reduced. This provides a means of reporting reduced services without disturbing the identification of the basic service. **Note:** For hospital outpatient reporting of a previously scheduled procedure/service that is partially reduced or cancelled as a result of extenuating circumstances or those that threaten the well-being of the patient prior to or after administration of anesthesia, see modifiers '73' and '74' (see modifiers approved for ASC hospital outpatient use).

53 Discontinued Procedure: Under certain circumstances, the physician may elect to terminate a surgical or diagnostic procedure. Due to extenuating circumstances or those that threaten the well being of the patient, it may be necessary to indicate that a surgical or diagnostic procedure was started but discontinued. This circumstance may be reported by adding the modifier '53' to the code reported by the physician for the discontinued procedure. **Note:** This modifier is not used to report the elective cancellation of a procedure prior to the patient's anesthesia induction and/or surgical preparation in the operating suite. For outpatient hospital/ambulatory surgery center (ASC) reporting of a previously scheduled procedure/service that is partially reduced or cancelled as a result of extenuating circumstances or those that threaten the well being of the patient prior to or after administration of anesthesia, see modifiers '73' and '74' (see modifiers approved for ASC hospital outpatient use).

54 Surgical Care Only: When one physician performs a surgical procedure and another provides preoperative and/or postoperative management, surgical services may be identified by adding the modifier '54' to the usual procedure number.

55 Postoperative Management Only: When one physician performed the postoperative management and another physician performed the surgical procedure, the postoperative component may be identified by adding the modifier '55' to the usual procedure number.

56 Preoperative Management Only: When one physician performed the preoperative care and evaluation and another physician performed the surgical procedure, the preoperative component may be identified by adding the modifier '56' to the usual procedure number.

57 Decision for Surgery: An evaluation and management service that resulted in the initial decision to perform the surgery may be identified by adding the modifier '57' to the appropriate level of E/M service.

58 Staged or Related Procedure or Service by the Same Physician During the Postoperative Period: The physician may need to indicate that the performance of a procedure or service during the postoperative period was: a) planned prospectively at the time of the original procedure (staged); b) more extensive than the original procedure; or c) for therapy following a diagnostic surgical procedure. This circumstance may be reported by adding the modifier '58' to the staged or related procedure. **Note:** This modifier is not used to report the treatment of a problem that requires a return to the operating room. See modifier '78.'

59 Distinct Procedural Service: Under certain circumstances, the physician may need to indicate that a procedure or service was distinct or independent from other services performed on the same day. Modifier '59' is used to identify procedures/services that are not normally reported together, but are appropriate under the circumstances. This may represent a different session or patient encounter, different procedure or surgery, different site or organ system, separate incision/excision, separate lesion, or separate injury (or area of injury in extensive injuries) not ordinarily encountered or performed on the same day by the same physician. However, when another already established modifier is appropriate it should be used rather than modifier '59.' Only if no more descriptive modifier is available, and the use of modifier '59' best explains the circumstances, should modifier '59' be used.

62 Two Surgeons: When two surgeons work together as primary surgeons performing distinct part(s) of a procedure, each surgeon should report his/her distinct operative work by adding the modifier '62' to the procedure code and any associated add-on code(s) for that procedure as long as both surgeons continue to work together as primary surgeons. Each surgeon should report the co-surgery once using the same procedure code. If additional procedure(s) (including add-on procedure(s) are performed during the same surgical session, separate code(s) may also be reported with the modifier '62' added. **Note:** If a co-surgeon acts as an assistant in the performance of additional procedure(s) during the same surgical session, those services may be reported using separate procedure code(s) with the modifier '80' or modifier '82' added, as appropriate.

63 Procedure Performed on Infants less than 4 kg: Procedures performed on neonates and infants up to a present body weight of 4 kg may involve significantly increased complexity and physician work commonly associated with these patients. This circumstance may be reported by adding the modifier '63' to the procedure number. **Note:** Unless otherwise designated, this modifier may only be appended to procedures/services listed in the 20000-69999 code series. Modifier '63' should not be appended to any CPT codes listed in the **Evaluation and Management Services, Anesthesia, Radiology, Pathology/Laboratory, or Medicine** sections.

66 Surgical Team: Under some circumstances, highly complex procedures (requiring the concomitant services of several physicians, often of different specialties, plus other highly skilled, specially trained personnel, various types of complex equipment) are carried out under the "surgical team" concept. Such circumstances may be identified by each participating physician with the addition of the modifier '66' to the basic procedure number used for reporting services.

76 Repeat Procedure by Same Physician: The physician may need to indicate that a procedure or service was repeated subsequent to the original procedure or service. This circumstance may be reported by adding the modifier '76' to the repeated procedure/service.

77 Repeat Procedure by Another Physician: The physician may need to indicate that a basic procedure or service performed by another physician had to be repeated. This situation may be reported by adding modifier '77' to the repeated procedure/service.

78 Return to the Operating Room for a Related Procedure During the Postoperative Period: The physician may need to indicate that another procedure was performed during the postoperative period of the initial procedure. When this subsequent procedure is related to the first, and requires the use of the operating room, it may be reported by adding the modifier '78' to the related procedure. (For repeat procedures on the same day, see '76'.)

79 Unrelated Procedure or Service by the Same Physician During the Postoperative Period: The physician may need to indicate that the performance of a procedure or service during the postoperative period was unrelated to the original procedure. This circumstance may be reported by using the modifier '79'. (For repeat procedures on the same day, see '76'.)

80 Assistant Surgeon: Surgical assistant services may be identified by adding the modifier '80' to the usual procedure number(s).

81 Minimum Assistant Surgeon: Minimum surgical assistant services are identified by adding the modifier '81' to the usual procedure number.

82 Assistant Surgeon (when qualified resident surgeon not available): The unavailability of a qualified resident surgeon is a prerequisite for use of modifier '82' appended to the usual procedure code number(s).

90 Reference (Outside) Laboratory: When laboratory procedures are performed by a party other than the treating or reporting physician, the procedure may be identified by adding the modifier '90' to the usual procedure number.

91 Repeat Clinical Diagnostic Laboratory Test: In the course of treatment of the patient, it may be necessary to repeat the same laboratory test on the same day to obtain subsequent (multiple) test results. Under these circumstances, the laboratory test performed can be identified by its usual procedure number and the addition of the modifier '91'. **Note:** This modifier may not be used when tests are rerun to confirm initial results; due to testing problems with specimens or equipment; or for any other reason when a normal, one-time, reportable result is all that is required. This modifier may not be used when other code(s) describe a series of test results (eg, glucose tolerance tests, evocative/suppression testing). This modifier may only be used for laboratory test(s) performed more than once on the same day on the same patient.

99 Multiple Modifiers: Under certain circumstances two or more modifiers may be necessary to completely delineate a service. In such situations modifier '99' should be added to the basic procedure, and other applicable modifiers may be listed as part of the description of the service.

Anesthesia Physical Status Modifiers

The Physical Status modifiers are consistent with the American Society of Anesthesiologists ranking of patient physical status, and distinguishing various levels of complexity of the anesthesia service provided. All anesthesia services are reported by use of the anesthesia five-digit procedure code (00100-03108) with the appropriate physical status modifier appended.

Example: 00100-P1

Under certain circumstances, when another established modifier(s) is appropriate, it should be used in addition to the physical status modifier.

Example: 00100-P4-53

Physical Status Modifier P1: A normal healthy patient

Physical Status Modifier P2: A patient with mild systemic disease

Physical Status Modifier P3: A patient with severe systemic disease

Physical Status Modifier P4: A patient with severe systemic disease that is a constant threat to life

Physical Status Modifier P5: A moribund patient who is not expected to survive without the operation

Physical Status Modifier P6: A declared brain-dead patient whose organs are being removed for donor purposes

Modifiers Approved for Ambulatory Surgery Center (ASC) Hospital Outpatient Use

CPT Level I Modifiers

25 Significant, Separately Identifiable Evaluation and Management Service by the Same Physician on the Same Day of the Procedure or Other Service: The physician may need to indicate that on the day a procedure or service identified by a CPT code was performed, the patient's condition required a significant, separately identifiable E/M service above and beyond the other service provided or beyond the usual preoperative and postoperative care associated with the procedure that was performed. The E/M service may be prompted by the symptom or condition for which the procedure and/or service was provided. As such, different diagnoses are not required for reporting of the E/M services on the same date. This circumstance may be reported by adding the modifier '25' to the appropriate level of E/M service. **Note:** This modifier is not used to report an E/M service that resulted in a decision to perform surgery. See modifier '57.'

27 Multiple Outpatient Hospital E/M Encounters on the Same Date: For hospital outpatient reporting purposes, utilization of hospital resources related to separate and distinct E/M encounters performed in multiple outpatient hospital settings on the same date may be reported by adding the modifier '27' to each appropriate level outpatient and/or emergency department E/M code(s). This modifier provides a means of reporting circumstances involving evaluation and management services provided by physician(s) in more than one (multiple) outpatient hospital setting(s) (eg, hospital emergency department, clinic). **Note:** This modifier is not to be used for physician reporting of multiple E/M services performed by the same physician on the same date. For physician reporting of all outpatient evaluation and management services provided by the same physician on the same date and performed in multiple outpatient setting(s) (eg, hospital emergency department, clinic), see **Evaluation and Management, Emergency Department, or Preventive Medicine Services** codes.

50 Bilateral Procedure: Unless otherwise identified in the listings, bilateral procedures that are performed at the same operative session should be identified by adding the modifier '50' to the appropriate five digit code.

52 Reduced Services: Under certain circumstances a service or procedure is partially reduced or eliminated at the physician's discretion. Under these circumstances the service provided can be identified by its usual procedure number and the addition of the modifier '52', signifying that the service is reduced. This provides a means of reporting reduced services without disturbing the identification of the basic service. **Note:** For hospital outpatient reporting of a previously scheduled procedure/service that is partially reduced or cancelled as a result of extenuating circumstances or those that threaten the well-being of the patient prior to or after administration of anesthesia, see modifiers '73' and '74'.

58 Staged or Related Procedure or Service by the Same Physician During the Postoperative Period: The physician may need to indicate that the performance of a procedure or service during the postoperative period was: a) planned prospectively at the time of the original procedure (staged); b) more extensive than the original procedure; or c) for therapy following a diagnostic surgical procedure. This circumstance may be reported by adding the modifier '58' to the staged or related procedure. **Note:** This modifier is not used to report the treatment of a problem that requires a return to the operating room. See modifier '78.'

59 Distinct Procedural Service: Under certain circumstances, the physician may need to indicate that a procedure or service was distinct or independent from other services performed on the same day. Modifier '59' is used to identify procedures/services that are not normally reported together, but are appropriate under the circumstances. This may represent a different session or patient encounter, different procedure or surgery, different site or organ system, separate incision/excision, separate lesion, or separate injury (or area of injury in extensive injuries) not ordinarily encountered or performed on the same day by the same physician. However, when another already established modifier is appropriate it should be used rather than modifier '59.' Only if no more descriptive modifier is available, and the use of modifier '59' best explains the circumstances, should modifier '59' be used.

73 Discontinued Out-Patient Hospital/Ambulatory Surgery Center (ASC) Procedure Prior to the Administration of Anesthesia: Due to extenuating circumstances or those that threaten the well being of the patient, the physician may cancel a surgical or diagnostic procedure subsequent to the patient's surgical preparation (including sedation when provided, and being taken to the room where the procedure is to be performed), but prior to the administration of anesthesia (local, regional block(s) or general). Under these circumstances, the intended service that is prepared for but cancelled can be reported by its usual procedure number and the addition of the modifier '73'. **Note:** The elective cancellation of a service prior to the administration of anesthesia and/or surgical preparation of the patient should not be reported. For physician reporting of a discontinued procedure, see modifier '53.'

74 Discontinued Out-Patient Hospital/Ambulatory Surgery Center (ASC) Procedure After Administration of Anesthesia: Due to extenuating circumstances or those that threaten the well being of the patient, the physician may terminate a surgical or diagnostic procedure after the administration of anesthesia (local, regional block(s), general) or after the procedure was started (incision made, intubation started, scope inserted, etc). Under these circumstances, the procedure started but terminated can be reported by its usual procedure number and the addition of the modifier '74'. **Note:** The elective cancellation of a service prior to the administration of anesthesia and/or surgical preparation of the patient should not be reported. For physician reporting of a discontinued procedure, see modifier '53.'

76 Repeat Procedure by Same Physician: The physician may need to indicate that a procedure or service was repeated subsequent to the original procedure or service. This circumstance may be reported by adding the modifier '76' to the repeated procedure/service.

77 Repeat Procedure by Another Physician: The physician may need to indicate that a basic procedure or service performed by another physician had to be repeated. This situation may be reported by adding modifier '77' to the repeated procedure/service.

78 Return to the Operating Room for a Related Procedure During the Postoperative Period: The physician may need to indicate that another procedure was performed during the postoperative period of the initial procedure. When this subsequent procedure is related to the first, and requires the use of the operating room, it may be reported by adding the modifier '78' to the related procedure. (For repeat procedures on the same day, see '76'.)

79 Unrelated Procedure or Service by the Same Physician During the Postoperative Period: The physician may need to indicate that the performance of a procedure or service during the postoperative period was unrelated to the original procedure. This circumstance may be reported by using the modifier '79'. (For repeat procedures on the same day, see '76'.)

91 Repeat Clinical Diagnostic Laboratory Test: In the course of treatment of the patient, it may be necessary to repeat the same laboratory test on the same day to obtain subsequent (multiple) test results. Under these circumstances, the laboratory test performed can be identified by its usual procedure number and the addition of the modifier '91'. **Note:** This modifier may not be used when tests are rerun to confirm initial results; due to testing problems with specimens or equipment; or for any other reason when a normal, one-time, reportable result is all that is required. This modifier may not be used when other code(s) describe a series of test results (eg, glucose tolerance tests, evocative/suppression testing). This modifier may only be used for laboratory test(s) performed more than once on the same day on the same patient.

Level II (HCPCS/National) Modifiers

E1 Upper left, eyelid

E2 Lower left, eyelid

E3 Upper right, eyelid

E4 Lower right, eyelid

F1 Left hand, second digit

F2 Left hand, third digit

F3 Left hand, fourth digit

F4 Left hand, fifth digit

F5 Right hand, thumb

F6 Right hand, second digit

F7 Right hand, third digit

F8 Right hand, fourth digit

F9 Right hand, fifth digit

FA Left hand, thumb

LC Left circumflex coronary artery (Hospitals use with codes 92980-92984, 92995, 92996)

LD Left anterior descending coronary artery (Hospitals use with codes 92980-92984, 92995, 92996)

LT Left side (used to identify procedures performed on the left side of the body)

QM Ambulance service provided under arrangement by a provider of services

QN Ambulance service furnished directly by a provider of services

RC Right coronary artery (Hospitals use with codes 92980-92984, 92995, 92996)

RT Right side (used to identify procedures performed on the right side of the body)

T1 Left foot, second digit

T2 Left foot, third digit

T3 Left foot, fourth digit

T4 Left foot, fifth digit

T5 Right foot, great toe

T6 Right foot, second digit

T7 Right foot, third digit

T8 Right foot, fourth digit

T9 Right foot, fifth digit

TA Left foot, great toe

Appendix B

Summary of Additions, Deletions, and Revisions

Appendix B shows the actual changes that were made to the code descriptors. New codes appear with a bullet (●) and are indicated as "Code added." Revised codes are preceded with a triangle (▲). Within revised codes, the deleted language appears with a ~~strikethrough~~, while new text appears <u>underlined</u>.

Revisions to the headings, notes, introductory paragraphs, and cross-references are not included in this Appendix, but are identified in the main text of the book with the "▶ ◀" symbols and presented in green. Codes listed as "Grammatical change" contain minor revisions that do not alter the original intent of the codes, and therefore are not preceded with a triangle (▲).

Note: This year the starred procedure designation was removed from the CPT book. The codes affected by this change are identified throughout this Appendix with the following language: "Starred procedure designation removed." If the code descriptor is revised, in addition to the removal of the starred procedure designation, then those codes are preceded with a triangle (▲), and retain the standard revised descriptor conventions.

Evaluation and Management

▲ **99293** Initial <u>inpatient</u> pediatric critical care, 31 days up through 24 months of age, per day, for the evaluation and management of a critically ill infant or young child

▲ **99294** Subsequent <u>inpatient</u> pediatric critical care, 31 days up through 24 months of age, per day, for the evaluation and management of a critically ill infant or young child

▲ **99295** Initial <u>inpatient</u> neonatal critical care, per day, for the evaluation and management of a critically ill neonate, 30 days of age or less

▲ **99296** Subsequent <u>inpatient</u> neonatal critical care, per day, for the evaluation and management of a critically ill neonate, 30 days of age or less

Anesthesia

▲ **00528** mediastinoscopy and diagnostic thoracoscopy <u>not utilizing one lung ventilation</u>

● **00529** Code added

~~**00544**~~ ~~pleurectomy~~

● **01173** Code added

● **01958** Code added

Surgery

10040* Starred procedure designation removed

10060* Starred procedure designation removed

10080* Starred procedure designation removed

10120* Starred procedure designation removed

10140* Starred procedure designation removed

10160* Starred procedure designation removed

11000* Starred procedure designation removed

11200* Starred procedure designation removed

11300* Starred procedure designation removed

11305* Starred procedure designation removed

11310* Starred procedure designation removed

11730* Starred procedure designation removed

11900* Starred procedure designation removed

11901* Starred procedure designation removed

▲ **11100** Biopsy of skin, subcutaneous tissue and/or mucous membrane (including simple closure), unless otherwise listed ~~(separate procedure)~~; single lesion

12001* Starred procedure designation removed

12002* Starred procedure designation removed

12004* Starred procedure designation removed

12011* Starred procedure designation removed

12013* Starred procedure designation removed

12031* Starred procedure designation removed

12032* Starred procedure designation removed

12041* Starred procedure designation removed

12051* Starred procedure designation removed

15786* Starred procedure designation removed

16020* Starred procedure designation removed

16025* Starred procedure designation removed

17000* Starred procedure designation removed

17110* Starred procedure designation removed

17250* Starred procedure designation removed

17260* Starred procedure designation removed

17270* Starred procedure designation removed

17280* Starred procedure designation removed

17340* Starred procedure designation removed

17360* Starred procedure designation removed

17380* Starred procedure designation removed

19000* Starred procedure designation removed

19100* Starred procedure designation removed

20000* Starred procedure designation removed

20206* Starred procedure designation removed

▲ **20240** Biopsy, bone, <u>open</u> ~~excisional~~; superficial (eg, ilium, sternum, spinous process, ribs, trochanter of femur)

20500* Starred procedure designation removed

20501* Starred procedure designation removed

20520*	Starred procedure designation removed
20525*	Starred procedure designation removed
▲ 20550*	Injection(s); single tendon sheath, or ligament, aponeurosis (eg, plantar "fascia")
▲ 20551	single tendon origin/insertion
▲ 20552	Injection(s); single or multiple trigger point(s), one or two muscle(s)
20600*	Starred procedure designation removed
20605*	Starred procedure designation removed
20610*	Starred procedure designation removed
20650*	Starred procedure designation removed
20665*	Starred procedure designation removed
20670*	Starred procedure designation removed
● 20982	Code added
21100*	Starred procedure designation removed
21315*	Starred procedure designation removed
21355*	Starred procedure designation removed
● 21685	Code added
● 22532	Code added
● 22533	Code added
+● 22534	Code added
23700*	Starred procedure designation removed
24640*	Starred procedure designation removed
26010*	Starred procedure designation removed
26011*	Starred procedure designation removed
▲ 26356	Repair or advancement, flexor tendon, in zone 2 digital flexor tendon sheath (eg, no man's land); primary, ~~or secondary~~ without free graft, each tendon
▲ 26357	secondary, without free graft, each tendon
27086*	Starred procedure designation removed
27256*	Starred procedure designation removed
27257*	Starred procedure designation removed
27275*	Starred procedure designation removed
27570*	Starred procedure designation removed
27605*	Starred procedure designation removed
27860*	Starred procedure designation removed
28001*	Starred procedure designation removed
28002*	Starred procedure designation removed
28190*	Starred procedure designation removed
28630*	Starred procedure designation removed
28635*	Starred procedure designation removed
28660*	Starred procedure designation removed
28665*	Starred procedure designation removed
30000*	Starred procedure designation removed
30020*	Starred procedure designation removed
30200*	Starred procedure designation removed
30210*	Starred procedure designation removed
30300*	Starred procedure designation removed
30560*	Starred procedure designation removed
30801*	Starred procedure designation removed
30901*	Starred procedure designation removed
30903*	Starred procedure designation removed
30905*	Starred procedure designation removed
30906*	Starred procedure designation removed
31000*	Starred procedure designation removed
31002*	Starred procedure designation removed
▲ 31622	Bronchoscopy, ~~(~~rigid or flexible~~)~~, with or without fluoroscopic guidance; diagnostic, with or without cell washing (separate procedure)
▲ 31625	with bronchial or endobronchial biopsy(s), single or multiple sites
▲ 31628	with transbronchial lung biopsy(s), single lobe~~, with or without fluoroscopic guidance~~
▲ 31629	with transbronchial needle aspiration biopsy(s), trachea, main stem and/or lobar bronchus(i)
+● 31632	Code added
+● 31633	Code added
⊘ 32000*	Starred procedure designation removed
32400*	Starred procedure designation removed
32420*	Starred procedure designation removed
32960*	Starred procedure designation removed
33010*	Starred procedure designation removed
33011*	Starred procedure designation removed
▲ 33310	Cardiotomy, exploratory (includes removal of foreign body, atrial or ventricular thrombus); without bypass
● 34805	Code added
● 35510	Code added
● 35512	Code added
● 35522	Code added
● 35525	Code added
+● 35697	Code added
36000*	Starred procedure designation removed
▲ 36400	Venipuncture, under age 3 years, necessitating physician's skill, not to be used for routine venipuncture; femoral or jugular vein
36405*	Starred procedure designation removed
▲ 36410*	Venipuncture, ~~child over~~ age 3 years or older ~~adult~~, necessitating physician's skill (separate procedure), for diagnostic or therapeutic purposes (not to be used for routine venipuncture)
36415*	Starred procedure designation removed
36440*	Starred procedure designation removed
36470*	Starred procedure designation removed
36471*	Starred procedure designation removed
⊖ ~~36488*~~	~~Placement of central venous catheter (subclavian, jugular, or other vein) (eg, for central venous pressure, hyperalimentation, hemodialysis, or chemotherapy); percutaneous, age 2 years or under~~

⊖ ~~36489~~*	~~percutaneous, over age 2~~
⊖ ~~36490~~*	~~age 2 years or under~~
⊖ ~~36491~~*	~~cutdown, over age 2~~
~~36493~~	~~Repositioning of previously placed central venous catheter under fluoroscopic guidance~~
36510*	Starred procedure designation removed
~~36530~~	~~Insertion of implantable intravenous infusion pump~~
~~36531~~	~~Revision of implantable intravenous infusion pump~~
~~36532~~	~~Removal of implantable intravenous infusion pump~~
~~36533~~	~~Insertion of implantable venous access device, with or without subcutaneous reservoir~~
~~36534~~	~~Revision of implantable venous access device and/or subcutaneous reservoir~~
~~36535~~	~~Removal of implantable venous access device and/or subcutaneous reservoir~~
~~36536~~	~~Mechanical removal of pericatheter obstructive material (eg, fibrin sheath) from central venous device via separate venous access~~
~~36537~~	~~Mechanical removal of intraluminal (intracatheter) obstructive material from central venous device through device lumen~~
● 36555	Code added
● 36556	Code added
● 36557	Code added
● 36558	Code added
● 36560	Code added
● 36561	Code added
● 36563	Code added
● 36565	Code added
● 36566	Code added
● 36568	Code added
● 36569	Code added
● 36570	Code added
● 36571	Code added
● 36575	Code added
● 36576	Code added
● 36578	Code added
● 36580	Code added
● 36581	Code added
● 36582	Code added
● 36583	Code added
● 36584	Code added
● 36585	Code added
● 36589	Code added
● 36590	Code added
● 36595	Code added
● 36596	Code added
● 36597	Code added
36600*	Starred procedure designation removed
⊘ 36660*	Starred procedure designation removed
● 36838	Code added
● 37765	Code added
● 37766	Code added
▲ 37785	Ligation, division, and/or excision of ~~recurrent or secondary~~ varicose vein~~s (~~cluster(s)~~)~~, one leg
▲ 38208	thawing of previously frozen harvest, without washing
▲ 38209	thawing of previously frozen harvest, with washing ~~of harvest~~
38300*	Starred procedure designation removed
40800*	Starred procedure designation removed
40804*	Starred procedure designation removed
41000*	Starred procedure designation removed
41005*	Starred procedure designation removed
41250*	Starred procedure designation removed
41251*	Starred procedure designation removed
41252*	Starred procedure designation removed
41800*	Starred procedure designation removed
42000*	Starred procedure designation removed
42300*	Starred procedure designation removed
42310*	Starred procedure designation removed
42320*	Starred procedure designation removed
42400*	Starred procedure designation removed
42650*	Starred procedure designation removed
42660*	Starred procedure designation removed
42700*	Starred procedure designation removed
● 43237	Code added
● 43238	Code added
▲ 43242	with transendoscopic ultrasound-guided intramural or transmural fine needle aspiration/biopsy(s) (includes endoscopic ultrasound examination of the esophagus, stomach, and either the duodenum and/or jejunum as appropriate)
▲ 43259	with endoscopic ultrasound examination, including the esophagus, stomach, and either the duodenum and/or jejunum as appropriate
43450*	Starred procedure designation removed
▲ 43752	Naso- or oro-gastric tube placement, ~~necessitating~~ requiring physician's skill and fluoroscopic guidance (includes fluoroscopy, image documentation and report)
43760*	Starred procedure designation removed
45900*	Starred procedure designation removed
45905*	Starred procedure designation removed
45915*	Starred procedure designation removed
46030*	Starred procedure designation removed
46050*	Starred procedure designation removed
46080*	Starred procedure designation removed
46320*	Starred procedure designation removed
46500*	Starred procedure designation removed
46900*	Starred procedure designation removed

46910*	Starred procedure designation removed
47000*	Starred procedure designation removed
47133	Grammatical change
~~47134~~	~~partial, from living donor~~
● 47140	Code added
● 47141	Code added
● 47142	Code added
48102*	Starred procedure designation removed
49080*	Starred procedure designation removed
49081*	Starred procedure designation removed
49180*	Starred procedure designation removed
49400*	Starred procedure designation removed
49420*	Starred procedure designation removed
50200*	Starred procedure designation removed
50390*	Starred procedure designation removed
50398*	Starred procedure designation removed
50688*	Starred procedure designation removed
51000*	Starred procedure designation removed
51005*	Starred procedure designation removed
51600*	Starred procedure designation removed
51700*	Starred procedure designation removed
51705*	Starred procedure designation removed
51710*	Starred procedure designation removed
● 53500	Code added
53600*	Starred procedure designation removed
53601*	Starred procedure designation removed
53620*	Starred procedure designation removed
53621*	Starred procedure designation removed
53660*	Starred procedure designation removed
53661*	Starred procedure designation removed
54050*	Starred procedure designation removed
54055*	Starred procedure designation removed
54200*	Starred procedure designation removed
55000*	Starred procedure designation removed
55100*	Starred procedure designation removed
56405*	Starred procedure designation removed
56420*	Starred procedure designation removed
56605*	Starred procedure designation removed
+ 56606*	Starred procedure designation removed
56720*	Starred procedure designation removed
57020*	Starred procedure designation removed
57100*	Starred procedure designation removed
57150*	Starred procedure designation removed
57160*	Starred procedure designation removed
57400*	Starred procedure designation removed
57410*	Starred procedure designation removed
● 57425	Code added
57452*	Starred procedure designation removed
57454*	Starred procedure designation removed
57500*	Starred procedure designation removed
57511*	Starred procedure designation removed
57800*	Starred procedure designation removed
58100*	Starred procedure designation removed
58300*	Starred procedure designation removed
▲ 58340*	Catheterization and introduction of saline or contrast material for ~~hysterosonography~~ saline infusion sonohysterography (SIS) or hysterosalpingography
58350*	Starred procedure designation removed
59000*	Starred procedure designation removed
59020*	Starred procedure designation removed
59030*	Starred procedure designation removed
● 59070	Code added
● 59072	Code added
● 59074	Code added
● 59076	Code added
● 59897	Code added
60000*	Starred procedure designation removed
60100*	Starred procedure designation removed
61000*	Starred procedure designation removed
61001*	Starred procedure designation removed
61020*	Starred procedure designation removed
61026*	Starred procedure designation removed
61050*	Starred procedure designation removed
61055*	Starred procedure designation removed
61070*	Starred procedure designation removed
61105*	Starred procedure designation removed
⊘ 61107*	Starred procedure designation removed
⊘ 61210*	Starred procedure designation removed
● 61537	Code added
▲ 61538	for lobectomy, temporal lobe, with electrocorticography during surgery~~, temporal lobe~~
▲ 61539	for lobectomy, other than temporal lobe, partial or total, with electrocorticography during surgery~~, other than temporal lobe, partial or total~~
● 61540	Code added
▲ 61543	for partial or subtotal (functional) hemispherectomy
● 61566	Code added
● 61567	Code added
~~61862~~	~~Twist drill, burr hole, craniotomy, or craniectomy for stereotactic implantation of one neurostimulator electrode array in subcortical site (eg, thalamus, globus pallidus, subthalamic nucleus, periventricular, periaqueductal gray); with use of intraoperative microelectrode recording~~
● 61863	Code added

+● 61864	Code added
● 61867	Code added
+● 61868	Code added
62268*	Starred procedure designation removed
62269*	Starred procedure designation removed
62270*	Starred procedure designation removed
62272*	Starred procedure designation removed
62280*	Starred procedure designation removed
62281*	Starred procedure designation removed
62282*	Starred procedure designation removed
⊘ 62284*	Starred procedure designation removed
62290*	Starred procedure designation removed
62291*	Starred procedure designation removed
● 63101	Code added
● 63102	Code added
+● 63103	Code added
▲ 63173	to peritoneal or pleural space
64400*	Starred procedure designation removed
64402*	Starred procedure designation removed
64405*	Starred procedure designation removed
64408*	Starred procedure designation removed
64410*	Starred procedure designation removed
64412*	Starred procedure designation removed
64413*	Starred procedure designation removed
64415*	Starred procedure designation removed
64417*	Starred procedure designation removed
64418*	Starred procedure designation removed
64420*	Starred procedure designation removed
64421*	Starred procedure designation removed
64425*	Starred procedure designation removed
64430*	Starred procedure designation removed
64435*	Starred procedure designation removed
64445*	Starred procedure designation removed
● 64449	Code added
64450*	Starred procedure designation removed
64505*	Starred procedure designation removed
64508*	Starred procedure designation removed
64510*	Starred procedure designation removed
● 64517	Code added
64520*	Starred procedure designation removed
64530*	Starred procedure designation removed
▲ 64680	Destruction by neurolytic agent, ~~celiac plexus,~~ with or without radiologic monitoring; celiac plexus
● 64681	Code added
65205*	Starred procedure designation removed
65210*	Starred procedure designation removed
65220*	Starred procedure designation removed
65222*	Starred procedure designation removed
65270*	Starred procedure designation removed
65410*	Starred procedure designation removed
65430*	Starred procedure designation removed
65435	Starred procedure designation removed
● 65780	Code added
● 65781	Code added
● 65782	Code added
65800*	Starred procedure designation removed
65805*	Starred procedure designation removed
66020*	Starred procedure designation removed
66030*	Starred procedure designation removed
67500*	Starred procedure designation removed
67515*	Starred procedure designation removed
67700*	Starred procedure designation removed
67710*	Starred procedure designation removed
67715*	Starred procedure designation removed
67810*	Starred procedure designation removed
67820*	Starred procedure designation removed
67825*	Starred procedure designation removed
67840*	Starred procedure designation removed
67850*	Starred procedure designation removed
● 67912	Code added
▲ 67916	~~blepharoplasty,~~ excision tarsal wedge
▲ 67917	~~blepharoplasty,~~ extensive (eg, ~~Kuhnt-Szymanowski or~~ tarsal strip operations)
▲ 67923	~~blepharoplasty,~~ excision tarsal wedge
▲ 67924	~~blepharoplasty,~~ extensive (eg, ~~Wheeler operation~~ tarsal strip or capsulopalpebral fascia repairs operation)
68135*	Starred procedure designation removed
68200*	Starred procedure designation removed
● 68371	Code added
68440*	Starred procedure designation removed
68801*	Starred procedure designation removed
68810*	Starred procedure designation removed
68840*	Starred procedure designation removed
68850*	Starred procedure designation removed
69000*	Starred procedure designation removed
69020*	Starred procedure designation removed
69420*	Starred procedure designation removed
69421*	Starred procedure designation removed
69433*	Starred procedure designation removed

Radiology

▲ 70250 Radiologic examination, skull; less than four views~~, with or without stereo~~

▲ 70260 complete, minimum of four views~~, with or without stereo~~

● 70557 Code added

● 70558 Code added

● 70559 Code added

▲ 72270 Myelography, ~~entire spinal canal~~ two or more regions (eg, lumbar/thoracic, cervical/thoracic, lumbar/cervical, lumbar/thoracic/cervical), radiological supervision and interpretation

▲ 75860 Venography, venous sinus (eg, petrosal and inferior sagittal) or jugular, catheter, radiological supervision and interpretation

✚● 75998 Code added

✚● 76082 Code added

✚● 76083 Code added

✚ ~~76085~~ ~~Digitization of film radiographic images with computer analysis for lesion detection and further physician review for interpretation, mammography (List separately in addition to code for primary procedure)~~

▲ 76362 ~~Computerized~~ Computed ~~axial~~ tomographi~~c~~y guidance for, and monitoring of, visceral tissue ablation

76375 Grammatical Change

▲ 76394 Magnetic resonance guidance for, and monitoring of visceral tissue ablation

~~76490~~ ~~Ultrasound guidance for, and monitoring of, tissue ablation~~

● 76514 Code added

▲ 76831 ~~Hysterosonography~~ Saline infusion sonohysterography (SIS), ~~with or without~~ including color flow Doppler, when performed

▲ 76872 ~~Echography~~ Ultrasound, transrectal;

✚● 76937 Code added

● 76940 Code added

▲ 78800 Radiopharmaceutical localization of tumor or distribution of radiopharmaceutical agent(s); limited area

▲ 78802 whole body, single day imaging

● 78804 Code added

▲ 79100 Radiopharmaceutical therapy, polycythemia vera, chronic leukemia, each treatment by intravenous injection

▲ 79400 Radiopharmaceutical therapy, nonthyroid, nonhematologic by intravenous injection

● 79403 Code added

Pathology and Laboratory

▲ 83716 high resolution fractionation and quantitation of lipoproteins ~~cholesterols~~ including lipoprotein subclasses when performed (eg, electrophoresis, nuclear magnetic resonance, ultracentrifugation)

▲ 84155 Protein~~;~~, total, except by refractometry; serum

● 84156 Code added

● 84157 Code added

▲ 84160 Protein, total, ~~refractrometric~~ by refractometry, any source

▲ 84165 Protein, electrophoretic fractionation and quantitation

● 85055 Code added

● 85396 Code added

▲ 87040 Culture, bacterial; blood, aerobic, with isolation and presumptive identification of isolates (includes anaerobic culture, if appropriate)

▲ 87045 ~~feces~~ stool, aerobic, with isolation and preliminary examination (eg, KIA, LIA), Salmonella and Shigella species

▲ 87046 stool, aerobic, additional pathogens, isolation and ~~preliminary examination (eg, Campylobacter, Yersinia, Vibrio, E. coli 0157), each plate~~ presumptive identification of isolates

▲ 87070 any other source except urine, blood or stool, aerobic, with isolation and presumptive identification of isolates

▲ 87075 any source, except blood, anaerobic with isolation and presumptive identification of isolates

● 87269 Code added

▲ 87272 cryptosporidium~~/giardia~~

▲ 87328 cryptosporidium~~/giardia~~

● 87329 Code added

● 87660 Code added

● 88112 Code added

✚▲ 88312 Special stains (List separately in addition to code for ~~surgical pathology examination~~ primary service); Group I for microorganisms (eg, Gridley, acid fast, methenamine silver), each

▲ 88342 ~~Immunocytochemistry~~ Immunohistochemistry (including tissue immunoperoxidase), each antibody

▲ 88358 tumor (eg, DNA ploidy)

● 88361 Code added

▲ 89055 Leukocyte assessment ~~count~~, fecal, qualitative or semiquantitative

● 89220 Code added

● 89225 Code added

● 89230 Code added

● 89235 Code added

● 89240 Code added

▲ 89250 Culture ~~and fertilization~~ of oocyte(s)/embryo(s), less than 4 days;

▲ 89251 with co-culture of oocyte(s)/embryo(s)

~~89252~~ ~~Assisted oocyte fertilization, microtechnique (any method)~~

~~89256~~ ~~Preparation of cryopreserved embryos for transfer (includes thaw)~~

▲ 89258 Cryopreservation; embryo(s)

● 89268 Code added

● 89272 Code added

● 89280 Code added

● 89281 Code added

● 89290 Code added

● 89291 Code added

● 89335 Code added

● 89342 Code added

● 89343 Code added

● **89344** Code added

● **89346** Code added

~~89350~~ ~~Sputum, obtaining specimen, aerosol induced technique (separate procedure)~~

● **89352** Code added

● **89353** Code added

● **89354** Code added

~~89355~~ ~~Starch granules, feces~~

● **89356** Code added

~~89360~~ ~~Sweat collection by iontophoresis~~

~~89365~~ ~~Water load test~~

~~89399~~ ~~Unlisted miscellaneous pathology test~~

Medicine

⊘● **90655** Code added

⊘▲ **90657** Influenza virus vaccine, split virus, for children 6-35 months of age ~~dosage~~, for intramuscular ~~or jet~~ ~~injection~~ use

⊘▲ **90658** Influenza virus vaccine, split virus, for use in individuals 3 years of age and above ~~dosage~~, for intramuscular ~~or jet~~ ~~injection~~ use

⊘ **~~90659~~** ~~Influenza virus vaccine, whole virus, for intramuscular or jet injection use~~

⊘▲ **90693** Typhoid vaccine, acetone-killed, dried (AKD), for subcutaneous ~~or jet injection~~ use (U.S. military)

● **90698** Code added

⊘▲ **90703** Tetanus toxoid adsorbed, for intramuscular ~~or jet injection~~ use

⊘▲ **90704** Mumps virus vaccine, live, for subcutaneous ~~or jet injection~~ use

⊘▲ **90705** Measles virus vaccine, live, for subcutaneous ~~or jet injection~~ use

⊘▲ **90706** Rubella virus vaccine, live, for subcutaneous ~~or jet injection~~ use

⊘▲ **90707** Measles, mumps and rubella virus vaccine (MMR), live, for subcutaneous ~~or jet injection~~ use

⊘▲ **90708** Measles and rubella virus vaccine, live, for subcutaneous ~~or jet injection~~ use

● **90715** Code added

⊘▲ **90718** Tetanus and diphtheria toxoids (Td) adsorbed for use in individuals seven years or older, for intramuscular ~~or jet injection~~ use

⊘▲ **90727** Plague vaccine, for intramuscular ~~or jet injection~~ use

⊘▲ **90733** Meningococococcal polysaccharide vaccine (any group(s)), for subcutaneous ~~or jet injection~~ use

● **90734** Code added

● **91110** Code added

95990 Grammatical change

● **95991** Code added

▲ **97537** Community/work reintegration training (eg, shopping, transportation, money management, avocational activities and/or work environment/modification analysis, work task analysis, use of assistive technology device/adaptive equipment), direct one-on-one contact by provider, each 15 minutes

● **97755** Code added

▲ **99024*** Postoperative follow-up visit, normally included in the surgical package, to indicate that an evaluation and management service was performed during a postoperative period for a reason(s) related to the original procedure ~~included in global service~~

~~99025*~~ ~~Initial (new patient) visit when starred surgical procedure constitutes major service at that visit~~

▲ **99050** Services requested after posted office hours in addition to basic service

▲ **99512** Home visit for hemodialysis~~, per diem~~

~~99551~~ ~~Home infusion for pain management (intravenous or subcutaneous), per visit~~

~~99552~~ ~~Home infusion for pain management (epidural or intrathecal), per visit~~

~~99553~~ ~~Home infusion for tocolytic therapy, per visit~~

~~99554~~ ~~Home infusion for hematopoietic hormones (eg, erythropoietin, G-CSF, GM-CSF) or platelets, per visit~~

~~99555~~ ~~Home infusion for chemotherapy, per visit~~

~~99556~~ ~~Home infusion for antibiotics/antifungals/antivirals, per visit~~

~~99557~~ ~~Home infusion of continuous anticoagulant therapy (eg, heparin), per visit~~

~~99558~~ ~~Home infusion of immunotherapy, per visit~~

~~99559~~ ~~Home infusion of peritoneal dialysis, per visit~~

~~99560~~ ~~Home infusion of enteral nutrition, per visit~~

~~99561~~ ~~Home infusion of hydration therapy, per visit~~

~~99562~~ ~~Home infusion of total parenteral nutrition, per visit~~

~~99563~~ ~~Home administration of aerosolized pentamidine, per visit~~

~~99564~~ ~~Home infusion for anti-hemophilic agents (eg, Factor VIII), per visit~~

~~99565~~ ~~Home infusion of alpha-1-proteinase inhibitor (eg, Prolastin), per visit~~

~~99566~~ ~~Home infusion for uninterrupted, long-term intravenous treatment (eg, epoprostenol), per visit~~

~~99567~~ ~~Home infusion of sympathomimetic agents (eg, dobutamine), per visit~~

~~99568~~ ~~Home infusion of miscellaneous drugs, per visit~~

✚ **~~99569~~** ~~Home infusion, each additional therapy given on same day (List separately in addition to code for primary visit)~~

● **99601** Code added

✚● **99602** Code added

Category II Codes

● **0001F** Code added

● **0002F** Code added

● **0003F** Code added

● **0004F** Code added

● **0005F** Code added

● **0006F** Code added

● **0007F** Code added

● **0008F** Code added

● **0009F** Code added

● **0010F** Code added

● **0011F** Code added

Category III Codes

0001T	Grammatical change
~~0002T~~	~~aorto-uni-iliac or aorto-unifemoral prosthesis~~
~~0025T~~	~~Determination of corneal thickness (eg, pachymetry) with interpretation and report, bilateral~~
0044T	Grammatical change
● 0045T	Code added
● 0046T	Code added
● 0047T	Code added
● 0048T	Code added
+● 0049T	Code added
● 0050T	Code added
● 0051T	Code added
● 0052T	Code added
● 0053T	Code added
+● 0054T	Code added
+● 0055T	Code added
+● 0056T	Code added
● 0057T	Code added
● 0058T	Code added
● 0059T	Code added
● 0060T	Code added
● 0061T	Code added

Appendix C

Clinical Examples

As described in *CPT 2004*, clinical examples of the CPT codes for Evaluation and Management (E/M) services are intended to be an important element of the coding system. The clinical examples, when used with the E/M descriptors contained in the full text of *CPT*, provide a comprehensive and powerful tool for physicians to report the services provided to their patients.

The American Medical Association is pleased to provide you with these clinical examples for *CPT 2004*. The clinical examples that are provided in this supplement are limited to Office or Other Outpatient Services, Hospital Inpatient Services, Consultations, Critical Care, Prolonged Services and Care Plan Oversight.

These clinical examples do not encompass the entire scope of medical practice. Inclusion or exclusion of any particular specialty group does not infer any judgment of importance or lack thereof; nor does it limit the applicability of the example to any particular specialty.

Of utmost importance is that these clinical examples are just that: examples. A particular patient encounter, depending on the specific circumstances, must be judged by the services provided by the physician for that particular patient. Simply because the patient's complaints, symptoms, or diagnoses match those of a particular clinical example, does not automatically assign that patient encounter to that particular level of service. The three key components (history, examination, and medical decision making) must be met and documented in the medical record to report a particular level of service.

Office or Other Outpatient Services

New Patient

99201 Initial office visit for a 50-year-old male from out-of-town who needs a prescription refill for a nonsteroidal anti-inflammatory drug. (Anesthesiology)

Initial office visit for a 40-year-old female, new patient, requesting information about local pain clinics. (Anesthesiology/Pain Medicine)

Initial office visit for a 10-year-old girl for determination of visual acuity as part of a summer camp physical (does not include determination of refractive error). (Ophthalmology)

Initial office visit for an out-of-town patient requiring topical refill. (Dermatology)

Initial office visit for a 65-year-old male for reassurance about an isolated seborrheic keratosis on upper back. (Plastic Surgery)

Initial office visit for an out-of-state visitor who needs refill of topical steroid to treat lichen planus. (Dermatology)

Initial office visit for an 86-year-old male, out-of-town visitor, who needs prescription refilled for an anal skin preparation that he forgot. (General Surgery/Colon & Rectal Surgery)

Initial office visit for a transient patient with alveolar osteitis for repacking. (Oral & Maxillofacial Surgery)

Initial office visit for a patient with a pedunculated lesion of the neck which is unsightly. (Dermatology)

Initial office visit for a 10-year-old male, for limited subungual hematoma not requiring drainage. (Internal Medicine)

Initial office visit with an out-of-town visitor who needs a prescription refilled because she forgot her hay fever medication. (Allergy & Immunology/Internal Medicine)

Initial office visit with a 9-month-old female with diaper rash. (Pediatrics)

Initial office visit with a 10-year-old male with severe rash and itching for the past 24 hours, positive history for contact with poison oak 48 hours prior to the visit. (Family Medicine)

Initial office visit with a 5-year-old female to remove sutures from simple wound placed by another physician. (Plastic Surgery)

Initial office visit for a 22-year-old male with a small area of sunburn requiring first aid. (Dermatology/Family Medicine/Internal Medicine)

Initial office visit for the evaluation and management of a contusion of a finger. (Orthopaedic Surgery)

99202 Initial office visit for a 13-year-old patient with comedopapular acne of the face unresponsive to over-the-counter medications. (Family Medicine)

Initial office visit for a patient with a clinically benign lesion or nodule of the lower leg which has been present for many years. (Dermatology)

Initial office visit for a patient with a circumscribed patch of dermatitis of the leg. (Dermatology)

Initial office visit for a patient with papulosquamous eruption of elbows. (Dermatology)

Initial office visit for a 9-year-old patient with erythematous, grouped, vesicular eruption of the lip of three days' duration. (Pediatrics)

Initial office visit for an 18-year-old male referred by an orthodontist for advice regarding removal of four wisdom teeth. (Oral & Maxillofacial Surgery)

Initial office visit for a 14-year-old male, who was referred by his orthodontist, for advice on the exposure of impacted maxillary cuspids. (Oral & Maxillofacial Surgery)

Initial office visit for a patient presenting with itching patches on the wrists and ankles. (Dermatology)

Initial office visit for a 30-year-old male for evaluation and discussion of treatment of rhinophyma. (Plastic Surgery)

Initial office visit for a 16-year-old male with severe cystic acne, new patient. (Dermatology)

Initial office evaluation for gradual hearing loss, 58-year-old male, history and physical examination, with interpretation of complete audiogram, air bone, etc. (Otolaryngology)

Initial evaluation and management of recurrent urinary infection in female. (Internal Medicine)

Initial office visit with a 10-year-old girl with history of chronic otitis media and a draining ear. (Pediatrics)

Initial office visit for a 10-year-old female with acute maxillary sinusitis. (Family Medicine)

Initial office visit for a patient with recurring episodes of herpes simplex who has developed a clustering of vesicles on the upper lip. (Internal Medicine)

Initial office visit for a 25-year-old patient with single season allergic rhinitis. (Allergy & Immunology)

Initial office visit to plan transient dialysis for a 56-year-old stable dialysis patient who has accompanying records. (Nephrology)

99203 Initial office visit for a 76-year-old male with a stasis ulcer of three months' duration. (Dermatology)

Initial office visit for a 30-year-old female with pain in the lateral aspect of the forearm. (Physical Medicine & Rehabilitation)

Initial office visit for a 15-year-old patient with a four-year history of moderate comedopapular acne of the face, chest, and back with early scarring. Discussion of use of systemic medication. (Dermatology)

Initial office visit for a patient with papulosquamous eruption of the elbow with pitting of nails and itchy scalp. (Dermatology)

Initial office visit for a 57-year-old female who complains of painful parotid swelling for one week's duration. (Oral & Maxillofacial Surgery)

Initial office visit for a patient with an ulcerated non-healing lesion or nodule on the tip of the nose. (Dermatology)

Initial office visit for a patient with dermatitis of the antecubital and popliteal fossae. (Dermatology)

Initial office visit for a 22-year-old female with irregular menses. (Family Medicine)

Initial office visit for a 50-year-old female with dyspepsia and nausea. (Family Medicine)

Initial office visit for a 53-year-old laborer with degenerative joint disease of the knee with no prior treatment. (Orthopaedic Surgery)

Initial office visit for a 60-year-old male with Dupuytren's contracture of one hand with multiple digit involvement. (Orthopaedic Surgery)

Initial office visit for a 33-year-old male with painless gross hematuria without cystoscopy. (Internal Medicine)

Initial office visit for a 55-year-old female with chronic blepharitis. There is a history of use of many medications. (Ophthalmology)

Initial office visit for an 18-year-old female with a two-day history of acute conjunctivitis. Extensive history of possible exposures, prior normal ocular history, and medication use is obtained. (Ophthalmology)

Initial office visit for a 14-year-old male with unilateral anterior knee pain. (Physical Medicine & Rehabilitation)

Initial office visit of an adult who presents with symptoms of an upper-respiratory infection that has progressed to unilateral purulent nasal discharge and discomfort in the right maxillary teeth. (Otolaryngology, Head & Neck Surgery)

Initial office visit of a 40-year-old female with symptoms of atopic allergies including eye and sinus congestion, often associated with infections. She would like to be tested for allergies. (Otolaryngology, Head & Neck Surgery)

Initial office visit of a 65-year-old with nasal stuffiness. (Otolaryngology, Head & Neck Surgery)

Initial office visit for initial evaluation of a 48-year-old man with recurrent low back pain radiating to the leg. (General Surgery)

Initial office visit for evaluation, diagnosis and management of painless gross hematuria in a new patient, without cystoscopy. (Internal Medicine)

Initial office visit with couple for counseling concerning voluntary vasectomy for sterility. Spent 30 minutes discussing procedure, risks and benefits, and answering questions. (Urology)

Initial office visit of a 49-year-old male with nasal obstruction. Detailed exam with topical anesthesia. (Plastic Surgery)

Initial office visit for evaluation of a 13-year-old female with progressive scoliosis. (Physical Medicine & Rehabilitation)

Initial office visit for a 21-year-old female desiring counseling and evaluation of initiation of contraception. (Family Practice/Internal Medicine/Obstetrics & Gynecology)

Initial office visit for a 49-year-old male presenting with painless blood per rectum associated with bowel movement. (Colon & Rectal Surgery)

Initial office visit for a 19-year-old football player with three-day-old acute knee injury; now with swelling and pain. (Orthopaedic Surgery)

99204 Initial office visit for a 13-year-old female with progressive scoliosis. (Orthopaedic Surgery)

Initial office visit for a 34-year-old female with primary infertility for evaluation and counseling. (Obstetrics & Gynecology)

Initial office visit for a 6-year-old male with multiple upper respiratory infections. (Allergy & Immunology)

Initial office visit for a patient with generalized dermatitis of 80 percent of the body surface area. (Dermatology)

Initial office visit for an adolescent who was referred by school counselor because of repeated skipping school. (Psychiatry)

Initial office visit for a 50-year-old machinist with a generalized eruption. (Dermatology)

Initial office visit for a 45-year-old female who has been abstinent from alcohol and benzodiazepines for three months but complains of headaches, insomnia, and anxiety. (Psychiatry)

Initial office visit for a 60-year-old male with recent change in bowel habits, weight loss, and abdominal pain. (Abdominal Surgery/General Surgery)

Initial office visit for a 50-year-old male with an aortic aneurysm who is considering surgery. (General Surgery)

Initial office visit for a 17-year-old female with depression. (Internal Medicine)

Initial office visit of a 40-year-old with chronic draining ear, imbalance, and probable cholesteatoma. (Otolaryngology, Head & Neck Surgery)

Initial office visit for initial evaluation of a 63-year-old male with chest pain on exertion. (Cardiology/Internal Medicine)

Initial office visit for evaluation of a 70-year-old patient with recent onset of episodic confusion. (Internal Medicine)

Initial office visit for a 7-year-old female with juvenile diabetes mellitus, new to area, past history of hospitalization times three. (Pediatrics)

Initial office visit of a 50-year-old female with progressive solid food dysphagia. (Gastroenterology)

Initial office visit for a 34-year-old patient with primary infertility, including counseling. (Obstetrics & Gynecology)

Initial office visit for evaluation of a 70-year-old female with polyarthralgia. (Rheumatology)

Initial office visit for a patient with papulosquamous eruption involving 60 percent of the cutaneous surface with joint pain. Combinations of topical and systemic treatments discussed. (Dermatology)

99205 Initial office visit for a patient with disseminated lupus erythematosus with kidney disease, edema, purpura, and scarring lesions on the extremities plus cardiac symptoms. (Dermatology/General Surgery/Internal Medicine)

Initial office visit for a 25-year-old female with systemic lupus erythematosus, fever, seizures, and profound thrombocytopenia. (Rheumatology/Allergy & Immunology)

Initial office visit for an adult with multiple cutaneous blisters, denuded secondarily infected ulcerations, oral lesions, weight loss, and increasing weakness refractory to high dose corticosteroid. Initiation of new immunosuppressive therapy. (Dermatology)

Initial office visit for a 28-year-old male with systemic vasculitis and compromised circulation to the limbs. (Rheumatology)

Initial office visit for a 41-year-old female new to the area requesting rheumatologic care, on disability due to scleroderma and recent hospitalization for malignant hypertension. (Rheumatology)

Initial office visit for a 52-year-old female with acute four extremity weakness and shortness of breath one week post-flu vaccination. (Physical Medicine & Rehabilitation)

Initial office visit for a 60-year-old male with previous back surgery; now presents with back and pelvic pain, two-month history of bilateral progressive calf and thigh tightness and weakness when walking, causing several falls. (Orthopaedic Surgery)

Initial office visit for an adolescent referred from ER after making suicide gesture. (Psychiatry)

Initial office visit for a 49-year-old female with a history of headaches and dependence on opioids. She reports weight loss, progressive headache, and depression. (Psychiatry)

Initial office visit for a 50-year-old female with symptoms of rash, swellings, recurrent arthritic complaints, and diarrhea and lymphadenopathy. Patient has had a 25 lb. weight loss and was recently camping in the Amazon. (Allergy & Immunology)

Initial office visit for a 34-year-old uremic Type I diabetic patient referred for ESRD modality assessment and planning. (Nephrology)

Initial office visit for a 75-year-old female with neck and bilateral shoulder pain, brisk deep tendon reflexes, and stress incontinence. (Physical Medicine & Rehabilitation)

Initial office visit for an 8-year-old male with cerebral palsy and spastic quadriparesis. (Physical Medicine & Rehabilitation)

Initial office visit for a 73-year-old male with known prostate malignancy, who presents with severe back pain and a recent onset of lower extremity weakness. (Physical Medicine & Rehabilitation)

Initial office visit for a 38-year-old male with paranoid delusions and a history of alcohol abuse. (Psychiatry)

Initial office visit for a 12-week-old with bilateral hip dislocations and bilateral club feet. (Orthopaedic Surgery)

Initial office visit for a 29-year-old female with acute orbital congestion, eyelid retraction, and bilateral visual loss from optic neuropathy. (Ophthalmology)

Initial office visit for a 70-year-old diabetic patient with progressive visual field loss, advanced optic disc cupping and neovascularization of retina. (Ophthalmology)

Initial office visit for a newly diagnosed Type I diabetic patient. (Endocrinology)

Initial office evaluation of a 65-year-old female with exertional chest pain, intermittent claudication, syncope and a murmur of aortic stenosis. (Cardiology)

Initial office visit for a 73-year-old male with an unexplained 20 lb. weight loss. (Hematology/Oncology)

Initial office evaluation, patient with systemic lupus erythematosus, fever, seizures and profound thrombocytopenia. (Allergy & Immunology/Internal Medicine/Rheumatology)

Initial office evaluation and management of patient with systemic vasculitis and compromised circulation to the limbs. (Rheumatology)

Initial office visit for a 24-year-old homosexual male who has a fever, a cough, and shortness of breath. (Infectious Disease)

Initial outpatient evaluation of a 69-year-old male with severe chronic obstructive pulmonary disease, congestive heart failure, and hypertension. (Family Medicine)

Initial office visit for a 17-year-old female, who is having school problems and has told a friend she is considering suicide. The patient and her family are consulted in regard to treatment options. (Psychiatry)

Initial office visit for a female with severe hirsutism, amenorrhea, weight loss and a desire to have children. (Endocrinology/Obstetrics & Gynecology)

Initial office visit for a 42-year-old male on hypertensive medication, newly arrived to the area, with diastolic blood pressure of 110, history of recurrent calculi, episodic headaches, intermittent chest pain and orthopnea. (Internal Medicine)

Established Patient

99211 Office visit for an 82-year-old female, established patient, for a monthly B12 injection with documented Vitamin B12 deficiency. (Geriatrics/Internal Medicine/Family Medicine)

Office visit for a 50-year-old male, established patient, for removal of uncomplicated facial sutures. (Plastic Surgery)

Office visit for an established patient who lost prescription for lichen planus. Returned for new copy. (Dermatology)

Office visit for an established patient undergoing orthodontics who complains of a wire which is irritating his/her cheek and asks you to check it. (Oral & Maxillofacial Surgery)

Office visit for a 50-year-old female, established patient, seen for her gold injection by the nurse. (Rheumatology)

Office visit for a 73-year-old female, established patient, with pernicious anemia for weekly B12 injection. (Gastroenterology)

Office visit for an established patient for dressing change on a skin biopsy. (Dermatology)

Office visit for a 19-year-old, established patient, for removal of sutures from a two cm. laceration of forehead, which you placed four days ago in ER. (Plastic Surgery)

Office visit of a 20-year-old female, established patient, who receives an allergy vaccine injection and is observed for a reaction by the nurse. (Otolaryngology, Head & Neck Surgery)

Office visit for a 45-year-old male, established patient, with chronic renal failure for the administration of erythropoietin. (Nephrology)

Office visit for an established patient, a Peace Corps enlistee, who requests documentation that third molars have been removed. (Oral & Maxillofacial Surgery)

Office visit for a 69-year-old female, established patient, for partial removal of antibiotic gauze from an infected wound site. (Plastic Surgery)

Office visit for a 9-year-old, established patient, successfully treated for impetigo, requiring release to return to school. (Dermatology/Pediatrics)

Office visit for an established patient requesting a return-to-work certificate for resolving contact dermatitis. (Dermatology)

Office visit for an established patient who is performing glucose monitoring and wants to check accuracy of machine with lab blood glucose by technician who checks accuracy and function of patient machine. (Endocrinology)

Follow-up office visit for a 65-year-old female with a chronic indwelling percutaneous nephrostomy catheter seen for routine pericatheter skin care and dressing change. (Interventional Radiology)

Outpatient visit with 19-year-old male, established patient, for supervised drug screen. (Addiction Medicine)

Office visit with 12-year-old male, established patient, for cursory check of hematoma one day after venipuncture. (Internal Medicine)

Office visit with 31-year-old female, established patient, for return to work certificate. (Anesthesiology)

Office visit for a 42-year-old, established patient, to read tuberculin test results. (Allergy & Immunology)

Office visit for 14-year-old, established patient, to re-dress an abrasion. (Orthopaedic Surgery)

Office visit for a 45-year-old female, established patient, for a blood pressure check. (Obstetrics & Gynecology)

Office visit for a 23-year-old, established patient, for instruction in use of peak flow meter. (Allergy & Immunology)

Office visit for prescription refill for a 35-year-old female, established patient, with schizophrenia who is stable but has run out of neuroleptic and is scheduled to be seen in a week. (Psychiatry)

99212 Office visit for an 11-year-old, established patient, seen in follow-up for mild comedonal acne of the cheeks on topical desquamating agents. (Dermatology/Family Medicine/Pediatrics)

Office visit for a 10-year-old female, established patient, who has been swimming in a lake, now presents with a one-day history of left ear pain with purulent drainage. (Family Medicine)

Office visit of a child, established patient, with chronic secretory otitis media. (Otolaryngology, Head & Neck Surgery)

Office visit for an established patient seen in follow-up of clearing patch of localized contact dermatitis. (Family Medicine/Dermatology)

Office visit for an established patient returning for evaluation of response to treatment of lichen planus on wrists and ankles. (Dermatology)

Office visit for an established patient with tinea pedis being treated with topical therapy. (Dermatology)

Office visit for an established patient with localized erythematous plaque of psoriasis with topical hydration. (Dermatology)

Office visit for a 50-year-old male, established patient, recently seen for acute neck pain, diagnosis of spondylosis, responding to physical therapy and intermittent cervical traction. Returns for evaluation for return to work. (Neurology)

Office visit for an established patient with recurring episodes of herpes simplex who has developed a clustering of vesicles on the upper lip. (Oral & Maxillofacial Surgery)

Evaluation for a 50-year-old male, established patient, who has experienced a recurrence of knee pain after he discontinued NSAID. (Anesthesiology/Pain Medicine)

Office visit for an established patient with an irritated skin tag for reassurance. (Dermatology)

Office visit for a 40-year-old, established patient, who has experienced a systemic allergic reaction following administration of immunotherapy. The dose must be readjusted. (Allergy & Immunology)

Office visit for a 33-year-old, established patient, for contusion and abrasion of lower extremity. (Orthopaedic Surgery)

Office visit for a 22-year-old male, established patient, one month after I & D of "wrestler's ear." (Plastic Surgery)

Office visit for a 21-year-old, established patient, who is seen in follow-up after antibiotic therapy for acute bacterial tonsillitis. (Otolaryngology, Head & Neck Surgery)

Office visit for a 4-year-old, established patient, with tympanostomy tubes, check-up. (Otolaryngology, Head & Neck Surgery)

Office visit for an established patient who has had needle aspiration of a peritonsillar abscess. (Otolaryngology, Head & Neck Surgery)

Follow-up office examination for evaluation and treatment of acute draining ear in a 5-year-old with tympanotomy tubes. (Otolaryngology, Head & Neck Surgery)

Office visit, established patient, 6-year-old with sore throat and headache. (Family Medicine/Pediatrics)

Office evaluation for possible purulent bacterial conjunctivitis with one- to two-day history of redness and discharge, 16-year-old female, established patient. (Pediatrics/Internal Medicine/Family Medicine)

Office visit with a 65-year-old female, established patient, returns for three-week follow-up for resolving severe ankle sprain. (Orthopaedic Surgery)

Office visit, sore throat, fever and fatigue in a 19-year-old college student, established patient. (Internal Medicine)

Office visit with a 33-year-old female, established patient, recently started on treatment for hemorrhoidal complaints, for re-evaluation. (Colon & Rectal Surgery)

Office visit with a 36-year-old male, established patient, for follow-up on effectiveness of medicine management of oral candidiasis. (Oral & Maxillofacial Surgery)

Office visit for a 27-year-old female, established patient, with complaints of vaginal itching. (Obstetrics & Gynecology)

Office visit for a 65-year-old male, established patient, with eruptions on both arms from poison oak exposure. (Allergy & Immunology/Internal Medicine)

99213 Office visit for an established patient with new lesions of lichen planus in spite of topical therapies. (Dermatology)

Office visit for the quarterly follow-up of a 45-year-old male with stable chronic asthma requiring regular drug therapy. (Allergy & Immunology)

Office visit for a 13-year-old, established patient, with comedopapular acne of the face which has shown poor response to topical medication. Discussion of use of systemic medication. (Dermatology)

Office visit for a 62-year-old female, established patient, for follow-up for stable cirrhosis of the liver. (Internal Medicine/Family Medicine)

Office visit for a 3-year-old, established patient, with atopic dermatitis and food hypersensitivity for quarterly follow-up evaluation. The patient is on topical lotions and steroid creams as well as oral antihistamines. (Allergy & Immunology)

Office visit for an 80-year-old female, established patient, to evaluate medical management of osteoarthritis of the temporomandibular joint. (Rheumatology)

Office visit for a 70-year-old female, established patient, one year post excision of basal cell carcinoma of nose with nasolabial flap. Now presents with new suspicious recurrent lesion and suspicious lesion of the back. (Plastic Surgery)

Office visit for a 68-year-old female, established patient, with polymyalgia rheumatic, maintained on chronic low-dose corticosteroid, with no new complaints. (Rheumatology)

Office visit for a 3-year-old female, established patient, for earache and dyshidrosis of feet. (Pediatrics/Family Medicine)

Office visit for an established patient for 18 months post-operative follow-up of TMJ repair. (Oral & Maxillofacial Surgery)

Office visit for a 45-year-old male, established patient, being re-evaluated for recurrent acute prostatitis. (Urology)

Office visit for a 43-year-old male, established patient, with known reflex sympathetic dystrophy. (Anesthesiology)

Office visit for an established patient with an evenly pigmented superficial nodule of leg which is symptomatic. (Dermatology)

Office visit for an established patient with psoriasis involvement of the elbows, pitting of the nails, and itchy scalp. (Dermatology)

Office visit for a 27-year-old male, established patient, with deep follicular and perifollicular inflammation unable to tolerate systemic antibiotics due to GI upset, requires change of systemic medication. (Dermatology)

Office visit for a 16-year-old male, established patient, who is on medication for exercise-induced bronchospasm. (Allergy & Immunology)

Office visit for a 60-year-old, established patient, with chronic essential hypertension on multiple drug regimen, for blood pressure check. (Family Medicine)

Office visit for a 20-year-old male, established patient, for removal of sutures in hand. (Family Medicine)

Office visit for a 58-year-old female, established patient, with unilateral painful bunion. (Orthopaedic Surgery)

Office visit for a 45-year-old female, established patient, with known osteoarthritis and painful swollen knees. (Rheumatology)

Office visit for a 25-year-old female, established patient, complaining of bleeding and heavy menses. (Obstetrics & Gynecology)

Office visit for a 55-year-old male, established patient, with hypertension managed by a beta blocker/thiazide regime; now experiencing mild fatigue. (Nephrology)

Office visit for a 65-year-old female, established patient, with primary glaucoma for interval determination of intraocular pressure and possible adjustment of medication. (Ophthalmology)

Office visit for a 56-year-old man, established patient, with stable exertional angina who complains of new onset of calf pain while walking. (Cardiology)

Office visit for a 63-year-old female, established patient, with rheumatoid arthritis on auranofin and ibuprofen, seen for routine follow-up visit. (Rheumatology)

Office visit for an established patient with Graves' disease, three months post I-131 therapy, who presents with lassitude and malaise. (Endocrinology)

Office visit for the quarterly follow-up of a 63-year-old male, established patient, with chronic myofascial pain syndrome, effectively managed by doxepin, who presents with new onset urinary hesitancy. (Pain Medicine)

Office visit for the biannual follow-up of an established patient with migraine variant having infrequent, intermittent, moderate to severe headaches with nausea and vomiting, which are sometimes effectively managed by ergotamine tartrate and an antiemetic, but occasionally requiring visits to an emergency department. (Pain Medicine)

Office visit for an established patient after discharge from a pain rehabilitation program to review and adjust medication dosage. (Pain Medicine)

Office visit with 55-year-old male, established patient, for management of hypertension, mild fatigue, on beta blocker/thiazide regimen. (Family Medicine/Internal Medicine)

Outpatient visit with 37-year-old male, established patient, who is three years post total colectomy for chronic ulcerative colitis, presents for increased irritation at his stoma. (General Surgery)

Office visit for a 70-year-old diabetic hypertensive established patient with recent change in insulin requirement. (Internal Medicine/Nephrology)

Office visit with 80-year-old female, established patient, for follow-up osteoporosis, status-post compression fractures. (Rheumatology)

Office visit for an established patient with stable cirrhosis of the liver. (Gastroenterology)

Routine, follow-up office evaluation at a three-month interval for a 77-year-old female, established patient, with nodular small cleaved-cell lymphoma. (Hematology/Oncology)

Quarterly follow-up office visit for a 45-year-old male, established patient, with stable chronic asthma, on steroid and bronchodilator therapy. (Pulmonary Medicine)

Office visit for a 50-year-old female, established patient, with insulin-dependent diabetes mellitus and stable coronary artery disease, for monitoring. (Family Medicine/Internal Medicine)

99214 Office visit for an established patient now presenting with generalized dermatitis of 80 percent of the body surface area. (Dermatology)

Office visit for a 32-year-old female, established patient, with new onset right lower quadrant pain. (Family Medicine)

Office visit for reassessment and reassurance/counseling of a 40-year-old female, established patient, who is experiencing increased symptoms while on a pain management treatment program. (Pain Medicine)

Office visit for a 30-year-old, established patient, under management for intractable low back pain, who now presents with new onset right posterior thigh pain. (Pain Medicine)

Office visit for an established patient with frequent intermittent, moderate to severe headaches requiring beta blocker or tricyclic antidepressant prophylaxis, as well as four symptomatic treatments, but who is still experiencing headaches at a frequency of several times a month that are unresponsive to treatment. (Pain Medicine)

Office visit for an established patient with psoriasis with extensive involvement of scalp, trunk, palms, and soles with joint pain. Combinations of topical and systemic treatments discussed and instituted. (Dermatology)

Office visit for a 55-year-old male, established patient, with increasing night pain, limp, and progressive varus of both knees. (Orthopaedic Surgery)

Follow-up visit for a 15-year-old withdrawn patient with four-year history of papulocystic acne of the face, chest, and back with early scarring and poor response to past treatment. Discussion of use of systemic medication. (Dermatology)

Office visit for a 28-year-old male, established patient, with regional enteritis, diarrhea, and low-grade fever. (Internal Medicine)

Office visit for a 25-year-old female, established patient, following recent arthrogram and MR imaging for TMJ pain. (Oral & Maxillofacial Surgery)

Office visit for a 32-year-old female, established patient, with large obstructing stone in left mid-ureter, to discuss management options including urethroscopy with extraction or ESWL. (Urology)

Evaluation for a 28-year-old male, established patient, with new onset of low back pain. (Anesthesiology/Pain Medicine)

Office visit for a 28-year-old female, established patient, with right lower quadrant abdominal pain, fever, and anorexia. (Internal Medicine/Family Medicine)

Office visit for a 45-year-old male, established patient, four months follow-up of L4-5 diskectomy, with persistent incapacitating low back and leg pain. (Orthopaedic Surgery)

Outpatient visit for a 77-year-old male, established patient, with hypertension, presenting with a three-month history of episodic substernal chest pain on exertion. (Cardiology)

Office visit for a 25-year-old female, established patient, for evaluation of progressive saddle nose deformity of unknown etiology. (Plastic Surgery)

Office visit for a 65-year-old male, established patient, with BPH and severe bladder outlet obstruction, to discuss management options such as TURP. (Urology)

Office visit for an adult diabetic established patient with a past history of recurrent sinusitis who presents with a one-week history of double vision. (Otolaryngology, Head & Neck Surgery)

Office visit for an established patient with lichen planus and 60 percent of the cutaneous surface involved, not responsive to systemic steroids, as well as developing symptoms of progressive heartburn and paranoid ideation. (Dermatology)

Office visit for a 52-year-old male, established patient, with a 12-year history of bipolar disorder responding to lithium carbonate and brief psychotherapy. Psychotherapy and prescription provided. (Psychiatry)

Office visit for a 63-year-old female, established patient, with a history of familial polyposis, status post-colectomy with sphincter sparing procedure, who now presents with rectal bleeding and increase in stooling frequency. (General Surgery)

Office visit for a 68-year-old male, established patient, with the sudden onset of multiple flashes and floaters in the right eye due to a posterior vitreous detachment. (Ophthalmology)

Office visit for a 55-year-old female, established patient, on cyclosporin for treatment of resistant, small vessel vasculitis. (Rheumatology)

Follow-up office visit for a 55-year-old male, two months after iliac angioplasty with new onset of contralateral extremity claudication. (Interventional Radiology)

Office visit for a 68-year-old male, established patient, with stable angina, two months post myocardial infarction, who is not tolerating one of his medications. (Cardiology)

Weekly office visit for 5FU therapy for an ambulatory established patient with metastatic colon cancer and increasing shortness of breath. (Hematology/Oncology)

Follow-up office visit for a 60-year-old male, established patient, whose post-traumatic seizures have disappeared on medication and who now raises the question of stopping the medication (Neurology)

Office evaluation on new onset RLQ pain in a 32-year-old woman, established patient. (Urology/General Surgery/Internal Medicine/Family Medicine)

Office evaluation of 28-year-old, established patient, with regional enteritis, diarrhea and low-grade fever. (Family Medicine/Internal Medicine)

Office visit with 50-year-old female, established patient, diabetic, blood sugar controlled by diet. She now complains of frequency of urination and weight loss, blood sugar of 320 and negative ketones on dipstick. (Internal Medicine)

Follow-up office visit for a 45-year-old, established patient, with rheumatoid arthritis on gold, methotrexate, or immunosuppressive therapy. (Rheumatology)

Office visit for a 60-year-old male, established patient, two years post-removal of intracranial meningioma, now with new headaches and visual disturbance. (Neurosurgery)

Office visit for a 68-year-old female, established patient, for routine review and follow-up of non-insulin dependent diabetes, obesity, hypertension and congestive heart failure. Complains of vision difficulties and admits dietary noncompliance. Patient is counseled concerning diet and current medications adjusted. (Family Medicine)

99215 Office visit for an established patient who developed persistent cough, rectal bleeding, weakness, and diarrhea plus pustular infection on skin. Patient on immunosuppressive therapy. (Dermatology)

Office visit for an established patient with disseminated lupus erythematosus, extensive edema of extremities kidney disease, and weakness requiring monitored course on azathioprene, corticosteroid and complicated by acute depression. (Dermatology/Internal Medicine/Rheumatology)

Office visit for an established patient with progressive dermatomyositis and recent onset of fever, nasal speech, and regurgitation of fluids through the nose. (Dermatology)

Office visit for a 28-year-old female, established patient, who is abstinent from previous cocaine dependence, but reports progressive panic attacks and chest pains. (Psychiatry)

Office visit for an established adolescent patient with history of bipolar disorder treated with lithium; seen on urgent basis at family's request because of severe depressive symptoms. (Psychiatry)

Office visit for an established patient having acute migraine with new onset neurological symptoms and whose headaches are unresponsive to previous attempts at management with a combination of preventive and abortive medication. (Pain Medicine)

Office visit for an established patient with exfoliative lichen planus with daily fever spikes, disorientation, and shortness of breath. (Dermatology)

Office visit for a 25-year-old, established patient, two years post-burn with bilateral ectropion, hypertrophic facial burn scars, near absence of left breast, and burn syndactyly of both hands. Discussion of treatment options following examination. (Plastic Surgery)

Office visit for a 6-year-old, established patient, to review newly diagnosed immune deficiency with recommendations for therapy including IV immunoglobulin and chronic antibiotics. (Allergy & Immunology)

Office visit for a 36-year-old, established patient, three months status post-transplant, with new onset of peripheral edema, increased blood pressure, and progressive fatigue. (Nephrology)

Office visit for an established patient with Kaposi's sarcoma who presents with fever and widespread vesicles. (Dermatology)

Office visit for a 27-year-old female, established patient, with bipolar disorder who was stable on lithium carbonate and monthly supportive psychotherapy but now has developed symptoms of hypomania. (Psychiatry)

Office visit for a 25-year-old male, established patient with a history of schizophrenia who has been seen bi-monthly but is complaining of auditory hallucinations. (Psychiatry)

Office visit for a 62-year-old male, established patient, three years post-op abdominal perineal resection, now with a rising carcinoembryonic antigen, weight loss, and pelvic pain. (Abdominal Surgery)

Office visit for a 42-year-old male, established patient, nine months post-op emergency vena cava shunt for variceal bleeding, now presents with complaints of one episode of "dark" bowel movement, weight gain, tightness in abdomen, whites of eyes seem "yellow" and occasional drowsiness after eating hamburgers. (Abdominal Surgery)

Office visit for a 68-year-old male, established patient, with biopsy-proven rectal carcinoma, for evaluation and discussion of treatment options. (General Surgery)

Office visit for a 60-year-old, established patient, with diabetic nephropathy with increasing edema and dyspnea. (Endocrinology)

Office visit with 30-year-old male, established patient for three-month history of fatigue, weight loss, intermittent fever, and presenting with diffuse adenopathy and splenomegaly. (Family Medicine)

Office visit for restaging of an established patient with new lymphadenopathy one year post-therapy for lymphoma. (Hematology/Oncology)

Office visit for evaluation of recent onset syncopal attacks in a 70-year-old woman, established patient. (Internal Medicine)

Follow-up visit, 40-year-old mother of three, established patient, with acute rheumatoid arthritis, anatomical Stage 3, ARA function Class 3 rheumatoid arthritis, and deteriorating function. (Rheumatology)

Office evaluation and discussion of treatment options for a 68-year-old male, established patient, with a biopsy-proven rectal carcinoma. (General Surgery)

Follow-up office visit for a 65-year-old male, established patient, with a fever of recent onset while on outpatient antibiotic therapy for endocarditis. (Infectious Disease)

Office visit for a 75-year-old, established patient, with ALS (amyotrophic lateral sclerosis), who is no longer able to swallow. (Neurology)

Office visit for a 70-year-old female, established patient, with diabetes mellitus and hypertension, presenting with a two-month history of increasing confusion, agitation and short-term memory loss. (Family Medicine/Internal Medicine)

Hospital Inpatient Services

Initial Hospital Care

New or Established Patient

99221 Initial hospital visit following admission for a 42-year-old male for observation following an uncomplicated mandible fracture. (Plastic Surgery/Oral & Maxillofacial Surgery)

Initial hospital visit for a 40-year-old patient with a thrombosed synthetic arteriovenous conduit. (Nephrology)

Initial hospital visit for a healthy 24-year-old male with an acute onset of low back pain following a lifting injury. (Internal Medicine/Anesthesiology/Pain Medicine)

Initial hospital visit for a 69-year-old female with controlled hypertension, scheduled for surgery. (Internal Medicine/Cardiology)

Initial hospital visit for a 24-year-old healthy female with benign tumor of palate. (Oral & Maxillofacial Surgery)

Initial hospital visit for a 14-year-old female with infectious mononucleosis and dehydration. (Internal Medicine)

Initial hospital visit for a 62-year-old female with stable rheumatoid arthritis, admitted for total joint replacement. (Rheumatology)

Initial hospital visit for a 12-year-old patient with a laceration of the upper eyelid, involving the lid margin and superior canaliculus, admitted prior to surgery for IV antibiotic therapy. (Plastic Surgery)

Initial hospital visit for a 69-year-old female with controlled hypertension, scheduled for surgery. (Cardiology)

Hospital admission, examination, and initiation of treatment program for a 67-year-old male with uncomplicated pneumonia who requires IV antibiotic therapy. (Internal Medicine)

Hospital admission for an 18-month-old with 10 percent dehydration. (Pediatrics)

Hospital admission for a 12-year-old with a laceration of the upper eyelid involving the lid margin and superior canaliculus, admitted prior to surgery for IV antibiotic therapy. (Ophthalmology)

Hospital admission for a 32-year-old female with severe flank pain, hematuria and presumed diagnosis of ureteral calculus as determined by Emergency Department physician. (Urology)

Initial hospital visit for a patient with several large venous stasis ulcers not responding to outpatient therapy. (Dermatology)

Initial hospital visit for 21-year-old pregnant patient (nine weeks gestation) with hyperemesis gravidarum. (Obstetrics & Gynecology)

Initial hospital visit for a 73-year-old female with acute pyelonephritis who is otherwise generally healthy. (Geriatrics)

Initial hospital visit for 62-year-old patient with cellulitis of the foot requiring bedrest and intravenous antibiotics. (Orthopaedic Surgery)

99222 Initial hospital visit for a 50-year-old patient with lower quadrant abdominal pain and increased temperature, but without septic picture. (General Surgery/Abdominal Surgery/Colon & Rectal Surgery)

Initial hospital visit for airway management, due to a benign laryngeal mass. (Otolaryngology, Head & Neck Surgery)

Initial hospital visit for a 66-year-old female with an L-2 vertebral compression fracture with acute onset of paralytic ileus; seen in the office two days previously. (Orthopaedic Surgery)

Initial hospital visit and evaluation of a 15-year-old male admitted with peritonsillar abscess or cellulitis requiring intravenous antibiotic therapy. (Otolaryngology, Head & Neck Surgery)

Initial hospital visit for a 42-year-old male with vertebral compression fracture following a motor vehicle accident. (Orthopaedic Surgery)

Initial hospital visit for a patient with generalized atopic dermatitis and secondary infection. (Dermatology)

Initial hospital visit for a 3-year-old patient with high temperature, limp, and painful hip motion of 18 hours' duration. (Pediatrics/Orthopaedic Surgery)

Initial hospital visit for a young adult, presenting with an acute asthma attack unresponsive to outpatient therapy. (Allergy & Immunology)

Initial hospital visit for an 18-year-old male who has suppurative sialoadenitis and dehydration. (Oral & Maxillofacial Surgery)

Initial hospital visit for a 65-year-old female for acute onset of thrombotic cerebrovascular accident with contralateral paralysis and aphasia. (Neurology)

Initial hospital visit for a 50-year-old male chronic paraplegic patient with pain and spasm below the lesion. (Anesthesiology)

Partial hospital admission for an adolescent patient from chaotic blended family, transferred from inpatient setting, for continued treatment to control symptomatic expressions of hostility and depression. (Psychiatry)

Initial hospital visit for a 15-year-old male with acute status asthmaticus, unresponsive to outpatient therapy. (Internal Medicine)

Initial hospital visit for a 61-year-old male with history of previous myocardial infarction, who now complains of chest pain. (Internal Medicine)

Initial hospital visit of a 15-year-old on medications for a sore throat over the last two weeks. The sore throat has worsened and patient now has dysphagia. The exam shows large necrotic tonsils with an adequate airway and small palpable nodes. The initial mono test was negative. (Otolaryngology, Head & Neck Surgery)

Initial hospital evaluation of a 23-year-old allergy patient admitted with eyelid edema and pain on fifth day of oral antibiotic therapy. (Otolaryngology, Head & Neck Surgery)

Hospital admission, young adult patient, failed previous therapy and now presents in acute asthmatic attack. (Family Medicine/Allergy & Immunology)

Hospital admission of a 62-year-old smoker, established patient, with bronchitis in acute respiratory distress. (Internal Medicine/Pulmonary Medicine)

Hospital admission, examination, and initiation of a treatment program for a 65-year-old female with new onset of right-sided paralysis and aphasia. (Neurology)

Hospital admission for a 50-year-old with left lower quadrant abdominal pain and increased temperature, but without septic picture. (General Surgery)

Hospital admission, examination, and initiation of treatment program for a 66-year-old chronic hemodialysis patient with fever and a new pulmonary infiltrate. (Nephrology)

Hospital admission for an 8-year-old febrile patient with chronic sinusitis and severe headache, unresponsive to oral antibiotics. (Allergy & Immunology)

Hospital admission for a 40-year-old male with submaxillary cellulitis and trismus from infected lower molar. (Oral & Maxillofacial Surgery)

99223 Initial hospital visit for a 45-year-old female, who has a history of rheumatic fever as a child and now has anemia, fever, and congestive heart failure. (Cardiology)

Initial hospital visit for a 50-year-old male with acute chest pain and diagnostic electrocardiographic changes of an acute anterior myocardial infarction. (Cardiology/Family Medicine/Internal Medicine)

Initial hospital visit of a 75-year-old with progressive stridor and dysphagia with history of cancer of the larynx treated by radiation therapy in the past. Exam shows a large recurrent tumor of the glottis with a mass in the neck. (Otolaryngology, Head & Neck Surgery)

Initial hospital visit for a 70-year-old male admitted with chest pain, complete heart block, and congestive heart failure. (Cardiology)

Initial hospital visit for an 82-year-old male who presents with syncope, chest pain, and ventricular arrhythmias. (Cardiology)

Initial hospital visit for a 75-year-old male with history of arteriosclerotic coronary vascular disease, who is severely dehydrated, disoriented, and experiencing auditory hallucinations. (Psychiatry)

Initial hospital visit for a 70-year-old male with alcohol and sedative-hypnotic dependence, admitted by family for severe withdrawal, hypertension, and diabetes mellitus. (Psychiatry)

Initial hospital visit for a persistently suicidal latency-aged child whose parents have requested admission to provide safety during evaluation, but are anxious about separation from her. (Psychiatry)

Initial psychiatric visit for an adolescent patient without previous psychiatric history, who was transferred from the medical ICU after a significant overdose. (Psychiatry)

Initial hospital visit for a 35-year-old female with severe systemic lupus erythematosus on corticosteroid and cyclophosphamide, with new onset of fever, chills, rash, and chest pain. (Rheumatology)

Initial hospital visit for a 52-year-old male with known rheumatic heart disease who presents with anasarca, hypertension, and history of alcohol abuse. (Cardiology)

Initial hospital visit for a 55-year-old female with a history of congenital heart disease; now presents with cyanosis. (Cardiology)

Initial hospital visit for a psychotic, hostile, violently combative adolescent, involuntarily committed, for seclusion and restraint in order to provide for safety on unit. (Psychiatry)

Initial hospital visit for a now subdued and sullen teenage male with six-month history of declining school performance, increasing self-endangerment, and resistance of parental expectations, including running away past weekend after physical fight with father. (Psychiatry)

Initial partial hospital admission for a 17-year-old female with history of borderline mental retardation who has developed auditory hallucinations. Parents are known to abuse alcohol, and Child Protective Services is investigating allegations of sexual abuse of a younger sibling. (Psychiatry)

Initial hospital visit of a 67-year old male admitted with a large neck mass, dysphagia, and history of myocardial infarction three months before. (Otolaryngology, Head & Neck Surgery)

Initial hospital visit for a patient with suspected cerebrospinal fluid rhinorrhea which developed two weeks after head injury. (Otolaryngology, Head & Neck Surgery)

Initial hospital visit for a 25-year-old female with history of poly-substance abuse and psychiatric disorder. The patient appears to be psychotic with markedly elevated vital signs. (Psychiatry)

Initial hospital visit for a 70-year-old male with cutaneous T-cell lymphoma who has developed fever and lymphadenopathy. (Internal Medicine)

Initial hospital visit for a 62-year-old female with known coronary artery disease, for evaluation of increasing edema, dyspnea on exertion, confusion, and sudden onset of fever with productive cough. (Internal Medicine)

Initial hospital visit for a 3-year-old female with 36-hour history of sore throat and high fever; now with sudden onset of lethargy, irritability, photophobia, and nuchal rigidity. (Pediatrics)

Initial hospital visit for a 26-year-old female for evaluation of severe facial fractures (LeFort's II/III). (Plastic Surgery)

Initial hospital visit for a 55-year-old female for bilateral mandibular fractures resulting in flail mandible and airway obstruction. (Plastic Surgery)

Initial hospital visit for a 71-year-old patient with a red painful eye four days following uncomplicated cataract surgery due to endophthalmitis. (Ophthalmology)

Initial hospital visit for a 45-year-old patient involved in a motor vehicle accident who suffered a perforating corneoscleral laceration with loss of vision. (Ophthalmology)

Initial hospital visit for a 58-year-old male who has Ludwig's angina and progressive airway compromise. (Oral & Maxillofacial Surgery)

Initial hospital visit for a patient with generalized systemic sclerosis, receiving immunosuppressive therapy because of recent onset of cough, fever, and inability to swallow. (Dermatology)

Initial hospital visit for an 82-year-old male who presents with syncope, chest pain, and ventricular arrhythmias. (Cardiology)

Initial hospital visit for a 62-year-old male with history of previous myocardial infarction, comes in with recurrent, sustained ventricular tachycardia. (Cardiology)

Initial hospital visit for a chronic dialysis patient with infected PTFE fistula, septicemia, and shock. (Nephrology)

Initial hospital visit for a 1-year-old male, victim of child abuse, with central nervous system depression, skull fracture, and retinal hemorrhage. (Family Medicine/Neurology)

Initial hospital visit for a 25-year-old female with recent C4-5 quadriplegia, admitted for rehabilitation. (Physical Medicine & Rehabilitation)

Initial hospital visit for an 18-year-old male, post-traumatic brain injury with multiple impairment. (Physical Medicine & Rehabilitation)

Initial partial hospital admission for 16-year-old male, sullen and subdued, with six-month history of declining school performance, increasing self-endangerment, and resistance to parental expectations. (Psychiatry)

Initial hospital visit for a 16-year-old primigravida at 32 weeks gestation with severe hypertension (200/110), thrombocytopenia, and headache. (Obstetrics & Gynecology)

Initial hospital visit for a 49-year-old male with cirrhosis of liver with hematemesis, hepatic encephalopathy, and fever. (Gastroenterology)

Initial hospital visit for a 55-year-old female in chronic pain who has attempted suicide. (Psychiatry)

Initial hospital visit for a 70-year-old male, with multiple organ system disease, admitted with history of being aneuric and septic for 24 hours prior to admission. (Urology)

Initial hospital visit for a 3-year-old female with 36-hour history of sore throat and high fever, now with sudden onset of lethargy, irritability, photophobia, and nuchal rigidity. (Internal Medicine)

Initial hospital visit for a 78-year-old male, transfers from nursing home with dysuria and pyuria, increasing confusion, and high fever. (Internal Medicine)

Initial hospital visit for a 1-day-old male with cyanosis, respiratory distress, and tachypnea. (Cardiology)

Initial hospital visit for a 3-year-old female with recurrent tachycardia and syncope. (Cardiology)

Initial hospital visit for a thyrotoxic patient who presents with fever, atrial fibrillation, and delirium. (Endocrinology)

Initial hospital visit for a 50-year-old Type I diabetic who presents with diabetic ketoacidosis with fever and obtundation. (Endocrinology)

Initial hospital visit for a 40-year-old female with anatomical stage 3, ARA functional class 3 rheumatoid arthritis on methotrexate, corticosteroid, and nonsteroidal anti-inflammatory drugs. Patient presents with severe arthritis flare, new oral ulcers, abdominal pain, and leukopenia. (Rheumatology)

Initial hospital exam of a pediatric patient with high fever and proptosis. (Otolaryngology, Head & Neck Surgery)

Initial hospital visit for a 25-year-old patient admitted for the first time to the rehab unit, with recent C-4-5 quadriplegia. (Physical Medicine & Rehabilitation)

Hospital admission, examination, and initiation of treatment program for a previously unknown 58-year-old male who presents with acute chest pain (Cardiology)

Hospital admission, examination, and initiation of induction chemotherapy for a 42-year-old patient with newly diagnosed acute myelogenous leukemia. (Hematology/Oncology)

Hospital admission following a motor vehicle accident of a 24-year-old male with fracture dislocation of C5-6; neurologically intact. (Neurosurgery)

Hospital admission for a 78-year-old female with left lower lobe pneumonia and a history of coronary artery disease, congestive heart failure, osteoarthritis and gout. (Family Medicine)

Hospital admission, examination, and initiation of treatment program for a 65-year-old immunosuppressed male with confusion, fever, and a headache. (Infectious Disease)

Hospital admission for a 9-year-old with vomiting, dehydration, fever, tachypnea and an admitting diagnosis of diabetic ketoacidosis. (Pediatrics)

Initial hospital visit for a 65-year-old male who presents with acute myocardial infarction, oliguria, hypotension, and altered state of consciousness. (Cardiology)

Initial hospital visit for a hostile/resistant adolescent patient who is severely depressed and involved in poly-substance abuse. Patient is experiencing significant conflict in his chaotic family situation and was suspended from school following an attack on a teacher with a baseball bat. (Psychiatry)

Initial hospital visit for 89-year-old female with fulminant hepatic failure and encephalopathy. (Gastroenterology)

Initial hospital visit for a 42-year-old female with rapidly progressing scleroderma, malignant hypertension, digital infarcts, and oligurea. (Rheumatology)

Subsequent Hospital Care

99231 Subsequent hospital visit for a 65-year-old female, post-open reduction and internal fixation of a fracture. (Physical Medicine & Rehabilitation)

Subsequent hospital visit for a 33-year-old patient with pelvic pain who is responding to pain medication and observation. (Obstetrics & Gynecology)

Subsequent hospital visit for a 21-year-old female with hyperemesis who has responded well to intravenous fluids. (Obstetrics & Gynecology)

Subsequent hospital visit to re-evaluate post-op pain and titrate patient-controlled analgesia for a 27-year-old female. (Anesthesiology)

Follow-up hospital visit for a 35-year-old female, status post-epidural analgesia. (Anesthesiology/Pain Medicine)

Subsequent hospital visit for a 56-year-old male, post-gastrectomy, for maintenance of analgesia using an intravenous dilaudid infusion. (Anesthesiology)

Subsequent hospital visit for a 4-year-old on day three receiving medication for uncomplicated pneumonia. (Allergy & Immunology)

Subsequent hospital visit for a 30-year-old female with urticaria which has stabilized with medication. (Allergy & Immunology)

Subsequent hospital visit for a 76-year-old male with venous stasis ulcers. (Dermatology)

Subsequent hospital visit for a 24-year-old female with otitis externa, seen two days before in consultation, now to have otic wick removal. (Otolaryngology, Head & Neck Surgery)

Subsequent hospital visit for a 27-year-old with acute labyrinthitis. (Otolaryngology, Head & Neck Surgery)

Subsequent hospital visit for a 10-year-old male admitted for lobar pneumonia with vomiting and dehydration; is becoming afebrile and tolerating oral fluids. (Family Medicine/Pediatrics)

Subsequent hospital visit for a 62-year-old patient with resolving cellulitis of the foot. (Orthopaedic Surgery)

Subsequent hospital visit for a 25-year-old male admitted for supra-ventricular tachycardia and converted on medical therapy. (Cardiology)

Subsequent hospital visit for a 27-year-old male two days after open reduction and internal fixation for malar complex fracture. (Plastic Surgery)

Subsequent hospital visit for a 76-year-old male with venous stasis ulcers. (Geriatrics)

Subsequent hospital visit for a 67-year-old female admitted three days ago with bleeding gastric ulcer; now stable. (Gastroenterology)

Subsequent hospital visit for stable 33-year-old male, status post-lower gastrointestinal bleeding. (General Surgery/Gastroenterology)

Subsequent hospital visit for a 29-year-old auto mechanic with effort thrombosis of left upper extremity. (General Surgery)

Subsequent hospital visit for a 14-year-old female in middle phase of inpatient treatment, who is now behaviorally stable and making satisfactory progress in treatment. (Psychiatry)

Subsequent hospital visit for an 18-year-old male with uncomplicated asthma who is clinically stable. (Allergy & Immunology)

Subsequent hospital visit for a 55-year-old male with rheumatoid arthritis, two days following an uncomplicated total joint replacement. (Rheumatology)

Subsequent hospital visit for a 60-year-old dialysis patient with an access infection, now afebrile on antibiotic. (Nephrology)

Subsequent hospital visit for a 36-year-old female with stable post-rhinoplasty epistaxis. (Plastic Surgery)

Subsequent hospital visit for a 66-year-old female with L-2 vertebral compression fracture with resolving ileus. (Orthopaedic Surgery)

Subsequent hospital visit for a patient with peritonsillar abscess. (Otolaryngology, Head & Neck Surgery)

Subsequent hospital visit for an 18-year-old female responding to intravenous antibiotic therapy for ear or sinus infection. (Otolaryngology, Head & Neck Surgery)

Subsequent hospital visit for a 70-year-old male admitted with congestive heart failure who has responded to therapy. (Cardiology)

Follow-up hospital visit for a 32-year-old female with left ureteral calculus; being followed in anticipation of spontaneous passage. (Urology)

Subsequent hospital visit for a 4-year-old female, admitted for acute gastroenteritis and dehydration, requiring IV hydration; now stable. (Family Medicine)

Subsequent hospital visit for a 50-year-old Type II diabetic who is clinically stable and without complications requiring regulation of a single dose of insulin daily. (Endocrinology)

Subsequent hospital visit to reassesses the status of a 65-year-old patient post-open reduction and internal fixation of hip fracture, on the rehab unit. (Physical Medicine & Rehabilitation)

Subsequent hospital visit for a 78-year-old male with cholangiocarcinoma managed by biliary drainage. (Interventional Radiology)

Subsequent hospital visit for a 50-year-old male with uncomplicated myocardial infarction who is clinically stable and without chest pain. (Family Medicine/Cardiology/Internal Medicine)

Subsequent hospital visit for a stable 72-year-old lung cancer patient undergoing a five-day course of infusion chemotherapy. (Hematology/Oncology)

Subsequent hospital visit, two days post admission for a 65-year-old male with a CVA (cerebral vascular accident) and left hemiparesis, who is clinically stable. (Neurology/Physical Medicine and Rehabilitation)

Subsequent hospital visit for now stable, 33-year-old male, status post lower gastrointestinal bleeding. (General Surgery)

Subsequent visit on third day of hospitalization for a 60-year-old female recovering from an uncomplicated pneumonia. (Infectious Disease/Internal Medicine/Pulmonary Medicine)

Subsequent hospital visit for a 3-year-old patient in traction for a congenital dislocation of the hip. (Orthopaedic Surgery)

Subsequent hospital visit for a 4-year-old female, admitted for acute gastroenteritis and dehydration, requiring IV hydration; now stable. (Family Medicine/Internal Medicine)

Subsequent hospital visit for 50-year-old female with resolving uncomplicated acute pancreatitis. (Gastroenterology)

99232 Subsequent hospital visit for a patient with venous stasis ulcers who developed fever and red streaks adjacent to the ulcer. (Dermatology/Internal Medicine/Family Medicine)

Subsequent hospital visit for a 66-year-old male for dressing changes and observation. Patient has had a myocutaneous flap to close a pharyngeal fistula and now has a low-grade fever. (Plastic Surgery)

Subsequent hospital visit for a 54-year-old female admitted for myocardial infarction, but who is now having frequent premature ventricular contractions. (Internal Medicine)

Subsequent hospital visit for an 80-year-old patient with a pelvic rim fracture, inability to walk, and severe pain; now 36 hours post-injury, experiencing urinary retention. (Orthopaedic Surgery)

Subsequent hospital visit for a 17-year-old female with fever, pharyngitis, and airway obstruction, who after 48 hours develops a maculopapular rash. (Pediatrics/Family Medicine)

Follow-up hospital visit for a 32-year-old patient admitted the previous day for corneal ulcer. (Dermatology)

Follow-up visit for a 67-year-old male with congestive heart failure who has responded to antibiotics and diuretics, and has now developed a monoarthropathy. (Internal Medicine)

Follow-up hospital visit for a 58-year-old male receiving continuous opioids who is experiencing severe nausea and vomiting. (Pain Medicine)

Subsequent hospital visit for a patient after an auto accident who is slow to respond to ambulation training. (Physical Medicine & Rehabilitation)

Subsequent hospital visit for a 14-year-old with unstable bronchial asthma complicated by pneumonia. (Allergy & Immunology)

Subsequent hospital visit for a 50-year-old diabetic, hypertensive male with back pain not responding to conservative inpatient management with continued radiation of pain to the lower left extremity. (Orthopaedic Surgery)

Subsequent hospital visit for a 37-year-old female on day five of antibiotics for bacterial endocarditis, who still has low-grade fever.

Subsequent hospital visit for a 54-year-old patient, post MI (myocardial infarction), who is out of the CCU (coronary care unit) but is now having frequent premature ventricular contractions on telemetry. (Cardiology/Internal Medicine)

Subsequent hospital visit for a patient with neutropenia, a fever responding to antibiotics, and continued slow gastrointestinal bleeding on platelet support. (Hematology/Oncology)

Subsequent hospital visit for a 50-year-old male admitted two days ago for sub-acute renal allograft rejection. (Nephrology)

Subsequent hospital visit for a 35-year-old drug addict, not responding to initial antibiotic therapy for pyelonephritis. (Urology)

Subsequent hospital visit of an 81-year-old male with abdominal distention, nausea, and vomiting. (General Surgery)

Subsequent hospital care for a 62-year-old female with congestive heart failure, who remains dyspneic and febrile. (Internal Medicine)

Subsequent hospital visit for a 73-year-old female with recently diagnosed lung cancer, who complains of unsteady gait. (Pulmonary Medicine)

Subsequent hospital visit for a 20-month-old male with bacterial meningitis treated one week with antibiotic therapy; has now developed a temperature of 101.0. (Pediatrics)

Subsequent hospital visit for 13-year-old male admitted with left lower quadrant abdominal pain and fever, not responding to therapy. (General Surgery)

Subsequent hospital visit for a 65-year-old male with hemiplegia and painful paretic shoulder. (Physical Medicine & Rehabilitation)

99233 Subsequent hospital visit for a 38-year-old male, quadriplegic with acute autonomic hyperreflexia, who is not responsive to initial care. (Physical Medicine & Rehabilitation)

Follow-up hospital visit for a teenage female who continues to experience severely disruptive, violent and life-threatening symptoms in a complicated multi-system illness. Family/social circumstances also a contributing factor. (Psychiatry)

Subsequent hospital visit for a 42-year-old female with progressive systemic sclerosis (scleroderma), renal failure on dialysis, congestive heart failure, cardiac arrhythmias, and digital ulcers. (Allergy & Immunology)

Subsequent hospital visit for a 50-year-old diabetic, hypertensive male with nonresponding back pain and radiating pain to the lower left extremity, who develops chest pain, cough, and bloody sputum. (Orthopaedic Surgery)

Subsequent hospital visit for a 64-year-old female, status post-abdominal aortic aneurysm resection, with non-responsive coagulopathy, who has now developed lower GI bleeding. (Abdominal Surgery/Colon & Rectal Surgery/General Surgery)

Follow-up hospital care of a patient with pansinusitis infection complicated by a brain abscess and asthma; no response to current treatment. (Otolaryngology, Head & Neck Surgery)

Subsequent hospital visit for a patient with a laryngeal neoplasm who develops airway compromise, suspected metastasis. (Otolaryngology, Head & Neck Surgery)

Subsequent hospital visit for a 49-year-old male with significant rectal bleeding, etiology undetermined, not responding to treatment. (Abdominal Surgery/General Surgery/Colon & Rectal Surgery)

Subsequent hospital visit for a 50-year-old male, post-aortocoronary bypass surgery; now develops hypotension and oliguria. (Cardiology)

Subsequent hospital visit for an adolescent patient who is violent, unsafe, and noncompliant, with multiple expectations for participation in treatment plan and behavior on the treatment unit. (Psychiatry)

Subsequent hospital visit for an 18-year-old male being treated for presumed PCP psychosis. Patient is still moderately symptomatic with auditory hallucinations and is insisting on signing out against medical advice. (Psychiatry)

Subsequent hospital visit for an 8-year-old female with caustic ingestion, who now has fever, dyspnea, and dropping hemoglobin. (Gastroenterology)

Follow-up hospital visit for a chronic renal failure patient on dialysis who develops chest pain and shortness of breath and a new onset pericardial friction rub. (Nephrology)

Subsequent hospital visit for a 44-year-old patient with electrical burns to the left arm with ascending infection. (Orthopaedic Surgery)

Subsequent hospital visit for a patient with systemic sclerosis who has aspirated and is short of breath. (Dermatology)

Subsequent hospital visit for a 65-year-old female, status post-op resection of abdominal aortic aneurysm, with suspected ischemic bowel. (General Surgery)

Subsequent hospital visit for a 50-year-old male, post-aortocoronary bypass surgery, now develops hypotension and oliguria. (Cardiology)

Subsequent hospital visit for a 65-year-old male, following an acute myocardial infarction, who complains of shortness of breath and new chest pain. (Cardiology)

Subsequent hospital visit for a 65-year-old female with rheumatoid arthritis (stage 3, class 3) admitted for urosepsis. On the third hospital day, chest pain, dyspnea and fever develop. (Rheumatology)

Follow-up hospital care of a pediatric case with stridor, laryngomalacia, established tracheostomy, complicated by multiple medical problems in PICU. (Otolaryngology, Head & Neck Surgery)

Subsequent hospital visit for a 60-year-old female, four days post uncomplicated inferior myocardial infarction who has developed severe chest pain, dyspnea, diaphoresis and nausea. (Family Medicine)

Subsequent hospital visit for a patient with AML (acute myelogenous leukemia), fever, elevated white count and uric acid undergoing induction chemotherapy. (Hematology/Oncology)

Subsequent hospital visit for a 38-year-old quadriplegic male with acute autonomic hyperreflexia, who is not responsive to initial care. (Physical Medicine & Rehabilitation)

Subsequent hospital visit for a 65-year-old female post-op resection of abdominal aortic aneurysm, with suspected ischemic bowel. (General Surgery)

Subsequent hospital visit for a 60-year-old female with persistent leukocytosis and a fever seven days after a sigmoid colon resection for carcinoma. (Infectious Disease)

Subsequent hospital visit for a chronic renal failure patient on dialysis, who develops chest pain, shortness of breath and new onset of pericardial friction rub. (Nephrology)

Subsequent hospital visit for a 65-year-old male with acute myocardial infarction who now demonstrates complete heart block and congestive heart failure. (Cardiology)

Subsequent hospital visit for a 25-year-old female with hypertension and systemic lupus erythematosus, admitted for fever and respiratory distress. On the third hospital day, the patient presented with purpuric skin lesions and acute renal failure. (Allergy & Immunology)

Subsequent hospital visit for a 55-year-old male with severe chronic obstructive pulmonary disease and bronchospasm; initially admitted for acute respiratory distress requiring ventilatory support in the ICU. The patient was stabilized, extubated and transferred to the floor, but has now developed acute fever, dyspnea, left lower lobe rhonchi and laboratory evidence of carbon dioxide retention and hypoxemia. (Family Medicine/Internal Medicine)

Subsequent hospital visit for 46-year-old female, known liver cirrhosis patient, with recent upper gastrointestinal hemorrhage from varices; now with worsening ascites and encephalopathy. (Gastroenterology)

Subsequent hospital visit for 62-year-old female admitted with acute subarachnoid hemorrhage, negative cerebral arteriogram, increased lethargy and hemiparesis with fever. (Neurosurgery)

Consultations

Office or Other Outpatient Consultations

New or Established Patient

99241 Initial office consultation for a 40-year-old female in pain from blister on lip following a cold. (Oral & Maxillofacial Surgery)

Initial office consultation for a 62-year-old construction worker with olecranon bursitis. (Orthopaedic Surgery)

Office consultation with 25-year-old postpartum female with severe symptomatic hemorrhoids. (Colon & Rectal Surgery)

Office consultation with 58-year-old male, referred for follow-up of creatinine level and evaluation of obstructive uropathy, relieved two months ago. (Nephrology)

Office consultation for 30-year-old female tennis player with sprain or contusion of the forearm. (Orthopaedic Surgery)

Office consultation for a 45-year-old male, requested by his internist, with asymptomatic torus palatinus requiring no further treatment. (Oral & Maxillofacial Surgery)

99242 Initial office consultation for a 20-year-old male with acute upper respiratory tract symptoms. (Allergy & Immunology)

Initial office consultation for a 29-year-old soccer player with painful proximal thigh/groin injury. (Orthopaedic Surgery)

Initial office consultation for a 66-year-old female with wrist and hand pain, numbness of finger tips, suspected median nerve compression by carpal tunnel syndrome. (Plastic Surgery)

Initial office consultation for a patient with a solitary lesion of discoid lupus erythematosus on left cheek to rule out malignancy or self-induced lesion. (Dermatology)

Office consultation for management of systolic hypertension in a 70-year-old male scheduled for elective prostate resection. (Geriatrics)

Office consultation with 27-year-old female, with old amputation, for evaluation of existing above-knee prosthesis. (Physical Medicine & Rehabilitation)

Office consultation with 66-year-old female with wrist and hand pain, and finger numbness, secondary to suspected carpal tunnel syndrome. (Orthopaedic Surgery)

Office consultation for 61-year-old female, recently on antibiotic therapy, now with diarrhea and leukocytosis. (Abdominal Surgery)

Office consultation for a patient with papulosquamous eruption of elbow with pitting of nails and itchy scalp. (Dermatology)

Office consultation for a 30-year-old female with single season allergic rhinitis. (Allergy & Immunology)

99243 Initial office consultation for a 60-year-old male with avascular necrosis of the left femoral head with increasing pain. (Orthopaedic Surgery)

Office consultation for a 31-year-old woman complaining of palpitations and chest pains. Her internist had described a mild systolic click. (Cardiology)

Office consultation for a 65-year-old female with persistent bronchitis. (Infectious Disease)

Office consultation for a 65-year-old man with chronic low-back pain radiating to the leg. (Neurosurgery)

Office consultation for 23-year-old female with Crohn's disease not responding to therapy. (Abdominal Surgery/Colon & Rectal Surgery)

Office consultation for 25-year-old patient with symptomatic knee pain and swelling, with torn anterior cruciate ligament and/or torn meniscus. (Orthopaedic Surgery)

Office consultation for a 67-year-old patient with osteoporosis and mandibular atrophy with regard to reconstructive alternatives. (Oral & Maxillofacial Surgery)

Office consultation for 39-year-old patient referred at a perimenopausal age for irregular menses and menopausal symptoms. (Obstetrics & Gynecology)

99244 Initial office consultation for a 28-year-old male, HIV+, with a recent change in visual acuity. (Ophthalmology)

Initial office consultation for a 15-year-old male with failing grades, suspected drug abuse. (Pediatrics)

Initial office consultation for a 36-year-old factory worker, status four months post-occupational low back injury and requires management of intractable low back pain. (Pain Medicine)

Initial office consultation for a 45-year-old female with a history of chronic arthralgia of TMJ and associated myalgia and sudden progressive symptomatology over last two to three months. (Oral & Maxillofacial Surgery)

Initial office consultation for evaluation of a 70-year-old male with appetite loss and diminished energy. (Psychiatry)

Initial office consultation for an elementary school-aged patient, referred by pediatrician, with multiple systematic complaints and recent onset of behavioral discontrol. (Psychiatry)

Initial office consultation for a 23-year-old female with developmental facial skeletal anomaly and subsequent abnormal relationship of jaw(s) to cranial base. (Oral & Maxillofacial Surgery)

Initial office consultation for a 45-year-old myopic patient with a one-week history of floaters and a partial retinal detachment. (Ophthalmology)

Initial office consultation for a 65-year-old female with moderate dementia, mild unsteadiness, back pain fatigue on ambulation, intermittent urinary incontinence. (Neurosurgery)

Initial office consultation for a 33-year-old female referred by endocrinologist with amenorrhea and galactorrhea, for evaluation of pituitary tumor. (Neurosurgery)

Initial office consultation for a 34-year-old male with new onset nephrotic syndrome. (Nephrology)

Initial office consultation for a 39-year-old female with intractable chest wall pain secondary to metastatic breast cancer. (Anesthesiology/Pain Medicine)

Initial office consultation for a patient with multiple giant tumors of jaws. (Oral & Maxillofacial Surgery)

Initial office consultation for a patient with a failed total hip replacement with loosening and pain upon walking. (Orthopaedic Surgery)

Initial office consultation for a 60-year-old female with three-year history of intermittent tic-like unilateral facial pain; now constant pain for six weeks without relief by adequate carbamazepine dosage. (Neurosurgery)

Initial office consultation for a 45-year-old male heavy construction worker with prior lumbar disk surgery two years earlier; now gradually recurring low back and unilateral leg pain for three months, unable to work for two weeks. (Neurosurgery)

Initial office consultation of a patient who presents with a 30-year history of smoking and right neck mass. (Otolaryngology, Head & Neck Surgery)

Office consultation with 38-year-old female, with inflammatory bowel disease, who now presents with right lower quadrant pain and suspected intra-abdominal abscess. (General Surgery/Colon & Rectal Surgery)

Office consultation with 72-year-old male with esophageal carcinoma, symptoms of dysphagia and reflux. (Thoracic Surgery)

Office consultation for discussion of treatment options for a 40-year-old female with a two-centimeter adenocarcinoma of the breast. (Radiation Oncology)

Office consultation for young patient referred by pediatrician because of patient's short attention span, easy distractibility and hyperactivity. (Psychiatry)

Office consultation for 66-year-old female, history of colon resection for adenocarcinoma six years earlier, now with severe mid-back pain; x-rays showing osteoporosis and multiple vertebral compression fractures. (Neurosurgery)

Office consultation for a patient with chronic pelvic inflammatory disease who now has left lower quadrant pain with a palpable pelvic mass. (Obstetrics & Gynecology)

Office consultation for a patient with long-standing psoriasis with acute onset of erythroderma, pustular lesions, chills and fever. Combinations of topical and systemic treatments discussed and instituted. (Dermatology)

99245 Initial office consultation for a 35-year-old multiple-trauma male patient with complex pelvic fractures, for evaluation and formulation of management plan. (Orthopaedic Surgery)

Initial emergency room consultation for 10-year-old male in status epilepticus, recent closed head injury, information about medication not available. (Neurosurgery)

Initial emergency room consultation for a 23-year-old patient with severe abdominal pain, guarding, febrile, and unstable vital signs. (Obstetrics & Gynecology)

Office consultation for a 67-year-old female longstanding uncontrolled diabetic who presents with retinopathy, nephropathy, and a foot ulcer. (Endocrinology)

Office consultation for a 37-year-old male for initial evaluation and management of Cushing's disease. (Endocrinology)

Office consultation for a 60-year-old male who presents with thyrotoxicosis, exophthalmos, frequent premature ventricular contractions and congestive heart failure. (Endocrinology)

Initial office consultation for a 36-year-old patient, one year status post occupational herniated cervical disk treated by laminectomy, requiring management of multiple sites of intractable pain, depression, and narcotic dependence. (Pain Medicine)

Office consultation for a 58-year-old man with a history of MI and CHF who complains of the recent onset of rest angina and shortness of breath. The patient has a systolic blood pressure of 90mmHG and is in Class IV heart failure. (Cardiology)

Emergency room consultation for a 1-year-old with a three-day history of fever with increasing respiratory distress who is thought to have cardiac tamponade by the ER physician. (Cardiology)

Office consultation in the emergency room for a 25-year-old male with severe, acute, closed head injury. (Neurosurgery)

Office consultation for a 23-year-old female with Stage II A Hodgkins disease with positive supraclavicular and mediastinal nodes. (Radiation Oncology)

Office consultation for a 27-year-old juvenile diabetic patient with severe diabetic retinopathy, gastric atony, nephrotic syndrome and progressive renal failure, now with a serum creatinine of 2.7, and a blood pressure of 170/114. (Nephrology)

Office consultation for independent medical evaluation of a patient with a history of complicated low back and neck problems with previous multiple failed back surgeries. (Orthopaedic Surgery)

Office consultation for an adolescent referred by pediatrician for recent onset of violent and self-injurious behavior. (Psychiatry)

Office consultation for a 6-year-old male for evaluation of severe muscle and joint pain and a diffuse rash. Patient well until 4-6 weeks earlier, when he developed arthralgia, myalgias, and a fever of 102 for one week. (Rheumatology)

Initial Inpatient Consultations

New or Established Patient

99251 Initial hospital consultation for a 27-year-old female with fractured incisor post-intubation. (Oral & Maxillofacial Surgery)

Initial hospital consultation for an orthopaedic patient on IV antibiotics who has developed an apparent candida infection of the oral cavity. (Oral & Maxillofacial Surgery)

Initial inpatient consultation for a 30-year-old female complaining of vaginal itching, post orthopaedic surgery. (Obstetrics & Gynecology)

Initial inpatient consultation for a 36-year-old male on orthopaedic service with complaint of localized dental pain. (Oral & Maxillofacial Surgery)

99252 Initial hospital consultation for a 45-year-old male, previously abstinent alcoholic, who relapsed and was admitted for management of gastritis. The patient readily accepts the need for further treatment. (Addiction Medicine)

Initial hospital consultation for a 35-year-old dialysis patient with episodic oral ulcerations. (Oral & Maxillofacial Surgery)

Initial inpatient preoperative consultation for a 43-year-old woman with cholecystitis and well-controlled hypertension. (Cardiology)

Initial inpatient consultation for recommendation of antibiotic prophylaxis for a patient with a synthetic heart valve who will undergo urologic surgery. (Internal Medicine)

Initial inpatient consultation for possible drug induced skin eruption in 50-year-old male. (Dermatology)

Preoperative inpatient consultation for evaluation of hypertension in a 60-year-old male who will undergo a cholecystectomy. Patient had a normal annual check-up in your office four months ago. (Internal Medicine)

Initial inpatient consultation for 66-year-old patient with wrist and hand pain and finger numbness, secondary to carpal tunnel syndrome. (Orthopaedic Surgery/Plastic Surgery)

Initial inpatient consultation for a 66-year-old male smoker referred for pain management immediately status post-biliary tract surgery done via sub-costal incision. (Anesthesiology/Pain Medicine)

99253 Initial hospital consultation for a 50-year-old female with incapacitating knee pain due to generalized rheumatoid arthritis. (Orthopaedic Surgery)

Initial hospital consultation for a 60-year-old male with avascular necrosis of the left femoral heel with increasing pain. (Orthopaedic Surgery)

Initial hospital consultation for a 45-year-old female with compound mandibular fracture and concurrent head, abdominal and/or orthopaedic injuries. (Oral & Maxillofacial Surgery)

Initial hospital consultation for a 22-year-old female, paraplegic, to evaluate wrist and hand pain. (Orthopaedic Surgery)

Initial hospital consultation for a 40-year-old male with 10-day history of incapacitating unilateral sciatica, unable to walk now, not improved by bed rest. (Neurosurgery)

Initial hospital consultation, requested by pediatrician, for treatment recommendations for a patient admitted with persistent inability to walk following soft tissue injury to ankle. (Physiatry)

Initial hospital consultation for a 27-year-old previously healthy male who vomited during IV sedation and may have aspirated gastric contents. (Anesthesiology)

Initial hospital consultation for a 33-year-old female, post-abdominal surgery, who now has a fever. (Internal Medicine)

Initial inpatient consultation for a 57-year-old male, post lower endoscopy, for evaluation of abdominal pain and fever. (General Surgery)

Initial inpatient consultation for rehabilitation of a 73-year-old female one week after surgical management of a hip fracture. (Physical Medicine & Rehabilitation)

Initial inpatient consultation for diagnosis/management of fever following abdominal surgery. (Internal Medicine)

Initial inpatient consultation for a 35-year-old female with a fever and pulmonary infiltrate following cesarean section. (Pulmonary Medicine)

Initial inpatient consultation for a 42-year-old non-diabetic patient, post-op cholecystectomy, now with an acute urinary tract infection. (Nephrology)

Initial inpatient consultation for 53-year-old female with moderate uncomplicated pancreatitis. (Gastroenterology)

Initial inpatient consultation for 45-year-old patient with chronic neck pain with radicular pain of the left arm. (Orthopaedic Surgery)

Initial inpatient consultation for 8-year-old patient with new onset of seizures who has a normal examination and previous history. (Neurology)

99254 Initial hospital consultation for a 15-year-old patient with painless swelling of proximal humerus with lytic lesion by x-ray. (Orthopaedic Surgery)

Initial hospital consultation for evaluation of a 29-year-old female with a diffusely positive medical review of systems and history of multiple surgeries. (Psychiatry)

Initial hospital consultation for a 70-year-old diabetic female with gangrene of the foot. (Orthopaedic Surgery)

Initial inpatient consultation for a 47-year-old female with progressive pulmonary infiltrate, hypoxemia, and diminished urine output. (Anesthesiology)

Initial hospital consultation for a 13-month-old with spasmodic cough, respiratory distress, and fever. (Allergy & Immunology)

Initial hospital consultation for a patient with failed total hip replacement with loosening and pain upon walking. (Orthopaedic Surgery)

Initial hospital consultation for a 62-year-old female with metastatic breast cancer to the femoral neck and thoracic vertebra. (Orthopaedic Surgery)

Initial hospital consultation for a 39-year-old female with nephrolithiasis requiring extensive opioid analgesics, whose vital signs are now elevated. She initially denied any drug use, but today gives history of multiple substance abuse, including opioids and prior treatment for a personality disorder. (Psychiatry)

Initial hospital consultation for a 70-year-old female without previous psychiatric history, who is now experiencing nocturnal confusion and visual hallucinations following hip replacement surgery. (Psychiatry)

Initial inpatient consultation for evaluation of a 63-year-old in the ICU with diabetes and chronic renal failure who develops acute respiratory distress syndrome 36 hours after a mitral valve replacement. (Anesthesiology)

Initial inpatient consultation for a 66-year-old female with enlarged supraclavicular lymph nodes, found on biopsy to be malignant. (Hematology/Oncology)

Initial inpatient consultation for a 43-year-old female for evaluation of sudden painful visual loss, optic neuritis and episodic paresthesia. (Ophthalmology)

Initial inpatient consultation for evaluation of a 71-year-old male with hyponatremia (serum sodium 114) who was admitted to the hospital with pneumonia. (Nephrology)

Initial inpatient consultation for a 72-year-old male with emergency admission for possible bowel obstruction. (Internal Medicine/General Surgery)

Initial inpatient consultation for a 35-year-old female with fever, swollen joints, and rash of one-week duration. (Rheumatology)

99255 Initial inpatient consultation for a 76-year-old female with massive, life-threatening gastrointestinal hemorrhage and chest pain. (Gastroenterology)

Initial inpatient consultation for a 75-year-old female, admitted to intensive care with acute respiratory distress syndrome, who is hypersensitive, has a moderate metabolic acidosis, and a rising serum creatinine. (Nephrology)

Initial hospital consultation for patient with a history of complicated low back pain and neck problems with previous multiple failed back surgeries. (Orthopaedic Surgery/Neurosurgery)

Initial hospital consultation for a 66-year-old female, two days post-abdominal aneurysm repair, with oliguria and hypertension of one-day duration. (Nephrology/Internal Medicine)

Initial hospital consultation for a patient with shotgun wound to face with massive facial trauma and airway obstruction. (Oral & Maxillofacial Surgery)

Initial hospital consultation for patient with severe pancreatitis complicated by respiratory insufficiency, acute renal failure, and abscess formation. (General Surgery/Colon & Rectal Surgery)

Initial hospital consultation for a 35-year-old multiple-trauma male patient with complex pelvic fractures to evaluate and formulate management plan. (Orthopaedic Surgery)

Initial inpatient consultation for adolescent patient with fractured femur and pelvis who pulled out IVs and disconnected traction in attempt to elope from hospital. (Psychiatry)

Initial hospital consultation for a 16-year-old primigravida at 32 weeks gestation requested by a family practitioner for evaluation of severe hypertension, thrombocytopenia, and headache. (Obstetrics & Gynecology)

Initial hospital consultation for a 58-year-old insulin-dependent diabetic with multiple antibiotic allergies, now with multiple fascial plane abscesses and airway obstruction. (Oral & Maxillofacial Surgery)

Initial inpatient consultation for a 55-year-old male with known cirrhosis and ascites, now with jaundice, encephalopathy, and massive hematemesis. (Gastroenterology)

Initial hospital consultation for a 25-year-old male, seen in emergency room with severe, closed head injury. (Neurosurgery)

Initial hospital consultation for a 2-day-old male with single ventricle physiology and subaortic obstruction. Family counseling following evaluation for multiple, staged surgical procedures. (Thoracic Surgery)

Initial hospital consultation for a 45-year-old male admitted with subarachnoid hemorrhage and intracranial aneurysm on angiogram. (Neurosurgery)

Initial inpatient consultation for myxedematous patient who is hypoventilating and obtunded. (Endocrinology)

Initial hospital consultation for a 45-year-old patient with widely metastatic lung carcinoma, intractable back pain, and a history that includes substance dependence, NSAID allergy, and two prior laminectomies with fusion for low back pain. (Pain Medicine)

Initial hospital consultation for evaluation of treatment options in a 50-year-old patient with cirrhosis, known peptic ulcer disease, hypotension, encephalopathy, and massive acute upper gastrointestinal bleeding which cannot be localized by endoscopy. (Interventional Radiology)

Initial inpatient consultation in the ICU for a 70-year-old male who experienced a cardiac arrest during surgery and was resuscitated. (Cardiology)

Initial inpatient consultation for a patient with severe pancreatitis complicated by respiratory insufficiency, acute renal failure and abscess formation. (Gastroenterology)

Initial inpatient consultation for a 70-year-old cirrhotic male admitted with ascites, jaundice, encephalopathy, and massive hematemesis. (Gastroenterology)

Initial inpatient consultation in the ICU for a 51-year-old patient who is on a ventilator and has a fever two weeks after a renal transplantation. (Infectious Disease)

Initial inpatient consultation for evaluation and formulation of plan for management of multiple trauma patient with complex pelvic fracture, 35-year-old male. (General Surgery/Orthopaedic Surgery)

Initial inpatient consultation for a 50-year-old male with a history of previous myocardial infarction, now with acute pulmonary edema and hypotension. (Cardiology)

Initial inpatient consultation for 45-year-old male with recent, acute subarachnoid hemorrhage, hesitant speech, mildly confused, drowsy. High risk group for HIV+ status. (Neurosurgery)

Initial inpatient consultation for 36-year-old female referred by her internist to evaluate a patient being followed for abdominal pain and fever. The patient has developed diffuse abdominal pain, guarding, rigidity and increased fever. (Obstetrics & Gynecology)

Follow-up Inpatient Consultations

Established Patient

99261 Follow-up consultation for a 78-year-old female nursing home resident for evaluation of medical management of pruritus ani. (Colon & Rectal Surgery/Geriatrics/General Surgery)

Follow-up hospital consultation on first post-op day for a 64-year-old male who has undergone uneventful CABG. (Anesthesiology)

Follow-up inpatient consultation for a 67-year-old female admitted several days ago for bleeding ulcer; now stable. (Gastroenterology)

Follow-up hospital consultation for a 35-year-old female with history of mitral valve prolapse. (Cardiology)

Follow-up inpatient consultation to complete initial consultation for dental pain after review of radiographs. (Oral & Maxillofacial Surgery)

Follow-up inpatient consultation for evaluation of response to therapy for moniliasis. (Oral & Maxillofacial Surgery)

Follow-up inpatient consultation for a 22-year-old female with recurrent aphthous ulcers. (Oral & Maxillofacial Surgery)

Follow-up hospital consultation for a 37-year-old female to complete review of previously unavailable studies. (Therapeutic Radiology & Oncology)

Follow-up consultation for a highly functional 75-year-old female with urinary incontinence to review preliminary results of diagnostic evaluation. (Geriatrics)

Follow-up inpatient consultation for a 1-week-old premature female with patent ductus arteriosus. The murmur has disappeared. (Cardiology)

Follow-up hospital consultation to review the results of an audiogram. (Otolaryngology, Head & Neck Surgery)

Follow-up inpatient consultation with 35-year-old female with pulmonary embolism post-op cesarean section, now stable, for assessment of response to anticoagulation and recommended adjustment of heparin dose. (Pulmonary Medicine)

Follow-up inpatient consultation for a 74-year-old male whose postoperative facial paralysis after a cholecystectomy is now resolving. (Neurology)

Follow-up inpatient consultation with 67-year-old female, established patient, for review of diagnostic studies ordered at time of first contact. (Internal Medicine)

Follow-up inpatient consultation for 78-year-old female nursing home resident for evaluation of medical management of pruritis ani. (General Surgery/Colon & Rectal Surgery)

Follow-up inpatient consultation for a 36-year-old female two days after spontaneous passage of 3mm stone. (Urology)

Follow-up inpatient consultation for a 94-year-old male nursing home resident for re-evaluation of hemorrhoids following conservative therapy. (Colon & Rectal Surgery/General Surgery/Geriatrics)

Follow-up inpatient consultation for a 50-year-old male, asymptomatic with borderline ECG abnormality, needs preoperative opinion after a thallium exercise perfusion scan. (Cardiology)

99262 Follow-up inpatient consultation for a 6-year-old female, established patient, with endocarditis and changing heart murmur. (Cardiology)

Follow-up inpatient consultation on a 2-year-old male, one day postoperative ventricular septal defect closure with signs of tachycardia. (Cardiology)

Follow-up inpatient consultation for a 63-year-old man, established patient, with moderately severe pulmonary insufficiency, 10 days postoperative coronary artery bypass for unstable angina. Patient has developed severe dyspnea, fever, and a new exudative right pleural effusion. (Cardiology)

Follow-up inpatient consultation for a 67-year-old woman with lung cancer and syndrome of inappropriate secretion of antidiuretic hormone (SIADH) who has had a seizure following intravenous saline. (Endocrinology)

Follow-up inpatient consultation for a 22-year-old female, established patient, with steroid-dependent systemic lupus erythematosus, arthritis, and glomerulonephritis. Patient is re-evaluated for loss of consciousness and chest pain. (Rheumatology)

Follow-up inpatient consultation for a 75-year-old diabetic with fever, chills, a gangrenous heel ulcer, rhonchi, and dyspnea who appears lethargic and tachypneic. (Endocrinology)

Follow-up inpatient consultation for a 30-year-old, established patient, with intractable neck and low back pain, who is excessively sedated after institution of methadone therapy. (Pain Medicine)

Follow-up inpatient consultation for a 65-year-old man with a history of hypertension and MI who is five days post uncomplicated GI procedure with an unremarkable postoperative recovery. He has just been resuscitated from a cardiopulmonary arrest. (Cardiology)

Follow-up inpatient consultation with 72-year-old female, established patient with bullous pemphigoid on combined oral therapy steroids and immunosuppressive to evaluate progress of cutaneous care orders and adjustment of oral/parenteral therapy dosages. (Dermatology)

Follow-up inpatient consultation for a 71-year-old male who has developed a maculopapular skin rash while on antibiotics recommended for an uncomplicated pneumonia. (Infectious Disease)

Follow-up inpatient consultation with 68-year-old, incapacitated male with spinal stenosis and failure to respond to bedrest, analgesics, and PT. (Neurosurgery)

Follow-up inpatient consultation with 51-year-old male for evaluation and determination of the etiology of postoperative hyponatremia following TURP. (Family Medicine)

Follow-up inpatient consultation for re-evaluation of a stroke patient, and development of plan for initial rehabilitation services. (Neurology)

Follow-up inpatient consultation with 45-year-old male, established patient for discussion of CT scan which demonstrates a cavernous hemangioma. (Ophthalmology)

Follow-up inpatient consultation for an asymptomatic 35-year-old Type I diabetic patient with hyperkalemic, hyperchloremia acidosis, to review lab results. (Nephrology)

Follow-up inpatient consultation for an elderly male with a perioperative myocardial infarction requiring adjustment of vasoactive medications. (Anesthesiology)

99263 Follow-up hospital consultation of an AIDS patient admitted with a sore throat who now has enlarging neck mass. (Otolaryngology, Head & Neck Surgery)

Follow-up hospital consultation of a pansinusitis patient with sudden onset of proptosis. (Otolaryngology, Head & Neck Surgery)

Follow-up inpatient consultation for a 53-year-old man with known angina who develops crescendo angina post cholecystectomy. (Cardiology)

Follow-up inpatient consultation with 72-year-old male established patient admitted for management of alcohol withdrawal, now confused and febrile. (Addiction Medicine)

Follow-up inpatient consultation for an HIV+ patient with an increasing fever following 10 days of antibiotic therapy for pneumocystis carinii pneumonia. (Infectious Disease)

Follow-up inpatient consultation with 58-year-old diabetic female, with bacterial endocarditis, continued fever after two weeks of intravenous antibiotic therapy, and new onset ventricular ectopia. (Cardiology)

Follow-up inpatient consultation for a 90-year-old female with urinary incontinence who has a complicated medical history requiring reassessment of multiple medical problems, recommendations for placement, further recommendation for management of incontinence and reevaluation of cognitive status because of competency issues. (Geriatrics/Psychiatry)

Follow-up inpatient consultation for 42-year-old male with persistent gastrointestinal bleeding, etiology undetermined, not responding to conservative therapy of transfusions. (General Surgery/Colon & Rectal Surgery)

Follow-up inpatient consultation for a 62-year-old female with steroid-dependent asthma, diabetes mellitus, thyrotoxicosis, abdominal pain and possible vasculitis. (Rheumatology)

Follow-up inpatient consultation for a 62-year-old male, status post-op acute small bowel obstruction; now with acute renal failure. (Family Medicine)

Emergency Department Services

New or Established Patient

99281 Emergency department visit for a patient for removal of sutures from a well-healed, uncomplicated laceration. (Emergency Medicine)

Emergency department visit for a patient for tetanus toxoid immunization. (Emergency Medicine)

Emergency department visit for a patient with several uncomplicated insect bites. (Emergency Medicine)

99282 Emergency department visit for a 20-year-old student who presents with a painful sunburn with blister formation on the back. (Emergency Medicine)

Emergency department visit for a child presenting with impetigo localized to the face. (Emergency Medicine)

Emergency department visit for a patient with a minor traumatic injury of an extremity with localized pain, swelling, and bruising. (Emergency Medicine)

Emergency department visit for an otherwise healthy patient whose chief complaint is a red, swollen cystic lesion on his/her back. (Emergency Medicine)

Emergency department visit for a patient presenting with a rash on both legs after exposure to poison ivy. (Emergency Medicine)

Emergency department visit for a young adult patient with infected sclera and purulent discharge from both eyes without pain, visual disturbance or history of foreign body in either eye. (Emergency Medicine)

99283 Emergency department visit for a sexually active female complaining of vaginal discharge who is afebrile and denies experiencing abdominal or back pain. (Emergency Medicine)

Emergency department visit for a well-appearing 8-year-old who has a fever, diarrhea and abdominal cramps, is tolerating oral fluids and is not vomiting. (Emergency Medicine)

Emergency department visit for a patient with an inversion ankle injury, who is unable to bear weight on the injured foot and ankle. (Emergency Medicine)

Emergency department visit for a patient who has a complaint of acute pain associated with a suspected foreign body in the painful eye. (Emergency Medicine)

Emergency department visit for a healthy, young adult patient who sustained a blunt head injury with local swelling and bruising without subsequent confusion, loss of consciousness or memory deficit. (Emergency Medicine)

99284 Emergency department visit for a 4-year-old who fell off a bike sustaining a head injury with brief loss of consciousness. (Emergency Medicine)

Emergency department visit for an elderly female who has fallen and is now complaining of pain in her right hip and is unable to walk. (Emergency Medicine)

Emergency department visit for a patient with flank pain and hematuria. (Emergency Medicine)

Emergency department visit for a female presenting with lower abdominal pain and a vaginal discharge. (Emergency Medicine)

99285 Emergency department visit for a patient with a complicated overdose requiring aggressive management to prevent side effects from the ingested materials. (Emergency Medicine)

Emergency department visit for a patient with a new onset of rapid heart rate requiring IV drugs. (Emergency Medicine)

Emergency department visit for a patient exhibiting active, upper gastrointestinal bleeding. (Emergency Medicine)

Emergency department visit for a previously healthy young adult patient who is injured in an automobile accident and is brought to the emergency department immobilized and has symptoms compatible with intra-abdominal injuries or multiple extremity injuries. (Emergency Medicine)

Emergency department visit for a patient with an acute onset of chest pain compatible with symptoms of cardiac ischemia and/or pulmonary embolus. (Emergency Medicine)

Emergency department visit for a patient who presents with a sudden onset of "the worst headache of her life," and complains of a stiff neck, nausea, and inability to concentrate. (Emergency Medicine)

Emergency department visit for a patient with a new onset of a cerebral vascular accident. (Emergency Medicine)

Emergency department visit for acute febrile illness in an adult, associated with shortness of breath and an altered level of alertness. (Emergency Medicine)

Critical Care Services

99291 First hour of critical care of a 65-year-old man with septic shock following relief of ureteral obstruction caused by a stone.

First hour of critical care of a 15-year-old with acute respiratory failure from asthma.

First hour of critical care of a 45-year-old who sustained a liver laceration, cerebral hematoma, flailed chest, and pulmonary contusion after being struck by an automobile.

First hour of critical care of a 65-year-old woman who, following a hysterectomy, suffered a cardiac arrest associated with a pulmonary embolus.

First hour of critical care of a 6-month-old with hypovolemic shock secondary to diarrhea and dehydration.

First hour of critical care of a 3-year-old with respiratory failure secondary to pneumocystis carinii pneumonia.

Comprehensive Nursing Facility Assessments

New or Established Patient

99301 Annual nursing facility history and physical and MDS/RAI evaluation for a two-year nursing facility resident who is an 84-year-old female with multiple chronic health problems, including: stable controlled hypertension, chronic constipation, osteoarthritis, and moderated stable dementia.

Nursing facility visit for an assessment of a resident with non-insulin dependent diabetes, stable angina, and chronic obstructive pulmonary disease (COPD) one year after previous MDS/RAI.

99302 Nursing facility visit one year after previous MDS/RAI to assess an 80-year-old woman with Parkinson's disease, chronic hypertension, and degenerative arthritis. Visit reveals Stage II decubitus.

Nursing facility assessment of a 28-year-old diabetic, male resident with a new Stage IV pressure ulcer on his left lateral malleolus that is unresponsive to treatment, thus triggering the need for a new MDS/RAI and new medical plan of care.

Nursing facility assessment of an 88-year-old male resident with a permanent change in status following a new cerebral vascular accident (CVA) that has triggered the need for a new MDS/RAI and medical plan of care.

Nursing facility visit and assessment to take over the primary care of a 75-year-old diabetic, previously stable, who was on oral hypoglycemic agents, but who now requires initiation of insulin therapy, a new MDS/RAI, and medical plan of care.

Nursing facility visit and assessment for an 81-year-old female resident with dementia, who, under structured guidance and intensive nutritional support has regained significant levels of function in three activities of daily living and is now able to feed and dress herself and ambulate with appliance and who now thus requires a new MDS/RAI and medical plan of care.

99303 Initial nursing facility assessment (MDS/RAI and medical plan of care) of a 72-year-old insulin dependent diabetic amputee with hearing and visual impairments and possible dementia seen in the office the day before and judged to require nursing facility care.

Sub-acute nursing facility assessment of a previously independently living 90-year-old male who suffered a recent cerebral vascular accident (CVA) and is transferred to the hospital sub-acute rehabilitation unit for further rehabilitation supportive services.

Initial nursing facility visit to evaluate a 72-year-old woman found confused and wandering, admitted by Adult Protective Services without a qualifying hospital stay or inpatient diagnostic work. The patient lives alone and has no relatives or significant others in the community.

Nursing facility assessment and creation of medical plan of care upon readmission to the nursing facility of an 82-year-old male who was previously discharged. The patient has just been discharged from the hospital where he had been treated for an acute gastric ulcer bleed associated with transient delirium. The patient returns to the nursing facility debilitated, protein depleted, and with a Stage III coccygeal decubitus.

Subsequent Nursing Facility Care

New or Established Patient

99311 Scheduled follow-up visit for a known 70-year-old stable paraplegic with no status change noted during visit.

Scheduled monthly nursing home visit with a patient who has mild senile dementia, Alzheimers' type, with no change in status, stable hypertension, and who is ambulating with a walker one year past stroke.

Follow-up in skilled nursing facility with a 70-year-old patient following a 10-day treatment of a cellulitis of the foot.

99312 Scheduled follow-up visit to a resident with controlled dementia, hypertension, and diabetes. During visit, patient seems to exhibit flu symptoms.

Scheduled nursing facility visit with an afebrile demented resident who also has a mild cough, requiring no change in the medical plan of care.

Subsequent visit in a skilled nursing facility with a patient who is six months post stroke and now has a fever and mild cough.

Scheduled nursing facility visit for an 84-year-old male with chronic renal insufficiency, on digitalis and diuretics, requiring adjustment of medications and revision of medical plan of care.

Nursing facility visit of a resident with multiple chronic health problems who is six months post stroke and now has a fever and mild cough, to evaluate for possible pneumonia. Requires the development of a new medical plan of care, but not a revised MDS/RAI.

99313 Follow-up nursing facility visit to evaluate the reason for frequent falls by a 90-year-old ataxic resident, and to determine possible need for change in medications and medical care plan.

Re-admission of a 75-year-old man with stroke who was hospitalized with pneumonia for his illness and who returns to the nursing facility with no permanent change in status from his condition prior to hospitalization; no new MDS/RAI is required.

Nursing facility visit with a diabetic resident who has developed Stage II decubitus ulcers with cellulitis, requiring a revision in the medical plan of care.

Nursing facility visit to develop a new plan of care for an amputee with atherosclerosis obliterans who has refused to eat for three days and has developed decreased urinary output.

Nursing facility visit for a 78-year-old resident with chronic atrial fibrillation and a history of heart failure to evaluate an acute confusional state and to revise the medical plan of care.

Unscheduled nursing facility visit for evaluation of a patient with fever and obtundation who is determined not to require hospital admission or new MDS, but who does require workup and revision of medical plan of care.

Prolonged Services

Prolonged Physician Service With Direct (Face-to-Face) Patient Contact

Office or Other Outpatient

99354/ 99355 A 20-year-old female with history of asthma presents with acute bronchospasm and moderate respiratory distress. Initial evaluation shows respiratory rate 30, labored breathing and wheezing heard in all lung fields. Office treatment is initiated which includes intermittent bronchial dilation and subcutaneous epinephrine. Requires intermittent physician face-to-face time with patient over a period of 2-3 hours. (Family Medicine/Internal Medicine)

Inpatient

99356 A 34-year-old primigravida presents to hospital in early labor. Admission history and physical reveals severe preeclampsia. Physician supervises management of preeclampsia, IV magnesium initiation and maintenance, labor augmentation with pitocin, and close maternal-fetal monitoring. Physician face-to-face involvement includes 40 minutes of continuous bedside care until the patient is stable, then is intermittent over several hours until the delivery. (Family Medicine/Internal Medicine/Obstetrics & Gynecology)

Prolonged Physician Service Without Direct Patient (Face-to-Face) Contact

99358/ 99359 A 65-year-old new patient with multiple problems is seen and evaluated. After the visit, the physician requires extensive time to talk with the patient's daughter, to review complex, detailed medical records transferred from previous physicians and to complete a comprehensive treatment plan. This plan also requires the physician to personally initiate and coordinate the care plan with a local home health agency and a dietician. (Family Medicine/Internal Medicine)

Physician Standby Services

99360 A 24-year-old patient is admitted to OB unit attempting VBAC. Fetal monitoring shows increasing fetal distress. Patient's blood pressure is rising and labor progressing slowly. A primary care physician is requested by the OB/GYN to standby in the unit for possible cesarean delivery and neonatal resuscitation. (Family Medicine/Internal Medicine)

Care Plan Oversight Services

99375 First month of care plan oversight for terminal care of a 58-year-old woman with advanced intraabdominal ovarian cancer. Care plan includes home oxygen, diuretics IV for edema and ascites control and pain control management involving IV morphine infusion when progressive ileus occurred. Physician phone contacts with nurse, family, and MSW. Discussion with MSW concerning plans to withdraw supportive measures per patient wishes. Documentation includes review and modification of care plan and certifications from nursing, MSW, pharmacy, and DME. (Family Medicine/Internal Medicine)

Appendix D

Summary of CPT Add-on Codes

This listing is a summary of CPT add-on codes for *CPT 2004*. The codes listed below are identified in *CPT 2004* with a ✚ symbol.

0006T
0036T
0049T
0054T
0055T
0056T
01953
01968
01969
11001
11101
11201
11732
11922
13102
13122
13133
13153
15001
15101
15121
15201
15221
15241
15261
15343
15351
15401
15787
16036
17003
17310
19001
19126
19291
19295
22103
22116
22216
22226
22328
22522
22534
22585
22614
22632
26125
26861
26863
27358
27692
31632
31633
32501
33141
33225
33508
33530
33572
33924
33961
34808
34813
34826
35390
35400
35500
35572
35681
35682
35683
35685
35686
35697
35700
36218
36248
37206
37208
37250
37251
38102
38746
38747
43635
44015
44121
44128
44139
44203
44701
44955
47001
47550
48400
49568
49905
56606
58611
59525
60512
61316
61517
61609
61610
61611
61612
61795
61864
61868
62148
62160
63035
63043
63044
63048
63057
63066
63076
63078
63082
63086
63088
63091
63103
63308
64472
64476
64480
64484
64623
64627
64727
64778
64783
64787
64832
64837
64859
64872
64874
64876
64901
64902
66990
67225
67320
67331
67332
67334
67335
67340
69990
74301
75774
75946
75964
75968
75993
75996
75998
76082
76083
76125
76802
76810
76812
76937
78020
78478
78480
78496
87187
87904
88141
88155
88311
88312
88313
88314
90472
90474
90781
92547
92608
92973
92974
92978
92979
92981
92984
92996
92998
93320
93321
93325
93571
93572
93609
93613
93621
93622
93623
93662
95920
95962
95967
95973
95975
96412
96423
96570
96571
97546
99100
99116
99135
99140
99290
99292
99354
99355
99356
99357
99358
99359
99602

Appendix E

Summary of CPT Codes Exempt from Modifier '-51'

This listing is a summary of CPT codes that are exempt from the use of modifier '-51' but have NOT been designated as CPT add-on procedures/services. The codes listed below are identified in *CPT 2004* with a ⊘ symbol.

17004
17304
17305
17306
17307
20660
20690
20692
20900
20902
20910
20912
20920
20922
20924
20926
20930
20931
20936
20937
20938
20974
20975
22840
22841
22842
22843
22844
22845
22846
22847
22848
22851
31500
32000
32002
32020
33517
33518
33519
33521
33522
33523
35600
36620
36660
38792
44500
61107
61210
62284
90281
90283
90287
90288
90291
90296
90371
90375
90376
90378
90379
90384
90385
90386
90389
90393
90396
90399
90476
90477
90581
90585
90586
90632
90633
90634
90636
90645
90646
90647
90648
90655
90657
90658
90660
90665
90669
90675
90676
90680
90690
90691
90692
90693
90700
90701
90702
90703
90704
90705
90706
90707
90708
90710
90712
90713
90716
90717
90718
90719
90720
90721
90723
90725
90727
90732
90733
90735
90740
90743
90744
90746
90747
90748
90749
93501
93503
93505
93508
93510
93511
93514
93524
93526
93527
93528
93529
93530
93531
93532
93533
93539
93540
93541
93542
93543
93544
93545
93555
93556
93600
93602
93603
93610
93612
93615
93616
93618
93619
93620
93624
93631
93640
93641
93642
93650
93651
93652
93660
95900
95903
95904
99141
99142

Notes

Index

Instructions for the Use of the CPT Index

Main Terms

The index is organized by main terms. Each main term can stand alone, or be followed by up to three modifying terms. There are four primary classes of main entries:

1. Procedure or service.
   For example: Endoscopy; Anastomosis; Splint
2. Organ or other anatomic site.
   For example: Tibia; Colon; Salivary Gland
3. Condition.
   For example: Abscess; Entropion; Tetralogy of Fallot
4. Synonyms, Eponyms and Abbreviations.
   For example: EEG; Bricker Operation; Clagett Procedure

Modifying Terms

A main term may be followed by a series of up to three indented terms that modify the main term. When modifying terms appear, one should review the list, as these subterms do have an effect on the selection of the appropriate code for the procedure.

Code Ranges

Whenever more than one code applies to a given index entry, a code range is listed. If several non-sequential codes apply, they will be separated by a comma. For example:

Esophagus
    Reconstruction 43300, 43310, 43113

If two or more sequential codes apply, they will be separated by a hyphen. For example:

Debridement
    Burns 01951-01953, 16010-16030

Conventions

As a space saving convention, certain words infer some meaning. This convention is primarily used when a procedure or service is listed as a subterm. For example:

Knee
    Incision (of)

In this example, the word in parentheses (of) does not appear in the index, but it is inferred. As another example:

Pancreas
    Anesthesia (for procedures on)

In this example, as there is no such entity as pancreas anesthesia, the words in parentheses are inferred. That is, anesthesia for procedures on the pancreas.

The alphabetic index is NOT a substitute for the main text of *CPT*. Even if only one code appears, the user must refer to the main text to ensure that the code selection is accurate.

A

A Vitamin
See Vitamin, A

A-II
See Angiotensin II

Abbe-Estlander Procedure
See Reconstruction; Repair, Cleft Lip

Abdomen
Abdominal Wall
  Repair
    Hernia 49491-49496, 49501, 49507, 49521, 49590
  Tumor
    Excision 22900
  Unlisted Services and Procedures 22999
Abscess
  Incision and Drainage 49020, 49040
    Open 49040
    Percutaneous 49021
Angiography 74175, 75635
Artery
  Ligation 37617
Biopsy 49000
Bypass Graft 35907
Cannula/Catheter
  Removal 49422
Celiotomy
  for Staging 49220
CT Scan 74150-74175, 75635
Cyst
  Destruction/Excision 49200-49201
Drainage
  Fluid 49080-49081
Ectopic Pregnancy 59130
Endometrioma
  Destruction/Excision 49200-49201
Exploration 49000-49002
  Blood Vessel 35840
  Staging 58960
Incision 49000
  Staging 58960
Incision and Drainage
  Pancreatitis 48000
Injection
  Air 49400
  Contrast Material 49400
Insertion
  Catheter 49419-49421
  Venous Shunt 49425
Intraperitoneal
  Catheter Removal 49422
  Shunt
    Ligation 49428
    Removal 49429
Laparotomy
  Staging 49220
Magnetic Resonance Imaging (MRI) 74181-74183
Needle Biopsy
  Mass 49180
Peritoneocentesis 49080-49081
Radical Resection 51597
Repair
  Blood Vessel 35221
    with Other Graft 35281
    with Vein Graft 35251
  Hernia 49491-49525, 49560-49587
  Suture 49900
Revision
  Venous Shunt 49426
Suture 49900
Tumor
  Destruction/Excision 49200-49201
Ultrasound 76700-76705
Unlisted Services and Procedures 49999
Wound Exploration
  Penetrating 20102
X-Ray 74000-74022

Abdominal Aorta
See Aorta, Abdominal

Abdominal Aortic Aneurysm
See Aorta, Abdominal, Aneurysm

Abdominal Deliveries
See Cesarean Delivery

Abdominal Hysterectomy
See Hysterectomy, Abdominal

Abdominal Lymphangiogram
See Lymphangiography, Abdomen

Abdominal Paracentesis
See Abdomen, Drainage

Abdominal Radiographies
See Abdomen, X-Ray

Abdominal Wall
Reconstruction 49905
Surgery 22999
Tumor
  Excision 22900

Abdominohysterectomy
See Hysterectomy, Abdominal

Abdominopelvic Amputation
See Amputation, Interpelviabdominal

Abdominoplasty 15831

Ablation
Anal
  Polyp 46615
  Tumor 46615
Bone
  Tumor 20982
Colon
  Tumor 45339
CT Scan Guidance 76362
Endometrial 0009T, 58353, 58563
Endometrium
  Ultrasound Guidance 0009T
Heart
  Arrhythmogenic Focus 93650-93652
    See Cardiology; Diagnostic, Intracardiac Pacing and Mapping
Liver
  Tumor 47380-47382
    Laparoscopic 47370-47371
Magnetic Resonance Guidance 76394
Prostate 55873
Renal Cyst 50541
Renal Mass 50542
Turbinate Mucosa 30801-30802
Ultrasound Guidance 76940

Abortion
See Obstetrical Care
Incomplete 59812
Induced
  by Dilation and Curettage 59840
  by Dilation and Evacuation 59841
  by Saline 59850-59851
  by Vaginal Suppositories 59855-59856
  with Hysterectomy 59100, 59852, 59857
Missed
  First Trimester 59820
  Second Trimester 59821
Septic 59830
Spontaneous 59812
Therapeutic
  by Saline 59850
    with Dilation and Curettage 59851
    with Hysterectomy 59852

Abrasion
Skin
  Chemical Peel 15788-15793
  Dermabrasion 15780-15783
  Lesion 15786-15787
  Salabrasion 15810-15811

Abscess
Abdomen 49040-49041
  Incision and Drainage
    Open 49040
    Percutaneous 49021
Anal
  Incision and Drainage 46045-46050
Ankle 27603
Appendix
  Incision and Drainage 44900
    Open 44900
    Percutaneous 44901
Arm, Lower 25028
  Excision 25145
  Incision and Drainage 25035
Arm, Upper
  Incision and Drainage 23930-23935
Auditory Canal, External 69020
Bartholin's Gland
  Incision and Drainage 56420
Bladder
  Incision and Drainage 51080
Brain
  Drainage 61150-61151
  Excision 61514, 61522
  Incision and Drainage 61320-61321
Breast
  Incision and Drainage 19020
Carpals
  Incision, Deep 25035
Clavicle
  Sequestrectomy 23170
Drainage
  with X-Ray 75989
Ear, External
  Complicated 69005
  Simple 69000

Elbow
 Incision and Drainage 23930-23935
Epididymis
 Incision and Drainage 54700
Excision
 Olecranon Process 24138
 Radius 24136
 Ulna 24138
Eyelid
 Incision and Drainage 67700
Facial Bones
 Excision 21026
Finger 26010-26011
 Incision and Drainage 26034
Foot
 Incision 28005
Gums
 Incision and Drainage 41800
Hand
 Incision and Drainage 26034
Hematoma
 Incision and Drainage 27603
Hip
 Incision and Drainage 26990-26992
Humeral Head 23174
Humerus
 Excision 24134
 Incision and Drainage 23935
Kidney
 Incision and Drainage 50020
  Open 50020
  Percutaneous 50021
Leg, Lower
 Incision and Drainage 27603
Liver 47010
 Drainage
  Open 47010
 Injection 47015
 Repair 47300
Localization
 Nuclear Medicine 78806-78807
Lung
 Percutaneous Drainage 32200-32201
Lymph Node
 Incision and Drainage 38300-38305
Lymphocele Drainage 49062
Mandible
 Excision 21025
Mouth
 Incision and Drainage 40800-40801, 41005-41009, 41015-41018
Nasal Septum
 Incision and Drainage 30020
Neck
 Incision and Drainage 21501-21502
Ovarian
 Incision and Drainage 58820-58822
  Abdominal Approach 58822
  Vaginal Approach 58820
Ovary
 Drainage
  Percutaneous 58823
Palate
 Incision and Drainage 42000
Paraurethral Gland
 Incision and Drainage 53060
Parotid Gland Drainage 42300-42305
Pelvic
 Drainage
  Percutaneous 58823
Pelvis
 Incision and Drainage ...26990-26992, 45000
Pericolic
 Drainage
  Percutaneous 58823
Perineum
 Incision and Drainage 56405
Perirenal or Renal
 Drainage 50020-50021
  Percutaneous 50021
Peritoneum
 Incision and Drainage
  Open 49020
  Percutaneous 49021
Prostate
 Incision and Drainage 55720-55725
 Transurethral Drainage 52700
Radius
 Incision, Deep 25035
Rectum
 Incision and Drainage 45005-45020, 46040, 46060
Retroperitoneal 49060-49061
 Drainage
  Open 49060
  Percutaneous 49061
Salivary Gland
 Drainage 42300-42320
Scapula
 Sequestrectomy 23172
Scrotum
 Incision and Drainage 54700, 55100
Shoulder
 Drainage 23030
Skene's Gland
 Incision and Drainage 53060
Skin
 Incision and Drainage 10060-10061
 Puncture Aspiration 10160
Soft Tissue
 Incision 20000-20005
Subdiaphragmatic 49040-49041
Sublingual Gland
 Drainage 42310-42320
Submaxillary Gland
 Drainage 42310-42320
Subphrenic 49040-49041
Testis
 Incision and Drainage 54700
Thoracostomy 32020
Thorax
 Incision and Drainage 21501-21502
Throat
 Incision and Drainage 42700-42725
Tongue
 Incision and Drainage 41000-41006
Tonsil
 Incision and Drainage 42700
Ulna
 Incision, Deep 25035
Urethra
 Incision and Drainage 53040
Uvula
 Incision and Drainage 42000
Vagina
 Incision and Drainage 57010
Vulva
 Incision and Drainage 56405
Wrist
 Excision 25145
 Incision and Drainage 25028, 25035
X-Ray 76080

Abscess, Nasal
See Nose, Abscess

Abscess, Parotid Gland
See Parotid Gland, Abscess

Absorptiometry
Dual Energy
 Body Composition 0028T
 Bone 76075
  Appendicular 76076
  Axial Skeleton 76075
Dual Photon
 Bone 78351
Radiographic
 Photodensity 76078
Single Photon
 Bone 78350

Absorption Spectrophotometry, Atomic
See Atomic Absorption Spectroscopy

Accessory Nerve, Spinal
See Nerves, Spinal Accessory

Accessory, Toes
See Polydactyly, Toes

ACE
See Angiotensin Converting Enzyme (ACE), Performance Measures

Acetabuloplasty 27120-27122

Acetabulum
Fracture
 Closed Treatment 27220-27222
 Open Treatment 27226-27228
 with Manipulation 27222
 without Manipulation 27220
Reconstruction 27120
 with Resection, Femoral Head 27122
Tumor
 Excision 27076

Acetaldehyde
Blood 82000

Acetaminophen
Urine 82003

Acetic Anhydrides 84600

Acetone
Blood or Urine 82009-82010

Acetone Body 82009-82010

Acetylcholinesterase
Blood or Urine 82013

AcG
See Clotting Factor

Intermarginal
  Construction .67880
    Transposition of Tarsal Plate .67882
Intestinal
  Enterolysis .44005
    Laparoscopic .44200
Intracranial
  Lysis .62161
Intrauterine
  Lysis .58559
Labial
  Lysis .56441
Lungs
  Lysis .32124
Pelvic
  Lysis .58660, 58662, 58740
Penile
  Lysis
    Post-circumcision .54162
Preputial
  Lysis .54450
Urethral
  Lysis .53500

Adipectomy
See Lipectomy

ADL
See Activities of Daily Living

Administration
Immunization
  Each Additional Vaccine/Toxoid .90472, 90474
  One Vaccine/Toxoid .90471, 90473

ADP
See Adenosine Diphosphate

ADP Phosphocreatine Phosphotransferase
See CPK

Adrenal Cortex Hormone
See Corticosteroids

Adrenal Gland
Biopsy .60540-60545
Excision
  Laparoscopy .60650
  Retroperitoneal Tumor .60545
Exploration .60540-60545
Nuclear Medicine
  Imaging .78075

Adrenal Medulla
See Medulla

Adrenalectomy .60540
Anesthesia .00866
Laparoscopic .50545

Adrenalin
See Catecholamines
Blood .82383
Urine .82384

Adrenaline-Noradrenaline
Testing .82382-82384

Adrenocorticotropic Hormone (ACTH) .80400-80406, 80412, 80418, 82024
Blood or Urine .82024
Stimulation Panel .80400-80406

Adrenogenital Syndrome .56805, 57335

Adult T Cell Leukemia Lymphoma Virus I
See HTLV I

Advanced Life Support
See Emergency Department Services
Physician Direction .99288

Advancement
Genioglossus .21199
Tendon
  Foot .28238

Advancement Flap
See Skin, Adjacent Tissue Transfer

Aerosol Inhalation
See Pulmonology, Therapeutic
Pentamidine .94642

AFB
See Acid Fast Bacilli (AFB)

Afferent Nerve
See Sensory Nerve

AFP
See Alpha-Fetoprotein

After Hours Medical Services .99050-99054

Agents, Anticoagulant
See Clotting Inhibitors

Agglutinin
Cold .86156-86157
Febrile .86000

Aggregation
Platelet .85576

AHG
See Clotting Factor

AICD (Pacing Cardioverter-Defibrillator)
See Defibrillator, Heart; Pacemaker, Heart

Aid, Hearing
See Hearing Aid

AIDS Antibodies
See Antibody, HIV

AIDS Virus
See HIV-1

Akin Operation
See Bunion Repair

ALA
See Aminolevulinic Acid (ALA)

Alanine 2 Oxoglutarate Aminotransferase
See Transaminase, Glutamic Pyruvic

Alanine Amino (ALT) .84460

Alanine Transaminase
See Transaminase, Glutamic Pyruvic

Albarran Test
See Water Load Test

Albumin
Serum .82040
Urine .82042

Alcohol
Breath .82075
Ethyl
  Blood .82055
  Urine .82055
Ethylene Glycol .82693

Alcohol Dehydrogenase
See Antidiuretic Hormone

Alcohol, Isopropyl
See Isopropyl Alcohol

Alcohol, Methyl
See Methanol

Aldolase
Blood .82085

Aldosterone
Blood .82088
Suppression Evaluation .80408
Urine .82088

Alimentary Canal
See Gastrointestinal Tract

Alkaline Phosphatase .84075-84080
Leukocyte .85540
WBC .85540

Alkaloids
See Specific Drug
Urine .82101

Allergen Bronchial Provocation Tests
See Allergy Tests; Bronchial Challenge Test

Allergen Challenge, Endobronchial
See Bronchial Challenge Test

Allergen Immunotherapy
Allergen
  Prescription/Supply/Injection .95120-95125
  with Extract Supply .95144
    Injection .95115-95117
Antigens .95144
IgE .86003-86005
IgG .86001
Insect Venom
  Prescription/Supply .95145-95149
  Prescription/Supply/Injection .95130-95134
Prescription/Supply .95165
  Insect, Whole Body .95170
Rapid Desensitization .95180

Amputation, Nose
See Resection, Nose

Amylase
Blood .82150
Urine .82150

ANA
See Antinuclear Antibodies (ANA)

Anabolic Steroid
See Androstenedione

Anal Abscess
See Abscess, Anal

Anal Bleeding
See Anus, Hemorrhage

Anal Fistula
See Fistula, Anal

Anal Fistulectomy
See Excision, Fistula, Anal

Anal Fistulotomy
See Fistulotomy, Anal

Anal Sphincter
Dilation .45905
Incision .46080

Anal Ulceration
See Anus, Fissure

Analgesia .99141-99142
See Anesthesia; Sedation

Analgesic Cutaneous Electrostimulation
See Application, Neurostimulation

Analysis
Computer Data .99090
Electroencephalogram
Digital .95957
Electronic
Drug Infusion Pump .62367-62368
Pacing Cardioverter-Defibrillator .93741-93744
See Pacemaker, Heart
Pulse Generator .95970-95971
Physiologic Data, Remote .99091
Protein
Tissue
Western Blot .88372
Semen
Sperm Isolation .89260-89261

Analysis, Spectrum
See Spectrophotometry

Anaspadias
See Epispadias

Anastomosis
Arteriovenous Fistula
Direct .36821
with Bypass Graft .35686
with Graft .36825-36830, 36832
Artery
to Aorta .33606
to Artery
Cranial .61711
Bile Duct
to Bile Duct .47800
to Intestines .47760, 47780
Bile Duct to Gastrointestinal .47785
Broncho-Bronchial .32486
Caval to Mesenteric .37160
Colorectal .44620
Epididymis
to Vas Deferens
Bilateral .54901
Unilateral .54900
Excision
Trachea .31780-31781
Fallopian Tube .58750
Gallbladder to Intestines .47720-47740
Hepatic Duct to Intestines .47765, 47802
Ileo-Anal .45113
Intestines
Colo-anal .45119
Cystectomy .51590
Enterocystoplasty .51960
Resection
Laparoscopic .44202-44205
Intestine to Intestine .44130
Intrahepatic Portosystemic .37182-37183
Jejunum .43825
Microvascular
Free Transfer
Jejunum .43496
Nerve
Facial to Hypoglossal .64868
Facial to Phrenic .64870
Oviduct .58750
Pancreas to Intestines .48180, 48520-48540
Portocaval .37140
Pulmonary .33606
Renoportal .37145
Splenorenal .37180-37181
Stomach .43825
to Duodenum .43810, 43855
Revision .43850
to Jejunum .43820, 43860-43865
Tubotubal .58750
Ureter
to Bladder .50780-50785
to Colon .50810-50815
Removal .50830
to Intestine .50800, 50820-50825
Removal .50830
to Kidney .50727-50750
to Ureter .50727, 50760-50770
Vein
Saphenopopliteal .34530
Vein to Vein .37140-37160, 37182-37183

Anastomosis of Lacrimal Sac to Conjunctival Sac
See Conjunctivorhinostomy

Anastomosis of Pancreas
See Pancreas, Anastomosis

Anastomosis, Aorta-Pulmonary Artery
See Aorta, Anastomosis, to Pulmonary Artery

Anastomosis, Bladder, to Intestine
See Enterocystoplasty

Anastomosis, Hepatic Duct
See Hepatic Duct, Anastomosis

Anderson Tibial Lengthening .27715
See Ankle; Tibia, Osteoplasty, Lengthening

Androstanediol Glucuronide .82154

Androstanolone
See Dihydrotestosterone

Androstenedione
Blood or Urine .82157

Androstenolone
See Dehydroepiandrosterone

Androsterone
Blood or Urine .82160

Anesthesia
See Analgesia
Abbe-Estlander Procedure .00102
Abdomen
Abdominal Wall .00700-00730, 00800-00802, 00820-00836
Halsted Repair .00750-00756
Blood Vessels .00770, 00880-00882
Endoscopy .00740, 00810
Extraperitoneal .00860-00862, 00866-00870
Hernia Repair .00830-00836
Halsted Repair .00750-00756
Intraperitoneal .00790-00797, 00840-00842
Abdominoperineal Resection .00844
Abortion
Induced .01964
Achilles Tendon Repair .01472
Acromioclavicular Joint .01620
Adrenalectomy .00866
Amniocentesis .00842
Aneurysm
Axillary-Brachial .01652
Knee .01444
Popliteal Artery .01444
Angiography .01920
Ankle .00400, 01462-01522
Anorectal Procedure .00902
Anus .00902
Arm
Lower .00400, 01810-01820, 01830-01860
Upper .00400, 01710-01782
Arrhythmias .00410
Arteriography .01916
Arteriovenous Fistula .01432
Arthroplasty
Hip .01214-01215
Knee .01402
Arthroscopic Procedures
Ankle .01464
Elbow .01732-01740
Foot .01464
Hip .01202
Knee .01382, 01400
Shoulder .01622-01630
Wrist .01829-01830

Anesthesia Local
See Anesthesia, Local

Aneurysm Artery, Femoral
See Artery, Femoral, Aneurysm

Aneurysm Artery, Radial
See Artery, Radial, Aneurysm

Aneurysm Artery, Renal
See Artery, Renal, Aneurysm

Aneurysm Repair

Repair
  Achilles Tendon ... 27650-27654
  Ligament ... 27695-27698
  Tendon ... 27612, 27680-27687
Strapping ... 29540
Synovium
  Excision ... 27625-27626
Tenotomy ... 27605-27606
Tumor
  Excision ... 27615-27619
Unlisted Services and Procedures ... 27899
X-Ray ... 73600-73610
  with Contrast ... 73615

Ankylosis (Surgical)
See Arthrodesis

Anogenital Region
See Perineum

Anoplasty
Stricture ... 46700-46705

Anorectal Myectomy
See Myomectomy, Anorectal

Anorectal Procedure
Biofeedback ... 90911

Anorectovaginoplasty ... 46744-46746

Anoscopy
Ablation
  Polyp ... 46615
  Tumor ... 46615
Biopsy ... 46606
Dilation ... 46604
Exploration ... 46600
Hemorrhage ... 46614
Removal
  Foreign Body ... 46608
  Polyp ... 46610-46612
  Tumor ... 46610-46612

Antebrachium
See Forearm

Antecedent, Plasma Thromboplastin
See Plasma Thromboplastin, Antecedent

Antepartum Care
Cesarean Delivery ... 59510
  Previous ... 59610, 59618
Vaginal Delivery ... 59425-59426

Anterior Ramus of Thoracic Nerve
See Intercostal Nerve

Anthrax Vaccine
See Vaccines

Anthrogon
See Follicle Stimulating Hormone (FSH)

Anti Australia Antigens
See Antibody, Hepatitis B

Anti D Immunoglobulin
See Immune Globulins, Rho (D)

Anti-Human Globulin Consumption Test
See Coombs Test

Anti-Phospholipid Antibody
See Antibody, Phospholipid

Antiactivator, Plasmin
See Alpha-2 Antiplasmin

Antibiotic Administration
Injection ... 90788

Antibiotic Sensitivity ... 87181-87184, 87188
Enzyme Detection ... 87185
Minimum Bactericidal Concentration ... 87187
Minimum Inhibitory Concentration ... 87186

Antibodies, Thyroid-Stimulating
See Immunoglobulin, Thyroid Stimulating

Antibodies, Viral
See Viral Antibodies

Antibody
See Antibody Identification; Microsomal Antibody
Actinomyces ... 86602
Adenovirus ... 86603
Antinuclear ... 86038-86039
Antiphosphatidylserine (Phospholipid) ... 86148
Antiprothrombin ... 0030T
Antistreptolysin O ... 86060-86063
Aspergillus ... 86606
Bacterium ... 86609
Bartonella ... 86611
Beta 2 Glycoprotein I ... 86146
Blastomyces ... 86612
Blood Crossmatch ... 86920-86922
Bordetella ... 86615
Borrelia ... 86618-86619
Brucella ... 86622
Campylobacter ... 86625
Candida ... 86628
Cardiolipin ... 86147
Chlamydia ... 86631-86632
Coccidioides ... 86635
Coxiella Burnetii ... 86638
Cryptococcus ... 86641
Cytomegalovirus ... 86644-86645
Cytotoxic Screen ... 86807-86808
Deoxyribonuclease ... 86215
Deoxyribonucleic Acid (DNA) ... 86225-86226
Diphtheria ... 86648
Ehrlichia ... 86666
Encephalitis ... 86651-86654
Enterovirus ... 86658
Epstein-Barr Virus ... 86663-86665
Fluorescent ... 86255-86256
Francisella Tularensis ... 86668
Fungus ... 86671
Giardia Lamblia ... 86674
Growth Hormone ... 86277
Helicobacter Pylori ... 86677
Helminth ... 86682
Hemophilus Influenza ... 86684
Hepatitis
  Delta Agent ... 86692
Hepatitis A ... 86708-86709
Hepatitis B
  Core ... 86704
  IgM ... 86705
  Surface ... 86706
Hepatitis Be ... 86707
Hepatitis C ... 86803-86804
Herpes Simplex ... 86694-86696
Heterophile ... 86308-86310
Histoplasma ... 86698
HIV ... 86689, 86701-86703
HIV-1 ... 86701, 86703
HIV-2 ... 86702-86703
HTLV-I ... 86687, 86689
HTLV-II ... 86688
Influenza Virus ... 86710
Insulin ... 86337
Intrinsic Factor ... 86340
Islet Cell ... 86341
Legionella ... 86713
Leishmania ... 86717
Leptospira ... 86720
Listeria Monocytogenes ... 86723
Lyme Disease ... 86617
Lymphocytic Choriomeningitis ... 86727
Lymphogranuloma Venereum ... 86729
Microsomal ... 86376
Mucormycosis ... 86732
Mumps ... 86735
Mycoplasma ... 86738
Neisseria Meningitidis ... 86741
Nocardia ... 86744
Nuclear Antigen ... 86235
Other Virus ... 86790
Parvovirus ... 86747
Phospholipid ... 86147
Phospholipid Cofactor ... 0030T
Plasmodium ... 86750
Platelet ... 86022-86023
Protozoa ... 86753
Red Blood Cell ... 86850-86870
Respiratory Syncytial Virus ... 86756
Rickettsia ... 86757
Rotavirus ... 86759
Rubella ... 86762
Rubeola ... 86765
Salmonella ... 86768
Shigella ... 86771
Sperm ... 89325
Streptokinase ... 86590
Tetanus ... 86774
Thyroglobulin ... 86800
Toxoplasma ... 86777-86778
Treponema Pallidum ... 86781
Trichinella ... 86784
Varicella-Zoster ... 86787
White Blood Cell ... 86021
Yersinia ... 86793

Antibody Identification
Leukocyte Antibodies ... 86021
Platelet ... 86022-86023
Red Blood Cell
  Pretreatment ... 86970-86972
Serum
  Pretreatment ... 86975-86978

Antibody Neutralization Test
See Neutralization Test

Antibody Receptor
See FC Receptor

Anticoagulant
See Clotting Inhibitors

Antidiabetic Hormone
See Glucagon

Antidiuretic Hormone 84588

Antidiuretic Hormone Measurement
See Vasopressin

AntiDNA Autoantibody
See Antinuclear Antibodies (ANA)

Antigen
Allergen Immunotherapy 95144
Carcinoembryonic 82378
Prostate Specific 84152-84153

Antigen Bronchial Provocation Tests
See Bronchial Challenge Test

Antigen Detection
Direct Fluorescence 87265-87272, 87276, 87278, 87280, 87285-87290
  Bordetella 87265
  Chlamydia Trachomatis 87270
  Cryptosporidium 87272
  Cytomegalovirus 87271
  Enterovirus 87267
  Giardia 87269
  Influenza A 87276
  Legionella Pneumophila 87278
  Not Otherwise Specified 87299
  Respiratory Syncytial Virus 87280
  Treponema Pallidum 87285
  Varicella-Zoster 87290
Enzyme Immunoassay
  Adenovirus 87301
  Chlamydia Trachomatis 87320
  Clostridium Difficile 87324
  Cryptococcus Neoformans 87327
  Cryptosporidium 87328
  Cytomegalovirus 87332
  Entamoeba Histolytica Dispar Group 87336
  Entamoeba Histolytica Group 87337
  Escherichia coli 0157 87335
  Giardia 87329
  Helicobacter Pylori 87338-87339
  Hepatitis B Surface Antigen (HBsAg) 87340
  Hepatitis B Surface Antigen (HBsAg) Neutralization 87341
  Hepatitis Be Antigen (HBeAg) 87350
  Hepatitis Delta Agent 87380
  Histoplasma capsulatum 87385
  HIV-1 87390
  HIV-2 87391
  Influenza A 87400
  Influenza B 87400
  Multiple Step Method 87301-87449
    Polyvalent 87451
  Not Otherwise Specified 87449, 87451
  Respiratory Syncytial Virus 87420
  Rotavirus 87425
  Shigella-like Toxin 87427
  Single Step Method 87450
  Streptococcus, Group A 87430
Immunofluorescence 87260-87300
  Adenovirus 87260
  Herpes Simplex 87273-87274
  Influenza B 87275
  Legionella Micdadei 87277
  Not Otherwise Specified 87299
  Parainfluenza Virus 87279
  Pneumocystis Carinii 87281
  Polyvalent 87300
  Rubeola 87283

Antigen, Australia
See Hepatitis Antigen, B Surface

Antigen, CD4
See CD4

Antigen, CD8
See CD8

Antigens, CD142
See Thromboplastin

Antigens, CD143
See Angiotensin Converting Enzyme (ACE)

Antigens, E
See Hepatitis Antigen, Be

Antigens, Hepatitis
See Hepatitis Antigen

Antigens, Hepatitis B
See Hepatitis Antigen, B

Antihemophilic Factor B
See Christmas Factor

Antihemophilic Factor C
See Plasma Thromboplastin, Antecedent

Antihemophilic Globulin (AHG) 85240

Antihuman Globulin 86880-86886

Antimony 83015

Antinuclear Antibodies (ANA) 86038-86039

Antiplasmin, Alpha-2 85410

Antiplatelet Therapy
See Performance Measures

Antiprotease, Alpha 1
See Alpha-1 Antitrypsin

Antiprothrombin Antibody 0030T

Antistreptococcal Antibody 86215

Antistreptokinase Titer 86590

Antistreptolysin O 86060-86063

Antithrombin III 85300-85301

Antithrombin VI
See Fibrin Degradation Products

Antitoxin Assay 87230

Antiviral Antibody
See Viral Antibodies

Antrostomy
Sinus
  Maxillary 31256-31267

Antrotomy
Sinus
  Maxillary 31020-31032
Transmastoid 69501

Antrum of Highmore
See Sinus, Maxillary

Antrum Puncture
Sinus
  Maxillary 31000
  Sphenoid 31002

Anus
See Hemorrhoids; Rectum
Ablation 46615
Abscess
  Incision and Drainage 46045-46050
Biofeedback 90911
Biopsy
  Endoscopy 46606
Crypt
  Excision 46210-46211
Dilation
  Endoscopy 46604
Endoscopy
  Biopsy 46606
  Dilation 46604
  Exploration 46600
  Hemorrhage 46614
  Removal
    Foreign Body 46608
    Polyp 46610, 46612
    Tumor 46610, 46612
Excision
  Tag 46220, 46230
Exploration
  Endoscopy 46600
Fissure
  Destruction 46940-46942
  Excision 46200
Fistula
  Excision 46270-46285
  Repair 46706
Hemorrhage
  Endoscopic Control 46614
Hemorrhoids
  Clot Excision 46320
  Destruction 46934-46936
  Excision 46250-46262
  Injection 46500
  Ligation 46221, 46945-46946
  Suture 46945-46946
Imperforated
  Repair 46715-46742
Incision
  Septum 46070
Lesion
  Destruction 46900-46917, 46924
  Excision 45108, 46922
Manometry 91122
Placement
  Seton 46020
Reconstruction 46742
  Congenital Absence 46730-46740
  Sphincter 46750-46751, 46760-46762
  with Graft 46753
  with Implant 46762

Removal
- Foreign Body 46608
- Seton 46030
- Suture 46754
- Wire 46754

Repair
- Anovaginal Fistula 46715-46716
- Cloacal Anomaly 46748
- Fistula 46706
- Stricture 46700-46705

Sphincter
- Electromyography 51784-51785
- Needle 51785

Unlisted Services and Procedures 46999

Aorta
Abdominal
- Aneurysm 0001T, 34800-34805, 34825-34832, 35081-35103, 75952-75953
- Thromboendarterectomy 35331

Anastomosis
- to Pulmonary Artery 33606

Angiogram
- Radiologic Injection 93544
  - *See* Cardiac Catheterization, Injection

Angioplasty 35452
Aortography 75600-75630
Balloon 33967, 33970
Catheterization
- Catheter 36200
- Intracatheter/Needle 36160

Circulation Assist 33967, 33970
Conduit to Heart 33404
Excision
- Coarctation 33840-33851

Insertion
- Balloon Device 33967
- Graft 33330-33335
- Intracatheter/Needle 36160

Removal
- Balloon Assist Device 33968, 33971

Repair 33320-33322, 33802-33803
- Coarctation 33840-33851
- Graft 33860-33877
- Hypoplastic or Interrupted Aortic Arch
  - with Cardiopulmonary Bypass 33853
  - without Cardiopulmonary Bypass ... 33852
- Sinus of Valsalva 33702-33720

Suspension 33800
Suture 33320-33322
Thoracic
- Aneurysm 0033T-0034T, 0035T-0039T, 0040T

Valve
- Incision 33415
- Repair 33400-33403
  - Left Ventricle 33414
  - Supravalvular Stenosis 33417
- Replacement 33405-33413

X-Ray with Contrast 75600-75630

Aorta-Pulmonary ART Transposition
See Transposition, Great Arteries

Aortic Sinus
See Sinus of Valsalva

Aortic Stenosis
Repair 33415
- Supravalvular 33417

Aortic Valve
See Heart, Aortic Valve

Aortic Valve Replacement
See Replacement, Aortic Valve

Aortocoronary Bypass
See Coronary Artery Bypass Graft (CABG)

Aortocoronary Bypass for Heart Revascularization
See Artery, Coronary, Bypass

Aortography 75600-75605, 75630, 93544
See Angiography
Serial 75625
with Iliofemoral Artery 75630

Aortoiliac
Embolectomy 34151-34201
Thrombectomy 34151-34201

Aortopexy 33800

Aortoplasty
Supravalvular Stenosis 33417

AP
See Voiding Pressure Studies

Apert-Gallais Syndrome
See Adrenogenital Syndrome

Aphasia Testing 96105
See Neurology, Diagnostic

Apheresis
Therapeutic 36511-36516

Apical-Aortic Conduit 33404

Apicectomy
with Mastoidectomy 69605
- Petrous 69530

Apoaminotransferase, Aspartate
See Transaminase, Glutamic Oxaloacetic

Apolipoprotein
Blood or Urine 82172

Appendectomy 44950-44960
Laparoscopic 44970

Appendiceal Abscess
See Abscess, Appendix

Appendico-Vesicostomy
Cutaneous 50845

Appendix
Abscess
- Incision and Drainage
  - Open 44900
  - Percutaneous 44901

Excision 44950-44960

Application
Allergy Tests 95044

Bone Fixation Device
- Multiplane 20692
- Uniplane 20690

Caliper 20660
Cranial Tongs 20660
Fixation Device
- Shoulder 23700

Halo
- Cranial 20661
  - Thin Skull Osteology 20664
- Femoral 20663
- Maxillofacial Fixation 21100
- Pelvic 20662

Interdental Fixation Device 21110
Neurostimulation 64550
Radioelement 77761-77778
- Surface 77789
- with Ultrasound 76965

Stereotactic Frame 20660

Application of External Fixation Device
See Fixation Device, Application, External

APPT
See Thromboplastin, Partial, Time

Aquatic Therapy
See Physical Medicine/Therapy/Occupational Therapy

Aqueous Shunt
to Extraocular Reservoir 66180
- Revision 66185

Arch, Zygomatic
See Zygomatic Arch

Arm
See Radius; Ulna; Wrist

Lower
- Abscess 25028
- Amputation 24900-24920, 25900-25905, 25915
  - Cineplasty 24940
  - Revision 25907-25909
- Angiography 73206
- Artery
  - Ligation 37618
- Biopsy 25065-25066
- Bursa
  - Incision and Drainage 25031
- Bypass Graft 35903
- Cast 29075
- CT Scan 73200-73206
- Decompression 25020-25025
- Exploration
  - Blood Vessel 35860
- Fasciotomy 24495, 25020-25025
- Hematoma 25028
- Lesion, Tendon Sheath
  - Excision 25110
- Magnetic Resonance Imaging (MRI) 73218-73220, 73223
- Reconstruction
  - Ulna 25337
- Removal
  - Foreign Body 25248

Cannulization
for Extra Corporeal Circulation 36823
to Vein 36810-36815
Carotid
Aneurysm 35001-35002, 61697-61705
Vascular Malformation or Carotid
Cavernous Fistula 61710
Angiography 75660-75680
Bypass Graft 35501-35510, 35526,
35601-35606, 35626, 35642
Catheterization 36100
Decompression ..61590-61591, 61595-61596
Embolectomy 34001
Exploration 35701
Ligation 37600-37606, 61611-61612
Thrombectomy 34001
Thromboendarterectomy 35301, 35390
Transection 61611-61612
Celiac
Aneurysm 35121-35122
Bypass Graft 35531, 35631
Embolectomy 34151
Thrombectomy 34151
Thromboendarterectomy 35341
Chest
Ligation 37616
Coronary
Angiography 93556
Atherectomy 92995-92996
Bypass 33517-33519
Arterial 33533-33536
Bypass Venous Graft 33510-33516
Graft 33503-33505
Ligation 33502
Repair 33500-33506
Thrombectomy
Percutaneous 92973
Digital
Sympathectomy 64820
Ethmoidal
Ligation 30915
Extra Corporeal Circulation
for Regional Chemotherapy
of Extremity 36823
Extracranial
Vascular Studies
Non-Invasive, Physiologic 93875
Extremities
Vascular Studies 93922-93923
Extremity
Bypass Graft Revision 35879-35881
Catheterization 36140
Ligation 37618
Femoral
Aneurysm 35141-35142
Angioplasty 35456
Atherectomy 35483, 35493
Bypass Graft 35521, 35533, 35546,
35551-35558, 35566, 35621, 35646-35647,
35651-35661, 35666, 35700
Bypass In-Situ 35582-35585
Embolectomy 34201
Exploration 35721
Exposure 34812-34813
Thrombectomy 34201
Thromboendarterectomy 35371-35381
Great Vessel
Repair 33770-33781
Head
Angiography 75650
Hepatic
Aneurysm 35121-35122
Iliac
Aneurysm 35131-35132, 75954
Angioplasty 35454
Atherectomy 35482, 35492
Bypass Graft ...35541, 35563, 35641, 35663
Embolectomy 34151-34201
Exposure 34820, 34833
Graft 34900
Occulsion Device 34808
Thrombectomy 34151-34201
Thromboendarterectomy 35351,
35361-35363
Iliofemoral
Bypass Graft 35548-35549, 35565, 35665
Thromboendarterectomy 35355, 35363
X-Ray with Contrast 75630
Innominate
Aneurysm 35021-35022
Embolectomy 34001-34101
Thrombectomy 34001-34101
Thromboendarterectomy 35311
Leg
Angiography 75710-75716
Catheterization 36245-36248
Mammary
Angiography 75756
Maxillary
Ligation 30920
Mesenteric
Aneurysm 35121-35122
Bypass Graft 35531, 35631
Embolectomy 34151
Thrombectomy 34151
Thromboendarterectomy 35341
Neck
Angiography 75650
Ligation 37615
Nose
Incision 30915-30920
Other Angiography 75774
Other Artery
Aneurysm 35161-35162
Exploration 35761
Occlusive Disease 35161
Pelvic
Angiography 75736
Catheterization 36245-36248
Peripheral Arterial Rehabilitation 93668
Peroneal
Bypass Graft 35566-35571, 35666-35671
Bypass In-Situ 35585-35587
Embolectomy 34203
Thrombectomy 34203
Thromboendarterectomy 35381
Popliteal
Aneurysm 35151-35152
Angioplasty 35456
Atherectomy 35483, 35493
Bypass Graft ...35551-35556, 35571, 35623,
35651, 35656, 35671, 35700
Bypass In-Situ 35582-35583, 35587
Embolectomy 34203
Exploration 35741
Thrombectomy 34203
Thromboendarterectomy 35381
Pulmonary
Anastomosis 33606
Angiography 75741-75746
Repair 33690
Radial
Aneurysm 35045
Embolectomy 34111
Sympathectomy 64821
Thrombectomy 34111
Rehabilitation 93668
Reimplantation
Carotid 35691, 35694-35695
Subclavian 35693-35695
Vertebral 35691-35693
Visceral 35697
Renal
Aneurysm 35121-35122
Angiography 75722-75724
Angioplasty 35450
Atherectomy 35480, 35490
Bypass Graft 35536, 35560, 35631-35636
Embolectomy 34151
Thrombectomy 34151
Thromboendarterectomy 35341
Repair
Aneurysm 36834, 61697-61708
Angioplasty 75962-75968
Revision
Hemodialysis Graft or Fistula
with Thrombectomy 36833
without Thrombectomy 36832
Spine
Angiography 75705
Splenic
Aneurysm 35111-35112
Bypass Graft 35536, 35636
Subclavian
Aneurysm 35001-35002, 35021-35022
Angioplasty 35458
Bypass Graft 35506-35507, 35511-35516,
35526, 35606-35616, 35626, 35645
Embolectomy 34001-34101
Thrombectomy 34001-34101
Thromboendarterectomy 35301-35311
Unlisted Services and Procedures 37799
Superficial Palmar Arch
Sympathectomy 64823
Temporal
Biopsy 37609
Ligation 37609
Thoracic
Catheterization 36215-36218
Thrombectomy
Hemodialysis Graft or Fistula 36831
Other than Hemodialysis Graft
or Fistula 35875, 36870
Tibial
Bypass Graft 35566-35571,
35623, 35666-35671
Bypass In-Situ 35585-35587
Embolectomy 34203
Thrombectomy 34203
Thromboendarterectomy 35381

Artery Catheterization, Pulmonary

Arthrectomy

Arthrocentesis

Arthrodeses

Arthrodesis

Arthrography

Arthroplasties, Knee Replacement

Arthroplasty

Arthroplasty, Hip, Total

Arthroplasty, Shoulder

Arthropods

Arthroscopy

Arthroscopy of Ankle

Arthrotomy
Acromioclavicular Joint 23044
Ankle 27610-27612, 27620
Ankle Joint 27625-27626
Carpometacarpal Joint 26070
  with Biopsy, Synovium
    with Synovial Biopsy 26100
Elbow 24000
  Capsular Release 24006
  with Joint Exploration 24101
  with Synovectomy 24102
  with Synovial Biopsy 24100
Finger Joint 26075
  Interphalangeal
    with Synovial Biopsy 26110
  Metacarpophalangeal
    with Biopsy, Synovium 26105
Glenohumeral Joint 23040
Hip 27033
  for Infection
    with Drainage 27030
  with Synovectomy 27054
Interphalangeal Joint 26080, 26110
  Toe 28024, 28054
Intertarsal Joint 28020, 28050
Knee 27310, 27330-27335, 27403
Metacarpophalangeal Joint 26075, 26105
Metatarsophalangeal Joint 28022, 28052
Shoulder 23044, 23105-23107
Shoulder Joint 23100-23101
  Exploration and/or Removal of Loose or Foreign Body 23107
Sternoclavicular Joint 23044
Tarsometatarsal Joint 28020, 28050
Temporomandibular Joint 21010
with Biopsy
  Acromioclavicular Joint 23101
  Glenohumeral Joint 23100
  Hip Joint 27052
  Knee Joint 27330
  Sacroiliac Joint
    Hip Joint 27050
  Sternoclavicular Joint 23101
with Synovectomy
  Glenohumeral Joint 23105
  Sternoclavicular Joint 23106
Wrist 25040, 25100-25107

Arthrotomy for Removal of Prosthesis of Ankle
See Ankle, Removal, Implant

Arthrotomy for Removal of Prosthesis of Hip
See Hip, Removal, Prosthesis

Arthrotomy for Removal of Prosthesis of Wrist
See Prosthesis, Wrist, Removal

Articular Ligament
See Ligament

Artificial Abortion
See Abortion

Artificial Cardiac Pacemaker
See Heart, Pacemaker

Artificial Eye
See Prosthesis

Artificial Genitourinary Sphincter
See Prosthesis, Urethral Sphincter

Artificial Insemination 58976
See In Vitro Fertilization
Intra-Cervical 58321
Intra-Uterine 58322
Sperm Washing 58323

Artificial Knee Joints
See Prosthesis, Knee

Artificial Penis
See Penile Prosthesis

Artificial Pneumothorax
See Pneumothorax, Therapeutic

Arytenoid
Excision
  Endoscopic 31560-31561

Arytenoid Cartilage
Excision 31400
Repair 31400

Arytenoidectomy 31400
Endoscopic 31560

Arytenoidopexy 31400

Ascorbic Acid
Blood 82180

Aspartate Aminotransferase
See Transaminase, Glutamic Oxaloacetic

Aspergillus
Antibody 86606

Aspiration
See Puncture Aspiration
Amniotic Fluid
  Diagnostic 59000
  Therapeutic 59001
Bladder 51000-51010
Bone Marrow 38220
Brain Lesion
  Stereotactic 61750-61751
Bronchi
  Endoscopy 31645-31646
Bursa 20600-20610
Catheter
  Nasotracheal 31720
  Tracheobronchial 31725
Cyst
  Bone 20615
  Kidney 50390
  Pelvis 50390
  Spinal Cord 62268
  Thyroid 60001
Duodenal 89100-89105
Fetal Fluid 59074
Ganglion Cyst 20612
Hydrocele
  Tunica Vaginalis 55000
Joint 20600-20610
Laryngoscopy
  Direct 31515
Lens Material 66840
Liver 47015
Lung 32420
Nucleus of Disk
  Lumbar 62287
Orbital Contents 67415
Pelvis
  Endoscopy 49322
Pericardium 33010-33011
Pleural Cavity 32000-32002
Puncture
  Cyst
    Breast 19000-19001
Spinal Cord
  Stereotaxis 63615
Syrinx
  Spinal Cord 62268
Thyroid 60001
Trachea
  Nasotracheal 31720
  Puncture 31612
Tunica Vaginalis
  Hydrocele 55000
Vitreous 67015

Aspiration Lipectomies
See Liposuction

Aspiration of Bone Marrow from Donor for Transplant
See Bone Marrow, Harvesting

Aspiration, Chest
See Thoracentesis

Aspiration, Lung Puncture
See Pneumocentesis

Aspiration, Nail
See Evacuation, Hematoma, Subungual

Aspiration, Spinal Puncture
See Spinal Tap

Assay Tobramycin
See Tobramycin

Assay, Very Long Chain Fatty Acids
See Fatty Acid, Very Long Chain

Assisted Circulation
See Circulation Assist

AST
See Transaminase, Glutamic Oxaloacetic

Astragalectomy 28130

Astragalus
See Talus

Asymmetry, Face
See Hemifacial Microsomia

Ataxia Telangiectasia
Chromosome Analysis 88248

Ataxy, Telangiectasia
See Ataxia Telangiectasia

Atherectomies, Coronary
See Artery, Coronary, Atherectomy

Gross and Micro Exam 88020-88029
Gross Exam 88000-88016
Organ 88037
Regional 88036
Unlisted Services and Procedures 88099

Autotransfusion
Blood 86890-86891

Autotransplant
See Autograft

Autotransplantation
Renal 50380

AV Fistula
See Arteriovenous Fistula

AV Shunt
See Arteriovenous Shunt

Avulsion
Nails 11730-11732
Nerve 64732-64772

Axillary Arteries
See Artery, Axillary

Axillary Nerve
Injection
  Anesthetic 64417

Axis, Dens
See Odontoid Process

B

B Antibodies, Hepatitis
See Antibody, Hepatitis B

B Antigens, Hepatitis
See Hepatitis Antigen, B

B Complex Vitamins
B-12 Absorption 78270-78272

B-DNA
See Deoxyribonucleic Acid

b-Hexosaminidase 83080

B1 Vitamin
See Thiamine

B6 Vitamin
See Vitamin, B-6

B12 Vitamin
See Cyanocobalamin

Babcock Operation
See Ligation, Vein, Saphenous

Bacillus Calmette Guerin Vaccine
See BCG Vaccine

Back/Flank
Biopsy 21920-21925
Repair
  Hernia 49540
Strapping 29220
Tumor
  Excision 21930
  Radical Resection 21935
Wound Exploration
  Penetrating 20102

Backbone
See Spine

Bacterial Endotoxins 87176

Bacteria Culture
Additional Methods 87077
Aerobic 87040-87071
Anaerobic 87073-87076
Blood 87040
Other Source 87070-87075
Screening 87081
Stool 87045-87046
Urine 87086-87088

Bactericidal Titer, Serum 87197

Bacterium
Antibody 86609

BAER
See Evoked Potential, Auditory Brainstem

Baker Tube
Intestine Decompression 44021

Baker's Cyst 27345

Balanoplasty
See Penis, Repair

Baldy-Webster Operation
See Uterus, Repair, Suspension

Balkan Grippe
See Q Fever

Balloon Angioplasties, Coronary
See Percutaneous Transluminal Angioplasty

Balloon Angioplasty
See Angioplasty

Balloon Assisted Device
Aorta 33967-33974, 93727

Band, Pulmonary Artery
See Banding, Artery, Pulmonary

Banding
Artery
  Fistula 37607
  Pulmonary 33690

Bank, Blood
See Blood Banking

Bankart Procedure
See Capsulorrhaphy, Anterior

Barany Caloric Test
See Caloric Vestibular Test

Barbiturates
Blood or Urine 82205

Bardenheurer Operation
See Ligation, Artery, Chest

Barium 83015

Barium Enema 74270-74280

Barker Operation
See Talus, Excision

Barr Bodies 88130

Barr Procedure
See Tendon, Transfer, Leg, Lower

Bartholin's Gland
Abscess
  Incision and Drainage 56420
Cyst
  Repair 56440
Excision 56740
Marsupialization 56440

Bartonella
Antibody 86611

Bartonella Detection 87470-87472

Basic Life Services 99450

Basic Proteins, Myelin
See Myelin Basic Protein

Basilar Arteries
See Artery, Basilar

Batch-Spittler-McFaddin Operation
See Disarticulation, Knee

BCG Vaccine
See Vaccines

Be Antigens, Hepatitis
See Hepatitis Antigen, Be

Bed Sores
See Debridement; Pressure Ulcer (Decubitus); Skin Graft and Flap

Bekesy Audiometry
See Audiometry, Bekesy

Belsey IV Procedure
See Fundoplasty

Bender-Gestalt Test 96100

Benedict Test for Urea
See Urinalysis, Qualitative

Benign Cystic Mucinous Tumor
See Ganglion

Benign Neoplasm of Cranial Nerves
See Cranial Nerve

Bennett Fracture
See Phalanx; Thumb, Fracture

Bennett Procedure
See Repair, Leg, Upper, Muscle; Revision

Hemogram
- Added Indices ... 85025-85027
- Automated ... 85025-85027
- Manual ... 85032

Microhematocrit ... 85013
Red Blood Cells ... 85032-85041
Reticulocyte ... 85044-85045
T-Cells ... 86359-86361
White Blood Cells ... 85032, 85048, 89055

Blood Cell Count, Red
See Red Blood Cell (RBC), Count

Blood Cell Count, White
See White Blood Cell, Count

Blood Cell, Red
See Red Blood Cell (RBC)

Blood Cell, White
See Leukocyte

Blood Clot
Assay ... 85396
Clot Lysis Time ... 85175
Clot Retraction ... 85170
Clotting Factor ... 85250-85293
Clotting Factor Test ... 85210-85244
Clotting Inhibitors ... 85300-85302, 85305, 85307
Coagulation Time ... 85345-85348

Blood Coagulation Defect
See Coagulopathy

Blood Coagulation Disorders
See Clot

Blood Coagulation Factor
See Clotting Factor

Blood Coagulation Factor I
See Fibrinogen

Blood Coagulation Factor II
See Prothrombin

Blood Coagulation Factor III
See Thromboplastin

Blood Coagulation Factor IV
See Calcium

Blood Coagulation Factor VII
See Proconvertin

Blood Coagulation Factor VIII
See Clotting Factor

Blood Coagulation Factor IX
See Christmas Factor

Blood Coagulation Factor X
See Stuart-Prower Factor

Blood Coagulation Factor X, Activated
See Thrombokinase

Blood Coagulation Factor XI
See Plasma Thromboplastin, Antecedent

Blood Coagulation Factor XIII
See Fibrin Stabilizing Factor

Blood Coagulation Test
See Coagulation

Blood Component Removal
See Apheresis

Blood Count, Complete
See Complete Blood Count (CBC)

Blood Flow Check, Graft ... 15860, 90939-90940

Blood Gases
CO2 ... 82803
HCO3 ... 82803
O2 Saturation ... 82805-82810
pCO2 ... 82803
pH ... 82800-82803
pO2 ... 82803

Blood Letting
See Phlebotomy

Blood Lipoprotein
See Lipoprotein

Blood, Occult
See Occult, Blood

Blood Pool Imaging ... 78472-78473, 78481-78483, 78494-78496

Blood Pressure
See Performance Measures
Monitoring, 24 Hour ... 93784-93790
Venous ... 93770

Blood Products
Irradiation ... 86945
Pooling ... 86965
Splitting ... 86985

Blood Sample
Fetal ... 59030

Blood Serum
See Serum

Blood Smear ... 85060

Blood Syndrome
Chromosome Analysis ... 88245-88248

Blood Tests
Nuclear Medicine
- Iron Absorption ... 78162
- Iron Utilization ... 78170
- Iron, Chelatable ... 78172
- Plasma Volume ... 78110-78111
- Platelet Survival ... 78190-78191
- Red Cell Volume ... 78120-78121
- Whole Blood Volume ... 78122

Panels
- Electrolyte ... 80051
- General Health Panel ... 80050
- Hepatic Function ... 80076
- Hepatitis, Acute ... 80074
- Lipid Panel ... 80061
- Metabolic
  - Basic ... 80048
  - Comprehensive ... 80053
- Obstetric Panel ... 80055
- Renal Function ... 80069

Volume Determination ... 78122

Blood Transfusion, Autologous
See Autotransfusion

Blood Typing
ABO Only ... 86900
Antigen Screen ... 86903-86904
Crossmatch ... 86920-86922
Other RBC Antigens ... 86905
Paternity Testing ... 86910-86911
Rh (D) ... 86901
Rh Phenotype ... 86906

Blood Urea Nitrogen ... 84520-84525

Blood Vessels
See Artery; Vein
Angioscopy
- Non-Coronary ... 35400

Endoscopy
- Surgical ... 37500

Excision
- Arteriovenous Malformation ... 63250-63252

Exploration
- Abdomen ... 35840
- Chest ... 35820
- Extremity ... 35860
- Neck ... 35800

Great
- Suture ... 33320-33322

Harvest
- Endoscopic ... 33508
- Lower Extremity Vein ... 35572
- Upper Extremity Artery ... 35600
- Upper Extremity Vein ... 35500

Kidney
- Repair ... 50100

Repair
- Abdomen
  - *See* Aneurysm Repair; Fistula, Repair
  - with Composite Graft ... 35681-35683
  - with Other Graft ... 35281
  - with Vein Graft ... 35251
- Aneurysm ... 61705-61708
- Arteriovenous Malformation ... 61680-61692, 61705-61710, 63250-63252
- Chest
  - with Composite Graft ... 35681-35683
  - with Other Graft ... 35271-35276
  - with Vein Graft ... 35241-35246
- Direct ... 35201-35226
- Finger ... 35207
- Graft Defect ... 35870
- Hand ... 35207
- Lower Extremity ... 35226
  - with Composite Graft ... 35681-35683
  - with Other Graft ... 35281
  - with Vein Graft ... 35251
- Neck
  - with Composite Graft ... 35681-35683
  - with Other Graft ... 35261
  - with Vein Graft ... 35231
- Upper Extremity ... 35206
  - with Composite Graft ... 35681-35683
  - with Other Graft ... 35266
  - with Vein Graft ... 35236

Bone Spur
See Exostosis

Bone Wedge Reversal
Osteotomy 21122

Bone, Carpal
See Carpal Bone

Bone, Cheek
See Cheekbone

Bone, Facial
See Facial Bone

Bone, Hyoid
See Hyoid Bone

Bone, Metatarsal
See Metatarsal

Bone, Nasal
See Nasal Bone

Bone, Navicular
See Navicular

Bone, Scan
See Bone, Nuclear Medicine; Nuclear Medicine Imaging

Bone, Semilunar
See Lunate

Bone, Sesamoid
See Sesamoid Bone

Bone, Tarsal
See Ankle Bone

Bone, Temporal
See Temporal Bone

Bordetella
Antibody 86615
Antigen Detection
  Direct Fluorescence 87265

Borrelia
Antibody 86618-86619

Borrelia burgdorferi ab
See Antibody, Lyme Disease

Borreliosis, Lyme
See Lyme Disease

Borthen Operation
See Iridotasis

Bost Fusion
See Arthrodesis, Wrist

Bosworth Operation
See Acromioclavicular Joint, Dislocation; Arthrodesis, Vertebrae; Fasciotomy,

Bottle Type Procedure 55060

Botulinum Toxin
See Chemodenervation

Boutonniere Deformity 26426-26428

Bowel
See Intestine

Bowleg Repair 27455-27457

Boyce Operation
See Nephrotomy

Boyd Hip Disarticulation
See Amputation, Leg, Upper; Radical Resection; Replantation

Brace
See Cast
for Leg Cast 29358

Brachial Arteries
See Artery, Brachial

Brachial Plexus
Decompression 64713
Injection
  Anesthetic 64415-64416
Neuroplasty 64713
Release 64713
Repair/Suture 64861

Brachiocephalic Artery
See Artery, Brachiocephalic

Brachycephaly 21175

Brachytherapy 77761-77778, 77789
Dose Plan 77326-77328
Remote Afterloading
  1-4 Positions 77781
  5-8 Positions 77782
  9-12 Positions 77783
  Over 12 Positions 77784
  Over 4 Positions 77781-77784
Unlisted Services and Procedures 77799

Bradykinin
Blood or Urine 82286

Brain
See Brainstem; Mesencephalon; Skull Base Surgery
Abscess
  Drainage 61150-61151
  Excision 61514, 61522
  Incision and Drainage 61320-61321
Adhesions
  Lysis 62161
Anesthesia 00210-00218, 00220-00222
Angiography 70496
Biopsy 61140
  Stereotactic 61750-61751
Catheter
  Irrigation 62194, 62225
  Replacement 62160, 62194, 62225
Cisternography 70015
Computer Assisted
  Surgery 61795
Cortex
  Magnetic Stimulation 0018T
Craniopharyngioma
  Excision 61545
CT Scan 0042T, 70450-70470, 70496
Cyst
  Drainage 61150-61151, 62161-62162
  Excision 61516, 61524, 62162
Epileptogenic Focus
  Excision 61534, 61536
Excision
  Amygdala 61566
  Choroid Plexus 61544
  Hemisphere 61542-61543
  Hippocampus 61566
  Other Lobe 61323, 61539-61540
  Temporal Lobe 61537-61538
Exploration
  Infratentorial 61305
  Supratentorial 61304
Hematoma
  Drainage 61154
  Incision and Drainage 61312-61315
Implantation
  Chemotherapy Agent 61517
  Electrode 61850-61875
  Pulse Generator 61885-61886
  Receiver 61885-61886
Incision
  Corpus Callosum 61541
  Frontal Lobe 61490
  Mesencephalic Tract 61480
  Subpial 61567
Insertion
  Catheter 61210
  Electrode 61531-61533, 61850-61875
  Pulse Generator 61885-61886
  Receiver 61885-61886
  Reservoir 61210-61215
Lesion
  Aspiration Stereotactic 61750-61751
  Excision 61534, 61536, 61600-61608, 61615-61616
Magnetic Resonance Imaging (MRI) 70551-70553
  Intraoperative 70557-70559
Meningioma
  Excision 61512, 61519
Myelography 70010
Nuclear Medicine
  Blood Flow 78610-78615
  Cerebrospinal Fluid 78630-78650
  Imaging 78600-78607
    Vascular Flow 78610
Positron Emission Tomography 78608-78609
Removal
  Electrode 61535, 61880
  Foreign Body 61570, 62163
  Pulse Generator 61888
  Receiver 61888
  Shunt 62256-62258
Repair
  Dura 61618
  Wound 61571
Shunt
  Creation 62180-62192, 62200-62223
  Removal 62256-62258
  Replacement ... 62160, 62194, 62225-62230, 62256-62258
  Reprogramming 62252
Skull
  Transcochlear Approach 61596
  Transcondylar Approach 61597
  Transpetrosal Approach 61598
  Transtemporal Approach 61595

Bronchial Brush Biopsy
with Catheterization 31717

Bronchial Brushings/Protected Brushing 31623

Bronchial Challenge Test
See Allergy Tests
with Antigens, Gases 95070
with Chemicals 95071

Bronchial Provocation Tests
See Bronchial Challenge Test

Bronchioalveolar Lavage
See Lung, Lavage

Broncho-Bronchial Anastomosis 32486

Bronchoalveolar Lavage
See Lung, Lavage

Bronchography 71040-71060
Catheterization 31710
Injection
  Transtracheal 31715
Instillation
  Contrast Material 31708
Segmental
  Injection 31656

Bronchoplasty 32501
See Reconstruction, Bronchi
Excision Stenosis and Anastomosis 31775
Graft Repair 31770

Bronchopneumonia, Hiberno-Vernal
See Q Fever

Bronchopulmonary Lavage
See Lung, Lavage

Bronchoscopy
Alveolar Lavage 31624
Aspiration 31645-31646
Biopsy 31625-31629, 31632-31633
Brushing/Protected Brushing 31623
Catheter Placement
  Intracavitary Radioelement 31643
Dilation 31630-31631
Exploration 31622
Fracture 31630
Injection 31656
Needle Biopsy 31629, 31633
Removal
  Foreign Body 31635
  Tumor 31640-31641
Stenosis 31641
Stent Placement 31631
X-Ray Contrast 31656

Bronchospasm Evaluation
See Pulmonology, Diagnostic, Spirometry

Bronkodyl
See Theophylline

Brow Ptosis
Repair 67900

Brucella 86000
Antibody 86622

Bruise
See Hematoma

Brunschwig Operation 58240
See Hip; Pelvis, Exenteration

Brush Biopsy
See Biopsy; Needle Biopsy
Bronchi 31717

Brush Border ab
See Antibody, Heterophile

Bucca
See Cheek

Buccal Mucosa
See Mouth, Mucosa

Bulbourethral Gland
Excision 53250

Bulla
Incision and Drainage
  Puncture Aspiration 10160
Lung
  Excision-Plication 32141
    Endoscopic 32655

BUN
See Blood Urea Nitrogen; Urea Nitrogen

Bunion Repair 28296-28299
Chevron Procedure 28296
Concentric Procedure 28296
Joplin Procedure 28294
Keller Procedure 28292
Lapidus Procedure 28297
Mayo Procedure 28292
McBride Procedure 28292
Mitchell Procedure 28296
Silver Procedure 28290
with Implant 28293

Burgess Amputation
See Disarticulation, Ankle

Burhenne Procedure
See Bile Duct, Removal, Calculi (Stone); Gallbladder

Burkitt Herpesvirus
See Epstein-Barr Virus

Burns
Allograft 15350-15351
Debridement 01951-01953, 15000-15001, 16010-16030
Dressings 16010-16030
Escharotomy 16035-16036
Excision 01951-01953, 15000-15001
Initial Treatment 16000
Tissue Culture Skin Grafts 15100-15121, 15342-15343
Xenograft 15400-15401

Burr Hole
Anesthesia 00214
Skull
  Biopsy Brain 61140
  Catheterization 61210
  Drainage
    Abscess 61150-61151
    Cyst 61150-61151
    Hematoma 61154-61156
  Exploration
    Infratentorial 61253
    Supratentorial 61250
  for Implant of Neurostimulator
  Array 61863-61868
  Injection, Contrast Media 61120
  Insertion
    Catheter 61210
    Reservoir 61210

Burrow's Operation
See Skin, Adjacent Tissue Transfer

Bursa
Ankle 27604
Arm, Lower 25031
Elbow
  Excision 24105
  Incision and Drainage 23931
Femur
  Excision 27062
Foot
  Incision and Drainage 28001
Hip
  Incision and Drainage 26991
Injection 20600-20610
Ischial
  Excision 27060
Joint
  Aspiration 20600-20610
  Drainage 20600-20610
  Injection 20600-20610
Knee
  Excision 27340
Leg, Lower 27604
Palm
  Incision and Drainage 26025-26030
Pelvis
  Incision and Drainage 26991
Shoulder
  Drainage 23031
Wrist 25031
  Excision 25115-25116

Bursectomy
See Excision, Bursa

Bursitis, Radiohumeral
See Tennis Elbow

Bursocentesis
See Aspiration, Bursa

Button
Nasal Septal Prosthesis
  Insertion 30220

Butyrylcholine Esterase
See Cholinesterase

Bypass Graft
Axillary Artery 35516-35522, 35533, 35616-35623, 35650, 35654
Brachial Artery 35510, 35512, 35522-35525
Carotid Artery 35501-35510, 35526, 35601-35606, 35626, 35642
Celiac Artery 35531, 35631
Coronary Artery
Angiography 93556
Arterial 33533-33536
Venous Graft 33510-33516
Excision
Abdomen 35907
Extremity 35903
Neck 35901
Thorax 35905
Femoral Artery 35521, 35533, 35546, 35551-35558, 35566, 35621, 35646-35647, 35651-35661, 35666, 35700
Harvest
Endoscopic 33508
Upper Extremity Vein 35500
Iliac Artery 35541, 35563, 35641, 35663
Iliofemoral Artery . . . 35548-35549, 35565, 35665
Mesenteric Artery 35531, 35631
Peroneal Artery 35566-35571, 35666-35671
Placement
Vein Patch 35685
Popliteal Artery 35551-35558, 35571, 35623, 35651, 35656, 35671, 35700
Renal Artery 35536, 35560, 35631-35636
Reoperation 35700
Repair
Abdomen 35907
Extremity 35903
Lower Extremity
with Composite Graft 35681-35683
Neck 35901
Thorax 35905
Revascularization
Extremity 35903
Neck 35901
Thorax 35905
Revision
Lower Extremity
with Angioplasty 35879
with Vein Interposition 35881
Secondary Repair 35870
Splenic Artery 35536, 35636
Subclavian Artery . . . 35506-35507, 35511-35516, 35526, 35606-35616, 35626, 35645
Thrombectomy
Other than Hemodialysis Graft or Fistula 35875-35876
Tibial Artery . . 35566-35571, 35623, 35666-35671
Vertebral Artery 35508, 35515, 35642-35645
with Composite Graft 35681

Bypass In-Situ
Femoral Artery 35582-35585
Peroneal Artery 35585-35587
Popliteal Artery 35582-35583, 35587
Tibial Artery 35585-35587

Bypass, Cardiopulmonary
See Cardiopulmonary Bypass

C

C Vitamin
See Ascorbic Acid

C-13
Urea Breath Test 83013-83014
Urease Activity 83013-83014

C-14
Urea Breath Test 78267-78268
Urease Activity 83013-83014

C-Peptide 80432, 84681

C-Reactive Protein 86140-86141

C-Section
See Cesarean Delivery

CABG
See Coronary Artery Bypass Graft (CABG)

Cadmium
Urine 82300

Calcaneal Spur
See Heel Spur

Calcaneus
Craterization 28120
Cyst
Excision 28100-28103
Diaphysectomy 28120
Excision 28118-28120
Fracture
Open Treatment 28415-28420
Percutaneous Fixation 28406
with Manipulation 28405-28406
without Manipulation 28400
Repair
Osteotomy 28300
Saucerization 28120
Tumor
Excision 27647, 28100-28103
X-Ray 73650

Calcareous Deposits
Subdeltoid
Removal 23000

Calcifediol
Blood or Urine 82306

Calcifediol Assay
See Calciferol

Calciferol
Blood or Urine 82307

Calcification
See Calcium, Deposits

Calciol
See Vitamin, D-3

Calcitonin
Blood or Urine 82308
Stimulation Panel 80410

Calcium
Blood
Infusion Test 82331
Deposits
See Removal, Calculi (Stone); Removal, Foreign Bodies
Ionized 82330
Total 82310
Urine 82340

Calcium-Binding Protein, Vitamin K-Dependent
See Osteocalcin

Calcium-Pentagastrin Stimulation 80410

Calculus
Analysis 82355-82370
Destruction
Bile Duct 43265
Pancreatic Duct 43265
Removal
Bile Duct 43264, 47554, 74327
Bladder 51050, 52310-52318, 52352
Kidney 50060-50081, 50130, 50561, 50580, 52352
Pancreatic Duct 43264
Ureter 50610-50630, 50961, 50980, 51060-51065, 52320-52325, 52352
Urethra 52310-52315, 52352

Calculus of Kidney
See Calculus, Removal, Kidney

Caldwell-Luc Procedure
See Sinus, Maxillary; Sinusotomy; Sternum, Fracture
Orbital Floor Blowout Fracture 21385
Sinusotomy 31030-31032

Caliper
Application/Removal 20660

Callander Knee Disarticulation
See Disarticulation, Knee

Callosum, Corpus
See Corpus Callosum

Calmette Guerin Bacillus Vaccine
See BCG Vaccine

Caloric Vestibular Test 92533

Calycoplasty 50405

Camey Enterocystoplasty 50825

CAMP
See Cyclic AMP

Campbell Procedure 27422

Campylobacter
Antibody 86625

Campylobacter Pylori
See Helicobacter Pylori

Canal, Ear
See Auditory Canal

Canal, Semicircular
See Semicircular Canal

Canaloplasty 69631, 69635

Candida
Antibody 86628
Skin Test 86485

Cannulation 36821
Arterial 36620-36625
Sinus
  Maxillary 31000
  Sphenoid 31002
Thoracic Duct 38794

Cannulation, Renoportal
See Anastomosis, Renoportal

Cannulization
See Catheterization
Arteriovenous 36145, 36810-36815
Declotting 36550, 36860-36861
ECMO 36822
External
  Declotting 36860-36861
Vas Deferens 55200
Vein to Vein 36800

Canthocystostomy
See Conjunctivorhinostomy

Canthopexy
Lateral 21282
Medial 21280

Canthoplasty 67950

Canthorrhaphy 67880-67882

Canthotomy 67715

Canthus
Reconstruction 67950

Cap, Cervical
See Cervical Cap

Capsule
See Capsulodesis
Elbow
  Arthrotomy 24006
  Excision 24006
Foot 28264
Interphalangeal Joint
  Excision 26525
  Incision 26525
Knee 27435
Metacarpophalangeal Joint
  Excision 26520
  Incision 26520
Metatarsophalangeal Joint
  Release 28289
Shoulder
  Incision 23020
Wrist
  Excision 25320

Capsulectomy
Breast
  Periprosthetic 19371

Capsulodesis
Metacarpophalangeal Joint 26516-26518

Capsulorrhaphy
Anterior 23450-23462
Multi-Directional Instability 23466
Posterior 23465
Wrist 25320

Capsulotomy
Breast
  Periprosthetic 19370
Foot 28260-28262
Hip
  with Release, Flexor Muscles 27036
Interphalangeal Joint 28272
Knee 27435
Metacarpophalangeal Joint 26520
Metatarsophalangeal Joint 28270
Toe 28270-28272
Wrist 25085

Captopril 80416-80417

Carbamazepine
Assay 80156-80157

Carbazepin
See Carbamazepine

Carbinol
See Methanol

Carbohydrate Deficient Transferrin 82373

Carbon Dioxide
Blood or Urine 82374

Carbon Monoxide
Blood 82375-82376

Carbon Tetrachloride 84600

Carboxycathepsin
See Angiotensin Converting Enzyme (ACE)

Carboxyhemoglobin 82375-82376

Carbuncle
Incision and Drainage 10060-10061

Carcinoembryonal Antigen
See Antigen, Carcinoembryonic

Carcinoembryonic Antigen 82378

Cardiac
See Coronary

Cardiac Arrhythmia, Tachycardia
See Tachycardia

Cardiac Atria
See Atria

Cardiac Catheterization
Combined Left and Right Heart 93526-93529
Combined Right and Retrograde Left
  Congenital Cardiac Anomalies 93531
Combined Right and Transseptal Left
  Congenital Cardiac Anomalies 93532-93533
for Biopsy 93505
for Dilution Studies 93561-93562
Imaging 93555-93556
Injection 93539-93545
  See Catheterization, Cardiac
Left Heart 93510-93524
Pacemaker 33210
Right
  Congenital Cardiac Anomalies 93530
Right Heart 93501-93503

Cardiac Electroversion
See Cardioversion

Cardiac Event Recorder
Implantation 33282
Removal 33284

Cardiac Magnetic Resonance Imaging (CMRI)
Complete Study 75554
Limited Study 75555
Morphology 75553
Velocity Flow Mapping 75556

Cardiac Massage
Thoracotomy 32160

Cardiac Muscle
See Myocardium

Cardiac Neoplasm
See Heart, Tumor

Cardiac Output
Indicator Dilution 93561-93562

Cardiac Pacemaker
See Heart, Pacemaker

Cardiac Rehabilitation 93797-93798

Cardiac Septal Defect
See Septal Defect

Cardiac Transplantation
See Heart, Transplantation

Cardiectomy
Donor 33930, 33940

Cardioassist 0049T, 92970-92971

Cardiolipin Antibody 86147

Cardiology
See Electrocardiography
Diagnostic
  Atrial Electrogram
    Esophageal Recording 93615-93616
  Cardio-Defibrillator
    Evaluation and Testing 93640-93642, 93741-93744
  Echocardiography
    Doppler 93303-93321, 93662
    Intracardiac 93662
    Transesophageal 93318
    Transthoracic 93303-93317, 93350

Wedging 29740-29750
Windowing 29730
Wrist 29085

Casting
Unlisted Services and Procedures 29799

Castration
See Orchiectomy

Castration, Female
See Oophorectomy

CAT Scan
See CT Scan

Cataract
Excision 66830
Incision 66820-66821
  Laser 66821
  Stab Incision 66820
Removal/Extraction
  Extracapsular 66982, 66984
  Intracapsular 66983

Catecholamines 80424, 82382-82384
Blood 82383
Urine 82382

Cathepsin-D 82387

Catheter
See Cannulization; Venipuncture
Aspiration
  Nasotracheal 31720
  Tracheobronchial 31725
Bladder 51701-51703
  Irrigation 51700
Breast
Cytology 0046T-0047T
Declotting 36550
Exchange
  Arterial 37209, 75900
  Peritoneal 49423
Intracatheter
  Irrigation 99507
  Obstruction Clearance 36596
Pericatheter
  Obstruction
    Clearance 36595
Placement
  Bronchus
    for Intracavitary Radioelement
    Application 31643
Removal
  Central Venous 36589
  Peritoneum 49422
  Spinal Cord 62355
Repair
  Central Venous 36575
Replacement
  Central Venous 36580-36581, 36584
Repositioning 36597

Catheterization
See Catheter
Abdomen 49420-49421
Abdominal Artery 36245-36248
Aorta 36160-36215
Arterial
  Cutdown 36625
  Intracatheter/Needle 36100-36140
  Percutaneous 36620
Arteriovenous Shunt 36145
Bile Duct 47530
  Change 47525
  Percutaneous 47510
Bladder 51010, 51045
Brachiocephalic Artery 36215-36218
Brain 61210
  Replacement 62160, 62194, 62225
Bronchography 31710
Cardiac
  Combined Left and Right
  Heart 93526-93529
  Combined Right and Retrograde Left
    for Congenital Cardiac Anomalies 93531
  Combined Right and Transseptal Left
    for Congenital Cardiac
    Anomalies 93532-93533
  Flow Directed 93503
  for Biopsy 93505
  for Dilution Studies 93561-93562
  Imaging 93555-93556
  Injection 93539-93545
  Left Heart 93510-93524
  Pacemaker 33210
  Right Heart 36013, 93501
    for Congenital Cardiac Anomalies 93530
Central 36555-36566
Cerebral Artery 36215
Cystourethroscopy
  Ejaculatory Duct 52010
  Ureteral 52005
Ear, Middle 69405
Eustachian Tube 69405
Fallopian Tube 58345, 74742
Intracardiac
  Ablation 93650-93652
Jejunum
  for Enteral 44015
Kidney
  Drainage 50392
  with Ureter 50393
Legs 36245-36248
Nasotracheal 31720
Newborn
  Umbilical Vein 36510
Pelvic Artery 36245-36248
Peripheral 36568-36571
Placement
  Arterial Coronary Conduit
    without Concomitant Left Heart
    Catheterization 93508
  Coronary Artery
    without Concomitant Left Heart
    Catheterization 93508
  Venous Coronary Bypass Graft
    without Concomitant Left Heart
    Catheterization 93508
Portal Vein 36481
Pulmonary Artery 36013-36015
Radioelement Application 55859
Removal
  Fractured Catheter 75961
  Obstructive Material
    Intracatheter 36596
    Pericatheter 36595
Salivary Duct 42660
Skull 61107
Spinal Cord 62350-62351
Thoracic Artery 36215-36218
Tracheobronchi 31725
Transglottic 31700
Umbilical Artery 36660
Umbilical Vein 36510
Ureter
  Endoscopic 50553, 50572, 50953, 50972, 52005
  Injection 50394, 50684
  Manometric Studies 50396, 50686
Uterus
  Radiology 58340
Vena Cava 36010
Venous
  Central Line 36555-36556, 36568-36569, 36580, 36584
  First Order 36011
  Intracatheter/Needle 36000
  Organ Blood 36500
  Second Order 36012
  Umbilical Vein 36510
Ventricular 61020-61026, 61210-61215

Cauda Equina
See Spinal Cord
Decompression 63005-63011, 63017, 63047-63057, 63087-63091
Exploration 63005-63011, 63017

Cauterization
Anal Fissure 46940-46942
Cervix 57522
  Cryocautery 57511
  Electro or Thermal 57510
  Laser Ablation 57513
Chemical
  Granulation Tissue 17250
Everted Punctum 68705
Lower Esophageal Sphincter
  Thermal
    via Endoscopy 0057T
Nasopharyngeal Hemorrhage 42970
Nose
  Hemorrhage 30901-30906
Skin Lesion 11055-11057, 17000-17004
Skin Tags 11200-11201
Turbinate Mucosa 30801-30802

Cavernitides, Fibrous
See Peyronie Disease

Cavernosography
Corpora 54230

Cavernosometry 54231

Cavities, Pleural
See Pleural Cavity

Cavus Foot Correction 28309

CBC
See Blood Cell Count; Complete Blood Count (CBC)

CCL4
See Carbon Tetrachloride

Choanal Atresia
Repair 30540-30545

Cholangiography
Injection 47500-47505
Intraoperative 74300-74301
Percutaneous 74320
with Laparoscopy 47560-47561
Postoperative 74305
Repair
with Bile Duct Exploration 47700
with Cholecystectomy .. 47563, 47605, 47620

Cholangiopancreatography 43260
See Bile Duct; Pancreatic Duct
Repair
See Bile Duct; Pancreatic Duct
with Biopsy 43261
with Surgery 43262-43267, 43269

Cholangiostomy
See Hepaticostomy

Cholangiotomy
See Hepaticostomy

Cholecalciferol
See Vitamin, D-3

Cholecystectomy 47562-47564, 47600-47620
Any Method 47562-47564
with Cholangiography .. 47563, 47605, 47620
with Exploration Common Duct 47564, 47610

Cholecystenterostomy 47570, 47720-47741

Cholecystography 74290-74291

Cholecystotomy 47480, 48001
Percutaneous 47490

Choledochoplasty
See Bile Duct, Repair

Choledochoscopy 47550

Choledochostomy 47420-47425

Choledochotomy 47420-47425

Choledochus, Cyst
See Cyst, Choledochal

Cholera Vaccine
Injectable 90725

Cholesterol
Measurement 83721
Serum 82465
Testing 83718-83719

Choline Esterase I
See Acetylcholinesterase

Choline Esterase II
See Cholinesterase

Cholinesterase
Blood 82480-82482

Cholylglycine
Blood 82240

Chondroitin Sulfate 82485

Chondromalacia Patella
Repair 27418

Chondropathia Patellae
See Chondromalacia Patella

Chondrosteoma
See Exostosis

Chopart Procedure 28800-28805
See Amputation, Foot; Radical Resection; Replantation

Chordotomies
See Cordotomy

Chorioangioma
See Lesion, Skin

Choriogonadotropin
See Chorionic Gonadotropin

Choriomeningitides, Lymphocytic
See Lymphocytic Choriomeningitis

Chorionic Gonadotropin 80414, 84702-84703
Stimulation 80414-80415

Chorionic Growth Hormone
See Lactogen, Human Placental

Chorionic Tumor
See Hydatidiform Mole

Chorionic Villi
See Biopsy, Chorionic Villus

Chorionic Villus
Biopsy 59015

Choroid
Destruction
Lesion 0016T, 67220-67225

Choroid Plexus
Excision 61544

Christmas Factor 85250

Chromaffinoma, Medullary
See Pheochromocytoma

Chromatin, Sex
See Barr Bodies

Chromatography
Column/Mass Spectrometry 82541-82544
Gas Liquid or HPLC 82486, 82491-82492
Paper 82487-82488
Thin-Layer 82489

Chromium 82495

Chromogenic Substrate Assay . 85130

Chromosome Analysis
See Amniocentesis
Added Study 88280-88289
Amniotic Fluid 88267-88269
Culture 88235
Biopsy Culture
Tissue 88233
Bone Marrow Culture 88237
Chorionic Villus 88267
5 Cells 88261
15-20 Cells 88262
20-25 Cells 88264
45 Cells 88263
Culture 88235
for Breakage Syndromes 88245-88249
Fragile-X 88248
Lymphocyte Culture 88230
Skin Culture
Tissue 88233
Tissue Culture 88239
Unlisted Services and Procedures 88299

Chromotubation 58350
Oviduct 58350

Chronic Erection
See Priapism

Chronic Interstitial Cystitides
See Cystitis, Interstitial

Ciliary Body
Cyst
Destruction
Cryotherapy 66720
Cyclodialysis 66740
Cyclophotocoagulation 66710
Diathermy 66700
Nonexcisional 66770
Lesion
Destruction 66770
Repair 66680

Cimino Type Procedure 36821

Cinefluorographies
See Cineradiography

Cineplasty
Arm, Lower or Upper 24940

Cineradiography
Esophagus 74230
Pharynx 70371, 74230
Speech Evaluation 70371
Swallowing Evaluation 74230
Unlisted Services and Procedures .. 76120-76125

Circulation Assist
Aortic 33967, 33970
Balloon 33967, 33970
External 33960-33961

Circulation, Extracorporeal
See Extracorporeal Circulation

Circulatory Assist
See Circulation Assist

Circumcision
Repair 54163
Surgical Excision 54161
Newborn 54160
with Clamp or Other Device 54152
Newborn 54150

Cisternal Puncture 61050-61055

Cisternography 70015
Nuclear 78630

Citrate
Blood or Urine 82507

Clagett Procedure
See Chest Wall, Repair, Closure

Clavicle
Craterization 23180
Cyst
  Excision 23140
    with Allograft 23146
    with Autograft 23145
Diaphysectomy 23180
Dislocation
  Acromioclavicular Joint
    Closed Treatment 23540-23545
    Open Treatment 23550-23552
  Sternoclavicular Joint
    Closed Treatment 23520-23525
    Open Treatment 23530-23532
  without Manipulation 23540
Excision 23170
  Partial 23120, 23180
  Total 23125
Fracture
  Closed Treatment
    with Manipulation 23505
    without Manipulation 23500
  Open Treatment 23515
Pinning, Wiring 23490
Prophylactic Treatment 23490
Repair Osteotomy 23480-23485
Saucerization 23180
Sequestrectomy 23170
Tumor
  Excision 23140, 23146, 23200
    with Autograft 23145
  Radical Resection 23200
X-Ray 73000

Clavicula
See Clavicle

Claviculectomy
Partial 23120
Total 23125

Claw Finger Repair 26499

Cleft Cyst, Branchial
See Branchial Cleft, Cyst

Cleft Foot
Reconstruction 28360

Cleft Hand
Repair 26580

Cleft Lip
Repair 40700-40761
Rhinoplasty 30460-30462

Cleft Palate
Repair 42200-42225
Rhinoplasty 30460-30462

Cleft, Branchial
See Branchial Cleft

Clinical Act of Insertion
See Insertion

Clinical Chemistry Test
See Chemistry Tests, Clinical

Clinical Pathology
See Pathology, Clinical

Clitoroplasty
Intersex State 56805

Closed [Transurethral] Biopsy of Bladder
See Biopsy, Bladder, Cystourethroscopy

Clostridial Tetanus
See Tetanus

Clostridium Botulinum Toxin
See Chemodenervation

Clostridium Difficile
Antigen Detection
  Enzyme Immunoassay 87324
by Immunoassay
  with Direct Optical Observation 87803

Clostridium Tetani ab
See Antibody, Tetanus

Closure 12001-13160
Anal Fistula 46288
Atrioventricular Valve 33600
Cystostomy 51880
Enterostomy 44625-44626
Lacrimal Fistula 68770
Lacrimal Punctum
  Plug 68761
  Thermocauterization, Ligation or Laser
  Surgery 68760
Rectovaginal Fistula 57300-57308
Semilunar Valve 33602
Septal Defect 33615
Sternotomy 21750
Ventricular Tunnel 33722

Closure of Esophagostomy
See Esophagostomy, Closure

Closure of Gastrostomy
See Gastrostomy, Closure

Closure, Atrial Septal Defect
See Heart, Repair, Atrial Septum

Closure, Cranial Sutures, Premature
See Craniosynostosis

Closure, Fistula, Vesicouterine
See Fistula, Vesicouterine, Closure

Closure, Meningocele Spinal
See Meningocele Repair

Closure, Vagina
See Vagina, Closure

Clot 34401-34490, 35875-35876, 50230
See Thrombectomy; Thromboendarterectomy

Clot Lysis Time 85175

Clot Retraction 85170

Clotting Disorder
See Coagulopathy

Clotting Factor 85210-85293

Clotting Inhibitors ...85300-85305, 85307

Clotting Operation
See Excision, Nail Fold

Clotting Test
Protein C 85303, 85307
Protein S 85306

Clotting Time
See Coagulation Time

Clubfoot Cast 29450
Wedging 29750

CMG
See Cystometrogram

CMRI
See Cardiac Magnetic Resonance Imaging

CMV
See Cytomegalovirus

CNPB
See Continuous Negative Pressure Breathing (CNPB); Pulmonology, Therapeutic

Co-Factor I, Heparin
See Antithrombin III

CO2
See Carbon Dioxide

Coagulation
Unlisted Services and Procedures 85999

Coagulation Defect
See Coagulopathy

Coagulation Factor
See Clotting Factor

Coagulation Factor I
See Fibrinogen

Coagulation Factor II
See Prothrombin

Coagulation Factor III
See Thromboplastin

Coagulation Factor IV
See Calcium

Coagulation Factor VII
See Proconvertin

Coagulation Factor VIII
See Clotting Factor

Coagulation Factor IX
See Christmas Factor

Reconstruction
  Bladder from 50810
Removal
  Foreign Body 44025, 44390, 45379
  Polyp 44392
Repair
  Diverticula 44605
  Fistula 44650-44661
  Hernia 44050
  Malrotation 44055
  Obstruction 44050
  Ulcer 44605
  Volvulus 44050
  Wound 44605
Stoma Closure 44620-44625
Suture
  Diverticula 44605
  Fistula 44650-44661
  Plication 44680
  Stoma 44620-44625
  Ulcer 44605
  Wound 44605
Tumor
  Destruction 45383
X-Ray with Contrast
  Barium Enema 74270-74280

Colon-Sigmoid
See Colon
Biopsy
  Endoscopy 45331
Dilation
  Endoscopy 45340
Endoscopy
  Ablation
    Polyp 45339
    Tumor 45339
  Biopsy 45331
  Dilation 45340
  Exploration 45330, 45335
  Hemorrhage 45334
  Needle Biopsy 45342
  Placement
    Stent 45327, 45345
  Removal
    Foreign Body 45332
    Polyp 45333, 45338
    Tumor 45333, 45338
  Ultrasound 45341-45342
  Volvulus 45337
Exploration
  Endoscopy 45330, 45335
Hemorrhage
  Endoscopy 45334
Needle Biopsy
  Endoscopy 45342
Removal
  Foreign Body 45332
Repair
  Volvulus
    Endoscopy 45337
Ultrasound
  Endoscopy 45341-45342

Colonna Procedure
See Acetabulum, Reconstruction

Colonoscopy
Biopsy 45380
Collection Specimen 45380
  via Colotomy 45355
Destruction
  Lesion 45383
  Tumor 45383
Dilation 45386
Hemorrhage Control 45382
Injection
  Submucosal 45381
Placement
  Stent 45387
Removal
  Foreign Body 45379
  Polyp 45384-45385
  Tumor 45384-45385
via Stoma 44388-44390
  Biopsy 44389
  Destruction
    of Lesion 44393
    of Tumor 44393
  Exploration 44388
  Hemorrhage 44391
  Placement
    Stent 44397
  Removal
    Foreign Body 44390
    Polyp 44392, 44394
    Tumor 44392, 44394

Color Vision Examination 92283

Colorrhaphy 44604

Colostomy 44320, 45563
Abdominal
  Establishment 50810
Home Visit 99505
Intestine, Large
  with Suture 44605
Perineal
  Establishment 50810
Revision 44340
  Paracolostomy Hernia 44345-44346

Colotomy 44025

Colpectomy
Partial 57106
Total 57110
with Hysterectomy 58275-58280
  with Repair of Enterocele 58280

Colpo-Urethrocystopexy 58152, 58267, 58293
Marshall-Marchetti-Krantz Procedure 58152, 58267, 58293
Pereyra Procedure 58267, 58293

Colpoceliocentesis
See Colpocentesis

Colpocentesis 57020

Colpocleisis 57120

Colpocleisis Complete
See Vagina, Closure

Colpohysterectomies
See Excision, Uterus, Vaginal

Colpoperineorrhaphy 57210

Colpopexy
Laparoscopic 57425
Open 57280

Colpoplasty
See Repair, Vagina

Colporrhaphy
Anterior 57240, 57289
Anteroposterior 57260-57265
  with Enterocele Repair 57265
Nonobstetrical 57200
Posterior 57250

Colposcopy
Biopsy 56821, 57421, 57454-57455, 57460
Cervix 57421, 57452-57461
Exploration 57452
Loop Electrode Biopsy 57460
Loop Electrode Conization 57461
Perineum 99170
Vagina 57420-57421
Vulva 56820
  Biopsy 56821

Colpotomy
Drainage
  Abscess 57010
Exploration 57000

Colprosterone
See Progesterone

Column Chromatography/Mass Spectrometry 82541-82544

Columna Vertebralis
See Spine

Combined Heart-Lung Transplantation
See Transplantation, Heart-Lung

Combined Right and Left Heart Cardiac Catheterization
See Cardiac Catheterization, Combined Left and Right Heart

Comedones
Removal 10040

Commissurotomy
Right Ventricle 33476-33478

Common Sensory Nerve
Repair/Suture 64834

Common Truncus
See Truncus Arteriosus

Communication Device
Non-speech-generating 92605-92606
Speech-generating 92606-92609

Community/Work Reintegration
Training 97537
  See Physical Medicine/Therapy/Occupational Therapy

Compatibility Test
Blood 86920

Corpora Cavernosa
Corpus Spongiosum Shunt 54430
Glans Penis Fistulization 54435
Injection 54235
Irrigation
  Priapism 54220
Saphenous Vein Shunt 54420
X-Ray with Contrast 74445

Corpora Cavernosa, Plastic Induration
See Peyronie Disease

Corpora Cavernosography 74445

Corpus Callosum
Transection 61541

Corpus Vertebrae (Vertebrale)
See Vertebral Body

Correction of Cleft Palate
See Cleft Palate, Repair

Correction of Lid Retraction
See Repair, Eyelid, Retraction

Correction of Malrotation of Duodenum
See Ladd Procedure

Correction of Syndactyly
See Syndactyly, Repair

Correction of Ureteropelvic Junction
See Pyeloplasty

Cortex Decortication, Cerebral
See Decortication

Cortical Mapping
Transection
  by Electric Stimulation 95961-95962

Corticoids
See Corticosteroids

Corticoliberin
See Corticotropic Releasing Hormone (CRH)

Corticosteroid Binding Globulin
See Transcortin

Corticosteroid Binding Protein
See Transcortin

Corticosteroids
Blood 83491
Urine 83491

Corticosterone
Blood or Urine 82528

Corticotropic Releasing Hormone (CRH) 80412

Cortisol 80400-80406, 80418-80420, 80436, 82530
Stimulation 80412
Total 82533

Cortisol Binding Globulin 84449

Costectomy
See Resection, Ribs

Costen Syndrome
See Temporomandibular Joint (TMJ)

Costotransversectomy 21610

Cothromboplastin
See Proconvertin

Cotte Operation 58400-58410
See Repair, Uterus, Suspension; Revision

Cotton Procedure
Bohler Procedure 28405

Counseling
See Preventive Medicine

Counseling and/or Risk Factor Reduction Intervention — Preventive Medicine, Individual Counseling
See Preventive Medicine, Counseling and/or Risk Factor Reduction Intervention, Individual Counseling, Performance Measures

Count, Blood Cell
See Blood Cell Count

Count, Blood Platelet
See Blood, Platelet, Count

Count, Cell
See Cell Count

Count, Complete Blood
See Complete Blood Count (CBC)

Count, Erythrocyte
See Red Blood Cell (RBC), Count

Count, Leukocyte
See White Blood Cell, Count

Count, Reticulocyte
See Reticulocyte, Count

Counterimmuno-electrophoresis 86185

Counters, Cell
See Cell Count

Countershock, Electric
See Cardioversion

Coventry Tibial Wedge Osteotomy
See Osteotomy, Tibia

Cowper's Gland
Excision 53250

Coxa
See Hip

Coxiella Burnetii
Antibody 86638

Coxsackie
Antibody 86658

CPAP
See Continuous Positive Airway Pressure

CPK
Blood 82550-82552

CPR (Cardiopulmonary Resuscitation) 92950

Cranial Bone
Halo
  Thin Skull Osteology 20664
Reconstruction
  Extracranial 21181-21184
Tumor
  Excision 61563-61564

Cranial Halo 20661

Cranial Nerve
See Specific Nerve
Avulsion 64732-64760, 64771
Decompression 61458, 64716
Implantation
  Electrode 64553, 64573
Incision 64732-64752, 64760, 65771
Injection
  Anesthetic 64400-64408, 64412
  Neurolytic 64600-64610
Insertion
  Electrode 64553, 64573
Neuroplasty 64716
Release 64716
Repair
  Suture, with or without Graft . . . 64864-64865
Section 61460
Transection 64732-64760, 64771
Transposition 64716

Cranial Nerve II
See Optic Nerve

Cranial Nerve V
See Trigeminal Nerve

Cranial Nerve VII
See Facial Nerve

Cranial Nerve X
See Vagus Nerve

Cranial Nerve XI
See Accessory Nerve

Cranial Nerve XII
See Hypoglossal Nerve

Cranial Tongs
Application/Removal 20660
Removal 20665

Craniectomy 61501
See Craniotomy
Decompression 61322-61323, 61340-61343
Exploratory 61304-61305
Extensive, for Multiple Suture
Craniosynostosis 61558-61559
for Electrode 61860-61875
Release Stenosis 61550-61552
Surgical 61312-61315, 61320-61323, 61440-61480, 61500-61516, 61518-61522

Craniofacial Procedures
Unlisted Services and Procedures 21299

Craniofacial Separation
Closed Treatment 21431
Open Treatment 21432-21436
Wire Fixation 21431

Craniomegalic Skull
Reduction 62115-62117

Craniopharyngioma
Excision 61545

Cranioplasty 62120
Encephalocele Repair 62120
for Defect 62140-62141, 62145
with Autograft 62146-62147
with Bone Graft 61316, 62146-62147

Craniostenosis
See Craniosynostosis

Craniosynostosis
Bifrontal Craniotomy 61557
Extensive Craniectomy 61558-61559

Craniotomy
See Burr Hole; Craniectomy; Drill Hole; Puncture
Bifrontal 61557
Decompression 61322-61323
Exploratory 61304-61305
for Craniosynostosis 61556-61557
for Encephalocele 62121
for Implant of Neurostimulators 61850-61875
Frontal 61556
Parietal 61556
Surgery 61312-61315, 61320-61323, 61440, 61490, 61546, 61570-61571, 61582-61583, 61590, 61592, 61760, 62120
with Bone Flap 61510-61516, 61526-61530, 61533-61545, 61566-61567

Cranium
See Skull

Craterization
Calcaneus 28120
Clavicle 23180
Femur 27070-27071, 27360
Fibula 27360, 27641
Hip 27070
Humerus 23184, 24140
Ileum 27070
Metacarpal 26230
Metatarsal 28122
Olecranon Process 24147
Phalanges
  Finger 26235-26236
  Toe 28124
Pubis 27070
Radius 24145, 25151
Scapula 23182
Talus 28120
Tarsal 28122
Tibia 27360, 27640
Ulna 24147, 25150

Creatine 82553-82554
Blood or Urine 82540

Creatine Kinase
Total 82550

Creatine Phosphokinase
Blood 82552
Total 82550

Creatinine
Blood 82565
Clearance 82575
Other Source 82570
Urine 82570-82575

Creation
Arteriovenous
  Fistula/Autogenous Graft 36825
Colonic Reservoir 45119
Complete Heart Block 93650
Defect 40720
Ileal Reservoir 44153, 45113
Lesion 61790, 63600
Mucofistula 44144
Pericardial Window 32659
Recipient Site 15000
Shunt
  Cerebrospinal Fluid 62200
  Subarachnoid
    Lumbar-Peritoneal 63740
  Subarachnoid-Subdural 62190
  Ventriculo 62220
Sigmoid Bladder 50810
Speech Prosthesis 31611
Stoma
  Bladder 51980
  Kidney 50395
  Renal Pelvis 50395
  Tympanic Membrane 69433-69436
  Ureter 50860
Ventral Hernia 39503

CRF
See Corticotropic Releasing Hormone (CRH)

CRH
See Corticotropic Releasing Hormone (CRH)

Cricoid Cartilage Split
Larynx 31587

Cricothyroid Membrane
Incision 31605

Cristobalite
See Silica

Critical Care Services 99289-99292
See Emergency Department Services; Prolonged Attendance
Evaluation and Management 99291-99292
Gastric Intubation 91105
Interfacility Transport 99289-99290
Ipecac Administration for Poison 99175
Neonatal
  Initial 99295
  Low Birth Weight Infant 99298-99299
  Subsequent 99296
Pediatric
  Initial 99293
  Interfacility Transport 99289-99290
  Subsequent 99294, 99299

Cross Finger Flap 15574

Crossmatch 86920-86922

Crossmatching, Tissue
See Tissue Typing

Cruciate Ligament
Arthroscopic Repair 29888-29889
Repair 27407-27409
  Knee
    with Collateral Ligament 27409

Cryoablation
See Cryosurgery

Cryofibrinogen 82585

Cryofixation
See Cryopreservation

Cryoglobulin 82595

Cryopreservation
Cells 38207-38209, 88240-88241
Embryo 89258
Freezing and Storage 38207, 88240
Oocyte 0059T
Ovarian Tissue 0058T
Sperm 89259
Testes 89335
Thawing
  Embryo 89352
  Oocytes 89353
  Reproductive Tissue 89354
  Sperm 89356

Cryosurgery 17000-17286, 47371, 47381
See Destruction
Labyrinthotomy 69801
Lesion
  Mouth 40820
  Penis 54056, 54065
  Vagina 57061-57065
  Vulva 56501-56515

Cryotherapy
Acne 17340
Destruction
  Ciliary Body 66720
Lesion
  Cornea 65450
  Retina 67208, 67227
Retinal Detachment
  Prophylaxis 67141
  Repair 67101
Trichiasis
  Correction 67825

Cryptectomy 46210-46211

Cryptococcus
Antibody 86641
Antigen Detection
  Enzyme Immunoassay 87327

Cryptococcus Neoformans
Antigen Detection
  Enzyme Immunoassay 87327

Cryptorchism
See Testis, Undescended

Cyst

Cyst Ovary

Cystatins, Kininogen

Cystectomy

D

Damus-Kaye-Stansel Procedure
See Anastomosis, Pulmonary

Dana Operation
See Rhizotomy

Dandy Operation
See Ventriculocisternostomy

Dark Adaptation Examination . . 92284

Dark Field Examination . . . 87164-87166

Darkroom Test
See Glaucoma, Provocative Test

Darrach Procedure
See Excision, Ulna, Partial

Day Test
See Blood, Feces

de Quervain's Disease Treatment . . . 25000

Death, Brain
See Brain Death

Debridement
Brain . . . 62010
Burns . . . 01951-01953, 16010-16030
Mastoid Cavity
  Complex . . . 69222
  Simple . . . 69220
Metatarsophalangeal Joint . . . 28289
Nails . . . 11720-11721
Nose
  Endoscopic . . . 31237
Pancreatic Tissue . . . 48005
Skin
  Eczematous . . . 11000-11001
  Full Thickness . . . 11041
  Infected . . . 11000-11001
  Partial Thickness . . . 11040
  Subcutaneous Tissue . . . 11042-11044
  with Open Fracture and/or Dislocation . . . 11010-11012
Sternum . . . 21627
Wound
  Non-Selective . . . 97602
  Selective . . . 97601

Debulking Procedure
Ovary/Pelvis . . . 58952-58954

Decompression
See Section
Arm, Lower . . . 24495, 25020-25025
Auditory Canal, Internal . . . 69960
Brainstem . . . 61575-61576
Cauda Equina . . . 63011, 63017, 63047-63048, 63056-63057, 63087-63091
Cranial Nerve . . . 61458
Esophagogastric Varices . . . 37181
Facial Nerve . . . 61590
  Intratemporal
    Lateral to Geniculate Ganglion . . . 69720, 69740
    Medial to Geniculate Ganglion . . . 69725, 69745
  Total . . . 69955
Finger . . . 26035
Gasserian Ganglion
  Sensory Root . . . 61450
Hand . . . 26035-26037
Intestines
  Small . . . 44021
Jejunostomy
  Laparoscopic . . . 44201
Leg
  Fasciotomy . . . 27600-27602
Nerve . . . 64702-64727
  Root . . . 63020-63103
Nucleus of Disk
  Lumbar . . . 62287
Optic Nerve . . . 67570
Orbit . . . 61330
  Removal of Bone . . . 67414, 67445
Skull . . . 61322-61323, 61340-61345
Spinal Cord . . . 63001-63017, 63045-63103
  Cauda Equina . . . 63005
Tarsal Tunnel Release . . . 28035
Volvulus . . . 45321, 45337
with Nasal/Sinus Endoscopy
  Optic Nerve . . . 31294
  Orbit Wall . . . 31292-31293
Wrist . . . 25020-25025

Decortication
Lung
  Endoscopic . . . 32651-32652
  Partial . . . 32225
  Total . . . 32220
  with Parietal Pleurectomy . . . 32320

Decubiti
See Pressure Ulcer (Decubitus)

Decubitus Ulcers
See Debridement; Pressure Ulcer (Decubitus); Skin Graft and Flap

Deetjeen's Body
See Blood, Platelet

Defect, Coagulation
See Coagulopathy

Defect, Heart Septal
See Septal Defect

Defect, Septal Closure, Atrial
See Heart, Repair, Atrial Septum

Deferens, Ductus
See Vas Deferens

Defibrillation
See Cardioversion

Defibrillator, Heart
See Pacemaker, Heart
Evaluation and Testing . . . 93640-93642
Insertion Single/Dual Chamber
  Electrodes . . . 33216-33217, 33224-33225, 33245-33249
  Pulse Generator . . . 33240, 33246
Removal Single/Dual Chamber
  Electrodes . . . 33243-33244
  Pulse Generator . . . 33241
Repair . . . 33218-33220
Repositioning Single/Dual Chamber
  Electrodes . . . 33215, 33226
Revise Pocket Chest . . . 33223

Deformity, Boutonniere
See Boutonniere Deformity

Deformity, Sprengel's
See Sprengel's Deformity

Degenerative, Articular Cartilage, Patella
See Chondromalacia Patella

Degradation Products, Fibrin
See Fibrin Degradation Products

Dehydroepiandrosterone . . . 82626

Dehydroepiandrosterone Sulfate . . . 82627

Dehydrogenase, 6-Phosphogluconate
See Phosphogluconate-6, Dehydrogenase

Dehydrogenase, Alcohol
See Antidiuretic Hormone

Dehydrogenase, Glucose-6-Phosphate
See Glucose-6-Phosphate, Dehydrogenase

Dehydrogenase, Glutamate
See Glutamate Dehydrogenase

Dehydrogenase, Isocitrate
See Isocitric Dehydrogenase

Dehydrogenase, Lactate
See Lactic Dehydrogenase

Dehydrogenase, Malate
See Malate Dehydrogenase

Dehydroisoandrosterone Sulfate
See Dehydroepiandrosterone Sulfate

Delay of Flap
Skin Graft . . . 15600-15630

Deligation
Ureter . . . 50940

Deliveries, Abdominal
See Cesarean Delivery

Delivery
See Cesarean Delivery; Vaginal Delivery

Delorme Operation
See Pericardiectomy

Denervation
Hip
  Femoral . . . 27035
  Obturator . . . 27035
  Sciatic . . . 27035

Denervation, Sympathetic
See Excision, Nerve, Sympathetic

Denis-Browne Splint . . . 29590

Dens Axis
See Odontoid Process

Tumor
Abdomen 49200-49201
Bile Duct 43272
Breast 0061T
Chemosurgery 17304-17310
Colon 45383
Intestines
Large 44393
Small 44369
Pancreatic Duct 43272
Rectum 45190, 46937-46938
Retroperitoneal 49200-49201
Urethra 53220
Tumor or Polyp
Rectum 45320
Turbinate Mucosa 30801-30802
Ureter 52354
Endoscopic 50957-50959, 50976-50978
Urethra 52214-52224, 52354
Prolapse 53275
Warts
Flat 17110-17111
with Cystourethroscopy 52354

Determination, Blood Pressure
See Blood Pressure

Developmental Testing 96110-96111

Device
Iliac Artery Occulsion Device
Insertion 34808
Venous Access
Collection of Blood Specimen 36540
Fluoroscopic Guidance 75998
Insertion
Central 36560-36566
Peripheral 36570-36571
Obstruction Clearance 36595-36596
Imaging 75901-75902
Removal 36590
Repair 36576
Replacement 36582-36583, 36585
Catheter 36578
Ventricular Assist
Extracorporeal Removal 0050T

Device Handling 99002

Device, Intrauterine
See Intrauterine Device (IUD)

Device, Orthotic
See Orthotics

DEXA
See Dual Energy X-Ray Absorptiometry (DEXA)

Dexamethasone
Suppression Test 80420

DHA Sulfate
See Dehydroepiandrosterone Sulfate

DHEA
See Dehydroepiandrosterone

DHEA Sulfate
See Dehydroepiandrosterone Sulfate

DHT
See Dihydrotestosterone

Diagnosis, Psychiatric
See Psychiatric Diagnosis

Diagnostic Amniocentesis
See Amniocentesis

Diagnostic Aspiration of Anterior Chamber of Eye
See Eye, Paracentesis, Anterior Chamber, with Diagnostic Aspiration of Aqueous

Diagnostic Radiologic Examination
See Radiology, Diagnostic

Diagnostic Skin and Sensitization Tests
See Allergy Tests

Diagnostic Ultrasound
See Echography

Diagnostic Ultrasound of Heart
See Echocardiography

Dialyses, Peritoneal
See Dialysis, Peritoneal

Dialysis
Arteriovenous Fistula
Revision
without Thrombectomy 36832
Arteriovenous Shunt 36145
Revision
with Thrombectomy 36833
Thrombectomy 36831
End Stage Renal Disease 90918-90925
Hemodialysis 90935-90937
Blood Flow Study 90939-90940
Hemoperfusion 90997
Patient Training
Completed Course 90989
Per Session 90993
Peritoneal 90945-90947
Unlisted Services and Procedures 90999

Dialysis, Extracorporeal
See Hemodialysis

Diaphragm
Repair
for Eventration 39545
Hernia 39502-39541
Laceration 39501
Resection 39560-39561
Unlisted Procedures 39599
Vagina
Fitting 57170

Diaphragm Contraception
See Contraception, Diaphragm

Diaphysectomy
Calcaneus 28120
Clavicle 23180
Femur 27360
Fibula 27360, 27641
Humerus 23184, 24140
Metacarpal 26230
Metatarsal 28122
Olecranon Process 24147
Phalanges
Finger 26235-26236
Toe 28124
Radius 24145, 25151
Scapula 23182
Talus 28120
Tarsal 28122
Tibia 27360, 27640
Ulna 24147, 25150

Diastase
See Amylase

Diastasis
See Separation

Diathermy 97024
See Physical Medicine/Therapy/Occupational Therapy
Destruction
Ciliary Body 66700
Lesion
Retina 67208, 67227
Retinal Detachment
Prophylaxis 67141
Repair 67101

Diathermy, Surgical
See Electrocautery

Dibucaine Number 82638

Dichloride, Methylene
See Dichloromethane

Dichlorides, Ethylene
See Dichloroethane

Dichloroethane 84600

Dichloromethane 84600

Diethylamide, Lysergic Acid
See Lysergic Acid Diethylamide

Diethylether 84600

Differential Count
See White Blood Cell Count

Differentiation Reversal Factor
See Prothrombin

Diffusion Test, Gel
See Immunodiffusion

Digestive Tract
See Gastrointestinal Tract

Digit
See Finger; Toe
Replantation 20816-20822

Digital Artery Sympathectomy 64820

Digital Slit-Beam Radiograph
See Scanogram

Digits
Pinch Graft 15050

Digoxin
Assay 80162

Dislocation
Acromioclavicular Joint
  Open Treatment 23550-23552
Ankle
  Closed Treatment 27840-27842
  Open Treatment 27846-27848
Carpal
  Closed Treatment 25690
  Open Treatment 25695
Carpometacarpal Joint 26670
  Closed Treatment
    with Manipulation 26675-26676
  Open Treatment 26685-26686
  Percutaneous Fixation 26676
Clavicle
  Closed Treatment 23540-23545
  Open Treatment 23550-23552
  with Manipulation 23545
  without Manipulation 23540
Closed Treatment
  Carpometacarpal Joint 26670-26675
  Metacarpophalangeal 26700-26706
  Thumb 26641
Elbow
  Closed Treatment 24600-24605, 24640
  Open Treatment 24615
Hip Joint
  Closed Treatment 27250-27252, 27265-27266
  Congenital 27256-27259
  Open Treatment .27253-27254, 27258-27259
  without Trauma 27265-27266
Interphalangeal Joint
  Closed Treatment 26770-26775
  Open Treatment 26785
  Percutaneous Fixation 26776
  Toe
    Closed Treatment 28660-28665
    Open Treatment 28675
    Percutaneous Fixation 26770-26776, 28666
  with Manipulation 26770
Knee 27560-27562
  Closed Treatment 27550-27552, 27560-27562
  Open Treatment 27556-27558, 27566
  Recurrent 27420-27424
Lunate
  Closed Treatment 25690
  Open Treatment 25695
  with Manipulation 25690, 26670-26676, 26700-26706
Metacarpophalangeal Joint
  Closed Treatment 26700-26706
  Open Treatment 26715
Metatarsophalangeal Joint
  Closed Treatment 28630-28635
  Open Treatment 28645
  Percutaneous Fixation 28636
Open Treatment 26685-26686
Patella
  Closed Treatment 27560-27562
  Open Treatment 27566
  Recurrent 27420-27424
Pelvic Ring
  Closed Treatment 27193-27194
  Open Treatment 27217-27218
  Percutaneous Fixation 27216
  without Manipulation 27193-27194
Percutaneous Fixation
  Metacarpophalangeal 26705
Peroneal Tendons 27675-27676
Radio-Ulnar Joint 25520-25526
Radius
  Closed Treatment 24640
  with Fracture
    Closed Treatment 24620
    Open Treatment 24635
Shoulder
  Closed Treatment with Manipulation 23650-23655
  Open Treatment 23660
  with Greater Tuberosity Fracture
    Closed Treatment 23665
    Open Treatment 23670
  with Surgical or Anatomical Neck Fracture
    Closed Treatment 23675
    Open Treatment 23680
Skin
  Debridement 11010-11012
Sternoclavicular Joint
  Closed Treatment
    with Manipulation 23525
    without Manipulation 23520
  Open Treatment 23530-23532
Talotarsal Joint
  Closed Treatment 28570-28575
  Open Treatment 28546
  Percutaneous Fixation 28576
Tarsal
  Closed Treatment 28540-28545
  Open Treatment 28555
  Percutaneous Fixation 28546
Tarsometatarsal Joint
  Closed Treatment 28600-28605
  Open Treatment 28615
  Percutaneous Fixation 28606
Temporomandibular Joint
  Closed Treatment 21480-21485
  Open Treatment 21490
Thumb
  Closed Treatment 26641-26645
  Open Treatment 26665
  Percutaneous Fixation 26650
  with Fracture 26645
    Open Treatment 26665
    Percutaneous Fixation 26650-26665
  with Manipulation 26641-26650
Tibiofibular Joint
  Closed Treatment 27830-27831
  Open Treatment 27832
Vertebra
  Additional Segment
    Open Treatment 22328
  Cervical
    Open Treatment 22326
  Closed Treatment 22305
    with Manipulation, Casting and/or Bracing 22315
    without Manipulation 22310
  Lumbar
    Open Treatment 22325
  Thoracic
    Open Treatment 22327
Wrist
  Closed Treatment 25660, 25675, 25680
  Intercarpal 25660
    Open Treatment 25670
  Open Treatment 25670, 25685
  Percutaneous Fixation 25671
  Radiocarpal 25660
    Open Treatment 25670
  Radioulnar
    Closed Treatment 25675
    Open Treatment 25676
    Percutaneous Fixation 25671
  with Fracture
    Closed Treatment 25680
    Open Treatment 25685
  with Manipulation 25660, 25675, 25680

Dislocation, Radiocarpal Joint
See Radiocarpal Joint, Dislocation

Disorder
Blood Coagulation
  See Coagulopathy
Penis
  See Penis
Retinal
  See Retina

Displacement Therapy
Nose 30210

Dissection
Hygroma, Cystic
  Axillary/Cervical 38550-38555
Lymph Nodes 38542

Dissection, Neck, Radical
See Radical Neck Dissection

Distention
See Dilation

Diverticula, Meckel's
See Diverticulum, Meckel's

Diverticulectomy 44800
Esophagus 43130-43135

Diverticulectomy, Meckel's
See Meckel's Diverticulum, Excision

Diverticulum
Bladder
  See Bladder, Diverticulum
Meckel's
  Excision 44800
Repair
  Urethra 53400-53405

Division
Muscle
  Foot 28250
Plantar Fascia
  Foot 28250

Division, Isthmus, Horseshoe Kidney
See Symphysiotomy, Horseshoe Kidney

Division, Scalenus Anticus Muscle
See Muscle Division, Scalenus Anticus

Dl-Amphetamine
See Amphetamine

DMO
See Dimethadione

DNA
Antibody 86225-86226

DNA Endonuclease
See DNAse

DNA Probe
See Cytogenetics Studies; Nucleic Acid Probe

DNAse
Antibody 86215

Domiciliary Services
See Nursing Facility Services
Discharge Services 99315-99316
Established Patient 99331-99333
New Patient 99321-99323

Donor Procedures
Conjunctival Graft 68371
Heart Excision 33940
Heart/Lung Excision 33930
Liver Segment 47140-47142
Stem Cells
Donor Search 38204

Dopamine
See Catecholamines
Blood 82383-82384
Urine 82382, 82384

Doppler Echocardiography 76827-76828, 93307-93308, 93320-93350
Extracranial 93875
Intracardiac 93662
Transesophageal 93318
Transthoracic 93303-93317

Doppler Scan
Arterial Studies, Extremities 93922-93924
Extremities 93965
Intracranial Arteries 93886-93888

Dorsal Vertebra
See Vertebra, Thoracic

Dose Plan
See Dosimetry

Dosimetry
Radiation Therapy 77300, 77331
Brachytherapy 77326-77328
Intensity Modulation 77301
Teletherapy 77305-77321

Double-Stranded DNA
See Deoxyribonucleic Acid

Doxepin
Assay 80166

DPH
See Phenytoin

Drainage
See Excision; Incision; Incision and Drainage
Abdomen
Abdomen Fluid 49080-49081
Abscess
Appendix 44900-44901
Percutaneous 44901
Brain 61150-61151
Eyelid 67700
Liver 47010-47011
Ovary
Percutaneous 58823
Pelvic
Percutaneous 58823
Pericolic
Percutaneous 58823
Perirenal or Renal 50020-50021
Percutaneous 50021
Prostate 52700
Retroperitoneal 49060-49061
Percutaneous 49061
Subdiaphragmatic or Subphrenic 49040-49041
Percutaneous 49040-49041
with X-Ray 75989
Amniotic Fluid
Diagnostic Aspiration 59000
Therapeutic Aspiration 59001
Bile Duct
Transhepatic 75980
Brain Fluid 61070
Bursa 20600-20610
Cerebrospinal Fluid 61000-61020, 61050, 61070, 62272
Cervical Fluid 61050
Cisternal Fluid 61050
Cyst
Bone 20615
Brain 61150-61151, 62161-62162
Breast 19000-19001
Ganglion 20612
Liver 47010-47011
Percutaneous 47011
Salivary Gland 42409
Sublingual Gland 42409
with Fistula 42325-42326
Extraperitoneal Lymphocele
Laparoscopic 49323
Open 49062
Eye
Anterior Chamber Paracentesis
with Diagnostic Aspiration of Aqueous 65800
with Therapeutic Release of Aqueous 65805
Removal Blood 65815
Removal of Vitreous and/or Discission Anterior Hyaloid Membrane 65810
Fetal Fluid 59074
Ganglion Cyst 20612
Hematoma
Brain 61154-61156
Vagina 57022-57023
Hematoma, Subungual 11740
Joint 20600-20610
Liver
Abscess or Cyst 47010-47011
Percutaneous 47011
Lymphocele
Endoscopic 49323
Onychia 10060-10061
Orbit 67405, 67440
Pancreas
See Anastomosis, Pancreas to Intestines
Pseudocyst 48510-48511
Percutaneous 48511
Paronychia 10060-10061
Pericardial Sac 32659
Pericardium
See Aspiration, Pericardium
Pseudocyst
Gastrointestinal, Upper
Transmural Endoscopic 43240
Pancreas 48510
Open 48510
Percutaneous 48511
Puncture
Chest 32000-32002
Skin 10040-10180
Spinal Cord
Cerebrospinal Fluid 62272
Subdural Fluid 61000-61001
Urethra
Extravasation 53080-53085
Ventricular Fluid 61020

Drainage Implant, Glaucoma
See Aqueous Shunt

Dressings
Burns 16010-16030
Change
Anesthesia 15852

DREZ Procedure
See Incision, Spinal Cord; Incision and Drainage

DRIL
see Revascularization, Distal

Drill Hole
Skull
Catheter 61107
Drain Hematoma 61108
Exploration 61105
Implant Electrode 61850, 61863-61868

Drinking Test for Glaucoma
See Glaucoma, Provocative Test

Drug
See Drug Assay; Specific Drug
Analysis
Tissue Preparation 80103
Confirmation 80102
Infusion 62360-62362

Drug Assay
Amikacin 80150
Amitriptyline 80152
Benzodiazepine 80154
Carbamazepine 80156-80157
Cyclosporine 80158
Desipramine 80160
Digoxin 80162
Dipropylacetic Acid 80164
Doxepin 80166
Ethosuximide 80168
Gentamicin 80170
Gold 80172
Haloperidol 80173
Imipramine 80174

E

Elbow
See Humerus; Radius; Ulna
Abscess
  Incision and Drainage 23930, 23935
Anesthesia 00400, 01710-01782
Arthrectomy 24155
Arthrocentesis 20605
Arthrodesis 24800-24802
Arthroplasty 24360
  Total Replacement 24363
  with Implant 24361-24362
Arthroscopy
  Diagnostic 29830
  Surgical 29834-29838
Arthrotomy 24000
  Capsular Release 24006
  with Joint Exploration 24101
  with Synovectomy 24102
  with Synovial Biopsy 24101
Biopsy 24065-24066, 24101
Bursa
  Incision and Drainage 23931
Dislocation
  Closed Treatment 24600-24605, 24640
  Open Treatment 24615
  Subluxate 24640
Excision 24155
  Bursa 24105
  Synovium 24102
Exploration 24000, 24101
Fracture
  Monteggia 24620-24635
  Open Treatment 24586-24587
Hematoma
  Incision and Drainage 23930
Implant
  Removal 24164
Incision and Drainage 24000
Injection
  Arthrography
    Radiologic 24220
Magnetic Resonance Imaging (MRI) 73221
Manipulation 24300
Radical Resection
  Capsule, Soft Tissue and Bone
    with Contracture Release 24149
Removal
  Foreign Body 24000, 24101, 24200-24201
  Implant 24160
  Loose Body 24101
Repair
  Epicondylitis 24350
  Fasciotomy 24350-24356
  Flexorplasty 24330
  Hemiepiphyseal Arrest 24470
  Ligament 24343-24346
  Muscle 24341
  Muscle Transfer 24301
  Tendon 24340-24342
    Lengthening 24305
    Transfer 24301
  Tennis Elbow 24350-24356
Steindler Advancement 24330
Strapping 29260
Tumor
  Excision 24075-24077
Unlisted Services and Procedures 24999
X-Ray 73070-73080
  with Contrast 73085

Elbow, Golfer
See Tennis Elbow

Elbows, Tennis
See Tennis Elbow

Electric Countershock
See Cardioversion

Electric Stimulation
See Electrical Stimulation

Electric Stimulation, Transcutaneous
See Application, Neurostimulation

Electrical Stimulation
Bone Healing
  Invasive 20975
  Noninvasive 20974
Brain Surface 95961-95962
Physical Therapy
  Attended, Manual 97032
  Unattended 97014

Electro-Hydraulic Procedure 52325

Electro-oculography 92270

Electroanalgesia
See Application, Neurostimulation

Electrocardiography
24 Hour Monitoring 93224-93237
Evaluation 93000, 93010, 93014
Patient-Demand Recording
  Transmission and Evaluation 93270
Patient-Demand Transmission and Evaluation
  Transmission and Evaluation
    Interpretation 93272
    Monitoring 93271
Rhythm
  Evaluation 93042
  Microvolt T-wave Alternans 93025
  Tracing 93041
  Tracing and Evaluation 93040
Signal Averaged 93278
Transmission 93012

Electrocautery 17000-17286
See Destruction

Electrochemistry
See Electrolysis

Electroconvulsive Therapy 90870-90871

Electrocorticogram
Intraoperative 95829

Electrode, Depth
See Depth Electrode

Electrodesiccation 17000-17286
Lesion
  Penis 54055

Electroejaculation 55870

Electroencephalography (EEG) 95816
Brain Death 95824
Coma 95822
Digital Analysis 95957
Electrode Placement 95830
Intraoperative 95955
Monitoring ...95812-95813, 95950-95953, 95956
  with Drug Activation 95954
  with Physical Activation 95954
  with WADA Activation 95958
Sleep 95822, 95827
Standard 95819

Electrogastrography 91132-91133

Electrogram, Atrial
Esophageal Recording 93615-93616

Electrolysis 17380

Electromyographs
See Electromyography, Needle

Electromyography
Anorectal with Biofeedback 90911
Fine Wire
  Dynamic 96004
Needle
  Extremities 95861-95864
  Extremity 95860
  Face and Neck Muscles 95867-95868
  Ocular 92265
  Other than Thoracic Paraspinal 95870
  Single Fiber Electrode 95872
  Thoracic Paraspinal Muscles 95869
Sphincter Muscles
  Anus 51784-51785
    Needle 51785
  Urethra 51784-51785
    Needle 51785
Surface
  Dynamic 96002-96004

Electron Microscopy 88348-88349

Electronic Analysis
Drug Infusion Pump 62367-62368
Implantable Loop Recorder System 93727
Neurostimulator Pulse Generator ...95970-95975
Pacing Cardioverter-Defibrillator ...93741-93744

Electrophoresis
Counterimmuno- 86185
Immuno- 86320-86327
Unlisted Services and Procedures 82664

Electrophysiology Procedure 93600-93660

Electroretinogram
See Electroretinography

Electroretinography 92275

Electrostimulation, Analgesic Cutaneous
See Application, Neurostimulation

Electrosurgery
Trichiasis
Correction 67825

Electroversion, Cardiac
See Cardioversion

Elevation, Scapula, Congenital
See Sprengel's Deformity

Elliot Operation
See Excision, Lesion, Sclera

Eloesser Procedure
See Thoracostomy, Empyema

Eloesser Thoracoplasty
See Thoracoplasty

Embolectomy
Aortoiliac Artery 34151-34201
Axillary Artery 34101
Brachial Artery 34101
Carotid Artery 34001
Celiac Artery 34151
Femoral 34201
Iliac 34151-34201
Innominate Artery 34001-34101
Mesentery Artery 34151
Peroneal Artery 34203
Popliteal Artery 34203
Pulmonary Artery 33910-33916
Radial Artery 34111
Renal Artery 34151
Subclavian Artery 34001-34101
Tibial Artery 34203
Ulnar Artery 34111

Embryo
Biopsy 89290-89291
Cryopreservation 89258
Cryopreserved
Preparation
Thawing 89352
Culture 89250
with Co-Culture Oocyte 89251
Hatching
Assisted
Microtechnique 89253
Preparation
for Transfer 89255
Storage 89342

Embryo/Fetus Monitoring
See Monitoring, Fetal

Embryo Implantation
See Implantation

Embryo Transfer
In Vitro Fertilization 58974-58976
Intrafallopian Transfer 58976
Intrauterine Transfer 58974

Embryonated Eggs
Inoculation 87250

Emergency Department Services 99281-99288
See Critical Care; Emergency Department Services
Anesthesia 99140
Physician Direction of Advanced Life Support 99288

Emesis Induction 99175

EMG
See Electromyography, Needle

EMI Scan
See CT Scan

Emission Computerized Tomography 78607

Emission-Computed Tomography, Single-Photon
See SPECT

Emmet Operation
See Vagina, Repair, Obstetric

Empyema
Closure
Chest Wall 32810
Thoracostomy 32020-32036

Empyema, Lung
See Abscess, Thorax

Empyemectomy 32540

Encephalitis
Antibody 86651-86654

Encephalitis Virus Vaccine 90735

Encephalocele
Repair 62120
Craniotomy 62121

Encephalon
See Brain

End Stage Renal Disease Services 90918-90925

End-Expiratory Pressure, Positive
See Pressure Breathing, Positive

Endarterectomy
Coronary Artery 33572
Pulmonary 33916

Endemic Flea-Borne Typhus
See Murine Typhus

Endobronchial Challenge Tests
See Bronchial Challenge Test

Endocavitary Fulguration
See Electrocautery

Endocrine System
Unlisted Services and Procedures ..60699, 78099

Endocrine, Pancreas
See Islet Cell

Endolymphatic Sac
Exploration
with Shunt 69806
without Shunt 69805

Endometrial Ablation 0009T, 58353
Exploration
via Hysteroscopy 58563

Endometrioma
Abdomen
Destruction/Excision 49200-49201
Retroperitoneal
Destruction/Excision 49200-49201

Endometriosis, Adhesive
See Adhesions, Intrauterine

Endometrium
Biopsy 58100, 58558

Endonuclease, DNA
See DNAse

Endoscopic Retrograde Cannulation of Pancreatic Duct (ERCP)
See Cholangiopancreatography

Endoscopies, Pleural
See Thoracoscopy

Endoscopy
See Arthroscopy; Thoracoscopy
Adrenal Gland
Biopsy 60650
Excision 60650
Anus
Biopsy 46606
Dilation 46604
Exploration 46600
Hemorrhage 46614
Removal
Foreign Body 46608
Polyp 46610, 46612
Tumor 46610, 46612
Bile Duct
Biopsy 47553
Destruction
Calculi (Stone) 43265
Tumor 43272
Dilation 43271, 47555-47556
Exploration 47552
Intraoperative 47550
Percutaneous 47552-47555
Removal
Calculi (Stone) 43264, 47554
Foreign Body 43269
Stent 43269
Specimen Collection 43260
Sphincter Pressure 43263
Sphincterotomy 43262
Tube Placement 43267-43268
Bladder 52000
Biopsy 52204, 52354
Catheterization 52005, 52010
Destruction 52354
Lesion 52400
Evacuation
Clot 52001

Excision
Bilateral 54861
Unilateral 54860
Exploration
Biopsy 54820
Hematoma
Incision and Drainage 54700
Lesion
Excision
Local 54830
Spermatocele 54840
Needle Biopsy 54800
Spermatocele
Excision 54840
Unlisted Services and Procedures 55899
X-Ray with Contrast 74440

Epididymograms 55300

Epididymography 74440

Epididymoplasty
See Repair, Epididymis

Epididymovasostomy
Bilateral 54901
Unilateral 54900

Epidural
Electrode
Insertion 61531
Removal 61535
Injection 62281-62282, 62310-62319, 64479-64484
Lysis 0027T, 62263-62264

Epidural Anesthesia
See Anesthesia, Epidural

Epidurography 72275

Epigastric
Hernia Repair 49572

Epiglottidectomy 31420

Epiglottis
Excision 31420

Epikeratoplasty 65767

Epilation
See Removal, Hair

Epinephrine
See Catecholamines
Blood 82383-82384
Urine 82384

Epiphyseal Arrest
Femur 20150, 27185, 27475, 27479-27485, 27742
Fibula 20150, 27477-27485, 27730-27742
Radius 20150, 25450-25455
Tibia .. 20150, 27477-27485, 27730, 27734-27742
Ulna 20150, 25450-25455

Epiphyseal Separation
Radius
Closed Treatment 25600
Open Treatment 25620

Epiphysiodesis
See Epiphyseal Arrest

Epiphysis
See Bone; Specific Bone

Epiploectomy 49255

Episiotomy 59300

Epispadias
Penis
Reconstruction 54385
Repair 54380-54390
with Exstrophy of Bladder 54390
with Incontinence 54380-54390

Epistaxis 30901-30906
with Nasal/Sinus Endoscopy 31238

EPO
See Erythropoietin

Epstein-Barr Virus
Antibody 86663-86665

Equina, Cauda
See Cauda Equina

ERCP
See Bile Duct; Cholangiopancreatography; Pancreatic Duct

ERG
See Electroretinography

Ergocalciferol
See Calciferol

Ergocalciferols
See Calciferol

Ergonovine Provocation Test 93024

Erythrocyte
See Red Blood Cell (RBC)

Erythrocyte ab
See Antibody, Red Blood Cell

Erythrocyte Count
See Red Blood Cell (RBC), Count

Erythropoietin 82668

Escharotomy
Burns 16035-16036

Escherichia coli 0157
Antigen Detection
Enzyme Immunoassay 87335

ESD
See Endoscopy, Gastrointestinal, Upper

Esophageal Acid Infusion Test
See Acid Perfusion Test

Esophageal Polyp
See Polyp, Esophagus

Esophageal Tumor
See Tumor, Esophagus

Esophageal Varices
Ligation 43205, 43400
Transection/Repair 43401

Esophagectomy
Partial 43116-43124
Total 43107-43113, 43124

Esophagoenterostomy
with Total Gastrectomy 43620

Esophagogastroduodenoscopies
See Endoscopy, Gastrointestinal, Upper

Esophagogastromyotomy
See Esophagomyotomy

Esophagogastrostomy 43320

Esophagojejunostomy 43340-43341

Esophagomyotomy .. 32665, 43330-43331

Esophagorrhaphy
See Esophagus, Suture

Esophagoscopies
See Endoscopy, Esophagus

Esophagostomy 43350-43352
Closure 43420-43425

Esophagotomy 43020, 43045

Esophagotracheal Fistula
See Fistula, Tracheoesophageal

Esophagus
Acid Perfusion Test 91030
Acid Reflux Tests 91032-91033
Biopsy
Endoscopy 43202
Cineradiography 74230
Dilation 43450-43458
Endoscopic 43220-43226, 43248-43249
Surgical 43510
Endoscopy
Biopsy 43202
Dilation 43220-43226
Exploration 43200
Hemorrhage 43227
Injection 43201, 43204
Insertion Stent 43219
Needle Biopsy 43232
Removal
Foreign Body 43215
Polyp 43216-43217, 43228
Tumor 43216, 43228
Ultrasound 43231-43232
Vein Ligation 43205
Excision
Diverticula 43130-43135
Partial 43116-43124
Total 43107-43113, 43124
Exploration
Endoscopy 43200
Hemorrhage 43227
Incision 43020, 43045
Muscle 43030

Injection
  Sclerosing Agent .43204
  Submucosal .43201
Insertion
  Stent .43219
  Tamponade .43460
  Tube .43510
Intubation with Specimen Collection .91000
Lesion
  Excision .43100-43101
Ligation .43405
Motility Study .78258, 91010-91012
Needle Biopsy
  Endoscopy .43232
Nuclear Medicine
  Imaging (Motility) .78258
  Reflux Study .78262
Reconstruction .43300, 43310, 43313
  Creation
    Stoma .43350-43352
  Esophagostomy .43350
  Fistula .43305, 43312, 43314
  Gastrointestinal .43360-43361
Removal
  Foreign Bodies .43020, 43045, 43215, 74235
  Lesion .43216
  Polyp .43216-43217, 43228
Repair .43300, 43310, 43313
  Esophagogastric Fundoplasty .43324-43325
    Laparoscopic .43280
  Esophagogastrostomy .43320
  Esophagojejunostomy .43340-43341
  Fistula .43305, 43312, 43314, 43420-43425
  Muscle .43330-43331
  Pre-existing Perforation .43405
  Varices .43401
  Wound .43410-43415
Suture .43405
  Wound .43410-43415
Ultrasound
  Endoscopy .43231-43232
Unlisted Services and Procedures .43289, 43499
Vein
  Ligation .43205, 43400
Video .74230
X-Ray .74220

Esophagus Neoplasm
See Tumor, Esophagus

Esophagus, Varix
See Esophageal Varices

Established Patient
Confirmatory Consultations .99271-99275
Domiciliary or Rest Home Visit .99331-99333
Emergency Department Services .99281-99285
Home Services .99347-99350
Hospital Inpatient Services .99221-99239
Hospital Observation Services .99217-99220
Initial Inpatient Consultations .99251-99255
Office and/or Other Outpatient Consultations . . . .
99241-99245
Office Visit .99211-99215
Outpatient Visit .99211-99215

Establishment
Colostomy
  Abdominal .50810
  Perineal .50810

Estes Operation
See Ovary, Transposition

Estlander Procedure .40525

Estradiol .82670
Response .80414

Estriol
Blood or Urine .82677

Estrogen
Blood or Urine .82671-82672
Receptor .84233

Estrone
Blood or Urine .82679

Ethanediols
See Ethylene Glycol

Ethanol
Blood .82055
Breath .82075
Urine .82055

Ethchlorovynol
See Ethchlorvynol

Ethchlorvinol
See Ethchlorvynol

Ethchlorvynol
Blood .82690
Urine .82690

Ethmoid
Fracture
  with Fixation .21340

Ethmoid, Sinus
See Sinus, Ethmoid

Ethmoidectomy .31200-31205
Endoscopic .31254-31255
Skull Base Surgery .61580-61581
with Nasal/Sinus Endoscopy .31254-31255

Ethosuccimid
See Ethosuximide

Ethosuximide .80168
Assay .80168

Ethyl Alcohol
See Ethanol

Ethylene Dichlorides
See Dichloroethane

Ethylene Glycol .82693

Ethylmethylsuccimide
See Ethosuximide

Etiocholanalone Measurement
See Etiocholanolone

Etiocholanolone .82696

ETOH
See Alcohol, Ethyl

Euglobulin Lysis .85360

European Blastomycosis
See Cryptococcus

Eustachian Tube
Catheterization .69405
Inflation
  Myringotomy .69420
    Anesthesia .69421
  with Catheterization .69400
  without Catheterization .69401
Insertion
  Catheter .69405

Eutelegenesis
See Artificial Insemination

Evacuation
Cervical Pregnancy .59140
Hematoma
  Brain .61312-61315
  Subungual .11740
Hydatidiform Mole .59870

Evaluation and Management
Assistive Technology
  Assessment .97755
Athletic Training
  Evaluation .97005
  Re-evaluation .97006
Basic Life and/or Disability
Evaluation Services .99450
Care Plan Oversight Services .99374-99380
  Home Health Agency Care .99374
  Hospice .99377-99378
  Nursing Facility .99379-99380
Case Management Services .99361-99373
Consultation .99241-99275
Critical Care .99291-99292
  Interfacility Pediatric Transport .99289-99290
Domiciliary or Rest Home .99321-99333
Emergency Department .99281-99288
Health Behavior
  Assessment .96150
  Family Intervention .96154-96155
  Group Intervention .96153
  Individual Intervention .96152
  Re-assessment .96151
Home Services .99341-99350
Hospital .99221-99233
  Discharge .99238-99239
Hospital Services
  Observation Care .99217-99220
Insurance Exam .99455-99456
Low Birthweight Infant .99298-99299
Medical
  with Individual Psychotherapy
    Hospital or Residential Care .90817,
    90819, 90822, 90824, 90827, 90829
    Office or Outpatient .90805, 90807, 90809
  with Individual Psychotherapy, Interactive
    Office or Outpatient .90811, 90813, 90815
Neonatal Critical Care .99295-99296
Newborn Care .99431-99440

Extrauterine Pregnancy
See Ectopic Pregnancy

Extravasation Blood
See Hemorrhage

Extremity
Lower
  Harvest of Vein for Bypass Graft 35500
  Harvest of Vein for Vascular Reconstruction 35572
  Revision 35879-35881
Upper
  Harvest of Artery for Coronary Artery Bypass Graft 35600
  Harvest of Vein for Bypass Graft 35500
  Repair
    Blood Vessel 35206
Wound Exploration
  Penetrating Wound 20103

Eye
See Ciliary Body; Cornea; Iris; Lens; Retina; Sclera; Vitreous
Biometry 76516-76519, 92136
Drainage
  Anterior Chamber
    Discission of Anterior Hyaloid Membrane 65810
    with Diagnostic Aspiration of Aqueous 65800
    with Removal of Blood 65815
    with Removal of Vitreous and/or with Therapeutic Release of Aqueous 65805
Endoscopy 66990
Goniotomy 65820
Incision
  Adhesions
    Anterior Synechiae 65860, 65870
    Corneovitreal Adhesions 65880
    Goniosynechiae 65865
    Posterior Synechiae 65875
  Anterior Chamber 65820
  Trabeculae 65850
Injection
  Air 66020
  Medication 66030
Insertion
  Implantation
    Drug Delivery System 67027
    Foreign Material for Reinforcement 65155
    Muscles Attached 65140
    Muscles, Not Attached 65135
    Reinsertion 65150
    Scleral Shell 65130
Interferometry
  Biometry 92136
Lesion
  Excision 65900
Nerve
  Destruction 67345
Paracentesis
  Anterior Chamber
    Removal of Blood 65815
    Removal or Vitreous and/or Discission Anterior Hyaloid Membrane 65810
    with Diagnostic Aspiration of Aqueous 65800
    with Therapeutic Release of Aqueous 65805
Radial Keratotomy 65771
Reconstruction
  Graft
    Conjunctiva 65782
    Stem Cell 65781
  Transplantation
    Amniotic Membrane 65780
Removal
  Blood Clot 65930
  Bone 65112
  Foreign Body
    Conjunctival Embedded 65210
    Conjunctival Superficial 65205
    Corneal with Slit Lamp 65222
    Corneal without Slit Lamp 65220
    Intraocular 65235-65265
  Implant 65175
    Anterior Segment 65920
    Muscles, Not Attached 65103
    Posterior Segment 67120-67121
Repair
  Conjunctiva
    by Mobilization and Rearrangement with Hospitalization 65273
    by Mobilization and Rearrangement without Hospitalization 65272
    Direct Closure 65270
  Cornea
    Nonperforating 65275
    Perforating 65280-65285
  Muscles 65290
  Sclera
    Anterior Segment 66250
    with Graft 66225
    with Tissue Glue 65286
    without Graft 66220
  Trabeculae 65855
  Wound
    by Mobilization and Rearrangement 65272-65273
    Direct Closure 65270
Shunt, Aqueous
  to Extraocular Reservoir 66180
Ultrasound 76511-76514
  Biometry 76516-76519
  Foreign Body 76529
Unlisted Services and Procedures
  Anterior Segment 66999
  Posterior Segment 67299
with Muscle or Myocutaneous Flap 65114
  Muscles Attached 65105
  Ocular Contents
    with Implant 65093
    without Implant 65091
  Orbital Contents 65110
    without Implant 65101
X-Ray 70030

Eye Allergy Test 95060
See Allergy Tests

Eye Evisceration
See Evisceration, Ocular Contents

Eye Exam
Established Patient 92012-92014
New Patient 92002-92004
with Anesthesia 92018-92019

Eye Exercises
Training 92065

Eye Muscles
Biopsy 67350
Repair
  Strabismus
    Adjustable Sutures 67335
    Exploration and/or Repair Detached Extraocular Muscle 67340
    on Patient with Previous Surgery ...67331
    One Vertical Muscle 67314
    Posterior Fixation Suture 67334
    Recession or Resection 67311-67312
    Release of Scar Tissue without Detaching Extraocular Muscle 67343
    Two or More Vertical Muscles 67316
    with Scarring Extraocular Muscles ..67332
    with Superior Oblique Muscle 67318
Transposition 67320
Unlisted Services and Procedures 67399

Eye Prosthesis
See Prosthesis

Eye Socket
See Orbit; Orbital Contents; Orbital Floor; Periorbital Region

Eyebrow
Repair
  Ptosis 67900

Eyeglasses
See Spectacle Services

Eyelashes
Repair Trichiasis
  Epilation
    by Forceps Only 67820
    by Other than Forceps 67825
  Incision of Lid Margin 67830
    with Free Mucous Membrane Graft .67835

Eyelid
Abscess
  Incision and Drainage 67700
Biopsy 67810
Blepharoplasty 15820-15823
Chalazion
  Excision 67805
    Multiple 67801-67805
    Single 67800
    with Anesthesia 67808
Closure by Suture 67875
Incision
  Canthus 67715
  Sutures 67710
Injection
  Subconjunctival 68200
Lesion
  Destruction 67850

Excision
Multiple 67801-67805
Single 67800
with Anesthesia 67808
without Closure 67840
Reconstruction
Canthus 67950
Total 67973-67975
Total Eyelid
Lower 67973-67975
Second Stage 67975
Upper 67974
Transfer of Tarsoconjunctival Flap from
Opposing Eyelid 67971
Removal
Foreign Body 67938
Repair 21280-21282
Blepharoptosis
Conjunctivo-Tarso-Muller's
Muscle-Levator Resection 67908
Frontalis Muscle Technique ..67901-67904
Reduction Overcorrection of Ptosis ..67909
Superior Rectus Technique with Fascial
Sling 67906
Ectropion
Blepharoplasty 67914
Suture 67914
Entropion
Excision Tarsal Wedge 67923
Extensive 67924
Suture 67921
Thermocauterization 67922
Excisional 67961
over One-Fourth of Lid Margin 67966
Lagophthalmos 67912
Lashes
Epilation, by Forceps Only 67820
Epilation, by Other than Forceps 67825
Lid Margin 67830-67835
Wound
Full Thickness 67935
Partial Thickness 67930
Repair with Graft
Retraction 67911
Skin Graft
Full Thickness 67961
Split 67961
Suture 67880
with Transposition of Tarsal Plate 67882
Tissue Transfer, Adjacent 67961
Unlisted Services and Procedures 67999

Eyelid Ptoses
See Blepharoptosis

F

Face
CT Scan 70486-70488
Lesion
Destruction 17000-17004, 17280-17286
Magnetic Resonance Imaging
(MRI) 70540-70543
Tumor Resection 21015

Face Lift 15824-15828

Facial Asymmetries
See Hemifacial Microsomia

Facial Bone
See Mandible; Maxilla
Tumor
Excision 21034

Facial Bones
Abscess
Excision 21026
Reconstruction
Secondary 21275
Repair 21208-21209
Tumor
Excision 21029-21030
Resection
Radical 21015
X-Ray 70140-70150

Facial Nerve
Anastomosis
to Hypoglossal 64868
to Phrenic Nerve 64870
to Spinal Accessory 64866
Avulsion 64742
Decompression 61590, 61596
Intratemporal
Lateral to Geniculate
Ganglion 69720, 69740
Medial to Geniculate
Ganglion 69725, 69745
Total 69955
Function Study 92516
Incision 64742
Injection
Anesthetic 64402
Mobilization 61590
Repair
Lateral to Geniculate Ganglion 69740
Medial to Geniculate Ganglion 69745
Repair/Suture
with or without Graft 64864-64865
Suture
Lateral to Geniculate Ganglion 69740
Medial to Geniculate Ganglion 69745
Transection 64742

Facial Nerve Paralysis
Graft 15840-15845
Repair 15840-15845

Facial Prosthesis
Impression 21088

Facial Rhytidectomy
See Face Lift

Factor I
See Fibrinogen

Factor II
See Prothrombin

Factor III
See Thromboplastin

Factor IV
See Calcium

Factor VII
See Proconvertin

Factor VIII
See Clotting Factor

Factor IX
See Christmas Factor

Factor X
See Stuart-Prower Factor

Factor X, Activated
See Thrombokinase

Factor Xa Inhibitor
See Antithrombin III

Factor XI
See Plasma Thromboplastin, Antecedent

Factor XII
See Hageman Factor

Factor XIII
See Fibrin Stabilizing Factor

Factor, ACTH-Releasing
See Corticotropic Releasing Hormone (CRH)

Factor, Antinuclear
See Antinuclear Antibodies (ANA)

Factor, Blood Coagulation
See Clotting Factor

Factor, Fitzgerald
See Fitzgerald Factor

Factor, Fletcher
See Fletcher Factor

Factor, Hyperglycemic-Glycogenolytic
See Glucagon

Factor Inhibitor Test 85335

Factor, Intrinsic
See Intrinsic Factor

Factor, Rheumatoid
See Rheumatoid Factor

Factor, Sulfation
See Somatomedin

Fallopian Tube
Anastomosis 58750
Catheterization 58345, 74742
Destruction
Endoscopy 58670
Ectopic Pregnancy 59121
with Salpingectomy and/or
Oophorectomy 59120
Excision 58700-58720
Ligation 58600-58611
Lysis
Adhesions 58740
Occlusion 58615
Endoscopy 58671

Tenotomy 26060, 26460
Flexor 26455
Tumor
Excision 26115-26117
Unlisted Services and Procedures 26989
X-Ray 73140

Finger Flap
Tissue Transfer 14350

Finger Joint
See Intercarpal Joint

Finney Operation
See Gastroduodenostomy

Fishberg Concentration Test
See Water Load Test

Fissure in Ano
See Anus, Fissure

Fissurectomy 46200

Fissurectomy, Anal
See Anus, Fissure, Excision

Fistula
Anal
Repair 46288, 46706
Autogenous Graft 36825
Bronchi
Repair 32815
Carotid-Cavernous
Repair 61710
Chest Wall
Repair 32906
Conjunctiva
with Tube or Stent 68750
without Tube 68745
Enterovesical
Closure 44660-44661
Kidney 50520-50526
Lacrimal Gland Closure 68770
Dacryocystorhinostomy 68720
Nose
Repair 30580-30600
Oval Window 69666
Postauricular 69700
Rectovaginal
Abdominal Approach 57305
Transperineal Approach 57308
with Concomitant Colostomy 57307
Round Window 69667
Sclera
Iridencleisis or Iridotasis 66165
Sclerectomy with Punch or Scissors
with Iridectomy 66160
Thermocauterization with Iridectomy ..66155
Trabeculectomy ab Externo in
Absence Previous Surgery 66170
Trabeculectomy ab Externo with
Scarring 66172
Trephination with Iridectomy 66150
Suture
Kidney 50520-50526
Ureter 50920-50930
Trachea 31755
Tracheoesophageal
Repair 43305, 43312, 43314
Speech Prosthesis 31611
Ureter 50920-50930
Urethra 53400-53405
Urethrovaginal 57310
with Bulbocavernosus Transplant 57311
Vesicouterine
Closure 51920-51925
Vesicovaginal
Closure 51900
Transvesical and Vaginal Approach ...57330
Vaginal Approach 57320
X-Ray 76080

Fistula Arteriovenous
See Arteriovenous Fistula

Fistulectomy
Anal 46060, 46270-46285
See Hemorrhoids

Fistulization
Conjunction
to Nasal Cavity 68745
Esophagus 43350-43352
Intestines 44300-44346
Lacrimal Sac
to Nasal Cavity 68720
Penis 54435
Pharynx 42955
Repair Salivary Cyst
Sublingual 42325-42326
Tracheopharyngeal 31755

Fistulization, Interatrial
See Septostomy, Atrial

Fistulotomy
Anal 46270, 46280

Fitting
Cervical Cap 57170
Contact Lens 92070, 92310-92313
See Contact Lens Services
Diaphragm 57170
Low Vision Aid 92354-92355
See Spectacle Services
Ocular Prosthesis 92330
Spectacle Prosthesis 92352-92353
Spectacles 92340-92342

Fitzgerald Factor 85293

Fixation
Interdental
without Fracture 21497

Fixation (Device)
See Application; Bone, Fixation; Spinal Instrumentation
Application
External 20690-20692
Pelvic
Insertion 22848
Removal
External 20694
Internal 20670-20680
Sacrospinous Ligament
Vaginal Prolapse 57282
Shoulder 23700
Skeletal
Humeral Epycondyle
Percutaneous 24566
Spinal
Insertion 22841-22847
Prosthetic 22851
Reinsertion 22849

Fixation Test, Complement
See Complement, Fixation Test

Fixation, External
See External Fixation

Fixation, Kidney
See Nephropexy

Fixation, Rectum
See Proctopexy

Fixation, Tongue
See Tongue, Fixation

Flank
See Back/Flank

Flap
See Skin Graft and Flap
Free
Breast Reconstruction 19364
Grafts 15574-15650, 15842
Latissimus Dorsi
Breast Reconstruction 19361
Omentum 49905
Omentum
Free
with Microvascular Anastomosis ...49906
Transverse Rectus Abdominis Myocutaneous
Breast Reconstruction 19367-19369

Flatfoot Correction 28735

Flea Typhus
See Murine Typhus

Fletcher Factor 85292

Flow Cytometry 88180-88182

Flow-Volume Loop
See Pulmonology, Diagnostic
Pulmonary 94375

Flu Vaccines 90645-90658, 90660

Fluid Collection
Incision and Drainage
Skin 10140

Fluid, Amniotic
See Amniotic Fluid

Fluid, Body
See Body Fluid

Fluid, Cerebrospinal
See Cerebrospinal Fluid

Fluorescein
Angiography, Ocular 92287
Intravenous Injection
Vascular Flow Check, Graft 15860

Fluorescein Angiography
See Angiography, Fluorescein

Free Skin Graft
See Skin, Grafts, Free

Free T4
See Thyroxine, Free

Frei Disease
See Lymphogranuloma Venereum

Frenectomy 40819, 41115

Frenectomy, Lingual
See Excision, Tongue, Frenum

Frenotomy 40806, 41010

Frenulectomy 40819

Frenuloplasty 41520

Frenum
Lip
Incision 40806
See Lip

Frenumectomy 40819

Frickman Operation
See Proctopexy

Frontal Craniotomy 61556

Frontal Sinus
See Sinus, Frontal

Frontal Sinusotomy
See Exploration, Sinus, Frontal

Frost Suture 67875

Frozen Blood Preparation 86930-86932

Fructose 84375
Semen 82757

Fruit Sugar
See Fructose

FSF 85290-85291

FSH
See Follicle Stimulating Hormone (FSH)

FSP
See Fibrin Degradation Products

FT-4 84439

Fulguration
See Destruction
Bladder 51020
Cystourethroscopy with 52214
Lesion 52224
Tumor 52234-52240
Ureter 50957-50959, 50976-50978
Ureterocele
Ectopic 52301
Orthotopic 52300

Fulguration, Endocavitary
See Electrocautery

Full Thickness Graft 15200-15261

Function Test, Lung
See Pulmonology, Diagnostic

Function Test, Vestibular
See Vestibular Function Tests

Function, Study, Nasal
See Nasal Function Study

Functional Ability
See Activities of Daily Living

Fundoplasty
Esophagogastric 43324-43325
Laparoscopic 43280
with Gastroplasty 43326

Fundoplication
See Fundoplasty, Esophagogastric

Fungus
Antibody 86671
Culture
Blood 87103
Identification 87106
Other 87102
Skin 87101
Tissue Exam 87220

Funnel Chest
See Pectus Excavatum

Furuncle
Incision and Drainage 10060-10061

Furuncle, Vulva
See Abscess, Vulva

Fusion
See Arthrodesis
Pleural Cavity 32005
Thumb
in Opposition 26820

Fusion, Epiphyseal-Diaphyseal
See Epiphyseal Arrest

Fusion, Joint
See Arthrodesis

Fusion, Joint, Ankle
See Ankle, Arthrodesis

Fusion, Joint, Interphalangeal, Finger
See Arthrodesis, Finger Joint, Interphalangeal

G

Gago Procedure
See Repair, Tricuspid Valve; Revision

Gait Training 97116
See Physical Medicine/Therapy/Occupational Therapy

Galactogram 76086-76088
Injection 19030

Galactokinase
Blood 82759

Galactose
Blood 82760
Urine 82760

Galactose-1-Phosphate
Uridyl Transferase 82775-82776

Gall Bladder
See Gallbladder

Gallbladder
See Bile Duct
Anastomosis
with Intestines 47720-47741
Excision 47562-47564, 47600-47620
Exploration 47480
Incision 47490
Incision and Drainage 47480
Nuclear Medicine
Imaging 78223
Removal
Calculi (Stone) 47480
Repair
with Gastroenterostomy 47741
with Intestines 47720-47740
Unlisted Services and Procedures 47999
X-Ray with Contrast 74290-74291

Galvanocautery
See Electrocautery

Galvanoionization
See Iontophoresis

Gamete Intrafallopian Transfer
See GIFT

Gamete Transfer
In Vitro Fertilization 58976

Gamma Camera Imaging
See Nuclear Medicine

Gamma Glutamyl Transferase 82977

Gamma Seminoprotein
See Antigen, Prostate Specific

Gammacorten
See Dexamethasone

Gammaglobulin
Blood 82784-82787

Gamulin Rh
See Immune Globulins, Rho (D)

Ganglia, Trigeminal
See Gasserian Ganglion

Ganglion
See Gasserian Ganglion
Cyst
Aspiration/Injection 20612
Drainage 20612
Wrist
Excision 25111-25112
Injection
Anesthetic 64505, 64510

Genotype Analysis
by Nucleic Acid
Infectious Agent
Hepatitis C Virus 87902
HIV-1 Protease/Reverse
Transcriptase 87901

Gentamicin 80170
Assay 80170

Gentamycin Level
See Gentamicin

Gentiobiase
See Beta Glucosidase

Genus: Human Cytomegalovirus Group
See Cytomegalovirus

German Measles
See Rubella

Gestational Trophoblastic Tumor
See Hydatidiform Mole

GGT
See Gamma Glutamyl Transferase

GI Tract
See Gastrointestinal Tract

Giardia
Antigen Detection
Immunofluorescence 87269
Enzyme Immunoassay 87329

Giardia Lamblia
Antibody 86674

Gibbons Stent 52332

GIF
See Somatostatin

GIFT 89250

Gill Operation 63012

Gillies Approach
Fracture
Zygomatic Arch 21356

Gingiva
See Gums

Gingiva, Abcess
See Abscess
Fracture
See Abscess, Gums; Gums
Zygomatic Arch
See Abscess, Gums; Gums, Abscess

Gingivectomy 41820

Gingivoplasty 41872

Girdlestone Laminectomy
See Laminectomy

Girdlestone Procedure
See Acetabulum, Reconstruction

Gla Protein (Bone)
See Osteocalcin

Gland
See Specific Gland

Gland, Adrenal
See Adrenal Gland

Gland, Bartholin's
See Bartholin's Gland

Gland, Bulbourethral
See Bulbourethral Gland

Gland, Lacrimal
See Lacrimal Gland

Gland, Mammary
See Breast

Gland, Parathyroid
See Parathyroid Gland

Gland, Parotid
See Parotid Gland

Gland, Pituitary
See Pituitary Gland

Gland, Salivary
See Salivary Glands

Gland, Sublingual
See Sublingual Gland

Gland, Sweat
See Sweat Glands

Gland, Thymus
See Thymus Gland

Gland, Thyroid
See Thyroid Gland

Glasses
See Spectacle Services

Glaucoma
Fistulization of Sclera 66150
Provocative Test 92140

Glaucoma Drainage Implant
See Aqueous Shunt

Glenn Procedure 33766-33767

Glenohumeral Joint
Arthrotomy 23040
with Biopsy 23100
with Synovectomy 23105
Exploration 23107
Removal
Foreign or Loose Body 23107

Glenoid Fossa
Reconstruction 21255

GLN
See Glutamine

Globulin
Antihuman 86880-86886
Immune 90281-90399
Sex Hormone Binding 84270

Globulin, Corticosteroid-Binding
See Transcortin

Globulin, Rh Immune
See Immune Globulins, Rho (D)

Globulin, Thyroxine-Binding
See Thyroxine Binding Globulin

Glomerular Procoagulant Activity
See Thromboplastin

Glomus Caroticum
See Carotid Body

Glossectomies
See Excision, Tongue

Glossopexy
See Tongue, Fixation

Glossorrhaphy
See Suture, Tongue

Glucagon 82943
Tolerance Panel 80422-80424
Tolerance Test 82946

Glucose ..80422-80424, 80430-80435, 95250
Blood Test 82947-82950, 82962
Body Fluid 82945
Interstitial Fluid
Continuous Monitoring 95250
Tolerance Test 82951-82952
with Tolbutamide 82953

Glucose Phosphate Isomerase
See Phosphohexose Isomerase

Glucose Phosphate Isomerase Measurement
See Phosphohexose Isomerase

Glucose-6-Phosphate
Dehydrogenase 82955-82960

Glucosidase 82963

Glucuronide Androstanediol ...82154

Glue
Cornea Wound 65286
Sclera Wound 65286

Glukagon
See Glucagon

Glutamate Dehydrogenase
Blood 82965

Glutamate Pyruvate Transaminase
See Transaminase, Glutamic Pyruvic

Glutamic Alanine Transaminase
See Transaminase, Glutamic Pyruvic

Glutamic Aspartic Transaminase
See Transaminase, Glutamic Oxaloacetic

Glutamic Dehydrogenase
See Glutamate Dehydrogenase

Glutamine 82975

Groin Area
Repair
  Hernia 49550-49557

Group Health Education 99078

Grouping, Blood
See Blood Typing

Growth Factors, Insulin-Like
See Somatomedin

Growth Hormone 83003
Human 80418, 80428-80430, 86277

Growth Hormone Release Inhibiting Factor
See Somatostatin

GTT
See Hydatidiform Mole

Guaiac Test
See Blood, Feces

Guanosine Monophosphate 83008

Guanosine Monophosphate, Cyclic
See Cyclic GMP

Guanylic Acids
See Guanosine Monophosphate

Guard Stain 88313

Gullet
See Esophagus

Gums
Abscess
  Incision and Drainage 41800
Alveolus
  Excision 41830
Cyst
  Incision and Drainage 41800
Excision
  Gingiva 41820
  Operculum 41821
Graft
  Mucosa 41870
Hematoma
  Incision and Drainage 41800
Lesion
  Destruction 41850
  Excision 41822-41828
Mucosa
  Excision 41828
Reconstruction
  Alveolus 41874
  Gingiva 41872
Removal
  Foreign Body 41805
Tumor
  Excision 41825-41827
Unlisted Services and Procedures 41899

Gunning-Lieben Test
See Acetone, Blood or Urine

Guthrie Test 84030

H

H Flu
See Hemophilus Influenza

H-Reflex Study 95934-95936

HAA (Hepatitis Associated Antigen)
See Hepatitis Antigen, B Surface

HAAb
See Antibody, Hepatitis

Haemoglobin F
See Fetal Hemoglobin

Haemorrhage
See Hemorrhage

Haemorrhage Rectum
See Hemorrhage, Rectum

Hageman Factor 85280

HAI Test
See Hemagglutination Inhibition Test

Hair
Electrolysis 17380
KOH Examination 87220
Microscopic Evaluation 96902
Transplant
  Punch Graft 15775-15776
  Strip Graft 15220-15221

Hair Removal
See Removal, Hair

Hallux
See Great Toe

Halo
Body Cast 29000
Cranial 20661
  for Thin Skull Osteology 20664
Femur 20663
Maxillofacial 21100
Pelvic 20662
Removal 20665

Haloperidol
Assay 80173

Halsted Mastectomy
See Mastectomy, Radical

Halsted Repair
See Hernia, Repair, Inguinal

Ham Test
See Hemolysins

Hammertoe Repair 28285-28286

Hamster Penetration Test 89329

Hand
See Carpometacarpal Joint; Intercarpal Joint
Amputation
  at Metacarpal 25927
  at Wrist 25920
    Revision 25922
  Revision 25924, 25929-25931
Arthrodesis
  Carpometacarpal Joint 26843-26844
  Intercarpal Joint 25820-25825
Bone
  Incision and Drainage 26034
Cast 29085
Decompression 26035-26037
Fracture
  Metacarpal 26600
Insertion
  Tendon Graft 26392
Magnetic Resonance Imaging (MRI) 73218-73223
Reconstruction
  Tendon Pulley 26500-26504
Removal
  Implantation 26320
    Tube/Rod 26390-26392, 26416
Repair
  Blood Vessel 35207
  Cleft Hand 26580
  Muscle 26591-26593
  Tendon
    Extensor 26410-26416, 26426-26428, 26433-26437
    Flexor 26350-26358, 26440
    Profundus 26370-26373
Replantation 20808
Strapping 29280
Tendon
  Excision 26390
    Extensor 26415
Tenotomy 26450, 26460
Tumor
  Excision 26115-26117
Unlisted Services and Procedures 26989
X-Ray 73120-73130

Hand Abscess
See Abscess, Hand

Hand Phalange
See Finger, Bone

Hand(s) Dupuytrens Contracture(s)
See Dupuytren's Contracture

Handling
Device 99002
Radioelement 77790
Specimen 99000-99001

Hanganutziu Deicher Antibodies
See Antibody, Heterophile

Haptoglobin 83010-83012

Hard Palate
See Palate

Harelip Operation
See Cleft Lip, Repair

Harii Procedure 25430

Harrington Rod
Insertion 22840
Removal 22850

Hartmann Procedure
Open 44143
Laparoscopic 44206

Harvesting
Bone Graft 20900-20902
Bone Marrow 38230
Cartilage Graft 20910-20912
Conjunctival Graft 68371
Eggs
In Vitro Fertilization 58970
Endoscopic
Vein for Bypass Graft 33508
Fascia Lata Graft 20920-20922
Intestines 44132-44133
Kidney 50300-50320, 50547
Liver 47133, 47140-47142
Lower Extremity Vein
for Vascular Reconstruction 35572
Stem Cell 38205-38206
Tendon Graft 20924
Tissue Grafts 20926
Upper Extremity Artery
for Coronary Artery Bypass Graft 35600
Upper Extremity Vein
for Bypass Graft 35500

Hauser Procedure 27420

Hayem's Elementary Corpuscle
See Blood, Platelet

Haygroves Procedure
See Reconstruction, Acetabulum; Revision

HBcAb
See Antibody, Hepatitis

HBeAb
See Antibody, Hepatitis

HBeAg
See Hepatitis Antigen, Be

HBsAb
See Antibody, Hepatitis

HBsAg (Hepatitis B Surface Antigen)
See Hepatitis Antigen, B Surface

HCG
See Chorionic Gonadotropin

HCO3
See Bicarbonate

HCV Antibodies
See Antibody, Hepatitis C

HDL
See Lipoprotein

Head
Angiography 70496, 70544-70546
CT Scan 70450-70470, 70496
Excision 21015-21070
Fracture and/or Dislocation 21300-21497
Incision 21010, 61316, 62148
Introduction or Removal 21076-21116
Lipectomy, Suction Assisted 15876
Magnetic Resonance Angiography
(MRA) 70544-70546
Nerve
Graft 64885-64886
Other Procedures 21299, 21499
Repair/Revision and/or
Reconstruction 21120-21296
Ultrasound Exam 76506, 76536
Unlisted Services and Procedures 21499
X-Ray 70350

Head Rings, Stereotactic
See Stereotactic Frame

Headbrace
Application 21100
Application/Removal 20661

Heaf Test
See TB Test

Health Behavior
See Evaluation and Management, Health Behavior

Health Risk Assessment Instrument
See Preventive Medicine

Hearing Aid
Bone Conduction
Implantation 69710
Removal 69711
Repair 69711
Replacement 69710

Hearing Aid Check 92592-92593

Hearing Aid Services
Electroacoustic Test 92594-92595
Examination 92590-92591

Hearing Evaluation 92510

Hearing Tests
See Audiologic Function Tests; Hearing Evaluation

Hearing Therapy 92507-92510, 92601-92604

Heart
Ablation
Ventricular Septum
Non-surgical 0024T
Angiography
Injection 93542-93543
See Cardiac Catheterization; Injection
Aortic Arch
with Cardiopulmonary Bypass 33853
without Cardiopulmonary Bypass 33852
Aortic Valve
Repair
Left Ventricle 33414
Replacement 33405-33413
Arrhythmogenic Focus
Catheter Ablation 93650-93652
Destruction 33250-33251, 33261
Atria
See Atria
Biopsy 93505
Imaging Guidance 76932
Ultrasound
Imaging Guidance 76932
Blood Vessel
Repair 33320-33322
Cardiac Output Measurements 93561-93562
Cardiac Rehabilitation 93797-93798
Cardioassist 92970-92971
Ventricular Assist Device
Extracorporeal 0049T
Cardiopulmonary Bypass
with Lung Transplant 32852, 32854
Catheterization 93501, 93510-93533
Combined Right and Retrograde Left
for Congenital Cardiac Anomalies ...93531
Combined Right and Transseptal Left
for Congenital Cardiac Anomalies ..93532-93533
Flow Directed 93503
Right
for Congenital Cardiac Anomalies ...93530
See Catheterization, Cardiac
Closure
Septal Defect 33615
Valve
Atrioventricular 33600
Semilunar 33602
Commissurotomy
Right Ventricle 33476-33478
Destruction
Arrhythmogenic Focus 33250, 33261
Electrical Recording
3-D Mapping 93613
Atria 93602
Atrial Electrogram, Esophageal
(or Trans-esophageal) 93615-93616
Bundle of His 93600
Comprehensive 93619-93622
Right Ventricle 93603
Tachycardia Sites 93609
Electroconversion 92960-92961
Electrophysiologic Follow-up Study 93624
Excision
Donor 33930, 33940
Tricuspid Valve 33460
Exploration 33310-33315
Fibrillation
Atrial 33253
Great Vessels
See Great Vessels
Heart-Lung Bypass
See Cardiopulmonary Bypass
Heart-Lung Transplantation
See Transplantation, Heart-Lung
Implantation
Artificial Heart
Intracorporeal 0051T
Total Replacement Heart System
Intracorporeal 0051T
Ventricular Assist Device 33976
Extracorporeal 0048T
Intracorporeal 33979
Incision
Atrial 33253
Exploration 33310-33315

Hematochezia
See Blood, Feces

Hematologic Test
See Blood Tests

Hematology
Unlisted Services and Procedures 85999

Hematoma
Ankle 27603
Arm, Lower 25028
Arm, Upper
  Incision and Drainage 23930
Brain
  Drainage 61154-61156
  Evacuation 61312-61315
  Incision and Drainage 61312-61315
Drain 61108
Ear, External
  Complicated 69005
  Simple 69000
Elbow
  Incision and Drainage 23930
Epididymis
  Incision and Drainage 54700
Gums
  Incision and Drainage 41800
Hip 26990
Incision and Drainage
  Neck 21501-21502
  Skin 10140
  Thorax 21501-21502
Knee 27301
Leg, Lower 27603
Leg, Upper 27301
Mouth 41005-41009, 41015-41018
  Incision and Drainage 40800-40801
Nasal Septum
  Incision and Drainage 30020
Nose
  Incision and Drainage 30000-30020
Pelvis 26990
Scrotum
  Incision and Drainage 54700
Shoulder
  Drainage 23030
Skin
  Puncture Aspiration 10160
Subdural 61108
Subungual
  Evacuation 11740
Testis
  Incision and Drainage 54700
Tongue 41000-41006, 41015
Vagina
  Incision and Drainage 57022-57023
Wrist 25028

Hematopoietic Stem Cell Transplantation
See Stem Cell, Transplantation

Hematopoietin
See Erythropoietin

Hematuria
See Blood, Urine

Hemic System
Unlisted Procedure .38999

Hemiepiphyseal Arrest
Elbow 24470

Hemifacial Microsomia
Reconstruction
  Mandibular Condyle 21247

Hemilaminectomy 63020-63044

Hemilaryngectomy 31370-31382

Hemipelvectomies
See Amputation, Interpelviabdominal

Hemiphalangectomy
Toe 28160

Hemispherectomy
Partial 61543
Total 61542

Hemocytoblast
See Stem Cell

Hemodialyses
See Hemodialysis

Hemodialysis 90935-90937
Blood Flow Study 90939-90940
Duplex Scan of Access 93990

Hemofiltration 90945-90947

Hemoglobin
Analysis
  O2 Affinity 82820
Antibody, Fecal 86683
Carboxyhemoglobin 82375-82376
Chromatography 83021
Concentration 85046
Electrophoresis 83020
Fetal 83030-83033, 85460-85461
Fractionation and Quantitation 83020
Glycated 83036
Methemoglobin 83045-83050
Non-Automated 83026
Plasma 83051
Sulfhemoglobin 83055-83060
Thermolabile .83065-83068
Urine 83069

Hemoglobin F
Fetal
  Chemical 83030
  Qualitative 83033

Hemoglobin, Glycosylated
See Glycohemoglobin

Hemogram
Added Indices 85025-85027
Automated 85025-85027
Manual 85014-85018, 85032

Hemolysins 85475
with Agglutinins 86940-86941

Hemolytic Complement
See Complement, Hemolytic

Hemolytic Complement, Total
See Complement, Hemolytic, Total

Hemoperfusion 90997

Hemophil
See Clotting Factor

Hemophilus Influenza
Antibody 86684

Hemorrhage
Abdomen 49002
Anal
  Endoscopic Control 46614
Bladder
  Postoperative 52606
Chest Cavity
  Endoscopic Control 32654
Colon
  Endoscopic Control 44391, 45382
Colon-Sigmoid
  Endoscopic Control 45334
Esophagus
  Endoscopic Control 43227
Gastrointestinal, Upper
  Endoscopic Control 43255
Intestines, Small
  Endoscopic Control 44366, 44378
Liver
  Control 47350
Lung 32110
Nasal
  Cauterization 30901-30906
  Endoscopic Control 31238
Nasopharynx 42970-42972
Oropharynx .42960-42962
Rectum
  Endoscopic Control 45317
Throat 42960-42962
Uterus
  Postpartum 59160
Vagina 57180

Hemorrhoidectomy
Complex 46260
  with Fissurectomy 46261-46262
External Complete .46250
Ligature 46221
Simple 46255
  with Fissurectomy 46257-46258

Hemorrhoids
Destruction .46934-46936
Incision
  External 46083
Injection
  Sclerosing Solution 46500
Ligation 46945-46946
Suture 46945-46946

Hemosiderin 83070-83071

Hemothorax
Thoracostomy 32020

Heparin 85520
See Clotting Inhibitors
Neutralization 85525
Protamine Tolerance Test 85530

Heparin Cofactor I
See Antithrombin III

Hepatectomy
Extensive 47122
Left Lobe 47125
Partial
  Donor 47140-47142
  Lobe 47120
Right Lobe 47130
Total
  Donor 47133

Hepatic Abscess
See Abscess, Liver

Hepatic Arteries
See Artery, Hepatic

Hepatic Artery Aneurysm
See Artery, Hepatic, Aneurysm

Hepatic Duct
Anastomosis
  with Intestines 47765, 47802
Exploration 47400
Incision and Drainage 47400
Nuclear Medicine
  Imaging 78223
Removal
  Calculi (Stone) 47400
Repair
  with Intestines 47765, 47802
Unlisted Services and Procedures 47999

Hepatic Haemorrhage
See Hemorrhage, Liver

Hepatic Portal Vein
See Vein, Hepatic Portal

Hepatic Portoenterostomies
See Hepaticoenterostomy

Hepatic Transplantation
See Liver, Transplantation

Hepaticodochotomy
See Hepaticostomy

Hepaticoenterostomy 47802

Hepaticostomy 47400

Hepaticotomy 47400

Hepatitis A and Hepatitis B 90636

Hepatitis A Vaccine
Adolescent/Pediatric
  2 Dose Schedule 90633
  3 Dose Schedule 90634
Adult Dosage 90632

Hepatitis Antibody
A 86708-86709
B
  B Core 86704-86705
  B Surface 86706
  Be 86707
C 86803-86804
Delta Agent 86692
IgG 86704, 86708
IgM 86704-86705, 86708-86709

Hepatitis Antigen
B 87515-87517
B Surface 87340-87341
Be 87350
C 87520-87522
Delta Agent 87380
G 87525-87527

Hepatitis B and Hib 90748

Hepatitis B Vaccine
Dosage
  Adolescent 90743
  Adult 90746
  Immunosuppressed 90740, 90747
  Pediatric/Adolescent 90744

Hepatitis B Virus E Antibody
See Antibody, Hepatitis

Hepatitis B Virus Surface ab
See Antibody, Hepatitis B, Surface

Hepatorrhaphy
See Liver, Repair

Hepatotomy
Abscess 47010-47011
  Percutaneous 47011
Cyst 47010-47011
  Percutaneous 47011

Hernia, Cerebral
See Encephalocele

Hernia, Rectovaginal
See Rectocele

Hernia Repair
Abdominal 49590
  Incisional 49560
  Recurrent 49565
Diaphragmatic 39502-39541
Epigastric 49570
  Incarcerated 49572
Femoral 49550
  Incarcerated 49553
  Recurrent 49555
  Recurrent Incarcerated 49557
Incisional
  Incarcerated 49561
Inguinal 49491, 49495-49500, 49505
  Incarcerated 49492, 49496, 49501, 49507, 49521
  Laparoscopic 49650-49651
  Recurrent 49520
  Sliding 49525
  Strangulated 49492
Lumbar 49540
Lung 32800
Orchiopexy 54640
Recurrent Incisional
  Incarcerated 49566
Spigelian 49590
Umbilicus 49580, 49585
  Incarcerated 49582, 49587
with Spermatic Cord 55540

Hernia, Umbilical
See Omphalocele

Heroin Screen 82486

Heroin, Alkaloid Screening 82101

Herpes Simplex
Antibody 86696
Antigen Detection
  Immunofluorescence 87273-87274
  Nucleic Acid 87528-87530
Identification
  Smear and Stain 87207

Herpes Smear and Stain 87207

Herpes Virus-4 (Gamma), Human
See Epstein-Barr Virus

Herpes Virus-6 Detection 87531-87533

Herpetic Vesicle
Destruction 54050-54065

Heteroantibodies
See Antibody, Heterophile

Heterograft
Skin 15400

Heterologous Transplant
See Xenograft

Heterologous Transplantation
See Heterograft

Heterophile Antibody 86308-86310

Heterotropia
See Strabismus

Hex B
See b-Hexosaminidase

Hexadecadrol
See Dexamethasone

Hexosephosphate Isomerase
See Phosphohexose Isomerase

Heyman Procedure 27179, 28264

Hg Factor
See Glucagon

HGB
See Hemoglobin, Concentration

HGH
See Growth Hormone, Human

HHV-4
See Epstein-Barr Virus

HIAA
See Hydroxyindolacetic Acid, Urine

Hib Vaccine
4 Dose Schedule
  HbOC 90645
  PRP-T 90648
PRP-D
  Booster 90646
PRP-OMP
  3 Dose Schedule 90647

Hibb Operation
See Spinal Cord; Spine, Fusion; Vertebra; Vertebral Body; Vertebral Process

Hickmann Catheterization
See Cannulization; Catheterization, Venous, Central Line; Venipuncture

Hidradenitis
See Sweat Gland
Excision 11450-11471
Suppurative
Incision and Drainage 10060-10061

High Density Lipoprotein
See Lipoprotein

High Molecular Weight Kininogen
See Fitzgerald Factor

Highly Selective Vagotomy
See Vagotomy, Highly Selective

Highmore Antrum
See Sinus, Maxillary

Hill Procedure 43324
Laparoscopic 43280

Hinton Positive
See RPR

Hip
See Femur; Pelvis
Abscess
Incision and Drainage 26990
Arthrocentesis 20610
Arthrodesis 27284-27286
Arthrography 73525
Arthroplasty 27130-27132
Arthroscopy 29860-29863
Arthrotomy 27030-27033
Biopsy 27040-27041
Bone
Drainage 26992
Bursa
Incision and Drainage 26991
Capsulectomy
with Release, Flexor Muscles 27036
Cast 29305-29325
Craterization 27070
Cyst
Excision 27065-27067
Denervation 27035
Echography
Infant 76885-76886
Endoprosthesis
See Prosthesis, Hip
Excision 27070
Exploration 27033
Fasciotomy 27025
Fusion 27284-27286
Hematoma
Incision and Drainage 26990
Injection
Radiologic 27093-27096
Reconstruction
Total Replacement 27130
Removal
Cast 29710
Foreign Body 27033, 27086-27087
Arthroscopic 29861
Loose Body
Arthroscopic 29861
Prosthesis 27090-27091
Repair
Muscle Transfer 27100-27105, 27111
Osteotomy 27146-27156
Tendon 27097
Saucerization 27070
Stem Prostheses
See Arthroplasty, Hip
Strapping 29520
Tenotomy
Abductor Tendon 27006
Adductor Tendon 27000-27003
Iliopsoas 27005
Total Replacement 27130-27132
Tumor
Excision 27047-27049, 27065-27067
Radical 27075-27076
Ultrasound
Infant 76885-76886
X-Ray 73500-73520, 73540
Intraoperative 73530
with Contrast 73525

Hip Joint
Arthroplasty 27132
Revision 27134-27138
Arthrotomy 27052
Biopsy 27052
Capsulotomy
with Release, Flexor Muscles 27036
Dislocation 27250-27252
Congenital 27256-27259
Open Treatment 27253-27254
without Trauma 27265-27266
Manipulation 27275
Reconstruction
Revision 27134-27138
Synovium
Excision 27054
Arthroscopic 29863
Total Replacement 27132

Hip Stem Prostheses
See Arthroplasty, Hip

Hippocampus
Excision 61566

Histamine 83088

Histamine Release Test 86343

Histochemistry 88318-88319

Histocompatibility Testing
See Tissue Typing

Histoplasma
Antibody 86698
Antigen 87385

Histoplasma capsulatum
Antigen Detection
Enzyme Immunoassay 87385

Histoplasmin Test
See Histoplasmosis, Skin Test

Histoplasmoses
See Histoplasmosis

Histoplasmosis
Skin Test 86510

History and Physical
See Evaluation and Management, Office and/or Other Outpatient Services
Pelvic Exam 57410

HIV
Antibody 86701-86703
Confirmation Test 86689

HIV-1
Antigen Detection
Enzyme Immunoassay 87390

HIV-2
Antigen Detection
Enzyme Immunoassay 87391

HK3 Kallikrein
See Antigen, Prostate Specific

HLA Typing 86812-86817

HMRK
See Fitzgerald Factor

HMW Kininogen
See Fitzgerald Factor

Hoffman Apparatus 20690

Hofmeister Operation
See Gastrectomy, Total

Holographic Imaging 76375

Holten Test
See Creatinine, Urine, Clearance

Home Services
Activities of Daily Living 99509
Catheter Care 99507
Enema Administration 99511
Established Patient 99347-99350
Hemodialysis 99512
Home Infusion Procedures 99601-99602
Individual or Family Counseling 99510
Intramuscular Injections 99506
Mechanical Ventilation 99504
New Patient 99341-99345
Newborn Care 99502
Postnatal Assessment 99501
Prenatal Monitoring 99500
Respiratory Therapy 99503
Sleep Studies 95805-95811
Stoma Care 99505
Unlisted Services and Procedures 99600

Home Visit
See House Calls

Homocystine 83090
Urine 82615

Homogenization, Tissue 87176

Homograft
Skin 15350

Homologous Grafts
See Graft

Homologous Transplantation
See Homograft

Homovanillic Acid
Urine 83150

Hormone Assay
ACTH 82024
Aldosterone
  Blood or Urine 82088
Androstenedione
  Blood or Urine 82157
Androsterone
  Blood or Urine 82160
Angiotensin II 82163
Corticosterone 82528
Cortisol
  Total 82533
Dehydroepiandrosterone 82626
Dihydroelestosterone 82651
Dihydrotestosterone 82651
Epiandrosterone 82666
Estradiol 82670
Estriol 82677
Estrogen 82671-82672
Estrone 82679
Follicle Stimulating Hormone 83001
Growth Hormone 83003
Hydroxyprogesterone 83498-83499
Luteinizing Hormone 83002
Somatotropin 83003
Testosterone 84403
Vasopressin 84588

Hormone Pellet Implantation 11980

Hormone, Adrenocorticotrophic
See Adrenocorticotropic Hormone (ACTH)

Hormone, Corticotropin-Releasing
See Corticotropic Releasing Hormone (CRH)

Hormone, Growth
See Growth Hormone

Hormone, Human Growth
See Growth Hormone, Human

Hormone, Interstitial Cell-Stimulating
See Luteinizing Hormone (LH)

Hormone, Parathyroid
See Parathormone

Hormone, Pituitary Lactogenic
See Prolactin

Hormone, Placental Lactogen
See Lactogen, Human Placental

Hormone, Somatotropin Release-Inhibiting
See Somatostatin

Hormone, Thyroid-Stimulating
See Thyroid Stimulating Hormone (TSH)

Hormone-Binding Globulin, Sex
See Globulin, Sex Hormone Binding

Hormones, Adrenal Cortex
See Corticosteroids

Hormones, Antidiuretic
See Antidiuretic Hormone

Hospital Discharge Services
See Discharge Services, Hospital

Hospital Services
Inpatient Services 99238-99239
  Discharge Services 99238-99239
  Initial Care
    New or Established Patient ..99221-99233
  Initial Hospital Care 99221-99223
  Newborn 99431-99433
  Prolonged Services 99356-99357
  Subsequent Hospital Care 99231-99233
Observation
  Discharge Services 99234-99236
  Initial Care 99218-99220
    New or Established Patient ..99218-99220
Same Day Admission
  Discharge Services 99234-99236
Subsequent Newborn Care 99433

Hot Pack Treatment 97010
See Physical Medicine and Rehabilitation

House Calls 99341-99350

Howard Test
See Cystourethroscopy, Catheterization, Ureter

HPL
See Lactogen, Human Placental

HTLV I
Antibody
  Confirmatory Test 86689
  Detection 86687

HTLV II
Antibody 86688

HTLV III
See HIV

HTLV III Antibodies
See Antibody, HIV

HTLV IV
See HIV-2

Hubbard Tank Therapy 97036
See Physical Medicine/Therapy/Occupational Therapy

Hue Test 92283

Huggin Operation
See Orchiectomy, Simple

Huhner Test 89300, 89320

Human Chorionic Gonadotropin
See Chorionic Gonadotropin

Human Chorionic Somatomammotropin
See Lactogen, Human Placental

Human Cytomegalovirus Group
See Cytomegalovirus

Human Growth Hormone (HGH) 80418, 80428-80430

Human Herpes Virus 4
See Epstein-Barr Virus

Human Immunodeficiency Virus
See HIV

Human Immunodeficiency Virus 1
See HIV-1

Human Immunodeficiency Virus 2
See HIV-2

Human Papillomavirus Detection 87620-87622

Human Placental Lactogen
See Lactogen, Human Placental

Human T Cell Leukemia Virus I
See HTLV I

Human T Cell Leukemia Virus I Antibodies
See Antibody, HTLV I

Human T Cell Leukemia Virus II
See HTLV II

Human T Cell Leukemia Virus II Antibodies
See Antibody, HTLV II

Humeral Epicondylitides, Lateral
See Tennis Elbow

Humeral Fracture
See Fracture, Humerus

Humerus
See Arm, Upper; Shoulder
Abscess
  Incision and Drainage 23935
Craterization 23184, 24140
Cyst
  Excision 23150, 24110
    with Allograft 23156, 24116
    with Autograft 23155, 24115
Diaphysectomy 23184, 24140
Excision 23174, 23184, 23195, 24134, 24140, 24150-24151
Fracture
  Closed Treatment 24500-24505
    with Manipulation 23605
    without Manipulation 23600
  Condyle
    Closed Treatment 24576-24577
    Open Treatment 24579
    Percutaneous Fixation 24582

Urethroplasty for Second Stage .54308-54316
Free Skin Graft 54316
Urethroplasty for Third Stage 54318

Hypothermia 99185-99186

Hysterectomy
Abdominal
Radical 58210
Resection of Ovarian Malignancy 58951, 58953-58954
Supracervical 58180
Total 58150, 58200
with Colpo-Urethrocystopexy 58152
with Partial Vaginectomy 58200
Cesarean
after Cesarean Delivery 59525
with Closure of Vesicouterine Fistula ..51925
Removal
Lesion 59100
Vaginal 58260-58270, 58290-58294, 58550, 58552-58554
Laparoscopic 58550
Radical 58285
Removal Tubes/Ovaries 58262-58263, 58291-58292, 58552, 58554
Repair of Enterocele .58263, 58292, 58294
with Colpectomy 58275-58280
with Colpo-Urethrocystopexy ..58267, 58293

Hysterolysis
See Lysis, Adhesions, Uterus

Hysteroplasty 58540

Hysterorrhaphy 58520, 59350

Hysterosalpingography 74740
Catheterization 58345
Injection Procedure 58340

Hysterosalpingostomy
See Implantation, Tubouterine

Hysteroscopy
Ablation
Endometrial 58563
Diagnostic 58555
Lysis
Adhesions 58559
Removal
Impacted Foreign Body 58562
Leiomyomata 58561
Resection
of Intrauterine Septum 58560
Surgical with Biopsy 58558
Unlisted Services and Procedures 58579

Hysterosonography
See Ultrasound; Sonohysterography

Hysterotomy 59100
See Ligation, Uterus
Induced Abortion
with Amniotic Injections 59852
with Vaginal Suppositories 59857

Hysterotrachelectomy
See Amputation, Cervix

I

I, Angiotensin
See Angiotensin I

I Antibodies, HTLV
See Antibody, HTLV-I

I, Coagulation Factor
See Fibrinogen

I, Heparin Co-Factor
See Antithrombin III

II, Coagulation Factor
See Prothrombin

II, Cranial Nerve
See Optic Nerve

IV, Coagulation Factor
See Calcium

IX Complex, Factor
See Christmas Factor

ICCE
See Extraction, Lens, Intracapsular

Ichthyosis, Sex Linked
See Syphilis Test

ICSH
See Luteinizing Hormone (LH)

Identification
Oocyte
from Follicular Fluid 89254
Sperm
from Aspiration 89257
from Tissue 89264

IDH
See Isocitric Dehydrogenase, Blood

IG
See Immune Globulins

IgE 86003-86005

IgG 86001

Ileal Conduit
Visualization 50690

Ileoscopy
via Stoma 44383

Ileostomy 44310, 45136
Continent (Kock Procedure) 44316
Revision 44312-44314

Iliac Arteries
See Artery, Iliac

Iliac Crest
Free Osteocutaneous Flap with Microvascular Anastomosis 20970

Iliohypogastric Nerve
Injection
Anesthetic 64425

Ilioinguinal Nerve
Injection
Anesthetic 64425

Ilium
Craterization 27070
Cyst
Excision 27065-27067
Excision 27070
Fracture
Open Treatment 27215, 27218
Saucerization 27070
Tumor
Excision 27065-27067

Ilizarov Procedure
Monticelli Type 20692
See Application, Bone Fixation Device

IM Injection
See Injection, Intramuscular

Imaging
See Vascular Studies

Imaging, Gamma Camera
See Nuclear Medicine

Imaging, Magnetic Resonance
See Magnetic Resonance Imaging (MRI)

Imaging, Ultrasonic
See Echography

Imbrication
Diaphragm 39545

Imidobenzyle
See Imipramine

Imipramine
Assay 80174

Immune Complex Assay 86332

Immune Globulin Administration 90780-90784

Immune Globulin E
See IgE

Immune Globulins
Antitoxin
Botulinum 90287
Diphtheria 90296
Botulism 90288
Cytomegalovirus 90291
Hepatitis B 90371
Human 90281-90283
Rabies 90375-90376
Respiratory Syncytial Virus 90378-90379
Rho (D) 90384-90386
Tetanus 90389
Unlisted Immune Globulin 90399
Vaccinia 90393
Varicella-Zoster 90396

Immunization Administration
Each Additional Vaccine/Toxoid 90472, 90474
One Vaccine/Toxoid 90471, 90473

Immunization, Mumps
See Mumps, Immunization

Incision and Drainage

Inspiratory Positive Pressure Breathing

Instillation

Instillation, Bladder

Instrumentation
See Application; Bone, Fixation; Spinal Instrumentation
Spinal
  Insertion 22840-22848, 22851
  Reinsertion 22849
  Removal 22850, 22852-22855

Insufflation, Eustachian Tube
See Eustachian Tube, Inflation

Insulin 80422, 80432-80435
Antibody 86337
Blood 83525
Free 83527

Insulin C-Peptide Measurement
See C-Peptide

Insulin Like Growth Factors
See Somatomedin

Insurance
Basic Life and/or Disability
Evaluation Services 99450
Examination 99450-99456

Integumentary System
Biopsy 11100-11101
Breast
  Excision 19100-19272
  Incision 19000-19030
  Metallic Localization Clip Placement ..19295
  Preoperative Placement of Needle
  Localization 19290-19291
  Reconstruction 19316-19396
  Repair 19316-19396
  Unlisted Services and Procedures 19499
Burns ..15000-15001, 15100-15121, 15342-15401
Debridement 11000-11044
Destruction
  See Dermatology
  Actinotherapy 96900
  Benign or Premalignant Lesion .17000-17250
  Chemical Exfoliation 17360
  Cryotherapy 17340
  Electrolysis Epilation 17380
  Malignant Lesion 17260-17286
    by Photodynamic Therapy 96567
  Mohs Micrographic Surgery ...17304-17310
  Photodynamic Therapy 96567-96571
  Unlisted Services and Procedures 17999
Drainage 10040-10180
Excision
  Benign Lesion 11400-11471
  Debridement 11000-11044
  Malignant Lesion 11600-11646
Incision 10040-10180
Introduction 11900-11977
  Drug Delivery Implant 11981, 11983
Nails 11720-11765
Paring 11055-11057
Pressure Ulcers 15920-15999
Removal
  Drug Delivery Implant 11982-11983
Repair
  Adjacent Tissue
  Transfer/Rearrangement 14000-14350
  Complex 13100-13160
  Flaps
    Other 15740-15776
  Free Skin Grafts 15000-15400
  Intermediate 12031-12057
  Other Procedures 15780-15879
  Simple 12001-12021
  Skin and/or Deep Tissue 15570-15738
Shaving of Epidermal or
Dermal Lesion 11300-11313
Skin Tags
  Removal 11200-11201

Integumentum Commune
See Integumentary System

Intelligence Test 96100

Intensive Care
Low Birthweight Infant
  Subsequent Care 99298-99299

Intercarpal Joint
Arthrodesis 25820-25825
Dislocation
  Closed Treatment 25660
Repair 25447

Intercostal Nerve
Destruction 64620
Injection
  Anesthetic 64420-64421
  Neurolytic 64620

Interdental Fixation
Device
  Application 21110
Mandibular Fracture
  Closed Treatment 21453
  Open Treatment 21462
without Fracture 21497

Interdental Papilla
See Gums

Interdental Wire Fixation
Closed Treatment
  Craniofacial Separation 21431

Interferometry
Eye
  Biometry 92136

Intermediate Care Facilities (ICFs)
See Nursing Facility Services

Intermediate Care Facility Visits 99301-99313

Intermittent Positive Pressure Breathing (IPPB)
See Continuous Negative Pressure Breathing (CNPB); Continuous Positive Airway Pressure (CPAP)

Internal Breast Prostheses
See Breast, Implants

Internal Ear
See Ear, Inner

Internal Rigid Fixation
Reconstruction
  Mandibular Rami 21196

Interphalangeal Joint
Arthrodesis 26860-26863
Arthroplasty 26535-26536
Arthrotomy 26080, 28054
Biopsy
  Synovium 26110
Capsule
  Excision 26525
  Incision 26525
Dislocation
  Closed Treatment 26770
  Open Treatment 26785
  Percutaneous Fixation 26776
  with Manipulation 26340
Exploration 26080
Fracture
  Closed Treatment 26740
  Open Treatment 26746
  with Manipulation 26742
Fusion 26860-26863
Great Toe
  Arthrodesis 28755
    with Tendon Transfer 28760
  Fusion 28755
    with Tendon Transfer 28760
Removal of Foreign Body 26080
Repair
  Collateral Ligament 26545
  Volar Plate 26548
Synovectomy 26140
Toe 28272
  Arthrotomy 28024
  Dislocation 28660-28665, 28675
    Percutaneous Fixation 28666
  Excision 28160
  Exploration 28024
  Removal
    Foreign Body 28024
    Loose Body 28024
  Synovial
    Biopsy 28054

Interruption
Vein
  Femoral 37650
  Iliac 37660
  Vena Cava 37620

Intersex State
Clitoroplasty 56805
Vaginoplasty 57335

Intersex Surgery
Female to Male 55980
Male to Female 55970

Interstitial Cell Stimulating Hormone
See Luteinizing Hormone (LH)

Interstitial Cystitides, Chronic
See Cystitis, Interstitial

Interstitial Cystitis
See Cystitis, Interstitial

Interstitial Fluid Pressure
Monitoring 20950

Interstitual Cell Stimulating Hormone
See Luteinizing Hormone (LH)

Intertarsal Joint
Arthrotomy 28020, 28050
Exploration 28020
Removal
  Foreign Body 28020
  Loose Body 28020
Synovial
  Biopsy 28050
  Excision 28070

Interthoracoscapular Amputation
See Amputation, Interthoracoscapular

Intertrochanteric Femur Fracture
See Femur, Fracture, Intertrochanteric

Intervertebral Chemonucleolysis
See Chemonucleolysis

Intervertebral Disk
Diskography
  Cervical 72285
  Lumbar 72295
  Thoracic 72285
Excision
  Decompression 63075-63078
  Herniated 63020-63044, 63055-63066
Injection
  Chemonucleolysis Agent 62292
  X-Ray 62290-62291

Intestinal Anastomosis
See Anastomosis, Intestines

Intestinal Invagination
See Intussusception

Intestinal Peptide, Vasoactive
See Vasoactive Intestinal Peptide

Intestine
Biopsy 44100
Lesion
  Excision 44110-44111
Unlisted Services and Procedures . . 44238, 44799

Intestines
Allotransplantation 44135-44136
Anastomosis 44625-44626
Bleeding Tube 91100
Closure
  Enterostomy
    Large or Small 44625-44626
  Stoma 44620-44625
Excision
  Donor 44132-44133
Exclusion 44700
Laparoscopic Resection
  with Anastomosis 44202-44208
Lysis of Adhesions
  Laparoscopic 44200
Nuclear Medicine
  Imaging 78290
Reconstruction
  Bladder 50820
  Colonic Reservoir 45119
Repair
  Diverticula 44605
  Obstruction 44615
  Ulcer 44605
  Wound 44605
Suture
  Diverticula 44605
  Stoma 44620-44625
  Ulcer 44605
  Wound 44605
Transplantation
  Donor Enterectomy 44132-44133

Intestines, Large
See Anus; Cecum; Colon; Rectum

Intestines, Small
Anastomosis 44130
Biopsy 44020
  Endoscopy 44361
Catheterization
  Jejunum 44015
Decompression 44021
Destruction
  Lesion 44369
  Tumor 44369
Endoscopy 44364
  Biopsy 44361, 44377
  Control of Bleeding 44366, 44378
    via Stoma 44382
  Destruction
    Lesion 44369
    Tumor 44369
  Diagnostic 44376
  Exploration 44360
  Hemorrhage 44366
  Insertion
    Stent 44370, 44379
    Tube 44379
  Pelvic Pouch 44385-44386
  Removal
    Foreign Body 44363
    Lesion 44365
    Polyp 44364-44365
    Tumor 44364-44365
  Tube Placement 44372
  Tube Revision 44373
  via Stoma 44380
Enterostomy 44300
Excision 44120-44128
  Partial with Anastomosis 44140
Exclusion 44700
Exploration 44020
Gastrostomy Tube 44373
Hemorrhage 44378
Hemorrhage Control 44366
Ileostomy 44310-44314, 45136
  Continent 44316
Incision 44020
  Creation
    Pouch 44316
    Stoma 44300-44310, 44314
  Decompression 44021
  Exploration 44020
  Revision
    Stoma 44312
    Stoma Closure 44620-44626
Insertion
  Catheter 44015
  Jejunostomy Tube 44372
Jejunostomy 44310
  Laparoscopic 44201
Lysis
  Adhesions 44005
Removal
  Foreign Body 44020, 44363
Repair
  Diverticula 44602-44603
  Enterocele
    Abdominal Approach 57270
    Vaginal Approach 57268
  Fistula 44640-44661
  Hernia 44050
  Malrotation 44055
  Obstruction 44050
  Ulcer 44602-44603
  Volvulus 44050
  Wound 44602-44603
Revision
  Jejunostomy Tube 44373
Specimen Collection 89100-89105
Suture
  Diverticula 44602-44603
  Fistula 44640-44661
  Plication 44680
  Ulcer 44602-44603
  Wound 44602-44603
X-Ray 74245, 74249-74251
  Guide Intubation 74355

Intestinovesical Fistula
See Fistula, Enterovesical

Intimectomy
See Endarterectomy

Intra Arterial Injections
See Injection, Intraarterial

Intra-Abdominal Voiding Pressure Studies 51797

Intra-Osseous Infusion
See Infusion, Intraosseous

Intracapsular Extraction of Lens
See Extraction, Lens, Intracapsular

Intracardiac Echocardiography 93662

Intracranial
Biopsy 61140
Extracranial 61623
Microdissection 69990

Intracranial Arterial Perfusion
Thrombolysis 61624

Intracranial Neoplasm, Acoustic Neuroma
See Brain, Tumor, Excision

Intracranial Neoplasm, Craniopharyngioma
See Craniopharyngioma

Intracranial Neoplasm, Meningioma
See Meningioma

Intrafallopian Transfer, Gamete
See GIFT

Intraluminal Angioplasty
See Angioplasty

Intramuscular Injection
See Injection, Intramuscular

Intraocular Lens
Exchange 66986
Insertion 66983
  Manual or Mechanical Technique 66982, 66984
  Not Associated with Concurrent Cataract Removal 66985

Intratracheal Intubation
See Insertion, Endotracheal Tube

Intrauterine Contraceptive Device
See Intrauterine Device (IUD)

Intrauterine Device (IUD)
Insertion 58300
Removal 58301

Intrauterine Synechiae
See Adhesions, Intrauterine

Intravascular Stent
See Transcatheter, Placement, Intravascular Stents
X-Ray 75960

Intravascular Ultrasound
Intraoperative 37250-37251

Intravenous Injection
See Injection, Intravenous

Intravenous Pyelogram
See Urography, Intravenous

Intravenous Therapy 90780-90781
See Injection, Chemotherapy
Pain Management 90783-90784

Intravesical Instillation
See Bladder, Instillation

Intravitreal Injection
Pharmacologic Agent 67028

Intrinsic Factor 83528
Antibody 86340

Introduction
Breast
  Metallic Localization Clip Placement 19295
  Preoperative Placement, Needle 19290-19291
Contraceptive Capsules
  Implantable 11975-11977
Drug Delivery Implant 11981, 11983
Gastrointestinal Tube 44500
  with Fluoroscopic Guidance 74340
Tissue Expanders
  Skin 11960-11971

Intubation
See Insertion
Endotracheal Tube 31500
Eustachian Tube
  See Catheterization, Eustachian Tube
Gastric 89130-89141, 91105
Specimen Collection
  Esophagus 91000
  Stomach 91055

Intubation Tube
See Endotracheal Tube

Intussusception
Barium Enema 74283
Reduction
  Laparotomy 44050

Invagination, Intestinal
See Intussusception

Inversion, Nipple
See Nipples, Inverted

Iodide Test
See Nuclear Medicine, Thyroid, Uptake

Iodine Test
See Starch Granules, Feces

Ionization, Medical
See Iontophoresis

Iontophoreses
See Iontophoresis

Iontophoresis 97033
Sweat Collection 89230

IP
See Allergen Immunotherapy

Ipecac Administration 99175

IPPB
See Intermittent Positive Pressure Breathing; Pulmonology, Therapeutic

Iridectomy
by Laser Surgery 66761
Peripheral for Glaucoma 66625
with Corneoscleral or Corneal Section 66600
with Sclerectomy with Punch or Scissors 66160
with Thermocauterization 66155
with Transfixion as for Iris Bombe 66605
with Trephination 66150

Iridencleisis 66165

Iridodialysis 66680

Iridoplasty 66762

Iridotasis 66165

Iridotomy
by Laser Surgery 66761
by Stab Incision 66500
Excision
  Optical 66635
  Peripheral 66625
  with Corneoscleral or Corneal Section 66600
  with Cyclectomy 66605
Incision
  Stab 66500
  with Transfixion as for Iris Bombe 66505
Optical 66635
Peripheral 66625
Sector 66630

Iris
Cyst
  Destruction 66770
Excision
  Iridectomy
    Optical 66635
    Peripheral 66625
    Sector 66630
    with Corneoscleral or Corneal Section 66600
    with Cyclectomy 66605
Incision
  Iridotomy
    Stab 66500
    with Transfixion as for Iris Bombe 66505
Lesion
  Destruction 66770
Repair
  with Ciliary Body 66680
    Suture 66682
Revision
  Laser Surgery 66761
  Photocoagulation 66762
Suture
  with Ciliary Body 66682

Iron 83540
Absorption 78162
Chelatable
  Total Body Iron 78172
Turnover Rate 78160
Utilization 78170

Iron Binding Capacity 83550

Iron Hematoxylin Stain 88312

Iron Stain 85536, 88313

Irradiation
Blood Products 86945

Irrigation
Bladder 51700
Catheter
  Brain 62194, 62225
Corpora Cavernosa
  Priapism 54220
Penis
  Priapism 54220
Peritoneal
  See Peritoneal Lavage
Rectum
  for Fecal Impaction 91123
Shunt
  Spinal Cord 63744

Sinus
  Maxillary 31000
  Sphenoid 31002
Vagina 57150

Irving Sterilization
See Ligation, Fallopian Tube, Oviduct

Ischial
Bursa
  Excision 27060
Tumor
  Excision 27078-27079

Ischiectomy 15941

Island Pedicle Flaps 15740

Islands of Langerhans
See Islet Cell

Islet Cell
Antibody 86341

Isocitrate Dehydrogenase
See Isocitric Dehydrogenase

Isocitric Dehydrogenase
Blood 83570

Isolation
Sperm 89260-89261

Isomerase, Glucose 6 Phosphate
See Phosphohexose Isomerase

Isopropanol
See Isopropyl Alcohol

Isopropyl Alcohol 84600

Isthmusectomy
Thyroid Gland 60210-60225

IUD
See Intrauterine Device (IUD)

IV
See Injection, Chemotherapy; Intravenous Therapy

IV Infusion Therapy
See Allergen Immunotherapy; Chemotherapy; Infusion; Injection, Chemotherapy

IV Injection
See Injection, Intravenous

IVC Filter
Placement 75940

IVF
See Artificial Insemination; In Vitro Fertilization

Ivy Bleeding Time 85002

J

Jaboulay Operation
See Gastroduodenostomy

Jaboulay Operation Gastroduodenostomy
See Gastroduodenostomy

Jannetta Procedure
See Decompression, Cranial Nerve; Section

Japanese, River Fever
See Scrub Typhus

Jatene Type 33770-33781

Jaw Joint
See Facial Bones; Mandible; Maxilla

Jaws
Muscle Reduction 21295-21296
X-Ray
  for Orthodontics 70355

Jejunostomy
Catheterization 44015
Insertion
  Catheter 44015
Laparoscopic 44201
Non-Tube 44310
with Pancreatic Drain 48001

Jejunum
Creation
  Stoma
    Laparoscopic 44201
Transfer
  with Microvascular Anastomosis
    Free 43496

Johannsen Procedure 53400

Johanson Operation
See Reconstruction, Urethra

Joint
See Specific Joint
Acromioclavicular
  See Acromioclavicular Joint
Arthrocentesis 20600-20610
Aspiration 20600-20610
Dislocation
  See Dislocation
Drainage 20600-20610
Finger
  See Intercarpal Joint
Fixation (Surgical)
  See Arthrodesis
Foot
  See Foot, Joint
Hip
  See Hip Joint
Injection 20600-20610
Intertarsal
  See Intertarsal Joint
Knee
  See Knee Joint
Ligament
  See Ligament
Metacarpophalangeal
  See Metacarpophalangeal Joint
Metatarsophalangeal
  See Metatarsophalangeal Joint
Nuclear Medicine
  Imaging 78300, 78315
Radiology
  Stress Views 76006
Sacroiliac
  See Sacroiliac Joint
Shoulder
  See Glenohumeral Joint
Sternoclavicular
  See Sternoclavicular Joint
Survey 76066
Temporomandibular
  See Temporomandibular Joint (TMJ)
  Dislocation Temporomandibular
    See Dislocation, Temporomandibular Joint
  Implant
    See Prosthesis, Temporomandibular Joint
Wrist
  See Radiocarpal Joint

Joint Syndrome, Temporomandibular
See Temporomandibular Joint (TMJ)

Jones and Cantarow Test
See Blood Urea Nitrogen; Urea Nitrogen, Clearance

Jones Procedure 28760

Joplin Procedure 28294

Jugal Bone
See Cheekbone

Jugular Vein
See Vein, Jugular

K

K-Wire Fixation
Tongue 41500

Kader Operation
See Incision, Stomach, Creation, Stoma; Incision and Drainage

Kala Azar Smear 87207

Kallidin I /Kallidin 9
See Bradykinin

Kallikrein HK3
See Antigen, Prostate Specific

Kallikreinogen
See Fletcher Factor

L

Lesion
Endoscopic 31512, 31578
Repair
Reinnervation Neuromuscular
Pedicle 31590
Stroboscopy 31579
Tumor
Excision 31300
Endoscopic 31540-31541
Unlisted Services and Procedures 31599
Vocal Cord(s)
Injection 31513, 31570-31571
X-Ray 70370
with Contrast 70373

Laser Surgery
Anal 46917
Lesion
Mouth 40820
Nose 30117-30118
Penis 54057

Laser Treatment 17000-17286, 96920-96922
See Destruction

Lateral Epicondylitis
See Tennis Elbow

Latex Fixation 86403-86406

LATS
See Thyrotropin Releasing Hormone (TRH)

Latzko Operation
See Repair, Vagina, Fistula; Revision

LAV
See HIV

Lav Antibodies
See Antibody, HIV

LAV-2
See HIV-2

Lavage
Colon 44701
Lung
Bronchial 31624
Total 32997
Mammary Duct 0046T-0047T
Peritoneal 49080

LCM
See Lymphocytic Choriomeningitis

LD
See Lactic Dehydrogenase

LDH 83615-83625

LDL
See Lipoprotein, LDL

Lead 83655

Leadbetter Procedure 53431

Lecithin-Sphingomyelin Ratio .83661

Lecithinase C
See Tissue Typing

Lee and White Test 85345

LEEP Procedure 57460

LeFort I Procedure
Midface Reconstruction 21141-21147, 21155, 21160
Palatal or Maxillary Fracture 21421-21423

LeFort II Procedure
Midface Reconstruction 21150-21151
Nasomaxillary Complex Fracture ...21345-21348

LeFort III Procedure
Craniofacial Separation 21431-21436
Midface Reconstruction 21154-21159

LeFort Procedure
Vagina 57120

Left Atrioventricular Valve
See Mitral Valve

Left Heart Cardiac Catheterization
See Cardiac Catheterization, Left Heart

Leg
Cast
Rigid Total Contact 29445
Lower
See Ankle; Fibula; Knee; Tibia
Abscess
Incision and Drainage 27603
Amputation 27598, 27880-27882
Revision 27884-27886
Angiography 73706
Artery
Ligation 37618
Biopsy 27613-27614
Bursa
Incision and Drainage 27604
Bypass Graft 35903
Cast 29405-29435, 29450
CT Scan 73700-73706
Decompression 27600-27602
Exploration
Blood Vessel 35860
Fasciotomy 27600-27602, 27892-27894
Hematoma
Incision and Drainage 27603
Lesion
Excision 27630
Magnetic Resonance Imaging (MRI) 73718-73720
Repair
Blood Vessel 35226
Blood Vessel with Other Graft 35286
Blood Vessel with Vein Graft 35256
Fascia 27656
Tendon 27658-27692
Splint 29515
Strapping 29580
Suture
Tendon 27658-27665
Tumor
Excision 27615-27619
Ultrasound 76880
Unlisted Services and Procedures 27899
Unna Boot 29580
X-Ray 73592
Upper
See Femur
Abscess 27301
Amputation 27590-27592
at Hip 27290-27295
Revision 27594-27596
Angiography 73706, 75635
Artery
Ligation 37618
Biopsy 27323-27324
Bursa 27301
Bypass Graft 35903
Cast 29345-29355, 29365, 29450
Cast Brace 29358
CT Scan 73700-73706, 75635
Exploration
Blood Vessel 35860
Fasciotomy 27305, 27496-27499, 27892-27894
Halo Application 20663
Hematoma 27301
Magnetic Resonance Imaging (MRI) 73718-73720
Neurectomy 27315-27320
Removal
Cast 29705
Foreign Body 27372
Repair
Blood Vessel with Other Graft 35286
Blood Vessel with Vein Graft 35256
Muscle 27385-27386, 27400, 27430
Tendon 27393-27400
Splint 29505
Strapping 29580
Suture
Muscle 27385-27386
Tenotomy 27306-27307, 27390-27392
Tumor
Excision 27327-27329
Ultrasound 76880
Unlisted Services and Procedures 27599
Unna Boot 29580
X-Ray 73592
Wound Exploration
Penetrating 20103

Leg Length Measurement X-Ray
See Scanogram

Legionella
Antibody 86713
Antigen 87277-87278, 87540-87542

Legionella Micdadei
Antigen Detection
Immunofluorescence 87277

Legionella Pneumophila
Antigen Detection
Direct Fluorescence 87278

Leiomyomata
Removal 58140, 58545-58546, 58561

Leishmania
Antibody 86717

Lengthening, Tendon
See Tendon, Lengthening

Lens
Extracapsular 66940
Intracapsular 66920
  Dislocated 66930
Intraocular
  Exchange 66986
  Reposition 66825
Prosthesis
  Insertion 66983
    Manual or Mechanical Technique 66982, 66984
    Not Associated with Concurrent Cataract Removal 66985
Removal
  Lens Material
    Aspiration Technique 66840
    Extracapsular 66940
    Intracapsular 66920-66930
    Pars Plana Approach 66852
    Phacofragmentation Technique 66850

Lens Material
Aspiration Technique 66840
Pars Plana Approach 66852
Phacofragmentation Technique 66850

Leptomeningioma
See Meningioma

Leptospira
Antibody 86720

Leriche Operation 64809
See Sympathectomy, Thoracolumbar

Lesion
See Tumor
Anal
  Destruction 46900-46917, 46924
  Excision 45108, 46922
Ankle
  Tendon Sheath .27630
Arm, Lower
  Tendon Sheath
    Excision 25110
Auditory Canal, External
  Excision
    Exostosis 69140
    Radical with Neck Dissection 69155
    Radical without Neck Dissection 69150
    Soft Tissue .69145
Bladder
  Destruction 51030
Brain
  Excision 61534, 61536, 61600-61608, 61615-61616
  Radiation Treatment 77432
Brainstem
  Excision 61575-61576
Breast
  Excision 19120-19126
Carotid Body
  Excision 60600-60605
Chemotherapy 96405-96406
  Destruction 67220-67225
Choroid
  Destruction 0016T
Ciliary Body
  Destruction 66770
Colon
  Destruction 44393, 45383
  Excision 44110-44111
Conjunctiva
  Destruction 68135
  Excision 68110-68130
    Over 1 cm 68115
    with Adjacent Sclera 68130
  Expression 68040
Cornea
  Destruction 65450
  Excision 65400
    of Pterygium 65420-65426
Destruction
  Ureter . . .52341-52342, 52344-52345, 52354
Ear, Middle
  Excision 69540
Epididymis
  Excision 54830
Esophagus
  Ablation 43228
  Excision 43100-43101
  Removal 43216
Excision 59100
  Bladder 52224
  Urethra .52224, 53265
Eye
  Excision 65900
Eyelid
  Destruction 67850
  Excision
    Multiple, Different Lids 67805
    Multiple, Same Lid 67801
    Single 67800
    Under Anesthesia 67808
    without Closure 67840
Facial
  Destruction 17000-17004, 17280-17286
Femur
  Excision 27062
Finger
  Tendon Sheath .26160
Foot
  Excision 28080, 28090
Gums
  Destruction 41850
  Excision 41822-41828
Hand Tendon Sheath 26160
Intestines
  Excision 44110
Intestines, Small
  Destruction 44369
  Excision 44111
Iris
  Destruction 66770
Leg, Lower
  Tendon Sheath .27630
Lymph Node
  Incision and Drainage 38300-38305
Mesentery
  Excision 44820
Mouth
  Destruction 40820
  Excision 40810-40816, 41116
  Vestibule
    Destruction 40820
    Repair 40830
Nerve
  Excision 64774-64792
Nose
  Intranasal
    External Approach 30118
    Internal Approach 30117
Orbit
  Excision 61333, 67412
Palate
  Destruction 42160
  Excision 42104-42120
Pancreas
  Excision 48120
Pelvis
  Destruction 58662
Penis
  Destruction
    Cryosurgery .54056
    Electrodesiccation 54055
    Extensive 54065
    Laser Surgery 54057
    Simple 54050-54060
    Surgical Excision 54060
  Excision 54060
    Penile Plague 54110-54112
Pharynx
  Destruction 42808
  Excision 42808
Rectum
  Excision 45108
Removal
  Larynx .31512, 31578
Resection 52354
Retina
  Destruction
    Extensive 67227-67228
    Localized 0017T, 67208-67210
  Radiation by Implantation of Source . . .67218
Sclera
  Excision 66130
Skin
  Abrasion 15786-15787
  Biopsy 11100-11101
  Destruction
    Benign 17000-17250
    Malignant 17260-17286
      by Photodynamic Therapy 96567
  Excision
    Benign 11400-11471
    Malignant 11600-11646
  Injection 11900-11901
  Paring or Curettement 11055-11057
  Shaving .11300-11313
Skin Tags
  Removal 11200-11201
Skull
  Excision . .61500, 61600-61608, 61615-61616
Spermatic Cord
  Excision 55520
Spinal Cord
  Destruction 62280-62282
  Excision 63265-63273
Stomach
  Excision 43611
Testis
  Excision 54512
Toe
  Excision 28092

Tongue
Excision 41110-41114
Uvula
Destruction 42145
Excision 42104-42107
Vagina
Destruction 57061-57065
Vulva
Destruction
Extensive 56515
Simple 56501
Wrist Tendon
Excision 25110

Lesion of Sciatic Nerve
See Sciatic Nerve, Lesion

Leu 2 Antigens
See CD8

Leucine Aminopeptidase 83670

Leukemia Lymphoma Virus I Antibodies, Human T Cell
See Antibody, HTLV-I

Leukemia Lymphoma Virus I, Adult T Cell
See HTLV I

Leukemia Lymphoma Virus II Antibodies, Human T Cell
See Antibody, HTLV-II

Leukemia Virus II, Hairy Cell Associated, Human T Cell
See HTLV II

Leukoagglutinins 86021

Leukocyte
See White Blood Cell
Alkaline Phosphatase 85540
Antibody 86021
Histamine Release Test 86343
Phagocytosis 86344
Transfusion 86950

Leukocyte Count
See White Blood Cell, Count

Levarterenol
See Noradrenalin

Levator Muscle Rep
See Blepharoptosis, Repair

LeVeen Shunt
Insertion 49425
Patency Test 78291
Revision 49426

Levulose
See Fructose

LGV
See Lymphogranuloma Venereum

LH
See Luteinizing Hormone (LH)

LHR
See Leukocyte Histamine Release Test

Lid Suture
See Blepharoptosis, Repair

Lidocaine
Assay 80176

Lift, Face
See Face Lift

Ligament
See Specific Site
Collateral
Repair
Knee
with Cruciate Ligament 27409
Dentate
Incision 63180-63182
Section 63180-63182
Injection 20550
Release
Coracoacromial 23415
Transverse Carpal 29848
Repair
Elbow 24343-24346
Knee Joint 27405-27409

Ligation
Artery
Abdomen 37617
Carotid 37600-37606
Chest 37616
Coronary 33502
Coronary Artery 33502
Ethmoidal 30915
Extremity 37618
Fistula 37607
Maxillary 30920
Neck 37615
Temporal 37609
Esophageal Varices 43204, 43400
Fallopian Tube
Oviduct 58600-58611, 58670
Gastroesophageal 43405
Hemorrhoids 46945-46946
Oviducts 59100
Salivary Duct 42665
Shunt
Aorta
Pulmonary 33924
Peritoneal
Venous 49428
Thoracic Duct 38380
Abdominal Approach 38382
Thoracic Approach 38381
Vas Deferens 55450
Vein
Clusters 37785
Esophagus 43205, 43244, 43400
Femoral 37650
Gastric 43244
Iliac 37660
Jugular, Internal 37565
Perforate 37760
Saphenous 37700-37735, 37780
Vena Cava 37620

Ligature Strangulation
Skin Tags 11200-11201

Light Coagulation
See Photocoagulation

Light Scattering Measurement
See Nephelometry

Light Therapy, UV
See Actinotherapy

Limb
See Extremity

Limited Lymphadenectomy for Staging
See Lymphadenectomy, Limited, for Staging

Limited Neck Dissection
with Thyroidectomy 60252

Limited Resection Mastectomies
See Breast, Excision, Lesion

Lindholm Operation
See Tenoplasty

Lingual Bone
See Hyoid Bone

Lingual Frenectomy
See Excision, Tongue, Frenum

Lingual Nerve
Avulsion 64740
Incision 64740
Transection 64740

Lingual Tonsil
See Tonsils, Lingual

Linton Procedure 37760

Lip
Biopsy 40490
Excision 40500-40530
Frenum 40819
Incision
Frenum 40806
Reconstruction 40525-40527
Repair 40650-40654
Cleft Lip 40700-40761
Fistula 42260
Unlisted Services and Procedures 40799

Lip, Cleft
See Cleft Lip

Lipase 83690

Lipectomies, Aspiration
See Liposuction

Lipectomy 15831-15839
Suction Assisted 15876-15879

Lipids
Feces 82705-82710

Lipo-Lutin
See Progesterone

Lipolysis, Aspiration
See Liposuction

Lipophosphodiesterase I
See Tissue Typing

Lipoprotein
Blood 0026T, 83715-83719
LDL 83716, 83721

Lipoprotein, Alpha
See Lipoprotein

Lipoprotein, Pre-Beta
See Lipoprotein, Blood

Liposuction 15876-15879

Lisfranc Operation
See Amputation, Foot; Radical Resection; Replantation

Listeria Monocytogenes
Antibody 86723

Lithium
Assay 80178

Litholapaxy 52317-52318

Lithotripsy
See Extracorporeal Shock Wave Therapy
Bile Duct Calculi (Stone)
  Endoscopy 43265
Bladder 52353
Kidney 50590, 52353
Pancreatic Duct Calculi (Stone)
  Endoscopy 43265
Ureter 52353
Urethra 52353
with Cystourethroscopy 52353

Lithotrity
See Litholapaxy

Liver
See Hepatic Duct
Ablation
  Tumor 47380-47382
    Laparoscopic 47370-47371
Abscess
  Aspiration 47015
  Incision and Drainage
    Open 47010
    Percutaneous 47011
  Injection 47015
Aspiration 47015
Biopsy 47100
Cyst
  Aspiration 47015
  Incision and Drainage
    Open 47010
    Percutaneous 47011
Excision
  Extensive 47122
  Partial ..47120, 47125-47130, 47140-47142
  Total 47133
Injection 47015
  Radiologic 47505
  X-Ray 47500
Lobectomy 47125-47130
  Partial 47120
Needle Biopsy 47000-47001
Nuclear Medicine
  Function Study 78220
  Imaging 78201-78216
  Vascular Flow 78206
Repair
  Abscess 47300
  Cyst 47300
  Wound 47350-47362
Suture
  Wound 47350-47362
Transplantation 47135-47136
Trisegmentectomy 47122
Unlisted Services and Procedures ..47379, 47399

Living Activities, Daily
See Activities of Daily Living

Lobectomy
Brain 61323, 61537-61540
Contralateral Subtotal
  Thyroid Gland 60212, 60225
Liver 47120-47130
Lung 32480-32482
  Sleeve 32486
Parotid Gland 42410-42415
Segmental 32663
Sleeve 32486
Temporal Lobe 61537-61538
Thyroid Gland Partial 60210-60212
  Total 60220-60225
Total 32663

Lobotomy
Frontal 61490

Local Excision Mastectomies
See Breast, Excision, Lesion

Local Excision of Lesion or Tissue of Femur
See Excision, Lesion, Femur

Localization of Nodule
Radiographic
  Breast 76096

Log Hydrogen Ion Concentration
See pH

Lombard Test
See Audiologic Function Test

Long Acting Thyroid Stimulator
See Thyrotropin Releasing Hormone (TRH)

Long Term Care Facility Visits
See Nursing Facility Services

Longmire Operation
See Anastomosis, Hepatic Duct to Intestines

Loopogram
See Urography, Antegrade

Loose Body
Removal
  Ankle 27620
  Carpometacarpal Joint 26070
  Elbow 24101
  Interphalangeal Joint 28020
    Toe 28024
  Knee Joint 27331
  Metatarsophalangeal Joint 28022
  Tarsometatarsal Joint 28020
  Toe 28022
  Wrist 25101

Lord Procedure
See Anal Sphincter, Dilation

Louis Bar Syndrome
See Ataxia Telangiectasia

Low Birth Weight Intensive Care Services 99298-99299

Low Density Lipoprotein
See Lipoprotein, LDL

Low Vision Aids
See Spectacle Services
Fitting 92354-92355
Supply 92392

Lower Extremities
See Extremity, Lower

Lower GI Series
See Barium Enema

LRH
See Luteinizing Releasing Factor

LSD
See Lysergic Acid Diethylamide

LTH
See Prolactin

Lumbar
See Spine
Aspiration, Disk
  Percutaneous 62287

Lumbar Plexus
Decompression 64714
Injection
  Anesthetic 64449
Neuroplasty 64714
Release 64714
Repair/Suture 64862

Lumbar Puncture
See Spinal Tap

Lumbar Spine Fracture
See Fracture, Vertebra, Lumbar

Lumbar Sympathectomy
See Sympathectomy, Lumbar

Lumbar Vertebra
See Vertebra, Lumbar

Lumen Dilation 74360

Lumpectomies
See Breast, Excision, Lesion

Lunate
Arthroplasty
  with Implant 25444
Dislocation
  Closed Treatment 25690
  Open Treatment 25695

Lung
Abscess
Incision and Drainage
Open 32200
Percutaneous 32200-32201
Aspiration 32420
Biopsy 32095-32100
Bullae
Excision 32141
Endoscopic 32655
Cyst
Incision and Drainage
Open 32200
Removal 32140
Decortication
Endoscopic 32651-32652
Partial 32225
Total 32220
with Parietal Pleurectomy 32320
Empyema
Excision 32540
Excision
Bronchus Resection 32486
Chest Resection 32520-32525
Completion 32488
Donor 33930
Emphysematous 32491
Lobe 32480-32482
Segment 32484
Total 32440-32445
Wedge Resection 32500
Endoscopic 32657
Foreign Body
Removal 32151
Hemorrhage 32110
Lavage
Bronchial 31624
Total 32997
Lysis
Adhesions 32124
Needle Biopsy 32405
Nuclear Medicine
Imaging, Perfusion 78580-78585
Imaging, Ventilation 78586-78594
Unlisted Services and Procedures 78599
Pneumocentesis 32420
Pneumolysis 32940
Pneumothorax 32960
Puncture 32420
Removal
Bronchoplasty 32501
Completion Pneumonectomy 32488
Extrapleural 32445
Single Lobe 32480
Single Segment 32484
Sleeve Lobectomy 32486
Sleeve Pneumonectomy 32442
Total Pneumonectomy 32440-32445
Two Lobes 32482
Volume Reduction 32491
Wedge Resection 32500
Repair
Hernia 32800
Segmentectomy 32484
Tear
Repair 32110
Thoracotomy
Biopsy 32095-32100
Cardiac Massage 32160
for Post-Op Complications 32120
Removal
Bullae 32141
Cyst 32140
Intrapleural Foreign Body 32150
Intrapulmonary Foreign Body 32151
Repair 32110
with Excision-Plication of Bullae 32141
with Open Intrapleural Pneumonolysis 32124
Transplantation 32851-32854, 33935
Unlisted Services and Procedures 32999

Lung Function Tests
See Pulmonology, Diagnostic

Lung Volume Reduction
Emphysematous 32491

Lupus Anticoagulant Assay 85705

Lupus Band Test
See Immunofluorescent Study

Luteinizing Hormone (LH) 80418, 80426, 83002

Luteinizing Releasing Factor 83727

Lutenizing Hormone
See Luteinizing Hormone (LH)

Luteotropic Hormone
See Prolactin

Luteotropin
See Prolactin

Luteotropin, Placental
See Lactogen, Human Placental

Lyme Disease 86617-86618

Lyme Disease ab
See Antibody, Lyme Disease

Lyme Disease Vaccine
See Vaccination

Lymph Duct
Injection 38790

Lymph Nodes
Abscess
Incision and Drainage 38300-38305
Biopsy 38500, 38510-38530, 38570
Needle 38505
Dissection 38542
Excision 38500, 38510-38530
Abdominal 38747
Inguinofemoral 38760-38765
Laparoscopic 38571-38572
Limited, for Staging
Para-Aortic 38562
Pelvic 38562
Retroperitoneal 38564
Pelvic 38770
Radical
Axillary 38740-38745
Cervical 38720-38724
Suprahyoid 38720-38724
Retroperitoneal Transabdominal 38780
Thoracic 38746
Exploration 38542
Hygroma, Cystic
Axillary/Cervical
Excision 38550-38555
Nuclear Medicine
Imaging 78195
Removal
Abdominal 38747
Inguinofemoral 38760-38765
Pelvic 38770
Retroperitoneal Transabdominal 38780
Thoracic 38746

Lymph Vessels
Abdomen
Lymphangiography 75805-75807
Arm
Lymphangiography 75801-75803
Leg
Lymphangiography 75801-75803
Nuclear Medicine
Imaging 78195
Pelvis
Lymphangiography 75805-75807

Lymphadenectomy
Abdominal 38747
Bilateral Inguinofemoral 54130, 56632, 56637
Bilateral Pelvic 51575, 51585, 51595, 54135, 55845, 55865
Total 38571-38572, 57531, 58210
Diaphragmatic Assessment 58960
Gastric 38747
Inguinofemoral 38760-38765
Inguinofemoral, Iliac and Pelvic 56640
Injection
Sentinel Node 38792
Limited Para-Aortic, Resection of Ovarian Malignancy 58951, 58954
Limited Pelvic 55842, 55862, 58954
Limited, for Staging
Para-Aortic 38562
Pelvic 38562
Retroperitoneal 38564
Mediastinal 21632
Peripancreatic 38747
Portal 38747
Radical
Axillary 38740-38745
Cervical 38720-38724
Pelvic 54135, 55845
Suprahyoid 38700
Regional 50230
Retroperitoneal Transabdominal 38780
Thoracic 38746
Unilateral Inguinofemoral 56631, 56634

Lymphadenitis
Incision and Drainage 38300-38305

Lymphadenopathy Associated Antibodies
See Antibody, HIV

Lymphadenopathy Associated Virus
See HIV

Lymphangiogram, Abdominal
See Lymphangiography, Abdomen

Lymphangiography
Abdomen 75805-75807
Arm 75801-75803
Injection 38790
Leg 75801-75803
Pelvis 75805-75807

Lymphangioma, Cystic
See Hygroma

Lymphangiotomy 38308

Lymphatic Channels
Incision 38308

Lymphatic Cyst
See Lymphocele

Lymphatic System
Unlisted Procedure 38999

Lymphatics
See Specific Procedure

Lymphoblast Transformation
See Blastogenesis

Lymphocele
Drainage
  Laparoscopic 49323
Extraperitoneal
  Open Drainage 49062

Lymphocoele
See Lymphocele

Lymphocyte
Culture 86821-86822
Toxicity Assay 86805-86806
Transformation 86353

Lymphocyte, Thymus-Dependent
See T-Cells

Lymphocytes, CD4
See CD4

Lymphocytes, CD8
See CD8

Lymphocytic Choriomeningitis
Antibody 86727

Lymphocytotoxicity 86805-86806

Lymphogranuloma Venereum
Antibody 86729

Lymphoma Virus, Burkitt
See Epstein-Barr Virus

Lynch Procedure 31075

Lysergic Acid Diethylamide . . . 80102-80103, 80299

Lysergide
See Lysergic Acid Diethylamide

Lysis
Adhesions
  Epidural 0027T, 62263-62264
  Fallopian Tube 58740
  Foreskin 54450
  Intestinal 44005
  Labial 56441
  Lung 32124
  Nose 30560
  Ovary 58740
  Oviduct 58740
  Penile
    Post-circumcision 54162
  Ureter 50715-50725
  Urethra 53500
  Uterus 58559
Euglobulin 85360
Labial
  Adhesions 56441
Nose
  Intranasal Synechia 30560

Lysozyme 85549

M

MacEwen Operation
See Hernia, Repair, Inguinal

Machado Test
See Complement, Fixation Test

MacLean-De Wesselow Test
See Blood Urea Nitrogen; Urea Nitrogen, Clearance

Macrodactylia
Repair 26590

Madlener Operation
See Tubal Ligation

Magnesium 83735

Magnet Operation
See Ciliary Body; Cornea; Eye, Removal, Foreign Body; Iris; Lens; Retina; Sclera; Vitreous

Magnetic Resonance
Unlisted Services and Procedures 76498

Magnetic Resonance Angiography (MRA)
Abdomen 74185
Arm 73225
Chest 71555
Head 70544-70546
Leg 73725
Neck 70547-70549
Pelvis 72198
Spine 72159

Magnetic Resonance Imaging (MRI)
Abdomen 74181-74183
Ankle 73721-73723
Arm 73218-73220, 73223
Bone Marrow Study 76400
Brain 70551-70553
  Intraoperative 70557-70559
Breast 76093-76094
Chest 71550-71552
Elbow 73221
Face 70540-70543
Finger Joint 73221
Foot 73718-73719
Foot Joints 73721-73723
Guidance
  Needle Placement 76393
  Visceral Tissue Ablation 76394
Hand 73218-73220, 73223
Heart 75552
  Complete Study 75554
  Flow Mapping 75556
  Limited Study 75555
  Morphology 75553
Joint
  Lower Extremity 73721-73723
  Upper Extremity 73221-73223
Knee 73721-73723
Leg 73718-73720
Neck 70540-70543
Orbit 70540-70543
Pelvis 72195-72197
Radiology
  Diagnostic
    Procedures 76499
Spectroscopy 76390
Spine
  Cervical 72141-72142, 72156-72158
  Lumbar 72148-72158
  Thoracic 72146-72147, 72156-72158
Temporomandibular Joint (TMJ) 70336
Toe 73721-73723
Wrist 73221

Magnetic Resonance Spectroscopy 76390

Magnetic Stimulation
Brain Cortex 0018T

Magnetoencephalography (MEG) 95965-95967

Magnuson Procedure 23450

Magpi Operation 54322

MAGPI Procedure
See Hypospadias, Repair

Major Vestibular Gland
See Bartholin's Gland

Malar Area
Augmentation 21270
Bone Graft 21210
Fracture
  Open Treatment 21360-21366
  with Bone Graft 21366
  with Manipulation 21355
Reconstruction 21270

Malar Bone
See Cheekbone

Interphalangeal Joint, Proximal 26742
Knee 27570
Osteopathic 98925-98929
Shoulder
  Application of Fixation Apparatus 23700
Spine
  with Anesthesia 22505
Tibial, Distal 27762

Manometric Studies
Kidney
  Pressure 50396
Rectum/Anus 91122
Ureter
  Pressure 50686
Ureterostomy 50686

Manometry
Rectum 90911

Mantoux Test
See TB Test, Skin Test

Manual Therapy 97140

Maquet Procedure 27418

Marcellation Operation
See Hysterectomy, Vaginal

Marrow, Bone
See Bone Marrow

Marshall-Marchetti-Krantz Procedure 51840-51841, 58152, 58267, 58293

Marsupialization 10040
Bartholin's Gland Cyst 56440
Cyst
  Sublingual Salivary 42409
Liver
  Cyst or Abscess 47300
Pancreatic Cyst 48500
Urethral Diverticulum 53240

Mass
Kidney
  Ablation 50542

Mass Spectrometry and Tandem Mass Spectrometry
Analyte
  Qualitative 83788
  Quantitative 83789

Massage
Cardiac 32160
Therapy 97124
  See Physical Medicine/Therapy/Occupational Therapy

Masseter Muscle/Bone
Reduction 21295-21296

Mastectomy
Gynecomastia 19140
Modified Radical 19240
Partial 19160-19162
Radical 19200-19220
Simple, Complete 19180
Subcutaneous 19182

Mastectomy, Halsted
See Mastectomy, Radical

Mastoid
Excision
  Complete 69502
  Radical 69511
    Modified 69505
    Petrous Apicectomy 69530
  Simple 69501
Obliteration 69670
Repair
  by Excision 69601-69603
  Fistula 69700
  with Apicectomy 69605
  with Tympanoplasty 69604

Mastoid Cavity
Debridement 69220-69222

Mastoidectomy
Osseointegrated Implant
  for External Speech Processor/Cochlear Stimulator 69715, 69718
with Apicectomy 69605
with Skull Base Surgery 61590, 61597
  Decompression 61595
  Facial Nerve 61595
with Tympanoplasty 69604, 69641-69646
  Cochlear Device Implantation 69930
  Complete 69502
    Revision 69601
  Ossicular Chain Reconstruction 69605
  Radical 69511
    Modified 69505
    Revision 69602-69603
  Simple 69501
  with Labyrinthectomy 69910
  with Labyrinthotomy 69802
  with Petrous Apicectomy 69530

Mastoidotomy 69635-69637
with Tympanoplasty 69635
  Ossicular Chain Reconstruction 69636
    and Synthetic Prosthesis 69636

Mastoids
Polytomography 76101-76102
X-Ray 70120-70130

Mastopexy 19316

Mastotomy 19020

Maternity Care
See Abortion; Cesarean Delivery; Ectopic Pregnancy; Obstetrical Care

Maternity Care and Delivery 59612-59622, 59898

Maxilla
See Facial Bones; Mandible
Bone Graft 21210
CT Scan 70486-70488
Cyst
  Excision 21048-21049
Excision 21030, 21032-21034
Fracture
  Closed Treatment 21345, 21421
  Open Treatment .21346-21348, 21422-21423
  with Fixation 21345-21347
Osteotomy 21206
Reconstruction
  with Implant 21245-21246, 21248-21249
Tumor
  Excision 21048-21049

Maxillary Arteries
See Artery, Maxillary

Maxillary Sinus
See Sinus, Maxillary

Maxillary Torus Palatinus
Tumor Excision 21032

Maxillectomy 31225-31230

Maxillofacial Fixation
Application
  Halo Type Appliance 21100

Maxillofacial Impressions
Auricular Prosthesis 21086
Definitive Obturator Prosthesis 21080
Facial Prosthesis 21088
Interim Obturator Prosthesis 21079
Mandibular Resection Prosthesis 21081
Nasal Prosthesis 21087
Oral Surgical Splint 21085
Orbital Prosthesis 21077
Palatal Augmentation Prosthesis 21082
Palatal Lift Prosthesis 21083
Speech Aid Prosthesis 21084
Surgical Obturator Prosthesis 21076

Maxillofacial Procedures
Unlisted Services and Procedures 21299

Maxillofacial Prosthetics 21076-21089
Unlisted Services and Procedures 21089

Maydl Operation 45563, 50810
See Colostomy

Mayo Hernia Repair
See Hernia, Repair, Umbilicus

Mayo Operation
See Varicose Vein, Removal

Mayo Procedure 28292

MBC
See Minimum Bactericidal Concentration

McBride Procedure 28292

McBurney Operation
See Hernia, Repair, Inguinal

McCannel Procedure 66682

McDonald Operation
See Repair, Cervix, Cerclage, Abdominal; Revision

McIndoe Procedure
See Vagina, Construction

Dislocation
Closed Treatment .26700
Open Treatment .26715
Percutaneous Fixation .26705-26706
with Manipulation .26340
Exploration .26075
Fracture
Closed Treatment .26740
Open Treatment .26746
with Manipulation .26742
Fusion .26516-26518, 26850-26852
Removal of Foreign Body .26075
Repair
Collateral Ligament .26540-26542
Synovectomy .26135

Metadrenaline
See Metanephrines

Metals, Heavy
See Heavy Metal

Metamfetamine
See Methamphetamine

Metanephrines .83835

Metatarsal
See Foot
Amputation .28810
Condyle
Excision .28288
Craterization .28122
Cyst
Excision .28104-28107
Diaphysectomy .28122
Excision .28110-28114, 28122, 28140
Fracture
Closed Treatment
with Manipulation .28475-28476
without Manipulation .28470
Open Treatment .28485
Percutaneous Fixation .28476
Free Osteocutaneous Flap with Microvascular Anastomosis .20972
Repair .28322
Lengthening .28306-28307
Osteotomy .28306-28309
Saucerization .28122
Tumor
Excision .28104-28107, 28173

Metatarsectomy .28140

Metatarsophalangeal Joint
Arthrotomy .28022, 28052
Cheilectomy .28289
Dislocation .28630-28635, 28645
Percutaneous Fixation .28636
Exploration .28022
Great Toe
Arthrodesis .28750
Fusion .28750
Removal
of Foreign Body .28022
of Loose Body .28022
Repair
Hallux Rigidus .28289
Synovial
Biopsy .28052
Excision .28072
Toe .28270

Methadone .83840

Methaemoglobin
See Methemoglobin

Methamphetamine
Blood or Urine .82145

Methanol .84600

Methbipyranone
See Metyrapone

Methemalbumin .83857

Methemoglobin .83045-83050

Methenamine Silver Stain .88312

Methopyrapone
See Metyrapone

Methoxyhydroxymandelic Acid
See Vanillylmandelic Acid

Methsuximide .83858

Methyl Alcohol
See Methanol

Methylamphetamine
See Methamphetamine

Methylene Bichloride
See Dichloromethane

Methylfluorprednisolone
See Dexamethasone

Methylmorphine
See Codeine

Metroplasty
See Hysteroplasty

Metyrapone .80436

MIC
See Minimum Inhibitory Concentration

Micro-Ophthalmia
Orbit Reconstruction .21256

Microalbumin
Urine .82043-82044

Microbiology .0023T, 87001-87999

Microdissection .88380

Microfluorometries, Flow
See Flow Cytometry

Microglobulin, Beta 2
Blood .82232
Urine .82232

Micrographic Surgery
Mohs Technique .17304-17310

Micrographic Surgery, Mohs
See Mohs Micrographic Surgery

Micropigmentation
Correction .11920-11922

Microscope, Surgical
See Operating Microscope

Microscopic Evaluation
Hair .96902

Microscopies, Electron
See Electron Microscopy

Microscopy
Ear Exam .92504

Microsomal Antibody .86376

Microsomia, Hemifacial
See Hemifacial Microsomia

Microsurgery
Operating Microscope .69990

Microvascular Anastomosis
Bone Graft
Fibula .20955
Other .20962
Fascial Flap, Free .15758
Muscle Flap, Free .15756
Osteocutaneous Flap with .20969-20973
Skin Flap, Free .15757

Microvite A
See Vitamin, A

Microwave Therapy .97020
See Physical Medicine/Therapy/Occupational Therapy

Midbrain
See Brain; Brainstem; Mesencephalon; Skull Base Surgery

Midcarpal Mediooccipital Joint
Arthrotomy .25040

Middle Ear
See Ear, Middle

Midface
Reconstruction
Forehead Advancement .21159-21160
with Bone Graft .21145-21160, 21188
without Bone Graft .21141-21143

Migration Inhibitory Factor (MIF) .86378

Mile Operation
See Colectomy, Total, with Proctectomy

Milia, Multiple
Removal .10040

Miller Procedure .28737

Miller-Abbott Intubation .44500, 74340

Minerva Cast .29035
Removal .29710

MPR
See Multifetal Pregnancy Reduction

MR Spectroscopy
See Magnetic Resonance Spectroscopy

MRA
See Magnetic Resonance Angiography

MRI
See Magnetic Resonance Imaging (MRI)

MSLT
See Multiple Sleep Latency Testing (MSLT)

Mucin
Synovial Fluid 83872

Mucocele
Sinusotomy
Frontal 31075

Mucopolysaccharides 83864-83866

Mucormycoses
See Mucormycosis

Mucormycosis
Antibody 86732

Mucosa
Ectopic Gastric Imaging 78290
Excision of Lesion
Alveolar, Hyperplastic 41828
Vestibule of Mouth 40810-40818
via Esophagoscopy 43228
via Small Intestinal Endoscopy 44369
via Upper GI Endoscopy 43258
Periodontal Grafting 41870
Urethra, Mucosal Advancement 53450
Vaginal Biopsy 57100-57105

Mucosa, Buccal
See Mouth, Mucosa

Mucous Cyst
Antibody
Hand or Finger 26160

Mucous Membrane
See Mouth, Mucosa
Cutaneous
Biopsy 11100-11101
Excision
Benign Lesion 11440-11446
Malignant Lesion 11640-11646
Layer Closure, Wounds 12051-12057
Simple Repair, Wounds 12011-12018
Excision
Sphenoid Sinus 31288
Lid Margin
Correction of Trichiasis 67835
Nasal Test 95065
Ophthalmic Test 95060
Rectum
Proctoplasty for Prolapse 45505

Mucus Cyst
See Mucous Cyst

MUGA (Multiple Gated Acquisition) 78472-78478, 78483

Muller Procedure
See Sleep Study

Multifetal Pregnancy Reduction 59866

Multiple Sleep Latency Testing (MSLT) 95805

Multiple Valve Procedures
See Valvuloplasty

Mumford Operation
See Claviculectomy, Partial

Mumford Procedure 29824

Mumps
Antibody 86735
Immunization 90704, 90707, 90710
Vaccine 90704
MMR 90707
MMRV 90710

Muramidase 85549

Murine Typhus 86000

Muscle
See Specific Muscle
Abdomen
See Abdominal Wall
Biopsy 20200-20206
Heart
See Myocardium
Neck
See Neck Muscle
Removal
Foreign Body 20520-20525
Repair
Forearm 25260-25274
Wrist 25260-25274
Revision
Arm, Upper 24330-24331
Transfer
Arm, Upper 24301, 24320
Elbow 24301
Femur 27110
Hip 27100-27105, 27111
Shoulder 23395-23397, 24301, 24320

Muscle Compartment Syndrome
Detection 20950

Muscle Denervation
See Denervation

Muscle Division
Scalenus Anticus 21700-21705
Sternocleidomastoid 21720-21725

Muscle Flaps 15732-15738
Free 15756

Muscle Grafts 15841-15845

Muscle Testing
Dynamometry, Eye 92260
Extraocular Multiple Muscles 92265
Manual 95831-95834

Muscle, Oculomotor
See Eye Muscles

Muscles
Repair
Extraocular 65290

Musculo-Skeletal System
See Musculoskeletal System

Musculoplasty
See Muscle, Repair

Musculoskeletal System
Unlisted Services and Procedures 20999, 24999, 25999, 26989, 27299, 27599, 27899
Unlisted Services and Procedures, Head 21499

Musculotendinous (Rotator) Cuff
Repair 23410-23412

Mustard Procedure
See Repair, Great Arteries; Revision

Myasthenia Gravis
Tensilon Test 95857-95858

Myasthenic, Gravis
See Myasthenia Gravis

Mycobacteria
Culture 87116
Identification 87118
Detection 87550-87562
Sensitivity Studies 87190

Mycoplasma
Antibody 86738
Culture 87109
Detection 87580-87582

Mycota
See Fungus

Myectomy, Anorectal
See Myomectomy, Anorectal

Myelencephalon
See Medulla

Myelin Basic Protein
Cerebrospinal Fluid 83873

Myelography
Brain 70010
Spine
Cervical 72240
Lumbosacral 72265
Thoracic 72255
Total 72270

Myelomeningocele
Repair 63704-63706

Myelotomy 63170

Myocardial
Perfusion Imaging 78460-78465, 78478-78480
See Nuclear Medicine
Positron Emission Tomography (PET) 78459

Unlisted Services and Procedures,
Surgery 21899
Urinary Bladder
See Bladder, Neck
Wound Exploration
Penetrating 20100
X-Ray 70360

Neck Muscle
Division
Scalenus Anticus 21700-21705
Sternocleidomastoid 21720-21725

Necropsy
Coroner's Exam 88045
Forensic Exam 88040
Gross and Micro Exam 88020-88029
Gross Exam 88000-88016
Organ 88037
Regional 88036
Unlisted Services and Procedures 88099

Needle Biopsy
See Biopsy
Abdomen Mass 49180
Bone 20220-20225
Bone Marrow 38221
Breast 19100
Colon-Sigmoid
Endoscopy 45342
CT Scan Guidance 76360
Epididymis 54800
Esophagus
Endoscopy 43232
Fluoroscopic Guidance 76003
Gastrointestinal, Upper
Endoscopy 43238, 43242
Kidney 50200
Liver 47000-47001
Lung 32405
Lymph Nodes 38505
Mediastinum 32405
Muscle 20206
Pancreas 48102
Pleura 32400
Prostate 55700
Retroperitoneal Mass 49180
Salivary Gland 42400
Spinal Cord 62269
Testis 54500
Thyroid Gland 60100
Transbronchial 31629, 31633

Needle Localization
Breast
Placement 19290-19291
with Lesion Excision 19125-19126
Magnetic Resonance Guidance 76393

Needle Manometer Technique 20950

Needle Wire
Introduction
Trachea 31730
Placement
Breast 19290-19291

Neer Procedure 23470

Neisseria gonorrheae 87590-87592, 87850

Neisseria Meningitidis
Antibody 86741

Neobladder
Construction 51596

Neonatal Critical Care
See Newborn Care
Initial 99295
Subsequent 99296

Neoplasm
Cancer Photoradiation Therapy
See Photochemotherapy
Cardiac
See Heart, Tumor
Colon
See Colon, Tumor
Esophageal
See Tumor, Esophagus
Spinal Cord
See Spinal Cord, Neoplasm
Unspecified Nature of Brain
See Brain, Tumor

Neoplastic Growth
See Tumor

Nephelometry 83883

Nephrectomy
Donor 50300-50320, 50547
Laparoscopic 50545-50548
Partial 50240
Laparoscopic 50543
Recipient 50340
with Ureters 50220-50236, 50546, 50548

Nephrolith
See Calculus, Removal, Kidney

Nephrolithotomy 50060-50075

Nephropexy 50400-50405

Nephroplasty
See Kidney, Repair

Nephropyeloplasty
See Pyeloplasty

Nephrorrhaphy 50500

Nephroscopy
See Endoscopy, Kidney

Nephrostogram 50394

Nephrostolithotomy
Percutaneous 50080-50081

Nephrostomy 50040
Change Tube 50398
Endoscopic 50562-50570
Percutaneous 52334
with Drainage 50040
X-Ray with Contrast
Guide Dilation 74485

Nephrostomy Tract
Establishment 50395

Nephrotomogram
See Nephrotomography

Nephrotomography 74415

Nephrotomy 50040-50045
with Exploration 50045

Nerve
Cranial
See Cranial Nerve
Facial
See Facial Nerve
Intercostal
See Intercostal Nerve
Lingual
See Lingual Nerve
Median
See Median Nerve
Obturator
See Obturator Nerve
Peripheral
See Peripheral Nerve
Phrenic
See Phrenic Nerve
Sciatic
See Sciatic Nerve
Spinal
See Spinal Nerve
Tibial
See Tibial Nerve
Ulnar
See Ulnar Nerve
Vestibular
See Vestibular Nerve

Nerve Conduction
Motor Nerve 95900-95903
Sensory Nerve or Mixed 95904

Nerve II, Cranial
See Optic Nerve

Nerve Root
See Cauda Equina; Spinal Cord
Decompression 63020-63103
Incision 63185-63190
Section 63185-63190

Nerve Stimulation, Transcutaneous
See Application, Neurostimulation

Nerve Teasing 88362

Nerve V, Cranial
See Trigeminal Nerve

Nerve VII, Cranial
See Facial Nerve

Nerve X, Cranial
See Vagus Nerve

Nerve XI, Cranial
See Accessory Nerve

Nerve XII, Cranial
See Hypoglossal Nerve

Neuroplasty 64712
Cranial Nerve 64716
Digital Nerve 64702-64704
Peripheral Nerve 64708-64714, 64718-64721

Neuropsychological Testing 96117

Neurorrhaphy 64831-64876
Peripheral Nerve
with Graft 64885-64907

Neurostimulation
Application 64550

Neurostimulators
Analysis 95970-95975
Insertion
Pulse Generator 64590
Receiver 64590
Removal
Pulse Generator 64595
Receiver 64595

Neurotomy, Sympathetic
See Gasserian Ganglion, Sensory Root, Decompression

Neurovascular Pedicle Flaps 15750

Neutralization Test
Virus 86382

New Patient
Confirmatory Consultations 99271-99275
Domiciliary or Rest Home Visit 99321-99323
Emergency Department Services 99281-99288
Home Services 99341-99345
Hospital Inpatient Services 99221-99239
Hospital Observation Services 99217-99220
Initial Inpatient Consultations 99251-99255
Initial Office Visit 99201-99205
See Evaluation and Management; Office and Other Outpatient
Office and/or Other Outpatient Consultations 99241-99245

Newborn Care 99431-99440, 99502
Attendance at Delivery 99436
Birthing Room 99431
Blood Transfusion 36450
See Neonatal Intensive Care
Circumcision
Clamp or Other Device 54150
Surgical Excision 54160
History and Examination 99431, 99435
Laryngoscopy 31520
Normal 99431-99433
Prepuce Slitting 54000
Preventive
Office 99432
Resuscitation 99440
Standby for Cesarean Delivery 99360
Subsequent Hospital Care 99433
Umbilical Artery Catheterization 36660

Nickel 83885

Nicolas-Durand-Favre Disease
See Lymphogranuloma Venereum

Nicotine 83887

Nidation
See Implantation

Nipples
See Breast
Inverted 19355
Reconstruction 19350

Nissen Operation
See Fundoplasty, Esophagogastric

Nissen Procedure 43324
Laparoscopic 43280

Nitrate Reduction Test
See Urinalysis

Nitroblue Tetrazolium Dye Test 86384

Nitrogen, Blood Urea
See Blood Urea Nitrogen

NMR Imaging
See Magnetic Resonance Imaging (MRI)

NMR Spectroscopies
See Magnetic Resonance Spectroscopy

No Man's Land
Tendon Repair 26356-26358

Noble Procedure
See Repair; Suture

Nocardia
Antibody 86744

Nocturnal Penile Rigidity Test 54250

Nocturnal Penile Tumescence Test 54250

Node Dissection, Lymph
See Dissection, Lymph Nodes

Node, Lymph
See Lymph Nodes

Nodes
See Lymph Nodes

Non-Invasive Vascular Imaging
See Vascular Studies

Non-Office Medical Services 99056

Non-Stress Test, Fetal 59025

Nonunion Repair
Femur
with Graft 27472
without Graft 27470
Metatarsal 28322
Tarsal Joint 28320

Noradrenalin
Blood 82383-82384
Urine 82384

Norchlorimipramine
See Imipramine

Norepinephrine
See Catecholamines
Blood 82383-82384
Urine 82384

Nortriptyline
Assay 80182

Norwood Procedure 33611-33612, 33619
See Repair, Heart, Ventricle; Revision

Nose
Abscess
Incision and Drainage 30000-30020
Artery
Incision 30915-30920
Biopsy
Intranasal 30100
Dermoid Cyst
Excision
Complex 30125
Simple 30124
Displacement Therapy 30210
Endoscopy
Diagnostic 31231-31235
Surgical 31237-31294
Excision
Rhinectomy 30150-30160
Fracture
Closed Treatment 21345
Open Treatment 21325-21336, 21338-21339, 21346-21347
Percutaneous Treatment 21340
with Fixation 21330, 21340, 21345-21347
Hematoma
Incision and Drainage 30000-30020
Hemorrhage
Cauterization 30901-30906
Insertion
Septal Prosthesis 30220
Intranasal
Lesion
External Approach 30118
Internal Approach 30117
Lysis of Adhesions 30560
Polyp
Excision
Extensive 30115
Simple 30110
Reconstruction
Cleft Lip/Cleft Palate 30460-30462
Dermatoplasty 30620
Primary 30400-30420
Secondary 30430-30450
Septum 30520
Removal
Foreign Body 30300
Anesthesia 30310
Lateral Rhinotomy 30320
Repair
Adhesions 30560
Cleft Lip 40700-40761
Fistula 30580-30600, 42260
Rhinophyma 30120

Hepatitis C 87520
Hepatitis G 87525
Herpes Simplex Virus 87528
Herpes Virus-6 87531
HIV-1 87534
HIV-2 87537
Legionella Pneumophila 87540
Multiple Organisms 87800
Mycobacteria avium-intracellulare 87560
Mycobacteria species 87550
Mycobacteria tuberculosis 87555
Mycoplasma pneumoniae 87580
Neisseria gonorrheae 87590
Not Otherwise Specified 87797
Papillomavirus, Human 87620
Streptococcus, Group A 87650
Trichomonas vaginalis 87660
Genotype Analysis
Infectious Agent
Hepatitis C Virus 87902
HIV-1 87901
In Situ Hybridization 88365
Phenotype Analysis
Infectious Agent
HIV-1 Drug Resistance 87903-87904
Quantification
Infectious Agent
Bartonella henselae 87472
Bartonella quintana 87472
Borrelia burgdorferi 87477
Candida species 87482
Chlamydia pneumoniae 87487
Chlamydia Trachomatis 87492
Cytomegalovirus 87497
Gardnerella Vaginalis 87512
Hepatitis B Virus 87517
Hepatitis C 87522
Hepatitis G 87527
Herpes Simplex Virus 87530
Herpes Virus-6 87533
HIV-1 87536
HIV-2 87539
Legionella Pneumophila 87542
Mycobacteria avium-intracellulare 87562
Mycobacteria species 87552
Mycobacteria tuberculosis 87557
Mycoplasma pneumoniae 87582
Neisseria gonorrheae 87592
Not Otherwise Specified 87799
Papillomavirus, Human 87622
Streptococcus, Group A 87652

Nucleolysis, Intervertebral Disk
See Chemonucleolysis

Nucleotidase 83915

Nursemaid Elbow 24640

Nursing Facility Discharge Services
See Discharge Services, Nursing Facility

Nursing Facility Services
Care Plan Oversight Services 99379-99380
Comprehensive Assessments
New or Established Patient 99301-99303
Discharge Services 99315-99316
Subsequent Care
New or Established Patient 99311-99313
See Domiciliary Services

Nuss Procedure
with Thoracoscopy 21743
without Thoracoscopy 21742

Nutrition Therapy
Group 97804
Home Infusion 99601-99602
Initial Assessment 97802
Reassessment 97803

Nystagmus Tests
See Vestibular Function Tests
Optokinetic 92534, 92544
Positional 92532, 92542
Spontaneous 92531, 92541

O

O2 Saturation
See Oxygen Saturation

Ober-Yount Procedure 27025
See Fasciotomy, Hip

Obliteration
Mastoid 69670

Obliteration, Total Excision of Vagina
See Excision, Vagina, Complete

Obliteration, Vaginal Vault
See Vagina, Closure

Oblongata, Medulla
See Medulla

Observation 99234-99236
See Evaluation and Management; Hospital Services

Obstetrical Care
Abortion
Induced
by Amniocentesis Injection 59850-59852
See Abortion; Cesarean Delivery; Ectopic Pregnancy
by Dilation and Curettage 59840
by Dilation and Evaluation 59841
Missed
First Trimester 59820
Second Trimester 59821
Spontaneous 59812
Therapeutic 59840-59852
Antepartum Care 59425-59426
Cesarean Delivery 59618-59622
Only 59514
Postpartum Care 59515
Routine 59510
with Hysterectomy 59525
Curettage
Hydatidiform Mole 59870
Evacuation
Hydatidiform Mole 59870
External Cephalic Version 59412
Miscarriage
Surgical Completion 59812-59821
Placenta Delivery 59414
Postpartum Care 59430, 59514
Septic Abortion 59830
Total (Global) 59400, 59610, 59618
Unlisted Services and Procedures 59898-59899
Vaginal
after Cesarean 59610-59614
Vaginal Delivery 59409-59410
Delivery after Cesarean 59610-59614

Obstruction
See Occlusion

Obstruction Clearance
Venous Access Device 36595-36596

Obstruction Colon
See Colon, Obstruction

Obturator Nerve
Avulsion 64763-64766
Incision 64763-64766
Transection 64763-64766

Obturator Prosthesis 21076
Definitive 21080
Insertion
Larynx 31527
Interim 21079

Occipital Nerve, Greater
Avulsion 64744
Incision 64744
Injection
Anesthetic 64405
Transection 64744

Occlusion
Extracranial
Intracranial 61623
Fallopian Tube
Oviduct 58615
Penis
Vein 37790
Umbilical Cord 59072

Occlusive Disease of Artery
See Repair, Artery; Revision

Occult Blood 82270
Penis
by Hemoglobin Immunoassay 82274

Occupational Therapy
Evaluation 97003-97004

Ocular Implant 65175
See Orbital Implant
Insertion
in Scleral Shell 65130
Muscles Attached 65140
Muscles, Not Attached 65135
Modification 65125
Reinsertion 65150
with Foreign Material 65155
Removal 65175

Ocular Muscle
See Eye Muscles

Ocular Orbit
See Orbit

Ocular Prostheses
See Prosthesis, Ocular

Oculomotor Muscle
See Eye Muscles

Oddi Sphincter
See Sphincter of Oddi

Odontoid Dislocation
Open Treatment/Reduction 22318
with Grafting 22319

Odontoid Fracture
Open Treatment/Reduction 22318
with Grafting 22319

Odontoid Process
Excision 22548

Oesophageal Neoplasm
See Tumor, Esophagus

Oesophageal Varices
See Esophageal Varices

Oesophagus
See Esophagus

Oestradiol
See Estradiol

Office and/or Other Outpatient Services
See History and Physical
Consultation
Confirmatory Consultations 99271-99275
Established Patient 99211-99215
New Patient 99201-99205
Normal Newborn 99432
Office Visit
Established Patient 99211-99215
New Patient 99201-99205
Outpatient Visit
Established Patient 99211-99215
New Patient 99201-99205
Prolonged Services 99354-99355

Office Medical Services
After Hours 99050-99054
Emergency Care 99058

Office or Other Outpatient Consultations
See Consultation, Office and/or Other Outpatient

Olecranon
See Elbow; Humerus; Radius; Ulna
Bursa
Arthrocentesis 20605
Cyst
Excision 24125-24126
Tumor
Cyst 24120
Excision 24125-24126

Olecranon Process
Craterization 24147
Diaphysectomy 24147
Excision 24147
Abscess 24138
Fracture
See Elbow; Humerus; Radius
Closed Treatment 24670-24675
Open Treatment 24685
Osteomyelitis 24138, 24147
Saucerization 24147
Sequestrectomy 24138

Oligoclonal Immunoglobulins .83916

Omentectomy 49255, 58950-58954
Laparotomy 58960
Oophorectomy 58943
Resection Ovarian Malignancy 58950-58954
Resection Peritoneal Malignancy . . .58950-58954
Resection Tubal Malignancy 58950-58954

Omentum
Excision 49255, 58950-58954
Flap 49904-49905
Free
with Microvascular Anastomosis . . .49906
Unlisted Services and Procedures 49999

Omphalectomy 49250

Omphalocele
Repair 49600-49611

Omphalomesenteric Duct
Excision 44800

Omphalomesenteric Duct, Persistent
See Diverticulum, Meckel's

Oncoprotein
HER-2/neu 83950

One Stage Prothrombin Time 85610-85611
See Prothrombin Time

Onychectomy
See Excision, Nails

Onychia
Drainage 10060-10061

Oocyte
Assisted Fertilization
Microtechnique 89280-89281
Biopsy 89290-89291
Cryopreservation 0059T
Culture
Extended 89272
Less than 4 Days 89250
with Co-Culture 89251
Identification
Follicular Fluid 89254
Insemination 89268
Retrieval
for In Vitro Fertilization 58970
Storage 89346
Thawing 89356

Oophorectomy .58262-58263, 58291-58292, 58552, 58554, 58661, 58940-58943
Ectopic Pregnancy
Laparoscopic Treatment 59120
Surgical Treatment 59120

Oophorectomy, Partial
See Excision, Ovary, Partial

Oophorocystectomy
See Cystectomy, Ovarian

Open Biopsy, Adrenal Gland
See Adrenal Gland, Biopsy

Operating Microscope 69990

Operation
Blalock-Hanlon
See Septostomy, Atrial
Blalock-Taussig Subclavian-Pulmonary Anastomosis
See Pulmonary Artery, Shunt, Subclavian
Borthen
See Iridotasis
Dana
See Rhizotomy
Dunn
See Arthrodesis, Foot Joint
Duvries
See Tenoplasty
Estes
See Ovary, Transposition
Foley Pyeloplasty
See Pyeloplasty
Fontan
See Repair, Heart, Anomaly
Fox
See Fox Operation
Gardner
See Meningocele Repair
Green
See Scapulopexy
Harelip
See Cleft Lip, Repair
Heine
See Cyclodialysis
Heller
See Esophagomyotomy
Iris, Inclusion
See Iridencleisis
Jaboulay Gastroduodenostomy
See Gastroduodenostomy
Johanson
See Reconstruction, Urethra
Keller
See Keller Procedure
Krause
See Gasserian Ganglion, Sensory Root, Decompression
Mumford
See Claviculectomy, Partial
Nissen
See Fundoplasty, Esophagogastric

Peet
See Nerves, Sympathectomy, Excision
Ramstedt
See Pyloromyotomy
Richardson Hysterectomy
See Hysterectomy, Abdominal, Total
Schanz
See Femur, Osteotomy
Schlatter Total Gastrectomy
See Excision, Stomach, Total
Smithwick
See Excision, Nerve, Sympathetic
Winiwarter Cholecystoenterostomy
See Anastomosis, Gallbladder to Intestines

Operation Microscopes
See Operating Microscope

Operculectomy 41821

Operculum
See Gums

Ophthalmic Mucous Membrane Test 95060
See Allergy Tests

Ophthalmology
Unlisted Services and Procedures 92499
See Ophthalmology, Diagnostic

Ophthalmology, Diagnostic
Color Vision Exam 92283
Computerized Scanning 92135
Computerized Screening 99172
Dark Adaptation 92284
Electro-oculography 92270
Electromyography, Needle 92265
Electroretinography 92275
Endoscopy 66990
Eye Exam
Established Patient 92012-92014
New Patient 92002-92004
with Anesthesia 92018-92019
Glaucoma Provocative Test 92140
Gonioscopy 92020
Ocular Photography
External 92285
Internal 92286-92287
Ophthalmoscopy 92225-92226
with Dynamometry 92260
with Fluorescein Angiography 92235
with Fluorescein Angioscopy 92230
with Fundus Photography 92250
with Indocyanine-green Angiography ..92240
Refractive Determination 92015
Sensorimotor Exam 92060
Tonography 92120
with Provocation 92130
Tonometry
Serial 92100
Visual Acuity Screen 99172-99173
Visual Field Exam 92081-92083
Visual Function Screen 99172

Ophthalmoscopy 92225-92226
See Ophthalmology, Diagnostic

Opiates 83925

Opinion, Second
See Confirmatory Consultations

Optic Nerve
Decompression 67570
with Nasal/Sinus Endoscopy 31294

Optokinetic Nystagmus Test
See Nystagmus Tests, Optokinetic

Oral Lactose Tolerance Test 82951-82953
See Glucose, Tolerance Test

Oral Mucosa
See Mouth, Mucosa

Oral Surgical Splint 21085

Orbit
See Orbital Contents; Orbital Floor; Periorbital Region
Biopsy 61332
Exploration 67450
Fine Needle Aspiration or Orbital Contents 67415
Orbitotomy without Bone Flap 67400
CT Scan 70480-70482
Decompression 61330
Bone Removal 67414, 67445
Exploration 61332, 67400, 67450
Lesion
Excision 61333
Fracture
Closed Treatment
with Manipulation 21401
without Manipulation 21400
Open Treatment 21406-21408
Blowout Fracture 21385-21395
Incision and Drainage 67405, 67440
Injection
Retrobulbar 67500-67505
Tenon's Capsule 67515
Insertion
Implant 67550
Lesion
Excision 67412, 67420
Magnetic Resonance Imaging (MRI) 70540-70543
Removal
Decompression 67445
Exploration 61334
Foreign Body 61334, 67413, 67430
Implant 67560
Sella Turcica 70482
Unlisted Services and Procedures 67599
X-Ray 70190-70200

Orbit Area
Reconstruction
Secondary 21275

Orbit Wall
Decompression
with Nasal/Sinus Endoscopy ...31292-31293

Orbital Contents
Aspiration 67415

Orbital Floor
See Orbit; Periorbital Region
Fracture
Blow Out 21385-21395

Orbital Hypertelorism
Osteotomy
Periorbital 21260-21263

Orbital Implant
See Ocular Implant
Insertion 67550
Removal 67560

Orbital Prosthesis 21077

Orbital Rim and Forehead
Reconstruction 21172-21180

Orbital Rims
Reconstruction 21182-21184

Orbital Transplant 67560

Orbital Walls
Reconstruction 21182-21184

Orbitocraniofacial Reconstruction
Secondary 21275

Orbitotomy
with Bone Flap
for Exploration 67450
Lateral Approach 67420
with Drainage 67440
with Removal Foreign Body 67430
with Removal of Bone for Decompression 67445
with Removal Foreign Body 67413
with Removal of Bone for Decompression .67414
without Bone Flap
for Exploration 67400
with Drainage Only 67405
with Removal Lesion 67412

Orchidectomies
See Excision, Testis

Orchidopexy
See Orchiopexy

Orchidoplasty
See Repair, Testis

Orchiectomy
Laparoscopic 54690
Partial 54522
Radical
Abdominal Exploration 54535
Inguinal Approach 54530
Simple 54520

Orchiopexy
Abdominal Approach 54650
Inguinal Approach 54640
Intra-Abdominal Testis 54692

Orchioplasty
See Repair, Testis

Organ Grafting
See Transplantation

Talus 28302
Tarsal 28304-28305
Tibia 27455-27457, 27705, 27709-27712
Ulna 25360
and Radius 25365, 25375
Multiple 25370
Vertebra
Additional Segment
Anterior Approach 22226
Posterior/Posterolateral Approach ..22216
Cervical
Anterior Approach 22220
Posterior/Posterolateral Approach ..22210
Lumbar
Anterior Approach 22224
Posterior/Posterolateral Approach ..22214
Thoracic
Anterior Approach 22222
Posterior/Posterolateral Approach ..22212
with Graft
Reconstruction
Periorbital Region 21267-21268

Otolaryngology
Diagnostic
Exam Under Anesthesia 92502

Otomy
See Incision

Otoplasty 69300

Otorhinolaryngology
Unlisted Services and Procedures 92700

Ouchterlony Immunodiffusion 86331

Outer Ear
See Ear, Outer

Outpatient Visit
See History and Physical; Office and/or Other Outpatient Services

Output, Cardiac
See Cardiac Output

Ova
Smear 87177

Oval Window
Repair Fistula 69666

Oval Window Fistula
See Fistula, Oval Window

Ovarian Cyst
See Cyst, Ovarian; Ovary, Cyst

Ovarian Vein Syndrome
Ureterolysis 50722

Ovariectomies
See Oophorectomy

Ovariolysis 58740

Ovary
Abscess
Incision and Drainage 58820-58822
Abdominal Approach 58822
Biopsy 58900
Cryopreservation 0058T
Cyst
Incision and Drainage 58800-58805
Excision 58662, 58720
Cyst 58925
Partial
Oophorectomy 58661, 58940
Ovarian Malignancy 58943
Peritoneal Malignancy 58943
Tubal Malignancy 58943
Wedge Resection 58920
Total 58940-58943
Laparoscopy 58660-58662, 58679
Lysis
Adhesions 58660, 58740
Radical Resection 58950-58952
Transposition 58825
Tumor
Resection 58950-58954
Unlisted Services and Procedures ..58679, 58999
Wedge Resection 58920

Oviduct
Anastomosis 58750
Chromotubation 58350
Ectopic Pregnancy 59120-59121
Excision 58700-58720
Fulguration
Laparoscopic 58670
Hysterosalpingography 74740
Laparoscopy 58679
Ligation 58600-58611
Lysis
Adhesions 58740
Occlusion 58615
Laparoscopic 58671
Repair 58752
Anastomosis 58750
Create Stoma 58770
Unlisted Services and Procedures ..58679, 58999
X-Ray with Contrast 74740

Ovocyte
See Oocyte

Ovulation Tests 84830

Ovum Implantation
See Implantation

Ovum Transfer Surgery
See GIFT

Oxalate 83945

Oxidase, Ceruloplasmin
See Ceruloplasmin

Oxidoreductase, Alcohol-Nad+
See Antidiuretic Hormone

Oximetry (Noninvasive)
See Pulmonology, Diagnostic
Blood O2 Saturation
Ear or Pulse 94760-94762

Oxoisomerase
See Phosphohexose Isomerase

Oxosteroids
See Ketosteroids

Oxycodinone 80102-80103, 83925

Oxygen Saturation 82805-82810

Oxygenation, Extracorporeal Membrane
See Extracorporeal Membrane Oxygenation

Oxyproline
See Hydroxyproline

Oxytocin Stress Test, Fetal 59020

P

P & P
See Proconvertin

P B Antibodies
See Antibody, Heterophile

P-Acetamidophenol
See Acetaminophen

Pacemaker, Heart
See Defibrillator, Heart
Conversion 33214
Electronic Analysis 93641-93642
Antitachycardia System 93724
Dual Chamber 93731-93732
Single Chamber 93734-93735
Insertion 33200-33208
Electrode 33210-33211, 33216-33217, 33224-33225
Pulse Generator Only 33212-33213
Removal 33233-33237
via Thoracotomy 33236-33237
Repair
Electrode 33218-33220
Replacement
Catheter 33210
Electrode 33210-33211, 33217
Insertion 33200-33208
Pulse Generator 33212-33213
Repositioning
Electrode 33215, 33226
Revise Pocket
Chest 33222
Telephonic Analysis 93733, 93736
Upgrade 33214

Pachymetry
Eye 75616-75619, 92136

Packing
Nasal Hemorrhage 30901-30906

Pain Management
See Injection, Chemotherapy
Epidural/Intrathecal 62351, 62360-62362, 99601-99602
Intravenous Therapy 90783-90784

Paralysis, Infantile
See Polio

Paranasal Sinuses
See Sinus; Sinuses

Parasites
Blood 87207
Examination 87169
Smear 87177

Parasitic Worms
See Helminth

Parathormone 83970

Parathyrin
See Parathormone

Parathyroid Autotransplantation 60512

Parathyroid Gland
Autotransplant 60512
Excision 60500-60502
Exploration 60500-60505
Nuclear Medicine
  Imaging 78070

Parathyroid Hormone 83970

Parathyroid Hormone Measurement
See Parathormone

Parathyroid Transplantation
See Transplantation, Parathyroid

Parathyroidectomy 60500-60505

Paraurethral Gland
Abscess
  Incision and Drainage 53060

Paravertebral Nerve
Destruction 64622-64627
Injection
  Anesthetic 64470-64484
  Neurolytic 64622-64627

Parietal Cell Vagotomies
See Vagotomy, Highly Selective

Parietal Craniotomy 61556

Paring
Skin Lesion
  Benign Hyperkeratotic
    More than Four Lesions 11057
    Single Lesion 11055
    Two to Four Lesions 11056

Paronychia
Incision and Drainage 10060-10061

Parotid Duct
Diversion 42507-42510
Reconstruction 42507-42510

Parotid Gland
Abscess
  Incision and Drainage 42300-42305
Calculi (Stone)
  Excision 42330, 42340
Excision
  Partial 42410-42415
  Total 42420-42426
Tumor
  Excision 42410-42426

Parotitides, Epidemic
See Mumps

Pars Abdominalis Aortae
See Aorta, Abdominal

Partial Colectomy
See Colectomy, Partial

Partial Cystectomy
See Cystectomy, Partial

Partial Esophagectomy
See Esophagectomy, Partial

Partial Gastrectomy
See Excision, Stomach, Partial

Partial Glossectomy
See Excision, Tongue, Partial

Partial Hepatectomy
See Excision, Liver, Partial

Partial Mastectomies
See Breast, Excision, Lesion

Partial Nephrectomy
See Excision, Kidney, Partial

Partial Pancreatectomy
See Pancreatectomy, Partial

Partial Splenectomy
See Splenectomy, Partial

Partial Thromboplastin Time
See Thromboplastin, Partial, Time

Partial Ureterectomy
See Ureterectomy, Partial

Particle Agglutination 86403-86406

Parvovirus
Antibody 86747

Patch
Allergy Tests 95044
  See Allergy Tests

Patella
See Knee
Dislocation 27560-27566
Excision 27350
  with Reconstruction 27424
Fracture 27520-27524
Reconstruction 27437-27438
Repair
  Chondromalacia 27418
  Instability 27420-27424

Patella, Chondromalacia
See Chondromalacia Patella

Patellar Tendon Bearing (PTB) Cast 29435

Patellectomy
with Reconstruction 27424

Paternity Testing 86910-86911

Patey's Operation
See Mastectomy, Radical

Pathologic Dilatation
See Dilation

Pathology
Clinical
  Consultation 80500-80502
Surgical 88355
  Consultation 88321-88325
    Intraoperative 88329-88332
  Decalcification Procedure 88311
  Electron Microscopy 88348-88349
  Gross and Micro Exam
    Level II 88302
    Level III 88304
    Level IV 88305
    Level V 88307
    Level VI 88309
  Gross Exam
    Level I 88300
  Histochemistry 88318-88319
  Immunocytochemistry 88342
  Immunofluorescent Study 88346-88347
  Morphometry
    Nerve 88356
    Skeletal Muscle 88355
    Tumor 88358-88361
  Nerve Teasing 88362
  Special Stain 88312-88314
  Staining 88312-88314
  Tissue Hybridization 88365
  Unlisted Services and Procedures 88399, 89240

Patterson's Test
See Blood Urea Nitrogen

Paul-Bunnell Test
See Antibody; Antibody Identification; Microsomal Antibody

PBG
See Porphobilinogen

PCP
See Phencyclidine

PCR
See Polymerase Chain Reaction

Peans' Operation
See Amputation, Leg, Upper, at Hip; Radical Resection; Replantation

Pectoral Cavity
See Chest Cavity

Pectus Carinatum
Reconstructive Repair 21740-21742
  with Thoracoscopy 21743

Pectus Excavatum
Reconstructive Repair 21740-21742
  with Thoracoscopy 21743

Peptide, Connecting
See C-Peptide

Peptide, Vasoactive Intestinal
See Vasoactive Intestinal Peptide

Peptidyl Dipeptidase A
See Angiotensin Converting Enzyme (ACE)

Percutaneous Abdominal Paracentesis
See Abdomen, Drainage

Percutaneous Atherectomies
See Artery, Atherectomy

Percutaneous Biopsy, Gallbladder/Bile Ducts
See Bile Duct, Biopsy

Percutaneous Discectomies
See Diskectomy, Percutaneous

Percutaneous Electric Nerve Stimulation
See Application, Neurostimulation

Percutaneous Lumbar Diskectomy 62287
See Aspiration, Nucleus of Disk, Lumbar; Puncture Aspiration

Percutaneous Lysis 62263-62264

Percutaneous Nephrostomies
See Nephrostomy, Percutaneous

Percutaneous Transluminal Angioplasty
Artery
  Aortic 35472
  Brachiocephalic 35475
  Coronary 92982-92984
  Femoral-Popliteal 35474
  Iliac 35473
  Pulmonary 92997-92998
  Renal 35471
  Tibioperoneal 35470
  Visceral 35471
Venous 35476

Percutaneous Transluminal Coronary Angioplasty
See Percutaneous Transluminal Angioplasty

Pereyra Procedure 51845, 57289, 58267, 58293

Performance Measures
ACE Inhibitor Therapy 0008F
Anginal Symptom Assessment 0009F-0010F
Antiplatelet Therapy 0011F
Beta-Blocker Therapy 0007F
Blood Pressure 0001F
Statin Therapy 0006F
Tobacco Use 0002F-0005F
  Assessment 0002F-0003F
  Counseling 0004F
  Pharmacologic Therapy 0005F

Performance Test 96100
See Physical Medicine/Therapy/Occupational Therapy
Physical Therapy 97750

Perfusion
Brain
  Imaging 0042T
Myocardial 78460-78465, 78478-78480
  Imaging 78466-78469
Positron Emission Tomography (PET)
  Myocardial Imaging 78491-78492

Perfusion Pump
See Infusion Pump

Perfusion, Intracranial Arterial
Thrombolysis 61624

Pericardectomies
See Excision, Pericardium

Pericardial Cyst
See Cyst, Pericardial

Pericardial Sac
Drainage 32659

Pericardial Window
for Drainage 33025

Pericardial Window Technic
See Pericardiostomy

Pericardiectomy
Complete 33030-33031
Subtotal 33030-33031
Total
  Endoscopic 32660

Pericardiocentesis 33010-33011
Ultrasound Guidance 76930

Pericardiostomy
Tube 33015

Pericardiotomy
Removal
  Clot 33020
  Foreign Body 33020

Pericardium
Cyst
  Excision 32661, 33050
Excision 32659, 33030-33031
Incision
  Removal
    Clot 33020
    Foreign Body 33020
  with Tube 33015
Incision and Drainage 33025
Puncture Aspiration 33010-33011
Removal
  Clot
    Endoscopic 32658
  Foreign Body
    Endoscopic 32658
Tumor
  Excision 32661, 33050

Peridural Anesthesia
See Anesthesia, Epidural

Peridural Injection
See Epidural, Injection

Perineal Prostatectomy
See Prostatectomy, Perineal

Perineoplasty 56810

Perineorrhaphy
Repair
  Rectocele 57250

Perineum
Abscess
  Incision and Drainage 56405
Colposcopy 99170
Removal
  Prosthesis 53442
Repair 56810
X-Ray with Contrast 74775

Perionychia
See Paronychia

Periorbital Region
Reconstruction
  Osteotomy with Graft 21267-21268
Repair-Osteotomy 21260-21263

Peripheral Artery Disease (PAD) Rehabilitation 93668

Peripheral Nerve
Repair/Suture
  Major 64856, 64859

Periprosthetic Capsulectomy
Breast 19371

Peristaltic Pumps
See Infusion Pump

Peritoneal Dialysis 90945-90947

Peritoneal Free Air
See Pneumoperitoneum

Peritoneal Lavage 49080

Peritoneocentesis 49080-49081

Peritoneoscopy
See Endoscopy, Peritoneum

Peritoneum
Abscess
  Incision and Drainage 49020
    Percutaneous 49021
Chemotherapy Administration 96445
  See Chemotherapy
Endoscopy
  Biopsy 47561
  Drainage
    Lymphocele 49323
  X-Ray 47560
Exchange
  Drainage Catheter 49423
Injection
  Contrast
    via Catheter 49424
Ligation
  Shunt 49428

Plexus Coeliacus
See Celiac Plexus

Plexus Lumbalis
See Lumbar Plexus

Plexus, Choroid
See Choroid Plexus

PLGN
See Plasminogen

Plication, Sphincter, Urinary Bladder
See Bladder, Repair, Neck

Pneumocentesis
Lung 32420

Pneumocisternogram
See Cisternography

Pneumococcal Vaccine
See Vaccines

Pneumocystis Carinii
Antigen Detection
  Immunofluorescence 87281

Pneumogastric Nerve
See Vagus Nerve

Pneumogram
Pediatric 94772

Pneumolysis 32940

Pneumonectomy 32440-32500
Completion 32488
Donor 32850, 33930
Sleeve 32442
Total 32440-32445

Pneumonology
See Pulmonology

Pneumonolysis 32940
Intrapleural 32652
Open Intrapleural 32124

Pneumonostomy 32200-32201

Pneumonotomy
See Incision, Lung

Pneumoperitoneum 49400

Pneumoplethysmography
Ocular 93875

Pneumothorax
Chemical Pleurodesis 32005
Pleural Scarification for Repeat 32215
Therapeutic
  Injection Intrapleural Air 32960
Thoracentesis with Tube Insertion 32002

Polio
Antibody 86658
Vaccine 90712-90713

Poliovirus Vaccine, Inactivated
See Vaccines

Pollicization
Digit 26550

Polya Gastrectomy
See Gastrectomy, Partial

Polydactylism
See Supernumerary Digit

Polydactylous Digit
Reconstruction 26587
Repair 26587

Polydactyly, Toes 28344

Polymerase Chain Reaction 83898

Polyp
Antrochoanal
  Removal 31032
Esophagus
  Ablation 43228
Nose
  Excision
    Endoscopic 31237-31240
    Extensive 30115
    Simple 30110
Sphenoid Sinus
  Removal 31051
Urethra
  Excision 53260

Polypectomy
Nose
  Endoscopic 31237
Uterus 58558

Polypeptide, Vasoactive Intestinal
See Vasoactive Intestinal Peptide

Polysomnography 95808-95811

Polyuria Test
See Water Load Test

Pomeroy's Operation
See Tubal Ligation

Pooling
Blood Products 86965

Popliteal Arteries
See Artery, Popliteal

Popliteal Synovial Cyst
See Baker's Cyst

Poradenitistras
See Lymphogranuloma Venereum

PORP (Partial Ossicular Replacement Prosthesis) 69633, 69637

Porphobilinogen
Urine 84106-84110

Porphyrin Precursors 82135

Porphyrins
Feces 84126-84127
Urine 84119-84120

Port Film 77417

Portal Vein
See Vein, Hepatic Portal

Porter-Silber Test
See Corticosteroid, Blood

Portoenterostomies, Hepatic
See Hepaticoenterostomy

Portoenterostomy 47701

Posadas-Wernicke Disease
See Coccidioidomycosis

Positional Nystagmus Test
See Nystagmus Tests, Positional

Positive End Expiratory Pressure
See Pressure Breathing, Positive

Positive-Pressure Breathing, Inspiratory
See Intermittent Positive Pressure Breathing (IPPB)

Positron Emission Tomography (PET)
Brain 78608-78609
Heart 78459
Myocardial Imaging
  Perfusion Study 78491-78492
Tumor 78810

Post-Op Visit 99024

Postauricular Fistula
See Fistula, Postauricular

Postcaval Ureter
See Retrocaval Ureter

Postmortem
See Autopsy

Postop Vas Reconstruction
See Vasovasorrhaphy

Postoperative Wound Infection
Incision and Drainage 10180

Postpartum Care
Cesarean Delivery 59515
  after Attempted Vaginal Delivery 59622
  Previous 59610, 59614-59618, 59622
Vaginal Delivery 59430
  after Previous Cesarean Delivery 59614

Potassium 84132
Urine 84133

Potential, Auditory Evoked
See Auditory Evoked Potentials

Potential, Evoked
See Evoked Potential

Potts-Smith Procedure 33762

Pouch, Kock
See Kock Pouch

PPP
See Fibrin Degradation Products

PRA
See Cytotoxic Screen

Prealbumin 84134

Prebeta Lipoproteins
See Lipoprotein, Blood

Pregl's Test
See Cystourethroscopy, Catheterization, Urethral

Pregnancy
Abortion
Induced 59855-59857
by Amniocentesis Injection 59850-59852
by Dilation and Curettage 59840
by Dilation and Evaluation 59841
Septic 59830
Therapeutic
by Dilation and Curettage 59851
by Hysterectomy 59852
by Saline 59850
Cesarean Delivery 59618-59622
Only 59514
Postpartum Care 59514-59515
Routine Care 59510
Vaginal Birth After 59610-59614
with Hysterectomy 59525
Ectopic
Abdominal 59130
Cervix 59140
Interstitial
Partial Resection Uterus 59136
Total Hysterectomy 59135
Laparoscopy
with Salpingectomy and/or Oophorectomy 59151
without Salpingectomy and/or Oophorectomy 59150
Tubal 59121
with Salpingectomy and/or Oophorectomy 59120
Miscarriage
Surgical Completion
Any Trimester 59812
First Trimester 59820
Second Trimester 59821
Molar
See Hydatidiform Mole
Multifetal Reduction 59866
Placenta Delivery 59414
Vaginal Delivery 59409-59410
after Cesarean Delivery 59610-59614
Antepartum Care 59425-59426
Postpartum Care 59430
Total Obstetrical Care ..59400, 59610, 59618

Pregnancy Test 84702-84703
Urinalysis 81025

Pregnanediol 84135

Pregnanetriol 84138

Pregnenolone 84140

Prekallikrein
See Fletcher Factor

Prekallikrein Factor 85292

Premature, Closure, Cranial Suture
See Craniosynostosis

Prenatal Procedure 59897
Amnioinfusion
Transabdominal 59070
Drainage
Fluid 59074
Occlusion
Umbilical Cord 59072
Shunt 59076

Prenatal Testing
Amniocentesis 59000
with Amniotic Fluid Reduction 59001
Chorionic Villus Sampling 59015
Cordocentesis 59012
Fetal Blood Sample 59030
Fetal Monitoring 59050
Interpretation Only 59051
Non-Stress Test, Fetal 59025, 99500
Oxytocin Stress Test 59020
Stress Test
Oxytocin 59020
Ultrasound 76801-76817
Fetal Biophysical Profile 76818-76819
Fetal Heart 76825

Prentiss Operation
See Orchiopexy, Inguinal Approach

Preparation
for Transfer
Embryo 89255
Thawing
Embryo
Cryopreserved 89352
Oocytes
Cryopreserved 89356
Reproductive Tissue
Cryopreserved 89354
Sperm
Cryopreserved 89353

Presacral Sympathectomy
See Sympathectomy, Presacral

Prescription
Contact Lens 92310-92317
See Contact Lens Services
Ocular Prosthesis 92330-92335
See Prosthesis, Ocular

Pressure Breathing
See Pulmonology, Therapeutic
Negative
Continuous (CNP) 94662
Positive
Continuous (CPAP) 94660

Pressure Measurement of Sphincter of Oddi
See Sphincter of Oddi, Pressure Measurement

Pressure Ulcer (Decubitus)
See Debridement; Skin Graft and Flap

Pressure Ulcers
Excision 15920-15999

Pressure, Blood
See Blood Pressure

Pressure, Venous
See Blood Pressure, Venous

Pretreatment
Red Blood Cell
Antibody Identification 86970-86972
Serum
Antibody Identification 86975-86978

Prevention & Control
See Prophylaxis

Preventive Medicine 99381-99397
See Immunization; Newborn Care, Normal; Office and/or Other Outpatient Services; Performance Measures, Prophylatic Treatment
Administration/Interpretation of Health Risk Assessment 99420
Counseling and/or Risk Factor Reduction Intervention 99401-99429
Group Counseling 99411-99412
Individual Counseling 99401-99404
Performance Measures 0001F-0011F
Established Patient 99382-99397
New Patient 99381-99387
Newborn Care 99432
Respiratory Pattern Recording 94772
Unlisted Services and Procedures 99429

Priapism
Repair
Fistulization 54435
with Shunt 54420-54430

Primidone
Assay 80188

PRL
See Prolactin

Pro-Insulin C Peptide
See C-Peptide

Proalbumin
See Prealbumin

Probes, DNA
See Nucleic Acid Probe

Probes, Nucleic Acid
See Nucleic Acid Probe

Procainamide
Assay 80190-80192

Procedure, Fontan
See Repair, Heart, Anomaly

Procedure, Maxillofacial
See Maxillofacial Procedures

Process, Odontoid
See Odontoid Process

Procidentia
Rectum
Excision 45130-45135
Repair 45900

Procoagulant Activity, Glomerular
See Thromboplastin

Proconvertin .85230

Proctectasis
See Dilation, Rectum

Proctectomy
Partial .45111, 45113-45116, 45123
Total .45110, 45112, 45119-45120
with Colon .45121
with Ileostomy .44212

Proctocele
See Rectocele

Proctopexy .45540-45541
with Sigmoid Excision .45550

Proctoplasty .45500-45505

Proctorrhaphy
See Rectum, Suture

Proctoscopies
See Anoscopy

Proctosigmoidoscopy
Ablation
Polyp or Lesion .45320
Biopsy .45305
Destruction
Tumor .45320
Dilation .45303
Exploration .45300
Hemorrhage Control .45317
Placement
Stent .45327
Removal
Foreign Body .45307
Polyp .45308-45315
Tumor .45315
Volvulus Repair .45321

Products, Gene
See Protein

Proetz Therapy
Nose .30210

Profibrinolysin
See Plasminogen

Progenitor Cell
See Stem Cell

Progesterone .84144

Progesterone Receptors .84234

Progestin Receptors
See Progesterone Receptors

Proinsulin .84206

Projective Test .96100

Prokallikrein
See Fletcher Factor

Prokallikrein, Plasma
See Fletcher Factor

Prokinogenase
See Fletcher Factor

Prolactin .80418, 80440, 84146

Prolapse
See Procidentia

Prolapse, Rectal
See Procidentia, Rectum

Prolastin
See Alpha-1 Antitrypsin

Prolonged Services .99354-99357, 99360
without Direct Patient Contact .99358-99359

Prophylactic Treatment
See Preventive Medicine
Femur .27495
Pinning .27187
Humerus
Pinning, Wiring .24498
Radius .25490, 25492
Nailing .25490, 25492
Pinning .25490, 25492
Plating .25490, 25492
Wiring .25490, 25492
Shoulder
Clavicle .23490
Humerus .23491
Tibia .27745
Ulna .25491-25492
Nailing .25491-25492
Pinning .25491-25492
Plating .25491-25492
Wiring .25491-25492

Prophylaxis
Retina
Detachment
Cryotherapy, Diathermy .67141
Photocoagulation .67145

Prostaglandin .84150
Insertion .59200

Prostanoids
See Prostaglandin

Prostate
Ablation
Cryosurgery .55873
Abscess
Drainage .52700
Incision and Drainage .55720-55725
Biopsy .55700-55705
Brachytherapy
Needle Insertion .55859
Coagulation
Laser .52647
Destruction
Cryosurgery .55873
Thermotherapy .53850-53853
Microwave .53850
Radio Frequency .53852
Excision
Partial .55801, 55821-55831
Perineal .55801-55815
Radical .55810-55815, 55840-55845
Retropubic .55831-55845
Suprapubic .55821
Transurethral .52601, 52612-52614
Exploration
Exposure .55860
with Nodes .55862-55865
Incision
Exposure .55860-55865
Transurethral .52450
Insertion
Radioactive Substance .55860
Needle Biopsy .55700
Thermotherapy
Transurethral .53850-53853
Ultrasound .76872-76873
Unlisted Services and Procedures .55899
Urinary System .53899
Urethra
Transurethral Balloon Dilation .52510
Vaporization
Laser .52648

Prostate Specific Antigen .84152-84154

Prostatectomy .52601
Laparascopic .55866
Perineal
Partial .55801
Radical .55810-55815
Retropubic
Partial .55831
Radical .55840-55845, 55866
Suprapubic
Partial .55821
Transurethral .52612-52614

Prostatic Abscess
See Abscess, Prostate

Prostatotomy .55720-55725

Prosthesis
Augmentation
Mandibular Body .21125
Auricular .21086
Breast
Insertion .19340-19342
Removal .19328-19330
Supply .19396
Check-Out .97703
See Physical Medicine/Therapy/Occupational Therapy
Cornea .65770
Facial .21088
Hernia
Mesh .49568
Hip
Removal .27090-27091
Intestines .44700
Knee
Insertion .27438, 27445
Lens
Insertion .66982-66985
Manual or Mechanical Technique .66982-66984
Not Associated with Concurrent Cataract Removal .66985
Mandibular Resection .21081
Nasal .21087
Nasal Septum
Insertion .30220

Pubis
Craterization 27070
Cyst
  Excision 27065-27067
Excision 27070
Saucerization 27070
Tumor
  Excision 27065-27067

Pudendal Nerve
Avulsion 64761
Destruction 64630
Incision 64761
Injection
  Anesthetic 64430
  Neurolytic 64630
Transection 64761

Puestow Procedure 48180

Pulled Elbow
See Nursemaid Elbow

Pulmonary Artery 33690
Catheterization
  See Catheterization, Pulmonary Artery
Embolism 33910-33916
  Excision 33910-33916
Percutaneous Transluminal
Angioplasty 92997-92998
Reimplantation 33788
Repair 33690, 33917-33920
  Reimplantation 33788
Shunt
  from Aorta 33755-33762, 33924
  from Vena Cava 33766-33767
  Subclavian 33750
Transection 33922

Pulmonary Function Test
See Pulmonology, Diagnostic

Pulmonary Haemorrhage
See Hemorrhage, Lung

Pulmonary Perfusion Imaging
Nuclear Medicine 78588

Pulmonary Valve
Incision 33470-33474
Repair 33470-33474
Replacement 33475

Pulmonary Vein
Repair 33730

Pulmonology
Diagnostic
  Airway Closing Volume 94370
  Bronchodilation 94664
  Carbon Dioxide Response Curve 94400
  Carbon Monoxide Diffusion Capacity .. 94720
  Expired Gas Analysis 0043T, 94250
    CO2 94770
    O2 and CO2 94681
    O2 Update, Direct 94680
    O2 Uptake, Indirect 94690
  Flow-Volume Loop 94375
  Function Study 78596
  Functional Residual Capacity 94240
  Hemoglobin O2 Affinity 82820
  Hypoxia Response Curve 94450
  Inhalation Treatment 94640
  Maldistribution of Inspired Air 94350
  Maximum Breathing Capacity 94200
  Maximum Voluntary Ventilation 94200
  Membrane Compliance 94750
  Membrane Diffusion Capacity 94725
  Nitrogen Washout Curve 94350
  Oximetry
    Ear or Pulse 94760-94762
  Resistance to Airflow 94360
  Spirometry 94010-94070
    Evaluation 94010-94070
    Patient Initiated with
    Bronchospasm 94014-94016
  Sputum Mobilization with
  Inhalants 94664
  Stress Test 94621
  Stress Test, Pulmonary 94620
  Thoracic Gas Volume 94260
Therapeutic
  Expired Gas Analysis 94250
  Inhalation
    Pentamidine 94642
  Inhalation Treatment .. 94640, 94664, 99503
  Manipulation of Chest Wall 94667-94668
  Pressure Ventilation
    Negative CNPB 94662
    Positive CPAP 94660
  Unlisted Services and Procedures 94799
  Ventilation Assist 94656-94657, 99504
Unlisted Services and Procedures 94799

Pulse Generator
Electronic Analysis 95970-95971
Heart
  Insertion/Replacement 33212-33213

Pulse Rate Increased
See Tachycardia

Pulsed Magnetic Neuromodulation
Urinary Incontinence 0029T

Pump
See Chemotherapy, Pump Services; Infusion Pump

Pump Services
Oxygenator/Heat Exchanger 99190-99192

Pump Stomach for Poison 91105

Pump, Infusion
See Infusion Pump

Punch Graft 15775-15776

Puncture
Artery 36600
Chest
  Drainage 32000-32002
Cisternal
  See Cisternal Puncture
Lumbar
  See Spinal Tap
Lung 32420
Pericardium 33010-33011
Pleural Cavity
  Drainage 32000-32002
Skull
  Drain Fluid 61000-61020
    Cistern 61050
  Inject Cistern 61055
  Inject Ventricle 61026
  Shunt
    Drain Fluid 61070
    Injection 61070
Spinal Cord
  Diagnostic 62270
  Drain Fluid 62272
  Lumbar 62270
Tracheal
  Aspiration and/or Injection 31612

Puncture Aspiration
Abscess
  Skin 10160
Bulla 10160
Cyst
  Breast 19000-19001
  Skin 10160
Hematoma 10160

Puncturing
See Puncture

Pure-Tone Audiometry
See Audiometry, Pure Tone

Pustules
Removal 10040

Putti-Platt Procedure 23450

PUVA
See Dermatology; Photochemotherapy; Ultraviolet Light Therapy

Pyelogram
See Urography, Intravenous; Urography, Retrograde

Pyelography 74400, 74425
Injection 50394

Pyelolithotomy 50130
Anatrophic 50075
Coagulum 50130

Pyeloplasty 50400-50405, 50544
Repair
  Horseshoe Kidney 50540
Secondary 50405

Pyeloscopy
with Cystourethroscopy 52351
  Biopsy 52354
  Destruction 52354
  Lithotripsy 52353
  Removal
    Calculus 52352
  Tumor Excision 52355

Pyelostogram 50394

Pyelostolithotomy
Percutaneous 50080-50081

Pyelostomy 50125, 50400-50405
Change Tube 50398

Q

R

Radioactive Substance
Insertion
  Kidney 50578
  Prostate 55860
  Ureteral Endoscopic 50978
  Urethral Endoscopic 50959

Radiocarpal Joint
Arthrotomy 25040
Dislocation
  Closed Treatment 25660

Radiocinematographies
See Cineradiography

Radioelement
Application 77761-77778
  Surface 77789
  with Ultrasound 76965
Handling 77790
Infusion 77750

Radioelement Substance
Catheter Placement
  Bronchus 31643
Catheterization 55859

Radiography
See Radiology, Diagnostic; X-Ray

Radioimmunosorbent Test
See Gammaglobulin, Blood

Radioisotope Brachytherapy
See Brachytherapy

Radioisotope Scan
See Nuclear Medicine

Radiological Marker
Preoperative Placement
  Excision of Breast Lesion 19125-19126

Radiology
Diagnostic
  Unlisted Services and Procedures 76499
Examination 70030
  Stress Views 76006
Therapeutic
  See Specific Procedure
  Field Set-up 77280-77290
  Planning 77261-77263, 77299
  Port Film 77417

Radionuclide CT Scan
See Emission Computerized Tomography

Radionuclide Imaging
See Nuclear Medicine

Radionuclide Therapy
Intra-articular 79440
Intravascular 79420
Intravenous Infusion 79403
Leukemia 79100
Other 79400
Polycythemia Vera 79100
Thyroid Gland 79000-79035
Unlisted Services and Procedures 79999

Radionuclide Tomography, Single-Photon Emission-Computed
See SPECT

Radiopharmaceutical Therapy
Heart 79440
Intravascular 79420
Intravenous Infusion 79403
Leukemia 79100
Other 79400
Polycythemia Vera 79100
Thyroid Gland 79020-79035
Unlisted Services and Procedures 79999

Radiotherapeutic
See Radiation Therapy

Radiotherapies
See Irradiation

Radiotherapy, Surface
See Application, Radioelement, Surface

Radioulnar Joint
Arthrodesis
  with Resection of Ulna 25830
Dislocation
  Closed Treatment 25675
  Open Treatment 25676
  Percutaneous Fixation 25671

Radius
See Arm, Lower; Elbow; Ulna
Arthroplasty 24365
  with Implant 24366, 25441
Craterization 24145, 25151
Cyst
  Excision 24125-24126, 25120-25126
Diaphysectomy 24145, 25151
Dislocation
  Partial 24640
  Subluxate 24640
  with Fracture
    Closed Treatment 24620
    Open Treatment 24635
Excision 24130, 24136, 24145, 24152-24153
  Epiphyseal Bar 20150
  Partial 25145
  Styloid Process 25230
Fracture 25605
  Closed Treatment 25500-25505, 25520, 25600-25605
    with Manipulation 25605
    without Manipulation 25600
  Distal 25600-25611
    Open Treatment 25620
  Head/Neck
    Closed Treatment 24650-24655
    Open Treatment 24665-24666
  Open Treatment 25515, 25525-25526, 25574
  Percutaneous Fixation 25611
  Shaft 25500-25526
    Open Treatment 25574
  with Ulna 25560-25565
    Open Treatment 25575
Implant
  Removal 24164
Incision and Drainage 25035
Osteomyelitis 24136, 24145
Osteoplasty 25390-25393
Prophylactic Treatment 25490, 25492
Repair
  Epiphyseal Arrest 25450-25455
  Epiphyseal Separation
    Closed 25600
    Closed with Manipulation 25605
    Open Treatment 25620
    Percutaneous Fixation 25611
  Malunion or Nonunion 25400, 25415
  Osteotomy 25350-25355, 25370-25375
    and Ulna 25365
  with Graft 25405, 25420-25426
Saucerization 24145, 25151
Sequestrectomy 24136, 25145
Tumor
  Cyst 24120
  Excision ..24125-24126, 25120-25126, 25170

Ramstedt Operation
See Pyloromyotomy

Ramus Anterior, Nervus Thoracicus
See Intercostal Nerve

Range of Motion Test
Extremities or Trunk 95851
Eye 92018-92019
Hand 95852

Rapid Heart Rate
See Tachycardia

Rapid Plasma Reagin Test 86592-86593

Rapid Test for Infection 86308, 86403-86406
Monospot Test 86308

Rapoport Test 52005

Raskind Procedure 33735-33737

Rat Typhus
See Murine Typhus

Rathke Pouch Tumor
See Craniopharyngioma

Rays, Roentgen
See X-Ray

Raz Procedure 51845
See Repair, Bladder, Neck

RBC
See Red Blood Cell (RBC)

RBC ab
See Antibody, Red Blood Cell

Reaction
Lip
  without Reconstruction 40530

Reaction, Polymerase Chain
See Polymerase Chain Reaction

Rectal Bleeding

Rectal Prolapse

Rectal Sphincter

Rectocele

Rectopexy

Rectoplasty

Rectorrhaphy

Rectovaginal Fistula

Rectovaginal Hernia

Rectum

Red Blood Cell (RBC)

Red Blood Cell ab

Reductase, Glutathione

Reductase, Lactic Cytochrome

Reduction

Repeat Surgeries

Replacement

Replantation

Report Preparation

Reposition

Repositioning

Reproductive Tissue

Reprogramming

Reptilase Test

Reptilase Time

Resection

Tarsal 28171
Tibia 27645
Ribs 32900
Synovial Membrane
See Synovectomy
Temporal Bone 69535
Ulna
Arthrosedis
Radioulnar Joint 25830
Ureterocele
Ectopic 52301
Orthotopic 52300
Vena Cava
with Reconstruction 37799

Resonance Spectroscopy, Magnetic
See Magnetic Resonance Spectroscopy

Respiration, Positive-Pressure
See Pressure Breathing, Positive

Respiratory Pattern Recording
Preventive
Infant 94772

Respiratory Syncytial Virus
Antibody 86756
Antigen Detection
Direct Fluorescence 87280
Enzyme Immunoassay 87420

Respiratory Syncytial Virus Immune Globulin
See Immune Globulins
Antigen Detection
See Immune Globulins, Respiratory Syncytial Virus

Response, Auditory Evoked
See Auditory Evoked Potentials

Rest Home Visit
See Domiciliary Services

Resuscitation
Cardiac
See Cardiac Massage
Cardio-Pulmonary
See Cardio-Pulmonary Resuscitation
Newborn 99440

Reticulocyte
Count 85044-85045

Retina
Incision
Encircling Material 67115
Lesion
Extensive
Destruction 67227-67228
Localized
Destruction 0017T, 67208-67218
Repair
Detachment
by Scleral Buckling 67112
Cryotherapy or Diathermy 67101
Injection of Air 67110
Photocoagulation 67105
Scleral Dissection 67107
with Vitrectomy 67108, 67112
Prophylaxis
Detachment 67141-67145
Retinopathy
Destruction
Cryotherapy, Diathermy 67227
Photocoagulation 67228

Retinacular
Knee
Release 27425

Retinopathy
Destruction
Cryotherapy, Diathermy 67227
Photocoagulation 67228

Retraction, Clot
See Clot Retraction

Retrieval
Transcatheter Foreign Body 37203

Retrocaval Ureter
Ureterolysis 50725

Retrograde Cholangiopancreatographies, Endoscopic
See Cholangiopancreatography

Retrograde Cystourethrogram
See Urethrocystography, Retrograde

Retrograde Pyelogram
See Urography, Retrograde

Retroperitoneal Area
Abscess
Incision and Drainage
Open 49060
Percutaneous 49061
Biopsy 49010
Cyst
Destruction/Excision 49200-49201
Endometriomas
Destruction/Excision 49200-49201
Exploration 49010
Needle Biopsy
Mass 49180
Tumor
Destruction/Excision 49200-49201

Retroperitoneal Fibrosis
Ureterolysis 50715

Retropubic Prostatectomies
See Prostatectomy, Retropubic

Revascularization
Distal Upper Extremity
with Interval Ligation 36838
Interval Ligation
Distal Upper Extremity 36838
Penis 37788
Transmyocardial 33140-33141

Reversal, Vasectomy
See Vasovasorrhaphy

Reverse T3
See Triiodothyronine, Reverse

Reverse Triiodothyronine
See Triiodothyronine, Reverse

Revision
See Reconstruction
Aorta 33404
Atrial 33253
Blepharoplasty 15820-15823
Bronchus 32501
Bypass Graft
Vein Patch 35685
Cervicoplasty 15819
Colostomy
See Colostomy, Revision
Cornea
Prosthesis 65770
Reshaping
Epikeratoplasty 65767
Keratomileusis 65760
Keratophakia 65765
Defibrillator Site
Chest 33223
Ear, Middle 69662
External Fixation System 20693
Eye
Aqueous Shunt 66185
Gastrostomy Tube 44373
Hip Replacement
See Replacement, Hip, Revision
Hymenal Ring 56700
Ileostomy
See Ileostomy, Revision
Infusion Pump
Intraarterial 36261
Intravenous 36576-36578, 36582-36583
Iris
Iridoplasty 66762
Iridotomy 66761
Jejunostomy Tube 44373
Lower Extremity Arterial Bypass 35879-35881
Pacemaker Site
Chest 33222
Rhytidectomy 15824-15829
Semicircular Canal
Fenestration 69840
Shunt
Intrahepatic Portosystemic 37183
Sling 53442
Stapedectomy
See Stapedectomy, Revsion
Stomach
for Obesity 43848
Tracheostomy
Scar 31830
Urinary-Cutaneous Anastomosis 50727-50728
Vagina
Sling
Stress Incontinence 57287
Venous Access Device 36576-36578, 36582-36583, 36585
Ventricle
Ventriculomyectomy 33416
Ventriculomyotomy 33416

Rh (D)
See Blood Typing

Rh Immune Globulin
See Immune Globulins, Rho (D)

S

Parotid
  Abscess ... 42300-42305
Unlisted Services and Procedures ... 42699
X-Ray ... 70380-70390
  with Contrast ... 70390

Salmonella
Antibody ... 86768

Salpingectomy ... 58262-58263, 58291-58292, 58552, 58554, 58661, 58700
Ectopic Pregnancy
  Laparoscopic Treatment ... 59151
  Surgical Treatment ... 59120
Oophorectomy ... 58943

Salpingo-Oophorectomy ... 58720
Resection Ovarian Malignancy ... 58950-58954
Resection Peritoneal Malignancy ... 58950-58954
Resection Tubal Malignancy ... 58950-58954

Salpingohysterostomy
See Implantation, Tubouterine

Salpingolysis ... 58740

Salpingoneostomy ... 58673, 58770

Salpingoplasty
See Fallopian Tube, Repair

Salpingostomy ... 58673, 58770
Laparoscopic ... 58673

Salter Osteotomy of the Pelvis
See Osteotomy, Pelvis

Sampling
See Biopsy; Brush Biopsy; Needle Biopsy

Sang-Park Procedure ... 33735-33737

Sao Paulo Typhus
See Rocky Mountain Spotted Fever

Saucerization
Calcaneus ... 28120
Clavicle ... 23180
Femur ... 27070, 27360
Fibula ... 27360, 27641
Hip ... 27070
Humerus ... 23184, 24140
Ileum ... 27070
Metacarpal ... 26230
Metatarsal ... 28122
Olecranon Process ... 24147
Phalanges
  Finger ... 26235-26236
  Toe ... 28124
Pubis ... 27070
Radius ... 24145, 25151
Scapula ... 23182
Talus ... 28120
Tarsal ... 28122
Tibia ... 27360, 27640
Ulna ... 24147, 25150

Saundby Test
See Blood, Feces

Scabies
See Tissue, Examination for Ectoparasites

Scalenotomy
See Muscle Division, Scalenus Anticus

Scalenus Anticus
Division ... 21700-21705

Scaling
See Exfoliation

Scalp
Tumor Resection
  Radical ... 21015

Scalp Blood Sampling ... 59030

Scan
See Specific Site, Nuclear Medicine
Abdomen
  See Abdomen, CT Scan
CT
  See CT Scan
MRI
  See Magnetic Resonance Imaging
PET
  See Positron Emission Tomography
Radionuclide
  See Emission Computerized Tomography

Scanning, Radioisotope
See Nuclear Medicine

Scanogram ... 76040

Scaphoid
Fracture
  Closed Treatment ... 25622
  Open Treatment ... 25628
  with Manipulation ... 25624

Scapula
Craterization ... 23182
Cyst
  Excision ... 23140
    with Allograft ... 23146
    with Autograft ... 23145
Diaphysectomy ... 23182
Excision ... 23172, 23190
  Partial ... 23182
Fracture
  Closed Treatment
    with Manipulation ... 23575
    without Manipulation ... 23570
  Open Treatment ... 23585
Ostectomy ... 23190
Repair
  Fixation ... 23400
  Scapulopexy ... 23400
Saucerization ... 23182
Sequestrectomy ... 23172
Tumor
  Excision ... 23140, 23210
    with Allograft ... 23146
    with Autograft ... 23145
  Radical Resection ... 23210
X-Ray ... 73010

Scapulopexy ... 23400

Scarification
Pleural ... 32215

Scarification of Pleura
See Pleurodesis

Schanz Operation
See Femur, Osteotomy

Schauta Operation
See Hysterectomy, Vaginal, Radical

Schede Procedure ... 32905-32906

Scheie Procedure
See Iridectomy

Schilling Test ... 78270
See Vitamin B-12 Absorption Study

Schlatter Operation Total Gastrectomy
See Excision, Stomach, Total

Schlicter Test ... 87197
See Bactericidal Titer, Serum

Schocket Procedure ... 66180
See Aqueous Shunt

Schonbein Test
See Blood, Feces

Schuchard Procedure
Osteotomy
  Maxilla ... 21206

Schwannoma, Acoustic
See Brain, Tumor, Excision

Sciatic Nerve
Decompression ... 64712
Injection
  Anesthetic ... 64445-64446
Lesion
  Excision ... 64786
Neuroma
  Excision ... 64786
Neuroplasty ... 64712
Release ... 64712
Repair/Suture ... 64858

Scintigraphy
See Nuclear Medicine
Computed Tomographic
  See Emission Computerized Tomography

Scissoring
Skin Tags ... 11200-11201

Sclera
Excision
  Sclerectomy with Punch or Scissors ... 66160
Fistulization
  Iridencleisis or Iridotasis ... 66165
  Sclerectomy with Punch or Scissors with Iridectomy ... 66160
  Thermocauterization with Iridectomy ... 66155
  Trabeculectomy ab Externo in Absence of Previous Surgery ... 66170
  Trephination with Iridectomy ... 66150
Incision
  Fistulization
    Iridencleisis or Iridotasis ... 66165
    Sclerectomy with Punch or Scissors with Iridectomy ... 66160

Thermocauterization with Iridectomy 66155
Trabeculectomy ab Externo in Absence of Previous Surgery ...66170
Trephination with Iridectomy ...66150
Lesion
Excision ...66130
Repair
Reinforcement
with Graft ...67255
without Graft ...67250
Staphyloma
with Graft ...66225
without Graft ...66220
with Glue ...65286
Wound
Operative ...66250
Tissue Glue ...65286

Scleral Buckling Operation
See Retina, Repair, Detachment

Scleral Ectasia
See Staphyloma, Sclera

Sclerectomy ...66160

Sclerotherapy
Venous ...36468-36471

Sclerotomy
See Incision, Sclera

Screening, Drug
See Drug Screen

Scribner Cannulization ...36810

Scrotal Varices
See Varicocele

Scrotoplasty ...55175-55180

Scrotum
Abscess
Incision and Drainage ...54700, 55100
Excision ...55150
Exploration ...55110
Hematoma
Incision and Drainage ...54700
Removal
Foreign Body ...55120
Repair ...55175-55180
Ultrasound ...76870
Unlisted Services and Procedures ...55899

Scrub Typhus ...86000

Second Look Surgery
See Reoperation

Second Opinion
See Confirmatory Consultations

Section
See Decompression
Cesarean
See Cesarean Delivery
Cranial Nerve ...61460
Spinal Access ...63191
Dentate Ligament ...63180-63182
Gasserian Ganglion
Sensory Root ...61450
Medullary Tract ...61470
Mesencephalic Tract ...61480
Nerve Root ...63185-63190
Spinal Accessory Nerve ...63191
Spinal Cord Tract ...63194-63199
Tentorium Cerebelli ...61440
Vestibular Nerve
Transcranial Approach ...69950
Translabyrinthine Approach ...69915

Sedation
with or without Analgesia ...99141-99142

Seddon-Brookes Procedure ...24320

Sedimentation Rate
Blood Cell
Automated ...85652
Manual ...85651

Segmentectomy
Lung ...32484

Seidlitz Powder Test
See X-Ray, with Contrast

Selective Cellular Enhancement Technique ...88112

Selenium ...84255

Self Care
See Physical Medicine/Therapy/Occupational Therapy
Training ...97535, 99509

Sella Turcica
CT Scan ...70480-70482
X-Ray ...70240

Semen
See Sperm

Semen Analysis ...89300-89321
Sperm Analysis
Antibodies ...89325
with Sperm Isolation ...89260-89261

Semenogelase
See Antigen, Prostate Specific

Semicircular Canal
Incision
Fenestration ...69820
Revised ...69840

Semilunar
Bone
See Lunate
Ganglion
See Gasserian Ganglion

Seminal Vesicle
Cyst
Excision ...55680
Excision ...55650
Incision ...55600-55605
Mullerian Duct
Excision ...55680
Unlisted Services and Procedures ...55899

Seminal Vesicles
Vesiculography ...74440
X-Ray with Contrast ...74440

Seminin
See Antigen, Prostate Specific

Semiquantitative ...81005

Sengstaaken Tamponade
Esophagus ...43460

Senning Procedure ...33774-33777
See Repair, Great Arteries; Revision

Senning Type ...33774-33777

Sensitivity Study
Antibiotic
Agar ...87181
Disc ...87184
Enzyme Detection ...87185
Macrobroth ...87188
MIC ...87186
Microtiter ...87186
MLC ...87187
Mycobacteria ...87190
Antiviral Drugs
HIV-1
Tissue Culture ...87904

Sensor, Fetal Oximetry
Insertion
Cervix ...0021T
Vagina ...0021T

Sensorimotor Exam ...92060

Sensory Nerve
Common
Repair/Suture ...64834

Sentinel Node
Injection Procedure ...38792

Separation
Craniofacial
Closed Treatment ...21431
Open Treatment ...21432-21436

Septal Defect
Repair ...33813-33814

Septectomy
Atrial ...33735-33737
Balloon (Rashkind Type) ...92992
Blade Method (Park) ...92993
Closed
See Septostomy, Atrial
Submucous Nasal
See Nasal Septum, Submucous Resection

Septic Abortion
See Abortion, Septic

Septoplasty ...30520

Septostomy
Atrial ...33735-33737
Balloon (Rashkind Type) ...92992
Blade Method (Park) ...92993

Septum, Nasal
See Nasal Septum

Sequestrectomy
Carpal . . . 25145
Clavicle . . . 23170
Humeral Head . . . 23174
Humerus . . . 24134
Olecranon Process . . . 24138
Radius . . . 24136, 25145
Scapula . . . 23172
Skull . . . 61501
Ulna . . . 24138, 25145

Serialography
Aorta . . . 75625

Serodiagnosis, Syphilis
See Serologic Test for Syphilis

Serologic Test for Syphilis . . . 86592-86593

Seroma
Incision and Drainage
  Skin . . . 10140

Serotonin . . . 84260

Serum
Albumin
  See Albumin, Serum
Antibody Identification
  Pretreatment . . . 86975-86978
CPK
  See Creatine Kinase, Total
Serum Immune Globulin . . . 90281-90283

Sesamoid Bone
Excision . . . 28315
Finger
  Excision . . . 26185
Foot
  Fracture . . . 28530-28531
Thumb
  Excision . . . 26185

Sesamoidectomy
Toe . . . 28315

Sever Procedure
See Contracture, Palm, Release

Severing of Blepharorrhaphy
See Tarsorrhaphy, Severing

Sex Change Operation
Female to Male . . . 55980
Male to Female . . . 55970

Sex Chromatin
See Barr Bodies

Sex Chromatin Identification . . . 88130-88140

Sex Hormone Binding Globulin . . . 84270

Sex-Linked Ichthyoses
See Syphilis Test

SGOT . . . 84450

SGPT . . . 84460

Shaving
Skin Lesion . . . 11300-11313

SHBG
See Sex Hormone Binding Globulin

Shelf Procedure
See Osteotomy, Hip

Shiga-like Toxin
Antigen Detection
  Enzyme Immunoassay . . . 87427

Shigella
Antibody . . . 86771

Shirodkar Operation
See Repair, Cervix, Cerclage, Abdominal

Shock Wave (Extracorporeal) Therapy . . . 0019T-0020T

Shock Wave Lithotripsy . . . 50590

Shock Wave, Ultrasonic
See Ultrasound

Shop Typhus of Malaya
See Murine Typhus

Shoulder
See Clavicle; Scapula
Abscess
  Drainage . . . 23030
Amputation . . . 23900-23921
Arthrocentesis . . . 20610
Arthrodesis . . . 23800
  with Autogenous Graft . . . 23802
Arthrography
  Injection
    Radiologic . . . 23350
Arthroscopy
  Diagnostic . . . 29805
  Surgical . . . 29806-29827
Arthrotomy
  with Removal Loose or Foreign Body . . . 23107
Biopsy
  Deep . . . 23066
  Soft Tissue . . . 23065
Blade
  See Scapula
Bone
  Excision
    Acromion . . . 23130
    Clavicle . . . 23120-23125
  Incision . . . 23035
  Tumor
    Excision . . . 23140-23146
Bursa
  Drainage . . . 23031
Capsular Contracture Release . . . 23020
Cast
  Figure Eight . . . 29049
  Removal . . . 29710
  Spica . . . 29055
  Velpeau . . . 29058
Disarticulation . . . 23920-23921
Dislocation
  Closed Treatment
    with Manipulation . . . 23650-23655
Exploration . . . 23107
Hematoma
  Drainage . . . 23030
Manipulation
  Application of Fixation Apparatus . . . 23700
Prophylactic Treatment . . . 23490-23491
Radical Resection . . . 23077
Removal
  Calcareous Deposits . . . 23000
  Cast . . . 29710
  Foreign Body
    Complicated . . . 23332
    Deep . . . 23331
    Subcutaneous . . . 23330
  Foreign or Loose Body . . . 23107
Repair
  Capsule . . . 23450-23466
  Ligament Release . . . 23415
  Muscle Transfer . . . 23395-23397
  Rotator Cuff . . . 23410-23420
  Tendon . . . 23410-23412, 23430-23440
  Tenomyotomy . . . 23405-23406
Strapping . . . 29240
Surgery
  Unlisted Services and Procedures . . . 23929
Tumor
  Excision . . . 23075-23077
Unlisted Services and Procedures . . . 23929
X-Ray . . . 73020-73030
X-Ray with Contrast . . . 73040

Shoulder Joint
See Clavicle; Scapula
Arthroplasty
  with Implant . . . 23470-23472
Arthrotomy
  with Biopsy . . . 23100-23101
  with Synovectomy . . . 23105-23106
Dislocation
  Open Treatment . . . 23660
  with Greater Tuberosity Fracture
    Closed Treatment . . . 23665
    Open Treatment . . . 23670
  with Surgical or Anatomical Neck Fracture
    Closed Treatment with Manipulation 23675
    Open Treatment . . . 23680
Excision
  Torn Cartilage . . . 23101
Exploration . . . 23040-23044
Incision and Drainage . . . 23040-23044
Removal
  Foreign Body . . . 23040-23044
X-Ray . . . 73050

Shunt(s)
Aqueous
  to Extraocular Reservoir . . . 66180
    Revision . . . 66185
Arteriovenous
  See Arteriovenous Shunt
Brain
  Creation . . . 62180-62223
  Removal . . . 62256-62258
  Replacement . . . 62160, 62194, 62225-62230, 62258
  Reprogramming . . . 62252

Skeletal Fixation
Humeral Epicondyle
Percutaneous 24566

Skeletal Traction
Insertion/Removal
Pin/Wire 20650

Skene's Gland
Abscess
Incision and Drainage 53060
Destruction 53270
Excision 53270

Skilled Nursing Facilities (SNFs)
See Nursing Facility Services

Skin
Abrasion 15786-15787
Chemical Peel 15788-15793
Dermabrasion 15780-15783
Salabrasion 15810-15811
Abscess
See Abscess, Skin
Adjacent Tissue Transfer 14000-14350
Allografts
See Allograft, Skin
Biopsy 11100-11101
Chemical Exfoliation 17360
Cyst
See Cyst, Skin
Debridement 11000-11044
Eczematous 11000-11001
Full Thickness 11041
Infected 11000-11001
Partial Thickness 11040
Subcutaneous Tissue 11042-11044
with Open Fracture and/or Dislocation 11010-11012
Decubitus Ulcer(s)
See Pressure Ulcer (Decubitus)
Desquamation
See Exfoliation
Destruction
Benign Lesions
Fifteen or More Lesions 17004
First Lesion 17000
Two - Fourteen Lesions 17003
Flat Warts 17110-17111
Lesions 17106-17108
Malignant Lesions 17260-17286
by Photodynamic Therapy 96567
Premalignant Lesions
by Photodynamic Therapy 96567
Fifteen or More Lesions 17004
First Lesion 17000
Two - Fourteen Lesions 17003
Excision
Debridement 11000-11044
Excess Skin 15831-15839
Hemangioma 11400-11446
Lesion
Benign 11400-11446
Malignant 11600-11646
Expanders
See Tissue, Expander
Fasciocutaneous Flaps 15732-15738
Grafts
Free 15000-15400, 15757
Homografts
See Homograft, Skin
Incision and Drainage 10040-10180
See Incision, Skin
Lesion
See Lesion; Tumor
Verrucous
See Warts
Muscle Flaps 15732-15738
Myocutaneous Flaps 15732-15738
Nose
Surgical Planing 30120
Paring 11055-11057
Photography
Diagnostic 0044T, 0045T
Removal
Skin Tags 11200-11201
Revision
Blepharoplasty 15820-15823
Cervicoplasty 15819
Rhytidectomy 15824-15829
Shaving 11300-11313
Tags
Removal 11200-11201
Tests
See Allergy Tests
Candida 86485
Coccidioidomycosis 86490
Histoplasmosis 86510
Other Antigen 86586
Tuberculosis 86580-86585
Unlisted Services and Procedures 17999
Wound Repair
Complex 13100-13160
Intermediate 12031-12057
Simple 12001-12021

Skin Graft and Flap
Allograft 15350-15351
Composite Graft 15760-15770
Cross Finger Flap 15574
Delay 15600-15630
Delay of Flap 15600-15630
Derma-Fat-Fascia 15770
Fascial
Free 15758
Fasciocutaneous 15732-15738
Formation 15570-15576
Free
Microvascular Anastomosis 15756-15758
Free Skin Graft
Full Thickness 15200-15261
Island Pedicle Flap 15740
Muscle 15732-15738, 15842
Free 15756
Myocutaneous 15732-15738, 15756
Pedicle Flap
Formation 15570-15576
Island 15740
Neurovascular 15750
Transfer 15650
Pinch Graft 15050
Platysmal 15825
Punch Graft 15775-15776
Punch Graft for Hair Transplant 15775-15776
Recipient Site Preparation 15000-15001
Skin
Free 15757
Split Graft 15100-15121
Superficial Musculoaponeurotic System 15829
Tissue Transfer 14000-14350
Tissue-Cultured 15100-15121, 15342-15343
Transfer 15650
Vascular Flow Check 15860
Xenograft 15400-15401

Skull
Burr Hole
Biopsy Brain 61140
Drainage
Abscess 61150-61151
Cyst 61150-61151
Hematoma 61154-61156
Exploration
Infratentorial 61253
Supratentorial 61250
Insertion
Catheter 61210
EEG Electrode 61210
Reservoir 61210
Intracranial
Biopsy 61140
with Injection 61120
Decompression 61322-61323, 61340-61345
Orbit 61330
Drill Hole
Catheter 61107
Drainage Hematoma 61108
Exploration 61105
Excision 61501
Exploration
Drill Hole 61105
Fracture 62000-62010
Closed Treatment 21300
Hematoma
Drainage 61108
Incision
Suture 61550-61552
Insertion
Catheter 61107
Lesion
Excision ..61500, 61600-61608, 61615-61616
Orbit
Biopsy 61332
Excision
Lesion 61333
Exploration 61332-61334
Removal Foreign Body 61334
Puncture
Cervical 61050
Cisternal 61050
Drain Fluid 61070
Injection 61070
Subdural 61000-61001
Ventricular Fluid 61020
Reconstruction 21172-21180
Defect 62140-62141, 62145
Reduction
Craniomegalic 62115-62117
Removal
Plate 62142
Prosthesis 62142

Stellate Ganglion
Injection
  Anesthetic 64510

Stem Cell
Cell Concentration 38215
Cryopreservation 38207, 88240
Donor Search 38204
Harvesting 38205-38206
Limbal
  Allograft 65781
Plasma Depletion 38214
Platelet Depletion 38213
Red Blood Cell Depletion 38212
T-cell Depletion 38210
Thawing 38208-38209, 88241
Transplantation 38240-38242
Tumor Cell Depletion 38211
Washing 38209

Stem, Brain
See Brainstem

Stenger Test 92565, 92577
See Audiologic Function Test; Ear, Nose and Throat

Stenosis
Aortic
  See Aortic Stenosis
Bronchi 31641
  Reconstruction 31775
Excision
  Trachea 31780-31781
Laryngoplasty 31582
Reconstruction
  Auditory Canal, External 69310
Repair
  Trachea 31780-31781
Tracheal
  See Trachea Stenosis
Urethral
  See Urethral Stenosis

Stensen Duct
See Parotid Duct

Stent
Indwelling
  Insertion
    Ureter 50605
Placement
  Bronchoscopy 31631
  Colonoscopy 45387
    via Stoma 44397
  Endoscopy
    Gastrointestinal, Upper 43256
  Enteroscopy 44370
  Proctosigmoidoscopy 45327
  Sigmoidoscopy 45345
  Ureteroneocystomy 50947-50948
Urethra
  Insertion 52282

Stent, Intravascular
See Transcatheter, Placement, Intravascular Stents

Stents, Tracheal
See Tracheal Stent

Stereotactic Frame
Application/Removal 20660

Stereotaxis
Aspiration
  Brain Lesion 61750
    with CT Scan and/or MRI 61751
  Spinal Cord 63615
Biopsy
  Aspiration
    Brain Lesion 61750
  Brain 61750
    with CT Scan and/or MRI 61751
  Breast 76095
  Spinal Cord 63615
Computer Assisted
  Brain Surgery 61795
  Orthopedic Surgery 0054T-0056T
Creation Lesion
  Brain
    Deep 61720-61735
    Percutaneous 61790
  Gasserian Ganglion 61790
  Spinal Cord 63600
  Trigeminal Tract 61791
CT Scan
  Aspiration 61751
  Biopsy 61751
Excision Lesion
  Brain 61750
  Spinal Cord 63615
Focus Beam
  Radiosurgery 61793
Localization
  Brain 61770
Radiation Therapy 77432
Stimulation
  Spinal Cord 63610

Sterile Coverings
See Dressings

Sternal Fracture
See Fracture, Sternum

Sternoclavicular Joint
Arthrotomy 23044
  with Biopsy 23101
  with Synovectomy 23106
Dislocation
  Closed Treatment
    with Manipulation 23525
    without Manipulation 23520
  Open Treatment 23530-23532
    with Fascial Graft 23532

Sternocleidomastoid
Division 21720-21725

Sternotomy
Closure 21750

Sternum
Debridement 21627
Excision 21620, 21630-21632
Fracture
  Closed Treatment 21820
  Open Treatment 21825
Ostectomy 21620
Radical Resection 21630-21632
Reconstruction 21740-21742, 21750
  with Thoracoscopy 21743
X-Ray 71120-71130

Steroid-Binding Protein, Sex
See Globulin, Sex Hormone Binding

Steroids
Anabolic
  See Androstenedione
Injection
  Urethral Stricture 52283
Ketogenic
  Urine 83582

STH (Somatotropic Hormone)
See Growth Hormone

Stimulating Antibody, Thyroid
See Immunoglobulin, Thyroid Stimulating

Stimulation
Electric
  See Electrical Stimulation
Lymphocyte
  See Blastogenesis
Spinal Cord
  Stereotaxis 63610
Transcutaneous Electric
  See Application, Neurostimulation

Stimulator, Long-Acting Thyroid
See Thyrotropin Releasing Hormone (TRH)

Stimulators, Cardiac
See Heart, Pacemaker

Stimulus Evoked Response 51792

Stoffel Operation
See Rhizotomy

Stoma
Creation
  Bladder 51980
  Kidney 50551-50561
  Stomach
    Neonatal 43831
    Temporary 43830-43831
  Ureter 50860
Ureter
  Endoscopy via 50951-50961

Stomach
Anastomosis
  with Duodenum 43810, 43850-43855
  with Jejunum 43820-43825, 43860-43865
Biopsy 43600-43605
Creation
  Stoma
    Temporary 43830-43831
  Temporary Stoma
    Laparoscopic 43653
Electrogastrography 91132-91133
Excision
  Partial 43631-43639
  Total 43620-43622
Exploration 43500
Gastric Bypass 43846
  Revision 43848

Incision 43830-43832
Exploration 43500
Pyloric Sphincter 43520
Removal
Foreign Body 43500
Intubation with Specimen Prep 91055
Nuclear Medicine
Blood Loss Study 78278
Emptying Study 78264
Imaging 78261
Protein Loss Study 78282
Reflux Study 78262
Vitamin B-12 Absorption 78270-78272
Reconstruction
for Obesity 43842-43847
Roux-En-Y 43846
Removal
Foreign Body 43500
Repair 48547
Fistula 43880
Fundoplasty 43324-43325
Laparoscopic 43280
Laceration 43501-43502
Stoma 43870
Ulcer 43501
Saline Load Test 91060
Specimen Collection 89130-89141
Stimulation of Secretion 91052
Suture
Fistula 43880
for Obesity 43842-43843
Stoma 43870
Ulcer 43840
Wound 43840
Tumor
Excision 43610-43611
Ulcer
Excision 43610
Unlisted Services and Procedures . .43659, 43999

Stomatoplasty
See Mouth, Repair

Stone, Kidney
See Calculus, Removal, Kidney

Stookey-Scarff Procedure
See Ventriculocisternostomy

Stool Blood
See Blood, Feces

Storage
Embryo 89342
Oocyte 89346
Reproductive Tissue 89344
Sperm 89343

Strabismus
Chemodenervation 67345
Repair
Adjustable Sutures 67335
Extraocular Muscles 67340
One Horizontal Muscle 67311
One Vertical Muscle 67314
Posterior Fixation Suture
Technique 67334-67335
Previous Surgery, Not Involving Extraocular
Muscles 67331
Release Extensive Scar Tissue 67343
Superior Oblique Muscle 67318
Transposition 67320
Two Horizontal Muscles 67312
Two or More Vertical Muscles 67316

Strapping
See Cast; Splint
Ankle 29540
Back 29220
Chest 29200
Elbow 29260
Finger 29280
Foot 29540, 29590
Hand 29280
Hip 29520
Knee 29530
Shoulder 29240
Thorax 29200
Toes 29550
Unlisted Services and Procedures 29799
Unna Boot 29580
Wrist 29260

Strassman Procedure 58540

Strayer Procedure
Leg, Lower 27687

Streptococcus pneumoniae Vaccine
See Vaccines

Streptococcus, Group A
Antigen Detection
Enzyme Immunoassay 87430
Nucleic Acid 87650-87652
Direct Optical Observation 87880

Streptococcus, Group B
by Immunoassay
with Direct Optical Observation 87802

Streptokinase, Antibody 86590

Stress Tests
Cardiovascular 93015-93024
Multiple Gated Acquisition (MUGA) .78472-78473
Myocardial Perfusion Imaging 78460-78465
Pulmonary 94620-94621
See Pulmonology, Diagnostic

Stricture
Repair
Urethra 53400-53405
Urethra
See Urethral Stenosis

Stricturoplasty
Intestines 44615

Stroboscopy
Larynx 31579

STS 86592-86593
See Syphilis Test

Stuart-Prower Factor 85260

Study, Color Vision
See Color Vision Examination

Sturmdorf Procedure 57520

Styloid Process
Radial
Excision 25230

Styloidectomy
Radial 25230

Stypven Time
See Russell Viper Venom Time

Subacromial Bursa
Arthrocentesis 20610

Subclavian Arteries
See Artery, Subclavian

Subcutaneous Injection
See Injection, Subcutaneous

Subcutaneous Mastectomies
See Mastectomy, Subcutaneous

Subcutaneous Tissue
Excision 15831-15839

Subdiaphragmatic Abscess
See Abscess, Subdiaphragmatic

Subdural Electrode
Insertion 61531-61533
Removal 61535

Subdural Hematonia
See Hematoma, Subdural

Subdural Puncture 61105-61108

Subdural Tap 61000-61001

Sublingual Gland
Abscess
Incision and Drainage 42310-42320
Calculi (Stone)
Excision 42330
Cyst
Drainage 42409
Excision 42408
Excision 42450

Subluxation
Elbow 24640

Submandibular Gland
Calculi (Stone)
Excision 42330-42335
Excision 42440

Submaxillary Gland
Abscess
Incision and Drainage 42310-42320

Submucous Resection of Nasal Septum
See Nasal Septum, Submucous Resection

Subperiosteal Implant
Reconstruction
Mandible 21245-21246
Maxilla 21245-21246

Subphrenic Abscess
See Abscess, Subdiaphragmatic

Substance S, Reichstein's
See Deoxycortisol

Subtrochanteric Fracture
See Femur, Fracture, Subtrochanteric

Sucrose Hemolysis Test
See Red Blood Cell (RBC), Fragility, Osmotic

Suction Lipectomies
See Liposuction

Sudiferous Gland
See Sweat Glands

Sugar Water Test
See Red Blood Cell (RBC), Fragility, Osmotic

Sugars 84375-84379

Sugiura Procedure
See Esophagus, Repair, Varices

Sulfate
Chondroitin
See Chondroitin Sulfate
DHA
See Dehydroepiandrosterone Sulfate
Urine 84392

Sulfation Factor
See Somatomedin

Sulphates
See Sulfate

Sumatran Mite Fever
See Scrub Typhus

Superficial Musculoaponeurotic System (SMAS) Flap
Rhytidectomy 15829

Supernumerary Digit
Reconstruction 26587
Repair 26587

Supply
Chemotherapeutic Agent 96545
See Chemotherapy
Contact Lenses 92391, 92396
Educational Materials 99071
Low Vision Aids 92392
See Spectacle Services
Materials 99070
Ocular Prosthesis 92393
Prosthesis
Breast 19396
Radionuclide 78990
Radionuclide Therapy 79900
Radiopharmaceutical 78990
Radiopharmaceutical Therapy 79900
Spectacle Prosthesis 92395
Spectacles 92390

Suppositories, Vaginal
See Pessary

Suppression 80400-80408

Suppression/Testing
See Evocative/Suppression Test

Suppressor T Lymphocyte Marker
See CD8

Suppurative Hidradenitides
See Hidradenitis, Suppurative

Suprahyoid
Lymphadenectomy 38700

Supraorbital Nerve
Avulsion 64732
Incision 64732
Transection 64732

Supraorbital Rim and Forehead
Reconstruction 21179-21180

Suprapubic Prostatectomies
See Prostatectomy, Suprapubic

Suprarenal
Gland
See Adrenal Gland
Vein
See Vein, Adrenal

Suprascapular Nerve
Injection
Anesthetic 64418

Suprasellar Cyst
See Craniopharyngioma

Surface CD4 Receptor
See CD4

Surface Radiotherapy
See Application, Radioelement, Surface

Surgeries
Breast-Conserving
See Breast, Excision, Lesion
Conventional
See Celiotomy
Laser
See Laser Surgery
Mohs
See Mohs Micrographic Surgery
Repeat
See Reoperation

Surgical
Avulsion
See Avulsion
Cataract Removal
See Cataract, Excision
Collapse Therapy; Thoracoplasty
See Thoracoplasty
Diathermy
See Electrocautery
Galvanism
See Electrolysis
Incision
See Incision
Microscopes
See Operating Microscope
Pathology
See Pathology, Surgical
Planing
Nose
Skin 30120
Pneumoperitoneum
See Pneumoperitoneum
Removal, Eye
See Enucleation, Eye
Revision
See Reoperation
Services
Post-Op Visit 99024

Surveillance
See Monitoring

Suspension
Aorta 33800
Kidney
See Nephropexy
Muscle
Hyoid 21685
Vagina
See Colpopexy

Suture
See Repair
Abdomen 49900
Aorta 33320-33322
Bile Duct
Wound 47900
Bladder
Fistulization 44660-44661, 45800-45805, 51880-51925
Vesicouterine 51920-51925
Vesicovaginal 51900
Wound 51860-51865
Cervix 57720
Colon
Diverticula 44604-44605
Fistula 44650-44661
Plication 44680
Stoma 44620-44625
Ulcer 44604-44605
Wound 44604-44605
Esophagus
Wound 43410-43415
Eyelid 67880
Closure of 67875
with Transposition of Tarsal Plate 67882
Wound
Full Thickness 67935
Partial Thickness 67930
Facial Nerve
Intratemporal
Lateral to Geniculate Ganglion 69740
Medial to Geniculate Ganglion 69745
Foot
Tendon 28200-28210
Gastroesophageal 0008T, 43405
Great Vessel 33320-33322
Hemorrhoids 46945-46946
Hepatic Duct
See Hepatic Duct, Repair
Intestine
Large
Diverticula 44605
Ulcer 44605
Wound 44605
Intestines
Large
Diverticula 44604
Ulcer 44604
Wound 44604

Synovial
Bursa
  See Bursa
Cyst
  See Ganglion
Membrane
  See Synovium
Popliteal Space
  See Baker's Cyst

Synovium
Biopsy
  Carpometacarpal Joint 26100
  Interphalangeal Joint 26110
  Knee Joint 27330
  Metacarpophalangeal Joint
    with Synovial Biopsy 26105

Syphilis ab
See Antibody, Treponema Pallidum

Syphilis Test 86592-86593

Syrinx
Spinal Cord
  Aspiration 62268

System
Endocrine
  See Endocrine System
Hemic
  See Hemic System
Lymphatic
  See Lymphatic System
Musculoskeletal
  See Musculoskeletal System
Nervous
  See Nervous System

T

T Cell Leukemia Virus I Antibodies, Adult
See Antibody, HTLV-I

T Cell Leukemia Virus I, Human
See HTLV I

T Cell Leukemia Virus II Antibodies, Human
See Antibody, HTLV-II

T Cell Leukemia Virus II, Human
See HTLV II

T Lymphotropic Virus Type III Antibodies, Human
See Antibody, HIV

T-3
See Triiodothyronine

T-4 .... 84436-84439, 86360

T-7 Index
See Thyroxine, Total

T-8
See CD8; T-Cells, Ratio

T-Cell T8 Antigens
See CD8

T-Cells
CD4
  Absolute 86361
Count 86359
Ratio 86360

T-Phyl
See Theophylline

T3 Free
See Triiodothyronine, Free

T4 Molecule
See CD4

T4 Total
See Thyroxine, Total

Taarnhoj Procedure
See Decompression, Gasserian Ganglion, Sensory Root; Section

Tachycardia
Heart
  Recording 93609

Tacrolimus
Drug Assay 80197

Tag, Skin
See Skin, Tags

Tail Bone
Excision 27080
Fracture 27200-27202

Takeuchi Procedure 33505

Talectomy
See Astragalectomy

Talotarsal Joint
Dislocation 28570-28575, 28585
  Percutaneous Fixation 28576

Talus
Arthrodesis
  Pantalar 28705
  Subtalar 28725
  Triple 28715
Arthroscopy
  Surgical 29891-29892
Craterization 28120
Cyst
  Excision 28100-28103
Diaphysectomy 28120
Excision 28120, 28130
Fracture
  Open Treatment 28445
  Percutaneous Fixation 28436
  with Manipulation 28435-28436
  without Manipulation 28430
Repair
  Osteochondritis Dissecans 29892
  Osteotomy 28302
Saucerization 28120
Tumor
  Excision 27647, 28100-28103

Tap
Cisternal
  See Cisternal Puncture
Lumbar Diagnostic
  See Spinal Tap

Tarsal
Fracture
  Percutaneous Fixation 28456

Tarsal Bone
See Ankle Bone

Tarsal Joint
See Foot
Arthrodesis 28730-28735, 28740
  with Advancement 28737
  with Lengthening 28737
Craterization 28122
Cyst
  Excision 28104-28107
Diaphysectomy 28122
Dislocation 28540-28545, 28555
  Percutaneous Fixation 28545-28546
Excision 28116, 28122
Fracture
  Open Treatment 28465
  with Manipulation 28455-28456
  without Manipulation 28450
Fusion 28730-28735, 28740
  with Advancement 28737
  with Lengthening 28737
Repair 28320
  Osteotomy 28304-28305
Saucerization 28122
Tumor
  Excision 28104-28107, 28171

Tarsal Strip Procedure 67917-67924

Tarsal Tunnel Release 28035

Tarsometatarsal Joint
Arthrodesis 28730-28735, 28740
Arthrotomy 28020, 28050
Dislocation 28600-28605, 28615
  Percutaneous Fixation 28606
Exploration 28020
Fusion 28730-28735, 28740
Removal
  Foreign Body 28020
  Loose Body 28020
Synovial
  Biopsy 28050
  Excision 28070

Tarsorrhaphy 67875
Median 67880
Severing 67710
  with Transposition of Tarsal Plate 67882

Tattoo
Cornea 65600
Skin 11920-11922

Tenomyotomy
Shoulder 23405-23406

Tenon's Capsule
Injection 67515

Tenoplasty
Anesthesia 01714

Tenorrhaphy
See Suture, Tendon

Tenosuspension
See Tenodesis

Tenosuture
See Suture, Tendon

Tenotomy
Achilles Tendon 27605-27606
Ankle 27605-27606
Arm, Lower 25290
Arm, Upper 24310
Finger 26060, 26455-26460
Foot 28230, 28234
Hand 26450, 26460
Hip
  Iliopsoas Tendon 27005
Hip, Abductor 27006
Hip, Adductor 27000-27003
Leg, Upper 27306-27307, 27390-27392
Toe 28010-28011, 28232-28234, 28240
Wrist 25290

TENS
See Application, Neurostimulation; Physical Medicine/Therapy/Occupational Therapy

Tensilon Test 95857-95858

Tension, Ocular
See Glaucoma

Tentorium Cerebelli
Section 61440

Terman-Merrill Test 96100

Termination, Pregnancy
See Abortion

Test
Antiglobulin
  See Coombs Test
Aphasia
  See Aphasia Testing
Bender Visual-Motor Gestalt
  See Bender-Gestalt Test
Binet
  See Binet Test
Blood
  See Blood Tests
Blood Coagulation
  See Coagulation
Breath
  See Breath Test
Cervical Mucus Penetration
  See Cervical Mucus Penetration Test
Clinical Chemistry
  See Chemistry Tests, Clinical
Complement Fixation
  See Complement, Fixation Test
Exercise
  See Exercise Stress Tests
Fern
  See Smear and Stain, Wet Mount
Fetal, Nonstress
  See Fetal Non-Stress Test
Function, Vestibular
  See Vestibular Function Tests
Gel Diffusion
  See Immunodiffusion
Glucose Tolerance
  See Glucose, Tolerance Test
Hearing
  See Audiologic Function Tests
Hemagglutination Inhibition
  See Hemagglutination Inhibition Test
Ink Blot
  See Inkblot Test
Intelligence
  See Intelligence Test
Lung Function
  See Pulmonology, Diagnostic
Neutralization
  See Neutralization Test
Papanicolaou
  See Pap Smears
Pregnancy
  See Pregnancy Test
Quick
  See Prothrombin Time
Radioimmunosorbent
  See Gammaglobulin, Blood
Rorschach
  See Rorschach Test
Schilling
  See Schilling Test
Skin
  See Skin, Tests
Stanford-Binet
  See Psychiatric Diagnosis
Tuberculin
  See Skin, Tests, Tuberculosis

Test Tube Fertilization
See In Vitro Fertilization

Tester, Color Vision
See Color Vision Examination

Testes
Cryopreservation 89335
Nuclear Medicine
  Imaging 78760-78761
Undescended
  See Testis, Undescended

Testicular Vein
See Spermatic Veins

Testimony, Medical 99075

Testing, Histocompatibility
See Tissue Typing

Testing, Neurophysiologic
Intraoperative 95920

Testing, Neuropsychological 96117

Testing, Range of Motion
See Range of Motion Test

Testis
Abscess
  Incision and Drainage 54700
Biopsy 54500-54505
Excision
  Laparoscopic 54690
  Partial 54522
  Radical 54530-54535
  Simple 54520
Hematoma
  Incision and Drainage 54700
Insertion
  Prosthesis 54660
Lesion
  Excision 54512
Needle Biopsy 54500
Repair
  Injury 54670
  Suspension 54620-54640
  Torsion 54600
Suture
  Injury 54670
  Suspension 54620-54640
Transplantation
  to Thigh 54680
Tumor
  Excision 54530-54535
Undescended
  Exploration 54550-54560
Unlisted Services and Procedures ..54699, 55899

Testosterone 84402
Response 80414
  Stimulation 80414-80415
Total 84403

Testosterone Estradiol Binding Globulin
See Globulin, Sex Hormone Binding

Tetanus 86280
Antibody 86774
Immunoglobulin 90389
Vaccine 90703

Tetrachloride, Carbon
See Carbon Tetrachloride

Tetralogy of Fallot ...33692-33697, 33924

Thal-Nissen Procedure 43325

Thawing
See Frozen Blood Preparation
Cryopreserved
  Embryo 89352
  Oocytes 89356
  Reproductive Tissue 89354
  Sperm 89353
Previously Frozen Cells 38208-38209

Thawing and Expansion
of Frozen Cell 88241

THBR
See Thyroid Hormone Binding Ratio

Theleplasty
See Nipples, Reconstruction

Incision
  Empyema 32035-32036
  Pneumothorax 32020
Incision and Drainage
  Abscess 21501-21502
  Deep 21510
  Hematoma 21501-21502
Strapping 29200
Tumor
  Excision 21555-21556
  Excision/Resection 21557
Unlisted Services and Procedures, Surgery . 21899

Three Glass Test
See Urinalysis, Glass Test

Three-Day Measles
See Rubella

Throat
See Pharynx
Abscess
  Incision and Drainage 42700-42725
Biopsy 42800-42806
Hemorrhage 42960-42962
Reconstruction 42950
Removal
  Foreign Body 42809
Repair
  Pharyngoesophageal 42953
  Wound 42900
Suture
  Wound 42900
Unlisted Services and Procedures 42999

Thrombectomy
See Thromboendarterectomy
Aortoiliac Artery 34151-34201
Arteriovenous Fistula
  Graft 36870
Axillary Artery 34101
Axillary Vein 34490
Brachial Artery 34101
Bypass Graft
  Other than Hemodialysis Graft or Fistula 35875-35876
Carotid Artery 34001
Celiac Artery 34151
Dialysis Graft
  without Revision 36831
Femoral 34201
Femoropopliteal Vein 34421-34451
Iliac 34151-34201
Iliac Vein 34401-34451
Innominate Artery 34001-34101
Mesentery Artery 34151
Percutaneous
  Coronary Artery 92973
Peroneal Artery 34203
Popliteal Artery 34203
Radial Artery 34111
Renal Artery 34151
Subclavian Artery 34001-34101
Subclavian Vein 34471-34490
Tibial Artery 34203
Ulnar Artery 34111
Vena Cava 34401-34451
Vena Caval 50230

Thrombin Inhibitor I
See Antithrombin III

Thrombin Time 85670-85675

Thrombocyte (Platelet)
See Blood, Platelet

Thrombocyte ab
See Antibody, Platelet

Thromboendarterectomy
See Thrombectomy
Aorta, Abdominal 35331
Aortoiliofemoral Artery 35363
Axillary Artery 35321
Brachial Artery 35321
Carotid Artery 35301, 35390
Celiac Artery 35341
Femoral Artery 35371-35381
Iliac Artery 35351, 35361-35363
Iliofemoral Artery 35355, 35363
Innominate Artery 35311
Mesenteric Artery 35341
Peroneal Artery 35381
Popliteal Artery 35381
Renal Artery 35341
Subclavian Artery 35301-35311
Tibial Artery 35381
Vertebral Artery 35301

Thrombokinase 85260

Thrombolysin
See Plasmin

Thrombolysis
Catheter Exchange
  Arterial 37209, 75900
Cerebral
  Intravenous Infusion 37195
Coronary Vessels 92975-92977
Cranial Vessels 37195

Thrombolysis Biopsy Intracranial
Arterial Perfusion 61624

Thrombolysis Intracranial 65205
See Ciliary Body; Cornea; Eye, Removal, Foreign Body; Iris; Lens; Retina; Sclera; Vitreous

Thrombomodulin 85337

Thromboplastin
Inhibition 85705
Inhibition Test 85347
Partial Time 85730-85732

Thromboplastin Antecedent, Plasma
See Plasma Thromboplastin, Antecedent

Thromboplastinogen
See Clotting Factor

Thromboplastinogen B
See Christmas Factor

Thumb
See Phalanx
Amputation 26910-26952
Arthrodesis
  Carpometacarpal Joint 26841-26842
Dislocation
  with Fracture 26645-26650
    Open Treatment 26665
  with Manipulation 26641
Fracture
  with Dislocation 26645-26650
    Open Treatment 26665
Fusion
  in Opposition 26820
Reconstruction
  from Finger 26550
  Opponensplasty 26490-26496
Repair
  Muscle 26508
  Muscle Transfer 26494
  Tendon Transfer 26510
Replantation 20824-20827
Sesamoidectomy 26185
Unlisted Services and Procedures 26989

Thymectomy 60520-60521
Sternal Split/Transthoracic Approach 60521-60522
Transcervical Approach 60520

Thymotaxin
See Beta-2-Microglobulin

Thymus Gland 60520
Excision 60520-60521

Thyramine
See Amphetamine

Thyrocalcitonin
See Calcitonin

Thyroglobulin 84432
Antibody 86800

Thyroglossal Duct
Cyst
  Excision 60280-60281

Thyroid Gland
Cyst
  Aspiration 60001
  Excision 60200
  Incision and Drainage 60000
  Injection 60001
Excision
  for Malignancy
    Limited Neck Dissection 60252
    Radical Neck Dissection 60254
  Partial 60210-60225
  Secondary 60260
  Total 60240, 60271
    Cervical Approach 60271
    Removal All Thyroid Tissue 60260
    Sternal Split/Transthoracic Approach 60270
    Transcervical Approach 60520
Metastatic Cancer
  Nuclear Imaging 78015-78018
Needle Biopsy 60100
Nuclear Medicine
  Imaging 78010
  Imaging for Metastases 78015-78018
  Imaging with Flow 78011
  Imaging with Uptake 78006-78007

Repair
Bunion 28290-28299
Muscle 28240
Tendon 28232-28234, 28240
Webbed 28280
Webbed Toe 28345
Tenotomy 28010-28011, 28232-28234
Unlisted Services and Procedures 28899

Toe Flap
Tissue Transfer 14350

Toes
Arthrocentesis 20600
Dislocation
See Specific Joint
Magnetic Resonance Imaging
(MRI) 73721-73723
Reposition to Hand 26551-26556
Strapping 29550
X-Ray 73660

Tolbutamide Tolerance Test 82953

Tolerance Test
Glucagon 82946
Glucose 82951-82952
with Tolbutamide 82953
Heparin-Protamine 85530
Insulin 80434-80435
Maltose 82951-82952
Tolbutamide 82953

Tomodensitometries
See CT Scan

Tomographic Scintigraphy, Computed
See Emission Computerized Tomography

Tomographic SPECT
Myocardial Imaging 78469

Tomographies, Computed X-Ray
See CT Scan

Tomography, Computerized Axial
Abdomen
See Abdomen, CT Scan
Head
See Head, CT Scan

Tomography, Emission Computed
See Positron Emission Tomography
Single Photon
See SPECT

Tompkins Metroplasty 58540
See Uterus, Reconstruction

Tongue
Abscess
Incision and Drainage ..41000-41006, 41015
Biopsy 41100-41105
Cyst
Incision and Drainage 41000-41006, 41015, 60000
Excision
Complete 41140-41155
Frenum 41115
Partial 41120-41135
with Mouth Resection 41150-41153
with Radical Neck 41135, 41145, 41153-41155
Fixation 41500
Hematoma
Incision and Drainage ..41000-41006, 41015
Incision
Frenum 41010
Lesion
Excision 41110-41114
Reconstruction
Frenum 41520
Repair
See Repair, Tongue
Laceration 41250-41252
Suture 41510
Suture 41510
Unlisted Services and Procedures 41599

Tonography 92120
with Provocation 92130

Tonometry, Serial 92100

Tonsil, Pharyngeal
See Adenoids

Tonsillectomy 42820-42826

Tonsils
Abscess
Incision and Drainage 42700
Excision 42825-42826
Lingual 42870
Radical 42842-42845
Tag 42860
with Adenoids 42820-42821
Lingual
Destruction 42870
Unlisted Services and Procedures 42999

Topiramate
Assay 80201

Torek Procedure
See Orchiopexy

Torkildsen Procedure 62180

TORP (Total Ossicular Replacement Prosthesis) 69633, 69637

Torsion Swing Test 92546

Torula
See Cryptococcus

Torus Mandibularis
Tumor Excision 21031

Total
Abdominal Hysterectomy
See Hysterectomy, Abdominal, Total
Bilirubin Level
See Bilirubin, Total
Catecholamines
See Catecholamines, Urine
Cystectomy
See Bladder, Excision, Total
Dacryoadenectomy
See Dacryoadenectomy, Total
Elbow Replacement
See Replacement, Elbow, Total
Esophagectomy
See Esophagectomy, Total
Gastrectomy
See Excision, Stomach, Total
Hemolytic Complement
See Complement, Hemolytic, Total
Hip Arthroplasty
See Hip, Total Replacement
Knee Arthroplasty
See Prosthesis, Knee
Mastectomies
See Mastectomy
Ostectomy of Patella
See Patellectomy
Splenectomy
See Splenectomy, Total

Touroff Operation 37615
See Ligation, Artery, Neck

Toxicology Screen 80100-80103

Toxin Assay 87230

Toxin, Botulinum
See Chemodenervation

Toxoplasma
Antibody 86777-86778

Trabeculectomies
See Trabeculoplasty

Trabeculectomy ab Externo
in Absence of Previous Surgery 66170
with Scarring Previous Surgery 66172

Trabeculoplasty
by Laser Surgery 65855

Trabeculotomy ab Externo
Eye 65850

Trachea
Aspiration 31720
Catheter 31720-31725
Catheterization 31700
Dilation 31630-31631
Endoscopy
via Tracheostomy 31615
Excision
Stenosis 31780-31781
Fistula
with Plastic Repair 31825
without Plastic Repair 31820
Fracture
Endoscopy 31630
Incision
Emergency 31603-31605
Planned 31600-31601
with Flaps 31610
Instillation
Contrast Material 31708
Introduction
Needle Wire 31730
Puncture
Aspiration and/or Injection 31612
Reconstruction
Carina 31766
Cervical 31750
Fistula 31755
Intrathoracic 31760

Repair
- Cervical 31750
- Fistula 31755
- Intrathoracic 31760
- Stoma 31613-31614

Revision
- Stoma
  - Scars 31830

Scar
- Revision 31830

Stenosis
- Excision 31780-31781
- Repair 31780-31781

Stoma
- Repair
  - with Plastic Repair 31825
  - without Plastic Repair 31820
- Revision
  - Scars 31830

Tumor
- Excision
  - Cervical 31785
  - Thoracic 31786

Unlisted Services and Procedures
- Bronchi 31899

Wound
- Suture
  - Cervical 31800
  - Intrathoracic 31805

Tracheal
Stent
- Placement 31631

Tubes
- *See* Endotracheal Tube

Trachelectomy 57530
Radical 57531

Tracheloplasty
See Cervicoplasty

Trachelorrhaphy 57720

Tracheo-Esophageal Fistula
See Fistula, Tracheoesophageal

Tracheobronchoscopy
through Tracheostomy 31615

Tracheoplasty
Cervical 31750
Intrathoracic 31760
Tracheopharyngeal Fistulization 31755

Tracheostoma
Revision 31613-31614

Tracheostomy
Emergency 31603-31605
Planned 31600-31601
Revision
- Scar 31830

Surgical Closure
- with Plastic Repair 31825
- without Plastic Repair 31820

Tracheobronchoscopy through 31615
with Flaps 31610

Tracheotomy
Tube Change 31502

Tracking Tests (Ocular) 92545
See Ear, Nose and Throat

Tract, Urinary
See Urinary Tract

Traction Therapy
See Physical Medicine/Therapy/Occupational Therapy
Manual 97140
Mechanical 97012

Tractotomy
Medulla 61470
Mesencephalon 61480

Training
Activities of Daily Living 97535, 99509
Biofeedback 90901-90911
Cognitive Skills 97532
Community/Work Reintegration 97537
Home Management 97535, 99509
Orthoptic/Pleoptic 92065
Orthotics 97504
Prosthetics 97520
Self Care 97535, 99509
Sensory Integration 97533
Walking (Physical Therapy) 97116
Wheelchair Management/Propulsion 97542

TRAM Flap
Breast Reconstruction 19367-19369

Trans-Scaphoperilunar
Fracture/Dislocation
- Closed Treatment 25680
- Open Treatment 25685

Transaminase
Glutamic Oxaloacetic 84450
Glutamic Pyruvic 84460

Transcatheter
Biopsy 37200
Closure
- Percutaneous
  - Heart 93580-93581

Embolization
- Percutaneous 37204
  - Cranial 61624-61626

Occlusion
- Percutaneous 37204
  - Cranial 61624-61626

Placement
- Intravascular Stents 0005T-0007T, 37205-37208

Therapy
- Embolization 75894
- Infusion 37201-37202, 75896-75898
- Perfusion
  - Cranial 61624-61626
- Retrieval 75961

Transcatheter Foreign Body
Retrieval 37203

Transcortin 84449

Transcutaneous Electric Nerve Stimulation
See Application, Neurostimulation

Transdermal Electrostimulation
See Application, Neurostimulation

Transection
Artery
- Carotid 61610, 61612

Blood Vessel
- Kidney 50100

Brain
- Subpial 61567

Carotid
- with Skull Base Surgery 61609

Nerve 64732-64772
- Vagus 43640-43641

Pulmonary Artery 33922

Transesophageal
Doppler Echocardiography 93312-93318

Transfer
Blastocyst
- *See* Embryo Transfer

Gamete Intrafallopian
- *See* GIFT

Jejunum
- with Microvascular Anastomosis
  - Free 43496

Preparation
- Embryo 89255
  - Cryopreserved 89352

Surgical
- *See* Transposition

Tendon
- *See* Tendon, Transfer

Toe to Hand 26551-26556

Transferase
Aspartate Amino 84450
Glutamic Oxaloacetic 84450

Transferrin 84466

Transformation
Lymphocyte 86353

Transfusion
Blood 36430
- Exchange 36450-36455
- Fetal 36460
- Push
  - Infant 36440

Blood Parts
- Exchange 36511-36516

Unlisted Services and Procedures 86999
White Blood Cells 86950

Transfusion of, Blood, Autologous
See Autotransfusion

Transluminal
Angioplasty
- Arterial 75962-75968

Atherectomies
- *See* Artery, Atherectomy

Coronary Balloon Dilatation
- *See* Percutaneous Transluminal Angioplasty

Transmyocardial Laser Revascularization 33140-33141

Transosteal Bone Plate
Reconstruction
  Mandible 21244

Transpeptidase, Gamma-Glutamyl
See Gamma Glutamyl Transferase

Transplant
See Graft
Bone
  See Bone Graft
Hair
  See Hair, Transplant

Transplantation
See Graft
Allogenic
  See Homograft
Autologous
  See Autograft
Bone Marrow 38240-38242
Cartilage
  Allograft
    Knee 0013T
  Autograft
    Knee 0012T
  Knee 0014T
Conjunctiva 65782
Cornea
  Autograft/Homograft
    Lamellar 65710
    Penetrating 65730-65755
  for Aphakia 65750
Eye
  Amniotic Membrane 65780
  Conjunctiva 65782
  Stem Cell 65781
Hair
  Punch Graft 15775-15776
  Strip 15220-15221
Heart 33945
Heart-Lung 33935
Heterologous
  See Heterograft
Intestines
  Allotransplantation 44135-44136
  Donor Enterectomy 44132-44133
Liver 47135
  Heterotopic 47136
Lung
  Anesthesia 00580
  Donor Pneumonectomy 32850
  Double, with Cardiopulmonary Bypass 32854
  Double, without Cardiopulmonary Bypass 32853
  Single, with Cardiopulmonary Bypass 32852
  Single, without Cardiopulmonary Bypass 32851
Muscle
  See Muscle Flaps
Pancreas 48160, 48550-48556
Parathyroid 60512
Renal
  Allotransplantation 50360
    with Recipient Nephrectomy 50365
  Autotransplantation 50380
  Donor Nephrectomy 50300-50320, 50547
  Recipient Nephrectomy 50340
  Removal Transplanted Renal Allograft . 50370
Skin
  See Dermatology
Stem Cells 38240-38242
  Cell Concentration 38215
  Cryopreservation 38207
  Harvesting 38205-38206
  Plasma Depletion 38214
  Platelet Depletion 38213
  Red Blood Cell Depletion 38212
  T-cell Depletion 38210
  Thawing 38208
  Tumor Cell Depletion 38211
  Washing 38209
Testis
  to Thigh 54680
Tissue, Harvesting
  See Graft, Tissue, Harvesting

Transpleural Thoracoscopy
See Thoracoscopy

Transposition
Arteries
  Carotid 0037T, 35691, 35694-35695
  Subclavian 0037T, 35693-35695
  Vertebral 35691-35693
Cranial Nerve 64716
Eye Muscles 67320
Great Arteries
  Repair 33770-33781
Nerve 64718-64721
Ovary 58825
Peripheral Nerve
  Major 64856
Vein Valve 34510

Transthoracic Echocardiography
See Echocardiography

Transthyretin
See Prealbumin

Transureteroureterostomy 50770

Transurethral Balloon Dilation
Prostatic Urethra 52510

Transurethral Fulguration
Postoperative Bleeding 52606

Transurethral Procedure
See Specific Procedure
Prostate
  Incision 52450
  Resection 52612-52614
  Thermotherapy 53850-53853
    Microwave 53850
    Radiofrequency 53852

Trapezium
Arthroplasty
  with Implant 25445

Travel, Unusual 99082

Treacher-Collins Syndrome
Midface Reconstruction 21150-21151

Treatment, Tocolytic
See Tocolysis

Trendelenburg Operation
See Varicose Vein, Removal, Secondary Varicosity

Trephine Procedure
Sinusotomy
  Frontal 31070

Treponema Pallidum
Antibody
  Confirmation Test 86781
Antigen Detection
  Direct Fluorescence 87285

TRH
See Thyrotropin Releasing Hormone (TRH)

Triacylglycerol
See Triglycerides

Triacylglycerol Hydrolase
See Lipase

Tributyrinase
See Lipase

Trichiasis
Repair 67825
  Epilation, by Forceps 67820
  Epilation, by Other than Forceps 67825
  Incision of Lid Margin 67830
    with Free Mucous Membrane Graft . 67835

Trichina
See Trichinella

Trichinella
Antibody 86784
Trichogram 96902

Trichomonas vaginalis
Antigen Detection
  Nucleic Acid 87660

Trichrome Stain 88313

Tricuspid Valve
Excision 33460
Repair 33463-33465
Replacement 33465
Repositioning 33468

Tridymite
See Silica

Trigeminal Ganglia
See Gasserian Ganglion

Trigeminal Nerve
Destruction 64600-64610
Injection
  Anesthetic 64400
  Neurolytic 64600-64610

Trigeminal Tract
Stereotactic
  Create Lesion 61791

Trigger Finger Repair 26055

Trigger Point
Injection
  One or Two Muscles 20552
  Two or More Muscles 20553

Triglyceridase
See Lipase

Triglyceride Lipase
See Lipase

Triglycerides 84478

Trigonocephaly 21175

Triiodothyronine
Free 84481
Reverse 84482
Total 84480
True 84480

Triolean Hydrolase
See Lipase

Trioxopurine
See Uric Acid

Tripcellim
See Trypsin

Trisegmentectomy 47122

Trocar Biopsy
Bone Marrow 38221

Trochanteric Femur Fracture
See Femur, Fracture, Trochanteric

Trophoblastic Tumor GTT
See Hydatidiform Mole

Troponin 84484
Qualitative 84512
Quantitative 84484

Truncal Vagotomies
See Vagotomy, Truncal

Truncus Arteriosus
Repair 33786

Truncus Brachiocephalicus
See Artery, Brachiocephalic

Trunk, Brachiocephalic
See Artery, Brachiocephalic

Trypanosomiases
See Trypanosomiasis

Trypanosomiasis 86171, 86280

Trypsin
Duodenum 84485
Feces 84488-84490

Trypsin Inhibitor, Alpha 1-Antitrypsin
See Alpha-1 Antitrypsin

Trypure
See Trypsin

Tsalicylate Intoxication
See Salicylate

TSH
See Thyroid Stimulating Hormone

TSI
See Thyroid Stimulating Immunoglobulin

Tsutsugamushi Disease
See Scrub Typhus

TT
See Thrombin Time

TT-3
See Triiodothyronine, True

TT-4
See Thyroxine, True

Tuba Auditoria (Auditiva)
See Eustachian Tube

Tubal Embryo Stage Transfer
See Embryo Transfer

Tubal Ligation 58600
Laparoscopic 58670
with Cesarean Delivery 58611

Tubal Occlusion
See Fallopian Tube
with Cesarean Delivery
  See Fallopian Tube, Occlusion; Occlusion
  Create Lesion
    See Fallopian Tube, Occlusion; Occlusion, Fallopian Tube

Tubal Pregnancy 59121
with Salpingectomy and/or Oophorectomy 59120

Tube Change
Tracheotomy 31502

Tube Placement
Endoscopic
  Bile Duct, Pancreatic Duct 43268
  Nasobiliary, Nasopancreatic
    for Drainage 43267
Gastrostomy Tube 43750
Nasogastric Tube 43752
Orogastric Tube 43752

Tube, Fallopian
See Fallopian Tube

Tubectomy
See Excision, Fallopian Tube

Tubed Pedicle Flap
Formation 15570-15576

Tubercle Bacilli
Culture 87116

Tubercleplasty
Tibia
  Anterior 27418

Tuberculin Test
See Skin, Tests, Tuberculosis

Tuberculosis
Antigen Response Test 0010T
Culture 87116
Skin Test 86580-86585

Tuberculosis Vaccine (BCG) 90585-90586

Tubes
Endotracheal
  See Endotracheal Tube
Gastrostomy
  See Gastrostomy Tube

Tudor 'Rabbit Ear'
See Urethra, Repair

Tuffier Vaginal Hysterectomy
See Hysterectomy, Vaginal

Tumor
See Craniopharyngioma
Abdomen
  Destruction/Excision 49200-49201
Abdominal Wall
  Excision 22900
Acetabulum
  Excision 27076
Ankle 27615-27619
Arm, Lower 25075-25077
Arm, Upper
  Excision 24075-24077
Back/Flank
  Excision 21930
  Radical Resection 21935
Bile Duct
  Destruction 43272
  Extrahepatic 47711
  Intrahepatic 47712
Bladder 52234-52240
  Excision 51530, 52355
Bone
  Ablation 20982
Brain 61510
  Excision 61518, 61520-61521, 61526-61530, 61545, 62164
Breast
  Excision 19120-19126
Bronchi
  Excision 31640
Calcaneus 28100-28103
  Excision 27647
Carpal 25130-25136
Cheekbone 21030, 21034
Chest Wall
  Excision 19260-19272
Clavicle
  Excision 23140, 23200
    with Allograft 23146
    with Autograft 23145
Coccyx 49215
Colon
  Destruction 44393, 45383
Cranial Bone
  Reconstruction 21181-21184
Destruction
  Chemosurgery 17304-17310
  Urethra 53220
Ear, Middle
  Extended 69554
  Transcanal 69550
  Transmastoid 69552
Elbow
  Excision 24075-24077

Tunica Vaginalis

Turbinate

U

Urethrocystopexy
See Vesicourethropexy

Urethromeatoplasty 53450-53460

Urethropexy 51840-51841

Urethroplasty 46744-46746
First Stage 53400
One Stage
Hypospadias 54322-54328
Reconstruction
Female Urethra 53430
Male Anterior Urethra 53410
Prostatic/Membranous Urethra
First Stage 53420
One Stage 53415
Second Stage 53425
Second Stage 53405
Hypospadias 54308-54316
Third Stage
Hypospadias 54318

Urethrorrhaphy 53502-53515

Urethroscopy
See Endoscopy, Urethra

Urethrostomy 53000-53010

Urethrotomy 53000-53010
Direct Vision
with Cystourethroscopy 52276
Internal 52601, 52647-52648
with Cystourethroscopy
Female 52270
Male 52275

Uric Acid
Blood 84550
Other Source 84560
Urine 84560

Uridyltransferase, Galactose-1-Phosphate
See Galactose-1-Phosphate, Uridyl Transferase

Uridylyltransferase, Galactosephosphate
See Galactose-1-Phosphate, Uridyl Transferase

Urinalysis 0041T, 81000-81099
Automated 81001, 81003
Glass Test 81020
Microalbumin 82043-82044
Microscopic 81015
Pregnancy Test 81025
Qualitative 81005
Routine 81002
Screen 81007
Semiquantitative 0041T, 81005
Unlisted Services and Procedures 81099
Volume Measurement 81050
without Microscopy 81002

Urinary Bladder
See Bladder

Urinary Catheter Irrigation
See Irrigation, Catheter

Urinary Concentration Test
See Water Load Test

Urinary Sphincter, Artificial
See Prosthesis, Urethral Sphincter

Urinary Tract
X-Ray with Contrast 74400-74425

Urine
Albumin
See Albumin, Urine
Blood
See Blood, Urine
Colony Count 87086
Pregnancy Test 81025
Tests 81001

Urobilinogen
Feces 84577
Urine 84578-84583

Urodynamic Tests
Bladder Capacity
Ultrasound 51798
Cystometrogram 51725-51726
Electromyography Studies
Needle 51785
Residual Urine
Ultrasound 51798
Stimulus Evoked Response 51792
Urethra Pressure Profile 51772
Uroflowmetry 51736-51741
Voiding Pressure Studies
Bladder 51795
Intra-Abdominal 51797

Uroflowmetry 51736-51741

Urography
Antegrade 74425
Infusion 74410-74415
Intravenous 74400-74415
Retrograde 74420

Uroporphyrin 84120

Urothromboplastin
See Thromboplastin

Uterine
Adhesion
See Adhesions, Intrauterine
Cervix
See Cervix
Endoscopies
See Endoscopy, Uterus
Haemorrhage
See Hemorrhage, Uterus

Uterus
Ablation
Endometrium 0009T, 58353
Biopsy
Endometrium 58100
Endoscopic 58558
Catheterization
X-Ray 58340
Chromotubation 58350
Curettage
Postpartum 59160
Dilation and Curettage 58120
Postpartum 59160
Ectopic Pregnancy
Interstitial
Partial Resection Uterus 59136
Total Hysterectomy 59135
Endoscopy
Endometrial Ablation 58563
Exploration 58555
Surgery 58558-58563
Treatment 58558-58563
Excision
Laparoscopic 58550
Partial 58180
Radical 58210, 58285
Removal of Tubes and/or
Ovaries 58262-58263, 58291-58293, 58552, 58554
Total ...58150-58152, 58200, 58953-58954
Vaginal 58260-58270, 58290-58294, 58550, 58552-58554
with Colpectomy 58275-58280
with Colpo-Urethrocystopexy 58267
with Repair of Enterocele ...58270, 58294
Hemorrhage
Postpartum 59160
Hydatidiform Mole
Excision 59100
Hydrotubation 58350
Hysterosalpingography 74740
Incision
Remove Lesion 59100
Insertion
Heyman Capsule
for Brachytherapy 58346
Intrauterine Device (IUD) 58300
Tandem
for Brachytherapy 57155
Laparoscopy 58578
Lesion
Excision 58545-58546, 59100
Reconstruction 58540
Removal
Intrauterine Device (IUD) 58301
Repair
Fistula 51920-51925
Rupture 58520, 59350
Suspension 58400
with Presacral Sympathectomy 58410
Sonohysterography 76831
Suture
Rupture 59350
Tumor
Excision
Abdominal Approach 58140, 58146
Vaginal Approach 58145
Unlisted Services and Procedures ..58578, 58999
X-Ray with Contrast 74740

UTP Hexose 1 Phosphate Uridylyltransferase
See Galactose-1-Phosphate, Uridyl Transferase

UV Light Therapy
See Actinotherapy

Uvula
Abscess
  Incision and Drainage 42000
Biopsy 42100
Excision 42140-42145
Lesion
  Destruction 42145
  Excision 42104-42107
Unlisted Services and Procedures 42299

Uvulectomy 42140

V

V Flap Procedure
One Stage Distal Hypospadias Repair 54322

V, Cranial Nerve
See Trigeminal Nerve

V-Y Operation, Bladder, Neck
See Bladder, Repair, Neck

V-Y Plasty
See Skin, Adjacent Tissue Transfer

Vaccination
See Allergen Immunotherapy; Immunization; Vaccines

Vaccines
Adenovirus 90476-90477
Anthrax 90581
Chicken Pox 90716
Cholera
  Injectable 90725
Diphtheria Toxoid 90719
Diphtheria, Tetanus (DT) 90702
Diphtheria, Tetanus, Acellular Pertussis (DTaP) 90700
Diphtheria, Tetanus, Acellular Pertussis and Hemophilus Influenza B (Hib) (DTaP-Hib) 90721
Diphtheria, Tetanus, Acellular Pertussis, Hepatitis B, and Inactivated Poliovirus (DTaP-HepB-IPV) 90723
Diphtheria, Tetanus, Whole Cell Pertussis (DTP) 90701
Diphtheria, Tetanus, Whole Cell Pertussis and Hemophilus Influenza B (Hib) (DTP-Hib) 90720
Encephalitis, Japanese 90735
Hemophilus Influenza b 90645-90648
Hepatitis A 90632-90634
Hepatitis A and Hepatitis B 90636
Hepatitis B 90740-90747
Hepatitis B and Hemophilus Influenza B (HepB-Hib) 90748
Influenza 90655-90658, 90660
Lyme Disease 90665
Measles 90705
Measles and Rubella 90708
Measles, Mumps and Rubella (MMR) 90707
Measles, Mumps, Rubella and Varicella (MMRV) 90710
Meningococcal 90733-90734
Mumps 90704
Plague 90727
Pneumococcal 90669, 90732
Poliovirus, Inactivated
  Subcutaneous 90713
Poliovirus, Live
  Oral 90712
Rabies 90675-90676
Rotavirus 90680
Rubella 90706
Tetanus and Diphtheria 90718
Tetanus Toxoid 90703
Tuberculosis (BCG) 90585-90586
Typhoid 90690-90693
Unlisted Vaccine/Toxoid 90749
Varicella (Chicken Pox) 90716
Yellow Fever 90717

Vagina
Abscess
  Incision and Drainage 57010
Amines Test 82120
Biopsy
  Colposcopy 57421
  Endocervical 57454
  Extensive 57105
  Simple 57100
Closure 57120
Colposcopy 57420-57421, 57455-57456, 57461
Construction
  with Graft 57292
  without Graft 57291
Cyst
  Excision 57135
Dilation 57400
Endocervical
  Biopsy 57454
  Exploration 57452
Excision
  Closure 57120
  Complete
    with Removal of Paravaginal Tissue 57111
    with Removal of Paravaginal Tissue with Lymphadenectomy 57112
    with Removal of Vaginal Wall 57110
  Partial
    with Removal of Paravaginal Tissue 57107
    with Removal of Paravaginal Tissue with Lymphadenectomy 57109
    with Removal of Vaginal Wall 57106
  Total 57110
  with Hysterectomy 58275-58280
    with Repair of Enterocele 58280
Exploration
  Endocervical 57452
  Incision 57000
Hematoma
  Incision and Drainage 57022-57023
Hemorrhage 57180
Hysterectomy 58290, 58550, 58552-58554
Incision and Drainage 57020
Insertion
  Ovoid
    for Brachytherapy 57155
  Packing for Bleeding 57180
  Pessary 57160
  Sensor, Fetal Oximetry 0021T
Irrigation 57150
Lesion
  Destruction 57061-57065
    Extensive 57065
    Simple 57061
Prolapse
  Sacrospinous Ligament Fixation 57282
Removal
  Foreign Body 57415
  Sling
    Stress Incontinence 57287
Repair 56800
  Cystocele 57240, 57260
    Combined Anteroposterior 57260-57265
    Posterior 57240
  Enterocele 57265
  Fistula 51900
    Rectovaginal 57300-57308
    Transvesical and Vaginal Approach 57330
    Urethrovaginal 57310-57311
    Vesicovaginal 51900, 57320-57330
  Hysterectomy 58267, 58293
  Incontinence 57284, 57288
  Obstetric 59300
  Paravaginal Defect 57284
  Pereyra Procedure 57289
  Prolapse 57282-57284
  Rectocele
    Combined Anteroposterior 57260-57265
    Posterior 57250
  Suspension 57280
    Laparoscopic 57425
  Urethral Sphincter 57220
  Wound 57200-57210
    Colpoperineorrhaphy 57210
    Colporrhaphy 57200
Revision
  Sling
    Stress Incontinence 57287
Septum
  Excision 57130
Suspension 57280
  Laparoscopic 57425
Suture
  Cystocele 57240, 57260
  Enterocele 57265
  Fistula 51900, 57300-57330
  Rectocele 57250-57260
  Wound 57200-57210
Tumor
  Excision 57135
Ultrasound 76830
Unlisted Services and Procedures 58999
X-Ray with Contrast 74775

Vaginal Delivery 59400, 59610-59614
after Previous Cesarean Delivery 59610-59612
  Attempted 59618-59622
Antepartum Care 59400
Cesarean Delivery after Attempted 59618
  Delivery Only 59620
  Postpartum Care 59622
Delivery after Previous
  Vaginal Delivery Only
    Postpartum Care 59614
Delivery Only 59409
External Cephalic Version 59412
Placenta 59414

Excision
Complete 56625, 56633-56640
Partial 56620, 56630-56632
Radical 56630-56631, 56633-56640
Complete 56633-56640
Partial 56630-56632
Simple
Complete 56625
Partial 56620
Lesion
Destruction 56501-56515
Perineum
Biopsy 56605-56606
Incision and Drainage 56405
Repair
Obstetric 59300

Vulvectomy
Complete 56625, 56633-56640
Partial 56620, 56630-56632
Radical 56630-56631, 56633-56640
Complete
with Bilateral Inguinofemoral Lymphadenectomy 56637
with Inguinofemoral, Iliac, and Pelvic Lymphadenectomy 56640
with Unilateral Inguinofemoral Lymphadenectomy 56634
Partial
with Bilateral Inguinofemoral Lymphadenectomy 56632
with Unilateral Inguinofemoral Lymphadenectomy 56631
Simple
Complete 56625
Partial 56620

VZIG
See Immune Globulins, Varicella-Zoster

W

W-Plasty
See Skin, Adjacent Tissue Transfer

WADA Activation Test 95958
See Electroencephalography

WAIS-R 96100

Waldius Procedure 27445

Wall, Abdominal
See Abdominal Wall

Walsh Modified Radical Prostatectomy
See Prostatectomy

Warts
Flat
Destruction 17110-17111

Washing
Sperm 58323

Wasserman Test
See Syphilis Test

Wassmund Procedure
Osteotomy
Maxilla 21206

Water Load Test 89235

Water Wart
See Molluscum Contagiosum

Waterston Procedure 33755

Watson-Jones Procedure 27695-27698

Wave, Ultrasonic Shock
See Ultrasound

WBC
See White Blood Cell

Webbed
Toe
Repair 28280

Wedge Excision
Osteotomy 21122

Wedge Resection
Ovary 58920

Well-Baby Care 99381, 99391, 99432

Wellness Behavior
See Evaluation and Management, Health Behavior

Wernicke-Posadas Disease
See Coccidioidomycosis

Westergren Test
See Sedimentation Rate, Blood Cell

Western Blot
HIV 86689
Protein 84181-84182
Tissue Analysis 88371-88372

Wheelchair Management/Propulsion
See Physical Medicine/Therapy/Occupational Therapy
Training 97542

Wheeler Knife Procedure
See Discission, Cataract

Wheeler Procedure
See Blepharoplasty, Entropion
Discission Secondary Membranous Cataract 66820

Whipple Procedure 48150

Whirlpool Therapy 97022
See Physical Medicine/Therapy/Occupational Therapy

White Blood Cell
Alkaline Phosphatase 85540
Antibody 86021
Count 85032, 85048, 89055
Differential 85004-85007, 85009
Histamine Release Test 86343
Phagocytosis 86344
Transfusion
See Leukocyte, Transfusion

Whitemead Operation
See Hemorrhoidectomy, Complex

Whitman Astragalectomy
See Talus, Excision

Whitman Procedure 27120

Wick Catheter Technique 20950

Widal Serum Test
See Agglutinin, Febrile

Window
Oval
See Oval Window
Round
See Round Window

Window Technic, Pericardial
See Pericardiostomy

Windpipe
See Trachea

Winiwarter Operation
See Anastomosis, Gallbladder to Intestines

Winter Procedure 54435

Wintrobe Test
See Sedimentation Rate, Blood Cell

Wire
See Pin
Insertion/Removal
Skeletal Traction 20650
Interdental
without Fracture 21497

Wiring
Prophylactic Treatment
Humerus 24498

Wirsung Duct
See Pancreatic Duct

Witzel Operation 43500, 43520, 43830-43832
See Incision, Stomach, Creation, Stoma; Incision and Drainage

Womb
See Uterus

Wood Alcohol
See Methanol

Work Hardening 97545-97546
See Physical Medicine/Therapy/Occupational Therapy

Work Related Evaluation Services 99455-99456

Worm
See Helminth

Wound
Debridement
Non-Selective 97602
Selective 97601
Dehiscence
Repair 12020-12021, 13160
Exploration
Penetrating
Abdomen/Flank/Back 20102
Chest 20101
Extremity 20103
Neck 20100
Penetrating Trauma 20100-20103
Infection
Incision and Drainage
Postoperative 10180
Repair
Complex 13100-13160
Intermediate 12031-12057
Simple 12001-12021
Urethra 53502-53515
Suture
Bladder 51860-51865
Kidney 50500
Trachea
Cervical 31800
Intrathoracic 31805
Urethra 53502-53515
Vagina
Repair 57200-57210

Wrist
See Arm, Lower; Carpal Bone
Abscess 25028
Arthrocentesis 20605
Arthrodesis 25800
with Graft 25810
with Sliding Graft 25805
Arthrography 73115
Arthroplasty 25332, 25443, 25447
Revision 25449
Total Replacement 25446
with Implant 25441-25442, 25444-25445
Arthroscopy
Diagnostic 29840
Surgical 29843-29848
Arthrotomy 25040, 25100-25105
for Repair 25107
Biopsy 25065-25066, 25100-25101
Bursa
Excision 25115-25116
Incision and Drainage 25031
Capsule
Incision 25085
Cast 29085
Cyst 25130-25136
Decompression 25020-25025
Disarticulation 25920
Reamputation 25924
Revision 25922
Dislocation
Closed Treatment 25660
Intercarpal 25660
Open Treatment 25670
Open Treatment 25670, 25676
Percutaneous Fixation 25671
Radiocarpal 25660
Open Treatment 25670
Radioulnar
Closed Treatment 25675
Percutaneous Fixation 25671
with Fracture
Closed Treatment 25680
Open Treatment 25685
with Manipulation 25259, 25660, 25675
Excision
Carpal 25210-25215
Cartilage 25107
Exploration 25040, 25101
Fasciotomy 25020-25025
Fracture 25645
Closed Treatment 25622, 25630
Open Treatment 25628
with Dislocation 25680-25685
with Manipulation 25259, 25624, 25635
Ganglion Cyst
Excision 25111-25112
Hematoma 25028
Incision 25040, 25100-25105
Tendon Sheath 25000-25001
Injection
Carpal Tunnel
Therapeutic 20526
X-Ray 25246
Joint
See Radiocarpal Joint
Lesion, Tendon Sheath
Excision 25110
Magnetic Resonance Imaging (MRI) 73221
Reconstruction
Capsulectomy 25320
Capsulorrhaphy 25320
Carpal Bone 25394, 25430
Realign 25335
Removal
Foreign Body 25040, 25101, 25248
Implant 25449
Loose Body 25101
Prosthesis 25250-25251
Repair 25447
Bone 25440
Carpal Bone 25431
Muscle 25260, 25270
Secondary 25263-25265, 25272-25274
Tendon 25260, 25270, 25280-25316
Secondary 25263-25265, 25272-25274
Tendon Sheath 25275
Strapping 29260
Synovium
Excision 25105, 25115-25119
Tendon Sheath
Excision 25115-25116
Tenodesis 25300-25301
Tenotomy 25290
Tumor 25130-25136
Excision 25075-25077
Unlisted Services and Procedures 25999
X-Ray 73100-73110
with Contrast 73115

X

X, Coagulation Factor
See Stuart-Prower Factor

X, Cranial Nerve
See Vagus Nerve

X-Linked Ichthyoses
See Syphilis Test

X-Ray
Abdomen 74000-74022
Abscess 76080
Acromioclavicular Joint 73050
Ankle 73600-73610
Arm, Lower 73090
Arm, Upper 73092
Artery
Atherectomy 75992-75996
Auditory Meatus 70134
Bile Duct
Guide Dilation 74360
Body Composition
Dual Energy Absorptiometry 0028T
Body Section 76100
Motion 76101-76102
Bone
Age Study 76020
Dual Energy Absorptiometry ...76075-76076
Length Study 76040
Osseous Survey 76061-76065
Ultrasound 76977
Breast 76090-76092
Localization Nodule 76096
with Computer-aided Detection 76085
Calcaneus 73650
Chest 71010-71035
Complete (Four Views)
with Fluoroscopy 71034
Insert Pacemaker 71090
Partial (Two Views)
with Fluoroscopy 71023
Stereo 71015
with Fluoroscopy 71090
Clavicle 73000
Coccyx 72220
Consultation 76140
Duodenum 74260
Elbow 73070-73080
Esophagus 74220
Eye 70030
Facial Bones 70140-70150
Fallopian Tube 74742
Femur 73550
Fibula 73590
Finger 73140
Fistula 76080

XIII, Coagulation Factor
See Fibrin Stabilizing Factor

Xylose Absorption Test
Blood .84620
Urine .84620

Y

Yeast
Culture .87106

Yellow Fever Vaccine .90717

Yersinia
Antibody .86793

Z

Ziegler Procedure
Discission Secondary Membranous Cataract .66820

Zinc .84630

Zinc Manganese Leucine Aminopeptidase
See Leucine Aminopeptidase

Zygoma
See Cheekbone

Zygomatic Arch
Fracture
- Open Treatment .21356-21366
- with Manipulation .21355